Psychology of Religion

Psychology and Christianity
Edited by David G. Benner

Psychology of Religion

Personalities, Problems, Possibilities

Edited by
H. Newton Malony

BAKER BOOK HOUSE
Grand Rapids, Michigan 49516

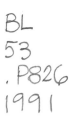
Copyright 1991 by
Baker Book House Company

Printed in the United States of America

Library of Congress Cataloging-in-Publication Data

Psychology of religion: personalities, problems, possibilities / H. Newton Malony, ed.
p. cm. –(Psychology and Christianity)
Includes index.
ISBN 0-8010-6268-3
1. Psychology, Religious. 2. Psychologists of religion. I. Malony, H. Newton. II. Series.
BL53.P826   1990
200'.1'9–dc20   90-38821
                                                                                      CIP

Scripture versions cited are the Good News Bible (GNB), the King James Version (KJV),
the New Jerusalem Bible (NJB), and the Revised Standard Version (RSV).

Videotaped interviews with many of the contributors to this volume can be rented or
purchased. In addition, a teaching manual with suggested projects and test questions is
available. For more information write:

Dr. H. Newton Malony
Fuller Theological Seminary
Graduate School of Psychology
180 North Oakland Avenue
Pasadena, CA 91101

To Walter Houston Clark
Professor Emeritus, Andover Newton Theological Seminary
Dean of American Psychology of Religion
whose 1958 book *The Psychology of Religion*
reintroduced the psychology of religion into mainline psychology
for the first time since its demise in 1930

Contents

Part 3 Personality Theory and Religion

Part 4 Psychopathology of Religion

Part 5 Research in the Psychology of Religion

Part 9 Clinical Psychology of Religion

Contributors

C. Daniel Batson is professor of psychology at the University of Kansas, Lawrence, Kansas.

Benjamin Beit-Hallahmi is associate professor of psychology at the University of Haifa, Israel.

Allen E. Bergin is professor of psychology and director of the clinical psychology program at Brigham Young University, Provo, Utah.

Laurence Binet Brown is professor and past chair in the department of psychology at the University of New South Wales, Sydney, Australia.

John D. Carter is professor at the Rosemead School of Psychology, Biola University, La Mirada, California.

Gary R. Collins is professor of counseling and psychology and dean of the Institute for International and Multicultural Counseling, Liberty University, Lynchburg, Virginia.

Jean-Pierre Deconchy is professor of social psychology at the University of Paris.

Andre Godin is retired professor of psychology of religion at the Institut Superieur des Sciences Religieuses, Charleroi, Belgium.

Richard L. Gorsuch is professor and director of research in the Graduate School of Psychology, Fuller Theological Seminary, Pasadena, California.

Nils G. Holm is professor of comparative religions at the Åbo Akademi, Helsinki, Finland.

Ralph W. Hood, Jr., is professor of psychology at the University of Tennessee at Chattanooga.

H. Newton Malony is professor and director of programs in the integration of psychology and theology in the Graduate School of Psychology, Fuller Theological Seminary, Pasadena, California.

11

Mary Jo Meadow is professor of psychology and director of religious studies at Mankato State University, Mankato, Minnesota.

David G. Myers is the John Dirk Werkman Professor of Psychology at Hope College, Holland, Michigan.

Raymond F. Paloutzian is professor and chair of the department of psychology at Westmont College, Santa Barbara, California.

Kenneth I. Pargament is associate professor of psychology at Bowling Green State University, Bowling Green, Ohio.

L. Rebecca Propst is associate professor of psychology at Lewis and Clark College, Graduate School of Professional Studies, Portland, Oregon.

Virginia Staudt Sexton is Distinguished Professor of Psychology at St. John's University, Jamaica, New York.

Edward P. Shafranske is associate professor in the Graduate School of Education and Psychology, Pepperdine University, Los Angeles, California.

Bernard Spilka is professor of psychology at the University of Denver, Colorado.

Hendrika Vande Kemp is a professor in the Graduate School of Psychology at Fuller Theological Seminary, Pasadena, California.

Jan van der Lans is professor of the psychology of religion at Catholic University of Nijmegen, The Netherlands.

Introduction to the Series

This volume is the fifth in the *Psychology and Christianity Series*, a collection of books published cooperatively by Baker Book House and the Christian Association for Psychological Studies (CAPS). Founded in 1952 in Grand Rapids, Michigan, by a group of psychologists, psychiatrists, and pastoral counselors, CAPS is an international society of Christian helping professions committed to the exploration of the relationship between psychology and Christian faith.

Books in this series draw on previous CAPS publications and supplement them with original articles written for each volume. The purpose of the series is to present psychological and theological reflection on the most important issues encountered in human relationships, particularly relationships of counseling, education, parenting, worship, and ministry.

Further information about the *Christian Association for Psychological Studies* may be obtained by contacting the head office:

Christian Association for Psychological Studies
P.O. Box 628
Blue Jay, CA 92317
(714) 337–5117

David G. Benner
Series Editor

Introduction

*P*sychology of Religion: Personalities, Problems, Possibilities, is the result of a long-held conviction. For some time I have been convinced that we study persons more than we study ideas. Persons make ideas come alive. This is no less true in the psychology of religion than in other fields. G. Stanley Hall, William James, Sigmund Freud, Erich Fromm, Walter Houston Clark, Gordon Allport, and Paul Pruyser are only a few among many 20th-century thinkers who have studied the psychology of religion. We remember them as much as their ideas. Their unique circumstances, their personal histories, and their special interests combine to make their thoughts intriguing.

Unfortunately, many texts in the psychology of religion fail to take this interest in persons into account. Their outlines focus on ideas rather than persons. While conversion, religious motivation, saintliness, and good works are attractive topics, I became convinced that a book organized around psychologists of religion themselves would be topically even more attractive.

This conviction about our interest in persons led me to edit a special issue of the *Journal of Psychology and Christianity* (1986) which included biographical sketches of many of the best-known psychologists of religion still living at that time. Readers found the material interesting and asked for more. This volume is an expanded version of that journal issue. Almost all of the noteworthy psychologists of religion—from the United States, France, Australia, Israel, The Netherlands, Belgium, and Finland—are represented.

These psychologists have emphasized a variety of themes in their academic and professional lives, and so this volume is organized thematically. Each part of the book examines such themes as history, personality, psychopathology, experimentation, or social influences. Each chapter includes a brief biography of a given psychologist and two essays by that psychologist. In most cases, one essay is a reprinted article illustrating the major aoncerns of the psychologist, and the other is the author's reflections on psychology of religion as a field of study.

15

The book is not intended to be read straight through from beginning to end; readers and students can selectively follow their interests in individuals or in topics. Teachers can plan courses around particular psychologists or special issues. A typical course might consider one psychologist each week. If the class meets for 3 hours, students might investigate the biography and background of the psychologist during the first hour. In the second hour they might consider the essay in which the psychologist reviewed her or his special interests and future concerns. The final hour might be built around the republished article included in this volume. Term projects could be developed around the bibliographies of the writers or comparisons of several authors and/or issues.

Incidentally, several years ago I videotaped 30-minute interviews with more than half of the psychologists in the book. (Interviews with the others are being prepared.) The tapes have been produced as "Vistas in the Psychology of Religion" and can be rented or purchased for use in courses or seminars (see the copyright page). A teaching manual with test questions is also available.

My concern for the psychology of religion is long-standing. I taught my first course on the topic more than 20 years ago, and my interest has never abated. If anything, it is stronger than ever. I am convinced of the importance of religion to life. Many psychologists agree with me. This book, which I hope will become a standard resource, is offered to all my colleagues who share this conviction and who want to know more about psychological understandings of religion. My wish is that the day might come when psychologists and citizens alike appreciate religious dynamics at a level higher than what they learned in Sunday school or acquired by an uninformed negative religious bias.

I express my appreciation to four excellent secretaries who have worked on this project with skill, thoroughness, and dedication. Without question, the names of Donna Meyer, Jeannine Masciola, Lynelle Bush, and Connie Loomer should appear alongside mine as coeditors of this volume. I salute and honor them.

H. Newton Malony

PART 1

Historical Developments

1

Virginia Staudt Sexton

Virginia Staudt Sexton is Distinguished Professor of Psychology at St. John's University in Jamaica, New York, and she is professor emerita of psychology at Herbert H. Lehman College of the City University of New York. She has also taught at Hunter College and Notre Dame College, both in New York. Her doctorate was from Fordham University. She is a member of Phi Beta Kappa, Sigma Xi, and Psi Chi, the national psychology honor society. In 1980 she received an honorary D.H.L. from Cedar Crest College.

Dr. Sexton has been very active in profession organizations, especially the American Psychological Association (APA). For a number of years she has been a member of the council, and she was twice (1983, 1986) a candidate for president. She has also served as president of several APA divisions, among them Division 36, Psychologists Interested in Religious Issues (its first president). She is chair of the oral history committee and a member of the task force on APA's centennial celebration (1992). Further, she has served as president of the International Council of Psychologists; she was also chair of the task force for the council's 50th anniversary celebration (1991). Her other professional affiliations are with the New York State Psychological Association, the Catholic Psychological Association (she has served as president of each), the American Association for the Advancement of Science, and the Association for Women in Psychology.

Dr. Sexton has coauthored six books in the area of the history of psychology. Of special interest to psychologists of religion is *Catholics in Psychology: A Historical Survey*, which she coauthored with Henryk Misiak (New York: McGraw-Hill, 1954). In addition, she has written about the philosophy of science, clinical psychology, psychology in other countries, and phenomenological, existential, and humanistic

19

psychologies. She has authored over 100 published articles including the following: "American Psychologists and Psychology Abroad," "Intimacy, a Historical Perspective," "Psychological Fulfillment for the Woman," "Pioneer Priest Psychologists," "Graduate Schools Out to Train Teachers of Psychology," "A Biometric Evaluation of the Somatotherapies in Schizophrenia," and "Psychology in Italy."

In her article "American Psychology and Philosophy, 1876–1976: Alienation and Reconciliation," Dr. Sexton traces the relationship between philosophy and psychology from the turn of the century to the present. Having charted the course of behaviorism from its inception as a reaction against anthropocentric, introspective psychology, she also notes the ascendancy of cognitive psychology, and with it a reaffirmation of the importance of the mind. Dr. Sexton suggests that the time has now come for us to rethink the meaning of psychology from a philosophic point of view. She calls for psychology to be primarily a study of persons—their inner experiences as well as their outward behavior.

In her essay "Psychology of Religion: Some Accomplishments and Challenges," Sexton reviews the history of the establishment of Division 36 of the APA, Psychologists Interested in Religious Issues. She notes changes in the negative attitude toward scientific psychology among Catholic educators over the last quarter century. On the 10th anniversary of Division 36, Sexton assesses various accomplishments and cites further work to be done. She calls for the inclusion of psychology of religion in introductory texts. And while noting the progress psychology of religion has made as a profession, Dr. Sexton challenges her peers to advance psychology of religion as a science.

American Psychology and Philosophy, 1876–1976: Alienation and Reconciliation

Introduction

It is just about 100 years since William James, the father of American psychology, introduced the German scientific psychology in his lectures at Harvard. Earlier, or pre-Jamesian, psychology in America was essentially a psychology of human conduct that had been successively nurtured in theology, moral philosophy, and mental philosophy. As customarily taught in the academies and colleges by philosophy professors who were almost invariably Protestant clergymen and theologians, this psychology aimed to inculcate moral virtues. It is, therefore, not surprising that the three pioneers of American psychology—James, Ladd, and Hall—had training in philosophy and that Ladd and Hall were trained in theology. In the subsequent wave of enthusiasm for science and science education in late 19th-century America, however, scientific psychology was readily accorded a hearty reception, and interest in the old philosophical psychology waned. Steadily thereafter in the 20th century American psychology made rapid strides as a science and as a profession.

Now in 1976, as Marx and Goodson recently observed, "Psychology is experiencing not revolution, but the inevitable pendulum swings that must be expected in any viable discipline" (v). Faith in the old scientific verities that buoyed psychologists in earlier years has been challenged in our day. Psychologists are questioning and doubting their research techniques and findings, theories, and indeed the very definition of their subject matter. Among the significant changes since the 1960s enumerated by Marx and Goodson are a revived interest in philosoph-

From *The Journal of General Psychology* 99 (1978): 3–18. Reprinted with permission of the Helen Dwight Reid Educational Foundation. Published by Heldref Publications, 4000 Albemarle St., N.W., Washington, D.C. 20016. Copyright © 1978.

ical issues and perspectives and a rediscovery of mind as central to the subject matter of psychology. American psychologists now seem to be coming to grips with some fundamental issues of their science which they had ignored or denied for several decades.

The purpose of this paper is to give a panoramic view of the psychology-philosophy relationship during the past 100 years of the existence of American scientific psychology and to trace some of the forces of alienation and reconciliation between the two disciplines.

Early American Psychology

The subject matter of the German scientific psychology imported by William James was the data of immediately lived experience inasmuch as this experience involves a subject which is characterized above all by activities such as knowing, feeling, willing. These data included sensory qualities and internal states, acts that exist only for the subject and can only be observed by the subject. Introspection was the method used to study man's mental life and his consciousness. Thus the German scientific psychology was an essentially subjective experimental science.

As a physician, philosopher, and humanist James sought to treat psychology as a natural science of mental life, distinct from the earlier American theology and moral and mental philosophy. In making a plea for psychology as natural science in 1892 James wrote, "I wished by treating psychology *like* a natural science, to help her to become one" (146). A little further on in the same article he observed that "We need a fair and square and explicit *abandonment* of such questions as that of the soul, the transcendental ego, the fusion of ideas or particles of mind stuff etc., by the practical man; and a fair and square determination on the part of philosophers to keep such questions out of psychology and treat them only in their widest possible connections, amongst the objects of an ultimate critical review of all the elements of the world" (149–50). In concluding his plea for psychology as natural science, James also stated:

> We never ought to doubt that Humanity will continue to produce all the types of thinkers which she needs. I myself do not doubt of the "final perseverance" or success of the philosophers. Nevertheless, if the hard alternative were to arise of a choice between "theories" and "facts" in psychology, between a merely rational and a merely practical science of the mind, I do not see how any man could hesitate in his decision. The kind of psychology which could cure a case of melancholy, or charm a chronic insane delusion away, ought certainly to be preferred to the most seraphic insight into the nature of the soul. And that is the sort of psychology which the men who care little or nothing for ultimate rationality, the biol-

ogists, nerve-doctors, and psychical researchers, namely, are surely tending, whether we help them or not, to bring about. (153)

Yet, for all his support of the new psychology, James intended no total rejection of philosophy. An empiricist rather than an experimentalist, James pursued the questions of psychology without losing a philosophical perspective. When he wrote his *Principles of Psychology* (1890), the philosophical influence was evident more as a persistent attempt to think critically and comprehensively than as a matter of doctrine. James tried to keep open the channels of communication between psychologists and philosophers. He admonished philosophers to ground their thinking in experience and to try to understand experience itself in terms of empirical inquiry. His pragmatism—a humanistic philosophy—stressed concreteness and life enhancement. He urged psychologists, too, to be critical of what they were doing and to recognize that the subject matter of psychology is carved out of a larger reality which cannot be ignored. As American psychology progressed in the late 19th century, James exhorted psychologists and philosophers not to be prejudiced by past history nor to be hostile toward each other, but rather to collaborate in the best interests of humankind. James's position was supported by James Mark Baldwin, who observed: "The traditional connection with philosophy is not severed by the new directions of our effort, but on the contrary they are made more close and reasonable" (1894, 389).

Despite James's and Baldwin's encouragement of a harmonious relationship between psychology and philosophy their advice seemed to go unheeded before 1900. Science was gaining prestige, and philosophy, especially the old moral and mental philosophy, was rapidly declining. In 1895 E. W. Scripture coined the phrase *armchair psychology* as a slogan to win converts for the new scientific psychology and to draw them away from the empirically nonverifiable metaphysical presuppositions prevalent among some American philosophers of that time. As Klein later observed, "the armchair taboo was to make psychology a 100 per cent laboratory science" (1942, 228). And yet it should be remembered that Wundt himself was not convinced that the experimental approach should be the exclusive scientific one for psychology. He did not believe, for example, that the higher mental processes could be studied experimentally.

By 1900 the new psychology in America came more and more to be a rigid laboratory study shunning reference to mental life and human nature. The empirical approach was thus narrowly restricted to the experimental approach, and nonexperimental data were classified as "armchair stuff." Klein summarized this early period as follows: "American founding fathers of psychology in the early twentieth century were rallying around the totem pole of laboratory psychology and proud of their loyalty to the armchair taboo" (1942, 228). In its protest against armchair psychology, the new psychology adopted the supercilious view toward philosophy held by the other empirical sciences in the 19th century. Terms like *philosopher* and *philosophy* became terms of opprobrium, synonymous with cloudy thinking and general muddleheadedness. Gradually James's eminence dimmed as he was dubbed an armchair psychologist. But, if indeed he was an armchair psychologist, he was, as Klein observed, "an armchair psychologist with his chair planted in the pulsating world of experience and not in the arid atmosphere of wordy metaphysical abstractions" (229).

The alienation of psychology and philosophy was also evidenced in the universities. Almost from the outset, as psychology was introduced into the American universities, separate chairs of psychology and departmental independence were the rule, in contrast to the 19th-century German universities. Wundt was strongly opposed to separate chairs of psychology because he felt that such a situation would create the danger of cutting psychology off completely from contact with philosophy, while psychology should be cultivated in close contact with philosophy. He appealed to the faculties of philosophy not to accept any candidate for habilitation who would only be an experimentalist and not well grounded in philosophy.

It was a critical period for American philosophers who taught psychology. They were expected to know more and more about laboratory psychology, but many philosophers remained aloof from psychologists' laboratory investigations, treating them with indifference, indulgence, or at times with contempt. Reviewing this period, Ogden reported in 1913 that philosophers regarded "a course in psychology which devotes two thirds of its time to a detailed study of the nervous system and the data of sensation, as a questionable introduction to the problems of logic, aesthetics, and metaphysics. Thus there has been dissatisfaction and a tendency to divorce psychology altogether from the course in philosophy with which it was formerly so narrowly allied" (183). This early alienation of psychology and philosophy was, therefore, as much the fault of philosophy as of psychology. It was a kind of mutual rejection.

A further factor—the popularity of psychology among students—also strained psychology's and philosophy's ties within the universities. Discussing the implications for education of the psychology-philosophy alienation Ogden stated: "Philosophy, in its turn, has doubtless suffered in the proportionate number of its students by the separation of psychology from its departmental regime. There are ordinarily no such large numbers taking logic, the usual introductory course, as take psychology" (1913, 183). All of us who are familiar with the academic scene and departments' competition for student registration can readily grasp the significance of that state of affairs. Such rivalry is not calculated to endear disciplines to each other. As late as 1913 Ogden, somewhat in the tradition of James and Baldwin, was still calling for a rapprochement and readjustment between psychology and philosophy, emphasizing especially the importance of psychology as a propaedeutic to philosophy. But that possibility was soon eliminated with the rise of behaviorism.

The Rise of Behaviorism

Little by little after 1900 in America a new orientation appeared which led to a basic change in the definition of the subject of psychology. From its beginnings as an essentially subjective science, psychology tended to become an objective study, an extension of the biological sciences. It now began to emphasize the biocentric and objective in contrast to the older anthropocentric, introspective psychology. The deliberate change to an aphilosophical orientation led ultimately to what became known as the science of behavior, a strictly objective psychology. A transitional stage in this transformation of psychology from an introspective to a behavioristic study was the functional point of view initially espoused by James and vigorously promoted by John Dewey. Functionalism supported objective methods, as well as introspection. It was John Watson's rebellion against functionalism in 1913 (as well as against the German subjective experimental psychology) which launched a veritable crusade for a fully mechanistic, objective science. Viewed in such light, psychology was to be the science of behavior rather than a science of mind or consciousness. As Woodworth (1948) pointed out, it was the negative emphasis of behaviorism that was novel. The program consisted mainly of a series of prohibitions: "Drop the mind, say no more about consciousness, cease introspecting, eliminate mentalistic concepts, stop speculating on what goes on in the brain" (71). Watson's behaviorism sought to sever any last remnants of the relations of psychology to mentalism and philosophical concerns. Philosophical terminology was abandoned. Philosophical problems and traditional subjects of study like consciousness yielded place to animal researches and studies of learning, conditioning, and the like.

By the early 1920s large numbers of American psychologists were following Watson's lead. In their laboratories they were eagerly studying the overt behavior of human and beast, manipulating them by applying some type of stimulus to the organism and by recording the ensuing response. In subscribing to the tenets and precepts of behaviorism, Watson's early followers felt that they were not only emancipating psychology from philosophy, but that they were establishing psychology firmly among the natural sciences.

Needless to say there were American psychologists at the advent of behaviorism who violently opposed its tenets, but they were a minority and their criticisms were not widely heeded. Among those who early cited some of the follies of this emancipated psychology was H. M. Johnson, who observed in a bitterly critical vein:

> It often happens that for a considerable time after his emancipation the libertine tends to exult in his liberty and to assert the right to practice more of it than he has yet learned to use. The newly emancipated psychologist has presented such a behavior-pattern. In adopting a new procedure, he had to rationalize his actions before he could proceed freely. Of course he overspoke himself. He proclaimed that experimentation, even in an undeveloped science, was not a supplement to analysis, but a substitute. It has become unscientific and undignified to work with one's head as soon as it became possible to work with one's hands. It was quite proper to rush into experimentation without first asking whether the question to be answered stated a genuine problem to which *any* experiment could yield a valid answer. As for logic—it was out of date. To violate its rules, and even to profess ignorance of them, only helped to prove that he was a scientist—by proving that he was not a philosopher. (1932, 293)

By way of remedy Johnson called for reaffirmation of the standards of ordinary logic and the submission of every inference in modern psychology to test by them. The result, he predicted, will be "treatises that are very much smaller than the ones we now have; our lists of solved problems will be greatly shortened; our lists of spurious problems, of absurd requirements, and of unsolved genuine problems will be lengthened; but the result will be both pleasing and valuable" (322).

By the 1930s, after the struggles and polemics of the schools of psychology, classical, or Watsonian, behaviorism was abandoned by most American psychologists. Although they rejected metaphysical behaviorism which denied the existence of mental states, a new behaviorist position emerged which tried to construct broad empirical theories based on physics. This post-Watsonian behavioristic psychology was greatly strengthened by developments in the philosophy of science.

It will be recalled that after the polemics of the 19th century occasioned by the emancipation of the various empirical sciences from philosophy (psychology being the last)—a new philosophy of science emerged whose goal was the critical review and supervision of the empirical sciences. Philosophers—reluctantly at first—began to study science. In 1926 R. B. Perry in *Philosophy of the Recent Past* described the beginnings of a reconciliation between philosophy and science, indicating that philosophers were showing great respect for science. They were cooperating more than formerly and were even manifesting "a tendency to reject externality and transcendence, and to think in terms of what is called 'experience'" (222). Ironically, this had been the ideal of William James.

The 1930s saw physical scientists become more philosophical. For example, Bohr and Heisenberg began to rediscover some of the problems of Locke, Hume, and Kant. During the 1920s and 1930s new movements, such as logical positivism, operationism, and physicalism, appeared. They tried to purify the language of science and to rid science of those "pseudoproblems" which arise when the scientist tries to translate the metaphysical, the unobservable, or the physically undemonstrable into the language of physical reality.

Later Behaviorists and Reactions to Them

These new movements of the 1920s and 1930s further strengthened behaviorism. Hull and Skinner were clearly and strongly influenced by the neopositivist philosophy of the Vienna Circle. Another spur to their thinking was Bridgman's operationism, which held that scientific concepts acquire their meaning from the methods used to derive them and that objective standards lead to validity. Thus methodological behaviorism replaced the old metaphysical behaviorism. Methodological behaviorism insisted that dependent and independent variables and theoretical constructs had to be defined in terms of public or intersubjectively agreed-upon events. The datum of psychology was behavior rather than mental states. However, even if an individual's behavior could not be explained by his state of mind because his private experience was not available to the observer's inspection, his report of his state—spoken or written—could be regarded as a public event. Then observers could agree on the verbal responses. This neobehaviorism has dominated American psychology in various forms or subschools from 1930 to the present.

The subschools headed by Tolman, Hull, and Skinner have been quite controversial, particularly in respect to their theories of learning. They have generated both extensive animal experimentation and theoretical discussion. Surely Tolman's purposive behaviorism, Hull's axiomatic system, and Skinner's descriptive, or radical, behaviorism are too well known to require review here. Suffice it to say that from the simple early stimulus-response (S-R) studies it was just a small step to more radical forms of behaviorism in which the S-R paradigm became more than a useful experimental method. It became the basis for all behavior of humans or lower animals. From the standpoint of Skinner and radical behaviorism the organism's responses to stimuli and drives and to reward and punishment ultimately were deemed adequate to explain all learning, emotions, all actions. In other words, operant conditioning with its schedules of reinforcement could account for all behavior. Skinner has gone on to demonstrate the applicability of his behaviorism in society in *Walden Two* and in *Beyond Freedom and Dignity*. When behaviorism was 50 years old, Skinner said, "Behaviorism, with the accent on the last syllable, is not the scientific study of behavior but a philosophy of science concerned with the subject matter and methods of psychology" (1963, 951).

While the post-Watsonians were developing their new behaviorism, major changes were occurring in the physical sciences, particularly in physics, after which psychology was patterning itself. One of these changes in the physical sciences was a rethinking of their methodology. Already in 1936 Winter noted:

> Formerly the tendency on the part of the physical sciences was to berate psychology on the ground of its inexactitude, lack of proper basis for predictability, and its tendency toward mysticism; and the hope and ambition of psychology was to develop toward the apparent perfection enjoyed by the physical sciences. Today the situation, as far as the physical scientists are concerned, is radically altered, if not completely reversed. The physical sciences are now beginning to admit the relative character of their postulates, the non-predictability of some of their principles and the reduction of some of their data to the level of mere probability, thus placing themselves in the situation formerly accorded to psychology. (131)

Winter reminded psychologists that if psychology wants to be scientific it should consider the prevailing trends in the physical sciences, and not continue to emulate an outmoded model of physics.

About the same time Williams commented that "It is the strangest anomaly of recent science that while an influential number of physicists, once supposed to be students of physical nature, are suggesting that only conscious experience exists, an equally influential number of psychologists, once supposed to be students of consciousness, have suggested that only physical nature exists" (1934, 461).

For four or five decades behavioristic psychologists who ignored consciousness and ruled out introspection held sway in the universities. Several generations of students were trained in the experimental tradition of behaviorism. They were taught rigid laboratory procedures to be used in studying behavior, usually animal behavior. Topics of human interest introduced by clinical psychology and psychoanalysis in the 1920s and 1930s were scorned and scrupulously avoided for many years because they could not be subjected to rigid experimentation. The clinical and psychoanalytical frames of reference concerned themselves with the central and subjective. They sought to know the inner man by both observational and intuitive approaches. Naturally the intuitive approach was frowned upon by behavioristic psychology. Thus most

American scientific psychologists became more and more removed from living issues and more abstract in the presentation of their subject matter. Their preoccupation was with method and with animal researches rather than with human behavior and human subjects. The subject's experiences were no longer of interest to the scientific psychologist.

Gordon Allport (1940) characterized the American psychology of 1940 as "empirical, mechanistic, nomothetic, analytic, and operational." He condemned those who demanded slavish subservience to such presuppositions. He urged that psychological science also be permitted to be "rational, ideological, qualitative, idiographic, and even non-rational." He reminded his fellow psychologists that the great insights of the past—those of Aristotle, Fechner, James, and Freud—stemmed from one or more of these currently unfashionable presuppositions. Finally, Allport stated, "My plea, therefore, is that we avoid authoritarianism, that we keep psychology from becoming a cult from which original and daring inquiry is ruled out by the application of one-sided tests of method" (26).

In a somewhat similar vein Gengerelli (1937) called psychologists' attention to the increasing recognition by the physical sciences of the unity of purpose of philosophy and science. He chided psychologists for their continuing failure to dispel their supercilious attitude toward philosophical speculation in their science. This failure he attributed to several factors including the triumph of specialization and fact-finding, 19th-century materialism, and behaviorism with its denial of consciousness. Gengerelli emphasized that there are two fundamental processes in science: the discovery of facts and relations and the organization of facts and relations into a conceptual framework of maximum simplicity, the latter being the concern of philosophy. He reminded psychologists that the nature of their experiments, the facts that they discover, and the significance assigned to them, all depend on the particular philosophical assumptions from which they originate. He urged them to realize that behaviorism itself is *one* philosophical point of view.

Five years later in 1942 Gengerelli could still complain that too many psychologists were still simply gathering facts about human nature without having any conceptual framework from which the large amount of data they accumulated could be suspended. In psychology, he insisted, there is an urgent need for philosophizing of the most rigorous sort and for posing hypotheses which are the essence of the scientific method, in order to reconcile contradictions and ambiguities.

About the same time Ericksen denounced the indiscriminate accumulation of experimental facts as "particularly meaningless in a science as complicated and disjointed as contemporary psychology" (1941, 80). "No experimentalist," he adds, "has completed his job until he has made his results meaningful in terms of some theoretical frame of reference" (80). Ericksen especially attacked the "pebble picking" character of all branches of psychological investigation. Pebble picking he describes as experimentation "which presents a specific problem together with solution within the limits of a single study. There are no true psychological problems as simple as that" (81). Ericksen concludes with the observation that "human experimentation too often becomes a display of remarkable apparatus and submissive subjects" (81). Strangely enough, 22 years later during the Rice Symposium on Behaviorism and Phenomenology, Joseph Royce in a banquet address entitled "Pebble Picking *vs.* Boulder Building" repeated the same criticism and urged psychologists to "promote a Zeitgeist of philosophic awareness and sophisticated theory building if we wish to develop a healthy basic and applied psychology" (1965, 450).

From this overview of the relations of psychology and philosophy from 1876 to World War II, we have noted repeated calls from within and from without psychology for its greater philosophic awareness and for a review of its philosophic assumptions and for a change of its focus. But in spite of all the rhetoric no significant alterations were made during these years while behavioristic psychology remained dominant in America. American psychology seemed unable to disentangle itself from its behavioristic moorings. The fact is that the behaviorists tried to divorce psychology from philosophy, but never really succeeded because they themselves represented a philosophical point of view. As Karl Jaspers has said in *Way to Wisdom*, "There is no escape from philosophy. The question is only whether a philosophy is conscious or not, whether it is good or bad, muddled or clear. Anyone who rejects philosophy is himself unconsciously practising a philosophy" (1951, 12). A comment by Royce in the previously mentioned paper is also in point here: "Psychology and philosophy were divorced in name only for the good of the children . . . it was, in fact, good for the children" (1965, 447). The good was that under the impetus of behaviorism American psychology established a strong experimental laboratory tradition between World War I and World War II. It gave psychology a solid base as science. Since World War II it has also provided valuable contributions in programmed learning, behavior modification, and the like. However, what behaviorism succeeded in doing that was not good for American psychology—as many of us have come to realize—was to alienate American psychology from philosophy for almost a half century in a way that restricted its growth as a human science. Behaviorism strove to meet the requirements of a strictly scientific psychology. The price for such an achievement was the loss of direct experience and a fostering of the view that scientific psychology must be reductionistic. Individual experience was either ignored or reduced to something else.

It became so totally objectified that the person whose experience it was, was ignored.

Challenges to Behavioristic Psychology: 1945 to Present

It is chiefly since World War II that the merits of behaviorism have been questioned, that the need for the reconciliation of psychology with philosophy has been increasingly felt, and that some steps in that direction have been taken. Various changes in the character of modern American psychology—we can only cite them briefly here—have generated a new state of affairs. These changes have not sought a return to the old speculative philosophy. They are rather urging upon psychology a different—or perhaps even an additional—frame of reference—that of a human science, and not merely a natural science.

One such source has been the rapid professionalization of psychology after 1945. Clinical psychology came into prominence and stands today as the largest field of specialization in American psychology. In the period between 1946 and 1976 the number of clinical psychologists has increased so much that they far exceed the number of academic psychologists, who characteristically have been the psychological scientists and researchers. Clinical psychology had little to learn about human personality in health or disease from the animal researches of the behaviorists. It demanded more information about humankind—its emotions, feelings, perceptions, motivations, and thought patterns. In its quest for this information it enlisted the aid of psychoanalysis and later of existential psychology which provided a base for such study of the individual and of human experience, which is so essential for the understanding and treatment of human problems.

Another related influence was the emergence of humanistic psychology spearheaded in 1954 by a disenchanted behaviorist, Abraham Maslow. This movement has chiefly succeeded in emphasizing the limitations of behaviorism for treating the subjects of its study as objects, and ignoring their humanity. Prompted by phenomenology and existential psychology, humanistic psychology has called for a change in psychological methodology, urging the study of human experience neglected by objective methodology—matters such as loneliness, suicide, attitudes toward death, values, and the like. To date, however, humanistic methodology still leaves much to be desired.

Impetus to the experimental study of experience has come, too, from phenomenological psychology as represented by Gestalt psychology, by MacLeod, Snygg, and Combs, and more recently by van Kaam, Giorgi, and others. They have sought to encourage the use of phenomenological methodology to tap areas of human behavior not accessible to the usual behavioristic procedures.

In addition one cannot overlook the contribution to philosophical issues in psychology by Jean Piaget, who became very popular in America after 1950. His contributions to such diverse areas as logic, epistemology, and ethics are well known and internationally acclaimed. One perhaps should recall here that in his invited address entitled "Analogy in Science" at the American Psychological Association (APA) convention in 1955, the noted theoretical physicist J. Robert Oppenheimer extolled the naturalistic observation and descriptive methods employed by Piaget at a time when many American psychologists were still skeptical about the worth of Piaget's exploratory work. Oppenheimer encouraged psychologists to pursue the Piagetian type of research rather than to model psychology after an outdated theory of science that physics had abandoned years before—namely, that in which predictability, causality, determinacy, objectivity, and measurement were the ideals.

In the 1960s the dominance of behaviorism waned, partly because of its barrenness and internal contradictions, and partly because it could not explain basic human phenomena such as language. At this period—scarcely a decade ago—there was much criticism of the limited contribution that decades of psychological research could offer in solving, for example, social problems—of the disadvantaged, of women, of alienated youth, of criminals, of the aged, and of marriage and the family. Moreover, the methods and motivations of scientists generally were scrutinized by American society. For example, the ethics of research which seemed to ignore the civil rights and personal integrity of its participants was questioned. In this milieu the older behavioristic psychology began to yield place to a more inner-directed cognitive psychology which has denounced behavioristic psychology for so long ignoring the inner wellsprings of behavior. It has criticized the S-R model as simplistic in its description of why people do what they do. (At this point it should be mentioned that only limited research had been done on cognition for decades. Between World War I and World War II it was mainly Gestalt psychology which represented the cognitive approach in experimental psychology.)

A new era was ushered in after World War II by the computer age along with cybernetics, information and communication theory, game theory, and the like. Then for the first time numerous concepts pertaining to the higher mental processes could be expressed in objective terminology and mathematical language. Interest in cognition became stronger. And so now, in the 1970s American psychology has rediscovered mind. This recent return of American psychology to the investigation of cognitive processes and development implies a basic psychophilosophical reorientation. In one sense we have come almost a full circle in the last 100 years.

In the 1976 issue of the *Annual Review of Psychology* there is a chapter devoted entirely to cognitive development—the first such chapter in the series which began in 1950. The authors Ginsburg and Koslowski attribute the revived interest in cognitive development to three factors: (a) Piaget's research to which we referred earlier; (b) Eleanor J. Gibson, who raised many fundamental issues concerning the nature of perceptual learning and initiated an influential body of research on perceptual development; and (c) psycholinguistics (as developed by theorists like G. A. Miller and inspired by Chomsky's work) which became a significant force in experimental psychology and furnished a new and rigorous framework for studying *mind,* its development and its organization. Ginsburg and Koslowski contend that "psycholinguistic theory provided a clear, concrete, and successful alternative to behaviorism in one area of study and thus conferred credibility on a cognitive approach in general" (30–31).

In consequence, as Beloff pointed out in 1973, "Cognitive psychology has now established itself as the current growing point of academic psychology and, in doing so, has ousted behaviouristics from this dominant position" (198). He further states that "with this shift of priorities, the human subject has once again come into his own in the psychological laboratory where for so long the white rat reigned supreme . . . animal psychology, in the future, can no longer be considered the *sine qua non* of a scientific psychology. Perhaps the present vogue for cognitive psychology is no more than a belated recognition by psychologists of the fact that man has a brain and that this brain is more than a switchboard coupling receptors and effectors. What exactly that something is forms the real point of departure for the cognitive psychologist" (198).

All of these forces which have been enumerated—to say nothing of the advances in the studies of the brain and recent studies of states of consciousness—have been encouraging a psychophilosophical reorientation and a growing appreciation of the mutual benefits arising from a philosophico-psychological dialogue. It would seem, therefore, that if ever in the last century there was a chance for a reconciliation between psychology and philosophy in America, now is the time. We are, however, only at the base of a mountain—a great distance from the resolution of age-old problems, such as the mind-body, free will, and the like. The challenge of detailing our present bases for advance will be up to us and to the students whom we teach.

In 1963—exactly 50 years after the formal beginning of behaviorism—the Division of Philosophical Psychology, Division 24, was established. The establishment of this division, itself a reflection of increased interest in philosophical issues among American psychologists, provides a platform at the annual American Psychological Association conventions for discussing such issues. Our involvement in the psychology of our time and within APA should now be greater and more dedicated to our purposes as described in our bylaws. As recently as 1973 one of our members L. La Fave wrote in our Divisional Newsletter, "That Division 24 presently fails to fulfill its mission, that it has 'missed the boat' is illustrated most dramatically in that it has been ignored by the brilliant Chomsky revolution against behaviorism. Nor has Division 24 succeeded in serving as a strong intradisciplinary thread interweaving itself between the other most relevant divisions. Nor has it progressed far as an interdisciplinary interweaver" (10).

While some may find such criticism generally unwarranted, or at least too harsh, it could serve for us as a "call to arms." In view of the changing Zeitgeist in American psychology we should take heart. We have an important job to do both as individuals and as a division devoted to philosophical psychology. I am not referring here to the writing of papers and books. They are important. But it seems to me that we must also take some practical steps. First and most importantly, we should press for revision of our undergraduate and graduate curricula to reflect the current emphasis on humankind, the revival of interest in mind, and the resurgence of interest in philosophical issues. This need for revision of psychological training was cited in 1974 by Koch:

> I do not think that what goes on in orthodox graduate and undergraduate education can continue much longer. Our students are asked to read and memorize a literature consisting of an endless set of advertisements for the emptiest concepts, the most inflated theories, the most trivial "findings," and the most fetishistic yet heuristically self-defeating methods in scholarly history—and all of it conveyed in the dreariest and most turgid prose that ever met the printed page. For these riches, they must exchange whatever curiosity about the human condition may have carried them into the field; whatever awe or humility they may feel before the human and organismic universe; whatever resources of imagination or observational sensitivity they may bring to the study of that complex universe; whatever openness to experience—their own or others'—they might have. Fine or ardent sensibilities will no longer seek out such debasement. When, by misfortune or misadvice, they arrive in such a field, they will soon abandon it—as they seem to be doing in increasing numbers. (27–28)

Clearly the psychology we teach must focus on humans. It must include inner experience, as well as overt behavior. It must cease to be a jumble of facts without any conceptual framework. Finally, we members of Division 24 should join with psychologists in other APA divisions and in our state and regional societies in establishing and refining ethical standards for research and practice, for example. To promote reconciliation with philosophy we should develop more dialogue with philosophers. Never before in the history of American psychology was a better opportunity provided for such reconciliation. Never in this century was there a more propitious time to redefine the subject matter, methodology, and practice of psychology—to broaden its scope and to liberate it from inhibiting tradition. Finally, as Deese stated in *Psychology as Science and Art* in 1972:

> With the development of a broader conception of knowledge, a less constraining notion of the scientific method, and an awareness of particular methods, psychology could indeed be the most important human science at the beginning of the twenty-first century. (117)

References

Allport, G. W. 1940. The psychologist's frame of reference. *Psychological Bulletin* 37: 1–28.

Baldwin, J. M. 1894. Psychology past and present. *Psychological Review* 1: 363–91.

Beloff, J. 1973. *Psychological sciences: A review of modern psychology.* New York: Harper and Row.

Deese, J. 1972. *Psychology as science and art.* New York: Harcourt Brace Jovanovich.

Ericksen, S. C. 1941. Unity in psychology: A survey of some opinions. *Psychological Review* 48: 73–82.

Gengerelli, J. A. 1937. The dichotomy of science and philosophy. *Psychological Review* 44: 117–37.

———. 1942. Facts and philosophers. *Scientific Monthly* 54: 431–40.

Ginsburg, H., and B. Koslowski. Cognitive development. In *Annual Review of Psychology,* ed. M. Rosenzweig and L. W. Porter, 27: 29–61.

James, W. 1892. A plea for psychology as a natural science. *Philosophical Review* 1: 146–53.

Jaspers, K. 1951. *Way to wisdom: An introduction to philosophy* Trans. R. Manheim. New Haven: Yale Univ. Press.

Johnson, H. M. 1932. Some follies of emancipated psychology. *Psychological Review* 39: 293–323.

Klein, D. B. 1942. Psychology's progress and the armchair taboo. *Psychological Review* 49: 226–34.

Koch, S. 1974. Psychology as science. In *Philosophy of Psychology,* ed. S. C. Brown, 3–40. New York: Harper and Row.

La Fave, L. 1973. What philosophical psychology ought not mean. *Philosophical Psychology* 8: 8–10.

Marx, M., and F. E. Goodson, eds. 1976. *Theories in contemporary psychology.* 2d ed. New York: Macmillan.

Ogden, R. M. 1913. The relation of psychology to philosophy and education. *Psychological Review* 20: 179–93.

Perry, R. B. 1926. *Philosophy of the recent past.* New York: Scribner.

Royce, J. R. 1965. Pebble picking *vs* boulder building. *Psychological Reports* 16: 447–50.

Skinner, B. F. 1963. Behaviorism at fifty. *Science* 140: 951–58.

Williams, D. C. 1934. Scientific method and the existence of consciousness. *Psychological Review* 41: 461–79.

Winter, J. E. 1936. The postulates of psychology. *Psychological Review* 43: 130–48.

Woodworth, R. S. 1948. *Contemporary schools of psychology.* Rev. ed. New York: Ronald.

Psychology of Religion:
Some Accomplishments and Challenges

During the century of its existence numerous historical surveys of the psychology of religion have been written. Most commemorate the contributions of the American pioneers, Edwin Starbuck, William James, G. Stanley Hall, James Pratt, George Coe, and James Leuba. In spite of attacks on these pioneers by theologians and by some of their fellow psychologists their work during the first two decades of the 20th century firmly established the importance of studying religious phenomena. The pioneering period, however, declined under the impact of scientism which sought to reject the authority of religion.

After a period of stagnation in the 1930s and 1940s during the glorious heyday of behaviorism, the volume of publications on religion increased noticeably in the 1950s. Since that time psychologists have turned again to the study of religious experience and motivation. Despite its ups and downs and its occasional brief spurts of interest, "The psychology of religion has manifested a fascinating and strangely persistent style of survival," as Strunk (1970, 90) has so aptly observed.

In recounting the history of the American psychology of religion, many authors have cited the establishment of Division 36 of the American Psychological Association (Psychologists Interested in Religious Issues) in 1976 as a milestone in that history. This year—1986—marks the 10th anniversary of its establishment. Since anniversaries are usually a time for a little looking back, as well as a time for planning ahead, I would like to state that, while the founding of Division 36 was perhaps significant professionally for American psychologists of religion, it was particularly meaningful for me personally and professionally because of the role which I played in obtaining the APA division for psychologists interested in religious issues. This historical beginning for our membership was the culmination for me of several years of effort toward clari-

From the *Journal of Psychology and Christianity* 5, no. 2 (1986): 79–83; reprinted by permission of the publisher and the author. Copyright 1986 by the Christian Association for Psychological Studies.

fying the roles of psychology and religion. In this paper I would like to chronicle some of my personal experiences in that process and speculate a little about the future of the psychology of religion on the American scene.

My interest in the psychology of religion grew out of my dissatisfaction early in my career with the negative attitudes toward psychology held by some of my fellow Catholics and especially by some of the church leaders in the 1940s. At that time Catholic psychologists were engaged in a major struggle to extricate and emancipate themselves from the domination of Catholic philosophy and theology. Some church leaders had a strong bias against psychology; others lacked the psychological sophistication to appreciate the way in which psychology could assist them. These negative attitudes of our coreligionists toward psychology motivated a group of us nationwide to organize the American Catholic Psychological Association (ACPA) in 1948 in order to promote the science and profession of psychology among American Catholics and to reduce the antipsychology bias.

About the same time a Fordham University colleague and fellow-historian of psychology, Henryk Misiak, and I decided to try to track down the roots of these hostile attitudes. Our efforts resulted in the volume *Catholics in Psychology: A Historical Survey* (1954), a review of the work of Catholic psychologists in various countries throughout the world who struggled to overcome opposition and to establish psychology in Catholic circles in their lands. Among them were Désiré Felicien Mercier of Belgium, Joseph Frobes in Germany, Agostino Gemelli in Italy, and Edward A. Pace in the United States. What was most remarkable was the fact that the eminent historian Edwin G. Boring generously accepted our invitation to write the foreword, "Science and Faith," after he graciously read the entire manuscript and offered numerous invaluable suggestions and criticisms.

Our survey revealed that from the outset Wundtian psychology was scrutinized by Catholic philosophical psychologists who soon took definite stands toward it. Most were suspicious of the new psychology, and many were vehemently opposed to it. Only a few accepted it. The negative attitudes toward scientific psychology in the early 20th century stemmed principally from the widely held view that psychology was the study of the soul and therefore a laboratory approach was impossible. Among some Catholic philosophers, such as Gruender (1922) in the United States, the new psychology was labeled the "psychology without a soul." There were also non-Catholic philosophers who held similar attitudes and who saw a real threat in scientific psychology to all religion because they believed that the new science undermined the notion of the spiritual and immortal soul. McDougall (1934) referred to this attitude when he wrote:

The sciences of life are widely reported to be more dangerous to religious belief in a higher degree than the physical sciences. Of all the sciences of life, psychology is, perhaps the most open to this reproach. It may, therefore, be of some general interest if I, who have devoted more than forty years to these sciences, testify while still pre-senile that these prolonged studies have led me to a position more favourable to religion than that from which I set out. They have, in fact, led me from agnosticism to religion.

While it was difficult to overcome the early opposition, gradually in the 1950s and 1960s psychology programs were developed in many Catholic and denominational colleges and universities. Pastoral psychology progressed rapidly, and in Catholic religious communities psychological assessment of candidates became very popular. By 1968 the governance of the American Catholic Psychological Association—after 20 years of its existence—decided that the time had come to disband the organization since it seemed to have achieved its objectives of reducing Catholic bias against psychology and of encouraging Catholics to pursue the science and profession of psychology. In 1971 the American Catholic Psychological Association reorganized under the name Psychologists Interested in Religious Issues (PIRI) and in the ecumenical spirit sought to recruit a broader membership. It was this expanded group with its varied religious representation and vigorous interdenominational interests which decided in 1974 to seek divisional status in the American Psychological Association. Accordingly, the late William C. Bier, S.J., of Fordham University, who had long been active in ACPA and PIRI governance, and I, who also had had some experience in APA governance, were asked to institute the necessary proceedings. We undertook the role of formal petitioners and organizers for APA status with enthusiasm and dedication.

The task of obtaining the division proved to be an enterprise that brought considerable pleasure and satisfaction. In order to secure the required number of petitioners we contacted many APA members, including clergy and lay persons of all faiths who were in clinical practice and/or teaching in denominational colleges, universities, seminaries, and the like. Most were very cooperative and eager to join the effort. Many wrote encouraging letters to us indicating that they had long hoped for such a division. But the task was not without its trials and tribulations. Several coreligionists and antireligionists within the American Psychological Association blocked our initial efforts to seek divisional status in September 1974 and January 1975. Some complained that there were already too many divisions and that there was too little convention time for the existing divisions. Others failed to see the need for a special division and argued that the proposed division should be subsumed in the Philosophical or Humanistic Psychology divisions.

However, with determination and perseverance we reapplied and finally acquired enough Council of Representatives support to be voted in as Division 36 in August 1975. In 1976 when the Division was formally organized and I became the first president several of our members told us that at last they felt as if they had found a "home" in APA.

Now after 10 years we may well ask what our membership has accomplished for the psychology of religion. Thanks to our divisional status we have achieved an identity in American psychology as psychologists interested in religious issues, and as such we have a voice and forum within our national organization. We have been able to meet at our annual conventions to discuss significant issues in our specialty and to share ideas. Moreover, there has been a noticeable increase in papers on religion written by our members, although there is still a dearth of such articles in the major APA publications. Several substantial textbooks on the psychology of religion have appeared in the last decade, and the number of college and university course offerings has also increased, which bodes well for the training of future specialists.

In respect of training there is an urgent matter that still demands attention. To date little or no mention of the psychology of religion is made in most introductory psychology textbooks. Since such textbooks are literally the gatekeepers of our science and profession, we need to encourage teachers and textbook writers to give due consideration to religious psychology along with other fields of psychology. Only when students—and their teachers, too—recognize that religious psychology deals with real human behavior and real human experience, like other applied fields of psychology, can they obtain a balanced perspective of the whole field of psychology. Moreover, those who review manuscripts for publishers and those who review books for journals should be alert to omissions of reference to the psychology of religion. Our writing of books and articles on the psychology of religion is fine, but it is not enough. The psychology of religion and its contributions have to be channeled into the mainstream of psychology and into its standard textbooks.

Probably the greatest progress for the psychology of religion has been made in respect to its application in counseling and clinical practice. Nearly all the major religious groups are represented among counseling and clinical psychologists. In fact, it seems safe to say that in Division 36 there are more psychologist-practitioners than psychologist-scientists. This situation, however, is not surprising because it reflects the general state of affairs in contemporary American psychology. The psychologist-practitioners have demonstrated considerable sensitivity and concern with the religious commitment of their patients. E. Mark Stern's recent publication of a series of papers written by practitioners entitled *The Religiously Committed Patient* (1985) is an excellent example of this concern with religion. In the introduction to this special issue of the *Psychotherapy Patient*, a journal of attribute-focused practice, editor Stern says that this issue "views the psycho-therapeutic process as a means of enhancing commitment rather than as a way of abrogating pain and discomfort" (xi). He further states that this issue "strives to make clear that religious commitment, as an attribute of many who seek psychiatric or psychological help, involves a special sort of urgency that prompts a willingness to invoke faith as a central healing modality" (xi).

Two additional volumes should also be cited here, namely, R. J. Lovinger's *Working with Religious Issues in Therapy* (1984) and M. H. Spero's (ed.) *Psychotherapy of the Religious Patient* (1985). Both were recently reviewed in *Contemporary Psychology* by Allen Bergin (1986, 85) who hails these volumes as marking "a turning point in the relationship between the field of professional psychotherapy and religion." Bergin commends them for taking religion "seriously as a potentially positive ingredient in personal change and adjustment, thus countering in a rigorous way the stigma associated with religiousness in much of the clinical literature" (85). It would seem, therefore, that clinical practitioners need to understand the helpful role that religion and religious values can play in psychotherapy. This psychological understanding of religion in psychopathology—and in normality—has become more essential than ever for mental health professionals. During the last few years religious thought and behavior seem to have emerged into the forefront of American cultural concerns. Several national surveys have demonstrated that the American people are admitting a more marked religious orientation. It is, therefore, important for our public to recognize that psychologists are concerned, too, about religion and religious behavior in human adjustment and development.

In my opinion, the psychology of religion as science does not seem to have progressed as well as the profession. Some, like Andrews (1979), have argued that the psychology of religion has been kept outside the gates of general psychology because it has not accepted the scientific paradigm and cannot speak the laboratory lingo. Certainly there is still some resistance to studying religion empirically, although this is probably more true of some religious orientations in the United States than of others. In Europe scientific studies in religious psychology seem to be more numerous. In the future the American psychology of religion needs to perfect and increase its research of religious behavior and experience. There is no dearth of issues and topics to be studied. Investigating religion scientifically, however, presents certain difficulties and complexities, as has been discussed elsewhere by Gorsuch (1984), McFarland (1984), and Arnold (1985). New improved methodologies for such experimentation and measurement, as well as sound theoretical perspectives, pose challenges for psychological investigators in this speciality.

It should also be pointed out that psychologists of religion, like ministers of religion, have tended to react slowly to studying the various contemporary social forces and changes which have been affecting individual behavior in modern society. Modernization has effected marked changes in traditional moral values and value systems relating to marriage, the family, sex, death, and even to religion itself, all of which are crucial to the well-being of the individual over the life span and for the stability of society. Many American psychologists have totally ignored religion's role in contemporary life and in human behavior today. Psychologists interested in religious issues should be leaders in demonstrating the significance of religious values at every stage of human development. We have not yet responded fully to society's urgent need for our expertise as scientists and practitioners in promoting human welfare.

On this 10th anniversary of Division 36, we, as psychologists interested in religious issues, might well rededicate ourselves to the objectives of our parent organization, the American Psychological Association, to advance psychology as a science, as a profession, and as a means of promoting human welfare. Our posture must be proactive and not simply reactive if we are to make our full contribution to those we serve and to American psychology and if our speciality is to be duly recognized by the year 2000. It is now time to include the psychology of religion in the education and training of psychologists!

References

Andrews, A. R. 1979. Religion, psychology, and science: Steps toward a wider psychology of religion. *Journal of Psychology and Theology* 7: 31–38.

Arnold, J. D. 1985. The psychology of religion: Placing paradigm in a historical and metatheoretical perspective. *American Psychologist* 40: 1060–62.

Bergin, A. E. 1986. Reviews of *Working with religious issues in therapy,* by R. J. Lovinger, and *Psychotherapy of the religious patient,* by M. H. Spero, ed. *Contemporary Psychology* 31: 85–87.

Gorsuch, R. L. 1984. Measurement: The boon and bane of investigating religion. *American Psychologist* 39: 228–36.

Gruender, H. 1922. *Psychology without a soul: A criticism.* 3d ed. St. Louis: Herder.

McDougall, W. 1934. *Religion and the sciences of life, with other essays on allied topics.* Durham, N.C.: Duke Univ. Press; London: Methuen.

McFarland, S. G. 1984. Psychology of religion: A call for a broader paradigm. *American Psychologist* 39: 321–34.

Misiak, H. and V. M. Staudt [Sexton]. 1954. *Catholics in psychology: A historical survey.* New York: McGraw-Hill.

Stern, E. M., ed. 1985. The religiously committed patient [Special issue]. *Psychotherapy Patient* 1, no. 3.

Strunk, O. 1970. Humanistic religious psychology: A new chapter in the psychology of religion. *Journal of Pastoral Care* 24: 90–97.

2

Hendrika Vande Kemp

Hendrika Vande Kemp is a professor in the Graduate School of Psychology at Fuller Theological Seminary, Pasadena, California. Professionally she has been particularly interested in the history of the psychology and religion interface and believes there is a rich historical heritage to be tapped for models of integration. Vande Kemp is listed in *The World Who's Who of Women, Outstanding Young Women in America, Who's Who in California, Who's Who in the West,* and the *Directory of Distinguished Americans,* among others.

Dr. Vande Kemp was the 1988–89 president of Division 36 of the American Psychological Association (APA), Psychologists Interested in Religious Issues. In the past she has been program chair and secretary-treasurer of this same division. She has also been secretary-treasurer of two other APA divisions: 24, Philosophical and Theoretical Psychology, and 26, History of Psychology. She is a fellow of both Divisions 26 and 36.

Dr. Vande Kemp has been a review editor for and frequent contributor to the *Journal of Psychology and Theology* and the *Journal of Psychology and Christianity.* She has reviewed articles for *Teaching of Psychology, American Psychologist, Journal for the Scientific Study of Religion,* and *Journal of the History of the Behavioral Sciences.* She collaborated with H. Newton Malony in editing *Psychology and Theology in Western Thought, 1672–1965: A Historical and Annotated Bibliography* (Millwood, N.Y.: Kraus International, 1984). Vande Kemp is coeditor with David G. Benner of a book series being published by Baker Book House, Explorations in Christian Psychology. Her first major contribution is an edited volume on family therapy, and she is currently completing a historical volume for the series.

45

In the article "An Early Attempt at Integration: The *Journal of Psychotherapy as a Religious Process*," Vande Kemp and Houskamp note that the interest in integrating theology and psychology has spawned a number of publications, not the least of which was the *Journal of Psychotherapy as a Religious Process*, which ceased publication in 1956 after only three years. They note the way in which the short-lived journal incorporated the best of the thinking of Otto Rank and included essays by such luminaries as Fritz Künkel, Paul Tournier, and Alphonse Maeder. The coauthors suggest that this journal, although it is seldom cited in bibliographies, provided seminal ideas for the burgeoning integration movement.

In "Dangers of Psychologism," Dr. Vande Kemp considers the philosophical underpinnings of psychotheological integration, specifically as it is represented in the motto "Christ in the heart of psychology." She suggests that while the thought conveyed by the motto might be commendable, the implications are troublesome. After analyzing the etymological history of the word *psychology,* she concludes by considering how the Christian psychologist might respond to the tension that exists between psychology and theology in a manner that does justice to both of them.

An Early Attempt at Integration:
The Journal of Psychotherapy
as a Religious Process

Man is born beyond psychology and he dies beyond it but he can
live beyond it only through vital experience of his own—in
religious terms, through revelation, conversion, or rebirth. (Rank
[1941] 1958, 14, 16)

T he integration of psychology and theology has emerged as a
strong specialty during the last two decades. With the founding of
the Graduate School of Psychology at Fuller Theological Seminary in 1964, the movement attained professional status, strengthened
by the later founding of the Rosemead Graduate School now at Biola
University and the Psychological Studies Institute in Atlanta. Like other
movements within psychology, integration led to the founding of a
number of journals. Primary among those surviving today are *Inward
Light: Journal of the Friends Conference on Religion and Psychology,*
founded in 1937; the *Journal of Religion and Health,* founded in 1961 by
the Institutes of Religion and Health; *Insight: Quarterly Review of
Religion and Mental Health,* founded in 1963 by the Franciscan, Fintan
McNamee; the *Journal of Psychology and Theology,* established by the
Rosemead Graduate School in 1973; the *Journal of Psychology and
Judaism,* launched in 1976 by the Center for the Study of Psychology
and Judaism, in Ottawa, Canada; and the *Journal of Psychology and
Christianity,* officially established in 1982 by the Christian Association
for Psychological Studies as an extension of its *Bulletin.* Two other sig-
nificant journals were published very briefly: *Psychotherapy: A Course*

Coauthored with Beth Houskamp. The authors are heavily indebted to the Reverend
William Rickel for his assistance. Many unacknowledged details of authorship and background were available exclusively in the nearly 200 pages of correspondence made available by Mr. Rickel. We are also indebted to David M. Wulff for background on G. P.
Zacharius.

   From the *Journal of Psychology and Theology* 14, no. 1 (1986): 3–14; reprinted by permission of the publisher and the authors. Copyright 1986 by Rosemead School of Psychology.

of Reading in Sound Psychology, Sound Medicine, and Sound Religion, a home-study course published by professionals associated with the Emmanuel Movement in 1908 and 1909; and the *Journal of Psychotherapy as a Religious Process* (referred to in this article as the *Journal*), published from 1954 through 1956 by the Institute for Rankian Psychoanalysis in Dayton, Ohio. The latter journal is the focus of this article.

The *Journal:* Its Origins and Founders

The *Journal of Psychotherapy as a Religious Process* was published by the Institute for Rankian Psychoanalysis, Inc., (IRP) in Dayton, Ohio. The Institute was incorporated as a nonprofit religious association on September 16, 1948, with its primary purpose the promotion of "a clearer understanding of the place of a sound and mature religion in the cure of emotional disturbances, and to indicate to the churches and ministers the place of Rankian insights and techniques in religion" (IRP 1948, 2). The Institute was Christian in its orientation, as stated in the Articles of Incorporation: "The basic point of view concerning human nature and the world, as understood by the Institute, is set forth *in part* in a book entitled *Beyond Psychology* and written by Otto Rank; and the Institute believes these insights to be in accord with the fundamental beliefs of the New Testament and particularly of the letters of St. Paul" ("The Articles" 1954, 94; Rickel 1950, 3).

The Institute offered psychoanalysis, counseling, diagnostic services, free counseling to ministers, seminars, speakers, a radio program, and training in Rankian psychoanalysis (Rickel 1949, 1950, 1952). In 1952, plans began for the publication of a journal. The editorial staff of the journal consisted of the Institute staff: William Rickel, Doris Mode, and Prescott Vernon (the latter for only the first volume). Rickel, Institute director and *Journal* editor, was a 1934 Harvard graduate in philosophy and psychology. He took additional training at the New York School of Social Work (1934–35), the University of Pennsylvania Graduate School of Social Work (1937–39), and Colgate-Rochester Divinity School, earning a B.D. in 1945. Rev. Rickel originally went to Dayton to found a new Congregational church. His wife, Doris Mode, was a graduate of the University of Chicago (1928), the Pennsylvania School of Social and Health Work (1933), and the University of Pennsylvania, earning her M.S.W. in 1937. Prescott Vernon was a graduate of the University of Denver (1935) and its Graduate School of Social Work (1935–37). Rickel and Mode, through their studies at Pennsylvania, were influenced both by Rank himself and by his famed follower, Jessie Taft, who was Mode's analyst (Doris Mode, letter to Rudolf Ekstein, March 7, 1953). While Rank was a strong influence on this group, they later regretted the Rankian emphasis in their name. Rickel wrote, "We subsequently wished we had called it the Institute for Relationship Therapy" (letter to the author, May 15, 1984) and "The Institute ought to have had another name, perhaps such as the Institute of Psychotherapy as a Religious Process" (letter to the author, October 19, 1984). In a letter to Fritz Künkel (June 12, 1953), he wrote: "We feel our view derived not only from Rank but in a general way from the views of Ferenczi and Jung. Right now, I'd say we are just ourselves."

The *Journal:* Its Contributors

In retrospect, the contributors to Rickel's *Journal* represent an auspicious group of leaders in the integration of psychology and theology/religion. Fritz Künkel's (1954) article on "The Integration of Religion and Psychology" apparently constitutes the first usage of "integration" in this context. Künkel himself used the phrase "the Integration of Christianity and Psychology" to describe his work after 1943 (Fritz Künkel, letter to William Rickel, October 19, 1953). The *Pastoral Psychology* "man of the month" biography of Künkel stated that "his major interest, based upon his conviction that only the religiously oriented counselor can be of real help to his people, has been the integration of psychology and religion, and the development of training facilities for counselors and psychotherapists in a religious orientation" ("The man" 1953). Künkel, the founder of We-psychology, was originally brought to America from Germany by the Quaker Douglas Steere to participate in the Pendle Hill Summer School, and taught for a year at the Pacific School of Religion (Douglas Steere, personal communication, February 15, 1984). In September, 1949, the Fritz Künkel School of We-Psychology was established at the First Congregational Church, Los Angeles. Later, probably in 1952, he established the Counseling Center of the Foundation for the Advancement of Religious Psychology. Publicity for these efforts described Künkel as "the well-known Christian psychologist and author" ("Announcing the Inauguration" 1949, 3). The dust jacket for Künkel's *Character Growth Education* ([1931] 1938) described him as "the most famous man in the field of child religious therapy today."

Paul Tournier is known to virtually every contemporary Christian psychologist and psychologically minded layperson. He was connected with Geneva's Ecumenical Institute of the World Council of Churches which in 1953 sponsored a series of seminars on psychotherapy and pastoral psychology. Tournier's first integrative contribution, *A Doctor's Casebook in the Light of the Bible* ([1951] 1954), appeared in English shortly after his debut in the *Journal.* A second Swiss contributor was Charles Baudouin, Privat-Dozent at the University of Geneva and active participant in the Catholic integrative dialogue. Baudouin's approach reflected deep roots in both scholastic and Jungian psychology. From Zurich a paper was contributed by Alphonse Maeder, an analyst whose Christian commitment reflected the strong pietistic Lutheranism of the Oxford Group Way. His integrative views were most clearly expressed in *Ways to Psychic Health* ([1944] 1953).

Representing the "New Vienna School" was Igor Caruso, a Louvain-trained Catholic who was a frequent contributor to *Cross Currents* and founder of the Vienna Working-Circle [or Research Group] for Depth-Psychology. Caruso's *Existential Psychology* ([1952] 1964) is one of the clearest statements of a depth psychology incorporating the philosophy of personalism. Caruso claimed that the analyst "must in some way correspond to his patient's 'Christ-archetype'" (163). His student Wilfried Daim, who contributed three articles, has become well known for his *Depth Psychology and Salvation* ([1954] 1963).

Several Jungians contributed to the *Journal*. Martha Jaeger, who did her first analytic work with Otto Rank, was attracted to him "because he called his approach dynamic relationship therapy" (Jaeger 1954, 85). While Jaeger was not a prolific writer, she was for many years an active force in the Friends' Conference on Religion and Psychology, serving on its executive committee. Two other Jungian contributors were Sheila Moon and Elizabeth Boyden Howes, both still practicing in San Francisco. With Luella Sibbald, they were involved in the founding of the Guild for Psychological Studies (Guild 1973, 4), devoted to "bringing about an intersection between the life and teachings of Jesus (teachings about choice, self-awareness, religious consciousness of meaning, ways to find these), and depth psychology" (2). Howes, who had studied under Künkel in Berlin, cooperated with Künkel in starting a series of seminars in 1942 at The Pines in southern California. These were devoted to the study of H. B. Sharman's *Records of the Life of Jesus* (1917). Howes was also co-editor of the anthology *The Choice Is Always Ours* (Phillips, Howes, and Nixon [1948] 1960/1975.). Both Moon and Howes have continued to make integrative contributions, although not in the Christian tradition (cf. Howes 1971; Howes and Moon 1962, 1973; Moon 1970, 1972).

Other contributors reflect the many facets of the integrative task. A. Aspiotis, the founder of the Institute of Medical Psychology and Mental Hygiene in Athens, felt that contemporary persons "must be helped in facing their various psychic problems within the Christian conception of life. . . . Now the period of psychology 'without a soul' is over, and it is time for the *Christian Soul* to appear with its content, its struggles, its oppositions and with its solution and salvation" (1954, 65–66). Roberto Assagioli was director of the Institute for Psychosynthesis and founder of the psychosynthesis movement (cf. Assagioli [1965] 1971). Aleck Dodd was by the mid-1950s a psychologist in private practice. However, he had been heavily involved in clinical pastoral education (Dodd 1954, 41), was professor of pastoral theology at Bangor Theological Seminary (1937–45), and director of the Department of Pastoral Services of the Toledo Council of Churches (1945–49). He also served on the board of IRP. A final contributor was Beatrice Burch (pseudonym, Beebe), a client of Künkel's and later friend of John Sanford and others in the Jungian community.

Rickel also used the *Journal* for networking purposes, including some of his correspondence with European psychotherapists ("Letters" 1954), attempting to establish a directory of religious psychotherapists ("A directory" 1954), and publishing information on study groups in psychology and religion ("Study groups" 1956). The European corre-spondents included (in addition to those who published in the *Journal*) J. H. van den Berg, professor of pastoral psychology and psychotherapy at the University of Utrecht; and [Gerhard] Paulus Zacharius, a Greek Orthodox priest who taught at the C. G. Jung Institute in Zurich as well as the Institute for Psychotherapy at Stuttgart. With a special interest in liturgy, Zacharius published a book under the title *Psyche and Mys-terium: The Significance of C. G. Jung's Psychology for Christian Theology and Liturgy* (1954; translation mine).

The *Journal:* Its Contents

The psychological theory inspiring the work of Rickel and his col-leagues was strongly rooted in the work of Otto Rank, as has already been documented. Rank was at one time Freud's favored disciple. How-ever, his inclination toward the philosophical, the artistic, and the cre-ative in ordinary persons led him to reject Freud's biological theory of pathogenesis. Ultimately, Rank's disagreements with Freud led to an irreparable breach in their once intimate relationship, and Rank departed from the stifling psychoanalytic "inner circle." This bitter sep-aration eventually led to an internationally pervasive blackballing of Rank, forcing him out of psychoanalytic circles into the field of social work (for more detailed discussion of the Freud/Rank relationship, see Roazen [1971] 1976; Lieberman 1985). Most likely he influenced Rickel and Mode directly through his formal connection with the Pennsylvania School for Social Work and his frequent lectures at the New York School for Social Work. Rank's psychology provided Rickel, Mode, and Vernon with a conceptual framework for the exploration of human nature as religious and subjective, providing an emphasis upon persons as "souls" and "psyches," a recognition of the necessity of the creative element, and a focus on the importance of the will as an avenue for rebirth through suffering.

The intimate connection between theology and psychology was clear in Rickel's (1956) article on Rank and Niebuhr. Rickel notes that while there are differences in terminology, there are also striking similarities between Rank and Niebuhr. Though Rank considers Christianity a myth, both thinkers begin with the realization of struggle, both acknowledge a spiritual element "beyond reason," and both identify power as the means for overcoming the struggle. Rank defined neurosis as "the result of excessive control on the part of the individual's will over his own nature" (Rickel 1956, 82). Similarly, Niebuhr asserts that sin is "man seeking to overcome his insecurity by a will-to-power which overreaches the limits of human creatureliness" (83). Rickel's thesis centers on his theory that the psychologist and the theologian are speaking about the same element of human nature. Rank's psychological theories, seen through the spectacles of theology, become a valuable tool for the religious therapist, despite Rank's lack of commitment to Christianity.

Rickel and Mode went "beyond" Rank both in making a Christian commitment *and* applying his ideas to the psychotherapy process. Rickel states, for example (letter to H. J. Urban, March 4, 1954):

> We have "gone beyond" this book and Dr. Rank in both our ideas concerning human nature and our practice of psychotherapy. I think that Otto Rank, a Jew, in his posthumous book, *Beyond Psychology*, did come to recognize that spiritual nature of man's emotional problems, and asserted that the "ideology of St. Paul" was the only answer to man's fundamental need for rebirth. But he was just beginning to reach this insight, and did not correlate it too closely with the practice of psychotherapy but presented his thinking more as an explanation of "social psychology," the "mass movement," the thinking of the cultural group.

And to Fritz Künkel (letter, June 12, 1953): "As to Rank, perhaps *Beyond Psychology*, privately printed in 1941, represents those views of his which best suggest religious psychotherapy—he had not gotten to the outlook earlier than that, and the book actually did not come out until two years after his untimely death." Doris Mode, in her letter to Rudolf Ekstein (March 7, 1953) also states: "*Beyond Psychology*, Rank's last book, indicated the religious areas of therapy but I do not believe he ever put this into his practice—certainly not in my day, and certainly Taft never did." Martha Jaeger (1955) said of Rank: "He stood on the brink longing for the experience of direct relationship, inherent in the Christian gospel of love. . . . [and] remained caught where many Westerners are, in the duality of life, the extremity of the opposites. He envisioned psycho-therapy as a religious process, but in his last work he admits his limitation: . . . He had the longing for but not the faith in the uniting power of the Spirit" (51, 56–57). In retrospect, Rank's ambivalence is not clear. Goldwert (1985) concludes that Rank "engaged in a religious psychotherapy in the last years of his life" and "praised to the sky the role of Christianity in history" (175). And he adds,

> Rank thus landed in the lap of God and religion. . . . Rank, the creative personality in conflict, loneliness, financial distress, and illness, began to argue that one must live the divine through conversion rather than being palsied in arid psychologizing. Believing that rational psychology was but a transitory stage in human history, Rank found God as a permanent reference-point for a sad world in flux. (176)

While Rank had been the primary influence for Rickel and his colleagues, many other influences may be detected in the *Journal*. Rickel observed that "the theological outlook undergirding the psychological theories of these European practitioners has as its source and inspiration the thinking of Karl Barth and Søren Kierkegaarde [sic] . . ." ("Letters" 1954, 88). Additional strands of philosophical, theological, and psychological thought stemming from such diverse sources as Edmund Husserl, Martin Heidegger, Edward Spranger, Karl Jaspers, Jean Piaget, Jean-Paul Sartre, C. G. Jung, Freud, and Sandor Ferenczi also appear. Thus, the articles present a diversity of articulations of the integrative task applied to the psychotherapeutic enterprise. In many ways the *Journal* represented a microcosm of the dynamic dialogue that has characterized this task for the ensuing three decades.

Rickel and his colleagues were especially interested in Rank's rejection of the biological/scientific elements in Freud. Rickel claimed that

> Neurosis can be understood only as an illness in the divine part of the self, arising through a break between the self and God. . . . Hence any human intervention by parent, foster-parent, parent-surrogate, or psychotherapist must reach out to the spiritual forces locked in the recesses of the personality, and draw them back into bond with God. That is the essence of the spiritual experience of rebirth. This is the task of psychotherapy. . . . Hence no discipline or profession which in its rationalistic or naturalistic limitation conceives of neuroses in its own limited terms can provide an adequate cure of the sick person. . . . The universal solvent is love, not scientific knowledge, and that love is the love of God. Hence therapy becomes a religious endeavor. (Rickel et al. 1956, 39)

Several *Journal* contributors focused on the process of rebirth through a struggle within the therapeutic relationship. Thus, Mode asserts that "the relationship of love or acceptance offers a basic support while [the client] is breaking down the neurotic structure and then reintegrating and finding the real self" (1954, 62). Elsewhere she states: "I believe that a basic caring is the important element, so perhaps we have become more Ferenczian than Rankian" (letter to Rudolf Ekstein, March 7,

1953). This emphasis on caring is especially obvious in the "creative" contributions to the *Journal*. In his narrative poem, Rickel (1955) poignantly describes the patient's journey on the "endless long road . . . into the valley of the self" (83) in which the resistance and the healing are encountered in the relationship with the analyst, who is a representative of God:

> You hate me because in me you find no escape
> From knowing knowledge of the self
> . . . .
> No one can know the anguish and the pain;
> And behind the desire and the pain, a deeper desire
> For comfort and love and protecting arms
> . . . .
> Dare I to ask for the love that was denied me before?
> . . . .
> Well now it looks as though his story ends
> Once more renewing the comradeship of life,
> Finding in God's love life's asymptote. (87–93)

Beebe's (1955) short story is told from the perspective of a client whose Freudian analyst not only refuses to acknowledge her as a creative, potentially religious individual searching desperately for meaning, but also repudiates the potential for genuine relatedness and love. Implicit is her critique of the Freudian analyst who remains dispassionately detached while fostering total dependency in the client. Beebe and Rickel both appear to have been influenced by Ferenczi, whose departure from Freud lay in his emphasis on "redemption by love" (see de Forest [1954] 1983, 179). De Forest, in her book on Ferenczi's therapy, commented that his "therapeutic genius as 'love' and the process as 'redemption' casts light on the similarity of psychotherapeutic love to that love which permeates the Judeo-Christian faith" (179).

Moon (1956) analyzed the themes of redemption and rebirth as they were exemplified in the Navajo creation myth (see also Moon 1970). She defined "psychological or religious redemption" as "the act of recovering for oneself an essential value or values which one knows to be one's own, and which one also recognizes as having been lost" (1956, 55). The myth reveals the same truth revealed in religious psychotherapy: that all psychological movement involves a descent into the depths and the conflict of opposites; that the heart's understanding is more important than the mind's; that what has been repressed and ignored must be recovered and assimilated into the present; that fuller creation requires prior destruction (thus, reintegration involves prior disintegration); that new values must be gradually incorporated lest they be perceived as alien or intrusive; that God and humans are interdependent. Paradoxically, "only through darkness, chaos, the unformed, the difficult, can light come into being" (55), and "the one who leads them is he who carries the idea of future redemption, of the healing of the separation in the psyche of man" (67).

While the religious nature of therapy is clear in Moon's exposition, it is even more prominent in the psychosynthesis of Assagioli, who regarded spiritual development as involving "a drastic purification and a complete transmutation of all the normal and purely 'human' elements of the personality" (1956, 31). Because this transformation is so fundamental, each stage may be "accompanied by various nervous, emotional, and even mental troubles" (31). He describes a spiritual realization process involving five stages. First, the person becomes aware that life no longer has meaning; this awareness may intensify into feelings of emptiness and annihilation, the awakening of conscience, suicidal ideation, and psychasthenia. Second, the channel between the person and the soul is bridged by illumination and there is an "interior perception of the *reality* of the Spirit and its intimate association and penetration with the human soul" (36). During this stage, the greatest danger is the confusion of the human spirit and the Spirit, the "confusion between absolute and relative truth; between the personal and metaphysical planes" (37), which Jung has described as the failure to distinguish the god-imago and God (1974, 64–65). Third, the person exists in a "state of grace" (Assagioli 1956, 39), which gradually diminishes and often results in "fits of depression, of despair and temptation to suicide" (40), and a rejection of the vision. Fourth, there is a gradual transformation of the personality often experienced as a "double life" in the old and new states. Here, the person is constantly tempted to "assist" the "spiritual elements in the work of inner regeneration" (42) rather than trust the Spirit to take its course. Finally, there is "the dark night of the soul," a "mystical crucifixion" or "mystical death," which "has a specific and spiritual cause and a great spiritual purpose" (43). Assagioli differentiated between ordinary symptoms, having a regressive character and requiring a *personal* psychosynthesis, and marks of spiritual development, having a progressive character and requiring *spiritual* psychosynthesis. Burch (1956), in a short story, describes the first-stage spiritual crisis that must begin this process, signaling the redemption that is possible for the person who first experiences the loss of meaning in "substanceless suffering" (73).

The depth psychologists who contributed to the *Journal* offered a variety of descriptions of psychotherapy as a religious process. Künkel (1954) contrasted religious therapy as art and teleology with psychology as a natural science concerned with causes and effects. He regarded therapy as a form of character development requiring a "dynamic answer" which grows within the client. This required discussing "the client's relationship to life as a whole and to the power behind his life which is God" (7). He felt that God was at work in this developing of religious consciousness, but that "apologetics do not enter into religious psychology" (10). He acknowledged that the development of religious consciousness does not entail healing, and the person may still be left with "a thorn in the flesh" (101).

Wilfried Daim (1954, 1955, 1956) was especially interested in the role of the will in personality. The will, a fundamental dynamic principle "entelechially aiming towards God" (1954, 34), must struggle with the person's object of fixation, its *idol*. The task of psychotherapy is to remove the objects of fixation and break up the system of idols, a process of deliverance. Thus, "analysis serves in all cases of liquidation of consequences of the original sin" (37) and is similar to actual grace, which brings about "enlightening of the mind and strengthening of the will" (37). Daim continued his focus on "idolization" in his second article (1955), assuming that "the inadequate attitude toward God leads to the inadequate reaction to reality as a whole" (26). Exploring salvation phenomenologically, he examines five of its characteristics: that *from which* the person seeks salvation; the *what* which is to be saved; that *towards which* the longing for salvation is directed; that which comes *before;* and that *by which* salvation is effected. Paralleling Assagioli's distinction between personal and spiritual psychosynthesis, Daim distinguished between partial and total salvation: psychoanalysis at best can lead to partial salvation, while Jesus Christ brings total salvation. Finally, Daim (1956) examines the darkening of will and restricting of intellect (note the Thomistic categories) in the analysand/client, resulting in "a conflict between the true and the false center of the self" (103). Again, he resorts to his idea of false absolutes, or idols, as substitutes for God. The therapeutic goal then becomes freedom *from* idols and freedom *for* God.

Baudouin and Caruso both represented the Catholic personalist tradition in their contributions. Echoing Assagioli and others, Baudouin (1956) asserted that often "the neurosis, the perturbations of the character and the vicissitudes of the religious sentiment together form a connected scheme" (11). Acknowledging his affinity with Jung, he confirms the fact that the symbols involved in the (re)construction of the self "are identified many times with those of an unquestionable religious realization" (14). Perhaps of most significance is Baudouin's assertion that ultimately religious and mystical claims are irrepressible. While out of consciousness, "they continue their own subterranean life. Repressed religious facts achieve a *regression* to primitive and barbarous religious stages, and then give birth to explosions often disconcerting. . . . Or else they will lead to *substitute productions* very absurd but often quite perfidious" (15). Citing Rene Laforgue, he raises "the question of sickness substituted for God. . . . Innumerable human beings are consecrated to forms of unconscious religious practices which have superseded current religion" (15–16). Baudouin likened the treatment of neurosis to "a re-education of the spirit of community" (17), also frequently expressed by religious symbols. Regarding therapy as a holistic process, he concludes that there is a "singular relationship between the conclusions of psychological healing and those of spiritual aspiration" (29), involving a dialectic of "reconciliation with the self and search for communion" (22).

While Baudouin's personalism integrates Jungian psychology, Caruso's (1955) is existential in nature. He begins with a definition of the *person* as "not only the point of encounter of the individual with God (an abstract God!) *but the living and real symbol of all possible encounters between a concrete God and a concrete man*" (p. 4, Caruso's italics). The person "can be realized only if one knows the personal mystery of the Trinity and of the Incarnation of the Son of God insofar as He is man" (4). Aligning himself with Daim, who was his student, Caruso denounces the "spiritualistic propaganda" of Frankl's logotherapy (6), while acknowledging that symbols have ever-higher levels of meaning. Repeating a by-now familiar theme, he warns against the transformation of symbols, which reveal the person in time, into "hypostasis" or "personifications" (8). Rejecting the interpretation of psychoanalysis as a "secularized caricature of the sacrament of penance" (16), he regards it as "secularized contemplation" in which *"each stage is also progress, each complex is an attempt at solution, each symbol successful realization of the archetypal forms"* (17–18, Caruso's italics). Caruso concludes that neurosis is, in part, "a religious drama" and that consequently psychotherapy is a religious process as well as a form of psychological medicine (18). For Caruso, religious experience is a comprehension of the foundation of the symbolic content that penetrates all persons striving for *"a way of knowing more perfect than others"* (19, Caruso's italics). Highly critical of Gnosticism (which included the alleged psychologism of Jung) and its depreciation of "the transcendant order to a mythological *system*" (23), Caruso nevertheless asserts that access to this order could only be accomplished through a new birth under the guidance of a psychotherapist who avoids interpretations that are merely biogenetic or merely spiritual (which was his problem with Frankl).

The therapeutic relationship itself was a focus for several contributors. Paul Tournier (1954) dissects the therapist's role into four functions: catharsis, resulting in confession and the genuine conviction of sin; transference, leading to a reconnection with God; bringing into consciousness of secret motives, directing the person to God's forgiving grace; and the philosophic function of encouraging existential questions. The process may lead not to complete healing, but to acceptance of the inevitable suffering of life. Maeder (1955) also discusses the psychotherapist's role. He stresses the fact that true empathy and compassion can only ensue if the therapist's profession becomes a vocation, through reestablished contact with the depths (and heights) experienced by what Nouwen (1972) later described as "the wounded healer." Portraying the therapist's role in explicitly Christian terms, Maeder focuses on the need to be Christ-like in order for spiritual healing to take place. He argues that to achieve true empathy, analysts must "be ready to take part in both the lives and sufferings of their patients, making themselves responsible for them and willing to carry the burden of such responsibility" (Maeder 1955, 39). Thus, the grace of God is essential to healing, and the religious component links "doctor and patient to that superpersonal, transcendental court of appeal which invokes the Savior's help and effects the sufferer's return to health" (39).

Aleck Dodd (1954) also believed that "healing in psychotherapy comes largely through the relationship which develops between therapist and patient" (42). Reflecting the influence of both Rank and Rogers, Dodd regards therapy as a process of releasing growth, which "is the activity of God, the very presence of God" (45). Patient and therapist together approach God in a search for truth. The surrender of defenses offers preparation for the surrender to God, the "giving up of self-sufficiency and adopting the Will of God" (46). He notes that only a will that is free can be surrendered, and stresses the fact that lowered defenses involve "an acceptance or forgiveness of oneself which is an essential in being forgiven" (48). But ultimately "it is the responsibility of the psychotherapist to help the patient realize him as a human being like himself, and to see that the help he is receiving really comes not from the therapist but through that relationship from 'beyond'" (48). *Agape* is experienced by the client who is able to say, "I have a strong feeling and certitude that there is some gracious power outside myself that loves me and has accepted me" (Rickel 1956, 90). Thus, the therapist becomes the channel for Christ's grace, but not a substitute for Christ. As Rickel (1954a) puts it: "The therapist . . . embodies *pro tempore* the love of God, for which he becomes only the vehicle transporting [love and understanding] from Life to the ailing person" (107).

For the most part, these authors rejected Rogerian notions of unconditional acceptance. Howes pointed out the moral responsibility coinciding with therapeutic guidance and tackled the difficult questions of the *ethics of self-fulfillment* that often emerge in the therapeutic process. However, she asserted that many persons have been conditioned to equate the "right" with the rigidly socially acceptable. For them, therapy involves evaluating options and making decisions based upon an emerging self, independent of previous learning, and requiring the nondirective approach of the midwife. Howes (1954) concludes that "it is questionable whether without a real struggle in the realm of values, with its uncertainties and its risks, any self is really actualized and dynamically operative" (30).

The moral and ethical were regarded as intricately ingrained in psychotherapy as a religious process. As this creative, philosophical, spiritual process bores deeper to the core, the person is inevitably confronted with religious issues. Rickel (1954b) describes the therapeutic experience as involving "moral, ethical, and valuational experiences" (68) and being "at heart religious" (69). In reviewing a therapeutic experience, Rickel notes that it was "one of re-birth, and was entirely religious in nature, not only because the component parts were ethical, but also because it ended in eventual reunion with God" (83). The latter component reflects Rickel's belief that "evil has always been seen as a break in the relationship of the person to God" (83) and that "psychotherapy is a modern, self-conscious and directed method through which a person can re-establish" this connection (83–84). Elsewhere, he described the psychotherapy which leads "beyond this life into eternity" as "the neoorthodox psychotherapy" ("Letters" 1954, 88). To enable this transcendent process, the therapist must be a Christian: "It is faith ultimately rooted in God and his relationship to God: if he does not have such a relationship, he cannot live in a state of expectation with respect to his patient" (Rickel 1954b, 71).

Thus, the three-cornered relationship among patient, therapist, and God was repeatedly emphasized. Mode (1956), in her examination of miracles, asserted that "the miracle is the re-establishment of relationship to God, even though another human stirs this into being because he too has the same divine spark and is willing to use it in the interest of serving God—for the patient's release" (51–52). Psychotherapy is a religious process in which the real miracle is "the discovery that the problem, and *therefore the answer,* is within the spiritual self; that is, in an area *beyond* the natural rather than related to the changing of the external set of circumstances or limitations" (51). Thus, again, we see the emphasis on spiritual transformation, or rebirth.

The *Journal:* Its Legacy

The *Journal of Psychotherapy as a Religious Process* was published for three years, reaching a circulation of approximately 700, which included about 100 library subscriptions. The decision to give up the journal (in 1957) and liquidate the Institute (1959) involved several factors (William Rickel, letter to the author, October 1984): the staff was taxed by the burden of carrying on full-time therapeutic practice; there were no financial resources to support trainees; hostility towards non-medical therapists was high; and much of the material submitted to the *Journal* was Jungian, and would have transformed its basic nature.

While Rickel donated unsold copies of the *Journal* to libraries (the most recent to Fuller Theological Seminary's McAlister Library), it apparently had little impact on the literature. Lieberman's (1985) recent biography of Rank fails to mention the *Journal* or the Institute. The Otto Rank Association apparently did not subscribe to the *Journal* or note its significance (Anita J. Faatz, letter to the author, March 4, 1981). My own efforts to "research" the *Journal* led to nothing but dead ends for nearly two years. It is probably true, as Beatrice Burch wrote (letter to the author, September 1, 1983), that "the Rickels, like Fritz Künkel, were a little too far in the forefront of what is now a widespread acceptance of the integration of psychology and religion." Rickel himself observed (letter to the author, August 17, 1984) in reflecting on those individuals who were concerned with "the relation of therapy and religion" in the 1950s, that it was "more a matter of a few inspired individuals, everywhere in the world, who saw the light, tried to do something about it; and who faced either indifference or outright opposition, especially from the medical group—and I think in a large measure still do. Though of course, there are so many persons who do see the relevance of the spiritual dimensions of the human needs that the opposition is less significant."

The opposition identified by Rickel is perhaps an understatement: the group was criticized by the psychiatrists who opposed "lay analysis," by psychologists who on this issue supported the medical establishment, and by leaders in the pastoral counseling movement, which was itself split between those who emphasized pastoral theology (and thus regarded counseling as one of the pastor's many tasks) and those who were developing a private practice model of pastoral care (for a more extensive discussion of these conflicts, see Vande Kemp 1985). Thus, the seed for the process of integration planted by Rickel and his colleagues in the 1950s lay dormant while interprofessional struggles aimed at resolution. Three decades later we can see that this "good seed," well-watered and lovingly tended, has come to fruition—though surrounded by no less a wilderness of opposition. Those of us engaged in the struggle today can claim in this work a legacy of hope—and continued challenge.

References

Announcing the Inauguration of the Fritz Künkel School of We-Psychology. 1949. First Congregational Church, 553 Hoover Street, Los Angeles.

The Articles of Incorporation of Institute for Rankian Psychoanalysis, Inc. 1954. *Journal of Psychotherapy as a Religious Process* 1: 94–95.

Aspiotis, A. 1954. The delivering endeavor of psychotherapy. *Journal of Psychotherapy as a Religious Process* 1: 64–66.

Assagioli, R. 1956. Spiritual development and nervous disease. *Journal of Psychotherapy as a Religious Process* 3: 30–46. (Originally published in *Hibbert Journal*.)

———. [1965] 1971. *Psychosynthesis: A manual of principles and techniques.* [New York: Hobbs Dorman.] Reprint. New York: Viking.

Baudouin, C. 1956. Unity and communion. Trans. W. Rickel and D. Mode. *Journal of Psychotherapy as a Religious Process* 3: 6–29.

Beebe, B. 1955. Lot's wife—a short story. *Journal of Psychotherapy as a Religious Process* 2: 58–79.

Burch, B. 1956. On the way to Damascus—a short story. *Journal of Psychotherapy as a Religious Process* 3: 73–76.

Caruso, I. A. [1952] 1964. *Existential psychology: From analysis to synthesis.* Trans E. Krapf. London: Darton, Longman and Todd. (Original German edition published 1952.)

———. 1955. Personalistic psychoanalysis and symbolic knowledge. Trans W. Rickel and D. Mode. *Journal of Psychotherapy as a Religious Process* 2: 2–23.

Daim, W. 1954. Depth-psychology and grace. Trans C. Ernst. *Journal of Psychotherapy as a Religious Process* 1: 31–40.

———. [1954] 1963. *Depth psychology and salvation.* Trans. K. F. Reinhardt. New York: Unger. (Original German edition published 1954.)

———. 1955. On depth-psychology and salvation. *Journal of Psychotherapy as a Religious Process* 2: 24–37.

———. 1956. Depth-psychology and freedom. Trans. C. Ernst. *Journal of Psychotherapy as a Religious Process* 3: 92–109.

de Forest, I. [1954] 1983. *The leaven of love: A development of the psychoanalytic theory and technique of Sandor Ferenczi.* New York: Harper. Reprint.

A directory of religious psychotherapists. 1954. *Journal of Psychotherapy as a Religious Process* 1: 92–93.

Dodd, A. D. 1954. Relationship therapy as religious. *Journal of Psychotherapy as a Religious Process* 1: 41–51.

Goldwert, M. 1985. Otto Rank and man's urge to immortality. *Journal of the History of the Behavioral Sciences* 21: 169–77.

Guild for Psychological Studies. 1973. *After thirty years. The history and purpose of the Guild for Psychological Studies, Inc.* San Francisco.

Howes, E. B. 1954. The ethics of self-fulfillment. *Journal of Psychotherapy as a Religious Process* 1: 22–30.

———. 1971. *Intersection and beyond.* San Francisco: Guild for Psychological Studies.

Howes, E. B., and S. Moon, eds. 1962. *And a time to die. Mark Pelgrin.* Montreal: Contact Press.

———. 1973. *Man, the choice maker.* Philadelphia: Westminster.

Institute for Rankian Psychoanalysis (IRP). 1948. Brochure. 135 North Perry Street, Dayton.

Jaeger, M. 1954. Letter from Switzerland. *Journal of Psychotherapy as a Religious Process* 1: 85–86.

———. 1955. Reflections on the work of Jung and Rank. *Journal of Psychotherapy as a Religious Process* 2: 47–57.

Jung, C. G. 1974. *Dreams.* Bollingen Series, vol. 20. Trans. R. F. C. Hull. Princeton, N.J.: Princeton Univ. Press.

Künkel, F. [1931] 1938. *Character growth education.* Trans. B. Keppel-Compton and B. Druitt. Philadelphia: Lippincott. (Original German edition published 1931.)

———. 1954. The integration of religion and psychology. *Journal of Psychotherapy as a Religious Process* 1: 3–11.

Letters from European psychotherapists. 1954. *Journal of Psychotherapy as a Religious Process* 1: 87–91.

Lieberman, E. J. 1985. *Acts of will: The life and work of Otto Rank.* New York: Free Press.

Maeder, A. [1944] 1953. *Ways to psychic health: Brief therapy from the practice of a psychiatrist.* Trans. T. Lit. New York: Charles Scribner's Sons. (Original German edition published 1944.)

———. 1955. A new concept of the psychotherapist's role. Trans. S. H. Kubie. *Journal of Psychotherapy as a Religious Process* 2: 38–46.

The man of the month. Fritz Künkel. 1953. *Pastoral Psychology* 4, no. 33: 8.

Mode, D. 1954. The meaning of religious psychotherapy. *Journal of Psychotherapy as a Religious Process* 1: 52–63.

———. 1956. A psychoanalytic view of miracles. *Journal of Psychotherapy as a Religious Process* 3: 47–52.

Moon, S. 1956. Some aspects of redemption in the Navajo creation myth. *Journal of Psychotherapy as a Religious Process* 3: 53–72.

———. 1970. *A magic dwells.* Middletown, Conn.: Wesleyan Univ. Press.

———. 1972. *Joseph's son.* Francestown, N.H.: Golden Quill.

Nouwen, H. 1972. *The wounded healer. Ministry in contemporary society.* New York: Doubleday.

Phillips, D. B., E. B. Howes, and L. M. Nixon. [1948] 1960/1975. *The choice is always ours: An anthology on the religious way.* [New York: Richard R. Smith.] Reprint and abridgement. New York: Harper; Wheaton: Re-Quest.

Rank, O. [1941] 1958. *Beyond psychology.* [Philadelphia: privately published.] Reprint. New York: Dover.

Rickel, W. 1949. *The Rankian method of psychoanalysis for the cure of personality problems. Being the first annual report of the Institute for Rankian Psychoanalysis, Inc., Dayton, Ohio, September 16, 1948 to September 16, 1949.* Dayton: Institute for Rankian Psychoanalysis.

————. 1950. *Undertaking psychoanalysis. Being the second annual report of the Institute for Rankian Psychoanalysis, Inc., Dayton, Ohio, September 1, 1949 to September 1, 1950.* Dayton: Institute for Rankian Psychoanalysis.

————. 1952. *Achieving inner strength and freedom. Being the combined third and fourth annual reports of the Institute for Rankian Psychoanalysis, Inc., Dayton, Ohio, covering the period from September 1, 1950 to September 1, 1952.* Dayton: Institute for Rankian Psychoanalysis.

————. 1954a. Editorial. *Journal of Psychotherapy as a Religious Process* 1: 2, 96–108.

————. 1954b. Psychotherapy as moral growth. *Journal of Psychotherapy as a Religious Process* 1: 67–84.

————. 1955. The backward river—a poem. *Journal of Psychotherapy as a Religious Process* 2: 80–93.

————. 1956. Concepts of power in personality as seen by Otto Rank and Reinhold Niebuhr. *Journal of Psychotherapy as a Religious Process* 3: 77–91.

Rickel, W., P. Tillich, C. R. Wise, J. A. P. Millet, R. L. Dicks, and A. T. Boisen. 1956. Reader's Forum: Is psychotherapy a religious process? *Pastoral Psychology* 7, no. 62: 36–46.

Roazen, P. [1971] 1976. *Freud and his followers.* [New York: Knopf.] Reprint. New York: New American Library.

Sharman, H. B. 1917. *Records of the life of Jesus.* New York: Association Press/Doran.

Study groups in psychology and religion. 1956. *Journal of Psychotherapy as a Religious Process* 3: 110–11.

Tournier, P. [1951] 1954. *A doctor's casebook in the light of the Bible.* Trans. E. Hudson. New York: Harper and Row. (Original French edition published 1951.)

————. 1954. The frontier between psychotherapy and soul-healing. *Journal of Psychotherapy as a Religious Process* 1: 12–21.

Vande Kemp, H. 1985. Integration in the 1950s: The *Journal of Psychotherapy as a Religious Process.* Paper presented at the annual meeting of the American Academy of Religion, November, Anaheim.

Zacharius, G. P. 1954. *Psyche und Mysterium: Die Bedeutung der Psychologie C. G. Jungs für die christliche Theologie und Liturgie.* Zurich: Rascher Verlag.

Dangers of Psychologism:
The Place of God in Psychology

In the pages that follow, I articulate a philosophical stance towards the task of psychotheological integration. As a faculty member in the Graduate School of Psychology at Fuller Theological Seminary, I have committed myself to that school's distinctive task: "Its attempt to integrate [psychology and theology] in theory, research, and practice" (Fuller Theological Seminary 1985, 104). As a historian of psychology, I have also maintained this focus, exploring the historical roots of integration from a variety of perspectives. The direct impetus to these reflections were Morton Kelsey's (1985) John G. Finch lectures, "Christianity as Psychology." I responded, orally and in writing, to Dr. Kelsey's first lecture: "The Place of God in Psychology." My response to Dr. Kelsey's lectures ultimately challenged the implicit questions, "What has been the place of God in psychology, and what should it be?" The reasons for this will be detailed, but my reflections had another impetus as well: the symbol and motto recently adopted informally by the Graduate School of Psychology. While the official stationery of Fuller Theological Seminary symbolizes the school with a cross at the center of a maze (a metaphorically "lean" symbol certainly deserving of obsolescence), the new symbol unites the Christian cross and the Greek psi, and is framed with text, "Christ in the heart of psychology." While the sentiment expressed there is one few Christian psychologists would misunderstand, the philosophical assumptions are more troublesome, creating serious questions for the psychologist familiar with the recurring ontological and epistemological quandaries of our discipline. The latter, when examined more closely, have serious implications recognized by many psychologists of religion, and deserving reexamination by contemporary students of integration.

I am indebted to William R. Woodward of the University of New Hampshire for directing me to the 19th-century German sources on psychologism and to Richard N. Williams of Brigham Young University for clarifying issues in contemporary phenomenology.

From the *Journal of Psychology and Theology* 14, no. 1 (1986): 97–109; reprinted by permission of the publisher and the author. Copyright 1986 by Rosemead School of Psychology.

The Emerging Meaning of "Psychology"

This inquiry logically begins with an etymological history of the term *psychology*, which reflects its changing nature as a discipline. While the subject matter of psychology is very old, the term itself was coined only in the 16th century, probably by the Yugoslavian Marco Marulic shortly before 1524 (Boring 1966; see also Lapointe 1970, 1972; Vande Kemp 1980, 1983). Prior to the 16th century, studies of the soul were shared by metaphysics, logic, and physics. Psychology acquired independent status as one of three branches of pneumatology, the doctrine of spirits. These three branches reflected the three levels of spiritual beings, and consisted of natural theology *(theologia naturalis)*, angelography and demonology *(angelographia, daemonologia)*, and psychology *(psychologia)*. Later in the 16th century, Otto Casmann coined the term *anthropologia* for the science of persons, dividing it into *psychologia*, the science of the human mind, and *somatologia*, the science of the human body. Christian von Wolff created the subdivisions of "rational" and "empirical" psychology, which in turn were borrowed and elaborated by Kant. Within this framework, there was no place for God within psychology per se, but by definition there was such a place within the realm of pneumatology. Thus, integration would have implied a dialogue between the sciences of human and divine spirits.

Wolff's distinction between rational and empirical psychology emerged as historically critical, as it conceived two still identifiable traditions. Rational psychology was a strong component of the moral and mental philosophies of the 19th century, which "cradled psychology when it was still an infant, and reared it until it could support itself" (Roback 1952, 97; see also Brennan 1945; Fay 1939; Misiak and Staudt 1954). It remained a strong element in the Catholic psychologies of the late 19th and early 20th centuries, represented by such writers as Michael Maher (1890), Désiré Felicien Mercier (1902), Edward Barrett (1911, 1921, 1925a, 1925b), Owen Aloysius Hill (1921), Robert Brennan (1925, 1937, 1941), Edward F. Murphy (1933), James H. Hoban (1939), Mark A. Gaffney (1942), William P. Witcutt (1943, 1946), Thomas V. Moore (1944, 1948, 1959), Anna Terruwe (1959, 1960), Peter Dempsey (1950, 1956), and Joseph Donceel (1955). Rational, philosophical psychologies generally had room for God, as they were a part of a more general speculative framework with a heritage rooted in Thomistic philosophy. Empirical psychology, which led to the experimental psychology emerging in the mid-19th century, had little room for speculative categories of any kind, as Wundt's "new psychology" adopted the scientific methods and assumptions of biology and physics. Thus, "the term psychology gained currency precisely at the time when psychology was about to become anything but the 'study of the soul'" (Lapointe 1970, 645).

With these emerging distinctions in mind, it is especially interesting to scrutinize Kierkegaard's use of the term *psychology*. The earliest use, *Repetition: An Essay in Experimental Psychology* ([1843] 1941), appears to be a self-conscious alignment with the new observation-based psychology and a departure from the speculative tradition. The second use, *The Concept of Dread: A Simple Deliberation on Psychological Lines in the Direction of the Dogmatic Problem of Original Sin* ([1844] 1944), appears to incorporate both empirical psychology (in its study of angst, or dread, a mental-emotional state) and rational psychology (in its study of faith, a spiritual dimension). The third use, *The Sickness unto Death: A Christian Psychological Exposition for Edification and Awakening* ([1849] 1941), is consistent itself with other "Christian psychologies" which emerged as a reaction against the "new psychology" (see, for example, the section on biblical and Christian psychologies in Vande Kemp 1984, 55–60).

This emergence of Christian or biblical psychology was one fascinating manifestation of the denotative transformation of *psychology*. An 1879 encyclopedia defined *biblical psychology* as "a term lately applied to the doctrines of Holy Scriptures on the subject, especially as to the distinction between the rational and immortal soul in man (pneuma), and the animal, sensitive and affectionate spirit (psyche)" (McClintock and Strong 1879, 769). These biblical psychologies were in fact Christian anthropologies reaffirming the original definition of psychology, as if the Christian psychologists were attempting to hold onto the rational (spiritual) principle, refusing the temptation to become, in effect, *somatologia*. These Christians included God in their "psychology" because secular psychology had, in a sense, "lost its soul," a phenomenon observed and lamented by many 20th-century psychologists (see, for example, Gruender 1911; Kearney 1985; Vande Kemp 1982). But the real concern was that secular psychologists of the late 19th century refused to define psychology as a subdivision of pneumatology—a refusal also applying to most psychologists of the 20th century. We cannot reverse the course of history and restore psychology to its previous disciplinary locus by "placing God in psychology." We *can* ask, "How does our psychology interact with a Christian faith commitment?"

The Dangers of Psychologism

Historical Development of the Philosophical Problem of Psychologism

One reason for this conservative demarcation of the psychological domain is the fact that including God, or theology, *within* psychology has repeatedly resulted in the error of *psychologism*. This term was first coined in Germany in the early 19th century to denote "a philosophical position based entirely on psychology" (Abbagnano 1967, 520). Associated primarily with the anti-Hegelianism of Jakob Friedrich Fries (1783–1843) and Friedrich Eduard Beneke (1798–1854), it involved the assumption that introspection was the only instrument available for philosophical inquiry and that truth could only be established by "reducing it to the subjective elements of self-observation" (520). Since then, *psychologism* has taken on various epistemological and ontological connotations. John Dewey ([1902] 1957), who defined the term for Baldwin's *Dictionary of Philosophy and Psychology*, offered the following definitions (the first attributed to Brownson):

> (1) The theory that "the soul can think without any real object, or with an object furnished by itself . . . that man is both intelligent and intelligible in himself, suffices for his own intelligence, without any dependence on any objective reality" . . . . (2) The doctrine of Fries and Beneke . . . , which translates the critical examination of reason (of Kant) into terms of empirical psychology. (382)

Dewey's first definition, linking psychologism implicitly with metaphysical idealism, does not appear to have dominated these early discussions, although it was of some significance (it is assumed by Dummett [1973] and challenged by Sluga [1980] in their discussions of Frege). Vincenzo Gioberti, for example, "branded as psychologism all of modern philosophy from Descartes on, referring to the philosophical procedure that claimed to go from man (that is, from experience) to God and contrasting it with ontologism, the movement from God to man" (Abbagnano 1967, 520; the contrast between psychologism and ontologism is also explored by Morgan 1985).

Most of the early discussions focused primarily on the relationship between psychology and logic. The psychologist Howard C. Warren emphasized the more common denotations:

> 1. the view that psychology is the basis of philosophy and of the sciences concerned with mankind (i.e., art, social customs, language, politics, religion, etc); 2. the view that the principles of the normative sciences (logic, ethics, esthetics) are subjective and empirical in origin; 3. the view that psychology is the basis of all science. ("Psychologism" 1934, 216)

Primary attention in the philosophical literature has been focused on Warren's latter two definitions, which are interrelated but contrasted, respectively, with logicism and subjectivism. Thus, psychologism is "the theory that psychology is the foundation of philosophy, and that introspection is the primary method of philosophical enquiry" ("Psychologism" 1979, 272), involving the thesis "that the categories of psychology can be used appropriately in philosophical analysis" ("Psychologism" 1980, 466), and the denial of "any inner dynamic" of logic (Stewart and Mickunas 1974, 17). Psychologism as the opposite of logicism is usually regarded pejoratively, as "the mistake of assuming that philosophical concepts and problems can be reduced to and resolved by psychological analysis" ("Psychologism" 1981, 229) and as "the failure to distinguish between psychological treatment of the origin of our knowledge in an activity of thinking and the nonpsychological structure, quality, and veracity of the content of that knowledge" ("Psychologism" [1958] 1972, 353). In this version of psychologism, "the factors, with which the empirical psychology explains the origin of human cognition, as a subjective occurrence, are also determinative for the truth value and the objectivity of the cognition" ("Psychologism" 1981, 229). Psychology as subjectivism wants the psychological point of view, whether introspective or experimental methodologically, "to dominate the specific viewpoints of other human sciences" (Borel 1972, 67–68).

A number of philosophical writers can be identified as major protagonists in the psychologism-antipsychologism debates. While Descartes was criticized for his psychologism, Kant was attacked by Fries and Beneke for his (idealist) rejection of psychologism. John Stuart Mill was also the focus of much of the controversy. In *A System of Logic* he explicitly stated "that introspection is the only basis of the axioms of mathematics and the principles of logic" (Abbagnano 1967, 521); in later writings Mill made logic a subdivision of psychology. Mill and other British empiricists became the focus of Edmund Husserl's critique of psychologism: "The psychological theories of Locke and his successors serve as continued admonitions against 'psychologism,' against any use of psychology for transcendental purposes" (see Popper 1962, 323 n. 19). Husserl "warned against the tendency to 'psychologize the eidetic'—that is, to identify the essences, which are the authentic objects of knowledge, with the simultaneous consciousness of these essences" (cited in Abbagnano 1967, 521). Husserl's genetic phenomenology was offered as an alternative: "It shows how objectivity is relative to consciousness through tracing the development of judgements from pre-predicative experience . . . but affirms that consciousness *reveals* the objective" (Bolton 1979, 169). David Katz, a well-known phenomenological psychologist, also clearly decried psychologism, the "tendency to make psychology 'the' fundamental basis of all other sciences" ([1937] 1970, 36).

Other more recent philosophers of science have revealed additional facets of the complex problem of psychologism. Jean Piaget described psychologism as the tendency by logicians to appeal to intuition or other psychological factors. Piaget paralleled "'psychologism,' . . . used by logicians to refer to insufficiently formalized logical theories," with "logicism," used by psychologists "to refer to psychological theories insufficiently tested by experience" (1957, 2; see also Piaget 1971). These errors led Piaget "to interpolate between psychology and axiomatic logic a *tertium quid*, a 'psycho-logic' or logico-psychology, related to these in the same way as mathematical physics is related to pure mathematics and experimental physics" (Piaget 1957, 25). Michael Polanyi used Piaget's work to affirm the necessity of making "a distinction between *normative* and *factual* problems" (Borel 1972, 68); "Psychology cannot distinguish by itself between true and false inferences, and hence is blind to logical principles; but it can throw light on the conditions under which the understanding and operation of correct logico-mathematical reasoning may develop, and it may supply an explanation for errors in reasoning. Indeed, an error in reasoning can never be the subject of logical demonstration; it can be understood only by psychological observations which reveal its causes" (Polanyi [1958] 1964, 39). Piaget and Polanyi support a Kantian distinction, positing a developmental process and adding an awareness that psychological observation (except when it involves introspection) involves another person subject to all the possible (psychological) errors of "thinking."

Rudolf Carnap also added distinctions that severely limited the role of the psychologist. He defined psychologism, in the context of deductive logic, as an enquiry process "where the problems are of an objective nature but the descriptions by which the author intends to give a general characterization of the problems are framed in subjectivist, psychological terms (like thinking)" (Carnap 1962, 39). A "qualified psychologism" in deductive logic is reflected by those who "say that logic is concerned with correct or rational thinking" (41). In inductive logic the problem of psychologism centers around the concept of probability, which involves theorems (logical probability), natural "facts" (empirical probability), and degree of belief. The latter, which may take the form of contrasting a person's "actual" belief (subjective probability) with "rational" belief (based on logical and empirical probability), may be a legitimate concern for the psychologist.

For Karl Popper, psychologism was "the theory that society depends on the 'human nature' of its members" (1966, 84). Its followers try "to explain imperatives as expressions of emotions, norms as habits, and standards as points of view" (234). Popper, whose critique of psychologism is a major thrust in *The Open Society and Its Enemies*, accuses Mill of believing that "the study of society, in the last analysis, must be reducible to psychology; that the laws of historical development must be explicable in terms of *human nature*, of the 'laws of the mind,' and in particular, of its progressiveness . . . that sociology must in principle be reducible to social psychology" (1962, 88). Psychologism makes the error of assuming that all social phenomena and regularities must be reduced to psychological phenomena and laws.

Thus, *psychologism* denotes and connotes a variety of errors associated with psychologists' confusion concerning the limits of their discipline. As we shall see, psychologists of religion have been prone to these errors, which are also a strong temptation to the Christian psychologist attempting the task of integration.

Psychologism in the Psychology of Religion

Psychologism as a construct was readily incorporated into the psychology of religion literature, where it experienced subtle changes in both denotative and connotative meaning. Wesley R. Wells (1918) offered one of the clearest early discussions, still closely linked to the philosophical concerns of the mathematicians and logicians. Wells was concerned with religious belief and its relationship to truth, an inquiry involving a clear juxtaposition of psychological and logical constructs. He asserted that

> fundamentally truth is a logical matter in which only propositions, theories, hypotheses, *etc.*, are involved, while the finding of these propositions, or the attempt to find them, and to verify them, is wholly a psychological matter, of which truth and falsity may not properly be predicated. This distinction between logical and nonlogical matters, between propositions and beliefs, allows for a clear-cut distinction between the values of beliefs "subjectively" considered, and the truth of propositions objectively considered; and it conforms both to popular and scientific usage of the word "truth." (270–71)

Wells was concerned with two kinds of errors made by psychologists of religion: (a) the *pragmatic fallacy,* which "consists of the identification of the value with the truth of religious beliefs, and of the acceptance of those religious beliefs, as true which are held to have value" (Wells 1918, 488; see also Wells 1917) and is "committed by those who maintain that the emotional effect of a belief upon an individual, of the biological effect of a belief upon a race, is a criterion of the truth of the propositions believed" (1918, 271) and (b) the *fallacy of false attribution,* "attributing the religious experience, so-called, to 'higher,' supernatural forces in cases where the experience is merely physiological in source—where it is from 'below' and not from 'above'" (Wells 1918, 498). Both "errors" involved extending the psychological data to unwarranted ontological and theological assertions, a temptation encountered frequently by psychologists of religion.

The many types of psychologistic errors in the psychology of religion were reviewed at length by R. H. Thouless in 1923. He discussed Wells's "pragmatic fallacy" as a "reduction of religious dogma to wish-fulfillment" (265), an error committed by both pro- and antireligionists. The proreligious, popular theologian "uses the fact that particular doctrines of Christianity fulfill mental needs as evidence for their truth" (264). That the "transition from psychology to metaphysics is not always easy to recognize" (Grensted 1952, 4) and thus readily becomes seductive is illustrated in the following quotation from Grace Croll Stuart (1938), in which psychology is used for apologetic purposes despite the author's previous caveat:

> It is not the business of psychology as a science, or of psychotherapy as an art, to prove the existence of God, and it could not if it would. The judgment that admits it is a judgment of trust and not a judgment of knowledge. God is not, and cannot be, a scientific hypothesis. But science can describe conditions which take on a new meaning when they are interpreted in the light of a theistic philosophy. And one can at least ask whether a God of the nature of the Christian hypothesis—a God, that is, of whose nature is to love, and to be active and seeking in that love—"whose nature it is to live in the perpetual giving of himself"—could fulfill human need and human hunger in ways which human love, even in the utmost of its desire and activity, cannot do? Or to ask whether—for it is the same question—the belief in such a God might render human love powerful and effective where otherwise it were weak and unavailing? (155)

Wells's "fallacy of false attribution reiterates an ontological and metaphysical maxim originally known as [William of] "Occam's Razor," reminding scientists not to "multiply causes unnecessarily" (Robinson 1976, 154) and implying that "explanatory entities or factors are not to be increased beyond necessity" (Klein 1970, 155). During the early 20th century, Occam's Razor dominated American and British psychology in the form of "Lloyd Morgan's Canon" (or the Law of Parsimony), focused on the dangers of anthropomorphism in animal psychology. It was this principle that led the early behaviorists to exclude "consciousness" from psychology and to prefer operationism to introspection. And it was this principle that led many psychologists of religion (quite appropriately) to exclude the supernatural from their psychological explanations.

Thus, the antireligionist often made the serious error of reducing the phenomena of faith (and God) to "nothing but" one of a multitude of psychological processes. Josef Rudin ([1960] 1968) addressed himself to this group:

> It is also *psychologism* when all manifestations of scientific, artistic, social, political, and religious life are too rashly seen from a psychological slant or simply labeled according to a certain doctrine of neurosis. This psychologism in particular has made enemies for psychology in many fields . . . Psychologism becomes most embarrassing when it leads to

almost *systematic dilution* of all metaphysical realities. The reality of the soul is certainly important and fascinating, but physical and metaphysical realities are likewise certain and significant. Perhaps some psychologists are not sufficiently aware that even the process of "projection" often has, as precondition, objective bases that ought to be taken seriously. (177–78)[1]

Both the pro- and antireligionist commit the error of unwarranted movement from psychology to ontology, an error repeatedly flagged by the early psychologists of religion. Lawrence W. Grensted (1952), in discussing the complex role of the psychologist of religion, concluded that "ultimate questions about the real existence of the constituents of our experience, in their own right and apart from their setting in that experience, cannot be decided, or even discussed, by psychological methods. But many psychologists, Freud and some of the leaders of American Behaviorism in particular, do in fact make pronouncements on such matters with great assurance, and it is hardly possible to name a psychologist who does not make occasional excursions beyond his proper field" (3).

Similarly, Wilfred Lawson Jones (1937) warned that "it would be manifestly unfair to expect a psychological investigation to provide an arbitrament for theological or metaphysical controversies. Psychological facts, of themselves, can neither necessitate nor invalidate any particular theological or metaphysical proposition" (6). Gordon W. Allport (1950) also cautioned that he made "no assumptions and no denials regarding the claims of revealed religion. Writing as a scientist I am not entitled to do either" (xi). John Pitts (1928), echoing Wells, asserted that "psychology may *explain* the mental laws to which religious experiences conform, but it does not *create* those experiences; it may set forth the psychological aspects of religion, but it can pronounce no judgment on the question of the ultimate truth of religion" (8). The absurdity of the negative form of the unwarranted movement from psychology to ontology was highlighted in William McDougall's (1934) criticism of Freud's [alleged] position. McDougall agreed with Freud "that the nature of man is such that he develops religious beliefs. The fact is obvious. If it were not so, man would not acquire religion, no matter how true its doctrines nor how obvious the evidences of them" (9). But he felt that this was no more an argument against the validity of religion than was

1. Rudin's critique applies, of course, to many classic works in the psychology of religion, whose authors have repeatedly taken the liberty of psychologizing, and have been criticized just as repeatedly. Some prominent critiques of early secular psychologies of religion include Rashdall (1914), Ellis (1922), Balmforth (1923), Berman (1972), Wickham (1928), Yellowlees (1930), and Hughes (1942).

the human tendency to reason an argument against the existence of reasonableness or lawfulness.

William Boothby Selbie (1924) concluded that "the psychology of religion . . . does not aim at any metaphysical or transcendental explanations, though it may provide materials for them" (14). This recalls Wells's observation that the *finding* of propositions and statements of truth is a *psychological* task. That the *psychology* of religion is a legitimate and significant *adjunct* to theology and the philosophy of religion was poignantly asserted by Paul Pruyser (1968) in his comments on this debate:

> It is a perfectly psychological question to ask why and on what grounds some people answer the ontological question about their god vigorously and in the affirmative, why some deny it, and why a third group say that they do not know. Particularly since the matter cannot be decided logically, as even some theologians admit, the psychology of knowledge, like the sociology of knowledge, may have some important contributions to make. The ontological question with capital letters is one thing: but every individual's way of coming to grips with it is quite a different thing. (7)

The ever-present danger, however, is that we stop seeing the psychology of religion as an *adjunct* to the ontological and theological disciplines, elevating it to a "superior" status. This is psychologism in the tradition of Mill, relegating philosophy and theology to subdisciplinary status. From within the realm of neo-Jungian psychologists, James Hillman (1975) has exposed this form of psychologism to detailed criticism and analysis. By way of definition, he observed that "psychologism means *only* psychologizing, converting all things into psychology. Psychology then becomes the new queen and—by taking itself and its premises literally—becomes a new metaphysics. When the insights of psychologizing harden into systematic arguments, becoming solid and opaque and monocentric, we have the metaphysical position of psychologism; there is only one fundamental discipline and ultimate viewpoint, psychology" (133).

Hillman observed that psychologism involves losing "the distinction between the activity of seeing through and the specific ideas by means of which [one] sees . . . The problem here is the ancient one of hypostasizing an idea into a literal thing. However, this is more than slipshod thinking, for it is inherent in *eidos*, idea, itself . . . idea implies both the tool by which we see and the thing we see. Psychologizing is in danger when it forgets that literalism is inherent in the very notion of idea. Then we begin to see ideas rather than seeing by means of them" (141).

Hillman here echoes Husserl's concern with the "tendency to 'psychologize the eidetic,'" and suggests that psychology, by its very nature, may be extremely vulnerable to reification.[2] As related to the psychology of religion, this has been aptly described by Viktor Frankl ([1946] 1955):

> What the whole problem comes down to is the fallacy of *psychologism*, for such we must call the pseudoscientific procedure which presumes to analyze every act for its psychic origin, and on that basis to decree whether its content is valid or invalid. Such an attempt is doomed to failure from the start. It is philosophical dilettantism to rule out, for example, the existence of a divine being on the ground that the idea of God arose out of primitive man's fear of powerful natural forces. It is equally false to judge the worth of a work of art by the fact that the artist created it in, say, a psychotic phase of his life. . . . (17)[3]

Hillman and Frankl remind us, respectively, of the positive and negative movement from psychology to ontology. It is my belief that such psychologism is an inevitable consequence of attempting to place "Christ in the heart of psychology." In fact, the most blatant and unrecognized form of psychologism may be the Christian layperson's suspicion of secular psychology, which is grounded in the belief that psychology *does* have the power to make metaphysical assertions. Professionals, unfortunately, are equally susceptible to this seductive fallacy. Perhaps the most poignant example of this lies in the work of

2. The most familiar source on reification for psychologists is Berger and Luckmann (1966). They add additional power to the antipsychologism argument by stressing the fact that psychology itself is based on presuppositions (and is thus always speculative, even if it is an empirical psychology): "Put simply, psychology always presupposes cosmology" (175).

3. Frankl was very sensitive to the issue of psychologism and clearly differentiated its epistemological and metaphysical aspects:

If only for exploratory purposes, therefore, we must continue to maintain that psychotherapy as such is exceeding its scope in dealing with philosophical questions alone, as we have shown, the special categories of psychopathology–namely "health" and "sickness"—have no bearing on the truth or validity of ideas. Once psychotherapy ventures a judgment in this regard, it instantly falls into the error of psychologism. If, therefore, we want to combat the psychologistic deviations of existing psychotherapy and put a stop to their dangerous invasions, it is necessary to supplement psychotherapy by a new procedure. In the field of philosophy, psychologism has been overcome by the critical methods of phenomenology; in the field of psychotherapy, psychologism must be overcome by a method which we shall call LOGOTHERAPY.

To this logotherapy would be assigned the task we have described as "psychotherapy in spiritual terms." Logotherapy must SUPPLEMENT psychotherapy; that is, it must fill the void whose existence we have mentioned. By the use of logotherapy we are equipped to deal with philosophical questions within their own frame of references, and can embark on objective discussion of the spiritual distress of human beings suffering from psychic disturbances. (Frankl 1955, 17)

Carl Gustav Jung, which is often used to support the antireligionist argument. Jung himself explicitly tried to avoid this leap from psychology to ontology, as he made clear in his 1937 Terry lectures:

> I approach psychological matters from a scientific and not from a philosophical standpoint. In as much as religion has a very important psychological aspect, I am dealing with it from a purely empirical point of view, that is, I restrict myself to the observation of phenomena and I refrain from any application of metaphysical or philosophical considerations. I do not deny the validity of other considerations, but I cannot claim to be competent to apply them correctly. (1938, 2)[4]
>
> The second inevitable mistake is psychologism: if god is anything, he must be an illusion derived from certain motives, from fear, for instance, from will to power, or from repressed sexuality. These arguments are not new. (103)

While Jung here was implicitly criticizing the (alleged) reductionism of Freud and Adler, he was equally suspicious of the positive versions of psychologism:

> It would be a regrettable mistake if anybody should understand my observations to be a kind of proof of the existence of God. They prove only the existence of an archetypal image of the Deity, which to my mind is the most we can assert psychologically about God. But it is a very important and influential archetype, its relatively frequent occurrence seems to be a noteworthy fact for any theologia naturalis. (73)

---

4. How vulnerable Jung was to accusations of "psychologism," despite his best efforts to avoid it, is especially clear in Buber (1952, 85–122). Igor Caruso ([1952] 1964) accuses Jung of "immanent psychologism" with "solipsist overtones" (100) and states that "Jung's complex psychology falters perceptibly only where the 'divine archetype' is concerned" (102). Caruso reveals his own tendency to psychologism (confusing psychology with ontology) when he quotes his student Wilfried Daim, who said: "we can but choose: either the life of the soul is meaningless, or there is psychological proof of God's existence" (102). Jung was interpreted quite differently by Victor White (1953), who states:
    It would take us too far away from our principal subject to discuss what may be called "pan-psychologism"—I mean the theory, more or less openly avowed, that religion, morality, indeed everything, is "nothing but" psychology, and which tends in practice to substitute psychological techniques for religion. It may be mentioned, incidentally, that pan-psychologism has been frequently and formally repudiated by C. G. Jung, and that it can easily be shown that it goes far beyond what is warranted by his own data and scientific postulates if they be rightly understood; but a certain tendency in this direction among some of his disciples, which can claim some measure of support from some of his own less careful writing, cannot easily be denied (147).
    Note how similar White's "pan-psychologism" is to "psychologism" as defined by Fries and Beneke.

Elaborating further on this in his book on dreams, Jung (1974) states:

> It is the fault of the everlasting contamination of object and imago that people can make no conceptual distinction between "God" and "God-image," and therefore think that when one speaks of the "God-image" one is speaking of God and offering "theological" explanations. It is not for psychology, as a science, to demand a hypostatization of the God-image. But the facts being what they are, it does have to reckon with the existence of a God-image. . . . It is equally clear that the God-image corresponds to a definite complex of psychological facts, and is thus a quantity which we can operate with; but what God is in himself remains a question outside the competence of all psychology. (64–65)

Freud apparently was also aware of the forementioned dangers of psychologism and tried to avoid them, a point stressed in Erich Fromm's Terry lectures:

> Freud himself states that the fact that an idea satisfies a wish does not mean *necessarily* that the idea is false. Since psychoanalysts have sometimes made this erroneous conclusion, I want to stress this remark of Freud's. Indeed, there are many true ideas as well as false ones which man has arrived at because he wishes his ideas to be true. . . . The criterion of validity does not lie in the psychological analysis of motivation but in the examination of evidence for or against a hypothesis within the logical framework of the hypothesis. (1950, 12n)

Fromm reminds us again of the psychologism/logicism distinction, and the subjectivist temptation to make psychology an arbiter of truth. He also hints at a related epistemological error to which Freud's metapsychology was extremely vulnerable, and against which every psychologist of religion must guard: "the psychologist's fallacy." This error was first described by William James, in the context of the introspective method, as "the *confusion of his own standpoint with that of the mental fact* about which he is making his report" ([1890] 1950, 196; note the similarity to what E. B. Titchener later terms the "stimulus error"). Thus, one may read into other minds what is true of one's own (as in anthropomorphizing; Baldwin [1902] 1957, 382), or attribute "to a mental process all the characteristics which seem . . . to be logically necessary from [one's] knowledge of the relations of the process" ("Psychologism" 1934, 216; this also raises the age-old question of "other minds"). Here, the psychologist is involved, not in the movement from psychology to ontology, but in a subjectivism that assumes self-knowledge is sufficient for the understanding of others. Allport deplored this tendency in psychologists of religion, referring to those writers who are "essentially autobiographical and unconsciously project their own del-

icate states of religious sensitivity upon all mankind" (1950, 5). Otto
Rank felt that this error was inevitable, attributing it to an inherent
dualism in the discipline of psychology: "the difference between psychology as self-knowledge and as a way of knowing others, or between
psychology as a doctrine of self-awareness and as a 'technique' for
understanding and controlling others" ([1930] 1950, 2). Rank felt that
objectivity was impossible, that psychology was at best "an interpretation of the attitude of the individual self, which we project on others
through the medium of so-called subjective psychology. Psychology is
an interpretation of self in others . . ." (195).

James's functionalism, Watson's behaviorism, and later experimental,
nomothetic approaches served as correctives to the psychologist's fallacy, but these approaches have themselves repeatedly succumbed to
other forms of psychologism. Thus, this error lurks everywhere for the
psychologist of religion not attuned to its ramifications. What, then,
should be the response of the Christian psychologist?

Psychology Practiced by the Committed Christian

Ultimately, the Christian psychologist is called to live with the same
tension and ambiguity that have haunted Christians for nearly two millennia: There is no "proof" for the existence of God that will forever
extinguish the seeds of doubt accompanying the leap of faith. Those
who want to "disprove" God will find through psychological analysis
innumerable plausible premises for their argument. Those who want to
"prove" the existence of God may, like Stuart and McDougall, find convincing evidence for human needs that can only be met if God exists.
Both groups, in very different ways, are reducing God to fit the categories of human understanding. Christian psychologists can do no
more than any other Christian: affirm the existence of God the Creator,
accept the redemption offered by Jesus Christ, and open our hearts to
the indwelling of the Holy Spirit. Given that affirmation, within the
context of a Christian worldview, we must pursue our work as psychologists with intellectual honesty and integrity true to our spiritual and
vocational calling and our professional training, and avoid the temptation to substitute for faith the intellectual pursuits of *either* psychology
or theology—for the latter is also an intellectual enterprise subject to
unique philosophical errors. We cannot look to our profession to alleviate the anguish of the leap of faith; nor can we expect from our professional pursuits affirmation for having made the leap. As psychologists
with "Christ in our hearts" and open to the process of sanctification,
our psychology will eventually be transformed into a Christian psychology, but as *psychology* it will have no power to "convict" others of
Christ. And those who are our clients and students must also be al-

lowed to evaluate psychology on its own merits, and taught to do so—a task in which the "maturity" of our own integration is of no small consequence. But they also must see that the leap of faith, while it may be psychologically understood, is fundamentally not a psychological matter; that Christian identity is a matter of ontology, not of psychology:

> Identity is not in what you do, no matter what you do,
>   nor how you feel about yourself, no matter how you feel
>   It's not a matter of psychology, it's a matter of theology
>
> . . . .
>
> God is not at the end of our searching;
>   it's "in the beginning, God."
> God calls you by your name
> not at the last but at the first,
> and from the beginning you're his "you."
> That identity you do not struggle toward or grope for,
>   You start with it
>   or not at all.
> If God is not Alpha he cannot be Omega,
>   If God is not in your premise,
>   he cannot be in your conclusion. . . .
> What havoc we play,
>   as by an unhappy human fallacy
>   we always put off to the end
>   what must be at the beginning
>   or it will not be at all. (Dykstra 1983, 6–8)

References

Abbagnano, N. 1967. Psychologism. In *The encyclopedia of philosophy*, ed. P. Edwards, trans. N. Langiulli, vol. 6, 520–21. New York: Macmillan.

Allport, G. W. 1950. *The individual and his religion: A psychological interpretation*. New York: Macmillan.

Baldwin, J. M. [1902] 1957. Psychologist's fallacy. In *Dictionary of philosophy and psychology*, ed. J. M. Baldwin, vol. 2, 382. Reprint. Gloucester, Mass.: Peter Smith.

Balmforth, H. 1923. *Is Christian experience an illusion? An essay in the philosophy of religion*. London: Student Christian Movement Press.

Barrett, E. J. B. 1911. *Motive-force and motivation tracks: A research in will psychology*. London: Longmans, Green.

———. 1921. *Psychoanalysis and Christian morality*. N.p.: Catholic Theological Society.

———. 1925a. *Man: His making and unmaking*. New York: T. Seltzer.

————. 1925b. *The new psychology: How it aids and interests.* New York: P. J. Kenedy.

Berger, P. L., and T. Luckmann. 1966. *The social construction of reality: A treatise in the sociology of knowledge.* New York: Doubleday.

Berman, L. 1927. *The religion called behaviorism.* New York: Boni and Liveright.

Bolton, N. 1979. Phenomenology and psychology. *In philosophical problems in psychology,* ed. N. Bolton, 158–75. London: Methuen.

Borel, M. J. 1972. Psychologism. In *Encyclopedia of psychology,* eds. H. J. Eysenck, W. Arnold, and R. Meili, 67–68. New York: Herder and Herder.

Boring, E. G. 1966. A note on the origin of the word psychology. *Journal of the History of the Behavioral Sciences* 2: 167.

Brennan, R. E. 1925. *Theory of abnormal cognitive processes according to St. Thomas Aquinas.* Washington, D.C.: Catholic Univ. of America.

————. 1937. *General psychology: An interpretation of the science of mind based on Thomas Aquinas.* New York: Macmillan.

————. 1941. *Thomistic psychology: A philosophic analysis of the nature of man.* New York: Macmillan.

————. 1945. *History of psychology from the standpoint of a Thomist.* New York: Macmillan.

Buber, M. 1952. *Eclipse of God: Studies in the relation between religion and philosophy.* New York: Harper.

Carnap, R. 1962. *Logical foundations of probability.* 2d ed. Chicago: Univ. of Chicago Press.

Caruso, I. A. [1952] 1964. *Existential psychology: From analysis to synthesis.* Trans. E. Krapf. London: Darton, Longman and Todd. (Original German edition published 1952.)

Dempsey, P. J. R. 1950. *The psychology of Sartre.* Westminster, England: Newman Press.

————. 1956. *Freud, psychoanalysis, Catholicism.* Chicago: H. Regnery.

Dewey, J. [1902] 1957. Psychologism. In *Dictionary of philosophy and psychology,* ed. J. M. Baldwin, vol. 2, 382. Reprint. Gloucester, Mass.: Peter Smith.

Donceel, J. F. 1955. *Philosophical psychology.* New York: Sheed and Ward.

Dummett, M. 1973. *Frege. The philosophy of language.* London: n.p.

Dykstra, D. I. 1983. *Who am I? And other sermons from Dimnent Memorial Chapel.* Holland, Mich.: Hope College.

Ellis, C. C. 1922. *The religion of religious psychology.* Philadelphia: S. S. Times.

Fay, J. W. 1939. *American psychology before William James.* New Brunswick, N.J.: Rutgers Univ. Press.

Frankl, V. [1946] 1955. *The doctor and the soul.* Trans. R. Winston and C. Winston. New York: Knopf. (Original German edition published 1946.)

Fromm, E. 1950. *Psychoanalysis and religion.* New Haven: Yale Univ. Press.

Fuller Theological Seminary. 1985. *Catalog for Fuller Theological Seminary. 1985–86.* Pasadena, Calif.

Gaffney, M. A. 1942. *The psychology of the interior senses.* St. Louis: Herder.

Grensted, L. W. 1952. *The psychology of religion.* London: Oxford Univ. Press.

Gruender, H. 1911. *Psychology without a soul: A criticism.* St. Louis: Herder.

Hill, O. A. 1921. *Psychology and natural theology.* New York: Macmillan.

Implicit in this title are the two subdivisions of pneumatology which are explicitly recognized as "two divisions of special metaphysics."

Hillman, J. 1975. *Re-visioning psychology.* New York: Harper and Row.

Hoban, J. H. 1939. *The Thomistic concept of person and some of its social implications.* Washington, D.C.: Catholic Univ. of America.

Hughes, T. H. 1942. *Psychology and religious truth.* London: George Allen and Unwin.

James, W. [1890] 1950. *The principles of psychology.* Vol. 1. Reprint. New York: Dover.

Jones, W. L. 1937. *A psychological study of religious conversion.* London: Epworth Press.

Jung, C. G. 1938. *Psychology and religion.* London: Oxford Univ. Press.

———. 1974. *Dreams.* Bollingen Series, vol. 20. Trans. R. F. C. Hull. Princeton, N.J.: Princeton Univ. Press.

Katz, D. [1937] 1970. Psychological needs. In *Human affairs,* eds. R. B. Cattell, J. Cohen, and R. M. W. Travers, 35–54. Reprint. Freeport, N.Y.: Books for Libraries.

Kearney, R. T. 1985. Psychology and the soul: An historical investigation. Ph.D. diss., Fuller Theological Seminary, Pasadena, Calif.

Kelsey, M. 1985. *Christianity as psychology: Psychology, philosophy, and the Christian faith.* Lectures presented at 15th annual John G. Finch Symposium on Christian Theology and the Human Sciences, January, Fuller Theological Seminary, Pasadena, Calif.

Kierkegaard, S. [1843] 1941. *Repetition: An essay in experimental psychology.* Trans. W. Lowrie. Princeton, N.J.: Princeton Univ. Press.

The original Danish version, published in 1843, uses the phrase *experimenterende Psychologi.*

———. [1844] 1944. *The concept of dread: A simple deliberation on psychological lines in the direction of the dogmatic problem of original sin.* Trans. W. Lowrie. Princeton, N.J.: Princeton Univ.

The original Danish version, published in 1844, uses the phrase *psychologiskpaapegende.*

———. [1849] 1941. *The sickness unto death: A Christian psychological exposition for edification and awakening.* Trans. W. Lowrie. Princeton, N.J.: Princeton Univ. Press.

The original Danish version, published in 1849, uses the phrase *christelig psychologisk.*

Klein, D. B. 1970. *A history of scientific psychology: Its origins and philosophical background.* New York: Basic.

Lapointe, F. H. 1970. Origin and evolution of the term "psychology." *American Psychologist* 25: 640–47.

————. 1972. Who originated the term "psychology"? *Journal of the History of the Behavioral Sciences* 8: 328–35.

McClintock, J., and J. Strong. 1879. *Cyclopaedia of biblical, theological, and ecclesiastical literature.* New York: Harper. 8:769.

McDougall, W. 1934. *Religion and the sciences of life, with other essays on allied topics.* London: Methuen.

Maher, M. 1890. *Psychology: Empirical and rational.* London: Longmans, Green.

Mercier, D. F. 1902. *The relation of experimental psychology to philosophy: Lecture delivered before the Royal Belgian Academy.* Trans. E. J. Wirth. New York: Benziger Brothers.

Misiak, H., and V. M. Staudt [Sexton]. 1954. *Catholics in psychology: A historical survey.* New York: McGraw-Hill.

Moore, T. V. 1944. *Personal mental hygiene.* New York: Grune.

————. 1948. *The driving forces of human nature and their adjustment: An introduction to the psychology and psychopathology of emotional behavior and volitional control.* New York: Grune.

————. 1959. *Heroic sanctity and insanity: An introduction to the spiritual life and mental hygiene.* New York: Grune.

Morgan, K. G. 1985. Intellect and will in psychology and theology in the nineteenth century. In *Anthropology revisited: Human nature and the absolute,* chair H. Vande Kemp. Symposium conducted for Division 26, The History of Psychology, at the meeting of the American Psychological Association, August, Los Angeles.

Murphy, E. F. 1933. *New psychology and old religion.* New York: Benziger Brothers.

As is implied in the title, Murphy emphasizes the close relationship between psychological and theological truths.

Piaget, J. 1957. *Logic and psychology.* New York: Basic.

————. 1971. *Psychology and epistemology.* Trans. A. Rosin. New York: Grossman.

Pitts, J. 1928. *Psychology and religion.* London: Kingsgate Press.

Polanyi, M. [1958] 1964. *Personal knowledge: Towards a post-critical philosophy.* Reprint. New York: Harper and Row.

Popper, K. R. 1962. *The open society and its enemies.* Vol. 2, *The high tide of prophecy: Hegel, Marx, and the aftermath.* New York: Harper and Row.

————. 1966. *The open society and its enemies.* Vol. 1, *The spell of Plato.* 5th ed. Princeton, N.J.: Princeton Univ. Press.

Pruyser, P. W. 1968. *A dynamic psychology of religion.* New York: Harper and Row.

Psychologism. 1934. In *Dictionary of psychology,* ed. H. C. Warren, 216. Boston: Houghton Mifflin.

Psychologism. [1958] 1972. In *New encyclopedia of philosophy,* ed. J. Grouten, trans. G. J. Steenbergen, ed. and rev. E. Van den Bossche, 353. Reprint. New York: Philosophical Library.

Psychologism. 1979. In *A dictionary of philosophy*, ed. A. Flew, 272. London: Pan Books.

Psychologism. 1980. In *Dictionary of philosophy and religion, Eastern and Western thought*, ed. W. L. Reese, 466–67. [No city given], N.J.: Humanities.

Psychologist's fallacy. 1934. In *Dictionary of psychology*, ed. H. C. Warren, 216–17. Boston: Houghton Mifflin.

Rank, O. 1950. *Psychology and the soul*. Trans. W. D. Turner. Philadelphia: Univ. of Pennsylvania Press. (Original German edition published 1930.)

Rashdall, H. 1914. *Is conscience an emotion? Three lectures on recent ethical theories*. Boston: Houghton Mifflin.

Roback, A. A. 1952. *History of American psychology*. New York: Library Publishers.

Robinson, D. N. 1976. *An intellectual history of psychology*. New York: Macmillan.

Rudin, J. [1960] 1968. *Psychotherapy and religion*. Trans. E. Reinecke and P. C. Bailey. Notre Dame, Ind., and London: Notre Dame Univ. Press. (Original German edition published 1960.)

Selbie, W. B. 1924. *The psychology of religion*. Oxford: Clarendon Press.

Sluga, H. D. 1980. *Gottlob Frege*. London: Routledge and Kegan Paul.

Stewart, D., and A. Mickunas. 1974. *Exploring phenomenology: A guide to the field and its literature*. Chicago: American Library Association.

Stuart, G. C. 1938. *The achievement of personality in the light of psychology and religion*. London: Student Christian Movement Press.

Terruwe, A. A. A. 1959. *Psychopathic personality and neurosis*. Trans. C. W. Baars and J. Aumann. New York: P. J. Kenedy. (Also published under the title *The priest and the sick in mind*. London: Burns and Oates.)

——. 1960. *The neurosis in the light of rational psychology*. Trans. C. W. Baars; ed. J. Aumann. New York: P. J. Kenedy.

Thouless, R. H. 1923. *An introduction to the psychology of religion*. Cambridge Univ. Press.

Vande Kemp, H. 1980. Origin and evolution of the term *psychology:* Addenda. *American Psychologist* 35: 774.

——. 1982. The tension between psychology and theology: An anthropological solution. *Journal of Psychology and Theology* 10: 205–11.

——. 1983. A note on the term "psychology" in English titles: Predecessors of Rauch. *Journal of the History of the Behavioral Sciences* 19: 185.

——. 1984. *Psychology and theology in Western thought, 1672–1965: A historical and annotated bibliography*. In collaboration with H. N. Malony. Bibliographies in the History of Psychology and Psychiatry: A Series. Millwood, N.Y.: Kraus International.

Wells, W. R. 1917. Two common fallacies in the logic of religion. *Journal of Philosophy, Psychology and the Scientific Methods* 14: 653–60.

——. 1918. On religious values: A rejoinder. *Journal of Philosophy, Psychology, and the Scientific Methods* 16: 270–71.

White, V. 1953. *God and the unconscious.* Chicago: H. Regnery.

Wickham, H. 1928. *The misbehaviorists: Pseudoscience and the modern temper.* New York: Dial.

Witcutt, W. P. 1943. *Catholic thought and modern psychology.* London: Burns, Oates and Washbourne.

————. 1946. *Blake: A psychological study.* London: Hollis and Carter.

Yellowlees, D. 1930. *Psychology's defence of the faith.* London: Student Christian Movement Press.

PART 2

Religious Experience

3

Ralph W. Hood, Jr.

R alph W. Hood, Jr., is professor of psychology at the University of Tennessee at Chattanooga. He began teaching at the university in 1970 and was recognized as Distinguished Psychology Professor in the late 1970s. Prior to this appointment, he taught at the University of South Dakota. His doctorate in social psychology was earned at the University of Nevada, where he was a half-time instructor during the late 1960s.

Dr. Hood's professional affiliations include the American Psychological Association (APA). In 1985 he received the William James Award from the APA's Division 36, Psychologists Interested in Religious Issues, for his contribution to the study of mysticism and for his numerous published research investigations in the psychology of religion. Prior to the award he had been elected a fellow by the association. In addition to the APA, Hood has been active in the Society for the Scientific Study of Religion (SSSR) and the Religious Research Association (RRA). He has been a consulting editor for journals published by these groups and has been a member of the council of the SSSR.

Hood has published more than 55 articles and given more than 35 presentations at professional meetings. A sample of the titles of his work attests to the breadth of his interest in psychology of religion: "The Social Psychology of Rural Religion," "Sin and Self in the Religious and Anti-religious Person," "Correlations between Reported Mystical Experience and Existential Psychological Health," "Forms of Religious Commitment and Intense Religious Experience," "Personality Correlates of the Report of Mystical Experience," "Social Psychology and Religious Fundamentalism," and "Empathy, Religious Orientation, and Social Desirability."

He was coauthor with Bernard Spilka and Richard L. Gorsuch of *The Psychology of Religion: An Empirical Approach* (Englewood Cliffs, N.J.: Prentice-Hall, 1985). This book is noteworthy for the reputation of its authors as well as for evidence from high-quality research used to support ideas. Hood's special contribution to the volume includes his analyses of religious experience in general and mystical experience in particular.

In his article "Religious Orientation and the Experience of Transcendence," Dr. Hood reports on a study in which persons who were very extrinsic and those who were very intrinsic in their religious orientation were questioned about their most significant personal experience. As predicted, persons who were categorized as intrinsic reported more experiences that were rated as transcendent than those who were categorized as extrinsic.

In his essay "Mysticism in the Psychology of Religion," Hood notes that mystical experiences have been of enduring interest to psychologists of religion, citing that researchers since the time of William James have regularly attempted to better understand these experiences. After noting current interest in and his support for measurement in the psychology of religion, Hood evaluates his own research of mysticism. Concluding that measurement per se is not sufficient to ensure truly meaningful research, he calls for a "methodological theism" that takes seriously religious claims to truth. Hood's suggestion that psychologists of religion must incorporate meaningful belief indicators in their research is noteworthy, as is his research, which shows the fruits of a narrow, well-defined subject of inquiry.

Religious Orientation
and the Experience of Transcendence

There is a recent well documented upsurge of interest in the psychological study of various altered forms of consciousness (Tart 1969). We see this reflected in the interests of "antipsychiatrists" such as Laing (1967) and Szasz (1961, 1970) in the nonpathological evaluation of states of consciousness, in the interests of a variety of researchers on the forms of consciousness produced by drugs (Featherstone and Simon 1959; Leary 1964; Pahnke and Richards 1966; Zaehner 1961), and in the interest of psychologists, theologians, and youth in non-Western thought (Murphy and Murphy 1968; Needleman 1972; Roszak 1969; Suzuki 1957; Watts 1961). It would appear then that interest in *experience* as opposed to mere behavior is being revived on a variety of levels, perhaps at least partially as a reaction to a narrow scientism (van Kaam 1966). Roszak has noted the point nicely:

> The exploration of the non-intellective powers assumes its greatest importance, not when the project becomes a free-for-all of pixilated dynamism, but when it becomes a critique of the scientific world view upon which the technocracy builds its citadel and in the shadow of which too many of the brightest splendors of our experience lie hidden. (1969, 83)

That such experiences lie hidden and are not eradicated is perhaps a testimony to a depth of human nature from which the potential for truly significant experience arises (Skorpen 1965). One such category of experience that has long been known is within the province of the mystic. Stace (1961) has done an excellent job in analyzing the phenomenological defining characteristics of mystical experiences. Of particular interest is his analysis of introvertive mystical experience which has as its unique defining characteristic a nontemporal, nonspatial, pure consciousness that is devoid of all content, including awareness of self. In addition this experience is also characterized by ineffability, paradoxi-

From the *Journal for the Scientific Study of Religion* 12 (1973): 441–48; reprinted by permission of the publisher and the author.

cality, sacredness, positive affect, and a sense of objectivity. Stace's analysis is consistent with other attempts to describe what is perhaps more generally termed an experience of transcendence (Johnson 1953; Otto 1960; Underhill 1955; Walker 1962). It also appears that this conceptualization of what we shall term *transcendent experience* is particularly relevant to recent empirical research concerned with identifying and measuring forms of religious experience.

Perhaps the most consistent effort to conceptualize and empirically identify experiential dimensions of religion has been that of Allport and his colleagues with respect to extrinsic and intrinsic religious orientation. Hunt and King (1971) have recently provided an excellent review of the development of these concepts over almost 20 years and their measurement problems in their currently operationalized form, the Religious Orientation Scale (ROS). In addition, Hood (1971) has demonstrated that the Intrinsic and Extrinsic subscales of the ROS cannot legitimately be combined to form a single scale, while Dittes (1971) has noted that the conceptualizations of intrinsic and extrinsic orientation are themselves confused and heavily loaded with value judgments. However, despite these problems the ROS continues to be a valuable research tool, especially when the Intrinsic and Extrinsic subscales are used as *independent* scales (Hood 1971; Hunt and King 1971; Dittes 1971).

At the conceptual level one important characteristic distinguishing between intrinsic and extrinsic religious orientation that has continued to be provocative is the definitional presumption that the intrinsically oriented person derives special experiential meanings from religion, something denied a utilitarian, extrinsically oriented counterpart. This presumption suggests a particular experiential awareness or consciousness characteristic of intrinsic persons (Allport 1960; Allport and Ross 1967). In several studies Hood (1970, 1971, 1972) has provided empirical data consistent with this presumption by consistently demonstrating a positive relationship between intrinsic religious orientation and reported religious experience. However, Hood measured religious experience by his "religious experience episodes measure" (REEM), which is essentially a paper-and-pencil instrument. This makes the relationship between presumed experiential states and intrinsic religious orientation less impressive since *both* variables are inferred from paper-and-pencil measures. Accordingly, the present study was designed to investigate the possibility of providing a more direct assessment of experiential religious states and their relationship to intrinsic and extrinsic religious orientations. The opportunity was provided by utilizing selective operationalized criteria of transcendent experiences modified from Stace's conceptualization of introvertive mysticism to directly assess significant personal experiences. The major intent was to relate such direct assessments to intrinsic and extrinsic religious orientation measured by appropriate independent use of Allport's Intrinsic and Extrinsic subscales (Hood 1971). The specific hypothesis tested was that groups of intrinsic religious persons would have more experiences codifiable as transcendent than would groups of extrinsic religious persons. This hypothesis is especially reasonable in light of the fact that several Intrinsic scale items specifically refer to experiential dimensions of religion, such as importance of meditation and awareness of the presence of God, that are likely to at least partially overlap our operationalization of the experience of transcendence. Support for this hypothesis would then provide important validation data for certain experiential assumptions Allport built into his definition of intrinsic religiosity and which are partially reflected in the Allport-Ross Intrinsic Scale.

Method

Subjects

The subjects were selected from 123 lower-division psychology students who volunteered to take Allport's Religious Orientation Scale during regularly scheduled classes in which the author was instructor. From these 123 subjects the 25 scoring highest on the Intrinsic subscale ($\overline{X}$ = 41.8, SD = 2.9) and the 25 scoring highest on the Extrinsic subscale ($\overline{X}$ = 49.2, SD = 3.7) were asked to volunteer for individual interviews which they were told would last approximately 1 hour and which would focus upon their most significant personal experience. Of the initial 25 intrinsic subjects scheduled for interview, four failed to show and one had her interview terminated due to emotional distress during the interview (in which she was describing the recent death of her brother). Of the 25 extrinsic subjects, three failed to show for their scheduled interview and one did not wish the interview to be recorded. Thus data were analyzed from 41 subjects (20 intrinsic, 21 extrinsic). The majority of subjects in both groups nominally identified themselves as fundamentalist Protestants.

Interviews

The actual interviews were conducted over a 3-week interval by a volunteer senior psychology student. The interviewer was unaware of the specific nature of the experiment and had no knowledge of subjects' intrinsic or extrinsic scores.

All 41 interviews were conducted in similar fashion and were tape-recorded with subjects' approval. Interviews varied in length from 20 to 75 minutes with an average length of approximately 35 minutes. Subjects were instructed that the interview was confidential and would only be heard by the author and his research assistants. They were told that the purpose of the study was to obtain a phenomenological classification system for personally significant experiences. Each subject was told that we were interested in a detailed description of his single most personal experience and was asked to think for a moment and then describe this experience in detail. The interviewer allowed the subject to explore his experience and was essentially nondirective until the subject exhausted his ability to describe his experience. At that point the interviewer prodded the subject further in terms of the five code categories used in this study, if they had not already been covered spontaneously by the subject. In addition, the interviewer obtained brief information as to the immediate antecedents of the experience and its immediate effects. In all cases the interviewer instructed the subject to focus upon the immediate nature of the experience itself and not on detailed personal interpretations. In cases where subjects talked about several experiences, the interviewer guided them to eventually focus upon the experience that was most significant, and in these cases only this experience was used for coding purposes. The interviewer was trained in 10 practice interview sessions. These practice interviews were not used in the data analysis, but excerpts were employed in training of the raters used to determine the reliability of our classification procedures for transcendent experiences.

Classification of Transcendent Nature of Subjects' Experience

The following five operational categories of the experience of transcendence were specified: ego quality, noetic quality, communicable quality, affective quality, and religious quality. These characteristics were basically derived from Stace's (1961, 41–133) criteria for introvertive mysticism with the exceptions that paradoxicality was excluded as a criterion of transcendence, since we found it could not be coded independently of other criteria, and the nontemporal, nonspatial criteria were excluded because in our opinion they are secondary defining characteristics of the transcendent experience. This is the case since an experience that is simply an awareness of an undifferentiated unity in which no sense of self is presented also necessarily lacks spatial and temporal parameters. All operational clarifications of the remaining five criteria are our own and do not always reflect complete agreement with Stace's own conceptualizations. Although it was not our primary intent, it appears that our operationalizations are quite compatible with transcendent experiences Christians are likely to report. Our operational categories are briefly presented in table 3.1.

The tape-recorded responses for each subject were judged by tallying each response indicative of one of the appropriate defining categories of transcendent experience. These tabulations were then summarized

Table 3.1

Interview Coding Categories

Operationalized Coding Criteria for the Experience of Transcendence

Transcendent Experience	**Nontranscendent Experience**

Ego Quality

Refers to the extent to which perception of the presence or absence of a sense of self is maintained during the experience.

Loss of self: The experience is in terms of maintaining consciousness but without consciousness of one's self. The experience is that of a void.	*Presence of self:* The experience is in terms of self that is continually maintained.

Noetic Quality

Refers to the extent to which the experience is perceived as affirming or revealing fundamental knowledge concerning reality.

Objective: The experience provides immediate, insightful knowledge concerning reality or affirms a previously held view of reality. The experience is characterized by an inner subjective certainty that its authority as a valid source of objective knowledge is beyond doubt.	*Subjective:* The experience is of a purely subjective nature indicating nothing valid concerning the nature of objective reality. The nature of the experience itself may not be doubted, but its authority as a valid source of objective knowledge is not entertained.

Communicable Quality

Refers to the extent to which the experience can be adequately expressed in words.

Incommunicable: The experience is characterized by ineffability. Statements about the experience are only indicative of the inherent impossibility of adequately communicating its true nature.	*Communicable:* The experience can be adequately described in words. Statements about the experience in fact adequately communicate its nature.

Affective Quality

Refers to the extent to which the experience is either emotionally positive or negative without regard to intensity.

Positive: The experience is in terms of positive affective states. These states may be joy, ecstasy, quietude, or peace but in all cases are positively experienced.	*Negative:* The experience is in terms of negative affective states. These states may be of fear, anxiety, depression, or despair but in all cases are negatively experienced.

Religious Quality

Refers to the extent to which the experience is perceived to be either sacred or profane.

Sacred: The experience is one of awe and reverence in the face of an engulfing mystery. The experience is perceived to transcend natural science categories.	*Profane:* The experience is within natural science categories. Nothing makes this experience, however significant, different *in kind* from other experiences.

and individual experiences were classified as either transcendent or nontranscendent on the basis of total tabulations across all five categories and for each category separately. The author served as rater for all interviews and was unaware of the intrinsic or extrinsic score of subjects prior to coding their interview.

Reliability

Three senior psychology students served as raters to determine the reliability of the classification procedure. Three training sessions of approximately 1 hour each were conducted in which the author's categories of transcendence were explained and illustrated with a variety of reading material and taped statements collected from the training interviews.

After subjects were familiar with the code categories 10 tapes were randomly selected from the completed 41 tapes and independently coded by these 3 raters. All raters were unaware of the intrinsic or extrinsic scores of the subjects interviewed in the tapes.

Interrater reliabilities were computed for each code category separately (ego, affective, communicable, noetic, and religious quality) and for the total category (transcendent vs. nontranscendent) after the fashion of Allen and Spilka (1967) in their study of committed and consensual religion. Agreement ranged from 92% for affective quality to 74% for ego quality. Agreement was 84% for the total category. Utilizing an analysis of variance technique the estimated reliability across categories was .87.

Results

The cross classification of intrinsic and extrinsic religious orientations by the presence or absence of transcendent experience is presented in table 3.2.

Examination of this table indicates significant differences for each category of the experience of transcendence as well as for the total. Inspection of table 3.2 also indicates that in all cases the difference between intrinsic and extrinsic subjects with respect to the code categories of the experience of transcendence as well as combined categories is in the predicted direction.

Discussion

These data clearly support the hypothesis that intrinsically oriented persons are more likely to have transcendent experiences than are extrinsically oriented persons. Each separate code category of the expe-

Table 3.2

Intrinsic and Extrinsic Religious Orientation and
Transcendent and Nontranscendent Experience Classification

Component	Intrinsic N = 20	Extrinsic N = 21	X2	Contingency Coefficient[1]
Total:				
Transcendent	15	3		
Nontranscendent	5	18	13.0***	.49
Ego Quality:				
Transcendent	14	3		
Nontranscendent	6	18	10.9***	.46
Noetic Quality:				
Transcendent	17	8		
Nontranscendent	3	13	7.6**	.39
Communicable Quality:				
Transcendent	19	4		
Nontranscendent	1	17	21.0***	.58
Active Quality:				
Transcendent	19	12		
Nontranscendent	1	9	6.0*	.36
Religious Quality:				
Transcendent	18	6		
Nontranscendent	2	15	13.8***	.56

[1]Upper limit of contingency coefficient = .71
*p<.02
**p<.01
***p<.001

rience of transcendence was more frequently represented in the most significant experience of intrinsically religious persons than in the most significant experience of extrinsically religious persons, as were these combined categories. These data are congruent with Allport's assertion that intrinsically oriented persons are likely to derive experiential benefits from their religious orientation and suggest that one specific benefit is in fact the experience of transcendence. To phrase this slightly differently, our data suggest that the most significant personal experiences of intrinsically religious persons are in fact transcendent experiences as operationally defined in this study. This interpretation is consistent with Allport's own assumption of unique experiential aspects of intrinsic religiosity and can thus be considered as at least partial validation of this assumption as operationalized in the Allport-Ross Intrinsic Scale. This interpretation also suggests the potential fruitfulness of analyzing the general concept of intrinsic orientation in terms of more specific measurable components (Hunt and King 1971). These data are also consistent with our previous research, utilizing other forms of measurement, indicating that intrinsically religious persons are more likely to report having significant religious experiences than are their extrinsically religious-oriented counterparts (Hood 1970, 1971, 1972). These data also support both Maslow's (1964) assertion that "peak experiences" and Laski's (1968) assertion that "ecstasies" are more common than previous research suggests and that their occurrence can be detected and studied outside of classically defined pathological syndromes.

However, cautious interpretation is required in view of the methodological limitations of our data. While intrinsic and extrinsic subjects did differentially distribute themselves within the category classifications as predicted, the level of measurement was essentially only nominal. This may have a tendency to accentuate differences among groups, especially groups selected for their extreme scores on the classification variables. More extensive research focusing upon more sophisticated levels of measurement among a wider range of subject types is certainly desirable.

The fact that intrinsically oriented persons do report significant personal experiences codifiable as experiences of transcendence is nevertheless most encouraging. It would appear that this great universal core of ultimate personal experiences (Stace 1961; Skorpen 1965) has not been eliminated even from "technocracy's children" (Roszak 1969). The determination of the exact parameters of this experience is a task that psychology must investigate with sympathetic methodologies. Certainly one must be patiently critical of persons who report an experience of ego loss that is simultaneously affectively positive and sacred, and that in addition provides them with objective knowledge claimed to be ineffable! As for the explanation for this paradoxical psychological phenomenon and its historical persistence, one must be modest. Currently, it appears that both God and the unconscious are the major contending explanatory possibilities, and it is at this sensitive interface that theologians, philosophers, and psychologists can benefit from sympathetic dialogue. Perhaps as May (1969, 407) has so nicely noted, the way to resolve—as opposed to solve—questions is to transform them by means of deeper and wider dimensions of consciousness. Somehow it seems that the study of trancendent experiences may be reflexive.

References

Allen, R. O., and B. Spilka. 1967. Committed and consensual religion: A specification of religion-prejudice relationships. *Journal for the Scientific Study of Religion* 6: 191–206.

Allport, G. W. 1960. *Personality and social encounter.* Boston: Beacon Press.

Allport, G. W., and J. M. Ross. 1967. Personal religious orientation and prejudice. *Journal of Personality and Social Psychology* 5: 432–43.

Dittes, J. E. 1971. Typing the typologies: Some parallels in the career of church-sect and extrinsic-intrinsic. *Journal for the Scientific Study of Religion* 4: 375–83.

Featherstone, R. M., and R. Simon, eds. 1959. *A pharmacologic approach to the study of the mind.* Springfield, Ill.: C. C. Thomas.

Hood, R. W., Jr. 1970. Religious orientation and the report of religious experience. *Journal for the Scientific Study of Religion* 9: 285–91. (1971)

———. 1971. A comparison of the Allport and Feagin scoring procedures for intrinsic/extrinsic religious orientation. *Journal for the Scientific Study of Religion* 10: 370–74.

———. 1972. Normative and motivational determinants of reported religious experience in two Baptist samples. *Review of Religious Research* 13: 192–96.

Hunt, R. A., and M. B. King. 1971. The intrinsic-extrinsic concept: A review and evaluation. *Journal for the Scientific Study of Religion* 10: 339–56.

Johnson, R. C. 1953. *The imprisoned splendor: An approach to reality based upon the significance of data drawn from the fields of natural science, psychical research, and mystical experience.* New York: Harper.

Laing, R. C. 1967. *The politics of experience.* New York: Ballantine.

Laski, M. 1968. *Ecstasy: A study of some secular and religious experiences.* New York: Greenwood.

Leary, T. 1964. The religious experience: Its production and interpretation. *Psychedelic Review* 1: 324–46.

Maslow, A. H. 1964. *Religions, values, and peak experiences.* Columbus: Ohio State Univ. Press.

May, R. 1969. *Love and will.* New York: Norton.

Murphy, G., and L. B. Murphy, eds. 1968. *Asian psychology.* New York: Basic.

Needleman, J. 1972. *The new religions.* Rev. ed. New York: Doubleday.

Otto, R. 1960. *Mysticism East and West.* Trans. B. L. Bracey and R. C. Payne. New York: Macmillan.

Pahnke, W. N., and W. A. Richards. 1966. Implications of LSD and experimental mysticism. *Journal of Religion and Health* 5: 175–208.

Roszak, T. 1969. The making of a counter culture. New York: Anchor.

Skorpen, E. 1965. The whole man. *Main Currents in Modern Thought* 22: 10–16.

Stace, W. T. 1961. *Mysticism and philosophy.* Philadelphia: Lippincott; London: Macmillan.

Suzuki, D. T. 1957. *Mysticism: Christian and Buddhist.* New York: Harper.

Szasz, T. S. 1961. *The myth of mental illness: Foundations of a theory of personal conduct.* New York: Hoeber-Harper.

———. 1970. *The manufacture of madness.* New York: Harper and Row.

Tart, C. T., ed. 1969. *Altered states of consciousness.* New York: Wiley.

Underhill, E. 1955. *Mysticism: A study of the nature and development of man's spiritual consciousness.* New York: Meridan.

van Kaam, A. 1966. *Existential foundations of psychology.* Pittsburgh: Duquesne Univ. Press.

Walker, K. 1962. *The conscious mind: A commentary on the mystics.* London: Rider.

Watts, A. W. 1961. *Psychotherapy East and West.* New York: Ballantine.

Zaehner, R. C. 1961. *Mysticism: sacred and profane, an inquiry into some varieties of praeternatural experiences.* New York: Galaxy Books.

Mysticism in the Psychology of Religion

Interest in mysticism has always been a central focus of the psychology of religion. Not surprisingly, the earliest investigators in psychology not only had an interest in religion, but wrote heavily on mysticism. Perhaps James ([1902] 1961, 329) put the issue most succintly when he stated, "In mystic states we both become one with the Absolute and we become aware of our oneness. This is the everlasting and triumphant mystical tradition, hardly altered by differences of clime or creed."

It comes as no surprise then that resurgence of interest in the psychology of religion provides a climate hospitable to the study of mysticism. Clearly my own efforts in the psychology of religion center primarily around mysticism. Yet if there has been a change from the earliest concerns with mysticism in the psychology of religion and present concerns, it is clearly focused upon issues of measurement. Recently Gorsuch (1984) has persuasively argued that the dominant paradigm in the contemporary psychology of religion is a measurement paradigm—one that operationalizes concepts of concern to the investigator and assesses them in a variety of methodological contexts, whether correlational, quasi-experimental, or even occasionally, true experimental designs. In this light, my own efforts to study mysticism illustrate Gorsuch's claim well. They also emphasize the distinction between contemporary research and the earliest work on mysticism. Since my own efforts in this area are reviewed in several readily available sources (Hood 1985; Hutch 1982; Spilka, Hood, and Gorsuch 1985; Preston 1984), I shall use this opportunity to attempt to assess the value of my own research in light of my concern with the psychology of religion in general. And while it may seem curious, given my own identification with the measurement paradigm, I want to express in this brief paper a concern with the too narrow focus upon measurement in the

From the *Journal of Psychology and Christianity* 5, no. 2 (1986): 32–37; reprinted by permission of the publisher and the author. Copyright 1986 by the Christian Association for Psychological Studies.

psychology of religion, divorced from theological considerations. I do this despite my strong agreement that measurement is essential in the psychology of religion. I merely want to insist that it be meaningful as well.

Promiscuous Empiricism

It has been more than a decade since Dittes, retiring as editor of the *Journal for the Scientific Study of Religion,* noted that much of the empirical psychology of religion was rooted in a "promiscuous empiricism" (1971, 393). By this he meant, among other things, that much of the empirical psychology of religion, while methodologically sound, reached essentially shallow conclusions. In the specific article in which Dittes (1971) made these comments, he was responding to an empirically adequate study (after all, Dittes as editor had accepted the study for publication) in which the perpetual claim that religion was related to "deprivation" was once again empirically tested. Dittes noted appropriately that the status of this claim was at least as old as the Old Testament itself and, given the proper choice of indices, could hardly fail to be "proven." Hence, despite the rigors of empirical investigation, the outcome is at best trivial and at worst uninformative.

I have kept Dittes's article filed in the back of my mind all these years and wonder about my own empirical research on mysticism in light of his charge of "promiscuous empiricism." Indeed, otherwise favorable comments on my own research have suggested a similar charge (Hutch 1982; Preston 1984). Put simply, has the empirical study of mysticism and religious experience truly been illuminating? If I were to answer that question in terms of my own research, the answer is less favorable. For example, much of my research can be summarized in terms of three major areas. First, intrinsic, devout persons are most likely to report religiously interpreted mystical experiences, and such experiences are not necessarily reported only by church committed persons, especially when the experiences are not religiously interpreted. Second, indicators of psychopathology, if unbiased, do not relate to mysticism. Third, various conditions trigger mystical experiences depending upon the beliefs of the persons involved. Perhaps this is a too brief summary of my work, but not all that unfair (e.g., Hood 1985). And yet, while I would argue that my research has been empirically sound, I am not as sure I can argue that it has been equally illuminating. Is this not, then, "promiscuous empiricism"? After all, if we do not know significantly more about mysticism after empirical research within the measurement paradigm, is measurement per se sufficient to provide truly meaningful research? The answer is clearly no.

If there is a hidden agenda in my empirical research efforts, it is in the careful measurement of reported mystical experiences derived from an explicit philosophical perspective. In all my studies of mysticism, I treat my measurement of mysticism as operational *indicators* and not as operational *definitions*. The distinction, simply put, is that operational indicators are always to be judged by their reasonableness in indicating some measurable aspects of a phenomenon, itself never directly assessed. This is to be distinguished from simple claims to operational definitions whereby the measurement is itself synonymous with the phenomenon. My own commitment to a conceptualization of mysticism, advocated most clearly by Stace (1961), is well documented. As such, two claims are implicit in my empirical research. First, interpretations of experience can be separated from experience itself, even though, paradoxically, no experience is uninterpreted. Second, mysticism is the fundamental experiential basis upon which religions ultimately rest. Succinctly summarized, I want to argue that mystical experience is a human universal variously confronted within and without religious traditions. As such, one can seek to empirically identify the report of mystical experience and its incorporation and structuring within various interpretative schemes. Indeed, I think contemporary concern with attribution theory is on the right track insofar as attributions are intepretative schemes rooted in certain experiences. Specifically with respect to mysticism, given my claim to its universality as a human characteristic, religions are inevitable as they form at least one major interpretative frame for understanding this experience. As Spilka, Shaver, and Kirkpatrick (1985) have recently noted, one reason religious attributions are made is that religions exist! To which I merely wish to add that the religions exist because of the necessity to adequately express people's inalienable mystical natures. If this is accepted, then I think the case can be made for an escape from "promiscuous empiricism" in a manner I tried to resist for a long time, but I think no longer wise. That is to say, the empirical study of religion must proceed under the guidance of a "methodological theism" (Hood 1985).

Methodological Theism

The case for a methodological theism cannot be totally made here, but is the direction I think the contemporary psychology of religion ought to take and the study of mysticism must take. In the simplest sense, methodological theism merely notes that religious claims to truth must be taken seriously and operational indicators formed that are theologically meaningful. It does not mean that one can "empirically test" a religion. Yet it does mean that if religions are claims to truth and are to be taken seriously, critical theory must incorporate theologically informed variables. The interface between theology and psychology is precisely in the former's guidance of relevant operational indices to be used by the latter.

Concluding Example

In a seldom-noted work, Bowker (1973) traces the various scientific claims to the origin of the sense of god and notes wryly that no investigator has really taken seriously that the origin of the sense of god might be God! This I think to be a perceptive point in many senses. I shall conclude, however, while focusing only upon one of these senses and using as my example Buber's telling criticism of Jung's psychology of religion. I do so, as I hope will be apparent, to illustrate how it is that empiricism can be more than promiscuous.

As is well known, Jung repeatedly argued that he was an empiricist. In his sense, this meant referring only to phenomena as they appeared to human consciousness (what perhaps loosely can be called a "phenomenological orientation"). As such, Jung rested securely in a curious interpretation of Kant—namely, that one could study appearances only (Kant's phenomena). For Jung this meant that all attributions to God have their origin purely in human mental processes. Yet as Buber rightly notes, such a claim is curious in that it equates for psychological purposes God with self as if self in the psychological sense was also God. As Buber notes correctly, this is gnosticism. Now I have no argument with Jung's gnostic commitments except insofar as he purports to thereby escape theological issues by claims to mere empiricism. As Buber also notes correctly, to equate the phenomena of religious and mystical experience as having origins only within human consciousness, as if such were mere phenomena in the Kantian sense, is erroneous. In Buber's (1952, 80) terse and telling criticism:

> It is thus unequivocally declared here that what the believer ascribes to God has its origin in his own soul. How this assertion is to be reconciled with Jung's assurance that he means by all this "approximately the same thing Kant meant when he called the thing in itself a 'purely negative, borderline concept'" is to me incomprehensible. Kant has explained that the things in themselves are not to be recognized through any categories because they are not phenomena, but are only to be conceived of as an unknown something. However, that that phenomenon, for example, which I call the tree before my window originates not in my meeting with an unknown something but in my own inner self Kant simply did not mean.

Buber's concern with Jung is relevant to my concerns suggested in this paper. Buber links religious experience to the reality of God and finds a psychology that ignores this reality incomplete. Would not theology suggest operational indicators from which a rigorous empirical psychology could be developed that Buber would find more adequate? If the psychology of religion is to be other than reductionistic with respect to theology, it can be neither a disguised theology nor a psychology devoid of theological influence. The distinction between the two is narrow yet essential.

Psychologists must entertain seriously claims to truth on the part of religions and incorporate theologically meaningful operational indicators in their empirical research. Theologically informed indicators mean that the psychology of religion can rise to critical theory and build upon empirical foundations rigorously substantiated from an empirical perspective, yet linked as indicators to the religious traditions within which their meaning resides. In this sense, the empirical study of mysticism will of necessity take a particular route in which specific experiences of mystical phenomena will gain their meaning and empirical validity from the traditions within which they are cultivated (Almond 1982). The study of mysticism will be no less empirical, but this empiricism will be of interest in illuminating and being illuminated by theologies which substantiated them. Put bluntly, psychologists will have to take the possibility of God more seriously as a truth claim if their research is to be meaningful in something other than a promiscuous sense. And that realm within which attributions to and about God are taken seriously as claims to truth is theology.

References

Almond, P. C. 1982. *Mystical experience and religious doctrine*. Berlin: Mouton.

Bowker, J. 1973. *The sense of God*. Oxford: Clarendon Press.

Buber, M. 1952. *Eclipse of God: Studies in the relation between religion and philosophy*. New York: Harper.

Dittes, J. E. 1971. Conceptual deprivation and statistical rigor. *Journal for the Scientific Study of Religion* 10: 393–95.

Gorsuch, R. L. 1984. Measurement: The boon and bane of investigating religion. *American Psychologist* 39: 228–36.

Hood, R. W., Jr. 1985. Mysticism. In *The sacred in a secular age*, ed. P. E. Hammond, 285–97. Berkeley and Los Angeles: Univ. of California Press.

Hutch, R. A. 1982. Are psychological studies of religion on the right track? *Religion* 12: 277–99.

James, W. [1902] 1961. *The varieties of religious experience: A study in human nature*. Reprint. London: Collins.

Preston, J. J. 1984. Empiricism and the phenomenology of religious experience. *Mentalities* 2: 10–20.

Spilka, B., R. W. Hood, Jr., and R. L. Gorsuch. 1985. *The psychology of religion: An empirical approach.* Englewood Cliffs, N.J.: Prentice-Hall. 175–98.

Spilka, B., P. Shaver, and L. A. Kirkpatrick. 1985. A general attribution theory for the psychology of religion. *Journal for the Scientific Study of Religion* 24: 1–20.

Stace, W. T. 1961. *Mysticism and philosophy.* Philadelphia: Lippincott; London: Macmillan.

4

Andre Godin

A ndre Godin, S.J., was born in Gembloux, Belgium, in 1915. He entered the Society of Jesus in 1933 and was ordained a Jesuit priest in 1946. Godin received his Ph.D. in philosophy from Brussels Central Jury (le Jury Central) in 1942, an M. A. in theology (License en Théologie) from the Jesuit Theologate at Leuven, Belgium, in 1947, and an M.A. in psychology from Fordham University in New York in 1951. Dr. Godin, a practicing psychotherapist, began his long and distinguished career as professor and writer at the Universita Gregoriana in Rome, where he taught educational and pastoral psychology from 1948 to 1956. Since 1968 he has been a visiting professor at this university and a visiting professor of psychology of religion at Universite Laval, Quebec, Canada. He is retired professor of psychology of religion at the Institute Superieur des Sciences Religieuses at Charleroi, Belgium. He continues to teach at Centre Universite (Charleroi) in the open faculty.

Dr. Godin has lectured widely in Europe and North America over the years, and has trained psychologists in Brussels for over 25 years. In 1957 he became a member of the Belgian Psycho-analytic Society. From 1955 to 1965 he was assistant editor of *Lumen Vitae;* from 1961 to 1975, editor of *Studies in Religious Psychology.* From 1960 until the present Godin has been secretary of the International Commission for the Scientific Psychology of Religion. In 1979, he was honored with the William James Award for his conceptual and theoretical contributions to the psychology of religion by Division 36, Psychologists Interested in Religious Issues, of the American Psychological Association. He is recognized as one of the world's leading authorities on psychology of religion.

Among Godin's publications are many books and articles. A sampling of his book titles follows: *The Psychological Dynamics of Religious Experience* (Birmingham, Ala.: Religious Education, 1985); *Death and Presence* (Brussels: International Center for Studies in Religious Education, 1972) *From Cry to Word* (1968), and *The Pastor as Counselor* (New York: Holt, Rinehart and Winston, 1965). His articles include "Psychologie de la mort" ("Psychology of death") in *Bulletin de la Societe de Thanatologie* (1987), "L'ecoute et le conseil" ("Listening and counseling in spiritual guidance") in *Initiation a la pratique de la theologie* (1988), "Quand le miracle fait defaut (San Gennaro, Naples, 1976)" ("When miracle fails [San Gennaro, Naples, 1976]") in *Journal de Psychologie* (1980), "Some Development Tasks in Christian Education" in M. P. Strommen's *Research on Religious Development* (1971), "Genetic Development of the Symbolic and Hermeneutic Function" in *Lumen Vitae* (1969), and "Transference in Pastoral Counseling" in *Theology Digest* (1961).

In the essay "One Religion Could Hide Another," Godin explores the question of how human wish fulfillment relates to religious experience. He notes the manner in which human wishes for safety, security, and special favor dominate in religion. He contrasts this with another type of religion, seen chiefly in Christianity, in which the issues are less what God can do for persons and more on what persons can do to promote the trinitarian project (kingdom of God) following the divine wishes as revealed in the New Testament. These two types of religion are seen by Godin as existing side by side and as interpenetrating each other. He calls for psychologists of religion to study these issues more scientifically.

As a practicing psychoanalyst on one hand and a professor of the scientific psychology of religion on the other, Godin has been confronted with some Freudian assertions: Religion is useful a) as a projection of wishful thinking b) leading to the idealization of historical founders (either Moses or Jesus) c) very often not open to a true sublimation with a complete acceptation of reality. Unlike most Christian scholars in this field, Godin is convinced that the question asked by Freud was and remains the true question, open perhaps to a different answer. For historical reasons, Freud has been "a good Jewish atheist," but he did not face the specific elements of the Christian revelation. Godin is also convinced that some prophetic utterances, attitudes, and practices of Jesus of Nazareth are psychologically quite distinct from wishful thinking. This distinguishes him from the Jewish tradition of the Sanhedrin—up to the point of being rejected and condemned to death. If psychologists want to study the concrete beliefs, attitudes, and praxis of Christian people today, they cannot do it without knowing at least *some* of these specific differences, which they have to rediscover using their own methods.

In his Nash lecture entitled "Some Psychological Dynamics in Religious Experience," Dr. Godin contrasts functional with revelational religion. He questions whether the general term *god* can be assumed to mean the same thing to every person who completes questionnaires given by psychologists of religion. Offering the same doubts about the term *experience,* Godin conceives it to include the whole gamut of human happenings, but to others it refers only to unexpected emotional events. His essay discusses many implications of these differences as seen in recent research.

One Religion Could Hide Another, or How Does Religion Talk to Desire?

In the first place the best scientific psychological studies on religion have not been precise about such concepts as God, religion, or even faith. Renouncing philosophical or theological definitions, they treat these concepts as empty categories, as words whose meanings would emerge and would be different from person to person. Thus, in approaching religious or nonreligious phenomena, researchers have not tried to understand or interpret them. However, they have discounted these manifestations (behavioral or verbal) as dynamics that were clearly psychic (conscious or unconscious), or eventually psychosocial.

Over the last 50 years, some works have produced methodologically valuable results. Recently, Batson and Ventis (1982), Deconchy (1980), Lerner (1980), Paloutzian (1983), and Vergote and Tamayo (1981) have published scientific volumes of great value, as can be seen in the creativity of their instrumental approach or in their critical reflection of presupposed theories. These efforts have achieved impact. The psychology of religion has found respect in the scientific field, as noted in an article that Gorsuch published in the *American Psychologist* (1984).

But aside from these major works, we frequently find more modest research works which are inspired by the same spirit. To this point these have been culturally limited to the North Atlantic (Germany and Sweden) and the Mediterranean basin—societies marked by a Judeo-Christian culture. It seemed to me that I discovered, while reading certain observations in these works, some unusual manifestations upon which researchers have seldom commented. Working in the midst of Christian, and later of Jewish, subgroups, researchers thought they were studying certain aspects of *one* religion but, without being very aware of it, they discovered at least *two*.

I don't wish to speak of the unlimited variety of positive or negative opinions about God found in the subjects or groups studied. I don't

From the *Journal of Psychology and Christianity* 5, no. 2 (1986): 32–37; reprinted by permission of publisher and author. Copyright 1986 by the Christian Association for Psychological Studies.

allude to *dimensions*—somewhat fundamental—on the basis of which certain people live their religion, practice their faith, speak profanely, or experience religion. Nor do I mean the double trend of living religion, for example, in the extrinsic or intrinsic mode (in the writing of Allport).

The duality meant in this article will give you some examples resulting from a psychic structure, sometimes unconscious but also apparent in some behavior or in reactions to some questionnaires. This duality can be found in each of four dimensions (rites, beliefs, creeds, and experiences) as well as in the double modality of extrinsic and intrinsic. It emanates from antinomies or dissonances (cognitive and affective) in the way to assimilate or to react to some fragments of an objective religion. These conflicting elements reveal a duality or deep divergences which are structural. They will appear to you, I hope, as they have to me, as soon as they are superimposed on certain results from published research. You will ask yourself what seems to me to be a psychologically obvious fact: How does this religion (established or taught) address desires in the person? And from what desires does religious experience come?

The Religion before the Desire

A religion presented in childhood, as part of a culture inheritance, causes a noticeable inside game that manifests a somewhat conflicting duality. The desires of children, youth, adults, and the aged possess certain symbolic elements from which they receive some satisfactions. It could mean linguistic fragments (God, Providence, resurrection), rituals (communion, confession, penitence), or history becoming mythical by idealization (the cross, the Virgin Mary, such and such saint). This functional assimilation, by the desire, constitutes a sensible separation within the observer who is somewhat knowledgeable about Christian symbols, whether or not he is a believer. Impoverishment? Distortion? Subversion? It is not up to the psychologist to judge. And if he's familiar with the New Testament and theology, he will have to particularly be on guard. Strong conviction in his judgments usually results from some degree of puritanism in the one that expresses it. For a psychologist, the reality can be seen, or be understood, from certain dimensions of desire.

Here are some examples of these discordances. They are taken from published research concerning believers or Christian groups. The limitations of this article do not allow me to completely describe the context of each study, as one can find the references in a recently translated volume (Godin 1985).

Some Interventions from God

The essential question regarding religious beliefs is, God acts in human affairs in a way that certain events can be attributed to him, but which ones and how?

Miraculous Eucharist

That morning two little girls were in Mass. Martha took communion. Paula didn't take communion. On the sidewalk outside of church, a speeding motorcyclist hit both of them. One is cut and hurt, the other is not. . . .

If you tell this story to 10 children from 7 to 9 years old well-versed in catechism, you will hear from certain children (more than half in the published research) that they knew immediately who was hurt (Paula) and who was not (Martha). This attribution of a protecting effect to the eucharistic communion is atonishing, since, according to all probability, it had never been taught to the children. It is psychologically the spontaneous product of a desire: the desire to be protected by God and joining that protection with taking the sacrament. This authorizes the psychologist to speak of a religious desire. But which God is in question?

Dissonance in the Desire

In the preceding example, undoubtedly the children do perceive a religious story without the Christian doctrine justifying or even suggesting such an interpretation. Yet it happens that some adults pray in a similar manner and ask, during the sacraments, for favors or change of course, to their advantage, intentionally attributing the result to God in case the wishes are met. There is then discord between hopeful religion lived consciously and the symbolic significance presented by the Christian religion (commemoration that reactualizes the making of bread and wine on the eve of the final night before the death of Jesus). Within this dissonance is found a deep interplay between the desire, even religious, of these believers and the desire of love, in the sharing of which, until his death, the Son expressed the love of the Father. This interplay, of which one pole is ignored or unknown, permits the "religious phenomenon" (psychologically considered) to exist by itself, to be built without a real meeting with another desire, specifically the Christian one. This verification of a broken symbolism is also part of the psychology of religion.

Providence versus Hazard

Putting aside divine action, there is a creative presence which sustains the cosmic and human universe (philosophical concepts or mystic accounts of many religions). Which human events, exterior or interior to the person, or most frequently considered as assigned to a divine responsibility? According to Gorsuch and Smith (1983), these are somewhat rare events, when the impact whether good or bad is very great and the cause is neither well known nor controllable. Most of these events can also be attributed to hazard (good or bad luck), or considered as results of chance. In the described situations (through a questionnaire), the attribution to God is very significantly related to beliefs stemming from a fundamental theology which states that the religious feeling is marked by God's proximity. On the contrary, attribution to chance is common in nonfundamentalists and in believers less likely to affirm this proximity of God. These results, while confirming others, suggest that at the simple level of vocabulary used some words such as *Providence* or *God* easily take the place of the word *chance*, which is evidently more charged with anxiety yet related to the human condition. The wish to escape hazard may support religion as much as it supports science.

Resurrection against Death

A word from the religious and Christian lexicon easily becomes another theme which lessens distressing effects. *Resurrection,* according to Christian significance, is a mystery, a hope, seen as a certitude for the believer. But this word assumes death. It doesn't suppress the character of broken dialogue communications if one is grieved or mourning. A brief study, preliminary to ongoing research, shows the evidence of separate answers to the simple question, According to you, is Jesus of Nazareth really dead? More often than not, Christians, that is, the practicing believers, respond no! In conversation, they even say that their answer is evident—since he is resurrected. The psychologically religious answer is seen as pious, but marked by a penchant to use one word to reduce the hard reality of a fact obviously bound to the human condition. The duality of dissonant inspirations is here even more clear, lessening or denying the real death of Jesus, the Son ("It is better that I leave you" [John 16:7]). In this way, the plain significance of the coming of the Holy Spirit ("If I do not leave, he will not come to you" [John 16:7]) is compromised or missed.

So, the idea of resurrection, similar to Providence, raises a reaction in human desire that takes possession of its own end. It exercises a vaguely protective function, which satisfies the religious desire of which the believer is aware and for which he is thankful to God. This psychological reflection lets us also understand that this religiosity exercises at the same time a defensive function against the reality of accidentally disastrous events or against the finality of death. The believer is not directly conscious of this defensive function, nor of the dissonance that he introduces into his own conception of the Spirit.

Supplemental Action of the Spirit
or the Experience of Humanity Receiving Love

A religious experience, as a product of desire looking for group satisfaction, interferes also with the idea that certain persons become Christians as a result of divine action. More specifically, they become Christians as a result of the Holy Spirit (among Christians of the charismatic family) encountering human behavior, which becomes interpreted and changed. The idea that God (or the Spirit) intervenes or supplements where man's action fails is naturally attractive in many religions and religious prayers. When Christianity is presented, or only perceived, as a revelation of divine love, without introducing more knowledge of the mystery of the Trinity according to its own adoptive wishes, it is likely to reinforce the idea of a personal action from God. It also favors, according to a more spiritual language, a conception of love where the stress flows easily towards a passive reception, towards a religion of inner happiness or towards forms of worship in which warm feelings are interpreted as an effect of the presence of the Holy Spirit.

Well then, the human religious feeling, so interlaced with desire, may be largely produced by a somewhat clever leadership in the conduct of meetings which ignore conflicting ideas. This was the case in many prayer groups in the beginning years of the renewal of the charismatic movement, before its rapid propagation. The fascination of the sects with this desire can be understood in this manner. However, it exists also as nostalgia or as an attraction in some churches which function according to an authoritative and simplified manner. They impose submission to some orthopraxis (moral, liturgical, and political) in a dependent climate that owes its origins more to the Old Testament than the New.

In the Netherlands and Germany, there have been some attempts to understand "the new religious movements"; see, for instance, the comparative approach by J. M. van der Lans ([1980] 1983). They were just studied from a bipolar perspective: the subjects were allured and converted by the need of submission, their free will becoming insensible to the sometimes vulgar manipulations, or totally to the contrary, the subjects were allured by an alternative need whereby the individual is himself active in the formation of his identity. Van der Lans, after noting that the passive model seems more convenient, found that the total acceptance of a guru is possible only when one renounces the ancient system of belief or when the previous model of identification was mainly Jesus. There is much to say psychologically about this and much research yet to be done on Jesus as a model of identification. Note, that when Jesus the Son is cut off from his Father's relationship, or from the Holy Spirit still to come who doesn't speak but gives man the power of speaking, Christian action in church can even become antisocial or violent.

Modifying Intervention or Modifying Identification

In Sweden, some research of great sensitivity showed two types of Christian psychological expectations. In some, the intervention of models (biblical people, or hagiography) is supposed to modify to people's benefit situations similar to those in which the historical heroes found themselves. But other people identify more with historical people and so receive from God (or from the saints) an inspiration by which they themselves modify the chain of events in their present situation (Wikström 1975). In Belgium, another researcher, in working more on "belief as a system of living relations," discovers a clear polarization between some people (more frequent in low economic groups) who strongly depend on obedience to the divine will and other people who emphasize identification with the person of Jesus Christ as the ideal example (Hutsebaut 1980).

These psychological expectations result in a desire to see ancient divine interventions repeat themselves or in a wish for peaceful submission without indentification with the ancient model. In the first two groups of each study mentioned, the desire stays fixed on a dependence, sometimes imaginatively fixed on an ancient model, sometimes abandoned in obedience to the divine will received from outside (directives of church, discernment accomplished by a spiritual director, and so on). On the contrary, in the two other groups of each study mentioned, personal activity is emphasized, either as inspiration orienting the action or as identification allowing the reactualizing of the attitudes of Jesus according to his Spirit.

The act of identification seems, then, psychologically crucial. How could it not be that for so long Christianity has presented itself as a gospel of love (brotherly adoption). In every loving union, is there not a progressive interior interaction of partially divergent wishes? A duality, partially conflicting, remains the source of desired love, even in agape love.

Application

1. Does God heal following a prayer we address to him? Fulfillment of religious wish: literal repetition of that on which Jesus' contemporaries waited. Miracle, yes. But sign of what?
2. The Christian (charismatic or not) is one who is invited to take things in his own hands. In Christian prayer groups, the healing ministry is mediated through knowledge of what Jesus said and did—*thaumaturgist* and prophet? Active digging from wish to some other desire that must be laboriously reactualized through touch and mistakes. Even without a miracle, the sign is shown.

The first attitude is religious. At Lourdes, it inspired the "Bureau of Verifications." It corresponds to the expectation of the majority of the crowds at Fatima and thaumaturgic places of pilgrimage. A divine action would be verified if doctors affirm that the modification is not medically explicable. It can be found outside of Christianity. It is shocking in some people's psychology to find this arbitrary God (this mother Mary), who sometimes heals and most of the time does not.

The second attitude, more specifically Christian, actually inspires the renewed charismatic trend, raises in each one the thaumaturge which is ignored: laying on of hands; saying, "Your faith has saved you"; and the looking to God for the result, whatever it may be!

The first attitude is religious. The second is in search of conforming to the Spirit, the only comforter. It's up to the theologian to judge, or to some churches' authorities to arbitrate. The psychologist will maintain that it is undoubtedly a duality of desires. Nothing less!

We must get to know better the origin and the structure of these two systems of desire, also their interaction in the resistance, the conflict, the alienation, and sometimes the rejection. In a clinical perspective, Freud surely posed certain problems, encumbered by his personal situation, which was not clearly elucidated. The analysis of results from some research helps us to discover them occasionally. A path seems opened which allows opposites to be brought back together. In a more scientific perspective (descriptive or even experimental), the question of the double system of desire can be seen in their effects and in their strictly psychological dynamic. This is true just as much for the ones that reject as for the ones that accept a prophetic religion, a religion of the Word announcing itself between desire and reality.

Summary and Prospective

One religion can hide another. This evidence progressed as I, a teacher of the psychology of religion, required myself to read numerous research studies. I consciously began from certain concepts of philosophy or theology acceptable to the interior of a religion. For example, in Christianity, it is supposed that the sacramental mentality (object of many works) is different from the magical mentality. So we build instruments of psychological research on the base of the polarity between two epistemologically distinct concepts, putting oneself in the service of the demand from the Christian point of view. Indeed, this corresponds to a problematic tradition in the catechism and in pastoral Christianity. These works remain valuable, eventually useful to already Christianized thought. But, conceived in this perspective, they do not allow a psychology of religion to be built from its own questions utilizing certain conceptual categories that already proved themselves in the profane domain. Thus, an attitude of "game" could find support with children (but also with certain adults) from some behavior that was sacramental and some that was magical. An equidistant concept of the spoken categories in a religious vocabulary (Christian in this example) would probably be promising and more creative with scientific instrumentality. And even regarding the responsibility of the churches, the results of such research would elucidate otherwise unclear situations and would help us understand them. Apart from all apologetics, it would be left to these authorities to discover the religious phenomenon, psychologically studied, in this new light.

Some apparently secular concepts have already been proposed: the "locus of control" (J. B. Rotter), religion "as a quest" (C. D. Batson), "belief" inferred from the behaviors (M. J. Lerner), "orthodoxy" protecting the social cohesion (J.-P. Deconchy). Those conceptualizations, epistemologically secular and equidistant from belief and unbelief, already have furnished works of great scientific rigor. Not dominated by the representatives of institutionalized churches, they could initially provoke some reticence to accept them. Over time it could be that the results might reveal themselves to be more complete and more durable than many others, by having immediately useful objectives. In vocational religious psychology, this has been validated. These psychometric efforts designed to discern non-religious determinants in numerous candidates actually appear less useful than the discovery of the major influence of the maternal figure on youths (boys or girls) in the making of the choice of a profession including celibacy. This dominant influence brought many negative effects. This knowledge has allowed authorities to correct this serious problem.

I attempted in this article to share with the reader my conviction that certain psychological observations confront us with two systems of desire in the origin of religious experience: the one of filled desire functionally assimilated by fragments of speech, of ritual conduct, of idealization of mystic heroes, while introducing some discrepancies in the relationship of the symbolism at stake, and the other desire, partially frustrated, forcing us to dig deeper, reacts by resistance, sometimes even repressed, comparable to what we establish at the birth of the bond of love.

In the volume entirely devoted to this question (Godin 1985), the structure of desires in a functional religion seems coherent. The all-powerful desire of the child magically transferred toward a god that would prolong it eventually would come from the anguish which is tied to hazard or to death, appeasement of fault idealization more than true sublimity. Superseding this structure, the coherence of inner symbolism directed towards the foundational words of a prophetic religion (Judaism, Christianity, Islam) is equally very strong: a kind of reality proposed to desire. Historically and socially, some dogmas and practices of institutional religion have tended to impose themselves as imperatives, by restraints, intimidations, and orthopraxis. They have not been presented as transitional procedures stemming from the loving inspiration of desires of the founder who these religions seek to emulate. In the case of Christianity, the proposal of an adoptive affiliation, which proclaims the unconditional pardon of sins, is based in a revelation of the mystery of the Trinity where the divine identity is the base of the union of all differences. The total aim in their saving activities is for the liberation of humanity from captivity to its own religious desires.

How does a religion speak, in fact, to religious desires? How do religious desires take possession of fragments of one religion to annul the embarrassing difference? These questions are not new. It seems to me that human sciences, psychology and also sociology and history, are now able to bring them closer via their own perspectives. Freud wrote that "a belief is an illusion when its motivation is predominantly the realization of a wish and so no heed is paid to the links of that belief with reality, just as an illusion itself does not seek confirmation in the real" (1927). As a Christian, it seems to me that this problem and the dynamic of the unconscious invite religious psychology to better understand the observable reactions between two religions and the manifested resistance in the inner game of desire and reality. But also it seems to me that all psychologists, even nonreligious ones, could become interested in the scientific approach to a tension (desire—reality) that has played such a great role in the history of humanity.

References

Batson, C. D., and W. L. Ventis. 1982. *The religious experience: A social-psychological perspective*. New York: Oxford Univ. Press.

Deconchy, J.-P. 1980. *Orthodoxie religieuse et sciences humanes*. Paris: Mouton.

Freud, S. 1927. *The future of an illusion.* Vienna: Internationaler Psychoanalytischer Verlag.

Godin, A. 1985. *The psychological dynamics of religious experience.* Trans. M. Turton. Birmingham, Ala.: Religious Education.

———. 1983. Meditation: A comparative and theoretical analysis. *The Annual Review for the Social Sciences* 6: 133–52. Original edition, 1980, *Religieuze ervaring en meditate (Religious experience and meditation).* Deventer: Van Loghum Slaterus.

Gorsuch, R. L. 1984. Measurement: The boon and bane of investigating religion. *American Psychologist* 39: 228–36.

Gorsuch, R. L., and C. S. Smith. 1983. Attribution of responsibility to God: An interaction of religious beliefs and outcomes. *Journal for the Psychology of Religion* 22: 340–52.

Hutsebaut, D. 1980. Belief as lived relations. *Psychologica Belgica* 20, no. 1: 33–47.

Lerner, M. J. 1980. *The belief in a just world: A fundamental delusion.* New York: Plenum.

Paloutzian, R. F. 1983. *Invitation to the psychology of religion.* Glenview, Ill.: Scott, Foresman.

van der Lans, J. M. 1977. Religious experience: An argument for a multi-disciplinary approach. *Annual Review of the Social Sciences of Religion* 1: 133–45.

Vergote, A., and A. Tamayo, eds. 1981. *The parental figures and the representation of God: A psychological and cross-cultural study.* The Hague and New York: Mouton.

Wikström, O. 1975. *Guds ledning.* Psychologia Religionum 4. Uppsala, Sweden: Acta Universitatis Upsaliensis.

Some Psychological Dynamics
in Religious Experience:
The Point of Resistance

In reading the fourth Nash lecture presented in 1981 by Arthur McGovern, professor of philosophy at the University of Detroit, I realized how tremendous is the honor of your invitation to speak this evening at Campion College. If Father McGovern wrote that he was "privileged for having been invited far from his native land" (1981, 1), how much more do I feel privileged for having been chosen among many European psychologists, including several Jesuits like Father Louis Beirnaert, who died last April in Paris,[1] and so invited to discover the wonderfully white snow of this autumn in Regina.

I

One day a friend of mine—let us call him George—asked me to tell him in a few words what was the most important discovery made by the psychology of religion since its beginnings 85 years ago,[2] a question,

From *Some Psychological Dynamics in Religious Experience: The Point of Resistance* (Regina: Campion College Press, 1985), 1–20; reprinted by permission of the publisher and the author. Copyright 1985 by Campion College Press.

1. Louis Beirnaert, who died in Paris on 21 April 1985, was born on 2 April 1906. His influence, as a pioneer on the frontier between psychoanalysis and the theology, has been great. From his numerous articles, an anthology of 30 among the best has been published under the title *Expérience chrétienne et psychologie* (1964).

2. Two different beginnings of the psychology of religion took place on the either sides of the North Atlantic with W. James and T. Flournoy. The former developed interviews describing the varieties of subjective religious experiences, and as such "he remains our giant and our despair" (Goodenough 1965, XI). Flournoy opened the way towards a more scientific approach to human religious manifestations with his basic principles in *Les principes de la psychologie religieuse* (1902). But it took more than 25 years before psychologists of religion started using for religion the same instrument of research (Thurstone, for instance) which had proved useful in studying psychological reactions in general—attitudes, semantics, and so forth—either empirically or experimentally. In recent years, a good example of an empirical design in presented by A. Vergote and A. Tamayo in the *Parental Figures and the Representation of God* (1981). An application of an experimental design has been presented and discussed by C. Daniel Batson in *The Religious Experience* (1982) and by J.-P. Deconchy in *Orthodoxie religieuse et sciences humaines* (1980).

118

as you see, typical of amateur students when they are in a hurry. "Well," I said, "since you (my old friend George) ask me that, I'll try to tell you in one sentence. Listen: the psychologists of religion have gradually discovered, but are not yet fully aware of it, that most people in the samples they have studied think that they have one religion (or perhaps that they are without or against such a thing as religion) while, in fact, they have (or they have missed or rejected) two religions, at least." At this point, George looked at me and said, "I don't understand." "Well," I said, "how much time do you give me to explain it?" "Three minutes," said George. "Thank you. Then listen to this story."

> That morning, two little girls went to mass. Paula did not take communion, Martha did. As they left the church, a motorcyclist mounted the pavement at speed and knocked both girls down. One was injured, the other escaped.[3]

"Well, if you tell that story individually to 50 seven- to nine-year-olds in a catechism class, you will find that a good half of them already know which one was injured (Paula) and which not (Martha). So a protective effect is being attributed to the taking of communion. This is an astonishing attribution, if you think about it, because the children have not been taught."

They are not taught, at least not in school, that the Eucharist protects against accidents, and they probably do not hear that kind of thing said in the family either. So where does the idea come from? I would say, like many psychologists, that this response is the product of a human desire, the desire to be protected against life's dangers, applied here to the sacramental encounter, which involves "God." This word obliges me, as a psychologist, to speak of a religious desire. But what God are we dealing with? A good question! So then you discover that you have here the trace of a religion that does not conform to that "revelational religion" (Christianity) that the children are being taught. The response can be considered as expressing a "functional religion" because it corresponds to the desire (to be protected) even if it diverges from the "revelational religion" as it is taught. You see, on reexamining certain results of observations, research, surveys and even systematic experimentation, we discover that there is not just one "religion" (that we have believed, since Allport, that we could study directly in its motivations or effects, according to a classic distinction) but maybe two. One of the two, at least, corresponds to human desires. The other not necessarily so. But if we are to discover that, we must bear in mind the question which is psychologically central: how does a religion (beliefs,

---

3. This story was a part of the method used in some old research but designed with quite a different purpose. Cf. Marthe and Godin (1965).

rites, sacred stories, or sacralized persons) speak to desire?[4] Do you understand?"

To this question George answered, "I am sorry: not really." "Well," I said, "how much time can you give me now?" George looked at his watch, seemed to hesitate a few seconds and said, "Fifty-five minutes." "All right," I said. "Let us try. But don't forget the key question (for a psychologist): how does a religion speak to desire?"

II

Methodologically, of course, I agree with several statements that are generally admitted by every scientifically minded psychologist of religion. *God* is a word very often used by so-called religious people and obviously figuring in the vocabulary of most established religions in the world (not all, however, Buddhism being a controversial case). Philosophically, *theos* (the Greek word for God or even the gods) is quite defendable. But concretely and historically, *Yahweh* or *Elohim* or *Adonai* are not the same reference when compared with the trinitarian inspiration which founded a revelational religion like Christianity. Psychologically, we must consider that God is an empty category so long as we do not know what it means to the people or groups under investigation or experimentation. I even wonder whether or not God is a good word to use in our questionnaires or other instruments of research. Religion is also only a word until we discover, by our own methods, how the core of its symbolic content relates to human wishes.

Belief obviously cannot pretend to be exclusively used in the matter of religion. Many religious unbelievers believe in something or in some fundamental values ("ultimate meaning" of life) like freedom, love, justice, and so on.

Psychology is not just a science of behavior (seen from the outside, as any good observer, possibly a sociologist, could do) but the science of the conduct of individuals or groups. Conduct is behavior plus its meaning, meaning being sometimes and in part conscious, but never totally. The psychologist of religion, perhaps more than in any other field of psychology, must be able to listen, and listen again to people or groups. If he is involved in some sort of language, instrumentally, he should take the greatest care not to introduce the very religious vocabulary he is supposed to be discovering from the people studied, starting

4. The central nature of the question, even in the sociology of religion, has been underlined by Jacques Maître in his "Psychoanalyse et sociologie religieuses" (1972): "L'emprise de la religion repose sur l'articulation entre le renforcement qu'elle procure aux idéologies des groupes les plus divers et le langage de désir qu'elle tient aux sujets individuels" (129).

from their own words. Many instruments or devices used in our field have failed to meet this epistemological prerequisite that should become clear later. Nevertheless, many researchers, although deficient in their construct, have produced interesting results, provided they are reexamined from another angle.

Finally the word *experience* is very ambiguous, in both the English and the French languages. What a delightful surprise I had 2 years ago to read some quotations from a book published by Lewis Wolfgang Brandt (1982), professor at the University of Regina. I quote: "The 'lack of interest among Anglo-American psychologists in the psychology of thinking [on one side] and the psychology of subjective experience [on the other side] . . . may be explained by . . . the difficulty of explaining to a unilingual English speaker the difference between [in German] an *Erlebnis* and an *Erfahrung.*'"[5] Doubtless the psychologists of religion, since the time of William James, have not neglected subjective experience, often as a starting point or an inspiration for their measurements. But several of them have restricted *religious experience* (meaning *Erlebnis*) to a broad gamut of subjective emotional states: sudden (as in some cases of conversion), intense, unexpected, exceptional, culminating ("peak experiences"). They have admitted sometimes that motivations, attitudes, and ideologies could be scientifically measured and analyzed, even in religious phenomena, but they have contended that some immediate experiences (meaning *Erlebnis*, passive-emotion experience) were privileged in procuring a direct contact with the sacred. In my last book (Godin 1985), on the contrary, I revived the use of the word *experience* for the whole gamut of human happenings or events (outside and inside) which people consider as religious (including the winning of $10,000 in a bingo game after many prayers of petition), provided we avoid confusion between deep but passive emotional experience *(Erlebnis)* and active-synthesis experience *(Erfahrung)*, the latter being essential in any specifically Christian experience (as we shall see at the end of this lecture).

The preceding remarks, as semantic as they look, will perhaps appear methodologically important in concretely reexamining three psychological theories with some results of recent research, namely: attribution theory related to religious beliefs; psychological or magical efficacy in ritual experience: and idealization and identification at the service of the ego in the so-called mystical element (Freud) of religious contemplation and life.

5. Words in brackets quoted from a review by Reuben Abel (1983).

III

At the beginning of an interesting piece of research on the "Attributions of Responsibility to God," Richard L. Gorsuch wrote, "In the Judeo-Christian heritage, a central component of belief is that God acts in human affairs" (Gorsuch and Smith 1983, 340). I invite you to submit that statement to further reflection after having heard this true story.

> At the end of a nice autumn weekend, a family, father, mother, and two children, decided to leave the small town of Dinant to come back to Brussels. They fixed the time at 4:45 P.M. and decided to return by driving along the left bank of the Meuse River. At a spot on the road, overhung by picturesque rocks, a boulder, undermined by recent heavy rains, hurtled down on top of the car. The outcome: the father is killed, the boy is severely paralyzed, the mother and daughter are safe and sound. This human accident produced a religious event: 2 years later, the mother sought out a priest, told him of her long grief and sufferings, also of her doubts. "I used to have faith," she said, "all our family was so obviously blessed by divine providence. But now after all that, how could I still believe in God? If God is good and all powerful as people say, how could he allow this to happen?"

To explain the accident, a fortuitous happening, two different causes must be taken into consideration: the physically conditioned factors (rain, poorly controlled previous erosion perhaps, stone, law of gravity, etc.), the free human decisions (to leave at 4:45, to follow the left shore rather than the right), plus chance (bad luck, if you will, in this case). What is chance? Is it nothing? Certainly it is not a force, nothing intentional, not a person. Chance is the fortuitous crossing of two series of causality: physical and intentional in this case. Any mature human being must sometimes use the category of chance (or hazard, bad luck, good luck) to qualify adequately the nature of some happenings in human existence. Chance is part of the hard reality of life: anxiety-provoking, of course, since we cannot control chance, nor can we accuse or condemn it.

The human fortuitous accident enters into an interaction during the grief process of that mother in such a way as to become a religious conflictual event. She used a religious vocabulary (divine providence, God, all-powerful). She was shocked. She mentioned God and two philosophical attributes of deity. She did not reject her belief since she went to a priest to explain her sorrow and discuss the matter in religious terms: God (which one?), Providence (but *pronoia* in a Judeo-Christian Bible is hardly mentioned). The human fortuitous accident has not been perceived as such but reveals that divine providence did not act in her own family as she had vaguely expected it would, and as we all would wish and will keep on wishing until our death. If we use the word *God* (or divine providence), it is with a vague and latent hope that God not only "acts in human affairs" (as Gorsuch wrote) but that he would act to modify causalities or intentionalities in the physical world or personal relations. Our wish is, and will always be if we are simply religious, that God (or Providence) will suppress or control or reduce chance.

I suggest that the category of modification is essential for a study of the interaction between our simply religious wishes (Providence might serve as wish fulfillment, reducing the anxiety of living in a world where we are confronted with chance happenings) and the beliefs derived from a revelational religion like Christianity. Is there something in the revelation of the Father, by his Son, prolonged by the Spirit's action that would ground the idea of a divine action modifying our human conditions in its struggle with chance, with death? If after much meditating on the Gospels you say no, then your responses to the questionnaire designed by Gorsuch will refuse to attribute "to God" (which one?) several outcomes of stories used in his research. You will increase the number of attributions to luck or to other factors, not because you are perhaps among the persons classified as being "far from God" (as found by Gorsuch and Smith 1983, 347), but simply because you are Christians close to the gospel.

Obviously this is a point of resistance: the so-called God is not modifying our human condition as we would wish or imagine he does. Perhaps in Jesus Christ he found some other ways to be with us in our sufferings. If we, psychologists of religion, want to take into account the revelational aspects of Christianity as they appear in the life of Jesus of Nazareth, the prophet, in his words, his practice, his attitudes, we should be ready to design our instruments of measurement in some other way. Since the first edition of my book, I have discovered a piece of research published by Jean D. Souyris (1969) showing how slow the process of acquiring a correct use of the word *chance* (or hazard) is between the ages of 5 and 15 years. A semantic approach, more complete, would reveal that a tendency to introduce the word *providence* in some propositions or interpretations of stories, where the word *chance* would be more appropriate and effectively used by adults, is responsible for some of the delay in this acquisition among children educated in religious families and schools. The word *Providence* introduces itself as a substitute and superposes itself in place of *chance*. In the sixties, Melvin Ezer (1973) had already noted a slowing down, due to religious education, in right answers to questions involving physical causality, substituted for by divine intentional interpretations.

Semantic or linguistic research could produce some interesting surprises in the psychology of beliefs. In helping to prepare a sociological survey of beliefs, I suggested that this statement be introduced: "Jesus of Nazareth is really dead." Even testing the whole questionnaire with a small sample of people who agreed to discuss their answers, it was found that more devout and practicing Roman Catholics than other persons failed to endorse the statement. Moreover they were quite convinced that their response was clear and obvious "because he is risen from the dead" or "since I believe in the Resurrection." This is a second case where a belief expressed by the word *resurrection* tends to deny or attenuate the hard reality expressed by another word, *death:* namely, the suppression of all reciprocal communication, the end of any form of dialogue in this life. The reality of the death of Jesus at the end of his trial is a fact (which every Christian repeats in his creed). The apostles' grief at having lost Jesus is reported with a certain insistence in the first chapter of the Acts of the Apostles. It is good theology (and psychology) to recognize that their process of grief permitted the pentecostal presence of the Spirit (the second *pneuma* of Jesus).[6]

Another example: the most ambitious and successful attempt to measure the semantic differentials of mother and father figures, cross-culturally, and how Christian people use the socially predominant parental figures in their evocation of God is the project initiated by A. Vergote at the Center for the Psychology of Religion in both universities of Leuven and Louvain-la-Neuve in 1962, and finally published in 1981 (Vergote and Tamayo 1981). The book includes applications of the same scale of parental traits to more than 25 different populations from India to Moncton, with professor Alvaro Tamayo, and from unbelievers to seminarians and women religious. Factorial analyses, strictly applied sample by sample, to the 3,333 very diverse answers, reveal that the psychological evocation of God uses a well-structured variety of maternal traits (like welcoming, tenderness, always waiting for me) grouped under the label of "availability," and of paternal traits (like firmness, initiative, authority, one who maintains order) grouped under the label of "law." The official and even dogmatic language of Christianity suggests that the father figure is a good, if not the best, ground to symbolize God. In a sense the analysis of the results in most samples (especially since several paternal qualities are attributed to God with a higher degree of intensity than even to the human father) seems to confirm that theologically derived assumption. On the other hand, several samples, especially among seminarians and women religious, show a high degree of idealization of the mother whose qualities are dominant when attributed to God and even to the father. Without any doubt, after read-

---

6. For a psychological rereading of some words and behavior in the Acts of the Apostles, see Godin (1981).

ing the results of that monumental inquiry, we face the fact that the representation of God (among Christians or unbelievers in a Christian cultural area) may be grounded not only on the basis of a "magnified father," as Freud wrote, but as well in some individuals or groups on the basis of a "magnified mother," an unconscious product of an idealized father or mother at the service of the ego. The outstanding publication of Vergote and his associates, nevertheless, left entirely open the theological question: Is the Father, revealed by his firstborn son, Jesus Christ, simply similar or analogous to the empirically or culturally familiar father figure *(secundum carnem)*? Is he not a father of another kind acting or reacting as a natural father would never act? It seems that the parable of the father who had two sons (the so-called parable of the prodigal son) would suggest the paradoxical image of the Father announced by Jesus, objectively unjust for his second son in order to introduce a new system of relations, that of a new justice. Of course, the same question is raised by the maternal image or figure with its numerous traits so well connected with our human psychological wish for unconditional love. But there is a more radical question: Is the structure of parenthood psychologically proper to evoke the specifically Christian concept of "adoptive sonship" when it is presented, offered, and not imposed by the gospel, as Saint Paul, the first theologian, interpreted the foundation of the new alliance? Professor Vergote is quite conscious of this since he wrote, "The essential element of the Christian message about divine paternity is not present" in this kind of research (Vergote and Tamayo 1981, 220).

Quite recently this year, Bernard Spilka and two associates have proposed a complete formal theory of attribution concepts from past results in various inquiries and for future research in the psychology of religious beliefs. Such an effort to operationalize empirical observations is always promising. However, the rational emphasis on "three basic needs or desires: a sense of meaning, control over outcomes, and self-esteem" (Spilka, Shaver, and Kirkpatrick 1985) is probably too narrow or too conceptual to confront the possibility of a dynamic conflict, partly conscious, partly unconscious between the "religiosity" they aim to analyze (a functional one, fulfilling human wishes as they are philosophically described) and another religion, if any, provoking some inner resistances against another kind of desires or wishes which is a part of the Christian heritage. A too exclusively rational approach, not using a simple knowledge of Christian theology, will always miss this point of resistance. Any rational analysis of a belief (for instance "God is always acting in the world") leaves aside the double meaning and equivocal character of *acting,* namely, the modifying or not modifying character of God's action (meaning: Father, Son, and their Spirit), and the true agents of their project for the world (if any). A semantic and linguistic approach to the interferences of some Christian beliefs with and in human language or ideology would perhaps be more revealing in our way to encounter both Christian beliefs, theologically grounded, and resistances or distortions in their symbolic use. The act of Christian rebirth by personal free affiliation is structurally different from being born from parents in a cultural system of parenthood. Hence its symbolic system of beliefs is also very different from both the Judaic symbolic system and from general religiosity.

IV

On the ritual dimension, the presence or even the divergence of psychological religiosity (wish fulfillment) and established religion has been more frequently recognized. Magical mentality, for instance, has been studied in its opposition "versus" sacramental efficacy (symbolic and real efficacy), as in the research by Sister Marthe already mentioned in the beginning of this lecture. In the case of prayers of petition, directed to obtain favors (thus some modifications in the outside world or inner dispositions), L. B. Brown (1966, 1968, 1973, 1985) has published the results of many studies conducted in three continents—Australia, Europe, North America—with young adult Christians of several denominations. The main conclusion, well-confirmed in many samples of population tested by different methods, indicates that prayers of petition were accompanied by more and more doubts about their material effects. During adolescence (12 to 20 years old in every denomination), the opinion that prayers of petition do in fact modify reality decreases continuously with age. But on the other hand, the opinion that it is "all right" to pray in certain circumstances (described in a questionnaire) hardly changes with age. An evident preference is given to another form of prayer, that is, to offer an action, to unite with other people and so forth, and then abandon the idea of a divine intervention to modify the situation.

It seems that very few studies have been conducted on ritual prayers, especially prayers involving the mediation of an object, gestures, some deprivations or sufferings in the body, a musical or other kind of artistic support. The psychological dynamics of the rite in relation to an object has been beautifully illustrated by Flournoy, quoting in 1915 a childhood memory from an autobiography by Mlle. Vé. It deserves careful reading:

> One of my earliest memories relates to my mother. She was very ill and had been in bed for weeks. A nurse told me that there was no doubt she would die in a few days. I must have been four or five years old. *My most precious possession* was a little brown wooden horse, covered with "real

hair," as I used to say, and with a saddle and bridle that I could take off and put on again. The horse had as its stable a little ladder of waxed wood in the corridor. In bed, I refused energetically to say my evening prayer because Mummy was not there to listen. But *I began praying to the horse, kneeling in front of the ladder* and reciting the few phrases of our evening prayer in German very quickly and without understanding them at all. *I was sure* that my mother's recovery depended on *my faithfulness in praying thus*. As the recovery was delayed, a curious thought grew in my mind: *that I had to give up my horse* so that my mother could recover. It was not accomplished in one go; it cost me agonies; I began by throwing the bridle and saddle on the fire, thinking that "when he is very ugly I shall be able to keep him after all." I don't remember the order of the events exactly, but I know that, in great despair, I finally smashed my horse and that, seeing my mother on her feet in a few days later, *I was convinced for a long time* that in some mysterious way my sacrifice had cured her.

Let us examine the dynamic aspects of the elements entering into what we could call the birth of an idol. Isolated from her mother by an illness said to be mortal, the little girl felt a deep anguish. Between 4 and 5 years old, her prayers were just a ritual memorized recitation (without understanding them at all), and their value for her came from saying them each evening in the presence of her mother who listened. If the mother is not there, what can she do? Invent a presence in an object ("my most precious possession") which is symbolic through its great value and also is a game, as will be seen in the continuation of the story: the child will be able to exercise her mastery of the little horse, firstly as a cult object, an idol, then as an object to be destroyed insofar as it resists her wish, and as a possession to be sacrificed. In her mother's absence, the child takes an important step toward her human and perhaps religious maturity. From a ritual formula learned by heart and recited in her mother's presence but not addressed to her mother, the child moves on to a request still implicit in that routinely directed to the idol ("I began praying to the horse"). Of course she does not ask the horse for anything directly, and yet she is certain ("I was sure") that if she keeps it up for long enough ("my faithfulness in praying thus") her wish will be fulfilled. On the archaic base of the all-powerfulness of the wish, a decisive test in her maturation will be played out. But the reality of her mother's illness resists her wish, breaches the effective illusion of all-powerfulness. A dull anger is then turned against her "precious possession," this horse placed in the position of an idol. Thus "a curious thought" grows: the destruction of the object, which after all is only a possession. This time the wish involves the child herself; it distances her from a prayer which may be magic, but also from the object as a symbolic prop. It is going to be a question of real sacrifice at the level of play, a sacrifice, however, that the child will connect mysteriously with her mother's recovery for a long time but not forever. When she is writing her story, Mademoiselle Vé has given up believing in the magical aspect including a causality of this granting of what she then wished, one of the most essential wishes of a child: that her mother should live, and if necessary that the idol should perish!

The dynamics that we have just described are the same which a psychoanalyst, Donald Winnicott (1971), analyzed in the so-called transitional object. The child, 6 to 9 months old, in order to acquire the capacity of remaining alone, plays sometimes in the presence of his mother or father with an object (any kind of rag, scrap of paper, piece of wood) able to be manipulated, even destroyed, which follows the child's fantasies but with no damage to his own body as was the case in the preceding stage with thumb sucking or endlessly rocking to and fro. In an analogous way, the mediation of a ritual object should be considered as a way of filling the gap between an absent all-powerful God and the wish to maintain a contact with him, a sense of presence materialized outside the body before a verbal contact or dialogue could take place. Thanks to the transitional ritual objects, even before or outside of a revelational religion, an interplay of aggressiveness, of guilt, of expected love can operate even unconsciously without damaging the very body of the praying people, unlike what we observe in many manifestations of popular religion corresponding to a primary impulsion to suffer (flagellation, tattooings, sacred incisions or mutilations, and other various ways of marking the body) sometimes supported by a dolorist ideology.

Has the Vé child just had an experience of God? No. In her evening prayer and then in her conduct towards the idol, has she had a religious experience? Psychologically, we must say that is so and, to be more exact, in the following sense. The Vé child has just confronted the all-powerfulness of her wish with the resistance of reality by involving the mediation of prayer. From an initial ritual position, accompanied by the production of an idol-object, she has proceeded to a sacrificial destruction with an interposed object, more expressive of her want and anger than really symbolic. Even if she had not been gratified, these items of religious conduct would still have "functioned" by reducing her initial anxiety.

Whereas the Vé child was using her idol-object for private ends in the absence of a sick mother, religions offer so many idol-objects to children and adults alike that they hardly need to be searched for, still less invented in order to find in them something onto which to support their religious demands, to express their cries for help and sustain their spontaneous claims to modify reality by objects that should remain transitional: amulets, talismans, medals, candles, scapulars, relics, phials of blood, images mysteriously imprinted on shrouds, sanctuaries with miraculous inscriptions. All these objects, rites, and even painful behavior could serve as mediations on the road to an encounter with God, or the gods. In this sense the whole universe would be a store of sacramentalizable objects, and bodily activities would provide an inexhaustible source of appeals to a more or less personalized other. But these can also serve to promote, soothe, or defer men's needs by maintaining them religiously at a primary stage of the religious wish, namely, that "My will be done with the help of. . . ." By what force? With whom? God or gods? Just as the child wishes for milk or the magical breast before it can address its demands to its mother, through language, and in exchanging its wishes and its mother's answers, wishes, or denials, it will enter into a cultural world where *symbols* mean "encounters," in a strict sense and etymologically, through demands expressing wishes from both sides. This is the only way of suppressing the ambiguity of any ritual object.

In any revelational religion, as in Christian sacraments, the educational task should provide a passage from an egocentric use of the rites to a performing use of them in conformity with the meaning proper to each one: the meaning of the Eucharist is not to protect against accidents. Any child, any adult is invited to participate more and more fully and share with others the symbolic encounter presented in any specifically Christian rite. Otherwise the new birth, as promised in the gospel, can hardly produce its effects. The man, Christian or not, remains alone and unchanged in some rituals where only his own wishes are expressed.

Very little psychological research, to my present knowledge, has been conducted along this line, at least with adults. In developmental psychology, we have at least the work published by Anne Dumoulin and Jean-Marie Jaspard (1973) on religious mediations in the world of children. They have found that the eucharistic rite and the person of the priest are progressively perceived with their specific Christian meanings from the ages of 6 to 12. But they have discovered that the process followed by boys is different when compared to the progress as obtained by girls. Girls are, even at the beginning, very prompt to have a sense of human presence, while boys from the beginning perceive the rite in the line of an action to accomplish, a rule of conduct. Their book has received the Quinquennial Award (1973) given by the International Commission for the Scientific Religions Psychology. But new observations have been published with commentaries by Jaspard in 1980 as a chapter of the proceedings of the First International Conference on Moral and Religious Development.

At the end of this little piece of clinical analysis on an observation presented as a memory by Mademoiselle Vé, you probably understand better how the differences between two kinds of religion (two at least, since we should never forget some Judaic components in our own Christian imagery) do enter into an unavoidable but fruitful interplay in the Christian development through human and religious experiences.[7]

V

But how does a revelational religion reach men and women psychologically in their individual development and the changing cultures of human history? We all know the answer, and the history of religions confirms it. Even before oral traditions have begun to be written down, religions are handed down on the basis of tales (narratives) in the form of myths which give meaning to rites, by the words and acts of persons (soon made sacred) with whom our relation takes on a timeless quality, through characters who died more or less heroically but whose action (praxis) have inspired communities which continue to live by them and proclaim their message. That message, consisting of *founding* words, is initially prophetic but is threatened constantly with impoverishment in orthodoxies or orthopraxies whose main function then is to preserve or restore the cohesion of the groups who live by it.[8]

Psychologically, every religion that is established and founded on a revelation develops a symbolic corpus whose rational coherence is insufficient to maintain and promote its affective dynamic. It is all the more difficult to transmit if the founding words have introduced or grafted certain desires or projects which diverge from specifically human desires, even from religious desires in the broad sense of the word.

If you miss the symbolic articulation of any Christian experience (belief, sacramental rite, spiritual attitude, or discernment), you construct a scientific design for research that isolates either the rational aspect of it or the subjective emotional component (experience as *Erleb-*

7. In his last book, in French at present, A. Vergote concluded a chapter on ritual efficacy with these lines: "In fact, the practices varied in their position along a continuum between, at one extreme, a position with a minimal symbolic action, that includes a maximal imaginary belief, and at the other, an asymptotic position of perfect conformity with symbolic action, where the human wish would be entirely transformed by the pregnancy of the message" (1983, 303). In his view, the "perfect conformity" and the complete transformation are presented as a desirable aim in Christian life. I would be inclined to speak of a permanent co-existence of two systems of desires, only partially superposed, maintained in active interaction through love. And on this point, the human love would be structured as is the Trinitarian divine *agape*.

8. On this opposition between conceptual orthodoxy and prophetic inspiration, see the convincing results obtained in several experimental designs by J.-P. Deconchy (1980) and also the historico-social volumes on messianisms old and new (1973) admirably condensed by Henri Desroche.

nis), or maybe both. Ronald Goldman (1964) missed the symbolic articulation, although his main publication remains a landmark in discovering the developmental aspect of a capacity to uncover the intellectual
meanings of certain symbolic stories, like those of Moses confronted
with a burning bush, the crossing of the Red Sea, or the temptations of
Jesus. Much influenced by Piaget's three levels of conceptualization,
Goldman has established, usefully for catechetical purposes, that it is
not possible before the age of 13 or 14 to find a meaning for today in
the majority of biblical stories. What Goldman studied is not the symbolic function but a kind of hermeneutic function, namely, the capacity
to decode what is written in a religious style, a wonderful narrative, into
a meaningful transcription valid for today, in an intellectual style combining the Bultmann theological and quasi-philosophical interpretations of Jesus' life and teaching.

In order to study the perception of symbols when they are presented
in religious stories, or images, or rites, or sacred persons living in the
past (Jesus, Mary, and so on), more refined methods should be
employed, taking into account the fact that a symbol might reach an
unconscious but dynamic emotional level in a personality where some
resistances may be revealed. To be clear, let us remember that there are
at least two kinds of symbolism, quite observable in children and at a
very early age. When John (1 year and 10 months old) pretends that a
shell pulled along on top of a box is a cat walking on a wall, he is perfectly conscious of the symbolic meaning of his play, so much so that
the shell has been transformed by him for his play and placed creatively
in a symbolic relationship with the cat. But we observe also in some
cases the interplay of a secondary symbolism of whose significance the
child is not fully aware and which he is certainly unable to express
directly. This is the case, for instance, when Jane (also 1 year and 10
months old) likes to play with two dolls of different size and repeatedly
makes the little one leave on a long journey while the bigger one
remains with the mother. To your minds, perhaps, the interpretation
already occurs that Jane may be somewhat jealous after the birth of a
little brother or sister. In certain conditions, depending on the information you have, your interpretation might be correct. This unconscious
symbolism is sometimes called *secondary:* it does not correspond to a
pure construction of the girl's wish, but to a compromise between her
wish to remain alone with her mother and the unavoidable hard reality
of the new baby's presence and the repressed feeling of aggressiveness.

Now let us turn to some research, partially published in 1968 by
Godelieve de Valensart. She has been able to prove that when very
young children (5 to 6 years old) are shown Christian pictures three at
a time and asked to choose amongst them, they are perfectly capable of
perceiving certain signs used by the artist with a symbolic intention,

but those signs become a reason for immediately rejecting the picture that contains them in favor of the other two. For instance, from three pictures of the nativity, they immediately reject one where the Virgin Mary is sitting on a poor chair of straw while, in an upper corner, a luxurious throne is provided for King Herod. The same goes for the picture in which they see tiny, sharp, black knives by the plates in front of each apostle, on the table prepared for the Last Supper. In the first case, they claim that it is not fitting for the Virgin Mary to be sitting on an ugly, uncomfortable straw chair like that; and in the second case, that the black knives are too dangerous or ugly for a joyful and peaceful last supper with Jesus. Thus those children do perceive the symbolic details, but they spontaneously reject the disturbing sign as not fitting in with their inner wish to honor the Virgin Mary as an idealized person or to imagine the Last Supper as a meeting of good friends, a wish which was aptly ridiculed in some of the songs in the musical *Jesus Christ Superstar*. It is so obvious that a correct perception of the signs requires an introduction to the fundamental gospel message on poverty and a catechesis where some of the conflictual aspects of Jesus' life, both for himself and in his relations with his disciples, are not ignored but commented on, in order to obtain a Christian experience; *Erfahrung* of the *Nachfolge Christi* today. In other words, Christian symbolism is not spontaneous or natural as a mystery accessible to agnostic interpretation. It is learned and received as a divine trinitarian project, proposed to human love, not imposed on it. It is an *agape*, a mystery not of unity but of union maintained first between three persons and then between them and mankind as a new project in the matter of love. Christian symbolism does not start, psychologically, in an inner experience— *Erlebnis* (although it might be achieved that way)—but only in an experience *(Erfahrung)* today in the Spirit as it took place in the past for the disciples of Jesus. As Saint Augustine wrote, "They have seen the man [Jesus] and they have believed in the God [the Word]." This active synthesis is structural in any specifically Christian experience. It should be studied that way and by psychological methods too.

But how can Christian experience be studied that way? Since 1968 and the experiment conducted by de Valensart, I am convinced that it can, provided we admit that the point of resistance should not be neglected in psychological research. Ambivalence, by which I mean a mixed feeling of attraction and aggressiveness, is a good sign that a new love is about to be born, perhaps beyond mere reciprocal sexual desires. As long as the love *(agape)* is perceived as a mere fulfillment of human desires, it easily produces a lot of intense experiences *(Erlebnisse)* where the subject is passively expecting or receiving God's gift. It may also possibly produce some doctrinal assents or heroic commitments. But the encounter with Jesus' spirit could be missed with his own desire to be the poorest, the most oppressed or rejected of mankind. The active identification with him in this kind of horizontal atonement is ignored. In its place, an idealization is produced that heightens the ideal-ego, without any real opening up to reality. Symbolism is destroyed for the benefit of imagination and wishful thinking.

The main challenge of Freud to religion is there. In the final analysis, Freud thought that religions are unable to contribute to man's maturity by directing him towards the dominance of the "reality principle." Sublimation is not achieved as it may be in sciences and art. "The artist," Freud wrote, "finds the way back to reality from his world of fantasy by making use of special gifts to mold his fantasies into objects of a new kind which are valued by men as precious reflections of reality. . . . Those other men feel the same dissatisfaction as he does. . . . That dissatisfaction is itself part of the reality" (1911, 223). Psychological dissatisfaction means also a resistance against accepting the way out towards reality. Instead, according to Freud, idealization produces many kinds of illusions or beliefs which serve to repress aggressiveness, to avoid active identification with some religious figures, and to keep man under the dominance of the pleasure principle until his death.

Some recent psychological research has been conducted taking into account the point of resistance: false or partial interpretation of parables, displacement of identification. For instance, after hearing the story of the good shepherd, an identification is produced with the lost sheep or with the group of other children temporarily deprived of their mother, not with the metaphorical actor of the story, Jesus himself.[10]

In Sweden, O. Wikström (1975) studied the feeling of being or having been led by God using some stories from the written traditions, the Bible, and the lives of the saints. He discovered "two different ways of linking the written story with the religious experience" of 27 Christian believers between 68 and 80 years of age.[11] For some of them, God's guidance is conceived as an intervention by him which for their benefit might repeat a modification of the situation in which the hero of the story found himself in the past. In that way they obtained a restructured view of their own situation. They were able to expect God would play his part as he had done in history: the past story, metaphorically conceived, might indeed be of great help in difficult situations. But other persons conceived God's guidance differently. They identified themselves to a greater extent with the historical personality or character who received through God's intervention the means of modifying the chain of events itself. In the metaphorical interpretation, God's guid-

9. For a more complete discussion of this point, see Godin (1969).

10. For further details and other attempts to differentiate several types of identification with Jesus, see Godin (1985, 209–35).

11. Quotation from the English summary, p. 207.

ance is a gift passively received; in the second case, an active identification is produced leading to a truly symbolic interpretation of God's guidance and possibly to several experiences *(Erfahrungen)* of active synthesis between an inner attitude and the difficult situation outside.

In social psychology, an excellent research project by Melvin J. Lerner at the University of Waterloo has produced after more than 15 years of systematic applications a set of observations which might be a sound methodological inspiration for psychologists of religion. Published 6 years ago, his volume *The Belief in a Just World* (1980) is obviously not a research on the psychology of religion, in spite of a few correlational attempts to establish a bridge with religious believers, but its indirect contribution to the discovery of latent belief, as a mental scheme to interpret and diminish the impact of the hard reality of unjust situations, is a new invitation to introduce some religious interpretations of the victims' suffering in a broader context than pseudo-explanations using a religious vocabulary (like Job's friends). More ethical than religious in their inspiration, Lerner and his associates have ingeniously developed several quasi-experimental methods of measuring the reactions of people invited to observe a microcosm of unjustly punished or badly treated persons. Their constructs lead to amazing observations such as distorted perceptions of real behavior, to the point of victimizing the victims in their own judgment: that person is less attractive or I would not like to cooperate with him, and so on. The root of these reactions is interpreted in the light of a kind of general presupposition, that is, the belief in a just world, a kind of secular way of denying or reducing the crude and disturbing facts presented to the observers. This is sometimes reinforced by religious statements concerning, for example, the fate of a world conducted according to a divine plan. Some answers even go as far as to affirm that suffering itself is a particular way of finding or making justice. These last findings, allusive and secondary for Lerner, demonstrate once more the functional aspect of some religious statement or ideologies, like dolorism in Christian life. They are the product of wishful thinking, like the belief in a just world in Lerner's interpretation of his observations, a means of restoring a kind of psychological homeostasis (equilibrium) in the very perception of disturbing injustices and sufferings. But of course the same methodology could also be used to evaluate the numerous resistances to accepting many narratives or parables in the Gospels, especially when they provoke a conflict between Jesus and the disciples, between Mary and Joseph, and so on. Job's friends speak to him from their own functional religious inspiration. But at least they do not have the last word.

Finally, when a revelational religion is confronted with a functional religion, rooted in human wishes, is there such a thing as a last word?

My last story will illustrate the fact that in a deeply Christian woman with a true knowledge of the gospel, the anxiety of an unbearable event can produce temporarily a movement of religious regression at a functional level which is accompanied by repression. Thus there are two religions in a few months, or more precisely, two different ways of relating to the Virgin Mary: idealization (anxiety-reducing but useless in facing reality) and the return to sublimation by a truly symbolic identification (opening up to a double anchorage in reality). This is the story of Mrs. Pilgrim, the woman who had two mothers.

Mrs. Pilgrim, a Catholic with a lively, confident, richly spontaneous faith, is going through one of the most painful ordeals possible for a mother. One of her two sons has been mortally injured by a blow in a scuffle during a student demonstration he was taking part in, supporting immigrants in Belgium. The 23-year-old victim is in the hospital, and the doctors despair of his life. Mrs. Pilgrim discusses with her husband and younger son an idea that came to her when praying: suppose they joined a trainload of sick people due to leave for Lourdes in a week's time? The younger son is not very keen to do this, the husband more than unwilling. He objects that the doctors advise against a journey, in the course of which their son might die.

Desperately worried, Mrs. Pilgrim tells me all this. "And your son?" I ask her. "What does he want?"

He is not against it. In fact, she adds, he is too weak to decide. My comment makes her think that her husband's opinion has some weight. She gets up and decides that under these circumstances her husband and son will remain at the hospital while she herself will go to Lourdes to implore the Virgin. As she leaves, she utters this magnificent and surprising statement, "You see, we mothers understand each other better!"

I got a card from Lourdes asking me to pray with her. Shortly after her return, the elder son dies. Six months later, Mrs. Pilgrim comes to see me again. She is slowly getting over her bereavement. But fortunately, she says, there is faith in the resurrection. Then too, there is her other son. I talk about the dead son again and recall the circumstances in which he received the fatal blow. She says that she has often thought about it and, as a Christian, she feels proud of her son. The journey to Lourdes is mentioned. "Yes," I say, "mothers understand each other." She asks me why I say that. I remind her that those were her own words. "Did I really say that?" she asks. There is a long silence and she seems upset, almost distressed. Then suddenly she gets up as abruptly as the previous time. "How awful!" she says with a faint smile. "How could I have prayed like that? Never mind. I shall go there again."

Another card reached me from Lourdes, signed this time by her husband as well with these words: "We are here together. This time the Virgin has really helped us."

All this shows, first, that distress brings us back to spontaneous religion, to the prayer that tries to enlist the services of the Virgin for our wish, to *have* her for our own ends. Secondly, that it shows in this case there was a genuine repression of something that was well known. The Mother to whom the prayer was addressed lost her son, too. "We mothers understand one another" can only lead to confusion in these conditions. The imagined Mother has lost a part of her past true story. Thirdly, it shows that spontaneous religious *attachment* ensures continuity in the transition (here a return of what was repressed) to the more complete identification. Fourthly, it also shows that roughly analogous *concrete* circumstance (the son's wish to be identified with the immigrants, by at least marching alongside them) intervenes effectively in the identification achieved during the second journey to Lourdes accompanied by the dead boy's father. Finally, that this mutation of attachment into love, with identification with the wish of Jesus, the indirect cause of his death, is not totally dysfunctional since this time "prayer has really helped us." Thus her prayer has become (again) a Christian *experience*. But at what cost!

VI

"Well, George, how do you feel now?"

"A little tired," he said. Then: "Your stories are fine."

"Thank you, George. The stories are observations made by the so-called clinical psychologist. Perhaps the dynamics discovered by clinical psychologists could inspire more creative research in the scientific psychology of religion. . . . Apart from the stories, what do you think?"

"I think that religious experiences do not fall from heaven. Even in the case of Jesus."

"Right, George, and then?"

"Christian experience may be a conflict in love, a conflict of wishes with some points of resistance."

"Right, George. Anything else?"

"You seem critical when you discuss some of the published American research. Be careful, André, criticism is easy but genuine production is difficult."

"You are right, George. That's why there are so few really worthwhile works in this field, maybe three every 10 years in Europe as well as in North America."

"Did you say that the situation is the same in Europe as in North America?"

"Yes, George."

"If you are ever invited over there, don't forget, André, to insist on this point."

"OK, George, you can be sure I will."

So, dear friends, I insist on this point: the situation is the same in Europe. No more than three good pieces of research in 10 years. After all, it is not so bad. Now, goodbye to George and many thanks for your attention.

Thank you.

References

Abel, R. 1983. Review of *Psychologists caught: A psycho-logic of psychology,* by L. W. Brandt. *Contemporary Psychology* 28: 964.

Batson, C. D., and W. L. Ventis. 1982. *The religious experience: A social-psychological perspective.* New York: Oxford Univ. Press.

Beirnaert, L. 1964. *Expérience chrétienne et psychologie.* Paris: Epi.

Brandt, L. W. 1982. *Psychologists caught: A psycho-logic of psychology.* Toronto: Univ. of Toronto Press.

Brown, L. B. 1966. Egocentric thought in petitionary prayer: A cross-cultural study. *Journal of Social Psychology* 68: 197–210.

———. 1968. Some attitudes underlying petitionary prayer. In *From cry to word,* ed. A. Godin, 65–84. Brussels: Lumen Vitae.

———. 1973. *Psychology and religion: Selected readings.* London: Penguin.

———. ed. 1985. *Advances in the psychology of religion.* Oxford: Pergamon.

Deconchy, J.-P. 1980. *Orthodoxie religieuse et sciences humaines.* Paris: Mouton.

Desroche, H. 1973. *Sociologie de l'espérance.* Paris: Calmann-Levy.

Dumoulin, A., and J.-M. Jaspard. 1973. *Les médiations religieuses dans l'univers de l'enfant (prêtre et Eucharistie dans la perception du divin et l'attitude religieuse de 6 a 12 ans).* Brussels: Lumen Vitae.

Ezer, M. 1973. The effect of religion upon children's responses to questions involving physical causality. In *Research in religious behavior: Selected readings,* ed. B. Beit-Hallahmi, 61–75. Monterey, Calif.: Brooks-Cole.

Flournoy, T. 1902. *Les principes de la psychologie religieuse.* Geneva: H. Kündig; Paris: Schleicher Frères; London: Williams and Norgate.

——— 1915. Une mystique moderne: Mlle. Vé. *Archives de Psychologie* 15: 57–58.

Freud, S. 1911. Formulations on the two principles of mental functioning. In *The standard edition of the complete psychological works of Sigmund Freud,* ed. and trans. J. Strachey, vol. 12.

Godin, A. 1969. Genetic development of the symbolic and hermeneutic function: Meaning and limits of the work of Goldman. *Lumen Vitae* 29: 95–106.

———. 1981. Histoire d'un deuil et d'un souffle nouveau. *Lumiére et Vie* 30: 153–54.

————. 1985. *The psychological dynamics of religious experience.* Trans. M. Turton. Birmingham, Ala.: Religious Education.

Goldman, R. 1964. *Religious thinking from childhood to adolescence.* London: Routledge and Kegan Paul.

Goodenough, E. R. 1965. *The psychology of religious experience.* New York: Basic.

Gorsuch, R. L., and C. S. Smith. 1983. Attributions of responsibility to God: An interaction of religious beliefs and outcomes. *Journal for the Scientific Study of Religion* 22: 340–52.

Jaspard, J.-M. 1980. The relation to God and the moral development of the young child. In *Toward moral and religious maturity,* ed. C. Brusselmans, 138–63. Morristown, N.J.: Silver Burdett.

Lerner, M. J. 1980. *The belief in a just world: A fundamental delusion.* New York: Plenum.

McGovern, A. F. 1981. *Education for justice: The mission of the church in the 1980s, The Nash lecture.* Regina: Campion College.

Maître, J. 1972. Psychoanalyse et sociologie religieuses. *Archives des sciences sociales des religions* 53: 111–34.

Marthe, Sr., and A. Godin. 1965. Magic mentality and sacramental life. In *Teaching the sacraments,* 121–39. Chicago.

Souyris, J.-D. 1969. Étude génétique d'une attitude "metaphysique" anti-hasard. *Psychologie Française* 14: 279–87.

Spilka, B., P. Shaver, and L. A. Kirkpatrick. 1985. A general attribution theory for the psychology of religion. *Journal for the Scientific Study of Religion* 24: 1–20.

Valensart, G. de. 1968. Modern religious picture: Spontaneous choice and understanding of symbols among children, five to twelve years old. In *From cry to word,* ed. A. Godin, 118–34. Brussels: Lumen Vitae.

Vergote, A. 1983. *Religion, foi et incroyance.* Brussels: Mardaga.

Vergote, A., and A. Tamayo, eds. 1981. *The parental figures and the representation of God: A psychological and cross-cultural study.* The Hague and New York: Mouton.

Wikström, O. 1975. *Guds ledning.* Psychologia Religionum 4. Uppsala, Sweden: Acta Universitatis Upsaliensis.

Winnicott, D. W. 1971. *Playing and reality.* London: Tavistock.

Part 3

Personality Theory and Religion

5

Bernard Spilka

Bernard Spilka has taught at the University of Denver since 1957 and has been professor of psychology since 1965. He received his undergraduate education at New York University and his doctorate from Purdue University.

Spilka's longtime interest in the psychology of religion is clear from his professional affiliations. He is past president of Division 36, Psychologists Interested in Religious Issues, of the American Psychological Association (APA) and has been recipient of the division's William James Award for his theoretical/empirical contributions to the psychology of religion. Spilka is a fellow of the APA (Divisions 26 and 36), the Society for the Scientific Study of Religion, and the Religious Research Association. He has also served on the executive council of the latter two organizations.

Dr. Spilka's publishing record is impressive in its length and variety. He has published over 108 articles with such titles as "Religion and Death: The Clerical Perspective," "Faith and Behavior: Religion in Introductory Psychology Texts of the 1950s and the 1970s," "Utilitarianism and Person Faith," "Religion and Mental Disorder: A Critical Review and Theoretical Perspective," "The Child's Conception of Prayer," "A General Attribution Theory for the Psychology of Religion" (with P. Shaver and L. A. Kirkpatrick), "The Role of Religion in the History of American Psychology," "Religion and Coping Behavior," and "How Breast Cancer Patients Cope Using Their Faith." In 1985, Spilka coauthored with Ralph W. Hood, Jr., and Richard L. Gorsuch *The Psychology of Religion: An Empirical Approach* (Englewood Cliffs, N.J.: Prentice-Hall). This volume, which will probably become a standard text in many graduate programs, is distinguished by its emphasis on sound research as the foundation for theory about religious behavior. With H.

141

Newton Malony he coedited the Oxford publication, *A Dynamic Psychology of Religion: The Contributions of Paul W. Pruyser*.

Spilka is also known widely as a stimulator of student research. He has published work on committed-consensual religion with Russel Allen and on God concepts with Peter Benson. Several of his students have become significant researchers in their own right.

In "Personal Religion and Psychological Schemata," which Spilka coauthored with Michael Mullin, it is noted that central to theology in the Judeo-Christian heritage are orientations toward the self, toward others, and toward ultimate significance. Samples of high school students, college students, and people in their middle years were surveyed to see if self-esteem, social concern, and God concepts are related to different forms of religiosity. The article illustrates the importance of the use of theology and theory in the psychology of religion.

In his essay "The Meaning of Personal Faith: A Continuing Research Odyssey," Spilka identifies his goal throughout 35 years of research as seeking to understand the role of religion in life. He reports that he has focused attention on two main issues: prejudice and death. Spilka describes how his search for reasons why religion and prejudice are correlated led him to a study of the complexity of personal religion. Gordon Allport's intrinsic-extrinsic scheme, which dominated the field, was subsequently augmented with a cognitive component through Spilka's and Allen's committed and consensual designations. Spilka asserts that the continued study of the different religious orientations will advance our understanding of how prejudice and religion are related. Spilka's research into death has revealed it to be a complex rather than a unitary phenomenon. He demonstrates how his study of terminally ill patients, their families, and associated professionals has led to some practical applications. In regard to future directions in the psychology of religion, Spilka suggests we need to continue to theorize about the general ways in which persons relate to religion. Arguing that these efforts need to be incorporated into mainline social-psychological theory, he mentions general attribution theory as a promising model for this development. Spilka feels that these efforts will open new doors for research as well as for practical applications of the psychology of religion.

Personal Religion and Psychological Schemata: A Research Approach to a Theological Psychology of Religion

In a previous paper in 1970, the view was advanced that research in the psychology of religion should be theologically informed and, therefore, relevant to theology itself (Spilka 1970b). It was shown here that the Judeo-Christian heritage (whether expressed in Judaism, Catholicism, or Protestantism) had taken three basic tenets as central in theology. These tenets dealt with the individual's orientation toward (a) the self, (b) others, and (c) ultimates. In the Aquinian tradition of Catholicism, for instance, these three orientations are hierarchically ordered in such a way that the first two of the three are at a "lower" level, while the third of the three (e.g., one's obligation to love God) takes precedence over all else.

This hierarchically ordered framework implies what can only be termed an "organized and meaningfully integrated personal religion" (or religious attitude) and, it would seem, necessitates a positive pattern of associations amongst these three levels within an individual. In other words, one should expect to find a positive, constructive pattern of *intra*personal perspectives and *inter*personal outlooks affiliated with an *overriding personal* religious commitment, which could be viewed as both progressive and actualizing. In contrast, persons who reveal what could be termed a "faith of convenience" (e.g., a "faith" of social opportunism and/or a "faith" of a self-seeking nature) would *not* manifest any such constructive integrative mode of either intrapersonal or interpersonal religious commitment to their faith.

Coauthored with Michael Mullin. From *Character Potential* 8 (1977): 57–66; reprinted by permission of the publisher and the authors.

Theoretical Considerations

In recent years, the measurement of religious orientations has resulted in the development of at least two dichotomous schemes, each of which seems to have been relatively successfully operationalized. The first of these schemes has been associated with the terms *intrinsic* and *extrinsic* as descriptive qualifiers of a religion (Allport and Ross 1967). The second of these schemes has been associated with the terms *committed* and *consensual* as descriptive qualifiers of a religion (Allen and Spilka 1967; Raschke 1973). Although these two schemes exhibit some degree of both conceptual and psychometric overlap, further refinement of research in the area of the psychology of religion suggests that *both* schemes should be used (which is why both schemes were used in the work to be reported here). That is, these two schemes (and the religious outlooks implicit in them!) were treated as dependent, or criterion variables.

The work previously carried out in this particular aspect of the psychology of religion suggests that the intrinsic and committed forms of religion provide an approximation to the Aquinian theological hierarchy, while the extrinsic and consensual types of religion provide a kind of counter dimension. In addition to instruments previously developed to measure the intrinsic-extrinsic scheme and the committed-consensual scheme, the 1973 work of Benson and Spilka indicated that it was useful to utilize God concepts as a further measure of the nature of one's religious faith. Therefore, a number of the scales originally developed by Gorsuch in 1968 and by Benson and Spilka in 1972 were employed in this study.

The theological-psychological perspective that Spilka originally discussed in his 1970 article in the *Review of Religious Research* focused, in positive terms, on the relationship of faith to both self-significance and other-significance. In regard to the relationship of faith to self-significance, the view advanced there suggests two overlapping emphases:

1. The recognition of the dignity and worth of the human spirit; and
2. The realization and acceptance of personal capability and individual determination.

Operationally, these two emphases may be translated into the two constructs of *self-esteem* and *powerlessness*. In this context, self-esteem connotes the value one places on the self and may be regarded as a cornerstone of one's self-obligation, as that idea has been handled by Aquinas, Brunner, Niebuhr, and others (Spilka 1970b, 177). The construct of powerlessness, however, implies a negation of one's personal capability and self-determination. Thus, *high* self-esteem and *low* powerlessness are to be regarded as fundamentals in the establishment and the maintenance of an intrinsic and a committed religious faith.

In regard to the relationship of faith to other-significance, or social significance, two dimensions may be readily perceived. For example, one's belief, or faith, in people, as expressed in one's willingness to trust others and, therefore, to see them in a hopeful light, realizes the religious prescription to "love thy neighbor as thyself." Such a belief in people also implies that one loves (or values) others for themselves rather than in terms of such extrinsics as money, prestige, or power. Therefore, how one relates to other people, in terms of physical distance, may well be a subtle indicator of one's sensitivity to and response to people that is relative *either* to their perceived inherent value *or* to how they are socially (i.e., structurally) defined. One may, then, invoke the concept of interpersonal schemata (or personal space) as well as seek a more direct measure of faith in people.

Methodology for the Study

Our report of the methodology for this study will be divided into two sections. First, we will describe the subjects used in our sample. Then, we will describe the materials we used in the study.

The Subjects in the Study

The broadest possible sample of subjects took place. Essentially, six identifiable, widely distributed groups were sampled, and their responses were combined. These groups provided a maximum number (N) of 689 for this study. However, some of the instruments could not be administered to all groups, and so there are some variations in sample size across analyses. These differences will, of course, be noted as those analyses are reported.

The six identifiable groups composing the total sample for this study consist of the following:

1. A Catholic high school provided 92 subjects (35 males and 57 females), with a mean chronological age of 16.3 years.
2. A Catholic college in the state of New Mexico provided 170 subjects (82 males and 88 females), with a mean chronological age of 23.3 years.
3. A private college in the Rocky Mountain region of the United States provided 80 subjects (29 males and 51 females), with a mean chronological age of 21.2 years.
4. A select sample of persons in their middle years provided 95 subjects (29 males and 66 females), with a mean chronological age of

27.8 years. This sample was gathered in Des Moines, Iowa, and in Elgin, Illinois, and represents persons who were elementary school-teachers, postal employees, insurance company personnel, members of a Veterans of Foreign Wars post, and members of a local bowling league.

5. A high school sample of Catholic youth, used previously in a study reported by Benson and Spilka in 1972, provided 153 subjects.

6. A high school sample of Lutheran youth, used previously in the same 1972 study, provided 99 subjects.

The Materials Used in the Study

Two measures of self-significance were used in this study. The first was an abbreviated version of Coopersmith's measure of self-esteem (1967). The second was Spilka's factor-analytically developed measure of powerlessness (1970a). This measure has demonstrated both great utility and validity in previous studies.

Two instruments were selected as measures of, or ways of evaluating, the individual's relationships with and perspectives on others. The first was Rosenberg's 1957 scale entitled Faith-in-People, which has shown both good validity and good reliability in studies with large numbers of subjects. The second was a modification of Duke and Nowicki's 1972 instrument to assess personal space. This instrument is entitled the Comfortable Interpersonal Distance Scale (CIDS) and is a device that permits one to indicate how close the subjects would be willing to allow others to approach them. Although it is a paper-and-pencil device, Duke and Nowicki have demonstrated that responses on the CIDS do correspond to the distances people maintain from one another in everyday situations. In this study, Duke and Nowicki's total distance index was supplemented by separate scores for both a front approach and a rear approach. In addition, for some of the sample groups, reference persons' sex, age, and social status were varied: this variation permitted analysis of the data in terms of these variables, as well as in terms of people in general.

Three types of instruments were selected as measures of personal religious orientations. The first of these was the Allport-Ross 1967 scales of intrinsic-extrinsic religion. The second type was made up of the Spilka instruments to assess committed-consensual religion. The third type was made up of a number of Gorsuch's 1968 devices for assessing God concepts. However, because of Raschke's 1973 article in the *Journal for the Scientific Study of Religion*, three scoring paradigms for the Committed-Consensual scales were extensively tested in this study. As a result, a new scoring procedure was developed and is used in this study for the first time.

In addition, this article refers to some earlier work in which a number of different measures were utilized. One such measure was the Self-Esteem Semantic Differential Schwartz and Tangri reported in 1965. That instrument, for instance, correlates with the Coopersmith measure of self-esteem in the range of .4 and .5, and since both measures were used in the initial work, it is possible to make comparisons between them. Rotter's 1968 Locus-of-Control scale was also a part of some earlier research (Rotter 1966). Since Spilka's measure of powerlessness was included in that research, the patterning of these two measures and the religious measures can be studied as well. Finally, Benson and Spilka's 1972 report involved a set of God concept scales, which they had built based upon the earlier (1964) work of Spilka, Armatas, and Nussbaum. Those scales conceptually overlap Gorsuch's 1968 scales, thus permitting a comparison between the data generated by the two sets of God-concept instruments.

Results of the Study and Discussion

The results of this study will be reported under three headings: *self*-significance, *other*-significance, and *ultimate*-significance. A discussion of the results will be included in each of these sections, rather than following them.

Results of the Study: Self-Significance

The correlations between the measures of (a) self-significance and (b) both the committed-consensual and the intrinsic-extrinsic forms of religious commitment are presented in table 5.1. Although all of these correlation coefficients are in the low-to-moderate range, they do suggest some apparently meaningful associations between self-orientations and the forms of personal religious commitment. Moreover, *most* of these observed relationships are in the hypothesized direction (although there is some evidence of contradiction present). For example, the Coopersmith Self-Esteem Inventory correlates positively (in one sample) with the committed form of personal religion ($r = .316$) while it also correlates (in another sample) negatively with the consensual form of personal religion ($r = -.203$). A rather borderline, albeit statistically significant, coefficient ($r = .161$) indicates a positive association between the Coopersmith inventory and the consensual form of personal religion: this coefficient, however, may be a chance phenomenon, or it may tap an aspect of conforming, socially approved behavior that is able to give one a sense of esteem through a sense of "fitting in" (or being adjusted to the status quo). In the sample where this coefficient appears, the committed form of personal religion appears to be independent of self-

Table 5.1

Correlation Coefficients for the Association Between Personal Religion and Measures of Self-Significance: Data from 3 Groups

Measures of Self-Esteem:		Measures of Personal Religion—			
		Committed	Consensual	Intrinsic	Extrinsic
Coopersmith's	(1)	.081	.161*	−.014	−.013
Self-Esteem	(2)	.316**	.054	n. a.	n. a.
Inventory:	(3)	.015	−.203*	n. a.	n. a.
Schwartz-Tangri	(1)	n. a.	n. a.	n. a.	n. a.
Self-Esteem	(2)	.178*	.086	n. a.	n. a.
Semantic Diff.:	(3)	.189*	.016	n. a.	n. a.
Spilka's Factor	(1)	−.002	.105	.057	.295**
Analytic Scale of	(2)	−.159*	.061	n. a.	n. a.
Powerlessness:	(3)	−.027	.144	n. a.	n. a.
Rotter's Locus-	(1)	n. a.	n. a.	n. a.	n. a.
of-Control	(2)	−.371**	−.165*	n. a.	n. a.
Measure:	(3)	−.248*	−.053	n. a.	n. a.

Where: * = statistically significant at the .05 level
      ** = statistically significant at the .01 level
and where: (1) = Coefficients generated by data from 170 College students.
         (2) = Coefficients generated by data from 153 Catholic H. S. students.
         (3) = Coefficients generated by data from 99 Lutheran H. S. students.

Note: The correlation coefficients for groups (2) and (3) for the association between the Coopersmith inventory and the Committeed and Consensul scale are based on the original scoring procedures, rather than the revised procedures developed during this study.

esteem (r = .081). However, further support for the general pattern of association is provided (in two of the three samples in table 5.1) by the correlation coefficients for the Schwartz-Tangri scale and the committed form of personal religion (r = .178, and r = .198). Both of these coefficients are in a theoretically expected direction. Still, in the sample in which the Coopersmith inventory failed to be obviously and "meaningfully" related to the measures of committed or consensual personal religion, the measures of intrinsic and extrinsic personal religion also failed to exhibit an association with the Coopersmith inventory that reached a level of statistical significance (r = −.014, and r = −.013).

In two of the three samples in table 5.1, Spilka's powerlessness scale was meaningfully tied to the measures of personal religion. Among the college students, extrinsic personal religion was positively and significantly correlated with powerlessness (r = −.259); while among the Catholic high school students, a committed personal religion was negatively and significantly correlated with powerlessness (r = −.159). Thus, table 5.1 suggests that there is a tie of some sort between what could be called an eternalized, security-giving personal religion that is cognitively restricted and personal feelings of helplessness and futility.

It is worth noting that of the 20 correlation coefficients reported in table 5.1 in the columns headed Committed and Consensual, nine are statistically significant and as expected, while only one is opposite to what was expected. Although often quite low, these correlation coefficients do imply some support for the proposition that "constructive" forms of personal religion are to be found associated with "positive" self-orientations.

Results of the Study: Other-Significance

As previously noted, two measures of perspective and relationships to others were used in this study: Rosenberg's Faith-in-People scale and a modification of Duke and Nowicki's Comfortable Interpersonal Distance Scale. The Rosenberg scale was used with the Catholic college sample ($N = 170$). With this sample no significant correlation coefficients were obtained for the association between this scale and the measures of committed, consensual, or extrinsic personal religion. However, a low but statistically significant (and theoretically meaningful!) correlation coefficient was found for the association with intrinsic personal religion ($r = .173, p < .05$). Thus, a slight tendency may exist for an intrinsic personal religion to be associated with "positive" regard for other people.

Since the associations with the Faith-in-People scale were so minimal, the main weight of our effort to understand the association (if any) between forms of personal religion and the significance of others for an individual rested on our analyses of data generated by the CIDS of Duke and Nowicki.

The correlation coefficients in table 5.2 are based on the association between CIDS and the 4 forms of personal religion, when the referent person for the CIDS is (a) a stranger of the same sex as the respondent, or (b) a stranger of the opposite sex as the respondent. Although generally low, a surprising pattern of associations is revealed in the coefficients of table 5.2. In only one instance does the committed form of personal religion relate to this measure of interpersonal distance, and that relationship involves total distance computed across the total for all samples. The correlation coefficient is low ($r = .138$) but statistically significant (.01 level), although one must note that this may be an artifact of the fairly large number involved in this total sample ($N = 437$). Thus, since there is no other statistically significant coefficient to support this particular association, one cannot rule out the possibility that the observed relation is essentially a chance occurrence. In contrast, in 16 instances the consensual form of personal religion and this measure of interpersonal distance are so related to one another that statistically significant coefficients are obtained. In addition, 4 similarly positive coefficients are obtained for the relation between intrinsic personal religion and interpersonal distance, while 12 such coefficients are obtained

Table 5.2

Correlation Coefficients for the Association Between Comfortable Interpersonal Distance, Forms of Personal Religion, and Other-Significance: Data from 4 Groups, Plus a Total Combined Sample

Comfortable Interpersonal Distance: (Samples)	Forms of Personal Religious Orientation:							
	Committed:		Consensual:		Intrinsic:		Extrinsic:	
	Same[1]	Other[1]	Same[1]	Other[1]	Same[1]	Other[1]	Same[1]	Other[1]
Front Distance[2]								
(Catholic H. S.)	−.021	.106	.086	.096	−.005	.124	−.125	−.060
(Catholic College)	−.146	−.072	.272**	.291**	.078	.183*	.183*	.049
(Private College)	.033	.119	.946**	.166	.139	.178	.183	.233*
(Middle Adults)	−.022	.186	.269	.306**	.007	.181	.186	.137
(Total Sample)	−.060	.057	.209**	.230**	.052	.169**	.142**	.079
Rear Distance[2]								
(Catholic H. S.)	.037	.129	−.032	−.032	.068	.161	.016	−.079
(Catholic College)	.043	.114	.241**	.229**	.049	.100	.177*	.146
(Private College)	.086	.095	.118	.184	.215	.217	.146	.215
(Middle Adult)	−.100	.018	.279**	.242**	−.098	−.005	.229**	.175
(Total Sample)	.019	.019	.180**	.169**	.051	.111*	.149**	.117*
Total Distance[2]								
(Catholic H. S.)	.007	.142	.025	.030	.024	.156	−.048	−.068
(Catholic College)	−.051	.110	.126	.190*	−.054	.057	.209**	.131
(Private College)	.119	.113	.166	.161	.178	.176	.233*	.217
(Middle Adult)	−.072	.102	.319**	.278**	−.048	.089	.272**	.171
(Total Sample)	−.030	.138**	.147**	.171**	−.012	.107*	.161**	.136**

Where: 1 =   "Same" indicates that CIDS referent person is *same sex* as respondent.
                  "Other" indicates that CIDS referent person is *opposite sex* to respondent.
           2 =   All distance measurements from CIDS were taken in 16ths of an inch.
           * =   Indicates statistical significance at the .05 level.
         ** =   Indicates statistical significance at the .01 level.

(Catholic H. S.)   =   Catholic high school sample with N of 92.
(Catholic College)   =   Catholic college sample with N of 170.
(Private College)   =   Private college sample with N of 80.
(Middle Adult)   =   Middle years adult sample with N of 95.
(Total Sample)   =   Total of 4 samples combined, an N of 437.

for the relation between extrinsic personal religion and interpersonal distance. However, the correlation coefficients under the column for the consensual personal religion are the greatest in their magnitude.

Quite clearly the weight of these findings suggests that persons who are consensually and extrinsically oriented in their personal religion tend to keep other people at a greater distance from themselves. The 4 similar correlation coefficients for the intrinsic personal religion orientation may very well be a function of certain common elements in our present measures of consensual and intrinsic personal religion. (For example: over all samples, the measures of consensual and intrinsic orientations have a positive correlation of .418.)

It seems that one can certainly hypothesize that the data picture a situation in which persons with a committed and, possibly, an intrinsic orientation, too, are "taking people as they come," probably evaluating each person more or less as an individual. In contrast, the data seem to picture a situation in which one might hypothesize that persons with either a consensually or an extrinsically oriented personal religion tie together their perceptions of others with the "cord" of a sense of a threat in general. If that be true, one might suspect that they would exhibit either poorer interpersonal relationships or a rather pervasive distrust, or suspicion of other people, either individually or collectively.

In a 1967 report of research, Allen and Spilka noted a cognitive structuring that was exhibited by the consensually oriented. Therefore, we hypothesized that the forms of personal religion would prove to be especially sensitive to variations in the social position categories that can be used to characterize people. Thus, we theorized that there should be evidence of a tendency to vary interpersonal distance, especially upon the part of the consensually and extrinsically oriented, as the referent persons in the CIDS were varied in age, sex, and status. Findings that support this hypothesized relation are to be found in table 5.3, which reports the results for the two samples in which the CIDS was administered with such variations in the referent persons.

As one can readily see, our findings were especially strong for the sample from the private college. The referent person's age was varied by making them either 40 years old or 60 years old. The status of the referent person was varied by identifying them as either a dean or school principal (high status), or as either a waiter or waitress (low status). The sex of the referent person was also varied, although we do not here offer any separate analysis of the results in terms of the various combinations of respondents' sex.

A total of 32 statistically significant correlation coefficients was found for the sample of students from the private college, while only 3 statistically significant correlation coefficients were found for the sample of students from a Catholic high school. Of these 35 coefficients some 32 were in the hypothesized direction. Only 3 coefficients were not in the predicted direction, and these occurred in the sample of students from the private college on the scale of intrinsic personal religion. (Again, common elements between the Intrinsic and the Consensual scales may account for this result since, in the sample of private college students, the correlation between these two scales is a rather high .598.) Moreover, 14 of the significant correlation coefficients come from the Consensual scale, while 15 such coefficients come from the Extrinsic scale, and 10 of these coefficients are for the same categories. In this sample, the Consensual scale and the Extrinsic scale correlate with one another positively ($r = .330$) at a level that is statistically significant, although this coefficient is low enough to indicate relatively little overlap for these two scales of personal religious orientation.

Table 5.3

Correlation Coefficients for the Association Between Comfortable Interpersonal Distance, Forms of Personal Religion, Other-Significance by Respondents' Sex and Age, with Referent Varied by Social Status: Data from 2 Groups

Comfortable Interpersonal Distance Scale Referent Persons: (Status/Age/Sex)	Forms of Personal Religious Orientation:							
	Committed:		Consensual:		Intrinsic:		Extrinsic:	
	PC:[1]	CHS:[2]	PC:[1]	CHS:[2]	PC:[1]	CHS:[2]	PC:[1]	CHS:[2]
(High/40 yrs/Male)								
Front Distance	.000	−.150	.056	−.085	.100	−.109	.177	−.030
Rear Distance	.125	−.131	.176	−.101	.160	−.095	.048*	−.128
Total Distance	.088	−.136	.118	−.108	.115	−.080	.198	−.097
(High/40 yrs/Female)								
Front Distance	.066	−.160	.080	−.058	.157	−.157	.340**	−.018
Rear Distance	.115	−.131	.237*	.001	.148	−.158	.372**	−.142
Total Distance	.080	−.159	.202	−.026	.068	−.142	.252**	−.092
(High/60 yrs/Male)								
Front Distance	.046	−.196	.110	−.043	.107	−.211	.164	−.074
Rear Distance	−.055	−.134	.092	−.075	.044	−.167	.242*	−.144
Total Distance	−.019	−.163	.120	−.067	.040	−.169	.313**	−.114
(High/60 yrs/Female)								
Front Distance	.155	−.165	.217*	.052	.191	−.253*	.194	−.082
Rear Distance	.164	−.077	.270*	.060	.209	−.174	.264*	−.132
Total Distance	.171	−.115	.265*	.053	.039*	−.212*	.286**	−.104
(Low/40 yrs/Male)								
Front Distance	.057	−.018	.248*	.124	.166	.032	.199	−.026
Rear Distance	.147	−.012	.282**	.106	.235*	.015	.239*	.012
Total Distance	.068	−.026	.238*	.132	.125	.026	.218*	−.012
(Low/40 yrs/Female)								
Front Distance	.074	−.118	.101	−.059	.072	−.074	.060	.071
Rear Distance	.071	.015	.190	−.019	.119	−.009	.059	−.088
Total Distance	.054	−.051	.218*	−.031	.091	−.028	.105	−.015
(Low/60 yrs/Male)								
Front Distance	.054	−.152	.302**	−.023	.116	−.078	.285**	−.087
Rear Distance	.000	−.176	.271*	−.037	.108	−.117	.204	−.022
Total Distance	.038	−.175	.315**	−.019	.112	−.094	.291**	−.040
(Low/60 yrs/Female)								
Front Distance	.106	−.105	.270*	−.105	.181	−.098	.233*	−.029
Rear Distance	.169	−.029	.345**	−.044	.257*	−.051	.255*	−.060
Total Distance	.118	−.049	.301**	−.096	.160	−.066	.146*	−.051

Where: 1 = "PC" indicates a *private college* sample
   2 = "CHS" indicates a *Catholic high school* sample
   * = Indicates statistical significance at the .05 level
   ** = Indicates statistical significance at the .01 level

We believe it worth noting that the students in the private college sample exhibited an association between a consensual personal religion orientation and increasing interpersonal distance from both older and lower status persons. The sex of the referent person on the CIDS did not appear to exhibit any meaningful variation. When we compared the findings from table 5.3 with those reported in table 5.1 for the private college sample, we could see no meaningful relationships when the CIDS referent person was the same age, sex, or (implicitly) status as the respondent. The same is true where the referent person is the opposite sex, but the same age and (implicitly) status. In a word, introducing age, sex, and status variations into the situation does not appear to be relevant to the findings for consensual personal religion. Thus, our hypothesis gains some rather noteworthy support.

Almost identical findings can be observed for the extrinsic personal religion orientation. Apparently, to the extent that individuals do, in fact, possess a personal religion oriented consensually or extrinsically, one can presume that such persons are sensitive to and responsive to the significance of social position categories and social structures.

Although 3 statistically meaningful but hypothetically contradictory coefficients are evidenced in the private college student sample for the Intrinsic personal religion scale, these associations are balanced by 3 hypothetically expected coefficients (for this scale) evidenced by the students in the younger, high school student sample. Apparently there is some tendency among the younger subjects for an intrinsic personal religion orientation to be associated with a willingness to let other persons come closer to oneself. However, it should be noted that all of these correlations occur in relation to older, high status referent persons.

Since the findings for the Intrinsic personal religion scale for these two samples are not in agreement, a further evaluation of the hypothesis for this variable is necessary. On the other hand, the Committed personal religion scale revealed no statistically significant correlations with the measure of interpersonal distance. This finding seems to be in line with the findings reported earlier in table 5.1. Thus, it seems reasonable to infer that the individual with a committed personal religion judges (or tends to judge) each person on his or her merits, making social structural definitions simply irrelevant for the "committed" religionist.

Results of the Study: Ultimate-Significance

Almost by definition, God is the ultimate for consideration, contemplation, and devotion. At least, that is presumedly true for a "religious" person who identifies with an established church or synagogue. Therefore, it seems important to assess the relationship between a person's perspective on God and his or her form of personal religion. In order to do that, two approaches were employed in this study. First, a measure of the strength of one's belief in God was obtained, since faith defined in terms of a belief in God is a cornerstone of Christian theology. Second, the various concepts of God were evaluated, since many "images" of the divine coexist within our culture. For example, although Judaism counsels against efforts to either define or circumscribe God, biblical (and other) sources do provide a picture of a deity that seems to embody almost all possible facets of outlook and describes almost all possible responses to that deity. In those sources one can read of God as vengeful, taking retribution on "enemies," and of God as loving, fatherly, a benevolent ruler, although God is also described as jealous. However, traditional Christianity seems to use the figure of Jesus as a primary model. As a model, Jesus seems to stress God's justice, equity, forgiveness, and love. Variation is obvious, and should be expected.

In order to measure individual God images, two means were used in this study. Both of these means, however, were based upon the work of Spilka, Armatas, and Nussbaum in the early 1960s, especially their factor analyses of respondents' God concepts (1968). The first means involved six of Gorsuch's (1968) God Concept scales, which resulted from his replication, refinement, and extension of the original research of Spilka, Armatas, and Nussbaum. These six Gorsuch scales were used with the Catholic college student sample. The second means involved utilizing the previous work of Benson and Spilka, which had developed a series of God images, constructed variations upon these, and used a semantic differential approach to measurement (1972, 1973). The data from these earlier studies were available and pertinent to the topic, which is why they are included in this study. In table 5.4, these data are reported for two high school samples: a Catholic sample ($N = 153$), and a Lutheran sample ($N = 99$).

Theoretically, the committed and the intrinsic forms of personal religion should be positively associated with "favorable" images of God, as well as with a strong belief in the deity. In contrast, if the theory presented earlier were followed, the consensual and the extrinsic forms of personal religion should be positively associated with "unfavorable" images of God: for example, images of a punitive, controlling God or images of a God not involved in human affairs (Spilka and Reynolds 1965). This theoretical set of expectations can be addressed in terms of the data displayed in table 5.4.

A consideration of the correlation coefficients reported in table 5.4 will, we believe, support our set of theoretical expectations. More specifically, we think the following patterns are of importance.

The Catholic College Sample of 170 Students

In this sample, a positive and statistically significant relationship is observed between both the committed and the intrinsic forms of per-

Table 5.4

Correlation Coefficients for the Association Between Forms of Personal Religion and Specific God Concepts: Data from 3 Groups

God Concept Scales: (Gorsuch) (Benson & Spilka)	Forms of Personal Religious Orientation:			
	Committed:	Consensual:	Intrinsic:	Extrinsic:
Catholic College Sample (N = 170)				
Wrathful[1]	−.004	.151*	.010	.276**
Traditional Christian	.277**	.219**	.361**	.082
Kindliness	.308**	.231**	.334**	.000
Omni-ness	.104	−.015	.130	−.059
Deistic	−.270**	−.160*	−.318**	.099
God Belief	.525**	.249**	.557**	−.029
Catholic High School[2] Sample (N = 153)				
Vindictive God[3]	−.106	.170*	n. a.	n. a.
Stern Father	−.018	.043	n. a.	n. a.
Impersonal Allness	−.187*	−.122	n. a.	n. a.
Impersonal Distant	−.317**	.011	n. a.	n. a.
Kindly Father	.130	−.190*	n. a.	n. a.
Matchless-Timeless	−.089	.004	n. a.	n. a.
Impersonal Ruler	−.024	.091	n. a.	n. a.
Loving God	.155	−.214*	n. a.	n. a.
Controlling God	−.149	.146	n. a.	n. a.
God Belief	.412**	.177*	n. a.	n. a.
Lutheran High School[4] Sample (N = 99)				
Vindictive God[3]	.040	.038	n. a.	n. a.
Stern Father	.071	−.297**	n. a.	n. a.
Impersonal Allness	.007	−.172	n. a.	n. a.
Impersonal Distant	−.012	.160	n. a.	n. a.
Kindly Father	.119	−.119	n. a.	n. a.
Matchless-Timeless	.301**	.059	n. a.	n. a.
Impersonal Ruler	−.021	.167	n. a.	n. a.
Loving God	.031	−.201	n. a.	n. a.
Controlling God	−.048	.003	n. a.	n. a.
God Belief	.377**	.081	n. a.	n. a.

Where: 1 = The six Gorsuch scales of God concept

2 = Sample size for correlations was either 153 or 141; however, significance reported for appropriate N. Original scoring used for Committed and Consensual scales

3 = The ten God concepts scales of Benson & Spilka

4 = Sample size for correlations was either 99 or 87; however, significance reported for appropriate N. Original scoring used for the committed and consensual scales

* = Indicates statistical significance at the .05 level

** = Indicates statistical significance at the .01 level

sonal religion and what the Gorsuch scales call a Traditional Christian concept of God ($r_{c.tc}$ = .277; $r_{i.tc}$ = .361). That scale uses a series of descriptive adjectives, such as "creative," "gracious," "blessed," and "majestic," to describe God. A parallel finding is the relationship observed between these two forms of personal religion and what is called a Kindliness concept of God ($r_{c.k}$ = .308; $r_{i.k}$ = .334). The negative and statistically significant relationship between these two forms of personal religion and what is called a Deistic concept of God is also in line with our theoretical expectations ($r_{c.d}$ = -.270; $r_{i.d}$ = -.318). Apparently, the committed and intrinsic forms of personal religion deny a concept of God as uninvolved in human affairs! (Gorsuch's Deistic scales uses a series of descriptive words, such as "distant," "inaccessible," and "impersonal.") Further support for our theoretical expectation is to be found in the strong, positive, and statistically significant relationship between the committed and the intrinsic forms of personal religion and the scale called God Belief ($r_{c.gb}$ = .525; $r_{i.gb}$ = .557).

Our theoretical expectations receive further support from the pattern of correlation coefficients observed between the consensual and the extrinsic forms of personal religion and the several God concept scales of Gorsuch. Although there is some obvious overlap in God concepts with the committed and intrinsic forms of personal religion, the coefficients for the consensual and the extrinsic forms of personal religion are consistently of a lesser magnitude. As we have suggested earlier in this article, these overlaps are undoubtedly a function of the common components found in these several forms of personal religion. Thus, it is not surprising to observe lower, albeit statistically significant, coefficients for the relationship between the consensual form of personal religion and the Gorsuch scales called Traditional Christian, Kindliness, and Deistic ($r_{cn.tc}$ = .219; $r_{cn.k}$ = .231; $r_{cn.d}$ = -.160). Similarly, the God Belief scale and the consensual form of personal religion are obviously related, but at a lower level of magnitude ($r_{cn.gb}$ = .249). However, much more directly supportive of our theoretical expectation is the observed relationship between the scale called Wrathful and both the consensual and the extrinsic forms of personal religion ($r_{cn.w}$ = .151; $r_{e.w}$ = .276). This support is obvious when one notes that the relationship between the Wrathful scale and either the committed or the intrinsic forms of personal religion is essentially of a zero order ($r_{c.w}$ = -.004; $r_{i.w}$ = .010). Apparently only those holding a consensual or extrinsic form of personal religion are, by virtue of their form of personal religion, likely to also hold a concept of God as "wrathful."

The Catholic and Lutheran High School Samples of 153 and 99 Students

An examination of the results obtained earlier in studies by Benson and Spilka, using similar but not identical God Concept scales, indicates similar findings. For example, in both the Catholic high school and in the Lutheran high school samples the committed form of personal religion is positively and statistically significantly related to a scale called God Belief ($r_{c(chs).gb}$ = .412; $r_{c(lhs).gb}$ = .377). In both samples the consensual form of personal religion is also positively related to the God Belief scale, but the association is weaker ($r_{cn(chs).gb}$ = .177; ($r_{cn(lhs).gb}$ = .081).

In the Lutheran high school sample, a scale entitled Matchless-Timeless, which is akin to the view measured by Gorsuch's Traditional Christian scale, had a strong, positive, and statistically significant relationship with the committed form of personal religion ($r_{c(lhs).mt}$ = .301). In the Catholic high school sample there is also evidence that the committed form of personal religion tends to counter God concepts involving impersonal "allness" or impersonally "distant" from the individual ($r_{c(chs).ia}$ = -.187; $r_{c(chs).id}$ = -.317). Although there appear to be denominationally related differences for each of these scales, here we are most interested in signs of support for a theoretical expectation associated with differing forms of personal religion across denominational milieus.

In the Catholic high school sample, the consensual form of personal religion is positively and statistically significantly related to the scale entitled Vindictive God, while it is negatively and statistically significantly related to the scales entitled Kindly Father and Loving God ($r_{cn(chs).vg}$ = .170; $r_{cn(chs).kf}$ = -.190; $r_{cn(chs).lg}$ = -.214). The coefficients for the Lutheran high school sample are all in the same direction, but do not reach the level of statistical significance. In fact, the data from this sample of Lutheran high school students are not at all clear. The only statistically significant coefficient for the consensual form of personal religion is a negative one for the scale entitled Stern Father, which suggests that (in this sample) a consensual form of personal religion is associated with a denial of a God concept that could be described as that of a Stern Father ($r_{cn(lhs).sf}$ = .297).

A review of all of the correlation coefficients reported in table 5.4 for the association of forms of personal religion with various God concepts seems to definitely support the theoretical expectations we have advanced. The weight of the statistically significant correlation coefficients, therefore, supports the theoretical framework from which we drew those expectations. The intrinsic/committed orientation in a personal religion appears to be consonant with (a) a strong belief in the existence of a deity and (b) a concept of that deity as one possessing "loving" and "positive" qualities. Although it may be slightly less evident, it also seems that a consensual solidus extrinsic orientation in a personal religion is more likely to be associated with a concept of the deity as one possessing qualities best described as "wrathful," "vindictive," or "impersonal." Apparently the form of one's personal religion varies with the concept of God one holds.

A Summary and Concluding Remarks

The research reported in this study was carried out as part of a larger investigation, which has been concerned with refining the measurement techniques for the kinds of personal religion, or faith, individuals possess. This study represents the results of an opportunity to conduct an initial test of a broad theoretical framework suggested somewhat earlier by the senior author (Spilka 1970b). There he advocated the directing of theory in the field of the psychology of religion by explicit theological reference. In this study, that perspective upon the psychology of religion was, in something of a broad outline, tentatively evaluated.

According to the suggested theoretical framework, the expectation was that a faith, or personal religion, of commitment which, in other quarters, is termed an "intrinsic faith," would reveal affiliation with a desirable and constructive pattern of psychological orientations toward the self, others, and God. Moreover, these orientations would be in line with what both theologians and religionists generally have, for centuries, thought of as the goals of a spiritual allegiance and religious involvement. As here conceived, one could easily argue that these goals represent more what is called the "spirit of the word" than they do the "letter" of doctrine, which can so easily be quite narrowly conceived.

In contrast, the consensual form of personal religion, or faith, was viewed as more likely to be intellectually, emotionally, and spiritually either restricted or confining. As defined in this study, the consensual and the extrinsic forms of personal religion would, we expected, affiliate with less favorable psychological orientations toward the self, others, and God. This seems to be evident in the data we have reported here.

In summary, then, we recognize clearly the need for further psychometric development and refinement in this area of study, but the data seem to be quite clearly supportive of the hypotheses our theoretical framework suggested to us. The manner in which one is oriented toward the self, toward others, and toward God does appear to relate all of these domains to one another. It is possible, therefore, to imagine theology and psychology united in a common endeavor.[1]

1. The authors wish to express their deep appreciation for the supportive help provided by Ms. Cynthia Beattle, the Reverend Joseph Carbone, Ms. Shirley Greenspoon, Ms. Marguerite Rosensohn, Ms. Nanci Appleman, and Ms. Jean Hamman.

The text of this article is based upon a paper presented at the 1974 convention of the Society for the Scientific Study of Religion in Washington, D.C., on October 26, 1974.

References

Allen, R. O., and B. Spilka. 1967. Committed and consensual religion: A specification of religion-prejudice relationships. *Journal for the Scientific Study of Religion* 6: 191–206.

Allport, G. W., and J. M. Ross. 1967. Personal religious orientation and prejudice. *Journal of Personality and Social Psychology* 5: 432–43.

Benson, P., and B. Spilka. 1972. God image as a function of self-esteem and locus of control. Paper presented at the International Congress of Learned Societies in the Field of Religion, September 5, Los Angeles.

———. 1973. God image as a function of self-esteem and locus of control. *Journal for the Scientific Study of Religion* 12: 297–310.

Coopersmith, S. 1967. *The antecedents of self-esteem.* San Francisco: Freeman.

Duke, M. P., and S. Nowicki, Jr. 1972. A new measure and social learning model for interpersonal distance. *Journal of Experimental Research in Personality* 6: 119–32.

Gorsuch, R. L. 1968. The conceptualization of God in attitude ratings. *Journal for the Scientific Study of Religion* 1: 56–64.

Raschke, V. 1973. Dogmatism and committed and consensual religiosity. *Journal for the Scientific Study of Religion* 12: 339–44.

Rotter, J. B. 1966. Generalized expectancies for internal versus external control of reinforcement. *Psychological Monographs* 80, no. 1, whole no. 609: 1–28.

Schwartz, M., and S. S. Tangri. 1965. A note on self-concept as insulator against delinquency. *American Sociological Review* 30: 922–26.

Spilka, B. 1970a. *Alienation and achievement among Oglala Sioux secondary school students: A final report.* A final report for Project MH 11232. Washington, D.C.: National Institute of Mental Health, August.

———. 1970b. Images of man and dimensions of personal religion: Values for an empirical psychology of religion. *Review of Religious Research* 11: 171–82.

Spilka, B., and J. F. Reynolds. 1965. Religion and prejudice: A factor-analytic study. *Review of Religious Research* 6: 163–68.

Spilka, B., P. Armatas, and J. Nussbaum. 1964. The concept of God: A factor-analytic approach. *Review of Religious Research* 6: 28–36.

The Meaning of Personal Faith:
A Continuing Research Odyssey

Some years ago a Hasidic rabbi told the author that there is one religious duty—to search for the truth. In essence, this is the task that confronts all of us who are researchers in the psychology of religion. We have faith that the truth can be found and that we must pursue this elusive goal to the best of our capabilities.

Over the past 35 years, I would like to think that my concern has been to understand the role of religion in life. This view is based on the assumption that a faith that remains totally individual and seems to stay "inside" people is simply not possible. It must always find expression in daily living through the outlooks we have on ourselves, others, and the world (Spilka 1970, 1976). Such a perspective is by no means unique, but rather has underlain the work of most psychologists of religion over the past century.

Such an orientation stresses the functional–dysfunctional nature of personal faith, and, though a scientific psychological approach necessitates the development and utilization of assessable theoretical perspectives, my long-range hope is that the information that research could provide would not only feed back into theory and, thus, stimulate more research, but would also find expression in the applied realm. Unhappily this is a most difficult aspiration to achieve, for it relies on others who have both the knowledge and power to see how research ideas can be translated from what so often resembles the proverbial ivory tower to the domain of hard experience.

Although virtually every aspect of the psychology of religion seems to be inherently interesting, there has to be some semblance of a focus in one's work. No one selects the problems which they study with dispassion, and, though I have tentatively put forth a research finger into a number of different areas, my main efforts have been directed toward two issues of great personal importance—prejudice and death. They

From the *Journal of Psychology and Christianity* 5, no. 2 (1986): 85–90; reprinted by permission of the publisher and the author. Copyright 1986 by the Christian Association for Psychological Studies.

may not appear to be closely related, but might be through the way people express their faith. This is suggested by research. Still, as topics for research involvement, they were arrived at independently of each other, but both have led me on extremely gratifying intellectual journeys into the meaning of faith for individuals, religious institutions, and our social order.

Religion in Life: The Problem of Prejudice

My initial concern was the problem that conceptually religiosity and prejudice should be negatively associated, but empirically the data revealed the opposite—they tended to be positively correlated (Allport and Kramer 1946; Allport 1954; Struening and Spilka 1953).

The solution was already being formulated, namely, that religiousness was not a simple, single dimension, but rather consisted of a number of different expressions (Allport 1954, 1959, 1966; Fromm 1950). Increasingly empirical support for this idea was appearing, and the work of Gordon Allport and his students was in the forefront of operationalizing such distinctions (Allport and Ross 1967; Feagin 1964; Wilson 1960). Allport's designation of intrinsic and extrinsic forms of faith were exciting innovations that rapidly dominated work in the psychology of religion, and still exerts a powerful influence 25 years after their introduction. My efforts along similar lines were by no means as successful until the concepts of committed and consensual religion were advanced (Allen and Spilka 1967). Nevertheless, it soon became evident that this dichotomy fundamentally added a cognitive facet to the intrinsic–extrinsic framework, further affirming the validity of Allport's ideas.

The multidimensionality of personal religion is now an acknowledged fact and represents an avenue that merits increasing attention plus further development. That these different orientations have been fruitful both in research and in extending our understanding of the role of religion in life cannot be questioned (King and Hunt 1971; Spilka, Hood, and Gorsuch 1985). The future holds the prospect of increasing our knowledge of the nature of the intrinsic and extrinsic orientations, and uncovering additional dimensions. Work is proceeding along both lines. Donahue's (1985) review and meta-analysis both constitutes a summary of the past and opens some new directions for the future.

The issue of new dimensions is currently a controversial one. Batson's proposal of a quest form of faith defines faith as doubt and self-examination (Batson and Ventis 1982). The work of Batson and his students suggests a need for an extensive evaluation of the quest idea and a reevaluation of the intrinsic–extrinsic dichotomy (Batson 1976; Batson and Gray 1981; Batson and Raynor-Prince 1983). Much of this work is currently in process.

What appeared to be a solution to the religion–prejudice relationship some two decades ago has been challenged (Batson, Naifeh, and Pate 1978). The scene has now shifted to possible biases in the measures we use; thus, our old problem had appeared clothed in a newer fashion. All signs point to the likelihood that it will be with us for some time to come (Donahue 1985). These questions, of course, point graphically to the fact that we are still far from being able to apply what we know, but one hopes this continues to be a realistic goal.

Religion in Life: The Ultimate Problem of Death

One cannot study religion without being aware of its concern with death. It may be the oldest problem with which religion has dealt. Not a few thinkers have claimed that death created religion (Dewey 1960; Malinowski 1965). Whether or not such an inference is true, for most people death does seem to focus their thoughts on religious matters, particularly with respect to the existence of an afterlife. Contradiction, however, seems to have dominated this research literature up to the early 1970s. Researchers kept attempting to find relationships between death fear or anxiety and religious motivation, beliefs, and behavior. Lester (1967, 1972) and Martin and Wrightsman (1965) pointed to a host of conceptual and methodological shortcomings in this work, not the least of which was the treatment of religion as an undimensional phenomenon. Magni (1972) and Kahoe and Dunn (1975) corrected this shortcoming by introducing intrinsic and extrinsic forms of faith into this research area. Both showed that an intrinsic orientation relates to low death anxiety, and their agreement opened a new avenue for research on this very significant topic.

Though virtually all of the instruments used to assess death fear and concern treat this realm as if it were unitary, evidence that people think about death in a rather complex manner had been accumulating for some time. Prior to the construction of most of the measures of feelings about death, Murphy (1959) discussed seven attitudes toward death, but his insights were not operationalized until Hooper (1962) developed eight death-perspective scales. In further efforts (Hooper and Spilka 1970; Minton and Spilka 1976; Spilka, Stout, Minton, and Sizemore 1977), these were refined, and intrinsic and extrinsic inclinations were shown to relate differentially to the various death perspectives. A number of other researchers have either confirmed these earlier findings or, by advancing other schemes, extended research in this area (Cerny and Carter 1977; Hoelter and Epley 1979; Leming 1979).

There is no doubt that improved measurement and theoretical speculation will further clarify issues in death research, but like all real-life problems, at some point, they have to be dealt with on the level of application. To realize such a possibility we studied professionals who deal with death, namely, physicians, nurses, and clergy, and, of course, those with whom they work. In our research these were cancer patients and the families of children with cancer.

At first, we stressed the feelings, perspectives, and actions of clergy (Spilka, Spangler, Rea, and Nelson 1981, Spilka, Spangler, and Rea 1981) and then worked with the patients and their families (Spilka, Spangler, and Nelson 1983). These studies show some of the strengths and weaknesses of clergy when they relate to the terminally ill and their families, how death perspectives are part of this picture, but most of all those actions of some clergy and hospital chaplains that appear to help or hurt patients and their families. That such findings have import for pastoral training programs goes without saying, and action research that follows trainees still needs to be undertaken so that curricula may be continually improved. Though we must continue to develop and assess theoretical formulations about death and religion, some of the findings of this work are finding their way into the realm of practice. The relationship of religion and death will continue to be around indefinitely, but it is presently conceptualized in a considerably different way than it was a short time ago. We can be sure more changes are in the offing.

Some Future Directions

The issue of the multidimensionality of personal faith and the ramifications of possessing varying degrees of the different forms is currently a pressing one. The immediate problem is to establish the meaning of intrinsic, extrinsic, and quest forms. Donahue (1985) has raised some central questions about quest religion, and research is in process to assess a number of Batson's assertions (Spilka, Kojetin, and McIntosh 1985). We can expect new challenges, replies, and rejoinders to fill journal columns and convention programs for some time to come.

Of broader significance are efforts to develop general theories of the way individuals relate to religion. A number of such approaches have been advanced by psychologists and sociologists (Glock 1962, 1964; Stark and Bainbridge 1980; Spilka 1982; Spilka, Shaver, and Kirkpatrick 1985). Especially noteworthy about this literature is (1) its attempt to study both the motivation for and expression of "individual" religion in its social context and (2) its utilization of concepts from the mainstream of social-psychological theory. Glock (1964) stresses the role of deprivation in religious activity, tying faith to the core of tension-reduction motivational formulations. Stark and Bainbridge (1980) develop the same basic theme further by embracing Homans's (1950, 1974) idea of social exchange, which is basically a view of human behavior premised on economic considerations of reward and cost. Spilka (1982) still on a rather broad level, added the possibility of growth motivation rather than simply what Maslow (1964) terms "deficiency motivation." The latter underlies the frameworks advanced by Glock and Stark and Bainbridge. More recent work has, however, attempted to present an attributional framework that includes both motivational and cognitive factors (Proudfoot and Shaver 1975; Spilka, Shaver, and Kirkpatrick 1985).

The enthusiasm with which scholars have embraced attribution theory testifies to its heuristic utility, leading this worker to believe it may be one of the prime guides for future research in the psychology of religion. This position has already proven productive in terms of what Dienstbier (1979) has denoted "emotion-attribution theory." This focuses on labeling the causes of emotional states when some degree of ambiguity is present. Stated most clearly relative to religion by Proudfoot and Shaver (1975), this view has stimulated work by Imhoff and Malony (1978) and Spradlin and Malony (1981). This perspective seems particularly appropriate to the investigation of religious experience.

Emotion-attribution theory has been placed in a broader systematic conceptualization: general attribution theory, which is concerned with the overall explanatory framework people use to explain life events. Given evidence and speculation that spans more than two centuries that individuals need to derive meaning and maintain and enhance personal control and self-esteem, our orientation suggests how these motives are realized through religion (Spilka, Shaver, and Kirkpatrick 1985). The research potential of this approach is stressed through the explicit formulation of axioms and derivations that include characteristics of the attributor and the event in question. Attention is also afforded the contexts of these two factors.

Independent of our work with these notions (Spilka and Schmidt 1983), similar directions have been taken by Gorsuch and Smith (1983), relative to the attribution of responsibility to God, and Pargament and Sullivan (1981) on control attributions. More work is in progress to tie together such attributor characteristics as form of personal faith to attributions of power and control (Spilka, Kojetin, and McIntosh 1985).

Also distinct from our efforts and those of the other psychologists of religion cited above, new theoretical possibilities have been advanced relative to control attributions (Folkman 1984; Lazarus and Folkman 1984; Rothbaum, Weisz, and Snyder 1982; Weisz, Rothbaum, and Blackburn 1984). Meaning enters the picture through the proposal of primary and secondary forms of cognitive appraisal—the first dealing with well-being (hence its relevance to esteem), while the latter focuses on coping options (Folkman 1984).

With regard to these and the question of control, this realm is also analyzed into primary and secondary forms. Primary control is concerned with changing existing realities, while secondary control stresses self-change. Four different forms of secondary control are posited that are particularly cogent to religion (Rothbaum, Weisz, and Snyder 1982). Though religion can be seen as pointing in both directions, Weisz, Rothbaum, and Blackburn (1984) explicitly suggest the role of secondary control in Buddhism and Christianity. The next step may be to extend these ideas to what we know about the nature of the kind of personal faith one embraces, for example, intrinsic-extrinsic.

To return to one of the first considerations suggested in this paper, namely, the functional-dysfunctional potential on religion, my inclination is to perceive the preceding formulations as opening new doors to meaningful research and application in the psychology of religion. One's faith is conceived as being an integral part of coping with everyday living. Our problem is to emphasize how people cognitively deal with their personal worlds, the place of religion within such systems, and what these imply for behavior. In essence, we have "a continuing research odyssey."

References

Allen, R. O., and B. Spilka. 1967. Committed and consensual religion: A specification of religion-prejudice relationships. *Journal for the Scientific Study of Religion* 6: 191–206.

Allport, G. W. 1954. *The nature of prejudice.* Cambridge, Mass.: Addison-Wesley.

———. 1959. Religion and prejudice. *Crane Review* 2: 1–10.

———. 1966. The religious context of prejudice. *Journal for the Scientific Study of Religion* 5: 447–57.

Allport, G. W., and B. M. Kramer. Some roots of prejudice. *Journal of Psychology* 22: 9–39.

Allport, G. W., and J. M. Ross. 1967. Personal religious orientation and prejudice. *Journal of Personality and Social Psychology* 5: 432–43.

Batson, C. D. 1976. Religion as prosocial: Agent or double agent? *Journal for the Scientific Study of Religion* 15: 29–45.

Batson, C. D., and R. A. Gray. 1981. Religious orientation and helping behavior: Responding to one's own or to the victim's needs. *Journal of Personality and Social Psychology* 40: 511–20.

Batson, C. D., and L. Raynor-Prince. 1983. Religious orientation and complexity of thought about existential concerns. *Journal for the Scientific Study of Religion* 22: 38–50.

Batson, C. D., and W. L. Ventis. 1982. *The religious experience: A social-psychological perspective.* New York: Oxford Univ. Press.

Batson, C. D., S. J. Naifeh, and S. Pate. 1978. Social desirability, religious orientation, and racial prejudice. *Journal for the Scientific Study of Religion* 17: 31–41.

Cerny, L. J., II, and J. D. Carter. 1977. Death perspectives and religious orientation as a function of Christian faith. Paper presented at the 1977 Convention of the Society for the Scientific Study of Religion, October, Chicago, Ill.

Dewey, J. 1960. *The quest for certainty.* New York: Capricorn.

Dienstbier, R. A. 1979. Emotion-attribution theory: Establishing roots and exploring future perspectives. In *Nebraska symposium on motivation 1978,* ed. R. A. Dienstbier, 237–306. Lincoln: Univ. of Nebraska Press.

Donahue, M. J. 1985. Intrinsic and extrinsic religiousness: Review and meta-analysis. *Journal of Personality and Social Psychology* 48: 400–419.

Feagin, J. R. 1964. Prejudice and religious types: A focused study of southern fundamentalists. *Journal for the Scientific Study of Religion* 4: 3–13.

Folkman, S. 1984. Personal control and stress and coping processes. A theoretical analysis. *Journal of Personality and Social Psychology* 46: 839–52.

Fromm, E. 1950. *Psychoanalysis and religion.* New Haven: Yale Univ. Press.

Glock, C. Y. 1962. On the study of religious commitment. *Religious Education Research Supplement* 57, no. 4: 98–110.

———. The role of deprivation in the origin and evolution of religious groups. In Religion and social conflict, ed. R. Lee and M. E. Marty, 24–36. New York: Oxford Univ. Press.

Gorsuch, R. L., and C. S. Smith. 1983. Attributions of responsibility to God: An interaction of religious beliefs and outcomes. *Journal for the Scientific Study of Religion* 22: 340–52.

Hoelter, J. W., and R. J. Epley. 1979. Religious correlates of fear of death. *Journal for the Scientific Study of Religion* 18: 404–11.

Homans, G. C. 1950. *The human group.* New York: Harcourt, Brace.

———. 1974. *Social behavior: Its elementary forms.* Rev. ed. New York: Harcourt Brace Jovanovich.

Hooper, W. T. 1962. Personal values and meanings of future time and death among college students. Unpublished dissertation, University of Denver.

Hooper, W. T., and B. Spilka. 1970. Some meanings and correlates of future time and death perspectives among college students. *Omega* 1: 49–56.

Hunt, R. A., and M. B. King. 1971. The intrinsic-extrinsic concept: A review and evaluation. *Journal for the Scientific Study of Religion* 10: 339–56.

Imhoff, M., and H. N. Malony. 1978. Physiological arousal, environmental cues, and the report of religious experience: A test of attribution theory. Paper presented at the annual meeting of the Society for the Scientific Study of Religion, October, Hartford, Conn.

Kahoe, R. D., and R. F. Dunn. 1975. The fear of death and religious attitudes and behavior. *Journal for the Scientific Study of Religion* 14: 379–82.

Lazarus, R. S., and S. Folkman. 1984. *Stress, appraisal, and coping.* New York: Springer Publishing.

Leming, M. R. 1979. The effects of personal and institutionalized religion upon death attitudes. Paper presented at the 1979 Convention of the Society for the Scientific Study of Religion, October, San Antonio, Tex.

Lester, D. 1967. Experimental and correlational studies of the fear of death. *Psychological Bulletin* 67: 27–36.

———. 1972. Religious behaviors and attitudes toward death. In *Death and presence,* ed. A. Godin, 107–24. Brussels: International Center for Studies in Religious Education.

Magni, K. C. 1972. The fear of death. In *Death and presence,* ed. A. Godin, 125–38. Brussels: International Center for Studies in Religious Education.

Malinowski, B. 1965. The role of magic and religion. In *A reader in comparative religion,* ed. W. A. Lessa and E. Z. Vogt, 63–72. New York: Harper and Row.

Martin, D., and L. S. Wrightsman. 1965. The relationship between religious behavior and concern about death. *Journal of Social Psychology* 65: 317–23.

Maslow, A. H. 1964. *Religions, values, and peak experiences.* Columbus: Ohio State Univ. Press.

Minton, B., and B. Spilka. 1976. Perspectives on death in relation to powerlessness and form of personal religion. *Omega* 1: 261–68.

Murphy, G. 1959. Discussion in *The meaning of death,* ed. H. Feifel, 317–40. New York: McGraw-Hill.

Pargament, K. I., and M. Sullivan. 1981. Examining attributions of control across diverse personal situations: A psychosocial perspective. Paper presented at the convention of the American Psychological Association, August, Los Angeles.

Proudfoot, W., and P. Shaver. 1975. Attribution theory and the psychology of religion. *Journal for the Scientific Study of Religion* 14: 317–30.

Rothbaum, F., J. R. Weisz, and S. S. Snyder. 1982. Changing the world and changing the self: A two-process model of perceived control. *Journal of Personality and Social Psychology* 42: 5–37.

Spilka, B. 1970. Images of man and dimensions of personal religion: Values for an empirical psychology of religion. *Review of Religious Research* 11: 171–82.

———. 1976. The compleat person: Some theoretical views and research findings for a theological-psychology of religion. *Journal of Psychology and Theology* 4: 15–24.

———. 1982. Theory in the psychology of religion. William James Award lecture given at the convention of the American Psychological Association, August, Washington, D.C.

Spilka, B., and G. Schmidt. 1983. General attribution theory for the psychology of religion: The influence of event-character on attributions to God. *Journal for the Scientific Study of Religion* 22: 326–39.

Spilka, B., R. W. Hood, Jr., and R. L. Gorsuch. 1985. *The psychology of religion: An empirical approach.* Englewood Cliffs, N.J.: Prentice-Hall.

Spilka, B., B. Kojetin, and D. McIntosh. 1985. Forms and measures of personal faith: Questions, correlates and distinctions. *Journal for the Scientific Study of Religion* 24: 437–42.

Spilka, B., P. Shaver, and L. A. Kirkpatrick. 1985. A general attribution theory for the psychology of religion. *Journal for the Scientific Study of Religion* 24: 1–20.

Spilka, B., J. D. Spangler, and C. Nelson. 1983. Spiritual support in life-threatening illness. *Journal of Religion and Health* 22: 98–104.

Spilka, B., J. D. Spangler, and M. P. Rea. 1981. The role of theology in pastoral care for the dying. *Theology Today* 38: 16–29.

Spilka, B., J. D. Spangler, M. P. Rea, and C. Nelson. 1981. Religion and death: The clerical perspective. *Journal of Religion and Health* 20: 299–306.

Spilka, B., L. Stout, B. Minton, and D. Sizemore. 1977. Death and personal faith: A psychometric investigation. *Journal for the Scientific Study of Religion* 16: 169–78.

Spradlin, W. H., and H. N. Malony. 1981. Psychological state deviation, personal religiosity, setting variation, and the report of religious experience. Paper presented at the annual meeting of the Society for the Scientific Study of Religion, October, Baltimore.

Stark, R., and W. S. Bainbridge. 1980. Towards a theory of religious commitment. *Journal for the Scientific Study of Religion* 19: 114–28.

Struening, E. L., and B. Spilka. 1953. A study of certain social and religious attitudes of university faculty members. *Psychological Newsletter* 43: 1–18.

Weisz, J. R., F. M. Rothbaum, and T. C. Blackburn. 1984. Standing out and standing in: The psychology of control in America and Japan. *American Psychologist* 39: 955–69.

Wilson, W. C. 1960. Extrinsic religious values and prejudice. *Journal of Abnormal and Social Psychology* 60: 286–88.

Benjamin Beit-Hallahmi

B enjamin Beit-Hallahmi, currently associate professor of psychology a the University of Haifa, was born in Tel-Aviv in 1943. In
1966 he graduated from the Hebrew University, majoring in psychology and sociology, and in 1970 received a Ph.D. in clinical psychology from Michigan State University. Since then he has held full-time
appointments at the University of Michigan and the University of Haifa
and visiting appointments at Hebrew University, Tel-Aviv University, the
Israel Institute of Technology, the University of Pennsylvania, Michigan
State University, Central Michigan University, Vassar College, Columbia
University, and New York University.

Dr. Beit-Hallahmi is a fellow of the American Psychological Association (APA) and is also an active member of the Society for the Scientific
Study of Religion and the European Symposium for the Psychology of
Religion. He is a reviewer for *The International Journal for the Psychology of Religion* and the *Journal for the Scientific Study of Religion*.

Beit-Hallahmi has authored *Psychoanalysis and Religion: A Bibliography* (Norwood, Penn.: Norwood Editions, 1978), *Prolegomena to the
Psychological Study of Religion* (Lewisburg, Penn: Bucknell Univ. Press,
1989), and *Dictionary of Modern Religious Movements* (New York:
Richards Rosen, 1990). He has coauthored *The Social Psychology of
Religion* (with Michael Argyle, London: Routledge and Kegan Paul,
1975), *Twenty Years Later: Kibbutz Children Grown Up* (with A. I. Rabin,
New York: Springer Publishing, 1982), and *The Kibbutz Bibliography*
(with S. Shur, J. R. Blasi, and A. I. Rabin, 1981). In addition to editing
Research in Religious Behavior (Monterey, Calif.: Brooks-Cole, 1973), Dr.
Beit-Hallahmi has published 75 articles and book chapters. Besides his
publications in psychology, Beit-Hallahmi has written widely about

169

political affairs, including his books *The Israeli Connection: Who Israel Arms and Why* (New York: Pantheon, 1987), and *Original Sins* (1990).

In his essay "Religion as Art and Identity," Beit-Hallahmi joins William James in stating that the uniqueness of religion lies in its content, not in the psychological processes involved. Believing that religion shares basic psychological processes with art, he uses metaphor to study religion as a form of art, concluding that illusion, which should be strongly differentiated from delusion, is common to both. Religion is also understood by Beit-Hallahmi to be intricately involved in the formation of individual and group identity. For this reason, he views religion as a form of art that makes claims about reality.

In the article "Goring the Sacred Ox: Toward a Psychology of Religion," Beit-Hallahmi shows, through historical analysis, how academic psychology has tried to distance itself from psychology of religion and how religion (i.e., theologians and philosophers) has tried to tame it. He calls for the deghettoization of the psychology of religion, outlining his own contributions to the cause.

Religion as Art and Identity

Introduction

A common theme in the literature on the psychology of religion is the search for psychological processes unique to religion. Here is a contrasting viewpoint, which states that religion is not unique in terms of process, but rather in terms of content. The psychological processes involved in religious activities can be found in other human activities, and art is one example of human activity in which processes similar to those operating in religion are involved. Through looking at the psychology of art, we may gain useful insights into the psychology of religion. This may be not just a useful way, but a major way, of understanding religion because religion, like art, is so readily recognized for being an expressive human activity, something which is noninstrumental, but nevertheless so pervasive. At the least, this would be a useful intellectual exercise, providing insights through the application of analogies. At the most, it would be a way of obtaining major new insights into religion. Art is simply the most similar to religion among all spheres of human activity. That is why we use it as our starting point. We definitely regard art as a general category, denoting a wide range of human activity, and religion as a more limited case, exemplifying the basic processes of the general category of art.

Presenting an analogy, or finding an analogy for something we are studying, is a way of gaining new understanding and insights. Scientific creativity consists of finding fruitful analogies and metaphors, normally referred to as models. Here I am suggesting a metaphor and a model, which will contribute to the development of a general theory of religion. The starting point, the moment of discovery, can be summarized as a metaphor, in the sense adopted by Black: "Metaphor is, at its simplest, a way of proceeding from the known to the unknown. It is a way of cognition in which the identifying qualities of one thing are transferred in an

From *Religion* 16 (1986): 1–17; reprinted by permission of the publisher and the author. Copyright 1986 by Academic Press Inc. (London) Ltd.

instantaneous, almost unconscious, flash of insight to some other thing that is, by remoteness, or complexity, unknown to us. . . . Metaphor is our means of effecting instantaneous fusion of two separated realms of experience into one illuminating, iconic, encapsulating image" (1962, 4).

This analogy between art and religion is based on the belief that both can be explained through basic and common psychological processes. The ideas expressed here are only a preliminary contribution, but the main point is intended to be taken quite seriously: looking at religion as a form of art may be a considerable advance over previous attempts to develop a coherent psychology of religion. Using art as a starting point in formulating our observations may help us in understanding the basic processes, the functions and the consequences, of religion.

The important theoretical contribution by Pruyser (1976) draws attention to various similarities between religion and art. In both art and religion we have universal psychological processes, the general experience of an imaginary world, together with specific cultural products and traditions, and the psychological response to both is similar. Both art and religion exist as social institutions for the same reasons: to provide gratification through fantasy. Art in practice, for both the artist and the audience, involves the combination of imagination and emotional arousal. So does religion. In religion, as in art, we have the involvement of producer-artists, products of the artists' work, and the audience which is responding to the artist through the product. Religion, as art, according to Pruyser, is the product of human imagination, being made possible by uniquely human qualities. The psychological process of responding to religion is similar to the process of responding to other forms of art. It includes the activation of the human capacity for imagination and fantasy and the involvement of such processes as identification, projection, displacement, and reaction-formation. While I take Pruyser's (1976) ideas as an important starting point, I intend to go much further, as will be seen in what follows.

To highlight the basic psychological similarities between the institution of art and the institution of religion in human society, we might say that both institutions are expressive, that is, noninstrumental, emotional, irrational, and "feminine." Religion, like art, is a form, and a product, of human labor. It is a system created by humans and a proof of human activity and genius. To put this claim in the strongest possible terms: religion is a work of art. It is (for believers, and even for nonbelievers) beautiful, harmonious, pleasing, and attractive. In a confused, confusing, and cruel world, where mankind feels helpless before nature and history, religion and art provide order and beauty. Religion and art are both comforting illusions in a world which makes such illusions necessary, to paraphrase Marx. Religion has inspired art much more naturally and easily, and with better results, than any kind of secular ideology, which may serve as another indication of their affinity. We will not deal here with the effect of religion on art as a source of inspiration, since this separate topic has been dealt with extensively in art history.

Turning to anthropological and sociological literature, we find both classical and contemporary expression of this notion. Malinowski, in his great work *Magic, Science, and Religion* (1925), which is really an important contribution to the psychology of religion, approvingly quotes Jane Harrison, who has said that "Art and religion alike spring from unsatisfied desire" (1911). Raymond Firth (1981, 584) has explicitly made the same claim I am making here regarding the basic nature of religion, and in clear enough language, as follows:

> Religion is really a form of human art, a symbolic product of human anxiety, desire, and imagination expressed in a social milieu. Like any art, religion is a product of tension—between the ideal and the actual, between the individual and the mass, between the urge to satisfaction and life, and recognition of the inevitability of suffering and death. A religion is distinguished from other arts by three main criteria. Its most effective expressions are generated, as in all arts, by individual creative effort, but they depend more than other arts upon tradition and membership of a community. Again, while every art has its forms and ceremonies to guard its practice, the rituals of religion tend to be so frequent, elaborate, evocative, and mandatory that they provide very strong guidelines for faith. Then, the rules of religious interpretation and conduct, unlike those of science and philosophy or the visual arts, are given a legitimacy of ultimate authority which is regarded as absolute and unchallengeable by those who subscribe to them. Now politics has been variously described as the art of the possible, or the art of the plausible. However this may be, one basic character of religion is clear—after a certain point it becomes the art of the implausible, in the sense of resting upon postulates which are non-empirical, which claim an inner rather than an outer appearance of truth, since they may run counter to what are ordinarily thought of as natural laws. In this promise to provide explanations which go beyond the world of sensory experience lies much of the appeal of religion.

In the literature of psychoanalysis, the Freudian notion of illusion is used to explain both art and religion in a way strikingly similar to Harrison's, as the fulfillment of unsatisfied or unattainable wishes through imaginary means. Kardiner (1939, 1945), combining psychoanalysis and anthropology, defines both art and religion as cultural projective systems. The psychological mechanism of projection is basic to our understanding of art, and it is basic in some theories of religion, notably Freud's and Marx's. According to psychoanalytic conceptions, religion is a projection of early family relations onto a cosmic screen. According to Marx, religion is an upside-down projection of social relations in the real world. In both cases there is a creative process involved.

Ego psychology views the whole of human behavior as adjustment efforts on the part of the ego and assumes that the ego's defense mechanisms and defense maneuvers are the basis for both art and religion. Art (and religion) are ways in which we turn away from directly coping with reality. Kris (1952) and others have referred to a "regression in the service of the ego." There are obvious reality limits on how much we can regress, and how often. That is why art may be regarded as a luxury, which we cannot always afford. Continuing the line developed by Kris, Brenner (1966) spoke of regression in the service of the ego, as it appears, in his words, "in intellectual and artistic creativity, in the enjoyment of works of art, in religious activities" (395).

Winnicott (1971) offers a fascinating conceptualization of the basic processes common to art and religion and refers explicitly to both, as he states: "I am therefore studying the substance of *illusion* [italics in the original], that which is allowed to the infant, and which in adult life is inherent in art and religion, and yet becomes the hallmark of madness when an adult puts too powerful a claim on the credulity of others . . ." (3). This substance of illusion is also the basis for "play, . . . artistic creativity and appreciation, . . . religious feelings, dreaming, fetishism, lying and stealing . . . and the talisman of obsessional rituals" (5). Winnicott arrived at this conception through the study of transitional objects, the infant's first possession, to which it is extremely attached, the proverbial "security blanket." The relationship to this object is the model for a special mode of experiencing. According to Winnicott:

> Transitional objects and transitional phenomena belong to the realm of illusion which is at the basis of initiation of experience. This early stage in development is made possible by the mother's special capacity for making adaptation to the needs of her infant, thus allowing the infant the illusion that what the infant creates really exists.
>
> The intermediate area of experience, unchallenged in respect of its belonging to inner or external (shared) reality, constitutes the greater part of the infant's experience, and throughout life is retained in the intense experiencing that belongs to the arts and to religion. . . . (14)

Religion as Art

Basic Elements

There are two major social roles in art: the role of the creator and the role of the audience (spectator, consumer). Kreitler and Kreitler (1972) suggest that concentrating on the role of the creator in art leads to the study of artistic motivation, creativity, uniqueness of artistic creativity, and the development of artistic creativity. Concentrating on the role of the audience in art leads to the study of the psychological processes involved in experiencing art, the development of the experience of art, and the effects of the experience of art. We can find exact parallels for the preceding concepts as we develop a psychology of religion.

We may describe great religious leaders and mystics as equivalent to great artists, theologians and philosophers of religion as equivalent to art historians and art critics, and the great mass of believers may be compared to art audiences and consumers. We can concentrate on religious creators (i.e., religious innovators, leaders, and saints), or we can examine the religious audience of common believers in their common experience of religion as a social reality. Truly creative individuals, in both art and religion, are few and far between. Spectators, in both art and religion, far outnumber creators.

The psychology of art assumes a certain unity of basic processes, which are involved in all forms of art. Now we suggest that the same processes are involved in religion. The process of artistic creation is a mode for understanding the process of religious creation. Individual (and group) reactions to religion can best be interpreted by looking at individual (and group) reactions to art. Both art and religion are based on imagination and emotional involvement (or emotional "arousal"). These are the necessary conditions for the existence of both. There are, of course, cognitive, conscious processes involved in the creation of art, which are as crucial as the presumed unconscious ones.

There is an individualistic bias in the psychology of religion, and a similar individualistic bias in the psychology of art. But the individual does not invent his own religion and does not come to experience it individually. Art, likewise, is not created, nor is it experienced, outside of social relations. A social system creates both religion and art. For the past 100 years there has been in the literature a common emphasis on the personal and private nature of the religious experience. And what is more private, personal, and ineffable than the aesthetic experience, which is much more common than the ecstatic "religious experience" described by James (1902)?

In religious ritual the artistic elements are most obvious and most conscious. The ritual is designed as a drama which enacts the relationship between the believer and the deity. Ritual is a highly structured repetition of a religious drama, designed to heighten emotions and commitments. The aesthetic nature of the experience is conscious and intentional. Much conscious effort is put into making ritual as artistically successful as possible. Even a sermon is first of all an artistic product, which has to capture attention and keep it, shed a new light on a common experience, and arouse strong feelings. When I participate in a religious ritual, or when I have a religious experience, I am an actor. The difference between ritual and individual experience is in the stage on which the drama is played out. Ritual provides ready-made structure. In individual experience I am both actor and playwright. Seguy (1977) has discussed the production of emotion and the control of emotion by various conscious and deliberate means, which he has termed "elements de spectacle," in religious ritual. He implies an awareness of the artistic process of ritual on the part of religious institutions. The goal of artistic technologies is to enable us, the audience, to put a distance between ourselves and our normal reality testing. That is why art needs special expressive styles, and the same expressive styles exist in religious rituals. Literary style, as opposed to everyday language, takes us away from reality. Poetry is less reality-related than prose, and special religious language has similar effects. The kind of coping which is represented by the two human activities of art and religion is characterized by being expressive, magical, or imaginary, and that special kind of coping, different from instrumental coping, is based on several basic psychological mechanisms.

Identification and Catharsis

Inspiration and identification are two terms crucial to the understanding of both art and religion. The mechanism of identification, which is so essential to art, operates selectively, according to given cultural constraints. Through identification, each member of the audience can participate in the unfolding drama on stage, and in the case of religion, each can participate in a drama set on a cosmic stage. Any religious myth is a fantasy, which has been created to serve the needs of both creator and audience. To be acceptable to the audience, it has to be reliable from a psychological point of view, not from any other viewpoint. This is the artistic, psychological truth of mythology.

There have been attempts to define religion or "religious experience" through a special form of emotional arousal, which is supposedly involved in it. Defining religion by emotion arousal, "emotionality," or "catharsis" is a "functional" definition, which is too broad to be useful. Emotional arousal, emotionality, or catharsis can be found in various human activities, most of which cannot be defined as religious. When we look closely at the process of emotional arousal in religion, we discover that it is indistinguishable from the process of emotional arousal in situations which would be defined as secular. Ecstasy is to be found among the participants in religious ceremonies, but it would also be found among participants in rock concerts, football games, and political rallies. The triggering of ecstasy by similar means, leading to very similar results, can be seen in three varieties of American popular culture: the revival meeting, the pop concert, and the college football game. In all three rituals we can see the effects of a mass setting, music, and group identification leading to a heightening of emotions and to ecstasy and exhilaration, warmth, joy, happiness—as the audience shares in this state of emotional arousal.

All religions offer us opportunities for joy and sadness. Religious rituals give us opportunities for ritual joy and for ritual mourning. We rejoice at victories, salvations, and promises of salvation. We mourn at the defeats of the just and faithful, of ancient destructions and massacres. The ritual experiencing of victories and defeats is capable of creating real catharsis, but there is an enormous range of individual reactions to religious stimuli, ranging from no response to sublime ecstasy.

There is a whole range of private experiences in both art and religion. Not every private aesthetic experience leads to ecstasy, nor does every private religious experience. Art is a good starting point for understanding the gradations of individual arousal in response to emotional stimuli. The gradations of emotional arousal related to both art and religion may be adumbrated through the following scale, from high to low: mystical experience, ecstasy, catharsis, relief of tension, anxiety reduction and a pleasant feeling. All of these terms describe levels of excitement and pleasure. All of them represent experiences which occur in response to both religious and artistic stimuli. In both religion and art, ecstatic experiences are rare. The notion of using "religious experience" as the starting point for the understanding of religion tends to obliterate this obvious fact. For most religious people, religion is experienced through routine rituals, rather than ecstasy. For most people, art is experienced as mildly pleasurable, rather than ecstatically cathartic. For most religious believers, religious activities and involvements are remarkably nondramatic. There are no miracles, no religious crises, and no mystical experiences in their own lives.

Illusion and Belief

From the nonbelieving observer's point of view, the question which creates the need for a psychology of religion goes as follows: "How can people believe in something which is so clearly an illusion?" One answer, which leads us to the task at hand, is "But in art they do it all the time, and nobody asks why." The suspension of disbelief is a precondition for the enjoyment of art and the acceptance of religion. (The enjoyment of religion as a form of art is not limited to believers. Even nonbelievers, such as myself, enjoy religious stories, symbols, and rituals as a source of aesthetic pleasure.) The basis for this experience is described by Taylor as follows:

> The fact that we have the ability to conceive of the "as if" is a central feature of human consciousness. Imagining, and being able to think of what is not the case, are clear instances of how fundamental this ability is to human thought. We can make it as though things are impinging upon

consciousness when they are not, and this ability is one we put to use in a variety of ways. One of the possibilities for us, in this respect, is the creation of "as if" worlds that there is the possibility of us entering for their own sake. We can create situations and objects that are not the same as other situations and objects but which are like them. Moreover, we can see and respond to the likenesses we create although knowing they are only likenesses. (1981, 177)

Unlike any other kind of art, a unique claim is made, in the case of religion, for the truth of the artistic message. The products of imagination are differentiated from the products of the secular artistic imagination by their special psychological status of holiness and are proclaimed to be true, while art is always recognized as illusion. Thus, religion can be defined as that form of art which is claimed to be not just beautiful, but also true. What may be unique in the artistic process through which religion is created is that the creators of religion ascribe their artistic achievements to divine sources. The question of "truth" is central to both religion and art, though in different ways. Adherents of a religion believe in the literal truth of its claims. Art audiences are likely to speak of "artistic truth," which is quite different. Following Freud ([1927] 1961) we may suggest that whatever truth there is in religion and art must be psychological truth.

One of the tasks of modern social science, since its beginnings in the 19th century, has been to explain the persistence and attraction of religion. The question of the persistence of religion in a rational world should be posed against the question of the persistence of art in the same. To the question "How does religion survive in this modern, rational, world?" we should reply with a parallel question: "How does art survive in this modern, rational, world?" The second question gives the answer to the first one. On the level of psychological theory, psychoanalytic ego psychology has suggested that there is a natural limit to the rational reality testing, and the tension of rationality is relieved by opportunities for regression in the service of the ego, which creates both art and religion.

Children tell and hear imaginary stories and act out roles and events. They talk to unseen objects, create symbols, and are taught to share in cultural symbols. This early experience prepares the child for participation in the cultural institutions of art and religion. Religion is most often transmitted and learned not as a belief system in abstract principles, but as a system of narrative (myths, stories). It is first learned through stories, not abstract principles (Pruyser 1976). The child is exposed to narratives and is told that these imaginary stories have special significance in regard to himself and in regard to the whole culture, or even the whole world. The normal course of acquiring religious beliefs, that is, the way in which children acquire religious beliefs inside the family, is by learning simple stories and rituals. Only later is there any cognitive involvement in beliefs and arguments in favor of certain beliefs. Religion is a collection of moving stories and moving rituals. The stories are wonderful because they can move us so deeply and touch us so deeply. Mythology presents us with moving dramatic stories into which we can, and do, project ourselves. The power of these moving stories is in creating powerful identification, and that is the power of art in every case.

Religious belief is, first and foremost, belief in certain narratives, which are experienced as true and significant. Beliefs are most often expressed as fantasies. Belief is a certainty that *something happened*, that a certain story is true. Religion does not exist in the abstract, as a general acceptance of supernaturalism. For most concrete human beings in most concrete human situations (with the exception of some philosophers and theologians who are attempting to defend supernaturalism by making it abstract; Kolakowski 1982), religion is a specific belief in a specific set of promises, claims, and stories. Psychology should aim at dealing with religion in the concrete reality of human history, the religion of real people rather than of the theologians (theologians are real, only their religion isn't). This means that the psychologist of religion deals with specific content, a specific text, if you will, which exists in the real world and calls for interpretation. I do not know better expression of the reality of religious faith than William Blake's lines (1905, 108):

> *Scoffers*
> Mock on, mock on, Voltaire, Rousseau;
> Mock on, mock on; 'tis all in vain!
> You throw the sand against the wind,
> And the wind blows it back again.
>
> And every sand becomes a gem
> Reflected in the beams divine;
> Blown back they blind the mocking eye,
> But still in Israel's path they shine.
>
> The Atoms of Democritus
> and Newton's Particles of Light
> Are sands upon the Red Sea shore,
> Where Israel's tents do shine and bright.

This is our subject matter, and our abstractions should grow out of it, and not above it. William Blake's unshakable belief in specific, concrete, and vivid stories is our datum.

The Audience

In the literature of the psychology of art, there is a common assumption of the basic similarities between creators and audiences in art, as far as basic psychological processes are concerned. As Berlyne (1960) stated, "The creator, the performer, and the audience of a work of art . . . must, at least in some measure, be actuated by common motivational factors and reinforced by common sources of reward value" (220). According to the psychoanalytical view, both the creation of art and the enjoyment of art are based on identical psychological mechanisms, especially sublimation and regression in the service of the ego.

There has to be, and there is, a basic psychological readiness for art, as there is a basic psychological readiness for religion, and the basic processes involved are identical. The psychological processes involved in responding to religion on the part of the audience are similar to the processes of responding to art. They include the activation of the imagination and the emotions and an identification with elements of the artifact presented to the audience. The artistic product creates in the individual member of the audience reverberations, which go deep into his or her unconscious. Readers do not participate in the process the novelist went through in creating the novel, but it reverberates through their unconscious responses and approaches the original process of creation.

There is a gap, perhaps an unbridgeable one, between artist and audience. A similar gap exists between the creators of religion and the audience of religion. Since religious rituals, like classical art, have been preserved over long periods of time, the connection between original intentions (by the creators) and present experience is unclear. The artistic audience's distance from Shakespeare, El Greco, or Bach is shorter than the religious audience's distance from credos, rituals, and prayers, sometimes dated more than a millennium, but preserved without changes. That is the gap between religion as given and religion as adopted. The official versions of religion, given by religious leaders and theologians, are always far removed from folk religion, the way in which people actually practice and (unofficially) create a living religious tradition. This gap can be compared to the parallel gap in art between high art and popular art. Routine religious activities can thus be compared not to high art but to entertainment, providing an easy, noncommittal outlet and emotional arousal. In the response to art we have two parallel systems. One belongs to the experts, the other one to the common audience. In religion we have a similar gap between experts and audience, with theologians and philosophers playing the role of art critics passing judgments on the merits of religious creations. The difference between the art critics and the theologians is, of course, that the critics pass judgment on artistic merits only, and not on truth values.

Art critics do not ever claim that a certain work of art has merits because it is veridical.

We may hypothesize that the number and characteristics of people in any society who are seriously involved in religion parallels the number and characteristics of people involved seriously in the arts. In both cases we are dealing with small minorities, and with a possible overlap between the two groups. An interesting similarity between the social institutions of art and religion is in the nature of their audience. In modern Western societies (and possibly in other societies) the audience for both religion and art is largely made up of women, while the creators of both art and religion are men. Women are the customers for religion in all forms, and for art in all its forms, more so than men (Argyle and Beit-Hallahmi 1975) because of their lack of political and social power. They may have to cope through the creative use of imagination, since their ability to change reality is limited. In this respect women may resemble other oppressed groups.

We are now in a position to explain various findings in the social psychology of religion, such as the differences in religious involvement on the basis of sex, age, and family status. We may hypothesize an inverse relationship between readiness and opportunity for instrumental coping on the one hand and involvement in religion and magic on the other hand.

The Question of Consequences

Looking at art and related processes may lead us to insights about one of the persistent questions in the contemporary psychology of religion: the question of effects. One of the common questions in the contemporary psychology of religion is that of consequences. The question is often asked with a degree of amazement: Why don't we find any behavioral effects of religious participation? Why doesn't going to church on Sunday have any effect on behavior during the rest of the week? (Argyle and Beit-Hallahmi 1975). This question will be asked with less amazement when the comparison to art is made. The effects of religious experience and rituals should be compared to the effect of artistic experience, since the processes involved are so similar. The effects of religious rituals and beliefs can be compared to the effects of art. There is an obviously satisfying quality about art, but we do not expect any of this satisfaction to linger on and to affect our behavior outside the specific situation of the art rituals, be it a theater or a museum. We do not expect any consequences after finding out that a certain individual attends chamber music concerts every Wednesday. We might be able to say something about him in terms of social background and education, but we will rarely venture a guess as to his moral qualities or personality structure. Has anybody ever been ruined (or saved) by listening to Beethoven, reading Proust, or looking at a Van Gogh painting?

The major function of art has been considered, since the days of Aristotle, that of catharsis, that is, the production of a (vicarious) emotional experience, through the arousal and ventilation of strong emotions. It is unclear whether such catharsis is likely to lead to other, instrumental behaviors. If we look at religion through the catharsis perspective, we can then understand its limited behavioral consequences. If we adopt a Marxian perspective, it becomes clear that religion exists to serve this cathartic function, thus supporting the existing social arrangements by providing an expressive outlet to instrumental frustrations.

There are many human activities that are engaged in for themselves, without any additional consequences expected, and such activities are indeed referred to as "art" or "entertainment." Do you expect any effects from a weekly visit to a museum or a concert similar to the ones you expect from religion? We do not expect any effects in subsequent behavior when people go to museums, theaters, or athletic events; why should we expect any effects when they go to church? Once this analogy is made, things become clearer. It is possible to have an emotional experience, a cathartic experience, or an ecstatic experience without any lasting, or even short-term, effects. One can recall numerous occasions of artistic catharsis or ecstasy which were not followed by any lasting changes in behavior (despite the presumed "ennobling effects" of art). Actually, the value of artistic experiences may lie in their temporariness. Remaining in a state of catharsis or ecstasy for long is something most of us cannot afford, psychologically and socially.

The puzzle of the presumed effects of catharsis is clarified once we realize that people search again and again for cathartic experiences, either in secular art or in religion. There is apparently no permanent or cumulative effect to catharsis. That is why the experience has to be repeated in various ways. People are ready to participate again and again in religious and artistic events which provide them with opportunities for emotional expression and ventilation. In other words, the effect of the experience is in the experience itself, when relief is provided. This relief, like all human satisfaction, is temporary and has to be attained repeatedly. There should be only minimal behavioral consequences to artistic experience, because it provides only an imaginary solution to behavioral problems. Art relieves tensions and neutralizes them, and thus should have some behavioral consequences. The imaginary relief of both art and religion should have some consequences, but their appreciation should be a matter of sensitive gauging. It may be that the behavioral consequences of art and religion are noticeable when there is an identity involvement or ego-involvement, and this carries us to the second element in this essay.

Religion as Identity

The lack of behavioral consequences following religious rituals and secular artistic rituals may be characteristic of specific situations, and not of all historical periods. It is a definite characteristic of both religion and art in modern society. Religion does, of course, have consequences on social levels, as a way of defining identity and belonging, but these can be separated from the psychological effects of religion (as experience and as ritual) on the individual.

Is there any religious activity which is not part of an institution? Are there any private creations in religion which reflect only an experience "in solitude," without reference to a tradition? Religion is both personal and social, individual and cultural. The questions are what and how does the individual add to the cultural tradition. The concept of identity seems to provide a bridge between the private and the public realms in religion, as an appropriate locus for that which connects the individual personality and the cultural matrix. An individual identity is made up of several subidentities, and the religious subidentity may be one of those.

The theoretical sources for the understanding of religion as art come from classical psychoanalysis. The theoretical sources for the understanding of religion as a form of identity and as a way of attachment come from social psychology, sociology, and anthropology. Identity and subidentity are useful social-psychological concepts which provide a bridge between individual personality and social tradition. The psychology of identity, as a social-psychological concept, should contribute to understanding the "persistence of religion" (Allport 1950). Religion is preserved not just because of its qualities as art, but is tied to those groups where social forces keep it as part of a group identity, and is often promoted as such.

Peter Berger has described identity in the following way:

> Every society contains a repertoire of identities that is part of the objective knowledge of its members. . . . As the individual is socialized, these identities are internalized. They are then not only taken for granted as constituents of an objective reality "out there" but as inevitable structures of the individual's own consciousness. The objective reality, as defined by society, is subjectively appropriated. In other words, socialization brings about symmetry between objective and subjective reality, objective and subjective identity. . . .
>
> Identity, with its appropriate attachments of psychological reality, is always identity with a specific, socially constructed world. . . . One iden-

tifies oneself, as one is identified by others, by being located in a common world. (1973, 275–77)

Social identity is structured by the culture and maintained in many different ways. Labels used to define religious affiliation structure one's identity in social space. Such labels are imposed from the outside, and may not lead to real ego-involvement. However, much effort is put into making the identity label into social reality. While in most cases the identity label is no more than a passive acceptance of a social convention, the religious community will make it into a central identity structure. Social group identity may be described as a loyalty structure, and as such it is reinforced and maintained by rituals of loyalty.

To use the term suggested by Mol (1978), religion sacralizes identity, and thus contributes to social integration. This sacralization is maintained by four mechanisms, as described by Mol (1976): objectification, in which the social order is projected beyond the temporal commitment; emotional investment; ritual; and myth. Religion becomes the basis for social identity by creating differences between groups, and it then becomes an ideology, a system of identity maintenance. The differences between religious groups in mythology, rituals, and customs all create barriers to social interaction, and serve to express existing social divisions. For most individuals, religion exists as part of their identity. They do not believe in a certain religious system. They are members of a religious group. They are Catholics, Jews, or Moslems. The only choice most individuals make, if they can make a choice at all regarding the dominant religious belief system in their group, is whether they will follow group tradition. Most individuals don't choose a religion; they are simply born into one. And they learn their religion in the same way they learn other aspects of their social identity. After they have acquired an identity, they have to discover (sometimes to their utter surprise) that they have also acquired a system of beliefs which is tied to that identity. Thus, being Catholic means believing in certain things, while being Jewish means believing in other things. And since religion is part of social identity, most people simply follow the religion they have learned. Only few people adopt a religion as a result of a conscious quest. For 99% of religious people all over the world, religion is part of a conventional identity.

The truth claims of religion are tied to identity. These beliefs are true not only because of their intrinsic merits, but also because they are a part of the self and the "me." And beliefs may serve an important function in enhancing self-esteem through social identity. Religion may compensate for objective suffering and inferiority by creating a group identity of the chosen, who are truly superior despite their worldly misery. The few may be chosen and superior because of their possession of the truth and their promised future salvation. There are endless examples of millenarian groups, which are secure in their expectation of imminent salvation and in their superiority feelings, despite the lack of any objective indications for those.

The uniqueness of religion as a system of beliefs and attitudes is often alleged to be its high degree of resistance to change and its high degree of emotionality. Both can best be explained in terms of the identity system. Religion as an individual belief system is so resistant to change because it is tied to a sense of identity. Every challenge to a religious belief is a threat to the personal identity system, and people react strongly to such threats. The religious groups make sure, through the process of religious socialization, that religious beliefs are indeed tied to one's sense of identity, so that one will be ready to defend these beliefs, if necessary. Identity then becomes the meeting ground for cognition and emotion, and these meetings have been known, of course, to lead also to battle grounds. When religious beliefs are part of the self system, every challenge to the religious system becomes a challenge to the self. Individual differences in the closeness of the religious system to the core of the self may explain individual differences in religious commitment.

Whereas there is little "instrumental" value in either art or religion, identity is more instrumental in the sense of having behavioral consequences. If we stated earlier that it is difficult to locate the behavioral consequences of religion as art, it is much easier, on the other hand, to locate the behavioral consequences of religion as identity. Social identity has social consequences in behavior, and these consequences are not hard to discover. When we can correlate voting patterns with religious affiliation, we are clearly dealing with the consequences of religious identity in social life. The political implications of religious identity are not hard to find nowadays in many parts of the world, and much current suffering can be tied to various consequences of religious identity claims (Beit-Hallahmi 1973).

Religion in its identity function supports the existence of human community, but the existence of multiple human identities and multiple human communities may be dysfunctional in the long run as it creates social divisions. Group identity, which exists to create social divisions, is a problem and an obstacle for both art and religion, indeed, for all of humanity. Particularistic identities have created both artistic and religious counter-identities, which aim at one universal human selfhood. The dream of a universal human identity exists in religion and in politics. Universal religions seek to unify all of humanity, while universalistic ideals, such as Marxism, seek to unify humanity on a secular basis. These dreams represent a natural yearning for overcoming human divisions, but the roots of group identity are deep and go back to early experiences in the human family, where every group identity begins. Identity on the individual level is a necessary support system for the ego, as the ego cannot survive without both ego-identity (Erikson 1950) and group identity, and as the ego cannot survive without structures around it, both ego-identity and social group identity serve as vital support structures.

Conclusion

The term *art* has been used here to circumscribe the individual level of involvement in religion, whereas the term *identity* has been used to refer to the social level of involvement and its consequences. The discussion of religion as art follows the classical historical emphasis on individual religious experience, which has dominated the psychology of religion since William James. The discussion of religion as identity follows the tradition of the social psychology of religion. The art and identity model is able to explain on the one hand the lack of visible consequences of religion on an individual level, and on the other hand the clearly visible consequences of religion on a social level.

Religion offers us a case of unique connection between art and identity. Religion is a form of art which is claimed to be representing reality, rather than reality transformed by imagination, and which is utilized to define and actualize an identity.

Viewing religion as representing social realities is a conception tied to the names of both Karl Marx and Emile Durkheim (both, incidentally, descended from distinguished rabbinical families). Durkheim has expressed this view most directly when stating that religion cannot be false, in a social sense, because it represents society and social relations. Against the psychological truth of religion, recognized by Freud, we may posit the social truth of religion, recognized by Durkheim. Carrying these two views one step further, within my framework here, I may say that Freud posits religion as art, while Durkheim posits it as social identity.

The psychoanalytic explanation for the function of both art and religion emphasizes gratification through fantasy. We go to church for the same reason that we go to the movies, because the fantasies presented at both places are gratifying. Going to church is in addition an expression of an identity, and identity may be just as important as fantasy for some individuals in determining religious behavior. One may venture a parallel between the intrinsic-extrinsic dichotomy, proposed by Allport and Ross (1967), and between the art and identity factors. The intrinsically religious individual responds to religion as art. The extrinsically religious responds to religion as identity. This analysis is, of course, historical. It is possible that in other times and other places the psychological context of religion was different. Today, in the age of secularization, religion has to compete very hard for its audience against other, more popular forms of art and entertainment, and its effect as an identity system is also diminishing.

We may want to go further in our usage of the two concepts, and we may want to use now a typology: a religion of art and a religion of identity. Based on the well-known distinctions between religious activity in different social groups (Argyle and Beit-Hallahmi 1975), we may want to suggest two kinds of involvement:

Religion of Art	*Religion of Identity*
Intense experience	Social activity
Intrinsic	Extrinsic
Sect	Church

The discussion of religion and identity brings us to a possibly more basic psychological tendency and a more basic source of religious feelings, and that is the process of, and the need for, attachment to human objects. Here lies the most basic urge of all human urges, which gives its energy to most human activities and human institutions. The basic psychological process of attachment operates in art, where there is attachment to imaginary objects, internalized and then externalized. It clearly operates in the case of social identity, where the underlying process is that of attachment to real objects.

We arrive at a new psychological definition of religion: religion is a form of art, about which a claim is made that it represents reality, and which also expresses both individual and group identity. It is the identity element which is responsible for the fact that this particular form of art is claimed to be true. It is claimed to be true because it is essential for the maintenance of a certain identity, like other kinds of ideology. Thus religion is both an art and an identity-maintenance serving as a basis for social divisions and social grouping.

References

Allport, G. W. 1950. *The individual and his religion: A psychological interpretation*. New York: Macmillan.

Allport, G. W., and J. M. Ross. 1967. Personal religious orientation and prejudice. *Journal of Personality and Social Psychology* 5: 432–43.

Argyle, M., and B. Beit-Hallahmi. 1975. *The social psychology of religion*. London: Routledge and Kegan Paul.

Beit-Hallahmi, B. 1973. Religion and nationalism in the Arab-Israeli conflict. *Il Politico* 38: 232–43.

Berger, P. L. 1973. Identity as a problem in the sociology of knowledge. In *Towards the sociology of knowledge*, ed. G. W. Remmling, 273–84. London: Routledge and Kegan Paul.

Berlyne, D. E. 1960. *Conflict, arousal, and curiosity*. New York: McGraw-Hill.

Black, M. 1962. *Models and metaphors: studies in language and philosophy*. Ithaca, N.Y.: Cornell Univ. Press.

Blake, W. 1905. *Poems of William Blake*. London: Routledge.

Brenner, C. 1966. The mechanism of repression. In *Psychoanalysis—A general psychology*, ed. R. M. Loewenstein, L. M. Newman, M. Schur, and A. J. Solnit, 395–99. New York: International Universities Press.

Erikson, E. H. 1950. *Childhood and society*. New York: Norton.

Firth, R. 1981. Spiritual aroma: Religion and politics. *American Anthropologist* 83: 582–601.

Freud, S. [1927] 1961. *The future of an illusion*. Reprint. New York: Norton.

Harrison, J. 1911. *Themis*. London: Cambridge Univ. Press.

James, W. 1902. *The varieties of religious experience: A study in human nature*. New York: Longmans.

Kardiner, A. 1939. *The individual and his society*. New York: Columbia Univ. Press.

———. 1945. *The psychological frontiers of society*. New York: Columbia Univ. Press.

Kolakowski, L. 1982. *Religion*. New York: Oxford Univ. Press.

Kreitler, H., and S. Kreitler, 1972. *Psychology of the arts*. Chapel Hill: Univ. of North Carolina Press.

Kris, E. 1952. *Psychoanalytic explorations in art*. New York: International Universities Press.

Malinowski, B. 1925. Magic, science and religion. In *Science, religion, and reality*, ed. J. Needham, 19–84. New York and London: Macmillan.

Mol, H. J. 1976. *Identity and the sacred*. Oxford: Basil Blackwell.

———. 1978. Introduction. In *Identity and religion*, ed. H. J. Mol. London: Sage.

Pruyser, P. W. 1976. Lessons from art theory for the psychology of religion. *Journal for the Scientific Study of Religion* 15: 1–14.

Seguy, J. 1977. Rationnel et emotionnel dans la pratique liturgique Catholique: Un modele theorique. *La Maison Dieu* 129: 73–92.

Taylor, R. 1981. *Beyond art*. Sussex: Harvester Press.

Winnicott, D. W. 1971. *Playing and reality*. London: Tavistock.

Goring the Sacred Ox:
Towards a Psychology of Religion

As psychologists studying religion, we often wonder why it is that we find ourselves on the margins of psychology. In a recent volume of 1,009 pages dealing with the development of psychology in the United States, the psychology of religion has earned a total of seven lines of text (Hilgard 1987). This is indeed a true measure of the alienation between psychology of religion and psychology in general.

Why should psychology be interested in studying religion? Why do I study religion? Religion is ideal subject matter for the psychologist. It is a system defined solely through the existence of beliefs and fantasies, a unique product of human cognitive capacities, a reflection of human flexibility, and a fascinating range of phenomen: creativity, imagination, and madness. What better way is there of looking at humankind?

Psychologists pursue a theoretical ideal of studying ahistorical, universal mental processes, and not mental content. There is nothing unique about religion in terms of psychological processes. What defines religion is a specific content, which is relative, historical, and constantly changing. We can make a claim on psychologists' time and energy when, and only when, the phenomena of religion evoke some theoretical connection. And indeed, these phenomena should be pertinent to theories of personality, psychopathology, social processes, group dynamics, and leadership.

Historically, the psychology of religion has been developing under two shadows—one of academic psychology, keeping its distance from it, and the other of religion, wishing to tame it. For the past 500 years, religion has been dealt severe blows by the developing sciences. The natural sciences demolished traditional religious cosmology, and the biological sciences demolished its view of humankind in the natural world. But it was left to the social sciences and psychology to examine the nature of religious beliefs, their development, and their relativity and in this way to deal probably the final blow to the credibility of religious claims (Cattell 1938).

189

The social sciences are a threat to religion because they take religion as an object of study, and not as a representation of a special reality or a special mode of knowledge. All social sciences (indeed all human sciences) are a threat to religion, inasmuch as they study changes in culture over time and space and show repeatedly that beliefs and customs, including religious ones, are relative and culturally conditioned. Psychology as the discipline that deals directly with the nature of human beliefs presents a most direct threat: (1) by challenging, and rejecting, the psychological notions of the soul and free will, which are part and parcel of all religious traditions and (2) by being a part of the historical rise of science, which challenges the supernatural premise and makes it less and less tenable.

The First Wave: The "Psychology of Religion Movement"

The history of the psychological study of religion is complex and paradoxical. Some of the best minds in the history of psychology have devoted considerable amounts of intellectual energy to the subject matter of religion, including Wilhelm Wundt, G. Stanley Hall, Sigmund Freud, John B. Watson, B. F. Skinner, James M. Cattell, Abraham Maslow, William James, O. Hobart Mowrer, and H. Guntrip.

What is most often noted in discussions of the history of the psychological study of religion is that the area enjoyed a period of much activity and attention at the end of the 19th century and at the beginning of the 20th century and then declined greatly in terms of research activity and publications. We can speak of a "psychology of religion movement," existing roughly between 1880 and 1930 and then disappearing as academic psychology became an established discipline (Beit-Hallahmi 1974, 1989).

Students of the movement agree that the main cause for its decline was its failure to separate itself from theology, philosophy of religion, and the general dogmatic and evangelistic tasks of religious institutions. The study of religion was conflictual for both researcher and subject because of their own personal investment in religion, which led to speculative and apologetic tendencies. The philosophical-theological approach could not have gained much respect for the psychology of religion among younger, and more critical, scholars. Despite the publication of several impressive studies, the naive theoretical approach limited the impact of the movement and separated it from the mainstream of academic research. The theoretical and ideological basis of the movement showed that the psychology of religion was basically a residue of the philosophical tradition in psychology.

Homans (1970) showed that the decline also coincided with the beginnings of both theological existentialism and psychoanalysis and with the appearance of pastoral psychology. The years between 1930 and 1960 were a low point (or the "dark ages") for publications dealing with psychology and religion. Since 1960, there has been a mild "revival" of psychological writings dealing with religion.

The Revival: Is History Repeating Itself?

Post-1960 literature in the psychology of religion represents three separate traditions:

1. a religious psychology, which focuses on religious apologetics,
2. a psychology of religion, which focuses on the psychological explanation of religious phenomena (e.g., Cavenar and Spaulding 1977; Spanos and Hewitt 1979; Ullman 1982),
3. a social psychology of religion, studying the social-psychological correlates of religion and religiosity (Argyle and Beit-Hallahmi 1975).

The difference between a religious psychology and a psychology of religion is that between defending religious beliefs and explaining them. Psychology of religion treats religion as a phenomenon for systematic psychological study, while religious psychology aims at promoting religion through the adaptation and use of psychological concepts. Dividing the literature into religious psychology, psychology of religion, and the social psychology of religion is not done *ad hominem*. The same individual can contribute to religious psychology, to the psychology of religion, and to the social psychology of religion, though in actuality this is not often the case. Gordon W. Allport, for example, has contributed to all three areas.

Although most psychologists are not committed to religion, either as a personal belief or as a topic of study, there exists a minority who are, and they are the ones responsible for most of the activity in the psychology of religion. As a result, what we have today is primarily a religious psychology of religion. The stereotype of the psychologist who is interested in religion, at least among his academic colleagues, embodies the notion of strong religious commitments or frustrated theological ambitions. This stereotype seems to have much truth (Ragan, Malony, and Beit-Hallahmi 1980). A close, or even a superficial, scrutiny of the personal histories, education, and writings of most of the contributors to the psychology of religion since 1960 shows that they come, in most cases, from religious backgrounds, which often included seminary education. Their commitment to religion is clear, and many of them see their main contribution in terms of helping religion become better and stronger. Personal statements by psychologists active in the psychology of religion show quite clearly that a commitment to a religious viewpoint is an important part of the motivation for their work (e.g., Dittes 1967, 1978). Many have been ordained as ministers or priests and are affiliated with divinity schools. (This is also a reflection of the fact that divinity schools are more hospitable to the psychology of religion than psychology departments.)

It seems that in most cases only a personal religious commitment can motivate a psychologist to break the strong norm against studying religion. Most psychologists of religion are religious, and in their cases personal involvement overrides disciplinary norms. Religious psychologists treat their subject matter differently because they accord a special status to religious claims, religious institutions, and individual religious experiences. The dominant perspective appears to be based on an interest in the preservation of religion. This creates a situation today in which those who study religion are committed to it, while those who are not show little interest in the area, or sometimes even a slight disdain.

Division 36 of the American Psychological Association, in existence since 1976 and officially titled Psychologists Interested in Religious Issues (PIRI), is the successor to the organization with the same name and represents the same interests. (Psychologists Interested in Religious Issues, Inc., was the nondenominational successor to the American Catholic Psychological Association.) Without a great effort at textual analysis one must note that the name does not identify religion as an object of study, only "Religious Issues." The existence and the activities of Division 36 tend to support the stereotype held by most academic psychologists about psychologists who are interested in religion as part of their professional activity.

If we compare the current "revival" in the psychology of religion with the 1880–1930 movement, we discover that history is not just being repeated. The post-1960 revival may be even more religious and religionist than the earlier one. The stereotype of the religious psychologist writing on the psychology of religion is truer today than ever before, with the inevitable result being a continuing alienation from serious academic psychology.

A Personal Agenda

If the insiders in the psychology of religion currently are the religionists, then I find myself in the position of an outsider, as a (secular) humanist commited to an analytical, "reductionist" approach, which takes religion as a phenomenon to be examined, and only that. I believe that the only serious questions to be answered here have to do with the universals in religion, questions asked by all the human sciences. Analysis demands taking the stand of the observer—not the partisan, and this is the normal stand in psychology. Taking the role of a partisan leads to inevitable ghettoization, which is currently the lot of our field.

My own modest contribution to the deghettoization of the psychology of religion has been in utilizing both psychoanalytic hypotheses (see Beit-Hallahmi 1978, 1989) and social-psychological, sociological, and historical data (see Argyle and Beit-Hallahmi 1975; Beit-Hallahmi 1990). The psychoanalytic interpretation of religion is diametrically opposed to the approach represented by the psychology of religion movement. It does not come to praise religion but to analyze it in every sense of the word, with demystification, which is the opposite of the apologetic impulse, as the final goal. Psychoanalysis remains a fountainhead of insights not only for psychology, but for all human sciences (see La Barre 1970).

My own current work focuses on fieldwork and historical research on new religious movements, which gives me an opportunity to study individual conversion, continuing the greatest tradition in the psychology of religion (see Beit-Hallahmi and Nevo 1987; Beit-Hallahmi 1990). Doing field observations gives me many occasions to test theories of personality and psychopathology, as well as social psychology. My clinical training stands me in good stead as well. It is in the examination of religious phenomena that we find material for understanding basic psychological processes, magnified and dramatized in the form of humankind's strongest attachments and wildest dreams.

References

Argyle, M., and B. Beit-Hallahmi. 1975. *The social psychology of religion*. London: Routledge and Kegan Paul.

Beit-Hallahmi, B. 1974. Psychology of religion 1880–1930: The rise and fall of a psychological movement. *Journal of the History of the Behavioral Sciences* 10: 84–90.

———. 1978. *Psychoanalysis and religion: A bibliography*. Norwood, Penn.: Norwood Editions.

———. 1989. *Prolegomena to the psychological study of religion*. Lewisburg, Penn.: Bucknell Univ. Press.

———. 1990. *Dictionary of modern religious movements*. New York: Richards Rosen.

Beit-Hallahmi, B., and B. Nevo. 1987. "Born-again" Jews in Israel: The dynamics of an identity change. *International Journal of Psychology* 22: 75–81.

Cattell, R. B. 1938. *Psychology and the religious quest*. London: Nelson.

Cavenar, J. C., Jr., and J. G. Spaulding. 1977. Depressive disorders and religious conversion. *Journal of Nervous and Mental Diseases* 165: 209–12.

Dittes, J. E. 1967. *The church in the way*. New York: Scribner.

———. 1978. Christian style in academics and administration. In *Psychology and faith: The Christian experience of eighteen psychologists*, ed. H. N. Malony, 212–18. Washington, D.C.: Univ. Press of America.

Hilgard, E. R. 1987. *Psychology in America: A historical survey*. San Diego: Harcourt Brace Jovanovich.

Homans, P. 1970. *Theology after Freud*. Indianapolis: Bobbs-Merrill.

La Barre, W. 1970. *The ghost dance*. New York: Dell.

Ragan, C. P., H. N. Malony, and B. Beit-Hallahmi. 1980. Psychologists and religion: Professional factors and personal belief. *Review of Religious Research* 21: 208–217.

Spanos, N. P., and E. C. Hewitt. 1979. Glossolalia: A test of the "trance" and psychopathology hypotheses. *Journal of Abnormal Psychology* 88: 427–34.

Ullman, C. 1982. Cognitive and emotional antecedents of religious conversion. *Journal of Personality and Social Psychology* 43: 183–92.

7

H. Newton Malony

H. Newton Malony is professor and director of programs in the integration of psychology and theology in the Graduate School of Psychology at Fuller Theological Seminary. He is a graduate of Birmingham-Southern College, Yale Divinity School, and George Peabody College of Vanderbilt University, from which he received the Ph.D. degree. Prior to his present position, he served as pastor of churches in Alabama, New York, and Tennessee; psychologist and chaplain in mental hospitals; and teacher of psychology at Tennessee Wesleyan College.

Dr. Malony, active in several organizations relating to the psychology of religion, has served on the councils of the Society for the Scientific Study of Religion, and the Religious Research Association. He has been chair of the governing board of the Institute for Religion and Wholeness. He has also been president of Division 36, Psychologists Interested in Religious Issues, of the American Psychological Association and of the Christian Association for Psychological Studies.

Dr. Malony has conducted research in a variety of areas of the psychology of religion including attribution theory and the report of religious experience, spiritual maturity, speaking in tongues, moral development, and secularism. He has also engaged in studies of religious leadership, church dynamics, ministerial effectiveness, and pastoral counseling. At Fuller, Malony has been the general chair of the John G. Finch Symposium on the Integration of Christian Theology and the Social Behavioral Sciences, which has published over a dozen volumes generally related to the psychology of religion.

A listing of some of Malony's published works makes clear the various interests he has had in psychology of religion. He edited *Current Perspectives in the Psychology of Religion* (Grand Rapids: Eerdmans,

1977), a volume of readings which has been adopted by a number of institutions. Dr. Malony is one of the editors of the *Dictionary of Pastoral Care and Counseling* (Nashville: Abingdon, 1990). He edited *Psychology and Faith: The Christian Experience of Eighteen Psychologists* (Washington, D.C.: Univ. Press of America, 1978) and *A Christian Existential Psychology: The Contributions of John G. Finch* (Washington, D.C.: Univ. Press of America, 1980). He has authored *Understanding Your Faith* (Nashville: Abingdon, 1978) and has coauthored *Speak Up! Christian Assertiveness* (with Randolph K. Sanders, Philadelphia: Westminster, 1985) and *Glossolalia: Behavioral Science Perspectives on Speaking in Tongues* (with A. Adams Lovekin, New York: Oxford Univ. Press, 1985). With Hendrika Vande Kemp he coedited probably the most complete available survey of the relationship between psychology and theology: *Psychology and Theology in Western Thought, 1672–1965: A Historical and Annotated Bibliography* (1984). Perhaps the most unique facet of Dr. Malony's work has been his efforts to produce a series of videotaped interviews with contemporary psychologists of religion, a number of whom are included in this publication. Out of an interest in teaching the psychology of religion, he has produced half-hour-long interviews, which may be used by teachers, along with related readings, as stimuli for learning.

In the article "Conversion: The Sociodynamics of Change" Dr. Malony deals with a controversial issue in the psychology of religion, namely, brainwashing. He cites evidence to show that most people who choose to be seriously religious do so less because they are coerced and more because religion meets their needs at the time. This is true for decisions to enter new religions as well as traditional ones.

In "The Excitement Never Ends" Dr. Malony notes the major themes that have dominated his professional interests. These have included a continuing concern for the nature of religious experience, a historical and conceptual interest in the relations of religion and science, an ongoing attempt to design a measure of religious maturity, and a preoccupation with the use of psychology of religion in the courtroom. The title of this article refers to Malony's long-held conviction that the psychology of religion is that field of psychology in which boredom never occurs.

Conversion:
The Sociodynamics of Change

A s of this date (February 1986) legal action involving conversion is taking place in California. Larry Wallersheim is suing the Church of Scientology for breach of promise and for making him mentally ill. Mr. Wallersheim became a member of Scientology while on a visit to San Francisco from the Midwest when he was 18 years old. He remained a member of this church for the next 11 years, until he was 29 years of age. During that time he availed himself of the church's training services and became part of the church's staff. Some time after leaving the church he became aware of what he felt was the ineffectiveness of Scientology's ministry to him. They had promised that his personality would improve and his intelligence would increase. In fact the reverse had occurred. He saw himself as mentally handicapped by his years in the church, and he decided to seek redress for his treatment by taking legal action against Scientology. He is suing the church for $18 million.

Expert witnesses for the plaintiff are asserting that Mr. Wallersheim was (1) an innocent, normal midwestern college lad in San Francisco on a midterm break; (2) physiologically and temperamentally hypersuggestible; (3) preyed upon by a seductive temptress; (4) falsely convinced by sales techniques of his need for what Scientology had to offer; (5) subtly coerced into joining the church; (6) influenced by brainwashing to stay in the church; (7) threatened with emotional and physical harm when he considered leaving; (8) continually promised beneficial change if he stayed with the group; and (9) made mentally ill by his 11-year experience in the church.

Because of the bad press which Scientology has received in the past decade, many would be inclined to suspect that all of the accusations were, indeed, true. However, it should be noted that social psychological processes are social psychological processes wherever they are found and that upon closer examination most of the procedures

From *Theology News and Notes*, June 1986, 16–19; reprinted by permission of the publisher and the author.

referred to in these accusations have their parallels in well-accepted evangelistic endeavors. They are similar to conversion experiences in a variety of settings. The case of the Church of Scientology is used here as a situation from which most readers can gain some distance, and therefore it is a case which will allow us to examine more closely many of the psychodynamics involved in conversion wherever it occurs.

The Psychophysiology of Conversion

One of the accusations made by expert witnesses in the Scientology case is that Larry Wallersheim was a physiologically hypersuggestible young man whose temperament made him unduly susceptible to being influenced by the sales pitch of the church—little matter that this assertion is based on an assessment of Wallersheim 15 years after the fact via the "eye roll test," which is widely discredited by professionals. The claim is made that at the time Larry did not have the psychological independence which one needs to make informed decisions. The inference is made that the church should assess this psychophysiological state in prospective members and should not attempt to influence persons who, like Larry, may be inclined temperamentally to accept the message of the church too easily.

This is not a new claim with regard to religious experience. William Sargant (1957) claimed some time ago that religious experience resulted in "reciprocal inhibition" of certain parts of the brain through "hyperexcitation" of other parts. Since religious experience tends to give one the feeling that all problems have been solved and that all the world looks new, Sargant felt this pervasive, different outlook had to be based on denial or repression. The ability to cut off from awareness certain parts of awareness, as one does when problems vanish in light of religious experience, Sargant felt was an ability which varied from person to person. Those who were hypersuggestible, whose brain receptors were physiologically weaker, who were "hysteric," were more inclined to have religious experiences.

Sargant's hypothesis has been widely accepted and tested. Kildahl (1972), for example, concluded among a sample of Lutherans that those who became glossolalic (i.e., spoke in tongues) were more inclined to score higher on the Hysteria scale of the Minnesota Multiphasic Personality Inventory (MMPI). However, no other research has been able to replicate these findings (cf. Malony and Lovekin 1985), and the possibility of finding more hysterics in churches than in the general population is extremely unlikely.

The contention that religious groups, such as Scientology or Christian churches, should be held responsible for assessing potential converts on their level of hypersuggestibility is very problematic. Would the expert witnesses who make this claim be willing to generalize this responsibility to used-car companies, department stores, resort developments, newspapers? I suspect the issues lie much deeper for these expert witnesses.

They speak of religion as "totalistic" in the sense that it provides answers to *all* of life. Gordon (1967, 1) agrees with this impression in his definition of conversion as "the process by which a person comes to adopt an all pervading world view." There is a general discomfort among Western social/behavioral scientists with institutions marketing a product which promises such a possibility. As Thomas Szasz has noted, the social behavioral sciences are entrenched servants of their culture and their tendency to counsel for "adjustment to society," is no accident. When one of the expert witnesses in the Scientology case reports that the former members of religious groups "take two years to readjust to society," she is making an implicit value judgment of approval for a society which esteems hyperindividualism and rationality about group commitment and overarching answers to life's problems.

I suspect that these scholars are uncomfortable with religion in general and that, had they the courage, they would challenge any and all conversions, be they to the Church of Scientology or to the United Presbyterian Church. Their singling out one group to accuse may be more a situational artifact than a matter of discrimination.

Suffice it to say, that neither the accusation of physiological hypersuggestibility among converts nor the claim that religious groups should screen out such persons are tenable propositions. Nevertheless, it should be said that a certain amount of susceptibility to social influence is necessary for any conversion to occur. Even such a private conversion as that of Donald Tweedie (reported in Malony 1975) was not complete until he sought out a church which offered him an invitation to become a Christian, which he accepted!

The Intrapersonal Dynamics of Conversion

The next claim that has been made about Larry Wallersheim is that he was an innocent, normal, 18-year-old, midwestern college lad on a spring break trip to San Francisco who was overwhelmed by the calculated seduction of a religious group. In my opinion, such a claim is patently untrue in this case and in almost all other cases where religious conversion occurs.

Persons are in need, or they would pay no attention to the sales talk of the evangelist—whether that evangelist be a representative of the Roman Catholic, the Southern Baptist, the Unification, the local, independent Bible church, or Scientology.

Larry Wallersheim was no exception to this rule of thumb. Prior to that fateful trip to San Francisco, his social history reveals that he was a lad who had dyed his hair purple while in high school, had left his Roman Catholic background and joined an Eastern religion, had walked nude around the office of his draft board to convince them of his instability, and had made failing grades in two colleges. Clearly this was a young man who was seeking answers to some major life issues.

The intrapersonal dynamics of converts require such a state if conversion is to occur. Jesus' statement about its being easier for a camel to crawl through the very low entrance to a sheepfold than for a rich man to get into heaven (cf. Matt. 19:24) is a testimony to this requirement. Jesus was saying that the rich tend to meet their life needs with money, and therefore, are cushioned against the disappointments and enigmas which provoke the need for religious answers. Of course, it is possible for camels to crawl into sheepfolds, and it is possible for the rich to be converted, but those with less wealth are more likely to listen when religion speaks.

The Lofland and Stark (1965) "problem-solving" model for conversion is a clear statement of these interpersonal dynamics. They call them "predisposing conditions." They suggest that the first condition is a state of tension, strain, frustration, or deprivation. This state, according to Lofland and Stark, has usually led to a problem-solving perspective which provokes preconverts to explore various solutions to the frustration they are experiencing. This results, in the third place, in a general mode of "seekership," which makes them oriented to answers. In other words, it makes them alert to those events in their environment which promise resolution of their tension. These intrapersonal dynamics make them susceptible to the "situational contingencies" in their environment. Thus, the fourth stage is a turning point, defined as an event that places them in a situation where conversion can occur. For Wallersheim this was his trip to San Francisco—an unfamiliar environment to which he went willingly even though unknowingly. This is similar to persons who go to church without clearly knowing why they are there.

The expert witnesses in the Scientology case present a "passive" model of the human being. They contend that humans are unsuspecting "sitting ducks" waiting to be shot by unscrupulous evangelists who use brainwashing and thought-control methods to overwhelm people.

This is questionable, at least in Western culture. As sociologist James Richardson suggests, ours is an "age of conversions" in which many, if not most, people could be best described as suffering from a hunger for meaning. Thus, people are continually seeking. They are not passively content and adjusted, as the expert witnesses would have us believe. In the words of theologian Paul Tillich, "Life poses the questions to which faith is the answer." And life is that which is lived by all persons—not just a few. Richardson (1980) suggests we study conversion "careers" rather than conversion "events."

Lifelong "careers" include a number of jobs. Conversion careers might include a variety of commitments to different religious groups. From this point of view, "alternation" might be a better term than "conversion." Many persons alternate between one group and another. They settle down in one group only after periods of soul-searching and identity seeking. It is still valid to think of these matters along a continuum in which "alternation" would refer to those transitions which were *pre*scribed or permitted within a person's former system of meaning (for example, a Methodist becoming an Episcopalian) and "conversion" would refer to those transitions to identities which were *pro*scribed or forbidden (for example, an Episcopalian becoming a Hare Krishna). But in *both* cases the person would best be thought of as an active seeker rather than a passive recipient. In fact, there is some warrant for hypothesizing that where the transition is more radical, as in Wallersheim's conversion from Roman Catholicism to Scientology, the decision will be *more* volitional and deliberate than in situations where the change is less so, as in a transfer of membership from the Presbyterian to the Baptist church.

The Sociodynamics of Conversion

While the expert witnesses in the Scientology case are in error in their view of the human being as passive, they are correct that the church promised radical transformation of Wallersheim's character. This is the model which religions always follow. For example, the Christian faith diagnoses the human condition as one of desperate sinfulness in need of a powerful savior. This judgment leads to the conviction in potential converts that they cannot save themselves. At this point the evangelist offers hope and redemption if they will accept the grace, or forgiveness, of God by faith in Jesus Christ. The promise is made that accepting God's grace through faith will result in the solving of all of life's basic problems.

The diagnosis of Wallersheim's condition and the recommended solution through accepting Scientology's service follows a similar pattern. Their belief that persons are contaminated by "thetans" which prevent them from using their full capacities is answered by offering potential converts the experience of "auditing"—a counseling-like procedure designed to "clear" persons of these contaminations and, thus, release their full capacities (personal, intellectual, and spiritual) for happy living. Although one may disagree with the content of such models as Scientology's, it is obvious that the format is very similar from religion to religion.

Therefore, the expert witnesses are correct in saying that Scientology made radical promises to Wallersheim—all religions do. They were also correct in saying that these ideas were mediated through persons who actively represented the church. Lofland and Stark (1965) termed these processes the "situational contingencies" of conversion. These situational contingencies involve 4 steps: (1) encounter with a religious group; (2) formation of affective, emotional attachments to those in the group; (3) reduction of contact with former associations; and (4) intensive interaction within the group. Lofland and Stark contended this was the normal process wherever conversion occurred.

However, the expert witnesses call this seduction, not normal social influence. In fact, Neil Duddy (1980) construed it as the "seduction syndrome" and contended that it characterized deviant religious groups such as the Unification Church, Scientology, and the Local Church, but not mainline churches. In support of this position, Richard Ofshe (1985), a sociologist who is one of the expert witnesses in the Wallersheim case, contends that there is a clear difference between "systematic" and "mundane" social influence. He asserts that systematic influence highly organizes the environment around the potential convert, exposes the individual to frequent and pervasive stimuli, and rewards the person with powerful rewards and punishments for acceptable performance. Mundane social influence, on the other hand, has fewer of these characteristics. While, at first glance, these characteristics sound as if they would support the contention that certain groups use deviant techniques while others do not, the expert witnesses have been unable to distinguish the methods used by such groups as Scientology from the highly sophisticated techniques of evangelism taught in major seminaries around the nation, much less the differences between negative systematic social influence and normal child rearing, newspaper advertisements, used car sales, training in the armed services, and graduate education.

One wonders whether the issue is so much one of a distinction between methods that are good or bad as a reluctance on the part of some group to put out the effort it takes to win converts. There are proven methods of social influence, and groups should not be criticized for using them. I suspect that most mainline churches who disapprove of such groups as the Moonies would have as much success were they willing to spend the time and energy the Moonies spent on design and execution of their method. That these groups follow proven methods—of this there can be no doubt. The experience of Larry Wallersheim follows Lofland and Stark's steps to the letter.

However, this does not mean that they are using "brainwashing" or "thought-coercion" techniques. Those expert witnesses who have claimed this relationship ignore one crucial difference between conversion in a free society and influence procedures used on captured prisoners. Converts to religious groups in our country are not physically imprisoned. This is an essential difference that obliterates for all time any comparison between the two. There is absolutely no way to claim that social influence without incarceration can be said to resemble change which occurs behind bars, in spite of what some expert witnesses may contend. The closest one could come to such a comparison would be those cases such as Constantine and the Roman Empire where a whole nation was declared Christian by fiat and where an ideology was forced on people who feared for their lives if they did not comply. The type of individual conversion that occurs in Western society is of a different genre.

I suspect that most of the criticism leveled at such groups as the Moonies, Hare Krishna, and Scientology is due to disagreement with their ideology rather than with their methods. Of course, such ideological disagreement is appropriate, but if we contend that the Christian faith is superior to all others, as I personally contend, such a contention deserves better than to be hidden underneath a false criticism of method. Once again, I further suspect that much of the expert witness testimony criticizing these groups is based more on a disapproval of *any* religion than on any clear-cut empirical distinction between good and bad methods of social influence.

In sum, all conversion has its sociodynamics. In fact, one could say that while tension and solution seeking are the necessary conditions, the situational contingencies are sufficient conditions for conversion. It may be that only when individuals affirm the ideology of a group and become a part of it can conversion be said to have occurred. This hypothesis has two implications: first, it implies that human beings may be so constructed that decisions made individually will not last and, second, it implies that the confirmation and support of others may be necessary for conversion to be effective. Whereas inner decision may be a first step (psychological conversion), it must be followed by attachment to a social group (structural conversion) for real-life change to occur.

Summary

This article has discussed the psychodynamics of conversion. Using the current case of *Wallersheim v. the Church of Scientology* as an example, the physiological, the intrapersonal, and the social dynamics of conversion were considered. A number of issues about which expert testimony in this case falsely presented the evidence were considered. While the article was meant in no wise to affirm the validity of Scientology beliefs, it was felt that the case revealed the tendency for those who disagree with the beliefs of a given religion to mistakenly criticize its methods when, in fact, they utilized the same approaches. It is hoped that the ideas presented here will help in better understanding the ways human beings function and the nature of the conversion process wherever and whenever it occurs.

References

Duddy, N. T. 1980. *The God men.* Downers Grove: Inter-Varsity.

Gordon, A. 1967. *The nature of conversion.* Boston: Beacon.

Kildahl, J. P. 1972. *The psychology of speaking in tongues.* New York: Harper and Row.

Lofland, J., and R. Stark. 1965. Becoming a world-saver: A theory of conversion to a deviant perspective. *American Sociological Review* 30: 862–74.

Malony, H. N. 1975. *Ways people meet God.* Nashville: Tidings Press.

Malony, H. N., and A. A. Lovekin. 1985. *Glossolalia: Behavioral science perspectives on speaking in tongues.* New York: Oxford Univ. Press.

Ofshe, R. J. 1985. Deposition taken in Wallersheim v. Church of Scientology. Document no. c 332 027. Superior Court of the State of California, for the County of Los Angeles, October 25.

Richardson, J. T. 1980. Conversion careers. *Society* (March/April): 47–50.

Sargant, W. 1957. *Battle for the mind: A physiology of conversion and brain washing.* New York: Doubleday.

The Excitement Never Ends

I well remember the excitement I experienced in reading the first paper on the initial program of the newly formed division for psychologists who were interested in religious issues at the annual meeting of the American Psychological Association (APA) in Washington, D.C., in the mid-1970s. I have always enjoyed history, and it felt like I was a part of a tradition in American psychology that had laid dormant for over 50 years. I knew that G. Stanley Hall's interest in the psychology of religion had been well received and that because of his and William James's impetus, papers such as mine had been read at meetings of the APA through the second half of this century. I was proud to be a part of the revival of that tradition: a tradition of having religion considered to be a legitimate interest and focus of the psychological profession.

The excitement that I felt that day in Washington, D.C., has not abated. It continues and, if anything, it has increased. Excitement has never been my problem. Focus has. However, for me involvement in the psychology of religion has not been entirely a scattered enterprise even though my interests have been varied. In the discussion to follow, I would like to mention several of these interests and indicate where I think the field is going in the next decade.

History has remained an interest of mine. The presentation I gave at the Washington, D.C., APA meeting was entitled "The Contribution of Gordon W. Allport to the Psychology of Religion." My Division 36 presidential address was entitled "G. Stanley Hall's Theory of Conversion." A subsequent APA presentation was entitled "From Galileo to Whitehead: Century Specific Questions of Interest to the Integration of Psychology and Theology." The ideas in these essays span the history of the science-religion dialogue since the 15th century and focus on the development of the psychology of religion in this century. It was no accident that I collaborated with Hendrika Vande Kemp in the publishing of an

From the *Journal of Psychology and Christianity* 5, no. 2 (1986): 51–54; reprinted by permission of the publisher and the author. Copyright 1986 by the Christian Association for Psychological Studies.

annotated bibliography of writings on these subjects between the early 18th and the mid-20th centuries.

I am convinced of the importance of history for our understanding of the present. In my opinion, one cannot be a good psychologist of religion without an appreciation for the development of this discipline from the time of Wilhelm Wundt and a depth understanding of how the interface of religion and psychology is grounded in the interaction of religionists with scientists over the last 500 years. I fear that too many of my colleagues ignore or are oblivious to these roots. I hope to continue to ground our discipline in the past. As Winston Churchill said, "Those who do not know history are bound to repeat its mistakes."

The second abiding interest I have had has been in the religion of psychologists. In my book (1978) detailing the religious pilgrimages of a number of psychologists, I report a survey of a random sample of psychologists in which I found that about 1% of the members of APA had either previous religious training or retained interest in religious issues. This survey, taken in the late 1960s, did not compare psychologists with others, but the results probably supported previous surveys of these issues, namely, that psychologists are the least religious of all other scientists—social, behavioral, or natural. Although the lastest of these surveys (Ragan, Malony, and Beit-Hallahmi 1980) reconfirmed these findings, a growing number of overtly religious psychologists was observed.

My interest in these matters has taken a little different turn than concern over whether psychologists were traditionally religious. I have served for several years on the California State Psychological Association's task force on psychotherapy and spirituality. We have published the results of two surveys which we made of psychologists in California. In the first survey (Shafranske and Gorsuch 1985) it was discovered that a much larger percentage than was previously thought considered themselves to be religious—but in a noninstitutional or nontraditional manner. In the second survey (Shafranske and Malony 1985) it was found that the majority of the psychologists felt that spiritual issues were important in counseling. Both these surveys were surpising in their results.

I would hope that the psychology of religion continues to attend to the religion of psychologists. I think it has import in two areas. First, there is the question of how religious or spiritual issues impact the counseling process. This is the applied side of the issue. Second, there is the question of how the religion of the psychologist impacts the research that is done and the conclusions that are drawn. This is the pure side of the issue. It is unsettled. Although my opinion is that those who are not religious do not know how to ask the proper questions, there is the possibility that religious psychologists may, in fact, be more subjective than they ought to be in these matters.

This leads me to mention my third continuing interest. I remain concerned about forensic psychology of religion, that is, psychology of religion in the courtroom. This involvement in what I would call *applied psychology of religion* came about for me as a result of testifying against another psychologist in a court case where a religious group was being called a cult. In this process I discovered two things. First, I discovered that there were religious persons who, intolerant of groups they did not understand, were willing to publish defamatory accusations which had no basis in fact. Second, I discovered that there were irreligious psychologists who were willing to join with these religious bigots and were eager to claim that "totalistic groups," such as religion, used brainwashing and thought control.

After studying the issues I came to the opinion that these other psychologists knew very little about religion and that they, most likely, were antireligious. I suspected that they were among that large percentage of psychologists who scored nonreligious in the national surveys which had been conducted earlier. I decided to testify against these intolerant religionists and these irreligious psychologists out of a concern for the freedom of religion and a concern that psychology not be used in an uninformed, prejudicial way. I have become convinced that there is no warrant for psychologists to prejudge religion unless they have been involved in it enough to minimally understand it.

I intend to remain involved in these legal battles. I hope other psychologists of religion will join in these efforts to protect religious freedom and guarantee that psychology not be misused. In the years ahead there will be many more legal suits filed against religion. While I would not want to be a party to protecting some group or person just because they were religious, I do think that religion is innocent until proven guilty and that religion will continue to have rationales for its practices that are not logical from society's point of view. My coedited book entitled *Clergy Malpractice* assumes this position in regard to religious leadership. I believe this will continue to be an issue for the psychology of religion in the years ahead.

The fourth issue which has been of concern to me has been to design a diagnostic procedure to measure religious maturity. While over 90% of Americans report believing in a divine being and while over 50% say they belong to a religious institution, the question of religion is scarcely considered when emotionally disturbed persons are evaluated by psychologists. Religion would appear to be an important, but unexamined, influence in the personality structure of people's lives. I have engaged in a serious attempt to design an interview schedule that would evaluate the degree to which religion was enhancing or confounding emotional adjustment. I reported this in an article entitled "Assessing religious maturity" (1985b).

Psychologists make three types of decisions in evaluating individuals. Initially, they attempt to diagnose the behaviors of the disturbed person and reach some conclusions as to what facets of the person's experience are impacting the diagnostic picture. Next, they seek, through a mental status examination, to determine the premorbid personality of the individual. Finally, they plan a treatment strategy. Since religion plays a part in so many people's lives, it is not unreasonable to think that it could play a part in the mental illness itself, the personality structure underlying the illness, and, finally, in the ability of the person to get well. Of course, the part that religion plays could be positive or negative. Persons' religion could or could not be one of the symptoms of the illness. Their religion could be a strength or weakness in their personality underlying the illness. Religion could be counted on to be a help or a hindrance in their getting well.

Over the last five years, my students have been working on an interview schedule which would assist psychologists in making these judgments about persons' religion. We call it the Religious Status Interview (RSI). It assumes that religion can be measured in a similar manner to intelligence and that an interview is a more valid assessment of this important part of people's lives than a paper-and-pencil test would be. Since we are Christians, we have designed the interview to assess Christian faith and decided it would not be helpful to assess religion in general. The interview attempts to evaluate how people's beliefs typically function in their daily lives as opposed to assessing *what* they believe. As with individual intelligence tests, we have assumed that what people spontaneously said in response to interview questions *was* their religious status. Finally, we have assumed that the more mature persons were in the appropriation of their faith into their daily lives, the less likely would religion be part of their mental illness, the more likely would religion be a personality strength, and the greater the possibility would be that religion could become a part of their getting well.

We have found support for these hypotheses. In addition to demonstrating that the interview could be administered reliably, we have found it able to discriminate hospitalized mental patients from their visitors and outpatients from inpatients. We have also found a relationship between ministers' nominations of mature and immature church members and scores on the RSI. Finally, more mature Christians tend to be less anxious and less depressed than those who scored less mature on the RSI.

My conviction is that we are just scratching the surface on this question of how religion impacts the emotional health of persons. Our research is continuing, and I look for these issues to be a significant part of the psychology of religion in the future years. If we are successful in further development of the RSI, it is possible that in the next few years psychologists will have available to them a reliable and valid tool for assessing these dynamics in a meaningful and helpful way. It does not seem too much to hope that psychological evaluations in the future will include an assessment of religious functioning on a routine basis.

The final interest that I have had has been in the nature of religious experience. My first book and my last book have been on this issue. In the early 1970s I collaborated with Walter Houston Clark in publishing *Religious Experience: Its Nature and Function in the Human Psyche*. In 1985 I collaborated with A. Adams Lovekin in publishing *Glossolalia: Behavioral Science Perspectives on Speaking in Tongues*. The psychosocial dynamics of what happens when persons report they have had a religious experience have been of significant concern to me during all these intervening years. Like William James, I have admitted to myself that my attempts to understand these phenomena were based on self-reports and were one step removed from the actual events. Most of life's important experiences are of this type, however, so that fact has not deterred me from the intriguing task of discovering these dynamics.

In the search for a better understanding of religious experience, I have assumed that psychology provided only one perspective and that the validity of these events was not subject to psychological analysis. Nevertheless, I have felt that, while my methods could not prove or disprove God, they could probe the channels by which the divinity was experienced, namely, humans' minds and bodies. Keeping this in mind, I have tried to be a good psychologist and a legitimate religious scholar in my formulations of religious experience. My article "An S-O-R Model of Religious Experience" sums up my thinking. In this essay, Christian religious experience is conceived under a stimulus-organism-response paradigm in which I accept the possibility that God is the stimulus which persons perceive and to which they respond by reconception and a decision to act on the basis of faith.

I am convinced that religious experience will neither go away nor be fully understood. I predict that the psychology of religion in the future will continue to be preoccupied with a study of its dynamics and that we will continue to make progress in its understanding.

I have attempted in this essay to trace several of my consuming interests as a psychologist of religion and to indicate how I believe them to be agendas for the future. I mentioned the religion of psychologists, psychology of religion in the courts, religious experience, the assessment of religious maturity, and the history of the science-religion dialogue. In whatever state the psychology of religion finds itself at the beginning of the 21st century, I am convinced it will include many of these themes.

References

Clark, W. H., and H. N. Malony. 1972. *Religious experience: Its nature and function in the human psyche.* Springfield, Ill.: C. C. Thomas.

Malony, H. N., ed. 1976. The contribution of Gordon W. Allport to the psychology of religion. Paper presented at the annual meeting of the American Psychological Association, September, Washington, D.C. Reprinted in *Journal of American Scientific Affiliation.*

————. 1978. *Psychology and faith: The Christian experience of eighteen psychologists.* Washington, D.C.: Univ. Press of America.

————. 1985a. An S-O-R model of religious experience. In *Advances in the psychology of religion,* ed. L. B. Brown, 113–26. Oxford: Pergamon.

————. 1985b. Assessing religious maturity. In *Psychotherapy and the religiously committed patient,* ed. E. M. Stern, 25–34. New York: Haworth Press.

Malony, H. N., and A. A. Lovekin. 1985. *Glossolalia: Behavioral science perspectives on speaking in tongues.* New York: Oxford Univ. Press.

Malony, H. N., T. L. Needham, and S. Southard, eds. 1986. *Clergy malpractice.* Philadelphia: Westminster.

Ragan, C. P., H. N. Malony, and B. Beit-Hallahmi. 1980. Psychologists and religion: Professional factors and personal belief. *Review of Religious Research* 21:208–17.

Shafranske, E. P., and R. L. Gorsuch. 1985. Factors associated with the perception of spirituality in psychotherapy. *Journal of Transpersonal Psychology* 16: 231–41.

Shafranske, E. P., and H. N. Malony. 1985. California Psychologists' religious and spiritual orientations and their practice of psychotherapy. Paper presented at the annual meeting of the American Psychological Association, August, Los Angeles.

Part 4

Psychopathology of Religion

8

Nils G. Holm

N ils G. Holm is full professor of comparative religion at the Åbo Akademi—the Swedish University—in Helsinki, Finland. He is also senior lecturer at the University of Helsinki and the University of Uppsala in Sweden and has lectured at Marburg in West Germany. Holm was educated at the Åbo Akademi and at Uppsala University, where he received a D.Th. in 1976.

Dr. Holm has been very active in international dialogues on religion and the social/behavioral sciences. He has been the Finnish representative to the organization committee for periodic European conferences on the psychology of religion, which have been held at the Catholic University of Nijmegen, the Netherlands, since 1979. He has also been the Nordic representative on the board of the International Conference of Sociology of Religion. He is vice president of Internationale Gesellschaft fur Religionpsychologie und Religionswissenschaft—the German organization for the psychology of religion. Holm is a member of the Association for the Sociology of Religion, the International Sociological Association, and the Society for the Scientific Study of Religion. He has presented papers at meetings of the International Congress of Psychology as well as at several conferences in the United States. He serves as a member of the editorial board for *Social Compass* and for *Temenos*—a yearbook for Nordic studies in comparative religion.

Dr. Holm is widely known for his writings about intense religious experiences such as glossolalia and mysticism. Among his writings are "Pentecostalism in Swedish-speaking Finland," "Functions of Glossolalia in the Pentecostal Movement," and *Glossolalia and Baptism in the Holy Spirit* (Uppsala, Sweden: Acta Universitatis Upsaliensis, 1976). In 1982 he wrote "Mysticism and Intense Experience," published in the

Journal for the Scientific Study of Religion, and edited *Religious Ecstasy* (Stockholm: Almqvist and Wiksell). In 1987 he authored the textbook *Scandinavian Psychology of Religion* (Helsinki: Åbo Akademi), and in 1988 he edited a special issue of *Social Compass* (35, no. 1) on the topic of religion in the Nordic countries. Among his articles in English are the following: "Ritualistic Pattern and Sound Structure of Glossolalia in Material Collected in the Swedish-speaking Parts of Finland" and "Recent Research into Revivalist Movements in Finland."

Holm's article "Sundén's Role Theory and Glossolalia" is an application of Hjalmar Sundén's theorizing about social reality, which has had a strong impact on Scandinavian psychology of religion. Sundén sees religious experience as a result of learning in a social community. Holm suggests that speaking in tongues can be understood as the playing of a social role within an environment in which expectation is high and the willingness to enter into an interpersonal drama is strong.

In the essay "Tradition, Upbringing, Experience," Dr. Holm attempts to describe the unique role of the psychology of religion in understanding religious experience. Contrary to sociology and history, the psychology of religion tries to comprehend religion in terms of individual psychological processes. He conceives this task to be one of fathoming how social traditions are incorporated into personal experience.

Sundén's Role Theory and Glossolalia

S ince the end of the 1960s, glossolalia has been my main area of research. This interest has not only been directed at the psychology of speaking in tongues, but also towards the history of this phenomenon in Finland, together with its linguistic and liturgical function. The results of my research have for the most part been published in articles and books in Swedish. There are also, however, a number of articles in English, listed among the references at the end of this essay.

When I began to be interested in the psychological aspects of glossolalia at the beginning of the seventies, it was difficult to find literature in this field, not to mention adequate theories. The main contribution I discovered was Hjalmar Sundén's role theory, which he published as early as the late fifties. His own discussion of speaking in tongues in his major work, *Religionen och rollerna* ([1959] 1966), applies a method of approach based on system theory, which in turn is linked with role theory. Sundén makes a distinction here between a weakly developed religious structure and a fully developed religious structure. If the structure, that is, the individually integrated group pattern, is weakly developed, there is a danger of popular hysteria and overacting. If, on the other hand, it is well developed, with its foundation in a given frame of tradition, it then produces, when confronted by collective suggestion mechanisms, a meaningful and integrative experience. The basis for this is the common role system which, with particular reference to speaking in tongues, may be found in the Bible, especially in the events of the first Pentecost. In my doctoral dissertation (Holm 1976) I analyzed interviews and field material from the point of view of role theory, and in the following pages I should like to discuss this approach and also point out the areas where research must go further.

From the *Journal for the Scientific Study of Religion* 26 (1987): 383–89; reprinted by permission of the publisher and the author. Copyright 1987 by the *Journal for the Scientific Study of Religion*.

The Major Concepts of Sundén's Role Theory

Sundén begins his theoretical considerations from the vantage point of social psychology. He indulges in mild polemics with the German school of psychology which tries above all to see religious experiences as the result of deep psychological structures in the human mind—the numinous feeling. In Sundén's opinion, a more meaningful approach is to look for structures in social reality which influence people and provide them with religious experience. He therefore comes to regard religious experience mainly as a consequence of social learning. The mainstay of all religion consists of mythological narratives which have been codified in sacred texts and which are therefore transmitted to ever new generations by learning processes. The distinctive elements of religious learning are the "holiness" of the object, the penetrative force of the myths or legends, and the connection with the social group. In this way the myths acquire a repetitive quality. New generations in succession can learn the holy tradition and thus find themselves integrated not only with their own time but also, retrospectively, with the conditions of the "original" congregation. At the same time, the religious person is presented with models for interpreting future phenomena. One acquires an eschatology.

The distinctive feature of Sundén's role theory is that he not only places religion in the context of social psychology, but that he also introduces perception psychology. Any mythological role description, for example, Abraham's relations with God, may function as a pattern of perception for a religious experience. If one has therefore learned the narrative in question—the roles—one is in possession of a set for a specific religious experience. One then carries a latent psychological propensity to experience the world in a religious manner. What is required for a concrete, specific religious experience to be released in a person is a situational resemblance and a motivating factor. If, from the individual's own perspective, there is a similarity between his own situation and a particular narrative in the holy tradition, the myth, a restructuring phenomenon can occur in that person so that the mythological reality also becomes reality for the individual in question. A person takes over the role of the human agent in the narrative—the myth—at the same time as he absorbs the role of the divine agent, that is, it comes to structure his field of experience. He thus experiences the external course of events as the actions of God. This happens for the individual in a manner which is as "direct" and unconscious as any everyday experience we undergo. But a person seldom remains for long within a religious experience, alternating instead with a more profane manner of experiencing the world. Sundén calls this *phase alternation*.

For a restructuring process of this kind to be released in the individual a special motivating factor is required. Not everyone who has absorbed mythological material allows the latter to structure the content of his life. If, however, the individual is subjected to internal or external pressure, if, for example, he encounters difficulties of various kinds, he then turns to alternative models of experience in order to solve his problems. In such a situation, latent religious narrative material can assume a structuring function with regard to the perception mechanisms. Such a person often feels that this "new" experience is given to him as a gift from the divine world. If a person lives in a religious environment with many mythological motives of high value and great restructuring potential, he can switch with relative ease to a religious model of interpretation.

The qualities which, according to Sundén, are most characteristic of religious experience are totality and intentionality. This means that when a strong religious experience occurs in an individual, the world is experienced as a unity, a totality, thus revealing a will, an intention, to the individual. The latter then enters into an I-thou relationship with the higher power, God. Thus for Sundén, religion is "the relation of a dialogue to existence as a totality, but this relationship is structured through roles and without roles it disappears" ([1959] 1966, 35).

Sundén thus sees religious experience principally as a function of learning in the social community, which is rich in role representations of the relationship with God. He conceives such a role as a pattern of perceptions which may be actualized and which may structure the stimuli coming from without. Thus, man is given one role and the supernatural, God, another. It is this latter role which summarizes the multiplicity of the world of experience and becomes totality and intention.

Glossolalia and Role Theory

My study of glossolalia has been carried out mainly in the Swedish-speaking part of the Pentecostal movement in Finland. The results I have published are based on almost 10 years of interviews and fieldwork. Before turning my attention to the psychological functions of glossolalia, I studied its liturgical significance and its linguistic structure. I analyzed dozens of authentic examples of glossolalia and discovered that one may distinguish two main categories of speaking in tongues. One is *supplicatory* glossolalia, often expressed in a group so that there is a general murmuring. The other is *prophetic* glossolalia, something uttered by individuals loudly and clearly so that everyone in the congregation can hear it. The normal practice is for some other person or the speaker himself to "interpret" the glossolalia, that is, to deliver the message in the language which everyone understands. There is no actual connection between the speaking in tongues and the message—the prophecy—from the linguistic point of view.

Linguistic analysis of glossolalia showed that speaking in tongues often reveals simple linguistic features. We may distinguish alliteration, assonance, rhyme, and so on. It proves to be based on a relatively small number of simple patterns which are varied from one occasion to another. One may also speak of different glossolalia dialects, or forms of speaking, which recur in several individuals in the same environment. Apparently, people adopt patterns of glossolalia from one another. Most of the phonemes occur in the speaker's mother tongue, but they are slightly more simplified with regard to combinations. Sometimes, however, exotic features are borrowed from completely foreign languages, for example, French or Swahili. In such cases, speaking in tongues may have a superficial resemblance to an actually extant language.

The conclusions I have been able to form from linguistic analysis are that glossolalia is based on the mother tongue, that it reveals simple linguistic patterns, and that it is influenced by the external linguistic environment. One may state that glossolalia is based on the universal human capacity for imitation. Children seem to be able to imitate the sounds of foreign languages very easily, while older people find it much more difficult. The fact that we do not use abracadabra language more may be ascribed to social conventions which forbid us to do this and also to the age factor. There is no need, in other words, to postulate any complicated or unhealthy psychological motives behind the use of glossolalia as such.

If one studies glossolalia among the Pentecostalists, however, one discovers that the phenomenon has a quite special significance for them. It is most frequently the external sign that the person in question has received the so-called baptism in the Spirit, that is, has been filled to overflowing with God's Holy Spirit. This experience has its biblical background in the events of the first Pentecost. In the same way as the apostles once did, later generations of Christians are to receive the Holy Spirit. The reception of the Holy Spirit is characterized by a manifest experience in individuals: baptism in the Spirit. The chief indication that this has occurred is precisely glossolalia.

We may thus speak of the role of baptism in the Spirit within the Pentecostal movement. It has its mythological basis in the Bible, but naturally also acquires a social basis in the devotional life of the congregation when private individuals practice glossolalia. Individuals, in other words, learn their role both from myth—the Bible—and in the social community. Since baptism in the Spirit is a highly desirable experience, every Pentecostalist soon learns the importance of this event and begins to anticipate receiving it. But not all members receive spiritual baptism immediately; they must sometimes wait a long time for it, if they ever receive it at all. How can one explain the latter phenomenon from a psychological point of view?

According to Pentecostal theology, God wishes to baptize people in the Holy Spirit as soon as possible after their conversion. The external sign of baptism in the Spirit is, as has been suggested, glossolalia. This means that glossolalia must be a gift from God, something which man cannot achieve by himself but something which is communicated to him in a supernatural way. The psychologically interesting aspect here is that individuals must enter a situation in which, when they begin to speak in tongues for the first time, this is experienced as a spiritual gift. Within the theology we thus find an "inhibiting" factor with regard to glossolalia. It must be produced in a situation and in such a way that the individual in question experiences it as a genuine "gift of grace," as the divinely inspired gift of tongues.

When I studied the situations in which Pentecostalists had received their baptism in the Spirit, it became apparent that about two-thirds of them had spoken in tongues for the first time in connection with inter-cessional prayer at some meeting. One-third, on the other hand, first spoke in tongues when alone, usually late in the evening as they were going to bed. The conclusion one can draw from this is that for the majority of Pentecostalists, the context of intercession at religious meet-ings provides the sort of occasion in their lives when glossolalia can be produced in what for them is a "genuine" manner. The group-dynamic aspects—intercession, loud shouts, songs, and exhortations—influence these individuals so that they can begin speaking in tongues. For those who received glossolalia while alone, relaxation of tension in connec-tion with going to bed apparently has great significance.

The interesting point, however, is that when the gift of tongues issues from the mouth of the expectant individual, this speech provides the impetus which releases the chain of perceptions leading the individual to interpret this speech as the gift of God. He takes over the role of the disciple at the same time as God's role is actualized and structures the field of perception. The individual enters fully into the role of baptism in the Spirit. The gift of tongues becomes a supernatural gift, and the feelings of spiritual happiness begin to flow. The frequent presence of "significant others" in the vicinity and their confirmation of the aural perception increase the speaker's certainty of the legitimacy of the bap-tism in the Spirit and the gift of tongues. There is, in other words, an interesting feedback mechanism between the situational factors and the outbreak of speaking in tongues. The situation must be opportune from the individual's own point of view at the same time as the outbreak of glossolalia "declares" the situation opportune.

It is naturally the case that the individual's capacity for self-criticism strongly affects the question of which point in time is the opportune one. The more intellectually oriented the individual, the harder he seems to find it to surrender to group-dynamic occurrences in the context of the religious meeting. Such people usually seem to receive the gift of tongues when alone. If the role of baptism in the Spirit is well learned, however, even in this case the individual perceives the gift of tongues in the same manner: as a spiritual gift of the God-given baptism in the Spirit. But other individuals seem to have the kind of mental constitution which makes it difficult to give way to abracadabra talk at all. Their mental mechanisms prevent them from adopting behavior which they hear and see among other people in their environment. People with a capacity for empathy thus produce glossolalia more quickly when they are in contact with the Pentecostal movement than those who do not have this aptitude. One conclusion I can draw from my studies is that it is therefore a perfectly natural thing to speak in tongues and thus receive baptism in the Spirit when one frequents a Pentecostal congregation. Specific psychological explanations are only required for those persons who, in spite of years of waiting for baptism in the Spirit, do not begin speaking in tongues.

Once individuals have become baptized in the Spirit, they continue to speak in tongues in the context of prayers. The same mental charge that was necessary on the first occasion is now no longer required. It is not unusual for glossolalia to be used at quite private prayer sessions, where it has an effect which corresponds to that of meditation for those who have learned a certain meditation technique. During this process of speaking in tongues a chain of associations is forged implying holiness, signs of grace, and relaxation. That speaking in tongues at the purely linguistic level is a "cleansing" of the mind is quite possible, although this still remains to be proved. In optimal conditions in the spiritual community, therefore, glossolalia assumes a positive function for the individual.

Discussion

The application of role theory to glossolalia shows clearly what function this speech exercises in the individual's life. It makes way for the assumption of the role of baptism in the Spirit at the same time as this role, in its own way, "sanctifies" the speaking and structures the field of experience so that it becomes God who gives the gift of tongues. When individuals have come into contact with the Pentecostal movement and learned to appreciate the gift of tongues and baptism in the Spirit, this gives way to the waiting phase. A motivation with a clear social basis forms inside them. It is, in other words, social "group pressure" which becomes a motivating factor. Speaking in tongues becomes a function of the process committing one to becoming a true Pentecostalist.

Something I have not yet studied is how this socially given motivating factor interacts with individual wishes and motives. It is nevertheless clear from the interviews that, from the individual point of view, too, speaking in tongues acquires a quite special social function. In this context one may reckon with various forms of self-assertion, the need for social acceptance, and even self-destruction. In other words, we are approaching issues of depth psychology. How these interact with socially given motivating factors is still an unexplained question. I assume that it is on this plane above all that explanations must be sought for the various complications affecting individuals when they take over glossolalia or alternatively when they do not adopt this behavior.

If we consider Sundén's theory as a whole, it regards the motivating factor as the driving force in the restructuring of the field of perception. But Sundén does not provide any more precise indications of potential motives in individual cases. At this point we approach broad areas which must be carefully studied. I should like to point out that Sundén himself has by no means used role-theory arguments exclusively in his psychology of religion. He has also contributed many studies which apply Freudian and Jungian approaches. At least as far as glossolalia is concerned, a study of motivating factors would be of great interest.

Another point where more careful study is required is the question of whether religious experiences should be understood exclusively as socially conditioned phenomena. A rigid application of role theory would imply that all new thought was precluded. Religion would be transmitted and shaped solely by socially given patterns and roles. Even Sundén himself has already expressed reservations about such arguments. He points out that the roles are by no means fixed patterns which are taken over automatically. They are in fact flexible, are taken on in an individual manner, and sometimes combined in quite surprising ways. There is, however, always enough left of the structure of the roles for the experience in question to be identified and legitimized in relation to the sacred tradition. It creates continuity and firmness of faith. One may nevertheless ask whether rudimentary elements of religious experience also become manifest in individuals with a weak religious heritage or who consistently avoid such a subject. Something of this may be seen in experiences which we have usually called "general mysticism." How this "mysticism" provided by existence itself is coordinated with socially given roles is a question which I find worthy of scholarly attention. In Sundén's own works there are many impulses around this point, which could be developed in various ways.

One further matter which I would like to consider is the question of whether glossolalia, when interpreted in terms of role theory, loses all its spiritual content and value. Does it not become mere speech with which God has no connection? This is in fact a theological problem for those who wish to preserve speaking in tongues as a gift of the Spirit. What I should like to point out as a scholar is that role theory assumes an alternation between a total religious structuring and a more profane and mechanic interpretation. There is a complementary relationship between these two which it is difficult to bridge in terms of religious philosophy. Interesting from the point of view of the history of theology is the fact that comparable problems have existed before in the church, particularly with regard to the double nature of Christ and in the matter of the Eucharist. Here it is a question of "natural" elements which in a religious context are simultaneously given a quite different emphasis and significance. Solving problems in this field is something I regard as a challenge for theology today.

The Sundén version of role theory is based on observations from learning theory and perception psychology. It explains the nature of the relationship between an I and a thou—God. Moreover, it emphasizes the continuity in the transmission of tradition. It is this which provides individuals in each new generation with identity and security of faith. The creation of new elements in religions is explained by newly required combinations of the elements of tradition and the internal and external motives in people. As I see the matter, this is also a point where more thorough study could be carried out with great benefit.

One particular advantage of using Sundén's role theory is its compatibility with several other theories. I am thinking here of symbolic interactionism as a whole, as well as learning theory—particularly modeling—together with perception psychology (visions and auditions). I also find that there is no lack of reason for linking motivating factors to aspects of depth psychology. The important point, however, is that such links are not made superficially, but only after careful theoretical investigation and in connection with the interpretation of experiential material.

References

Holm, N. G. 1976. *Tungotal och andedop.* (Glossolalia and baptism in the Holy Spirit.) Psychologia Religionum 5. Uppsala, Sweden: Acta Universitatis Upsaliensis. (Summary in English.)

Sundén, H. [1959] 1966. *Religionen och rollerna.* (Religion and roles). [Stockholm: Svenska Kyrkans Diakonistyrelse Bokförlage.] Reprint in German. *Die Religion und die Rollen,* trans. H. Muller and S. Ohman. Berlin: Töpelmann.

Tradition, Upbringing, Experience: A Research Program for the Psychology of Religion

When we speak of religion, we think primarily of a historically and socially given quantity in which every individual in a society participates in some way or another. Within any major religion there may be a large number of different contributing traditions. There may be differences between sects and churches, between forms of expression in the towns and in the countryside, between family traditions in different areas, and so on. The first thing we may establish is that religion is always a social quantity existing prior to the individual in history. In various ways the individual is absorbed into a religion or into the traditions it represents.

Dimensions of Religion

Within the sociology of religion different dimensions of religiosity have been discussed. For the sake of simplicity, I distinguish here between only three factors within religion. Firstly we have *statements of belief,* or the cognitive element. It is possible to distinguish between various genres in the cognitive—linguistic material supplied by religion: among the genres are myths, legends, stories, and personal narratives (memoirs). In all these forms, metaphors, similes, and idealizations—symbolic means of expression—play an important role. The different genres normally correspond to a purely concrete *behavior situation,* at which point we then obtain the second important dimension within religion. Liturgies, prayers, and cultic acts of different kinds are encountered in all religions. Outside these major collective forms of worship we also find a great variety of narrative situations in which a union of the cognitive element and the behavioral occurs. Every time such a union takes place it is formed into a specific *experience* for the individuals involved. We may regard this experience as the third important dimension of religion.

In a genuinely religious situation we do not speak objectively about God, but rather allow God and other figures to associate with each other and engage in action. Religious traditions may be classified in accordance with the kind of material they allow to function in an experience, a cultic act. The Protestant communions are probably among those traditions which place the strongest emphasis on reflections, on discourse about God. On the other hand, there are religions which transform the cognitive subject matter into the material of concrete experience in a literal sense. A concrete unity between experience and mythological material may be found in prophetism and messianism. Muhammad's prophecies and Emanuel Swedenborg's visions may be regarded as examples of such a unity. The study of why there are different associations between message and experience is an important subject for research in the psychology of religion.

The study of the structure of different religious traditions is primarily the responsibility of the history and sociology of religion. It is important to acquire a valid understanding of the historically given conditions as well as of the function of a religion in relation to other social factors, be they economic, political, or group-dynamic. Without sufficient knowledge of these dimensions no interpretation based on the psychology of religion willl be either comprehensible or relevant.

The Task of Psychology of Religion

The question then becomes what is the special task of the psychology of religion in the context of research. The psychology of religion attempts to study forms of religious expression in relation to man's psychological processes. In contrast to the sociology of religion, the psychology of religion tries to study religion from a more individual perspective. It tries to take social factors into account, but studies how these are "crystalized" in a concrete individual, in a living human being. Many other variables then come into play, including hereditary ones, personality typologies, maturation, and the overall limitations and capacities implied by human beings' mental resources. I should, therefore, like to suggest that the main task of the psychology of religion is to study how the *macrotradition*—religion in the form of belief statements and behaviors—confronts the *microorganism* of man and how this encounter gives rise to new occurrences and genuine experience.

Every experience is unique from the individual's own point of view, but at the same time it must be recognizable and capable of being related to a familiar tradition for it to be felt as "real" and "true." How this dialectical relationship is formed today in different religions and religious traditions is, in my opinion, an important task for the psychology of religion. How people can live religiously in the harsh spiritual climate of the West is likewise a delicate issue for research. The dangers of manipulation and compromise in the religious sphere are manifold.

Transmission of Tradition

Much of this method of describing religion is found in the sociology of knowledge as it has been described, for example, in P. L. Berger's and T. Luckmann's famous book *The Social Construction of Reality* (1966). Here the process is described in terms of externalization, objectification, and internalization. Each tradition consists of typified ways of acting, or roles. These correspond to given ways of thinking, symbolic forms of expression, and legitimizing mechanisms. The unique task of the psychology of religion from this perspective is to study which different types of internalization models are to be found at the individual level. The single individual is of interest here, but so are various groups of individuals, since we assume that there are certain types of reception forms with regard to tradition. Berger's and Luckmann's account, like those of other sociologists of religion, is sociological by nature and does not, therefore, introduce personality-typological models for the adoption of religious tradition. Thus it is at this point that the psychologist of religion must make his entry, if we are to obtain as complete a picture as possible of the transmission of tradition. In the following I shall sketch some important elements in this process.

What Is Transmitted

We have stated that every individual gradually comes to participate in a tradition represented by parents and others close to him. Through linguistic transmission and participation in cultic acts of different kinds the newcomer becomes absorbed into the symbolic world of the macro-tradition. If one wishes to understand a single individual, one must consider the totality of the tradition of which he or she has just become a part. Here it is not merely a matter of confining oneself to grand, all-embracing statements, but one must actually descend to the individual level and try to find with which subdivision in a particular tradition the individual has lived. I am suggesting that it is important not merely to consider the broad expressions of principle within a religion, but also actually to study the subtradition which an individual encounters. Here we must specify between different sects and churches, between private religious forms and revivalist movements of different kinds. It is vital to describe and understand as small units as possible, perhaps on occasion one single family and its traditions. Only in this way can we avoid the mistake of believing that all individuals within a major religious organization face tradition in the same way. Specification regarding what the individual has learned is important.

Social Stratification

In the second place we may state that it is meaningful to obtain as clear an idea as possible of the structure in a society or a smaller community. Individuals do not occupy the same social positions, do not possess the same prestige, and do not practice the same roles. Every role also generally corresponds to different cognitive structures, and the experiential world is, therefore, dependent in different degrees on the social position an individual adopts. Thus there is a stratification of religious knowledge and religious experience. In the field of religion, certain individuals are specialists, such as theologians, shamans, and priests, while others are more receptive. In other words, a mapping of this social stratification is necessary.

How the Tradition Is Transmitted

The third important question is how the religious tradition is transmitted to a particular individual. Here we approach questions of learning psychology. We must consider the stages of cognitive maturation and the socially given models for learning; we must also study the actual situation in which learning takes place. We are dealing with matters of developmental psychology, categorizations of personality typologies, and different models for learning psychology (conditioning, reward, punishment, model learning, and so on). Not least, it is important to realize that every learning stage in adolescence as well as later contains, together with the actual cognitive material, an emotional element and a readiness for action. Particularly in childhood emotional ties are important, since these are stored in the memory and can subsequently color one's complete religious view (the halo effect).

In Sweden, the transmission of tradition has been described above all by Hjalmar Sundén, who distinguishes between three different categories of tradition bearers. The *unconfident transmitters* continue their tradition in an inadequate fashion. They themselves have problems with their attitudes towards religion and therefore frequently pass their tradition on to children in a fragmentary form, often only orally and with negative emotional conditioning. Trying to impress upon children ideas and behaviors that one has not adopted wholeheartedly oneself is often a negative experience for the receiving party. *Confident transmitters*, however, pass on their tradition in an emotionally harmonious form, allowing the children to participate in the experiential situations and providing instruction at the pace preferred by the receivers themselves. In this way, a total tradition is transmitted, not merely a verbal one with which the unconfident transmitters are readily identified.

There are also those who have been described as *overconfident transmitters* of tradition. Such people try, through intensive influence, to transmit their own opinions and ways of looking at things to the new generation. They are often extremely vigilant and demanding educators who actively crush any signs of deviation. A tradition model of this kind may lead to an impasse in the perception of religion so that no mature reflection, no flexible adaptation of the tradition material to new situations, and no new hypotheses can be achieved. Responsible management of tradition is prevented, frequently giving rise to a polarization between naive fundamentalism and emancipation from all forms of religion.

If this third way of transmitting tradition is combined with negative and destructive emotions, the resultant reaction patterns may be described in the following three ways. There are first of all those who wish to liberate themselves by becoming atheists of some kind. Often this is not some carefully considered life view, but merely an *inverted belief* when one reacts negatively to all memories of religious behavior. A second group reacts with an *Angst-filled and guilt-laden piety*. Such people have never felt themselves to be genuinely accepted for their own sakes in religious contexts. They carry out their duty out of respect to others, never feel that they are in the right place, and thus provide constant fuel for their own low self-esteem. It is possible to experience a certain relief if one looks up to spiritual idols with strong authority and an ideology of success. The third reaction pattern consists of a *strong identification* with patterns with which one was forced to live as a child. To escape the helplessness and mental paralysis they feel, such people try to get very close to the sources of the transmission of tradition and try to find acceptance and appreciation by an even more rigid application of the system. We may say that they cover up their aggressive attitude with *hyper-belief* instead. In Scandinavia we have begun to use the term *God's grandchildren* to describe people with personal difficulties emerging from the ways of transmitting the religious tradition.

An overview of the ways of transmitting religious tradition (and naturally other ideologies, too) suggests that there are, in principle, three different kinds of attitudes. We have, first of all, those who react to the absence of consistent and in-depth transmission of tradition. If an individual completely lacks, or has very conflicting ideas about, essential questions in life, it is easy to react with anxiety and despair. When one is faced by life's most profound and serious questions, one then has no ideology with which to confront them. One lacks the reassuring rituals that give life its meaning and context. Another possibility, which I have already suggested, is that the models one has observed are so rigid and negatively charged that it is not possible to liberate oneself from them. They shackle an individual in the process of maturation and growth. Not infrequently, they are combined with an emphasis on negative and censoring aspects in the conception of God. A third way is what might be characterized as the edifying and supportive system. If the religious motifs are transmitted in a way which allows variation, reflection, and flexibility, these can operate in different situations in life as healing and supportive symbols. Mythological material can then function in structural terms for one's own experience world and enrich one's life. People then adopt roles from the holy tradition and are thus given new experiences and interpretative models. The different situations in life are filled with meaningful material. Much of this has been developed by Sundén in his so-called role theory. In Scandinavia it has acquired great importance for the understanding of religious experiences in different traditions.

Role theory attempts to explain experiences as restructuring phenomena on the perceptual plane, beginning with the mythological models which are given by virtue of a holy tradition. An early adoption of these images and experience situations is important; at the same time an impasse should not be allowed to occur. From this perspective, material from the religious tradition should be conveyed to children at an early stage so that mature reflection at subsequent periods is not prevented. It is above all the emotional charge which is important, and not so much the purely cognitive grasp of the content. Similarity of situation and strong motivation allow the role-taking to occur. Once the role of God is adopted it will then function to structure the perception, and a religious experience will take place. In this way one can obtain a rich set of symbols and linguistic-mythological images for the interpretation of life situations.

Early Emotional Influences

One more significant point in the process of transmitting tradition may be added: the early emotional ties to father, mother, siblings and others to whom one is close. This dimension can be subsumed under the heading of depth psychology. The significance of early emotional influences for our personality and their association with mythological motifs, such as God, Jesus, Mary, and saints of various kinds, are fairly clear. Here I should like to draw attention to the research conducted, for example, by Antoine Vergote and Alvaro Tamayo (1981) in Belgium and also by scholars such as Ana-Maria Rizzuto (1981) who have begun from reasoning associated with object relation theory. It is of course difficult to establish clear and simple connections between religious assimilation and such deep emotional structures, but research suggests that a mutual influence exists. In this context, I can also refer to my own research on the connection between assimilation of religious tradition and psychosocial maturity. I (1987a) studied the popular author from Åland, Finland, Joel Pettersson, and was able to find clear connections between his image of God and his psychosocial development. To dedicate oneself to the doctrine of God as the forgiving father presumes, in the majority of cases, a purely personal and human experience of something similar. In addition, the lack of a female figure for the divinity sometimes seems, perhaps particularly for Protestants, to produce a feminization of the Jesus image on occasion together with an idealization of the Virgin Mary, particularly for Catholics.

Acquiring a qualified understanding of the connections between assimilation of tradition and the psychodynamic aspects is perhaps something which is difficult to do with large groups of people. Surveys of these relations only give the most superficial indications of the links. In this case, however, an in-depth study of individual cases is to be preferred. Only in this way may an appropriate differentiation be obtained. Clearly, the method has consequences for generalization, but this is something faced by all interpretative research in the area of depth psychology.

Summary

I have spoken of factors connected with learning psychology in understanding the transmission of tradition and have tried to show how important it is to have the right learning situation and solid transmitters of tradition. I have also indicated the significance of deep emotional ties which arise particularly during childhood. That these conditions have a mutual influence on each other and are, in practice, also difficult to distinguish seems clear. It is moreover a fact that the mythological motifs which have been codified for generations in myths, legends, and other narrative genres have analogies in the experiential structures which emerge in the interplay between children, other children, parents, and other adults. In a certain sense, we can say that religion has objectified experience motifs that are important for humans in general. The goal of religious education must therefore be to provide the symbols and motifs of tradition in such a way that every individual finds some correspondence between deep-lying motifs in his or her own world of experience and in the collective tradition. Only then can a religious motif acquire life and carry meaning in the deepest sense. The existence of different models for this synthesis is clear. We must allow for reinforcement, compensation, sublimation, and repression mechanisms. But all the major religions seems to have a rich set of motifs and symbols which go a long way to providing for individual needs. The ability to adopt these motifs from the tradition is not a simple process, however, especially in today's pluralistic and rationalistic world. Sometimes, however, sociopolitical conditions reinforce the process, something we can see today in militant Islam.

The research program for the psychology of religion which has been outlined here may appear extensive and difficult to arrange. There are many different subsidiary tasks within it, but the essential point would be to arrive gradually at psychological models for how the reception of the symbolic world of religion occurs in man together with how he can use and realize it; make it living in his own experiential life. Some may think, moreover, that the program does not correspond to all scientific demands of objectivity and evaluative freedom. I must emphasize that I am convinced that the actual research itself can be carried out without subjective evaluations but that, obviously, interpretation, in a broader perspective of the desirability of religion, depends on fundamental evaluations of worldviews. Scientific research in itself can make no pronouncements about ethical or philosophical values.

I should also like to stress that it is naturally very difficult to separate religious expression from other forms of human expression such as art, for example. The boundary is necessarily vague. One must therefore work with both substantial and functional definitions of religion. An extension of the parameters of definition is often desirable, at least from the general perspective of comparative religion. I also believe that we need considerably more cross-cultural studies. Material from religions other than Christianity must be seriously introduced into discussions of religious psychology. Only in this way will we see the symbol-bearing functions of humanity and, thus, of religion in the deepest sense.

References

Berger, P. L., and T. Luckmann. 1966. *The social construction of reality: A treatise in the sociology of knowledge.* New York: Doubleday.

Holm, N. G. 1987. Joels Gud. En religionspsykologisk studie av Joel Pettersson. (The God of Joel. A religio-psychological study of Joel Pettersson.) *Meddelanden från Ålands kulturstiftelse,* no. 2: 1–127.

Rizzuto, A.-M. 1981. *The birth of the living God: A psychoanalytic study.* Chicago: Univ. of Chicago Press.

Vergote, A., and A. Tamayo, eds. 1981. *The parental figures and the representation of God: A psychological and cross-cultural study.* The Hague: Mouton.

9

Mary Jo Meadow

Mary Jo Meadow is professor of psychology and director of religious studies at Mankato State University, Mankato, Minnesota. She received the Ph.D. in clinical psychology from the University of Minnesota.

Meadow has been active in several divisions of the American Psychological Association (APA). In Division 36, Psychologists Interested in Religious Issues, she has served as member of the division council, program chair, editor of the newsletter, APA council representative, and president. She has been involved in the leadership of Division 32, Humanistic Psychology, serving as secretary and president. She has also been a leader in Division 35, which is concerned with the psychology of women, and is one of the organizers of a proposed division of transpersonal psychology. Dr. Meadow is a member of the Society for the Scientific Study of Religion and has presented papers at many of its annual meetings. Active in the American Academy of Religion (AAR), she has served as board member, section chair, and president of the upper Midwest region. She is a consulting editor of the *Journal of Religion and Health*.

Meadow is coauthor (with Richard D. Kahoe) of *Psychology of Religion: Religion in Individual Lives* (New York: Harper and Row, 1984). One of several comprehensive texts written in the last decade, this volume is a significant contribution to the literature. In the book Meadow discusses an idea, presented earlier in an article entitled "The Cross and the Seed: Active and Receptive Spiritualities," that is one of the more innovative models to be suggested in recent theorizing. She notes that Jesus called for his followers to be like "seed which fall to the earth and die." She terms this the *receptive*, or *surrender*, mode of religion. Further, Jesus called for his followers to "take up their crosses and follow

231

him." Meadow terms this the *active*, or *ascetic*, mode of religion. She relates these options to introverted and extroverted personality traits resulting in a fourfold model, which is heuristically valuable: the "discipliner" (active/introverted), the "communer" (receptive/introverted), the "zealot" (active/extroverted), and the "neighbor" (receptive/extroverted). In addition to the volume on the psychology of religion, Meadow has written *Other People* (Philadelphia: Westminster, 1984) and has coedited with Carole A. Rayburn *A Time to Weep and a Time to Sing: Faith Journeys of Women Scholars of Religion* (Minneapolis: Winston, 1985).

In the article "The Dark Side of Mysticism," Dr. Meadow discusses the negative aspect of mystical experience. She notes that most religious mystics report darkness and despair, desolation as well as consolation. She describes this "dark night of the soul" and details a possible explanation for its occurrence. She illustrates these ideas by considering the lives of two mystics in particular—Simone Weil and Dag Hammarskjöld—and concludes the essay by relating mysticism to temperament, guilt, passivity, and loss.

In her essay "Current and Emerging Themes in the Psychology of Religion," Meadow identifies those areas in psychology of religion that attracted her attention early. She notes her long-standing interest in measuring the dimensions of religion. Pervasive interest, which resulted in the innovative model of active and receptive modes of religion, has been in personality and spirituality. Another has been sexism in religion, which is paralleled by an interest in religious development in adulthood. Addressing her current interests in the field, Meadow expresses much concern about the pragmatic use of religion, particularly in psychotherapy. She feels this use often distorts the therapeutic process and results in clients' acquiescing to therapists' desires; further, she eschews therapists acting as spiritual advisors. Meadow is also interested in religion and world peace, hoping to construct a foundation for peace out of religion's admonition to love one another. Dr. Meadow also identifies areas to which she will devote time in the future. These include further study of mysticism and of dogma-free religion. Most recently Meadow has become interested in Eastern psychologies, particularly those of Hindu yoga and Theravadan Buddhism. She studies Buddhist psychology academically as well as by participating in intensive meditation for up to 4 months of every year.

The Dark Side of Mysticism: Depression and "The Dark Night"

Most people writing about mysticism emphasize mystical exaltation, ecstasy and union with God, divinity, value. Such experiences—the crown of mystical endeavor—are surely important aspects of mysticism. However, mystics also acknowledge periods of dryness, darkness, and religious despair—the keenly felt absence of God. These features seldom receive scholarly consideration in spite of their importance in virtually all mystics' experience.

Psychologists have studied mystical states simply as altered states of consciousness, and also in relation to drug experience and psychotic episodes. Some writers consider both drugs and mysticism self-chosen ways of diving into the depths of the same inner sea in which the schizophrenic person struggles and drowns (Campbell 1972). The Group for the Advancement of Psychiatry, in their 1976 report "Mysticism: Spiritual Quest or Psychic Disorder?," concluded that distinguishing between mysticism and certain psychiatric disorders is virtually impossible (Goleman and Davidson 1979). Most psychological studies, spanning more than three-fourths of a century, emphasize mystical exaltation.

Psychologist William James ([1902] 1961) considered insanity the opposite side of the coin of mysticism. In both, there is the same sense of importance in small events, the same words having new and exciting meanings that other people do not discern, the same feeling of being controlled by external powers, the same sense of mission, the same exalted emotion. James also pointed out differences: in insanity, the emotion is pessimistic compared to mystical optimism; there are desolations instead of consolations; the meanings are dreadful instead of wonderful; and the powers are enemies rather than friends.

Recognized mystics also report desolation as well as consolation, dryness as well as the dew of mystical grace, yearning as well as fulfill-

From *Pastoral Psychology* 33, no. 2 (1984): 105–25; reprinted by permission of the publisher and the author. Copyright 1984 by Human Sciences Press.

ment, entombment in the awful continuing ordinariness of frustrated longing as well as upliftedness to a personal heaven. These aspects of mysticism might more aptly be compared to such psychological states as depression, despair, meaninglessness, or futility than to psychotic episodes. Here, there are not hidden meanings in things, but an apparent absence of meaning. There is no exalted emotion, but a deadly and despairing yearning for some emotional anointing, for watering of one's dryness. External powers seem to have withdrawn their presence or ceased to exist. Events do not have added importance, but seem to have lost all importance. Life itself lacks purpose or coherence, and is devoid of any sense of mission or direction.

This article explores relationships between mystical periods of aridity and suffering—"the dark night of the soul"—and clinical depression. Material from the lives and writings of two contemporary figures who were not formally associated with any religious tradition illustrates the discussion. Simone Weil and Dag Hammarskjöld are readily acknowledged to be mystics by most scholars in the field. The paper also discusses the possible necessity of mysticism in some lives.

The Mystical Dark Night

Although mystics give differing descriptions of their voyage, they apparently agree upon some commonalities. Five steps outline the general mystical voyage: (1) awakening, (2) purification, (3) illumination, (4) the dark night of the soul, and (5) the unitive state of spiritual marriage. This paper is concerned with the second and fourth steps. (General references for this material are Arintero 1949–51; Garrigou-LaGrange 1947–48; and Underhill 1955.)

The Early Mystical Life

The mystic's initial task is a conscious decision to purify life of aspects contrary to mystical endeavor. This consists of active striving against deliberate sin, cultivation of an awareness of God, practice of some meditative technique to focus consciousness on God, and various other ritual, ascetic, and spiritual disciplines according to the particular path being followed. The time of active striving involves some anguish over the costs of the voyage, but gives a sense of mastery over one's situation.

In the second stage, all sense of competence disappears. The individual feels overwhelmed by personal failure and inadequacy. Prayer becomes difficult, and consciousness focuses on subtle faults of which one was previously unaware. The individual feels overwhelmed by her or his own evilness, and may believe that God has withdrawn support.

Writers of mystical theology warn against mistaking this relatively benign trial for the more rigorously purging dark night of the soul, which is characteristic of a more advanced state. Perseverance in this initial trial leads to the first stages of mystical prayer. One enjoys scattered episodes of peace in being wordlessly in the presence of God. Virtue also becomes easier as the many outbreaks of anger, gluttony, greed, and other faults diminish.

The Later Mystical Life

The dark night of the soul reflects advanced spirituality. Here, the mystical path is complicated by the apparent loss of the very basis for spiritual endeavor itself; religious meaning disappears. The mystic feels completely abandoned by God, incapable of faith or hope, and heavily burdened by the demands of religious love and perseverance. Completely alone, bereft of any consolation, one faces the task of continuing on the path. Religious literature reflects the terrible anguish of this period: "How much longer will you forget me, Yahweh? Forever? How much longer will you hide your face from me? How much longer must I endure grief in my soul, and sorrow in my heart by day and by night?" (Ps. 13:1–2, NJB) Similarly: "God, you are my God, I am seeking you, my soul is thirsting for you, my flesh is longing for you, a land parched, weary and waterless" (Ps. 63:1).

The Indian poet Tagore describes the same experience: "The rain has held back for days and days, my God, in my arid heart. The horizon is fiercely naked—not the thinnest cover of a soft cloud, not the vaguest hint of a distant cool shower. . . . Call back, my lord, call back, this pervading silent heat, still and keen and cruel, burning the heart with dire despair" (Tagore [1913] 1971, 53–54). Also from Tagore: "Ah, love, why dost thou let me wait outside at the door all alone? . . . It is only for thee that I hope. If thou showest not thy face, if thou leavest me wholly aside, I know not how I am to pass these long, rainy hours. I keep gazing on the far away gloom of the sky, and my heart wanders wailing with the restless wind" (37).

Mystics consider perseverance in this often very prolonged period of distress necessary for the final crown of mystical attainment, the ecstasy that has been compared to drug experience and psychosis. Mystical literature often seems to suggest that sheer perseverance—should one attain the dark night—will necessarily lead to mystical union. This paper raises two questions concerning this contention. Does one who experiences an agony of longing for God necessarily eventually pass to mystical ecstasy? Is one who experiences this intense longing for God necessarily far advanced in the spiritual life?

Within a normal range, people differ in basic optimism—with feelings of confidence, happiness, and positive expectations of life and the future—and pessimism—with self-doubt, frequent "blue" feelings, forebodings of unhappiness, and dissatisfaction with life and the future. This paper is not concerned with temporary depression, reactions to particular events in life, but with individuals who appear to have a depressive life cycle.

Mental health professionals agree on the common symptoms of clinical depression. The typically depressed person is deeply sad and lonely. Life seems empty and lacks meaning; the future is bleak. Often, there is great fatigue and a general slowdown in thinking, speaking, and acting. Anxiety, shame, and guilt are also common. The depressed person likely has negative attitudes toward self, others, and the world. All tasks feel like a burden for which one is inadequate. Life holds no joy or delight.

As depression deepens, there may be severe problems with concentration and problem solving. Sleeping and eating disorders are common. Sometimes strong hypochondriacal concerns appear. An extremely negative attitude toward oneself—even to the point of seeing oneself as vile and despicable—is common. The depressed person may feel guilty of unpardonable sins. In extreme cases, delusions and/or suicide may occur.

Genetic/Biochemical Understanding of Depression

Psychologists disagree about the bases for depressive life-styles. Genetically based, biochemical factors seem clearly to be at work in some cases. Ancient documents attribute to Hippocrates and Galen classifications of people that include a biologically based melancholic group (Gray 1978, 173). Numerous other biologically based explanations of depression have since arisen. We also know that treatment with appropriate medications often reduces the wide mood swings of some individuals (Kolb 1977, 464–69) and that electroconvulsive therapy lifts some depressions. Four other explanations of depression consider depressive life-styles as learned behavior which can—theoretically, at least—be modified without somatic treatment.

Claiming Depression

Temporary depressions often seem triggered by some kind of loss: loss of love or emotional support, personal or economic failures, or the loss of security produced by new responsibilities (Cameron 1963, 415). Silvano Arieti (1978, 221–22) has described a depressive life-style focusing on poignant sensitivity to loss. In this "claiming depression," the depressed person lays claim to a "lost paradise," and any unfulfilled desire leads to depression. These people want to be dependent on some dominant other responsible for meeting their needs and keeping them from feeling deprived. They generally hold unexpressed hostility toward others failing to satisfy them and feel they do not get what they should have. Treatment consists of getting the person beyond using dependency and hostile expectations to get what she or he wants.

Self-Blaming Depression

Arieti (1978, 223–25) also described a "self-blaming" depression. This commonly accepted interpretation sees depression as anger turned inward against oneself. Freud postulated a "death instinct" which could either be turned inward against oneself or else manifest as aggression against others. Depression thus results from having turned aggressive impulses toward others inward against oneself (Gray 1978, 177). This produces strong feelings of guilt and unworthiness, and desire to punish oneself.

In self-blaming depression, concerns about sin, duty, punishment, and guilt dominate. One reacts to disappointments with self-accusation. Arieti maintains that such depressed people try to retrieve losses by expiating instead of insisting upon their right to certain goods. The person chooses guilt and suffering because they leave one feeling the power of self-redemption by suffering, instead of being dependent upon another. Treatment consists of getting the person to recognize how feelings of loss and anxiety are translated into self-blame; one then learns to face and deal with anxiety.

O. H. Mowrer (1961) believes self-blame in depression is usually related to the person's real guilt. Depressed people often blame themselves for small or insignificant peccadillos to avoid facing deeper underlying guilt. Mowrer's treatment begins with an opportunity for the person to confess what the real guilt is. Next comes admitting to important people in one's life the real truths about oneself, repairing—to the extent of one's ability—any damage done to others, and amending one's conduct in the future.

Helplessness and Depression

Arieti's models of depression consider emotion the basis of depression. Two other recent understandings emphasize the cognitive components of depression. Seligman's (1975) work views depression as learned helplessness. People who acquire a generalized expectancy that they are not able to control their outcome in life are especially prone to depression (Depue and Monroe 1978). Seligman (1975, 106) noted many symptom similarities between depressed persons and animals in whom learned helplessness had been experimentally induced: passivity, lack of aggression, negative cognitive sets, and disturbances of social, sexual, and eating behavior. Being unable to control one's outcomes prolongs feelings of powerlessness, hopelessness, and pessimism about the future. This model says treatment should consist of corrective learning experiences in which the depressed person exercises power with positive outcomes.

Attributions and Depression

Aaron Beck (1967) says that depression is best understood as resulting from cognitive distortions: the person incorrectly attributes certain characteristics to some of her or his experiences. These emphasize unfavorable aspects of oneself, others, the world, and the future. Trivial problems are magnified, difficulties seem unsolvable, and change is impossible. The depressed person has acquired a habit of automatically having negative cognitions which seem logical and irrefutable. Treatment consists of teaching the person to substitute other more optimistic cognitions in place of those leading to depression.

These four models are not meant by their proposers to be mutually exclusive; indeed, all can be seen as complementary and alternative frameworks for understanding. In actual work with clients, therapists often find different models particularly appropriate for different clients. All these models help focus on some aspects of depressive life-styles for which we can examine the lives of mystics.

Our Illustrative Figures

We now look briefly at the writings and lives of our mystics for themes related to various interpretations of depression.

Dag Hammarskjöld

Dag Hammarskjöld (1905–1961) had strong tendencies toward a mystical vision of life. Early in life, the study of philosophy and theology greatly interested him (Soderberg 1962, 36). He dedicated himself to serving causes greater than himself as a self-surrender without anxiety about outcomes (Miller 1961, 21–22). Hammarskjöld died in an airplane crash while on United Nations business. Shortly before the flight, he spoke with a friend about the demands of mystical love (Soderberg 1962, 97).

In a program for Edward R. Murrow's "This I Believe," Hammarskjöld stated his personal faith: "The full explanation of how man should live . . . I found in the writings of those great medieval mystics for whom 'self-surrender' had been the way to self-realization, and who in 'singleness of mind' and 'inwardness' had found strength to say *yes* also to every fate life had in store for them. . . . Love . . . meant simply an overflowing of the strength with which they felt themselves filled when living in true self-oblivion . . . whatever it brought them personally of toil, suffering—or happiness" (1962, 24). For the dedication of the meditation room of the United Nations, he stated, "When we come to our deepest feelings and urgings we have to be alone, we have to feel the sky and the earth, and hear the voice that speaks within us" (Miller 1961, 20). In a pamphlet explaining this room, he said, "It is for those who come here to fill the void with what they find in their center of stillness" (Hammarskjöld 1962, 161).

Hammarskjöld was deeply sensitive to loss and loneliness throughout his life; these themes dominate in his journal *Markings* (1964). He stated, "What makes loneliness an anguish is not that I have no one to share my burden, but this: I have only my own burden to bear" (85). Further: "Alone beside the moorland spring, once again you are aware of your loneliness—as it is and always has been. As it always had been—even when, at times, the friendship of others veiled its nakedness" (116). Loneliness led him to suicidal ruminations: "To be sure, you have to fence with an unbuttoned foil: but, in the loneliness of yesterday, did you not toy with the idea of poisoning the tip?" (8). Later, he wrote, "So *that* is the way in which you are tempted to overcome your loneliness—by making the ultimate escape from life" (86). His journal noted accounts of several suicides he had observed (27–28).

Hammarskjöld was also highly sensitive to his own failings. He once complained of himself: "So, once again, you chose for yourself—and opened the door to chaos. The chaos you become whenever God's hand does not rest upon your head" (Hammarskjöld 1964, 104). He wrote elsewhere, "When all becomes silent around you, and you recoil in terror—see that your work has become a flight from suffering and responsibility, your unselfishness a thinly disguised masochism. . . . Gaze steadfastly at the vision until you have plumbed its depths" (16).

Themes of helplessness also appear: "Slow and gray—He searches every face. But the people aimlessly streaming along the gray ditches of the streets are all like himself—atoms in whom the radioactivity is extinct, and force has tied its endless chain around nothing—In the dim light he searches every face, but sees only endless variations on his own meanness" (Hammarskjöld 1964, 24). Later he wrote, "How am I to find the strength to live as a free man, detached from all that was unjust in my past and all that is pretty in my present, and so, daily, to forgive myself?" (150).

Negative expectations of himself, others, and the future were common attributions made by Hammarskjöld: "Isn't the void which surrounds you when the noise ceases your just reward for a day devoted to preventing others from neglecting you?" (1964, 12). Similarly: "Your contempt for your fellow human beings does not prevent you, with a well-guarded self-respect, from trying to win their respect" (41). He noted: "What I ask for is absurd: that life shall have a meaning. What I strive for is impossible: that my life shall acquire a meaning. I dare not believe, I do not see how I shall ever be able to believe: that I am not alone" (86).

Simone Weil

Simone Weil (1909–1943) appears to have been born with an unusually deep sensitivity. Her awareness of other people's deprivations led her to practice austerities even as a child. She considered herself stupid and ugly, although she was clearly a brilliant intellectual. At 14, contemplating her own acute sense of absolute unworthiness, she was suicidal. Later in life, although her family was well able to support her, she insisted on taking jobs of exhausting physical labor to be with the common person. She was intensely concerned with the social and political problems of her times.

Reading a poem about the unworthiness of a guest at a feast precipitated Weil's first mystical experience. She had read nothing of the mystical literature before this time and later was grateful for her ignorance. She had refused to kneel until literally forced to her knees by a power from without stronger than her resistance. Throughout her life, she considered herself a reluctant and unworthy intimate of God. Weil daily recited the Lord's Prayer in Greek with a concentration that regularly transported her to mystical ecstasy. Her writings emphasize a theme of "waiting for God."

Another central theme in Weil's works is eating and not eating (Weil 1973, 35). Her spirituality stressed that one must be content to be externally hungry and welcome it, refusing to eat what is forbidden to make up for felt lack. Her concerns for social injustice and maintaining pure desire for God expressed themselves behaviorally in bouts of fasting and semistarvation. Weil died in England in a sanitarium for treatment of tuberculosis. The cause of death is given as starvation from refusing to eat because of mental imbalance. Some people with her during the last days report that she apparently tried to eat, but was unable to do so.

Weil was intensely alone throughout her life. She wrote: "It is not by chance that you have never been loved . . . To want to escape from being lonely is cowardice. Friendship ought not to cure the sorrows of loneliness but to double its joys. Friendship is not to be sought for, dreamed about, longed for, but exercised (it is virtue)" (Weil 1970, 43; Weil's punctuation). She wrote Father Perrin, a priest with whom she corresponded and counseled: "I think that, except you, all those human beings for whom I have made it easy to hurt me through my friendship have amused themselves by doing so. . . . They did not behave like this from malice, but as a result of . . . this animal nature within them" (Weil 1973, 92).

Weil strongly longed for passivity: "The most beautiful life possible has always seemed to me to be one where everything is determined, either by the pressure of circumstances or by impulses . . . where there is never any room for choice" (Weil 1973, 100). She claimed that "men can never escape from obedience to God. . . . The only choice given to me . . . is to desire obedience or not to desire it" (133). Forced compliance would appeal to her: "We experience the compulsion of God's pressure, on condition that we deserve to do so. . . . We have to abandon ourselves to that pressure" (44–45).

Weil's intense feelings of guilt and unworthiness lasted her lifetime. She wrote: "I am an instrument already rotten. I am too worn out. . . . I have never read the story of the barren fig tree without trembling. I think that it is a portrait of me" (Weil 1973, 100). Weil expected little good from herself, others, life, or the future. Another quotation indicates her understanding of Providence: "A blind mechanism, heedless of degrees of spiritual perfection, continually tosses men about and throws some of them at the very foot of the Cross. . . . It is in his Providence that God has willed that necessity should be like a blind mechanism" (124–25).

Spirituality and Temperament

At the turn of the century, psychologist William James ([1902] 1961) related basic emotional temperament to religiousness. He concluded that people with a proclivity to melancholy—whom he called "sick soul" types—are constituted to be far more religiously sensitive than those of more sanguine nature. Sick souls have a low threshhold for mental distress, are deeply sensitive to internal discord, suffer from negative feelings about themselves, and brood about possible future ills. James said that the most complete religions are essentially religions of deliverance in which the pessimistic elements are well developed; only sick souls can most fully appreciate the deliverance that they offer. The superficiality of the more "healthy-minded" insulates them from emotional contact with experience that predisposes one to religious or spiritual needs: lack, evil, suffering, anguish, and sorrow.

One can easily agree with James that some sensitivity to discord and anguish may be a precondition for deeply developed religiousness. Existential anxiety, "cosmic empathy," and awareness of life's darker aspects are probably prerequisite to mysticism. Individuals lacking such sensitivity can certainly be depressed though. Their depression would probably be related to minor losses and frustrations, crushed personal ambitions, petty matters of everyday life, and other such individual agendas. Such mundane depression might indicate an awareness of and capacity for suffering that could eventually become desire for God but, in itself, bears no relationship to the fully developed anguish of mystics. Maslow considered such suffering a sign of spiritual disorder if it did not transcend itself. He wrote, "It is better to consider neurosis as related rather to spiritual disorders, to loss of meaning, to doubts about the goal of life, to grief and anger over a lost love, to seeing life in a different way, to loss of courage or hope, to despair over the future, to dislike for oneself, to recognition that one's life is being wasted, or that there is no possibility of joy or love, etc. These are all falling away from full humanness" (Maslow 1971, 31).

Hammarskjöld and Weil surely fit James's "sick soul" type in some ways, whether their "depression" was neurotic or not. Weil said of herself: "If I am sad, it comes primarily from the permanent sadness that destiny has imprinted forever upon my emotions, where the greatest and purest joys can only be superimposed and that at the price of a great effort of attention" (1973, 76). From Hammarskjöld we have: "At least he knew this much about himself—I know what man is—his vulgarity, lust, pride, envy,—and longing. Longing—among other things, for the Cross" (1964, 55). Maslow summed up this idea in saying, "I have a vague impression that the transcenders are less 'happy' than the healthy ones. They can be more ecstatic, more rapturous, and experience greater heights of 'happiness' (a too weak word) than the happy and healthy ones. But I sometimes get the impression that they are *as* prone and maybe more prone to a kind of cosmic-sadness . . . over the stupidity of people, their self-defeat, their blindness, their cruelty to each other, their shortsightedness" (1971, 284).

While mystics show evidence of depression, Maslow has captured the flavor of an additional note that is struck. The anguish experienced, the loss felt, the guilt suffered, the meanings extinguished, the impotence endured—all must have as their referent something of the cosmic order, of yearning for divinity or God, to be considered mystical suffering. Guilt must be more than a fear of punishment; it must include awareness of being in opposition to cosmic order. The yearning must be for the Ultimate—not for petty satisfactions. The mystics have experienced Augustine's "our hearts were made for thee, O God, and they will not rest until they rest in thee."

Mysticism and Depression

We have seen in the lives of Hammarskjöld and Weil evidence that psychiatry could easily consider symptoms of depression. Are mystics chronically depressed individuals who manage occasionally to break through to mystical joy as scattered islands in their gloom? Can we develop any criteria to sort out the wheat from the chaff? These issues raise more questions than answers.

Mysticism and Loss

Mystics' intense awareness of ultimate human aloneness and emptiness shows their sensitivity to loss. They interpret their longings as an
absence of God rather than other goods, however. From Hammarskjöld
we have: "Did'st Thou give me this inescapable loneliness so that it
would be easier for me to give Thee all?" (1964, 166). Weil claimed,
"The longing to love the beauty of the world in a human being is essentially the longing for the Incarnation. . . . The Incarnation alone can satisfy it" (1973, 171).

If an expressed yearning for the Ultimate is a necessary prerequisite
for mysticism, it is not a sufficient one. Various longings can easily be
translated into longing for God. Some scholars (see Clark 1958, 278–84)
see mysticism as a sublimation of needs for sex, love, security, or
escape. Boisen pointed out that "the idea of God stands for something
which is operative in the lives of all men, even though they may not call
themselves religious. It is the symbol of that which is supreme in the
interpersonal relationships and . . . that fellowship without which he
cannot live" (1970, 203).

Thus, God may simply be the name under which other longings are
subsumed. Dag Hammarskjöld understood this: "Your cravings as a
human animal do not become prayer just because it is God whom you
ask to attend to them" (1964, 11). Psychologist Gordon Allport
described transformation of lesser desires: "Prayer is continuous with
hope, as hope is continuous with fear. Religious activity thus grows
imperceptibly out of desire. The mind finds itself gradually . . . seeking
to add to its natural powers a reasonable complement" ([1950] 1973,
56). As a counterpoint to Boisen and a continuation of Allport's theme,
Weil says, "If love finds no object, the lover must love his love itself, perceived as something external. Then one has found God" (1970, 260).
For this to be factually true in a given life, one's behavior should evidence that God is the true focus of desire. Weil claims that "all sins are
attempts to fill voids" (160) and insists that "anyone who, at the
moment when he is thinking of God, has not renounced everything,
without any exception, is giving the name of God to one of his idols"
(217).

Mysticism and Guilt

Mystics throughout history have been highly sensitive to their own
failings. A mystic's ethical sensitivity—as opposed to neurotic self-blaming—should be reflected in genuine efforts to govern one's life ethically.
This should result in transcending the preoccupation with one's own
guilt and lackingness that paralyzes appropriate conduct. Weil noted
that "the great obstacle to the loss of personality is the feeling of guilt.

One must lose it" (1970, 208). Her own success at this task is not pronounced, although somewhat implicit in such statements as "when we have the feeling that on some occasion we have disobeyed God, it simply means that for a time we have ceased to desire obedience" (Weil 1973, 133). If awareness of personal fault is "genuine" rather than neurotic, it should lead beyond mere confession to further events. Mowrer (1961) discussed continuing honesty about oneself with salient others, reparative expiation, and amendment of conduct. Weil certainly accomplished these further steps.

Failure to transcend preoccupation with personal ego-centered guilt is written of by James, who complains of those who go about professing their smallness and sinfulness with the greatest of pride. He pointed out in one saint "her voluble egotism; her sense, not of radical bad being, as the really contrite have it, but of her 'faults' and 'imperfections' in the plural; her stereotyped humility and return upon herself" (James, [1902] 1961, 276). This feeling of radical badness, rather than scattered particular flaws, is strongly apparent in our examples. Hammarskjöld noted: "Guilt—it is not the repeated mistakes, the long succession of petty betrayals . . . but the huge elementary mistake, the betrayal of that within me which is greater than I—in a complacent adjustment to alien demands" (1964, 47). Weil wrote of herself, "Even if I believed in the possibility of God's consenting to repair the mutilations of my nature, I could not bring myself to ask it of him" (1973, 100).

Traditionally, the mystics' awareness of personal guilt also extends to a general awareness of human foibles and a feeling for the common misery of humankind in attempting reasonable self-management. Hammarskjöld wrote, "We can reach the point where it becomes possible for us to recognize and understand Original Sin, that dark counter-center in our nature . . . that something within us which rejoices when disaster befalls the very cause we are trying to serve, or misfortune overtakes even those whom we love" (1964, 149).

In spite of their subjective feelings of failure, inadequacy, and sinfulness, the ethical imperative demands that mystics continue to meet obligations to others and their lifework. There may be brief periods of incapacitation because of intense suffering, but the life pattern as a whole should show consistent application of self to one's perceived duty. In more classically psychological terms, mytics should have transcended ego-centeredness, for task-centeredness. Such task-orientation is seen in Hammarskjöld's "Be grateful as your deeds become less and less associated with your name, as your feet ever more lightly tread the earth" (1964, 146). Also: *Dedicated*—for my destiny is to be used and used up according to Thy will" (123).

Weil wrote: "If still persevering in our love, we fall to the point where the soul cannot keep back the cry, 'My God, why hast thou forsaken me?' If we remain at this point without ceasing to love, we end by touching something that is not affliction, not joy, something that is the central essence . . . the very love of God" (1973, 89). This criterion of perseverance in one's tasks cannot seem as sufficient, however, for agreeing that one is a mystic. Hammarskjöld warns us: "Work as an anesthetic against loneliness, books as a substitute for people—! You say you are waiting, that door stands open. For what? . . . a fate beyond companionship?" (1964, 82). Work and business *can* be running away rather than dedicated service.

Mysticism and Passivity

The line between helpless passivity regarding one's life and general religious acceptance of all that befalls one is thin. We have already established that though our figures showed tendencies toward passivity and feelings of impotence, they also conducted their lives according to their understanding of duty. They were prestigious accomplishers in their endeavors.

Most mystics manifest a pronounced submission to life that extends even to welcoming and embracing pain, rather than fighting against it as something alien. Although James emphasized that deliverance features of religiousness attract the "sick soul," clearly, any religiousness which remains primarily a search for personal deliverance is not a developed religiousness. In mystics, the emphasis shifts from "may I be delivered" to "thy will be done," and even to delight in enduring all of one's lot as reflecting God's will. The poet Tagore captured this attitude: "If thou speakest not I will fill my heart with thy silence and endure it . . . head bent low with patience" ([1913] 1971, 37–38).

Willed and chosen passivity in relation to God is strong in both Weil and Hammarskjöld. The latter wrote: "It is not we who seek the Way, but the Way which seeks us. That is why you are faithful to it, even while you stand waiting, so long as you are prepared, and act the moment you are confronted by its demands" (1964, 120). Also: "You are not the oil, you are not the air—merely the lens in the beam. You can only receive, give, and possess the light as a lens does" (155). Maslow described the general attitude of acceptance common in mystical awareness: "Because he becomes more unmotivated, that is to say, closer to non-striving, non-needing, non-wishing, he asks less for himself. . . . The unmotivated human being becomes more god-like" (1964, 67).

Weil wrote: "Our misery gives us the infinitely precious privilege of sharing in this distance placed between the Son and his Father. . . . Even the distress of the abandoned Christ is a good. There cannot be a greater good for us on earth than to share it. God can never be perfectly present to us here below . . . but he can be almost in extreme application. This is the only possibility of perfection for us on earth" (1973, 127). Weil had reservations about acceptance. She said, "I believe in the value of suffering, so long as one makes every (legitimate) effort to escape it" (1970, 3; Weil's parentheses). She renounced the luxury of yielding responsibility for her life in a letter to Father Perrin: "There are times when I am tempted to put myself entirely in your hands and ask you to decide for me. But, when all is said and done, I cannot do this. I have not the right" (Weil 1973, 56). She commented further: "What Christ meant when he advised his friends to bear their cross each day was not, as people seem to think nowadays, simply that one should be resigned about one's little daily troubles—which, by an almost sacreligious abuse of language, people sometimes refer to as crosses . . . To bear one's cross is to bear the knowledge that one is entirely subject to . . . blind necessity in every part of one's being, except for one point in the soul which is so secret that it is inaccessible to consciousness" (Weil 1968, 185). Weil concludes: "Having absolutely relinquished every kind of existence, I accept existence, of no matter what kind, solely through conformity to God's will" (1970, 360).

Our figures expressed highly negative views of self, others, the world, and expectations for the future. Yet, in addition to those less sanguine interpretations, they tend to see all that happens in terms of ultimate divine purposes or goals, no matter how painful or distressing an event might appear. Mystics commonly impose higher order meanings upon the apparent chaos of life.

Hammarskjöld urged himself to keep alive his religious interpretations: "Never let success hide its emptiness from you, achievement its nothingness, toil its desolation. And so keep alive the incentive to push on further, that pain in the soul which drives us beyond ourselves" (1964, 55). He speculated: "Perhaps a great love is never returned. Had it been given warmth and shelter by its counterpart in the other, perhaps it would have been hindered from ever growing to maturity. It 'gives' us nothing. But in its world of loneliness, it leads us up to summits with wide vistas—of insight" (42).

Weil frequently interpreted pain in terms of her vision:

> This infinite distance between God and God, this supreme tearing apart, this agony beyond all others, this marvel of love, is the crucifixion. (1973, 123–24).
>
> He whose soul remains ever turned toward God though the nail pierces it finds himself nailed to the very center of the universe. . . . It is at the intersection of creation and its Creator. This point of intersection is the point of intersection of the arms of the Cross. (135–36)
>
> It is the purpose of affliction to provide the occasion for judging that God's creation is good. (1968, 193)

It is in affliction itself that the splendor of God's mercy shines, from its very depths, in the heart of its inconsolable bitterness. (1973, 89)

Such insistence on religious meaning could simply be a defense such as denial or isolation—ways of deceiving oneself in a partially unconscious fashion. Gordon Allport ([1950] 1973) noted that mature religiousness necessarily requires heuristic faith—that it acknowledges doubt. Hammarskjöld queried: "Is the bleakness of this world of mine a reflection of my poverty or my honesty, a symptom of weakness or of strength, an indication that I have strayed from my path, or that I am to follow it?—Will despair provide the answer?" (1964, 86).

Awareness of the "risk" of religious faith—even of the uncertainties associated with the mystical vision itself—was pondered by Weil. She commented: "The whole problem of mysticism and kindred questions is that of the degree of value of sensations of presence" (Weil 1970, 198). She reasoned: "If God should be an illusion from the point of view of existence, He is the sole reality from the point of view of the good. . . . I am in accord with the truth if I wrench my desire away from everything which is not a good, so as to direct it solely towards the good, without knowing whether the good exists or not" (157). Elsewhere, she expressed strong doubts about the survival of the soul (152).

The genuineness of investment in religious frameworks of meaning can be measured indirectly by conduct. However firm or uncertain one's belief may appear, behavior reflects the values one is trying to make operative in life. Allport ([1950] 1973, 145) noted that "sometimes we designate unrest that has not found its polarization of 'divine discontent.'" Yet, he was very clear in insisting that vividness of longing, or use of religious interpretation, does not constitute the religious intention. Desire may be the original impetus, but an intention requires productive striving.

William James, reflecting on the intricate connection between belief and behavior, said: "There are, then, cases where a fact cannot come at all unless a preliminary faith exists in its coming . . . *where faith in a fact can help create the fact.* . . . In truths dependent on our personal action, then, faith based on desire is . . . possibly an indispensable thing" (James 1897 [1969], 209). To believe or manifest commitment to a belief, "we need only in cold blood ACT as if the thing in question were real, and keep acting as if it were real and it will infallibly end by growing into such a connection with our life that it will become real" (James 1897 [1952], 661).

Hammarskjöld wrote of making goals operative: "O how much self-discipline, nobility of soul, lofty sentiments, we can treat ourselves to when we are well-off and everything we touch prospers—Cheap: Scarcely better than believing success is the reward of virtue" (1964,

56). He said further: "To reach perfection, we must all pass, one by one, through the death of self-effacement" (25). Characteristically for Weil, action-oriented faith involves waiting for God: "The only choice before man is whether he will or will not . . . stay motionless, without searching, waiting in immobility and without even trying to know what he waits . . . it is absolutely certain that God will come all the way to him" (Weil 1968, 159). However differently mystics might state it, they believe one must not merely mouth religious interpretations of life but also act in accord with them.

Necessity, Risks, and Demands of Mysticism

For some people, mysticism may be the most viable alternative to shipwreck. These individuals have intense spiritual needs, much as other individuals may have different strong needs.

Characteristics Likely Contributing to Mystical Need

Cosmic Sadness

A temperamental sadness appears to be an underlying note in mystics. They show great sensitivity to loss, transience, change, vulnerability, insecurity, and other "unsolvable" problems of life. A sufficiently keen sensitivity may, on its own, make mysticism necessary; the individual may find genuine comfort in nothing other than the ultimate satisfier: the divine. Weil echoed this position: "The man who has known pure joy, if only for a moment . . . is the only man for whom affliction . . . is no punishment; it is God himself holding his hand and pressing it rather hard. For, if he remains constant, what he will discover buried deep under the sound of his own lamentations is the pearl of the silence of God" (1968, 198). Awareness of such need is also strong in Hammarskjöld.

High-Motivational Intensity

Highly passionate individuals, who strongly feel motivational pushes, also likely need mysticism. Although some very passionate individuals find other outlets to absorb their energies, for some only the Ultimate may be sufficiently large. For high-intensity people, the option may be between utter depravity and sanctity. Highly charismatic or forceful people may distort aspirations for sanctity unless they maintain continuing awareness of that greater than self.

Hammarskjöld felt intensely his own strong inclinations: "Upon your continual cowardice, your repeated lies, sentence will be passed on the day when some exhibition of your weakness . . . deprives you of any further opportunities to make a choice—and justly. Do you at least feel grateful that your trial is permitted to continue, that you have not yet been taken at your word?" (1964, 72). Weil wrote: "One might conclude that there are some souls with a natural deficiency which irremediably unfits them for the service of God. And I am one of them. Is there any remedy? . . .The only way is, if a seed has fallen into a hollow place in a stone, to water it and keep on doing so whenever the water evaporates. . . . Detachment is even more rigorously necessary than for the souls which are good ground. For, if thorn and weed absorb a few drops of the water which has to be renewed continually, the wheat will inevitably shrivel. . . . Literally, it is total purity or death" (1970, 348).

Strong Abilities

Weil and Hammarskjöld had strong intellectual capabilities and high levels of talent. Some mystics have lacked these features, but ability probably adds to need for mysticism. As with motivational intensity, many high-ability people find other outlets. Ability heightens the temptation to an excessively narcissistic self-involvement though, and some people may avoid that pitfall only with the felt awareness of "smallness" that mysticism gives. The highly intelligent psychologist of religion Gordon Allport explained his own religious involvement: "Humility and some mysticism, I felt, were indispensable for me; otherwise I would be victimized by my own arrogance" (Boring and Lindzey 1967, 7). This exceptional man supports the contention being made here.

Awareness of being talented may also produce feelings of indebtedness. Maslow hypothesized that self-actualized individuals might further need to transcend self in some way. This need may be related to a heightened awareness of one's good fortune in having been blessed beyond the average of all persons. Hammarskjöld wrote: "Atonement, for the guilt you carry because of your good fortune: without pity for yourself or others, to give all you are, and thus justify, at least morally, what you possess, knowing that you only have a right to demand anything of others so long as you follow this course" (1964, 50).

Who Needs Mysticism?

Certainly not all individuals of heightened emotional sensitivity, strong motivational intensity, and high talent and/or capacity actually need mysticism. Such characteristics however, might interact multiplicatively with each other to raise one's level of need. Individuals high in only one of these characteristics may not be especially prone to such need; cosmic sadness is likely the most compelling single need. The interaction of moderate levels of two of these characteristics may produce considerable need. An individual with at least moderate to high levels of all these conditions should have considerable need.

William James, commenting on unappealing manifestations of religiousness, blamed them on relative deficiencies in other human attributes. He wrote: "It is hard to imagine an essential faculty too strong, if only other faculties equally strong be there to cooperate with it in action. . . . Spiritual excitement takes pathological forms whenever other interests are too few and the intellect too narrow" (James [1902] 1961, 271). Conversely, individuals of strong intellect, high talent, deep emotionality, and intense volition may be most able to "contain" mystical experience. They may further need it to prevent excessive grandiosity and self-preoccupation.

Clearly, Weil and Hammarskjöld showed characteristics suggesting they needed mysticism. They were poignantly aware of their need for spiritual involvement. In some ways, it was their "salvation." The same may well be true of other individuals of similar qualities.

The Demands and Risks of Mysticism

No mystics claim that the path is easy. That the results are not assured, fewer are willing to admit. An ancient Bengali saying states: "The sides of the mountain are strewn with the bones of those who fail to reach the top." Mystics note the risks of despair, failure to persevere, resentment, and being ground to pieces by suffering. Hammarskjöld admitted tendencies to resent being an "outsider" who could not enjoy life as simply as most people: "In spite of everything, your bitterness because others are enjoying what you are denied is always ready to flare up" (1964, 47). "I feel that it is necessary and ordained that I should be alone, a stranger and an exile in relation to every human circle without exception" (Weil 1973, 54).

Both Hammarskjöld and Weil were aware of having at some point said "yes" to their calling. Weil wrote: "Over the infinity of space and time, the infinitely more infinite love of God comes to possess us. . . . If we consent, God puts a little seed in us and he goes away again . . . no more to do . . . except to wait. We only have not to regret the consent we gave him" (1973, 133). Hammarskjöld reported: "I don't know Who—or what—put the question, I don't know when it was put. I don't even remember answering. But at some moment I did answer *Yes* to Someone—or Something—and from that hour . . . I have known what it means 'not to look back'" (1964, 205). He was aware of the cost of such a decision: "He who has surrendered himself to it knows that the Way ends on the Cross—even when it is leading him through the . . . triumphal entry in Jerusalem" (91).

Conclusions

Trying to evaluate these individuals in the different darknesses they inhabited produces awesome problems. Darkness has so many meanings. It stands simply for being bereft or alone, for loss, loneliness, and longing for satisfaction and closeness. Darkness also stands for being in sin, in error of conduct. How does one evaluate another's self-accusation in this regard, the attribution to oneself of guilt and unworthiness? Darkness also stands for ignorance and/or error, for misinterpreting or misunderstanding what is going on around oneself. Darkness stands for being in danger, for being helpless and impotent. These four connotations of darkness are mirrored in the theories of depression discussed above. Yet, the darkness inherent in human existence goes beyond simple theories of emotional disturbance to something far more radical and profound.

Darkness stands for other uncomfortable things. It stands for being confused, unable to see clearly, not knowing—a common experience for all mystics. Darkness eventually stands for death—death either as the ultimate of cut-offness, aloneness, loneliness, vulnerability, and extinction—or death as the termination of self-preoccupation, petty concerns, and seeking the tinsel rather than the gold of existence—as being born into the goodness of darkness.

Darkness thus also has positive connotations. It stands for a welcome solitude, a retreating within oneself to recharge and revitalize oneself. It stands for peace and rest—hard earned retirement from striving and effort. In the lives of mystics over the centuries, darkness stands for the visitation of God. For mystics, darkness means all of the above—both the positive and the negative. Darkness contained terrible aloneness, devastating self-knowledge, and the awareness of evil and personal impotence. Darkness also held the light of truth, intimacy with God, and perfect peace in the midst of terrible suffering; darkness revealed Goodness, Truth, and Beauty.

How can one judge that which comes in the darkness? Is it heavenly or diabolical? Is it merely a chemical imbalance in the brain? Is it truth or delusion? What can one know for sure? In the lives of the great mystics are both profound certainty and agonizing uncertainty. The common trial of the dark night is the terrible suffering in loss of the religious framework of meaning itself, in the inability to believe in the reality of their own experiences, the inability to hope and love. Well might one fear the darkness—the darkness in which devil and angel, insanity and God, both come. Well might one tremble at human limitation, fallibility, and vulnerability. Well might one pray: "Deliver us from evil."

One never reaches higher than one aims. Aspiration to the vision of God requires the attendant risks. One who prays, "Give us this day our daily bread"—give us the sustaining vision of God—must be prepared to drink the chalice drunk by other God-lovers. In "fear and trembling" they went forth, in courageous acceptance of risk they went, in openness to grace they went. They went forth; the silent attentiveness they trusted was nearness to God—into the darkness—and waited.

References

Allport, G. W. [1950] 1973. *The individual and his religion: A psychological interpretation.* [New York: Macmillan] Reprint. New York: Macmillan. (Citations from paperback edition.)

Arieti, S. 1978. *On schizophrenia, phobias, depression, psychotherapy, and the farther shores of psychiatry.* New York: Brunner-Mazel.

Arintero, J. G. 1949–51. *The mystical evolution.* 2 vols. Trans. J. Aumann. St. Louis: Herder.

Beck, A. T. 1967. *Depression: Causes and treatment.* Philadelphia: Univ. of Pennsylvania Press.

Boisen, A. T. 1970. Crises in personality development. In *Personality and religion,* ed. W. Sadler, 191–205. New York: Harper.

Boring, E. G., and G. Lindzey, eds. 1967. *A history of psychology in autobiography.* New York: Appleton-Century-Crofts. 5:1–25.

Cameron, N. 1963. *Personality development and psychopathology.* Boston: Houghton Mifflin.

Campbell, J. 1972. *Myths to live by.* New York: Viking.

Clark, W. H. 1958. *The psychology of religion: An introduction to religious experience and behavior.* New York: Macmillan.

Depue, R. A., and S. M. Monroe. 1978. Learned helplessness in the perspective of the depressive disorders: Conceptual and definitional issues. *Journal of Abnormal Psychology* 87: 3–20.

Garrigou-LaGrange, R. 1947–48. *The three ages of the interior life.* 2 vols. Trans. M. T. Doyle. St. Louis: Herder.

Goleman, D., and R. J. Davidson, eds. 1979. *Consciousness: Brain, states of awareness, and mysticism.* New York: Harper and Row.

Gray, M. 1978. *Neuroses: A comprehensive and critical view.* New York: Van Nostrand Reinhold.

Hammarskjöld, D. 1962. *Servant of peace.* Ed. W. Foote. New York: Harper.

———. 1964. *Markings.* Trans. L. Sjoberg and W. H. Auden. New York: Knopf.

James, W. [1897] 1952. The will to believe. In *The will to believe and other essays in popular philosophy.* [New York: Longmans, Green.] Cited from *Great books of the western world,* ed. J. K. Roth. Vol. 53, *William James.* Chicago: Encyclopaedia Britannica.

———. [1897] 1969. The will to believe. In *The will to believe and other essays in popular philosophy.* [New York: Longmans, Green.] Cited from *The moral philosophy of William James,* ed. J. K. Roth. New York: T. Y. Crowell.

———. [1902] 1961. *The varieties of religious experience: A study in human nature.* [New York: Longmans, Green.] Reprint. New York: Collier.

Jones, A., ed. 1966. *The new Jerusalem Bible.* Garden City, N.Y.: Doubleday.

Kolb, L. C. 1977. *Modern clinical psychiatry.* Philadelphia: Saunders.

Maslow, A. H. 1964. *Religions, values, and peak experiences.* Columbus: Ohio State Univ. Press.

———. 1971. *The farther reaches of human nature.* New York: Viking.

Miller, R. I. 1961. *Dag Hammarskjöld and crisis diplomacy.* Washington, D.C.: Oceania Publications.

Mowrer, O. H. 1961. *The crisis in psychiatry and religion.* Princeton, N.J.: Van Nostrand.

Petrement, S. 1976. *Simone Weil: A life.* Trans. R. Rosenthal. New York: Random.

Rees, R. 1966. *Simone Weil: A sketch for a portrait.* Carbondale, Ill.: Southern Illinois Univ. Press.

Seligman, M. 1975. *Helplessness: On depression, development, and death.* San Francisco: W. H. Freeman.

Soderberg, S. 1962. *Hammarskjöld: A pictorial biography.* New York: Viking.

Tagore, R. [1913] 1971. *Gitanjali.* [New York: Macmillan.] Reprint. New York: Macmillan.

Underhill, E. 1955. *Mysticism: A study in the nature and development of man's spiritual consciousness.* New York: Meridian.

Weil, S. 1968. *On science, necessity, and the love of God.* Ed. and trans. R. Rees. New York: Oxford Univ. Press.

———. 1970. *First and last notebooks.* Ed. R. Rees. New York: Oxford Univ. Press.

———. 1973. *Waiting for God.* Trans. E. Craufurd. New York: Harper and Row.

Current and Emerging Themes in the Psychology of Religion

Early Interests

My earliest interest in the psychology of religion was one that had also attracted considerable attention from other social science scholars. I wanted to develop an inventory to measure dimensions of religiousness. The King and Hunt inventory was appearing at regular intervals in the *Journal for the Scientific Study of Religion* while I was working on my doctoral dissertation, "Philosophical-Religious Attitudes Inventory: A Factor Analytic Study" (1977). My interest in the measurement of religious dimensions has continued, and this doctoral work was simplified and refined with a colleague, Richard D. Kahoe. Some of our work on this is described in our text, *Psychology of Religion: Religion in Individual Lives* (Meadow and Kahoe 1984).

Another pervasive interest—continuing to this day—is that of relationships between personality and spirituality. My first publication, "The Cross and the Seed: Active and Receptive Spiritualities" (1978), was on this topic. The basic typology outlined in this paper—four religious types defined by crossing the dimension of extraversion-introversion with an active-receptive (cross versus seed) one—still forms the basis of much of my thinking about personality and religion.

A third major interest was the recognition and assessment of sexism in religion. This interest led to my developing additional measuring instruments, three scales of religious sexism: one defining a hierarchical universe in which females are lower than males, one prescribing submissive and passive roles for women in religion, and a third relegating women to private rather than public functions in religion. My scales assess the extent to which an individual subscribes to each of these

From the *Journal of Psychology and Christianity* 5, no. 2 (1986): 56–60; reprinted by permission of the publisher and the author. Copyright 1986 by the Christian Association for Psychological Studies.

three stances. The sexist ends of the scales are positively correlated with general conservatism, dogmatism, authoritarianism, self-centered values, and personal ineffectiveness.

My fourth early interest to emerge was that of religious development in adulthood. Although *Psychology of Religion* contains some discussion of this, I have not yet written at length on this topic.

The Current Picture

Earlier Interests

I believe that psychologists' general interest in assessment of religiousness has declined greatly. Although I still remain somewhat interested, I, also, am not currently active in this area. I think few psychologists remain as interested as I am in personality styles and spirituality. This interest remains sufficiently strong so that I am planning a book on the topic, trying to relate a variety of approaches to spirituality with personality variables.

Most people now generally concede religion to be sexist. Some are dismayed by this, while others consider it the proper order of things. My interests in the area are now less in defining and assessing sexism in religion than in working on the development of spiritualities suitable to and helpful for women, since most spiritualities have an androcentric bias. My older interest has thus shaded off into a related but substantively different task. My third book, coedited with Carole A. Rayburn, reflects this interest; it is *A Time to Weep and a Time to Sing: Faith Journeys of Women Scholars of Religion* (1985). I have also prepared a 500-entry annotated bibliography of books related to women's spirituality and religiousness.

My interest in adult religious development remains high. Primary is concern for the unchurched who are unable to make established faith traditions "work" for them, yet who seek a spiritual life and want help with it. I am working on a book about spirituality for the unchurched.

Religion in Psychotherapy

I am engaged in a running "battle" or "dialogue" with several colleagues over the appropriateness of using specific religious content in therapy. I urge those psychologists who are also pastors to know which hat they are wearing when, and to stay within one role with any given client. For others, I urge abstinence. My concerns are several.

Any pragmatic use of religion disturbs me. When religion is put in the service of mental health goals, an inappropriate ordering of values seems present. One should put oneself in service to religious ideals: any healing "spillover" that occurs should be simply a by-product of living appropriately. The therapist's co-opting of religious ideas and practices to accomplish the task of psychological healing appears to me to encourage making religion a means to secular ends.

I also fear that particular faith positions will become tied to the client's mental stability. This is particularly a problem when cognitive restructuring pits the religious worldview against the psychopathological one held by the client. It may accomplish psychological healing, but one's mental and emotional equilibrium has gotten tied to particular religious ideas. Either one's religious understandings cease to change and grow in order to maintain psychological stability, or the bases upon which mental health is established erode with religious reevaluation. Religious growth requires continual discarding of relatively immature perspectives for more developed and thoughtful ones lest one engage in the idolatry of absolutizing partial and incomplete understandings which are all that any human being is capable of having. The needs of spiritual growth are thus sacrificed to those of mental stability when specific religious content is used in therapy.

Another problem is the heavyweight of the therapist's "sanction" of particular views. We cannot help that our clients tend to adopt our values when we work with them in therapy, but we can certainly avoid "endorsing" viewpoints that are outside our domain as psychologists— even if we and the client share similar attitudes. If we reflect on how inappropriate it would be for the therapist to spend the therapy hour confirming the client in, or wooing the client toward, particular political beliefs, we can begin to view similar behavior regarding religion in fresh light. Such behavior can also be strongly countertherapeutic since religion, with its cosmic language and cosmic significance, is easily misappropriated in psychopathological ways. For example, encouragement of a suffering person to identify with the sufferings of Jesus might lead to a harmful grandiosity or to masochism. Therapist-"ratified" religious content may be used to exacerbate existing pathology, inappropriately bolster faltering self-esteem, or justify faulty problem solving. The therapist's idea of how the religious content may be used is not necessarily how the client will adopt it, and the therapist's commitment to her or his own religious perspectives might make this difficult to see.

Psychological Spirituality

I have a related concern about psychologists who seem determined to act as if they were spiritual directors rather than therapists. Many of these people—not all—are ignorant of the great traditions of the world's developed spiritualities or else know only one, their own. They typically lack any training in the growing profession of spiritual direction; some consider generalized training in pastoral counseling adequate preparation. The latter are apt to impose on the client their own limited understandings of one spiritual tradition as representing the summation of spiritual knowledge. The former are likely to involve their clients in an incoherent mishmash of vague spiritual yearnings and philosophically unreasonable mental meanderings.

That clients may receive an appropriate blend of disciplined practice and openness to individual inspiration, in an intelligible context that recognizes the variety of historical spiritualities that have served people over the ages, I cannot urge psychotherapists too strongly to refer their spiritually inclined clients to those who are properly trained for spiritual direction. Although we need to see the person as a *unity* of various functions and components of personal life (such as spiritual, mental, and physical), I still believe in specialization of function for professional healers. In some cases, collaboration might be called for. Just as the wise therapist would make medical and legal referrals when appropriate, so also ought they do so regarding spiritual direction. Some therapists' own strong interests in this area suggest that they, too, could profit from such direction themselves. Some might thus be freed from excessively narrow and tradition-bound perspectives, while others may come to respect more fully the value of traditional wisdom.

Religion and World Peace

Little awareness of history is needed to recognize the crucial factor that religious differences have been in fostering warfare among people. I agree strongly with Gordon Allport that insistence upon such doctrines as revelation and divine election encourages a warring and prejudiced mentality in many religious people. Although religions preach love of others, this is frequently done with the underlying premise that one's own faith holds the truth, whereas others are in error or ignorance, and that one is among God's elect or "chosen" people, while those outside the fold lack that distinction. A true agape love seems to me to require a full respect for the opinions and religious practices of others, according them the same consideration and value that one accords one's own. Religious people must recognize that just because their ideas are their own ideas does not necessarily make them superior to anybody else's!

I believe that religious institutions are, in today's world, called upon to have the humility necessary to declare themselves seekers among other seekers. They must admit that subjective certainty regarding their own tradition is less a sign of its veracity than it is of the socialization procedures and emotional conditioning that undergird that certainty. Had one been born into other circumstances and another culture, one would likely be holding a different faith with just the same tenacity! Calling back one's judgments of other religions as less true or erroneous or poor-faithed is a necessary step to avoid religious support of international and intercultural tensions. One can be faithful to one's own tradition without having to see it as necessarily superior to others' traditions.

Looking to the Future

Expansion of Current Interests

My interests in religion and world peace are still growing. I made it the subject of my presidential address (August 1984) for Division 36 of the American Psychological Association. I expect to devote considerable time and attention to this issue in the future.

I also anticipate a continuing concern with the uses and abuses of religious content in psychotherapy and with "psychological spirituality." I will continue to urge psychotherapists to avoid the ego inflation of assuming themselves competent to engage in spiritual direction without specific training, and will try to interest them in referral to competent spiritual guides.

Spirituality and the Unchurched

My interest in spirituality for the unchurched is sufficiently strong that I expect it will be expressed in many other ways in addition to the book I am writing. I anticipate preparing additional papers on this topic, and probably organizing workshops about it. Many people are alienated from religions that make claims of exclusive possession of truth or that seem to have narrowly parochial interests in face of world problems. The spiritual needs of these people are not going to be met by poorly informed psychotherapists acting as spiritual guides nor by spokespersons for the traditions they cannot accept.

I am seeking out the underlying bases of agreement among world faiths that have solidly established spiritual traditions, trying to discern the core value in these bases. I want to evaluate them in the light of contemporary understandings of human inner life—without, however, constraining them by narrowly conceived psychological understandings—and offer them to the spiritually hungry as food they might wish to consider.

Religious Values in Psychotherapy

I also do see some place for religious values in psychotherapy. The values that religions have converged upon can be studied for ways to formulate their usefulness in psychological terms. I will be drawing upon my knowledge—both intellectual and practical—of the world's religious traditions in an effort to do this. For example, from Eastern traditions, some therapists have incorporated relaxation and meditation techniques, means of controlling autonomic processes of the body, and various other forms of mental control and restructuring. Helpful religious values should be distilled from a broad base of religious endorsement, and should be offered to clients free of exclusive truth claims or presentation in the language of a particular religious tradition.

In other words, what is psychologically helpful in religious practice—such as forgiving one's enemies (after suitable expression and understanding of the emotions and cognitions associated with the experience of being victimized, of course)—might be presented in terms of its psychological helpfulness and in the language of psychology to enhance and complete the client's healing. Please note that this is different from suggesting that one forgive an enemy because Jesus would have, or that one reinterpret one's sufferings in light of the sufferings of Jesus, and so on. Such suggestions may be appropriate ones for a pastor, but not a psychologist, to make. My suggested usage does not tie the psychologically healing practice to the concrete expressions of any particular religious tradition and involves clear understanding and psychological justification of why it is a helpful step to take. It should not be confounded with a person's religious practice by the therapist, although particular clients may conclude for themselves that a similarity exists between the teachings of their faith and psychologically helpful steps that the therapist suggests.

Spiritual Growth and Personality

I am involved in an extensive intellectual and practical study of different spiritual traditions of the world because of my interest in integrating understandings of these traditions with understandings of personality. In addition to the book that I plan in this area, I hope to provide practical aids for personal assessment or assessment by spiritual guides of individual factors relevant to spiritual growth. Different people seem to me to require different approaches to spirituality; the more that compatibility with particular approaches could be ascertained, the less time one would spend in practices that are not maximally conducive to their own development toward the Holy. Similarly, different tactics are called for at different levels of development. Methods of determining the particular needs of different persons would greatly aid them in their spiritual practice. I realize that this is an enormous task, and that I might expect to spend an entire lifetime on it with little gain. However, I believe the time has come for a spiritually informed psychology—necessarily informed in both praxis and intellectual grasp of *at least* several traditions—to offer its assistance in understanding the personal bases upon which spiritual development necessarily rests.

Mysticism and Psychopathology

Some years ago, the Group for the Advancement of Psychiatry declared that one cannot tell the difference between religious mysticism and certain psychopathological states. I want to take them on! Most mental health professionals have a poor understanding of religious mysticism. Some look only at experiences, which admittedly *do* have some factors in common with some psychopathological states, and neglect to consider that religious mysticism implies a radical, life-pervading reorientation of an individual—not just some "high" experiences. Many are incapable of considering certain altered states of consciousness other than in a context of psychopathology. Since I am trained as a clinical psychologist and have a deep interest in spirituality and mysticism, I believe that I am in an excellent position to debate this issue. This interest will also eventually result in a book.

Women's Spirituality

My interest in women's spirituality stems from my concern over the extent to which spiritual/religious traditions have been shaped and dominated by men. Women's experiences have been considered only in limited fashion—mostly in the meditative/mystical spiritualities. Even then, women have typically not been considered on equal footing with men.

I have the idea that women's experiences demand some differences in understanding from those of male-developed religiousness. Women's cardinal faults appear to differ somewhat from men's; for example, I believe women have been more in error from low self-esteem, failure to be assertive, and need to be loved or appreciated far more than from pride, anger, or envy. How much such differences might be temperamentally "feminine" and how much a result of socialization has yet to be determined. These issues need to be explored in depth, discussed with women and their spiritual guides, and worked through so that the best means for women to flourish and grow spiritually may be determined. This task will also occupy me in the future.

Implications/Value of My Work for Psychology of Religion

I believe the issues with which I am choosing to occupy myself are valid and important ones. In so saying, I am not denying that colleagues may have quite different issues that they find intriguing, and that these issues may also be very important ones. I am also aware that some of my more religiously "traditional" colleagues find some of my interests disconcerting. Just possibly, one of my functions may be as a helpful or necessary "devil's advocate" for the majority of Western psychologists of religion whose work lies mainly within the Judeo-Christian perspective.

Some common denominators run through my interest. They tie together my training as a clinical and personality psychologist with my background in religious studies (*not* the theology of *one* tradition), in which I have almost as much graduate study as in psychology. My interests all unite a broadly based study of people's religiousness with a psychological method and perspective, with an emphasis on those factors that make for human wholeness and on appreciating what can be learned from those persons or traditions that have been relatively neglected in psychology of religion. I want most to avoid parochial positions and the fostering of particular interest against the totality of human religiousness and wholeness.

My interests have slowly evolved over time in a manner that seems to me natural and harmonious. As I write this, I am about to leave for an intensive 3-month Buddhist vipassanā meditation retreat. I am seeking out training as a spiritual director and preparing for intensive study of women's spirituality in relation to the historical religious traditions. I do not foresee radical changes of direction for myself. What will be the ultimate value and meaning of my chosen life's tasks for humankind and for the psychology of religion is, of course, for others to evaluate after I have written my last word and delivered my last address.

References

Meadow, M. J. 1977. The structure of religious attitudes: A factor-analytic study. *Dissertations Abstracts International* 37: 6339B.

———. 1978. The cross and the seed: Active and receptive spiritualities. *Journal of Religion and Health* 17: 57–69.

Meadow, M. J., and R. D. Kahoe. 1984. *Psychology of religion: Religion in individual lives.* New York: Harper and Row.

Meadow, M. J., and C. A. Rayburn, eds. 1985. *A Time to weep and a time to sing: Faith journeys of women scholars of religion.* San Francisco: Harper and Row.

Part 5

Research in the Psychology of Religion

10

Richard L. Gorsuch

R ichard L. Gorsuch is professor and director of research in the
Graduate School of Psychology at Fuller Theological Seminary.
He is a social psychologist as well as an ordained minister in the
Disciples of Christ. He received the Ph.D. in psychology from the University of Illinois, where he studied with Raymond Cattell.

Dr. Gorsuch is a fellow of Division 36, Psychologists Interested in
Religious Issues, of the American Psychological Association (APA). He
has served on the councils of the APA and the Religious Research Association (RRA). Gorsuch has distinguished himself as one of the most
prominent researchers and theorists in the psychology of religion, having served for four years as editor of the *Journal for the Scientific Study
of Religion*. He is also a consulting editor for a number of journals,
including *Multivariate Behavioral Research* and *Review of Religious
Research*.

Dr. Gorsuch is the author of several books, including the first and
second editions of *Factor Analysis* (Hillsdale, N.J.: L. Erlbaum Associates, 1974, 1983) and *The Nature of Man: A Social Psychological Perspective* (Springfield, Ill.: C. C. Thomas, 1976). His most recent volume is
The Psychology of Religion: An Empirical Approach (Englewood Cliffs,
N.J.: Prentice-Hall, 1985), coauthored with Bernard Spilka and Ralph
W. Hood, Jr. This book is destined to become known as one of the most
thorough surveys of current research in the field.

Because of his expertise in the field, Dr. Gorsuch was recently asked
to write the section on the psychology of religion for the 1988 *Annual
Review of Psychology*. This is the first time that such a section has been
included in the *Annual Review* since early in the century. Gorsuch has
published over 60 articles, among which are the following: "Religion:
Its Role in Prevention and Treatment of Addiction," "Moral Obligation

265

and Attitudes: Their Relation to Behavioral Intentions" (coauthored with J. A. Ortberg), "Attributions of Responsibility to God: An Interaction of Religious Beliefs and Outcomes" (coauthored with C. S. Smith), and "Trait Anxiety and Intrinsic-Extrinsic Religiousness."

The 1984 article "Measurement: The Boon and Bane of Investigating Religion," which is reprinted here, is perhaps one of Gorsuch's most important publications, for it was the first article on the psychology of religion to appear recently in *American Psychologist*, the official publication of the APA. In the article, Dr. Gorsuch notes the progress that has been made in the development of psychometric scales to measure religion. He suggests that, with questionnaires the modal method of inquiry, measurement of religion in individuals has become the primary goal within the field. He concludes that an effort should be made to directly relate these questionnaires to behavior and warns that measurement should not be an end unto itself, but should lead to the study of the development and impact of religious phenomena.

In his essay "Psychology and Religion, Beliefs, and Values," Gorsuch notes his own educational heritage at the University of Illinois, where Raymond B. Cattell and O. Hobart Mowrer taught. Although both wrote about religion, Cattell did so under the rubric of "sentiments," whereas Mowrer was more explicit and historical in his emphases. In his historical tracing of developments in the field, Gorsuch speculates that the lack of interest in religious behavior during the second quarter of the 20th century was due to the separation of psychology from philosophy. He considers the revival of cognitive psychology a positive step and notes the importance of beliefs and values in contemporary research. Gorsuch suggests that the last two decades have seen a reuniting of philosophy with psychology, noting that the contemporary scene is marked by a reuniting of psychology of religion with mainstream psychology.

Measurement:
The Boon and Bane of Investigating Religion

easurement is a cornerstone of science and hence is a critical component of scientific investigations of religious phenomena. While measurement is defined before a given scientific investigation, measurement is also a result of the scientific process. Periodically, it behooves us to evaluate the product from that process for its strengths and weaknesses. This article provides one such examination of how religious phenomena are measured.

A critical examination of measurement in psychological studies of religion appears particularly apropos because a common paradigm has generally been accepted in this area. This is evidenced by the fact that articles published in the major journals cannot be identified by "schools." Nor are articles readily distinguishable by the journal in which they appear, nor by whether the journals are supported by the American Psychological Association, the Society for the Scientific Study of Religion, the Religious Research Association, or by sociological associations. For example, almost any article published in the recent readers in the psychology of religion—ranging from Brown (1973) to Malony (1977) to Tisdale (1980)—could be placed in one of the other readers or in any of the major journals with few if any paradigm problems. Although there continues to be psychoanalytic tradition, that tradition is peripheral and contributes mainly to theory rather than to psychological research. Our paradigm probably became truly established in the 1970s, and its first major product may well be Division 36 itself.

In addition to the similarity of articles published in major readers and journals, the area now has several investigators with established research programs. As is the case with most normal science when a paradigm is established, these investigators respect one another and use each other's results rather than being—as in the preparadigm states—in competing schools. The forerunner of such programs was conducted by Allport. His efforts ranged from early measurement of religion in All-

From the *American Psychologist* 39 (1984): 228–36; reprinted by permission of the publisher and the author. Copyright 1984 by the American Psychological Association, Inc.

port's and Vernon's (1931) *Study of Values* to investigating the relationship of religion and prejudice, and to redefining religion by intrinsic and extrinsic dimensions (e.g., Allport 1950; Allport and Ross 1967). Other research programs include Spilka's work investigating a broad range of phenomena, such as his series of studies concerned with religion and death (e.g., Spilka et al. 1977), and Hood's continuing work on mysticism (e.g., Hood 1970, 1975).

To exist and become accepted, a paradigm needs attractive features, or at least features that are more attractive than the other paradigms. These features are discussed first as an aid to defining the paradigm currently in existence. Their usefulness is then examined. Another attractive feature needed in a paradigm is sufficient open-endedness to allow for interesting new problems. Discussion of that aspect of the measurement paradigm occurs after the major elements of the paradigm are presented and their usefulness examined.

The Current Paradigm

The first task is to note briefly some of the major features of the contemporary paradigm for measuring religious phenomena. *Paradigm* is here used in the first of the two senses identified by Kuhn (1970, 175–87): the "entire constellation of beliefs, values, techniques, and so on, shared by the members of a given community" (175). Kuhn has also called this the "disciplinary matrix," which includes the shared symbolic generalizations and scientific laws, shared beliefs and particular models, shared values, and shared exemplar studies (180–82).

This is obviously a large task, and all of it will not, by any means, be covered within this single article. In particular, elements of the paradigm shared with social science in general and American psychology in particular will not be a focus of attention. There will be little discussion of the empirical, quantitative, scientific perspective that underlies the paradigm itself. Instead, the effort here will be to lift up those elements of the paradigm for measuring religious phenomena that are uniquely present or absent as compared to psychology in general. This means that approaches that are primarily of historical interest in the sense of only occasionally being reflected in current empirical research—such as Freud and Jung—are also not discussed.

One warning: as Kuhn has pointed out (1970, 80), having a common paradigm does not mean that there is universal harmony and agreement on any of its points. Indeed, the common paradigm itself is often a focus of continuing debate and disagreement. What makes it a common paradigm, however, is that all see the issues as important and are able to argue with each other in the same technical language. Such debate is possible only in the presence of a common paradigm that makes the arguments and debates meaningful to the parties involved.

The Importance of Measurement Issues

Perhaps central to the paradigm for measuring religious phenomena is the importance of measurement issues themselves. Even a brief scanning of the psychology of religion literature suggests that there are many articles in which at least one emphasis is on constructing, validating, or critiquing a measurement device. Indeed, an early leader in the area of measurement, Thurstone developed scales for religious phenomena (Thurstone and Chave 1929). (Parenthetically, these predate our contemporary paradigm. Despite their extensive and expert work, others have seldom utilized their scales. This is often the fate of scientific effort when there is no community sharing a common paradigm to use the results.)

An illustration of the importance of the measurement issue is found in the factor-analytic studies of religious phenomena. There have been many of these, with perhaps the most systematic, extended effort by King and Hunt. They have not only published initial factor analyses (King 1967) but also replicated and extended those analyses in different types of samples (e.g., King and Hunt 1969, 1972a, 1972b, 1975).

Factor-analytic articles are commonly published and appear to be taken seriously. For example, the fact that it has been difficult to find a single bipolar factor involving both extrinsic and intrinsic concepts has been a serious problem for a critique of the early developments of the intrinsic-extrinsic dimension (Hunt and King 1971). Further work in this area has proceeded so that, as noted subsequently, a variation of intrinsic and extrinsic factors can now be readily recognized in several studies.

Building on factor-analytic studies has not been a widely accepted tradition in psychology. Except for a few areas such as intelligence, factor-analytic studies are often difficult to publish in leading journals. But within the psychology of religion, factor-analytic studies are readily published. For example, Spilka factor analyzes the areas of death and of religion and then interrelates the factors in his studies (e.g., Spilka et al. 1977); Batson (1976) includes measures from past factor-analytic studies with hypothesized scales in a factor analysis to create factor scores for use in an experiment. Taking the measurement issue seriously means that the factor analyses are put to immediate use in the research studies themselves.

Reliance on Questionnaires

One of the more unusual defining elements of the current paradigm is the reliance on questionnaires for data collection. Although an occasional study has used other techniques (e.g., Cattell and Child 1975), this has been the exception rather than the rule. Our major conclusions about the definition and nature of religion result from questionnaires.

The content of the questionnaires is highly variable. "Beliefs" from a technical definition as the conviction that something exists—"God is real"—or that a particular historical event occurred—"Jesus died on a cross"—or that a particular state exists—"the church is an effective tool for helping the poor"—are often all intermixed in such questionnaires. "Values" from a technical definition as concern with ideal states—"the church should help the poor by supporting labor laws"—or as an evaluation of a current state—"the church is doing its work well"—may also be mixed in the same questionnaire. In addition, reports of personal experience—"God has answered my prayers"—may be mixed into the questionnaire as well. It is interesting that we do not seem to have competing views here. Despite the logical distinctions between these items, no one seems disturbed—as yet—when they are all mixed into the same questionnaire or factor analyzed in an indiscriminate manner.

There is, however, another approach to the use of questionnaires that appears to be distinctive: the functional approach where the emphasis is on the *use* of religion rather than *content* per se. Functional approaches are found in the intrinsic-extrinsic concepts (Allport and Ross 1967); the committed-consensual distinctions (Allen and Spilka 1967); the means, ends, and quest distinctions (Batson 1976); and the literal, mythological, and symbolic distinctions (Hunt 1972). These measuring attempts are distinctively different from the general belief/value/experience questionnaires since the content of faith is less important than the goals or style of religion.

One question seldom used for measurement by psychologists active in psychology of religion is religious membership (although this is widely used—misused?—by others). Although it might be included in a study, the assumption within the current paradigm seems to be that people who are members of the same religious group vary widely in their beliefs and approaches to religion. For that reason, measurement starts with each person's beliefs and not with his or her group membership. Perhaps this is also a function of our psychological perspective, which primarily focuses on the individual and not on the more sociological elements. But this may mean that we overlook social psychological dynamics of importance. The social psychological work on reference and membership groups and the research on opinion leaders both suggest group memberships remain important, if not for belief then for process reasons.

Usefulness of the Paradigm

Psychometric Qualities of Religious Questionnaires

Use of the questionnaire has been relatively successful. The questionnaires not only have been easy to construct, but also have been instruments with at least adequate reliabilities. Indeed, it seems that questionnaire measurement of religion is easier than with most areas of psychology. For example, consider the results of Scott (1965) when attempting to measure values. His procedures for item development and selection were the same in each value area. Two types of reliability coefficients for his value scales—homogeneity and stability—are shown in table 10.1 (along with the results of correlating questionnaires with open-ended questions to participants about their values). As can be seen, the religious scale had the highest internal consistency and the highest stability coefficient. When measured by open-ended questions, religion was tied for the second-highest stability coefficient. It is also interesting to note that the correlations across scale and open-ended forms, while not large, also indicate that religion is the second-highest coefficient. Accepting questionnaires as a basic part of the paradigm has been relatively successful from a psychometric viewpoint.

Table 10.1

Homogeneities of Value Scales, Correlations With Open-ended Question, and Stability Coefficients

Value	Scale Homogeneity (alpha)	Stability coefficients		Scale/ open-ended correlations
		Scale	Open-ended	
Intellectualism	.68	.64	.35	.15
Kindness	.66	.68	.39	.27
Social skills	.70	.74	.13	.19
Loyalty	.71	.58	.38	.10
Academic achievement	.69	.68	.49	.11
Physical development	.77	.74	.37	.16
Status (leadership)	.65	.70	.27	.17
Honesty	.61	.74	.51	.15
Religiousness	.78	.77	.49	.23
Self-control	.68	.72	.27	.10
Creativity	.64	.66	.46	.05
Independence	.55	.73	.26	.15
M	.67	.70	.36	.16

Note: The scales contained four to seven items, each rated on a three point scale; the open-ended question was a set of general questions about what is valuable, rated for whether each of the values was spontaneously mentioned. Data adopted from Scott (1956).

The success of the questionnaire approach is partially a function of the ease with which it produces the high level of results just noted. For example, a long-term project comparing several different questionnaire methods for measuring a particular religious content area is not necessary because it does not matter which scaling method is used. The several scaling methods that do exist all seem to produce much the same results. When Fishbein and Ajzen (1974) used five different methods for measuring religion, the intercorrelations among them were all about as high as reliabilities generally are (see table 10.2). It appears that the correlations are sufficiently high so that the several methods for questionnaire measurement of religion can be considered parallel forms of each other.

Table 10.2
Correlations of Verbal Attitude Measures of Religion

Verbal attitude scales	Verbal attitude scales				
	SR	**SD**	**G**	**L**	**T**
Self-report (SR)	—				
Semantic differential (SD)	.80	—			
Guttman (G)	.52	.64	—		
Likert (L)	.76	.76	.79	—	
Thurstone (T)	.58	.68	.74	.78	

Note: Abbreviations for verbal attitude scale are SR = self-report, SD = semantic differential, G = Guttman, L = Likert, T = Thurstone. Data adapted from Fishbein & Ajzen (1974).

The ease of developing useful questionnaires is also evidenced by carefully chosen single-item questions being as effective as long questionnaires. In table 10.2 the single-item self-report measure shows approximately the same median correlation (.76) with the other scales as do those full-length scales with each other. It has been suggested (Gorsuch and McFarland 1972) that such ease of use of the questionnaire results from religion being a widely discussed phenomenon in our culture. Hence, individuals have extensive practice in classifying themselves religiously.

The Relationship between Questionnaires and Behavior

Fishbein and Ajzen (1974) have provided interesting evidence that religious attitude measures relate well to reported religious behaviors provided a sufficiently sophisticated approach is taken. In this case, "sufficiently sophisticated" turns out to be rather simple: measuring attitude and behavior at the same level of generality. Since multiple-item scales for measuring religion usually include different facets of religion, the attitudes measured are relatively broad. Measures of behavior also must be relatively broad to match the generality of such scales. To test this hypothesis, Fishbein and Ajzen examined the correlations of five techniques for measuring religious attitudes with reports of single religious behaviors and with a broader multiple-item scale of religious behavior. The results for single items are given at the top of table 10.3, and show the typical—seemingly embarrassing—situation of a lack of prediction from questionnaires to an individual behavior.

Table 10.3
Correlations of Verbal Attitude Scales
with Religious Behavior

Criteria	Verbal attitude scales				
	SR	SD	G	L	T
Single act					
Average correlations with 100 single behaviors	.14	.15	.12	.14	.13
Multiple act					
Correlation with sum of 100 behaviors	.64*	.71*	.61*	.68*	.63*

Note: Abbreviations for verbal attitude scales are SR = self-report, SD = semantic differential, G = Guttman, L = Likert, T = Thurstone. Data adapted from Fishbein & Ajzen (1974). *$p < .10$.

But these are measures of a single behavior that are considerably narrower than either the attitude scales or a multiple-item scale of behavior. So Fishbein and Ajzen put together 100 behaviors into a total scale which was then correlated with each of the five attitude scales. The multiple-item scale results are also given in table 10.3 and show that religious behavior broadly defined correlates with the attitude scales—which also define religion broadly—almost as well as the attitude scales correlate with themselves. Religious attitudes are highly related to reports of religious behavior when appropriate methods are used to relate them.

Other social psychological approaches hypothesize moderator variables that influence the values–behavior relationship. Following Schwartz (1968), Aleshire and Gorsuch (1975) suggested religion would relate to behavior when people both accept responsibility for outcomes and think in terms of consequences. Table 10.4 shows that religion correlates well with behavior for those high on the two moderators when religion is the only value involved and poorly for those who do not accept responsibility or think of consequences. More complex situa-

Table 10.4

Value—Behavior Intention Correlations

	Ascription of responsibility (AR)		Awareness of consequences (AC)		AR/AC	
Behavioral intention	Low	High	Low	High	Low/low	High/high
Simple situation						
Contribution to church	.27[a]	.62**	.11[b]	.69**	.15[b]	.81*
Dual Situation						
Contribution/personal conflict	.26	.43**	.22	.35**	−.14[b]	.57

Note: Religious value measure is from Scott (1965); data adapted from Aleshire and Gorsuch (Note 1). *N = 40 for all groups except low/low and high/high groups, where n* = 20. For difference between correlations, superscripts are a = *p* < .05 and b = *p* < .01. **p* < .05. *** p* < .01.

tions would, of course, require more values to produce such a high correlation, as is also shown in table 10.4.

Puzzles and Problems

Kuhn (1970) notes that a paradigm is attactive in part because it offers a series of puzzles to solve. The paradigm is carried along by the activity that the puzzles generate. At some points, puzzles are solved and knowledge accumulates. At other points, puzzles become problems that lead to major revisions of paradigms or even to a new paradigm becoming established. Having briefly outlined some basic elements of the paradigm, it now seems appropriate to examine some of the puzzles of the current paradigm.

Score Meaningfulness

One puzzle is how to give more meaning to the scores developed from our scales. In psychology of religion—as in other similar areas of psychology—the scores are treated as only ordinal. The result is that median splits are often used to separate, for example, the extrinsically religious from the nonextrinsically religious. The problem with median splits is the lack of information whether the groups formed consist of truly extrinsic and nonextrinsic people. Pugh (letter, 1982) has found that different congregations vary widely in both mean and standard deviation for such scales. The differences are large enough for a group of "low extrinsics" based on a median split in Congregation A to have essentially the same mean and standard deviation as a group of "high extrinsics" from a median split in Congregation B. This may cause considerable confusion, for the same extrinsic score called high extrinsic in a study using Congregation A would be called low extrinsic in a study using Congregation B. Can we expect consistency of results across such studies? Are not terms such as *extrinsic* then ambiguous since the same people are differentially classified depending on the study?

One hopes this is not a major problem but more of an interesting puzzle to be solved. It is indeed possible to begin classifying people according to the number of items answered on one particular scale—or better yet, their average response to the average item—and begin reporting results by actual scale scores. Further studies should then, regardless of how the people are distributed in their own sample, reclassify people by the *same* scores. Translating from one scale to another can be done readily by appropriate studies that give regression equations between the scales. Hence, this should not be a problem if we are alert to it and consider it a puzzle that needs to be solved.

Dimensionality of Religion

An unresolved problem is the dimensionality of religion. Some investigators implicitly suggest it is unidimensional by using a single measure. Others use multidimensional measures. Is religion unidimensional? If not, what are its dimensions?

The resolution could be both/and rather than either/or. There may be a general religious dimension—as a unidimensionalist might assume—that can be subdivided into dimensions—as a multidimensionalist might assume.

Elsewhere (Gorsuch and McFarland 1972) we have suggested that in *our* culture it appears that religious people are distinguished from nonreligious by a general dimension. This dimension reflects an intrinsic commitment to a traditional, gospel-oriented interpretation of the Christian faith (which is not, however, identical to fundamentalism). This dimension can be measured with reasonable consistency by most scales concerned with creedal assent and related beliefs and attitudes.

It is also apparent that studies can subdivide the general religious dimension into more discrete factors. Some of these factors are due to methodology (Clayton 1971; Roof 1979; see Gorsuch 1983, chaps. 11, 14, and 16), but King and Hunt (1975), for example, have confirmed several such factors in appropriate samples. These include creedal assent, church attendance, and growth and striving. Although these can be distinguished, King and Hunt also report these factors all correlate positively, as is expected from a model that would suggest they share a general factor.

A uni/multidimensional approach to religion can be illustrated with Maranell's (1974) study across samples from eight separate populations. He began with eight a priori scales, which are listed in table 10.5 along with the results from two samples. (Other variables were included in the factor analyses but are excluded from table 10.5.) The several factor analyses consistently found two religious factors. The first one, as can be seen from table 10.5, is defined best by scales of fundamentalism and theism. The second is one of church orientation and ritualism. As is common in factor analyses, Maranell himself did not perform an oblique rotation. Hence, in his analyses he assumed (note the word *assumed*) that no general dimension existed. But the data presented do allow estimating what the correlations between these factors would be in an oblique version of Varimax, and that estimated correlation is given along with the estimated second-order factors that result. They show in both cases a general dimension underlying these two dimensions. So in these data an appropriate conceptualization has a general Christianity second-order factor subdividing into theism and church orientation factors. (The first-order factors could, if desired, be further subdivided into the scales loading each factor.)

Table 10.5
General Christianity and Church Orientation Factors

	Student sample			
	Southern		Midwestern	
First-order loadings	**I**	**V**	**II**	**X**
Church orientation	.44	.62	.69	.47
Ritualism	.38	.74	.27	.87
Altruism (Christian)	.74	.41	.76	.19
Fundamentalism	.84	.12	.87	.00
Theism	.87	.08	.88	−.01
Idealism	.28	−.03	.31	.05
Superstition	.70	.20	.36	.15
Mysticism	.81	.06	.62	.11
Estimated r between factors	.43		.21	
Estimated second-order loading	I .66		II .46	
	V .66		X .46	

Note: N = 137 for southern students and n = 140 for midwestern students. Data adapted from Maranell (1974).

If a second-order general factor is appropriate, one would expect the broad second-order factor to be predictive of many events (whereas the first-order factors would, as it were, predict the exceptions to the rule from the general factor). Some of Maranell's results did indeed follow the general factor, and in those situations knowledge about the first-order factors or the scales is not needed, for they all follow the same pattern. For example, in denominational differences, Unitarian-Universalists were lowest on the general factor, and they were also consistently lowest across all the scales, except for ritualism where they were tied for second lowest. Age differences were the same for every factor and scale, with older people being more religious than younger people. The individual scales or factors added no information to the conclusions based on the second-order factor in these areas. It is certainly better to say that religiousness is higher among older people and lower among Unitarian-Universalists than to report the same result for two first-order factors or for each of eight scales. A broad definition of Christianity operates well in relating to the broad characteristics of denomination and of age.

The religious scales were also correlated with political attitudes. Again, the results were accurately represented by the general second-order factor. When strong results were found, all the religious scales related in the same direction. In Maranell's (1974) table 5-3, whenever strong (more than 30 significant) relationships were found, the conclusions were the same regardless of the scale. A general conclusion can be reached based on the second-order general Christianity factor: religious people were more politically conservative in Maranell's study.

But with a more specific dependent variable, some individual factors may have greater accuracy than the general Christianity factor. Such results also occurred in Maranell's study. Examining factor scores occasionally produced important differences in the findings. For example, correlations with bigotry scales were positive for the variables representing the church orientation factor but generally negative for variables representing the theistic-Christian factor. So the first-order factors are important because they identify the *exceptions* to the conclusions about religion in general, as represented by the second-order general Christianity factor.

If the paradigm of religious measurement is to continue to provide the direction that is needed from a paradigm, then it is apparent that we need to resolve the issue of uni/multidimensionality as well as beginning to establish some common agreement on the nature of the dimensions. Common agreement would increase our effectiveness considerably because the research would then be focused on a fairly narrow area so that studies could be readily accumulated and used in a reasonable length of time. Such a series of efforts would then show the limitations of the approach, so that the paradigm could be developed further.

I suggest that we are ready, in terms of empirical data, for a new subparadigm that transcends the question of unidimensionality versus multidimensionality of religious phenomena. It is a paradigm that recognizes a higher order integration and provides us with both multidimensional and unidimensional perspectives, which can then each be related to theory and data as needed. The new paradigm consists of a general Christianity factor that can be subdivided into factors such as those found by King and Hunt and by Maranell.

Closed or Open-Ended Questions?

Using closed-ended questionnaires to measure religious phenomena may also create some puzzles. Closed-ended questionnaires produce somewhat different results from open-ended questionnaires, and we do not know what the relationship is between these two approaches. For example, in table 10.1 we presented the Scott religious scale, which was correlated with open-ended questions about a person's values, with the result being a low correlation across these two approaches to measuring values. That is typical; Vernon (1962) asked people directly how they would rate their feelings about religion in a closed-ended question. But he also asked people to list 20 different statements in response to the question, "Who am I?" Their statements were rated on the degree to which they showed religious identification. Both techniques identified about three-fifths to three-fourths of the people as having some type of religious orientation, but there was no relationship between the people identified as religious by the 20 questions and by the self-rating approaches. A different set of people was identified as religious by each procedure. So when is a closed-ended approach better than an open-ended one?

Mixing Different Types of Items on the Same Scale

I have a personal question about the paradigm, although I am not sure that it is widely shared by others in the field: the hodgepodge nature of our questionnaires which freely intermix beliefs, values, and reports of behavior. For example, the Allport and Ross (1967) intrinsic scale includes belief and value items along with a report of frequency of church attendance. Mixing these together suggests either that intrinsic religious beliefs automatically lead to church attendance or that attendance leads to associated beliefs. But are not the interrelationships among beliefs, attitudes, values, and behavior an empirical question for investigation? Our current composite scales, because they mix these several domains, provide no information on the interrelationships. (Interestingly, it is the distinction between beliefs and evaluations which Fishbein and Ajzen [1975; Gorsuch and Ortberg 1983] have found important in their social psychological theories regarding attitudes and behavior.)

Perhaps composite scales have worked because there is an underlying correlation between beliefs and values in the area of religion. This would result in factors extending across the two areas that are being measured by our contemporary questionnaires. The composite questionnaires do give broad predictions and are therefore useful in many cases.

For the exacting work of science, however, it may also be necessary to have instruments measuring either beliefs, attitudes, or values to produce greater accuracy for a particular question. With more specific instruments, we may find, as Fishbein and Ajzen argue, that the relationship between religiousness and behavior is better understood if we consider religious beliefs as distinct from religious values. Perhaps it is important not only to know whether a person is intrinsically or extrinsically oriented toward religion but also to know what type of religion the person is oriented toward.

Concluding Comments

Established Scales as a Boon

From this admittedly cursory description of the measurement paradigm, I would like to suggest some conclusions. First, it appears that the measurement area is a boon to the psychology of religion because we have produced reasonably effective instruments. We have good content and predictive validity as well as usable reliabilities. Scales are available in sufficient variety for most any task in the psychology of religion. We are ready to go beyond measurement to basic, enduring issues, and thus our measurement success should be a boon to the area. An important corollary conclusion is that few new scales are needed, and certainly no new scales are needed in most areas already being investigated. Instead, we need to extend and revise the current scales or dimensions insofar as it *then* seems necessary.

Three conditions must be met before anyone should even consider developing a new questionnaire in the area of religion. First, a detailed review of the literature must be carried out without finding a comparable scale. For example, Strommen, Brekke, Undewager, and Johnson (1972) have 78 scales published not only with the items but also with correlational analyses among them. Since numerous scales already exist, it is unlikely that any new scale would be better than one already in the literature, particularly one that is selected as being the best of its kind.

Second, a new scale should be developed only if it can be argued that a new concept has been developed which is unrelated to factors already found. There are more than enough measures of general traditional Christianity. A new scale should only be recommended after it is demonstrated to add unique information over and above scales already in existence. This means that every new scale should be included immediately in a study with several standard scales to see if it adds to those scales. An example of such an approach is given by Batson (1976). He hypothesized that another approach to religion—in addition to approaching it as a means to other goals (i.e., extrinsically) or as an end itself (i.e., intrinsically)—would be to approach religion as a quest. His research included past measures of extrinsicness and intrinsicness and showed that quest does predict certain types of helping behavior that are not predicted by the other two dimensions. Thus, Batson has shown both that quest is independent of past scales and that it is uniquely useful.

A further paradigm for this type of approach may be the work of Hood on mysticism. Several of his initial studies were concerned with identifying the components of the phenomena and with developing appropriate measuring instruments for them. He has since proceeded to relate the resulting mysticism scales both to other variables and to life experiences that may produce the mysticism phenomenon. If he had stopped after developing mysticism scales, then this work might have been in vain. Placing mysticism in the context of other variables is changing his work from interesting to interesting and important (e.g., Hood 1970, 1975).

Batson's approach may illustrate a third condition for the development of a new scale: there must be adequate resources available. Even a single, simple scale requires a considerable amount of time and empirical analysis to have any possibility of competing on psychometric grounds with previously existing scales. This means that scale development in the psychology of religion has progressed sufficiently so that it should be generally left to those with advanced training in the psychology of religion, in scale development, and in related topics such as factor analysis. Certainly, it is not a task for the average master's level project. Fortunately, religious measurement is sufficiently developed so that many studies can use existing measures rather than develop new ones.

Concern with Questionnaire Measurement as a Bane

But in some senses, the current measurement levels are also a bane for the psychology of religion. The first possibility for it being a bane comes from the interest causing its success. It is possible that psychologists studying religion will study the measurement of religion rather than religion itself. Religion does need further resolution in a paradigmatic sense of what the basic dimensions are, but this resolution is needed so that studies of the impact of religiousness and studies of the development of religiousness can be carried out using refined measurement techniques. Measurement is not a goal unto itself to provide with interesting studies, but rather a means to lay the background for studying the development and impact of religious phenomena. It is these latter studies, and not measurement per se, that are the prime focus of the psychology of religion and the end toward which we must be oriented. If we are engaged only in measurement studies—if dimensionality and other such topics are the ends of research programs—then the concern with measurement will be a bane to the area.

Two sets of investigations provide paradigms—in Kuhn's second sense of exemplars or models—of the appropriate role of measurement in the total psychology of religion effort. First historically is the work of Allport. He included religion within the values that he defined in his original scale with Vernon and later included such measures in his studies of prejudice. Thus, he began with an initial measurement attempt but immediately carried that measurement further in terms of relating to actual phenomena. As a result of those investigations on prejudice, he further redefined his measurement procedure. The result was a hypothesized distinction between intrinsic and extrinsic. Further studies followed where these scales were utilized with varying degrees of success and the concepts further revised. Hence, his work never involved measurement alone but instead involved measurement as a part of more general psychological problems.

A second possibility for current measurement being a bane for the psychology of religion arises from its success. Although the questionnaire approach is successful, it is still a questionnaire approach. Questionnaires may not be adequate to tap more basic motivaitonal levels; Cattell and Child (1975) note that the methods they use are relatively unrelated to questionnaire results. The personalistic approaches more akin to William James's (1902) *Varieties of Religious Experience* or Cattell's P-technique using nonquestionnaire data are as yet rarely researched. If the success of our current religious measurement paradigm prohibits research on other measurement techniques for too long, then its current success could be a long-term bane for the psychology of religion.

Hopefully, the current measurement paradigm will broaden in time into a more comprehensive paradigm that incorporates approaches currently functioning as competing paradigms for investigating religion. A spur for a more comprehensive paradigm could develop from the problems and possibilities generated by greater participation of psychologists from other cultures.

Perhaps psychologists of religion need to attend to Kuhn's (1970) message that science is not an individual affair and that scientific research does not automatically accumulate into a body of scientific knowledge. Instead, there is a sense in which knowledge results from the community interacting as a scientific community. Through discussions and dialogues within the community, a common paradigm develops. The existence of such a paradigm focuses the research so that a sufficient, critical body of knowledge can develop within an area. This means that our own research must take very seriously the research efforts of others, including their measurement techniques, and make every effort to reconcile our results and their results into a more comprehensive paradigm—thus turning banes into boons.

References

Aleshire, D., and R. L. Gorsuch. 1975. The influence of religious values on religious behavior: Testing a multivariate model of the relationship. Paper presented at the annual meeting of the Society for the Scientific Study of Religion, October.

Allen, R. O., and B. Spilka. 1967. Committed and consensual religion: A specification of religion-prejudice relationships. *Journal for the Scientific Study of Religion* 6: 191–206.

Allport, G. W. 1950. *The individual and his religion: A psychological interpretation.* New York: Macmillan.

Allport, G. W., and J. M. Ross. 1967. Personal religious orientation and prejudice. *Journal of Personality and Social Psychology* 5: 432–43.

Allport, G. W., and P. E. Vernon. 1931. A test for personal values. *Journal of Psychology* 22: 9–39.

Batson, C. D. 1976. Religion as prosocial: Agent or double agent? *Journal for the Scientific Study of Religion* 15: 29–45.

Brown, L. B. 1973. *Psychology and religion: Selected readings.* Baltimore: Penguin.

Cattell, R. B., and D. Child. 1975. *Motivation and dynamic structure.* New York: Wiley.

Clayton, R. R. 1971. 5-D or 1? *Journal for the Scientific Study of Religion* 10: 37–40.

Fishbein, M., and I. Ajzen. 1974. Attitudes toward objects as predictors of single and multiple behavioral criteria. *Psychological Review* 81: 59–74.

———. 1975. *Belief, attitude, intention, and behavior.* Menlo Park, Calif.: Addison-Wesley.

Gorsuch, R. L. 1983. *Factor analysis.* 2d ed. Hillsdale, N.J.: L. Erlbaum Associates.

Gorsuch, R. L., and S. G. McFarland. 1972. Single vs. multiple-item scales for measuring religious values. *Journal for the Scientific Study of Religion* 11: 53–64.

Gorsuch, R. L., and J. A. Ortberg. 1983. Moral obligation and attitudes: Their relation to behavioral intentions. *Journal of Personality and Social Psychology* 44: 1025–28.

Hood, R. W., Jr. 1970. Religious orientation and the report of religious experience. *Journal for the Scientific Study of Religion* 9: 285–92.

———. 1975. The construction and prelimi'nary validation of a measure of reported mystical experience. *Journal for the Scientific Study of Religion* 14: 29–41.

Hunt, R. A. 1972. Mythological-symbolic religious commitment: The LAM Scale. *Journal for the Scientific Study of Religion* 11: 42–52.

Hunt, R. A., and M. B. King. 1971. The intrinsic-extrinsic concept: A review and evaluation. *Journal for the Scientific Study of Religion* 10: 339–56.

James, W. 1902. *The varieties of religious experience: A study in human nature.* New York: Random.

King, M. B. 1967. Measuring the religious variable: Nine proposed dimensions. *Journal for the Scientific Study of Religion* 6: 173–90.

King, M. B., and R. A. Hunt. 1969. Measuring the religious variable: Amended findings. *Journal for the Scientific Study of Religion* 8: 321–23.

———. 1972a. *Measuring religious dimensions: Studies in congregational involvement.* Dallas: Southern Methodist Univ. Press.

———. 1972b. Measuring the religious variable: Replication. *Journal for the Scientific Study of Religion* 11: 240–51.

———. 1975. Measuring the religious variable: National replication. *Journal for the Scientific Study of Religion* 14: 13–22.

Kuhn, T. S. 1970. *The structure of scientific revolutions.* 2d ed. Chicago: Univ. of Chicago Press.

Malony, H. N., ed. 1977. *Current perspectives in the psychology of religion.* Grand Rapids: Eerdmans.

Maranell, G. M. 1974. *Responses to religion.* Lawrence, Kans.: Univ. Press of Kansas.

Roof, W. C. 1979. Concepts and indicators of religious commitment: A critical review. In *The religious dimension: New directions in quantitative research,* ed. R. Wuthnow, 17–45. New York: Academic Press.

Schwartz, S. 1968. Words, deeds, and the perception of consequences and responsibility in action situations. *Journal of Personality and Social Psychology* 10: 232–42.

Scott, W. A. 1965. *Values and organizations.* Chicago: Rand McNally.

Spilka, B., L. Stout, B. Minton, and D. Sizemore. 1977. Death and personal faith: A psychometric investigation. *Journal for the Scientific Study of Religion* 16: 169–78.

Strommen, M. P., M. L. Brekke, R. C. Undewager, and A. L. Johnson. 1972. *A study of generations.* Minneapolis: Augsburg.

Thurstone, L. L., and E. J. Chave. 1929. *The measurement of attitudes.* Chicago: Univ. of Chicago Press.

Tisdale, J. R., ed. 1980. *Growing edges in the psychology of religion.* Chicago: Nelson-Hall.

Vernon, G. M. 1962. Measuring religion: Two methods compared. *Review of Religious Research* 3: 159–65.

Psychology and Religion, Beliefs, and Values

My view of the relationship of psychology and religion of the past as well as the present is primarily based upon my personal involvements rather than a systematic review of the literature of each period. This has led me to particular beliefs about the interaction of people interested in psychology and religion which have, I believe, some import for the future. But since any discipline is ultimately determined by the people therein, as much or more than the subject matter per se, this somewhat personal presentation may be appropriate.

1950s–1960s

In retracing the past history of psychology of religion, it is important to note that events of 1960 and later could not occur without precursors in the 1950s. Major precursors were the textbooks by Clark (1958) and Johnson (1959), and Strunk's (1959) book of readings. These summarized the early research and the little research which was then being conducted. But more importantly, they at least gave a common information base for those who were interested in the psychology of religion.

But the psychology of religion was scarcely an accepted topic in psychology during that era. As a case study, consider the University of Illinois. To most psychologists there, the psychology of religion seemed a strange creature and part of "the superstitions of the past from which psychologists, as enlightened scientists, would naturally keep the distance." But there were two professors on the faculty who had some concerns about religion, and they illustrate the problems and possibilities for psychology of religion in that era and suggest why psychology of religion became a phoenix.

From the *Journal of Psychology and Christianity* 5, no. 2 (1986): 39–44; reprinted by permission of the publisher and the author. Copyright by the Christian Association for Psychological Studies.

One professor at the University of Illinois, Raymond B. Cattell, had a systematic approach to all psychology and a classical education background which included considerable philosophy and related areas (Gorsuch 1984). Part of his approach was concerned with morality and with "sentiments," that is, objects which came to have generalized reinforcement value because they are constantly associated with satisfaction of basic needs. In his research on sentiments, Cattell identified a "religious sentiment" along with sentiments to, for example, one's spouse and one's profession. Some interesting measurement techniques—including those designed to tap unconscious motivation—were included in those early studies but were not included in the standard measuring instruments which Cattell later published as the Motivation Analysis Test. That perhaps reflects his own personal view that religion has indeed been important as a topic for the popular people, even though he himself is not religious, but that it would not be significant enough to monitor in a standard test. From that perspective, social scientists have considerable respect for religion because of its strong historical role although they "would, of course, be beyond that sort of thing themselves."

In the case of Cattell and other psychologists of that era there was a curious anomaly that reflects strongly, I believe, on the history of psychology of religion: the lack of a place for beliefs. Beliefs, defined as cognitive conclusions regarding the truth probability of statements such as "God exists" or "I can swim well enough to cross the lagoon" were, despite the comprehensiveness of Cattell's system, not included. Indeed, when I raised the question with Cattell both as a graduate student and in recent years, the conversation immediately became strained because Cattell appears not to be able to utilize the term. And with beliefs not being a critical element in psychology, the psychology of religion becomes only a motivational matter dealt with, if at all, in a reductionistic manner.

Another professor at the University of Illinois interested in and writing about religion was O. H. Mowrer. He was both a clinical psychologist and a classical learning theory experimental psychologist who made his reputation as much in the latter as in the former. During the late 1950s and 1960s, Mowrer published a series of books and articles concerned with religion (e.g., Mowrer 1961). But the focus here was not on the psychology of religion per se but, rather, what classical statements within religion had to teach us regarding the nature of people with the implications of those lessons for clinical psychology. His basic position was that all nonphysiological abnormalities were primarily a result of inner personal immorality. He noted that the church had classically dealt with the concept *sin* and appropriated this term as a central point for therapy. As in the case of Cattell, this borders upon the psychology of religion but is not quite the psychology of religion because beliefs per se are ignored. Instead it is again the point that *historically* religion has had much to say to people and psychology could well learn from that.

Both Cattell and Mowrer had been trained in the post-World War I period after the psychology of religion had been dropped from a central place in psychology. What might have produced a generation of psychologists among whom Cattell and Mowrer were those *most* open to psychology and religion?

My personal speculation is that the demise of psychology of religion and the lack of a place for cognitive developments such as beliefs were a result of the separation of psychology from departments of philosophy. During William James's era, the principal place where any psychology was taught was in departments of philosophy, but psychology then, as a new discipline, separated out of philosophy. I suspect that was a considerable struggle and that early psychologists constantly had people interpreting them as philosophers rather than as scientists.

A natural response for developing identity as psychologists rather than philosophers was to strongly emphasize the differences between the two areas. The difference emphasized was that psychology was to be a natural science, and this led to psychology becoming "the science of behavior" rather than, for example, the science of the mind or spirit.

Behavior had the advantage that it avoided any topics which might cause a psychologist to be viewed as a philosopher rather than as a psychologist. Behavior was seldom talked about by philosophers and even less in terms of scientific perspectives. But other topics that had been important to psychologists earlier were topics which dealt with philosophy in some depth. These included the nature of the mind, the nature of cognitions, and the nature and role of religion. All these topics then came to be avoided by psychologists because of their desire to have an identity that could not be confused with philosophy. Hence my hypothesis is that the psychology of religion did not die out as a separate area but rather died out with other quasi-philosophical areas including beliefs and values. An understanding of the demise and rebirth of psychology of religion, then, needs to take into account the parallel movements in beliefs and values.

Cognitive psychology, including the nature and role of beliefs, also disappeared from psychology during the same period that psychology of religion was at its ebb. The same is true for values as well. While there were occasional psychologists who dealt in such areas—such as Gordon Allport—it can be reasonably safely stated that their reputation in psychology arose in spite of these interests rather than because of them.

Even as psychology of religion began to return in the 1950s and 1960s, so this era also marks a rebirth of cognitive psychology, including beliefs and values. Fishbein (1967), for example, based his reasoned action theory technically in beliefs. This both illustrates the fact that he was dealing with cognitions that would not have been acceptable in an earlier year—for what else is "reasoned action" research in psychology except an examination of the working of the mind? And Rokeach (1968) was beginning his series of studies reintroducing the concept of values, a concept which also, in theory, is based heavily upon beliefs. Even though the reliance upon beliefs was more verbal and theoretical than used in research, the fact that beliefs were recognized and that these topics were being investigated at all indicates the opening of the door to matters which had previously been "too philosophical" to be touched by an "empirical social science."

The 1950s and 1960s found the revival in cognitive psychology and psychology of religion because, I would like to suggest, a new generation of psychologists was moving to the forefront. The previous generation, that is, those trained between World War I and II, were trained by those who had gone through the struggle of separating psychology from philosophy. They were probably trained by example, as well as possibly by direct instruction, to fight for psychology to be a science with the implication of avoiding all that which was philosophical. And this they did. But those psychologists themselves did not, at least past the early days of their career, actually face a fight to establish psychology's identity. By the time of the 1950s, it was obvious that psychology had its own identity as a social and behavioral science. It is then not surprising that individuals trained after World War II would be more open to doing psychological research on matters which had been primarily considered philosophically previously. The identity of psychology was too well established to be threatened by quasi-philosophical matters such as beliefs and religion.

1960s–1970s

The rebirth of psychology of religion can be marked by the publishing of the *Review of Religious Research* (*RRR*—begun in 1959) and the *Journal for the Scientific Study of Religion* (*JSSR*—begun in 1961). These journals moved fairly quickly from being small, ad hoc publishers of a large percent of what was submitted to being major scientific journals undergirding the psychology and sociology of religion. Thus by the mid-1970s *JSSR* had a rejection rate of 80 percent, just as is found in the major journals sponsored by the American Psychological Association (APA). The articles published used the methodology of psychology and sociology and would, from that point of view, be virtually indistinguishable from those of other journals in these professions.

It was during this transitional time that psychology of religion began once again to have established research programs. These are found in people such as Allport, Batson, Hood, and Spilka, as well as in the work of others with broader interests, such as Malony and Brown. But I personally feel that it is too soon to speak of a growing empirical body of knowledge which was forming a paradigm during this transitional phase. Rather we have sets of individual investigators with their own paradigms which were not incompatible with each other and which were beginning to generate the necessary data to form a basis for an empirical psychology of religion.

In the transitional period it seems that many psychologists had begun to shake off the mantles placed upon their shoulders by those who had fought the battle to separate philosophy and psychology. Psychology of religion then became quasi-respectable and has, as will be noted, moved into some degree of respectability in the contemporary period.

But at this point I would like to suggest that there is another element in the interaction between psychology and religion in addition to the necessity to establish an identity separate from philosophy: the predominance of atheists and agnostics within the profession itself. Whereas the natural sciences such as physics now are among those having the highest percentage of Christians of academic disciplines, psychology and sociology generally are reported to have the lowest percentages. This creates special problems for the psychology of religion because to say that religion is important in life is, to an atheist psychologist, to say that they may have overlooked something in their personal life. Hence there may well be some natural inclinations to ignore religion even when it is a variable of some importance. Indeed, this is exactly what I have found in such areas as drug abuse (Gorsuch and Butler 1976). Many of the studies included religion as a background variable and, despite the fact that it might have been the most powerful variable in the study, invariably excluded religion from the discussion and the abstract of the paper. Hence the investigators often had blinders which seemed to prevent them from seeing religion even when it was a major variable in their own data analyses.

The Contemporary Era: 1970s–1980s

It is during the last decade or two that psychology of religion has reestablished itself as a legitimate topic within psychology per se. Part of this centered around the battles in establishing Division 36 of the American Psychological Association: Psychologists Interested in Religious Issues. While I had little personal contact with this movement at that time, I could see, as an outsider, at least two issues that were debated in the attempts to found the division. The first issue was one among the psychologists interested in religion. Some of those who had fought hard for the other two organizations—the Society for the Scientific Study of Religion (SSSR) and the Religious Research Association (RRA)—probably felt that forming a division would handicap our attempts in two ways. First, the establishment of a division would compete with SSSR and RRA. This is notwithstanding the fact that sociology of religion has always been the mainstay of those societies and the sociologists remain active in both types of organization. Even so, I feel that there has been partial truth in that position. Certainly I can afford only one "east of the Mississippi" trip each year and must choose when APA and RRA/SSSR both meet in the East.

A second major issue, as I saw it, in forming Division 36 was whether such a division would "ghettoize" psychologists of religion or whether it would bring them some degree of respectability within "the establishment." Certainly there are members of the division who feel that Division 36 has attracted more than its share of "people interested in strange phenomena." But I feel that it is also apparent that psychology of religion has come to have a greater increase in respectability in psychology per se, and I personally feel having the division as a part of APA has contributed to that.

Critical to the division's helping to establish psychology of religion as a legitimate activity is probably the factor that it did *not* establish a journal. If it had established a journal, then there would have been a strong push toward moving all psychology of religion to that journal (where it could safely be ignored by almost all the psychologists). Thus when Donahue (1985) wished to publish a review of the intrinsic-extrinsic work, the appropriate vehicle was the APA's *Journal of Personality and Social Psychology*. Likewise when it seemed apparent that psychology of religion had established a paradigm in the area of measurement, the resulting article was published in the *American Psychologist* rather than a specialty journal, and hence was sent to all APA members. It is this visibility for psychology of religion as a legitimate discipline that is absolutely essential for the psychology of religion to complete its rebirth into psychology per se and to encourage psychologists to take religion seriously as a variable.

Establishment of a journal by Division 36 would certainly decrease the impact of psychology of religion in general because then the articles will be overlooked by most psychologists. If that were the case, psychologists could continue to assume that religion is an unimportant variable of interest only to a few esoteric people.

With growth of the societies and Division 36, and with the development of people who were able to engage in psychology of religion across their career, there have been definite progresses toward establishing the subdiscipline of the psychology of religion. A subdiscipline might be said to be established when a fairly common paradigm is used for answering questions and a fairly common paradigm is used for establishing the important questions. I would also argue that such a paradigm comes into existence only when there is a clearly established body of fact as well. Please note that I am not including theory per se in this, for theory is a derivative function. Any scientific theory must begin by explaining a widely accepted body of facts that have already been established. To encourage theory before that body of facts is well established would produce talk without substance. One must have something to explain before theory can explain it. In that sense, psychology of religion is making rapid progress toward the establishment of a paradigm on which appropriate theories can then be based, as can be seen in the recent texts in the area (e.g., Spilka, Hood, and Gorsuch 1985).

The contemporary period can be seen as transitional between the reestablishment of psychology of religion with its own paradigm(s) and the development of a continuing science of psychology of religion. The former derives from acceptance of a common body of facts and the latter from theories to explain those facts. The former is almost established and will lead naturally to the latter in which theory comes to a more central role.

There are several factors of possible importance for continuing psychology of religion without a further relapse. Some of these are as follows:

1. Further moving into publishing in mainline psychology journals. This is necessary for several reasons. (a) We need publication outlets with the least cost possible. If we establish a journal of our own, then it will take at least one of our major researchers out of much of his or her research in order to edit that journal, a long-term disadvantage. But more importantly, (b) psychology of religion will be forced to take seriously the general paradigms of psychology in its own work if it avoids a specialty journal. Taking seriously those general paradigms means that we can build upon the research of others and not have to duplicate much of the groundbreaking research to establish paradigms that are important to the discipline per se. Further, (c) publishing in mainline psychology journals guarantees that we meet the methodological standards of our parental discipline. Without meeting those standards, psychology of religion will indeed become a "backwater" with little respect from the psychology per se. We must be methodologically strong to be

able to maintain the progress we have made within psychology and methodologically stronger to increase those gains.

2. It is necessary that we continue to have extensive interaction among those actively involved in the field. This is necessary in part to develop common paradigms, but it is also necessary for social support. And it is very important that those be "open-door" situations where we can involve people who may be entering the field as well as those already well established. Passing on to the new people ways we have found to survive in secular psychology departments is important.

If conditions such as these are met, we need to have no concern for psychology of religion in the future. The substantive agendas will naturally develop by themselves if we remain in dialogue, taking each other's work seriously.

References

Clark, W. H. 1958. *The Psychology of religion: An introduction to religious experience and behavior.* New York: Macmillan.

Donahue, M. J. 1985. Intrinsic and extrinsic religiousness: Review and meta-analysis. *Journal of Personality and Social Psychology,* 48: 400–419.

Fishbein, M., ed. 1967. *Readings in attitude theory and measurement.* New York: Wiley.

Gorsuch, R. L. 1984. R. B. Cattell: An Integration of psychology and ethics. *Multivariate Behavioral Research* 19: 209–20.

Gorsuch, R. L., and M. Butler. 1976. Initial drug abuse: A review of predisposing social psychology factors. *Psychological Bulletin* 83: 120–37. (Reprinted in *The effectiveness of drug abuse treatment,* ed. S. B. Sells, vol. 4 [Cambridge, Mass.: Ballinger Publishing, 1976]; in *Myths and realities: A book about drug realities,* ed. H. Shaffer [Hinghow, Mass.: Project Turnabout, 1977].)

Johnson, P. E. 1959. *Psychology of religion.* Rev., enl. ed. Nashville: Abingdon.

Mowrer, O. H. 1961. *The crisis in psychiatry and religion.* Princeton, N.J: Van Nostrand.

Rokeach, M. 1968. *Beliefs, attitudes, and values: A theory of organization and change.* San Francisco: Jossey Bass.

Spilka, B., R. W. Hood, Jr., and R. L. Gorsuch. 1985. *The psychology of religion: An empirical approach.* Englewood Cliffs, N.J.: Prentice-Hall.

Strunk, O., Jr., ed. 1959. *Readings in the psychology of religion.* Nashville: Abingdon.

11

Jan van der Lans

Jan van der Lans is professor of the psychology of religion on the faculty of the social sciences at Catholic University of Nijmegen in the Netherlands. His career began when, after having obtained his master's degree in psychology, van der Lans started teaching psychology to students of the theological faculty at Catholic University. In 1976 Dr. van der Lans received his doctoral degree from Catholic University of Nijmegen. In 1978 he became an assistant professor on the faculty of the social sciences at that institution, where he has remained.

Dr. van der Lans is a member of the board of the International Society of Psychology of Religion and Science of Religion (founded in 1916 in Germany) and the Commission Internationale de Psychologie Religieuse Scientifique (International Commission of the Scientific Psychology of Religion). In 1979 he originated a symposium of European psychologists of religion; the symposium has met at Nijmegen every three years since that date. The symposium in 1985 resulted in the book *Proceedings of the Third Symposium on the Psychology of Religion in Europe: Current Issues in the Psychology of Religion* (Amsterdam: Rodopi, 1986), which was edited by J. A. van Belzen and van der Lans.

With van der Lans in particular, it seems necessary to discuss his publications in conjunction with his research. While a research assistant to the psychology faculty at Nijmegen, he executed a survey-study into the role conflicts of Roman Catholic priests and Protestant ministers. This research resulted in the publication of "Ministers in the Netherlands: An Investigation into the Position, Task, and Profession of the Pastor" (1968). In the 1970s he became interested in the psychological and physiological effects of Zen meditation, which led to his doctoral dissertation "Religious Experience and Meditation." In the dissertation van der Lans described religious experience in terms of the information-processing paradigm and analyzed the meditation methods of Hinduism, Buddhism, Taoism, and Christian mysticism as structurally comparable techniques that switch off the profane frame of reference and activate a religious memory scheme. The work also reported a laboratory experiment in which he tested the hypothesis that religious experiences would come about in meditating subjects only if they had a religious memory program at their disposal. Articles written by van der Lans on meditation include "Meditation: A Comparative and Theoretical Analysis" and "The Value of Sundén's Role-Theory Demonstrated and Tested with Respect to Religious Experience in Meditation."

Attracted by the phenomena of many people starting to practice meditation or being converted to new religious movements, van der Lans, together with sociologist James T. Richardson and doctoral students, has made some comparative studies into the psychological factors underlying conversion to the Divine Light Mission, the Baghwan movement, the Unification Church, and Ananda Marga. He has now widened his scope to study the religious attitudes and beliefs of young adults in general. The focus of his research has become the psychological implications of the secularization process. In several studies he and his coworkers are investigating how religious people deal with the cognitive tension between religious and modern scientific representations of reality as well as how people who have abandoned religious beliefs deal with problems of ultimate meaning. One of the subgroups studied in this context are second-generation Muslim immigrants from Turkey and Morocco.

In the essay "Interpretation of Religious Language and Cognitive Style," van der Lans considers the question of whether persons who interpret religious language literally differ in their judgments of how God works in human life from those who interpret religious language metaphorically. He reports two studies which demonstrated that more literal persons think more intrinsically about God's actions and reason less imaginatively than metaphorical persons. He concludes that two distinct cognitive modes are apparent from the studies.

In the article on "What Is Psychology of Religion About?" van der Lans notes that, whereas the prime focus of the field at the beginning of the 20th century was Christianity, today the situation is more pluralistic. Islam and other religions have spread throughout the world, and much of the Western world has become unchurched. He suggests we broaden our definition of the field and investigate the ways people are meeting the needs out of which they were traditionally religious in the past.

Interpretation of Religious Language and Cognitive Style: A Pilot Study with the LAM Scale

Introduction

As we know, research studies in the psychology of religion deal with the construction of typologies of religious behavior and attitudes. I call it a remarkable fact that, except in four earlier empirical investigations (Hogge and Friedman 1967; Hunt 1972; Poythress 1975; Orlowski 1979), hardly any use has been made of the interpretation of religious language as a parameter, in spite of the fact that in many theological and philosophical studies (Tillich 1964; Barbour 1976; Fortmann 1965; Howe 1978; MacCormac 1983) it is suggested that this is a decisive factor in people's attitude towards religion.

It is not within the competence of psychologists of religion to judge whether a particular interpretation of religious language is right or wrong. However, in their empirical work they observe that people differ in the way they understand statements and representations of their religious tradition. Psychologists of religion also frequently observe that people reject religious belief statements, arguing that these are archaic and don't fit in a modern worldview. This obvious lack of competence to think in terms of complementary theories has been studied recently by Oser and Reich (1987; Reich 1987). The aspect of religious behavior at issue here is a basic one. In several studies of religious behavior the belief dimension has proved to account for a large percentage of the variance (Faulkner and De Jong, 1966; Clayton 1971). However, while the message of religious belief statements is unambiguous for some, it is polyinterpretable for others. Therefore psychologists of religion should construct measures that enable them to investigate the linguistic aspect of religious behavior and to study how it is linked with social and psychological factors.

From the *International Journal for the Psychology of Religion* 1, no. 2 (1991): 107–23; reprinted by permission of Lawrence Erlbaum Associates, Publishers.

Current belief scales seem useless for this purpose. Their items mostly reproduce statements from the Bible or the confession of faith. Their power is confined to measuring the degree to which people assent to a literal interpretation of the church doctrine. Although Richard Hunt as early as 1972 denounced this practice with the convincing argument that it misclassifies proreligious subjects who disagree with a literal conception of religious language as less religious or nonreligious, such belief scales are still in use (Donahue 1985).

In several projects of our research program we try to get insight into the strategies people use in solving the cognitive problem of the disparity between a religious and a profane worldview. That makes the interpretation of religious language one of the key variables. Recently, Frye (1981) in his linguistic study of the Bible distinguished two modes of interpreting religious language, which he labels as the *literal-descriptive* mode and the *metaphorical* mode. Although, according to Frye, the authors of the Bible had undoubtedly intended their text to be taken literally, they had not intended to write history or to exhibit facts objectively. Seen from the perspective of the history of language, the religious language of the Bible and of many other religious traditions gives expression to a collective experience. Consequently, metaphor is its leading stylistic device. When we were looking for an instrument that would enable us empirically to investigate the degree to which subjects prefer either of these modes of understanding religious language, it seemed obvious to hark back to the pioneer work of Richard Hunt, who in 1972 published the so-called LAM Scale.

Hunt's LAM Scale Revised and Translated

This scale is intended to be a combination of two measures since at the same time it explores both religious commitment and use of religious language. Three combinations of commitment and interpretation are represented. First, agreement with doctrinal statements that are taken at face value without questioning *(Literal position);* second, a rejection of belief statements with the argument that they sound primitive and unscientific *(Antiliteral position);* third, agreement with belief statements with a reinterpretation of them as mythological *(Mythological position).* Hunt's Literal (L), Antiliteral (A), and Mythological (M) Scale consists of 24 items, each of which has the format of a stem item with three alternative answers. For example:

I believe in God, the Father Almighty, maker of heaven and earth.
    1. Agree, since available evidence proves that God made everything.
    2. Disagree, since available evidence suggests some type of spontaneous creation for which it is unnecessary to assume a God to create.

3. Agree, but only in the sense that this is an anthropomorphical way of thinking about whatever Process, Being, or Ultimate Concern stands behind the creative process.

Subjects can be asked to rank each set of three alternatives or to choose one. Adding the scores of the L, A, and M alternatives separately produces three subscale scores. With the ranking method these subscales are ipsative and significantly intercorrelated. With the second scoring method, however, they are independent subscales according to Hunt.

The reliabilities of the subscales that Hunt reported are satisfactory (between .80 and .92). In a later study (Orlowski 1979), however, they were considerably lower, especially for the M and A scales (.67; .71). Using a multitrait, multimethod matrix, Orlowski also estimated the external construct validity of the scales. The validity coefficients for the L and M scales were significant, but not for the scale. Poythress (1975), who has modified the LAM Scale into a Likert format, has questioned the construct validity of the Mythological scale since he did not find support for Hunt's contention that mythology-oriented subjects differ from literally-oriented subjects in terms of personality characteristics.

To fit our purpose we thought it necessary to reformulate several items of the LAM Scale. First, Hunt's concept "mythological-symbolical interpretation of religious language," being the construct underlying his M scale, seems ambiguous. "Mythological" is not identical with "symbolical." Several items of the M scale suggest that Hunt's concept of *mythological* refers to the history of knowledge (i.e., the M alternative cited earlier), whereas the qualification *symbolical* in the context of religious language primarily refers to the fact that word meaning is multidimensional instead of unidimensional. In spite of the fact that Hunt explicitly says that his M scale is intended as a representation of the tendency to "reinterpret religious statements in order to seek their deeper symbolic meanings which lie beyond the literal wording," the wording is more rationalistic than symbolic (Hunt 1972, 43; cf. also Greeley 1972). Some of Hunt's M alternatives are not more than a sophisticated translation of the literal-fundamentalistic alternatives, mitigating their straight fundamentalistic style (e.g., items 2, 5, 9, 12, 15, 17). Most of them did not seem suitable to measure the metaphorical mode of interpreting religious language. So when we translated the LAM Scale into Dutch, nearly each of the M alternatives was rephrased. An example may give an idea of the differences between the M alternatives in Hunt's version and ours:

Item 17 (Hunt's original)
"We were made for fellowship with God and our hearts are restless until they rest in him."

M(ythological) interpretation
"Agree, although this is merely a way of talking about the ultimate nature of man's activities as being in some way related to God's purpose."

Item 17 (revised)
"Restless is my heart until it will find rest in God."
M(etaphorical) interpretation:
"Agree. This is a way of saying that finally we are longing for something greater that transcends human existence."

Also some of the Literal alternatives were rewritten. Finally, we removed item stems which refer not to biblical issues, but to ethical ones, and we added item stems with respect to resurrection and prayers.

In the instructions subjects are asked to indicate how they interpret each of the stem items by marking the alternative that most accurately represents their own view. We preferred this scoring method over a Likert format, as proposed by Poythress, since Orlowski has reported that his subjects indicated the Likert format was confusing and too complicated. The Likert format seems preferable from a psychometric viewpoint, however. As the structure of the revised scale remains similar to the original one of Hunt, we decided to maintain the label LAM Scale. The initial *M*, however, no longer stands for mythological but for metaphorical.[1]

In this paper results, which have been obtained with preliminary versions of the revised and translated scale, will be reported. In two pilot studies we tested its predictive and construct validity. Although it was Hunt's intention that the LAM Scale discriminate two different modes of being religious (Hunt 1972), it is remarkable that the scale scores have never been compared with other measures of religious behavior. Hunt also suggested that the symbolic approach to religion may be related to the complexity of cognitive functioning. In this paper we will explore whether the choice a respondent makes between alternative interpretations of the stem items is related to different styles of religious cognitive functioning. Since in these studies, in addition to the LAM Scale, data have been gathered with respect to spontaneous use of religious language, they make it possible to examine the construct validity of the scale.

1. As is the case with Hunt's LAM Scale, the Dutch version can be used only with Christian populations. In two other research projects, Hinduistic and Islamic versions of the LAM Scale were developed. The Hinduistic version is in English, the Islamic version in Dutch. A copy of these versions is available on request. (Hinduistic version: Mr. P. Eussen, c/o Subdepartment for Psychology of Culture and Religion, Psychological Laboratory, Catholic University, P. O. Box 9104, 6500 HE Nijmegen, Netherlands. Islamic version: Mrs. M. Rooyackers, same address.)

First Study

The first data set was gathered in interviews in which among other variables the development of religious judgment was studied utilizing the method designed by Oser (Oser 1980; Oser and Gmünder 1984). Data from this interview-study is borrowed in order to explore whether there is a relation between the way in which a subject conceives biblical concepts and statements on one hand and uses religious categories in a religious problem-solving task on the other.

In Oser's cognitive-developmental theory the term *religious judgment* does not refer to a statement about religion or God, but to the way in which a person conceives reality when facing a border situation that needs to be explained in order to restore his disturbed cognitive balance. Oser assumes that in such a situation everybody forms an idea about the relationship between himself and the transcendent. Oser is not interested in the content of a person's religious judgment but, like Piaget, in its structural characteristics or the cognitive operations by which one tries to master the situation. Through several investigations, in which he applied a Kohlbergian dilemma-method, Oser has succeeded in finding empirical evidence for five structurally different stages of religious judgment. At stage 1 persons conceive themselves as completely dependent on God, who is seen as an ultimate power, arbitrarily punishing and rewarding. At stage 2 people see themselves as capable of influencing the ultimate power; reality is structured by means of the categories *cause* and *effect*. Characteristic for stage 3 is the awakening of human autonomy. People feel a tension between the Ultimate and their own free will. At stage 4 this conflict is resolved by the idea that a person's autonomy is supported by God since it is founded in an eternal divine plan. Finally at stage 5 intersubjectivity becomes the source of religious judgment; the Ultimate is no longer approached as something outside and above the world, but as manifesting itself in intersubjective communication. Here the concept God is no longer used for causal attribution to explain life events but to give meaning.

Hypotheses

It may be evident that the way in which somebody interprets the concepts and representations of the religious tradition and the structure of his or her personal religious thinking (as defined by Oser) interact with each other. We hypothesized that subjects who prefer a literal-descriptive interpretation of the Bible (high score on the L scale of the LAM, low score on the M scale) will in their religious judgment predominantly demonstrate characteristics of stage 1 or 2. This expectation follows from the reference-frame theory. If subjects need or are invited to judge a situation from a religious perspective—as is done in Oser's religious judgment interview-schedule—they will use a cognitive scheme that results from their way of processing biblical information. One who interprets biblical stories descriptively is accustomed to a religious cognitive scheme in which facts are seen as directly attributable to God as actor. Another reason for this expectation might be that preference for a literal-descriptive reading of the Bible indicates that one has a need for cognitive clarity and wants to avoid cognitive complexity. It is unlikely that such persons will produce religious judgments of stage 4 or 5.

As an antiliteral score on the LAM Scale indicates a disposition to reject biblical representations because they are opposed to a scientific worldview, it is to be expected that persons with a high A score on the LAM Scale will demonstrate a religious judgment of stage 3. The idea that God could be involved in occurrences is experienced by them as a threat to human autonomy.

Finally, the religious judgments of people who interpret religious language metaphorically are expected to have the characteristics of stage 4 or 5. In their religious reference frame, biblical stories are not models of causal explanation. People who predominantly prefer metaphorical statements on the LAM Scale demonstrate a critical attitude toward the human tendency to form a concrete, anthropomorphical idea of God as final cause. It is, therefore, unlikely that their religious judgments will exhibit the characteristics of a person belonging to stages 1 or 2, who derives certainty from an external locus of authority. On the contrary, because they understand the meaning of biblical statements as not manifest but hidden, they will approach life events in a dialectical manner. They will not handle creedal statements as a straightforward key to disclose the meaning of life events, but will be sensitive to their polyinterpretability.

Method

In order to test these expectations, data were used from a small pilot study,[2] in which 19 Roman Catholic church visitors of various ages were interviewed with the aim of exploring the field of feelings, attitudes, and behavior with respect to liturgy. Of them, 5 were male, 14 female. The average age was 45.5 with a standard deviation of 16.0. Because of the length of the questionnaire, all subjects were visited twice. In the second interview, besides a 13-item LAM Scale, the so-called Paul dilemma was presented to them followed by the standard questions. Of the several dilemma-stories that Oser has constructed, the Paul-dilemma is most frequently used. It tells about Paul, a successful

---

2. Data were gathered by M. van den Munckhoff and analyzed and reported in her master's thesis (1988).

young medical doctor, who, traveling in a plane with a damaged engine, had promised God to give up his girlfriend and his career and to dedicate his life to poor people in Africa if he would be saved. After having returned home safely, a lucrative position was offered to him. Now Paul does not know what to do. It is the interviewer's task to make the respondent tell what Paul should do. The structure of the argumentation reveals, according to Oser, the developmental level of the respondent's religious judgment. The antiliteral alternatives of the LAM Scale had been left out in this study, because it was (wrongly) assumed that these statements would be irrelevant and disturbing to church visitors.

Results

In the analysis, 4 items of the LAM Scale have been eliminated since the majority of the respondents either had raised objections to the formulation or found it difficult to choose between the L and M alternatives. Also 4 respondents were eliminated because they had left 4 or more of the remaining 9 items unanswered. The data on the remaining subjects on the LAM Scale and the developmental stage of their religious judgment are recorded in table 11.1.

Table 11.1
LAM Scale Scores and Stage
of Religious Judgment

Respondent	Number of L Choice	Number of M Choice	Number of Unanswered Items	Stage of Religious Judgment	Age
11	7	1	1	2.5	71
6	6	1	2	3	50
15	5	3	1	2.5	62
9	3	4	2	4	58
5	3	6	0	2.5	33
8	2	5	2	3	59
18	2	5	2	3.5	28
12	1	5	3	4	24
3	1	6	2	3	50
1	1	8	0	3	50
13	1	8	0	3.5	25
10	0	6	3	2.5	52
14	0	6	3	3.5	17
16	0	7	2	3.5	45
19	0	7	2	3.5	49

Table 11.1 shows that of the 15 subjects in our analysis only 9 show a rather consistent pattern with respect to their choices between literal and metaphorical alternatives on the LAM Scale: 2 subjects are evidently literal, 7 metaphorical. The responses of the 6 remaining subjects fluctuate among the literal, metaphorical, and no-answer categories. A comparison of the columns in table 11.1 suggests that subjects with a clear preference for literal interpretations of the LAM Scale items gave evidence of a relatively low-developed structure of religious thinking in Oser's measure of religious judgment. Contrary to the third expectation, however, some subjects whose LAM Scale performance indicates a clear preference for a metaphorical interpretation have been categorized in a relatively low stage with respect to their religious judgment. When we arrange the subjects in order of their stage score, as is done in figure 11.1, and observe the average number of literal and metaphorical LAM Scale choices in each developmental stage . . . in each developmental stage the averages obviously change in the expected direction, although stage 4 apparently deviates from the pattern. This is caused mainly by one of the respondents in this stage category.

Fig. 11.1
Stages of Religious Judgment Compared
with Respect to LAM-Scale Answers

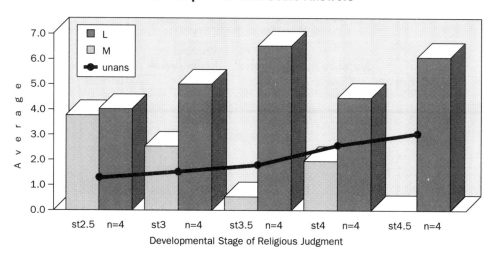

Unfortunately, it is not possible to test the second expectation. Retrospectively, the leaving out of the antiliteral alternatives in this study is regretted considering the high frequency of stage 3 subjects.

To test whether the data confirm the expectation that subjects who prefer a metaphorical interpretation of religious language are characterized by a more developed religious cognitive structure than subjects who prefer a literal interpretation, we have applied the Mann-Whitney U test (a powerful nonparametric test for very small samples) to the ranked stage scores of the 9 subjects with the most consistent LAM Scale response patterns. The difference between "literals" and "metaphoricals" in this respect is not significant, however (Mann-Whitney U = 2.5; Z corr = –.1.37; p = .17).

A further inspection of the data shows an unpredicted tendency which seems obliquely relevant in connection with our aim to evaluate the LAM Scale. We have already noticed the relatively high number of unanswered items, which caused us to omit the scores of 4 subjects from the analysis. Figure 11.1 suggests a relation between the number of items in which a subject could not decide to choose between the literal and the metaphorical interpretation and the subject's stage score for religious judgment. This relation is weak but significant (Kendall's t, corrected for ties = .41; p = .03).

The more differentiated a subject's religious cognitive structure, the more difficult it seems to make a choice between the LAM Scale alternatives. The fact that subjects have frequently used the "no-answer" category may have been caused by the instructions. The possibility of not making a choice between the alternatives was explicitly mentioned to the subjects. The interviewees were free to abstain from choosing. However, it is remarkable that subjects for whom a more differentiated cognitive structure seems to be characteristic espcially made use of this possibility. Explaining the difficulty in choosing, subjects remarked that sometimes they agreed with both alternatives, sometimes they could not agree with either of them, and sometimes the literal alternative could also be conceived metaphorically. This suggests that not only by preferring the metaphorical answers but also by not making a choice between the literal and the metaphorical interpretations, subjects demonstrated their conviction that religious language is not unequivocal. When the LAM Scale is used to measure a subject's sensitivity for the symbolic character of religious language, it is recommended that this possibility be taken into account.

Responses to the LAM Scale Compared with Age

The data in table 11.1 create the impression that there is a connection between age and answers to the LAM Scale. Some of the eldest subjects had a high preference for literal interpretations, whereas the literal answers were rarely chosen by respondents below the age of 30. We should not exclude the possibility that agreement or disagreement with the literal answers of the LAM Scale has more to do with the degree of the subjects' familiarity with the religious words than with their way of interpreting religious language. The relationship between age and preference for metaphorical answers is weaker. Age seemed not to be a better explanation for the choice between literal and metaphorical interpretations than stage of religious judgment, as neither the difference between "literal" and "metaphorical" subjects with respect to ranked age was significant. (Mann-Whitney U = 2; Z corr = –.1.49; p = .13). Obliquely we found that the stage scores of religious judgment seemed to be stronger related with age. The correlation between the ranks of all respondents on both variables was significant (r^s = .55; p = .03).

Conclusion

With respect to the presumed relation between preference for either a literal or a metaphorical interpretation of religious language and the style of religious thinking, the first study did not yield the expected results. Although subjects with a high preference for metaphorical interpretations averaged higher stage scores of religious judgment than subjects who preferred literal interpretations, the level of the latter subjects' religious judgment, according to Oser's criteria, obviously more elaborated than expected. Further, only one of the subjects who preferred metaphorical interpretations showed the predicted high level of religious thinking. The others were classified in stage 3 or in transition between stage 3 and 4, and one of them was even in the transitional stage 2.5.

Although the very small number of available subjects does not allow one to formulate any conclusions, the results suggest that subjects' scores on the LAM Scale cannot simply be conceived as an index of their developmental level of religious judgment. There are indications that age is an intervening variable. If it is true that religious judgments of older subjects showed characteristics of the lower stages in Oser's developmental theory, this is a puzzling phenomenon for the psychologist of religion and a challenge for Oser's theory as well.[3] However, in the context of this report we can leave it aside. The relation that we found between age and answers to the LAM Scale is less puzzling. It is conceivable that the literal alternatives were experienced as more familiar by older respondents since they represent the traditional religious discourse to which they have been accustomed from childhood. On the other hand it might be that the same traditional character of the literal alternatives was the reason why younger subjects preferred the metaphorical ones. This might be a cultural-psychological explanation for the obtained distribution of answers to the LAM Scale. Whether we may consider the LAM Scale a valid method for differentiating between styles of religious thinking is still an unsolved problem.

---

3. This age phenomenon might indicate that the obtained stage scores are based (more than Oser's theory presumes) on content learning or culturally conditioned performance than on development of cognitive structure.

Second Study

For a further exploration of this problem we have analyzed the data of a second study, which seems very suitable to our purpose because the subjects were all young adults. This makes it possible to investigate the relation between LAM Scale responses and cognitive functioning more directly without the intervening influence of the age variable. In order to know whether the LAM Scale is a valid operationalization of the underlying constructs, it is important to compare the subjects' reactions to the structured scale items with their spontaneous use of religious language. The data of this second study have been obtained in interviews in which subjects have been invited to free-associate to a series of photographs. The interviews were held in the context of a larger study of prayer behavior of young adults. As a first step in this study, 212 students of Advanced Nursing Schools completed a large questionnaire of which the LAM Scale formed a part. This version of the LAM Scale consisted of 14 items. As a second step, 10 subjects were selected from the larger sample and interviewed in order to further explore the relation between their praying behavior and their ability to perceive symbolic meanings of verbal and nonverbal stimuli. The selection of the interviewees was made on the basis of scores on the LAM Scale. Two homogeneous subgroups were formed, one group consisting of 5 subjects with a high preference for literal alternatives, and the other group consisting of the 5 subjects who scored lowest on the literal subscale and highest on the metaphorical. Both groups differed significantly with respect to their total number of literal and metaphorical choices on the LAM Scale (see table 11.2). With respect to average age the groups were comparable (19.8 and 20.4 respectively).[4]

Method

In the context of this paper we have analyzed the answers given in an association task. The interviewees had been asked to free-associate on 10 photographs, which either represented people in a manifestly religious act or in a situation that easily might have evoked in them a religious feeling.[5] The pictures were presented to the subjects successively. Each picture was followed by the question: "Which images or feelings

4. Data were gathered by Christen den Draak and analyzed and reported in her master's thesis (1989).

5. Pictures as a stimulus instrument for studying religious experience have been used earlier by Bachs and by Orens (Vergote 1984, 143–54). Like Bachs and Orens, we used pictures of human persons in a nature setting (for example, climbing a mountain, standing before a huge waterfall) and a picture of the first man on the moon, but unlike them, pictures of other settings (for example, cultic behavior [praying woman, ancestor-worship], human relationship [child holding hand of adult; mother with baby], existential crises [women around the bed of a deceased, a comfort-seeking soldier]).

Table 11.2
L and M Socres of Selected Interviewees

	L scale		M scale	
	Average	St.dev.	Average	St.dev.
subgroup 1 (n = 5)	13.2	1.0	0.6	0.9
subgroup 2 (n = 5)	4.0	1.9	10.0	1.9
Difference between groups	$t = 9.0$	$p < .001$	$t = -10.1$	$p < .001$

cross your mind when looking at this picture? Tell me as much as you can. The point is not to explain the picture, but to tell what it evokes in you." After the whole series had been shown, a set of questions was asked: "Which of these pictures make you think of God? And which don't? Can you tell me why?" The first question was asked to measure to what extent subjects, in processing visual information, were inclined to make use of various images, feelings, or memories. The answers to the set of questions revealed the style of the subjects' religious thinking. Following Piaget, Oser aimed to investigate religious problem solving. His method, the "Paul dilemma," reveals how the respondent uses concepts derived from the religious tradition as instruments in religious reasoning. The association task in this second study, however, more directly appeals to the respondent's sensitivity to the metaphorical quality of religious language. Through comparing the responses of subjects to the presented pictures with their preference scores on the LAM Scale, we wanted to test a twofold expectation:

1. Metaphors function as instruments of imaginative thinking. If the LAM Scale really measures competence with respect to metaphorical language, it is hypothesized that people with a high M score and a low L score on the LAM Scale will show a greater amount of imaginative thinking in a free-association task than people with a low M score and a high L score.

2. It was hypothesized that subjects with either a high metaphorical or a high literal score on the LAM Scale will not differ with respect to the tendency to connect religious meanings to a situation. However, subjects with a high literal score will be more inclined than subjects with a high metaphorical score to use religious language in making causal attributions. That is, in describing the religious meaning of a situation, these subjects will refer to God as cause, as creator, or as legislator. Subjects with a high M score on the LAM Scale will be more inclined than subjects with a high L score to use religious language in giving expression to the ambiguity of the meaning of a perceived situation.

Results

To be able to test the hypotheses, four scores were calculated:

the number of associative answers each of the respondents had given in response to the first question, being a measure of imaginative thinking. For this purpose, all answers were analyzed for content and put in either of two categories: responses that only described or explained a picture and responses that were free associations to it.[6]

the number of pictures that made the respondents think of God.

the number of religious-attributional associations. For example, "She radiates peace, which she could have gotten from God" (in response to picture F: a praying woman) equals causal attribution.

the number of religious-metaphorical associations. For example, "The light on her face is striking; the rest is dark, dead, but that light gives me a feeling of hope" (in response to same picture; answer qualified by respondent as religious).

Comparing the two groups with respect to the total number of real associations (in response to the first question), we learn that subjects with a low preference for a metaphorical interpretation and a high preference for a literal interpretation of religious language scored lower on the measure we employed for imaginative thinking (see fig. 11.2). According to Fisher's exact probability test, the difference between the two groups is highly significant ($p = .004$; two-tailed). This result confirms our first hypothesis.

With respect to the question of which photographs made the respondents think of God, we did not presume a difference between the groups. Figure 11.3 shows that each picture elicited this association in both groups, but that the subjects of the M group were slightly more receptive to this than the L group, with exception of picture E (child holding the hand of an adult and looking up to him). The discrepancy between the groups in this respect was greatest with pictures H (ancestor worship), and D (deathwatch). The average number of "God" associations made by each of the two groups was significantly different ($p = .05$).[7]

With respect to the type of religious association, the discrepancy between the groups was even larger (in the predicted direction). When

6. For example, "a walk through the snow in the mountains" = description; "perhaps the man tries to make contact with the deceased in the grave" (to the picture representing ancestor worship) = explanation; "gives me a feeling of mystery" (same picture) = association; "makes me think of oneness with nature" (waterfall) = association.

7. Average L = 4.8; st.dev. = 2.8; average M = 7.6; st.dev. = 2.6. t = -2.8.

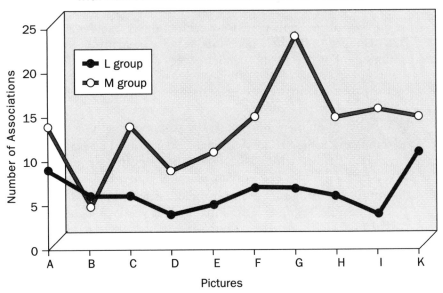

Fig. 11.2
Responses to LAM Scale Compared
with Number of General Associations to Pictures

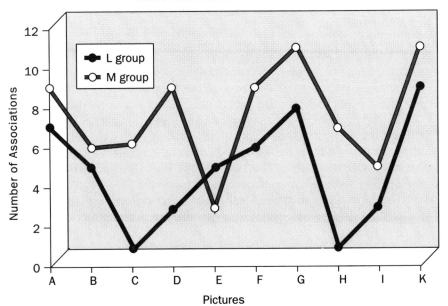

Fig. 11.3
Degree to Which Religious Meanings
Were Associated to Pictures

the subjects of the L group declared that pictures made them think of God and explained why, they far more than the M group used religious language in an objectifying manner. Frequently their religious associations had the character of causal attributions stating, for example, that a picture made them think of God because it represented something God had created. From figure 11.4 it is evident that two pictures in particular elicited such a response: G (waterfall) and K (mother with baby). This figure also demonstrates that, with exception of pictures A (mountain climbers) and B (girl with young deer), and E (astronaut on the moon), in the literal group the causal-attributional associations generally outnumbered metaphorical associations. The typical pattern in the other group is quite the opposite: few associations of the causal-attributional type and many of the metaphorical type. Conspicuous in the figure is that the attributional associations of the literal group are most numerous with those pictures that to the highest degree elicited metaphorical associations in the metaphorical group.

The results seem to confirm the hypotheses. Fisher's exact probability test has been applied to the classification of subscores of both the L group and M group above and below the median. This has been done with respect to each type of association (fig. 11.4). In both cases the two groups appeared to be significantly different (attributional type: $p = .05$; metaphorical type: $p = .004$).

Fig. 11.3
**LAM Scale Groups Compared with Respect
to Type of Religious Association**

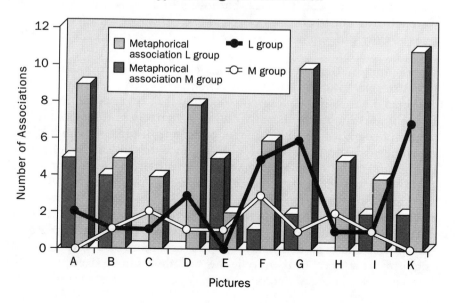

Summary

To summarize the results from the second study: in a small sample, where between subjects with a high preference for M alternatives and subjects with a high preference for L alternatives on the LAM Scale age differences did not exist, we have found evidence that these groups differ from each other with respect to a relevant aspect of general cognitive functioning and with respect to religious cognitive functioning. Subjects who prefer metaphorical alternatives on the LAM Scale showed a higher propensity for imaginative thinking in the association task. Also, while both M-type and L-type subjects appeared to be sensitive to the religious-symbolic character of shown pictures, these two groups obviously differed in the way they interpreted the pictures and described the religious meaning the pictures had for them.

Conclusion

As we have said in the introduction, the aim of the reported analyses was to test the predictive and construct validity of our translated and adapted version of Hunt's LAM Scale. Can the LAM Scale be considered a valid instrument to distinguish different styles of religious thinking? The data of our samples do not allow us to draw conclusions in regard to the A (antiliteral) alternatives. However, we obtained evidence of the discriminating power of the L and M scales with respect to the concepts of literal-descriptive and metaphorical use of religious language. Using Oser's measure of religious judgment as a criterion variable was not helpful in this respect. The fact that in the first study the respondents were left free not to choose between literal and metaphorical alternatives if they did not want to may have obscured the theoretically expected relation. But the results obtained in the second study confirm the assumption that these two linguistic modes on the domain of religion are related to differences in general cognitive functioning. The obtained data from the picture-association task suggest that interpreting religious language literally and descriptively is related to a low degree of cognitive flexibility. In comparison with subjects who prefer a metaphorical interpretation of biblical concepts, subjects preferring a literal interpretation showed a weaker sensitivity with respect to the multiplicity of meanings of perceived objects. Preference for a literal-descriptive interpretation of the LAM Scale items seems to be an aspect of a general tendency to structure the world along the trusted lines of clearcut traditional answers. On the contrary, people who prefer a metaphorical interpretation seem to possess a more elaborate religious cognitive structure. For them religious tradition is not a fixed system of facts and rules, not an ideology, but the symbolic expression of a view on world and life, meant as an inspiration instead of a ready-for-use solution, not relieving them of the responsibility to think for themselves. This general profile of their cognitive structure, which is derived from their performance on the cognitive tasks, supports the assumption that the forced-choice answering method of the LAM Scale may have been frustrating especially to these autonomously thinking people. Retrospectively, the Likert format, as proposed by Poythress (1975), seems to be preferable.

References

Barbour, I. 1976. *Myths, models and paradigms: The nature of religious and scientific language.* New York: Harper and Row.

Clayton, R. R. 1971. 5-D or 1? *Journal for the Scientific Study of Religion* 10: 37–40.

Donahue, M. J. 1985. Intrinsic and extrinsic religiousness: Review and meta-analysis. *Journal of Personality and Social Psychology* 48: 400–419.

Draak, C. den. 1989. Bidden en Gebedstaal. Psychologische studie naar aanleiding van onderzoek onder jongeren. (Praying and prayer-language. A psychological study on basis of a survey among youth.) Master's thesis, Catholic University of Nijmegen, Nijmegen, Netherlands.

Faulkner, J. E., and G. F. DeJong. 1966. Religiosity in 5-D: An empirical analysis. *Social Forces* 45: 246–54.

Fortmann, H. M. M. 1965. *Als Ziende de Onzienlijke. Een cultuurpsychologische studie over de religieuze waarneming en de zogenaamde religieuze projectie. (As if seeing the Unseeable. A cultural psychological study on religious perception and the so-called religious projection.)* Hilversum-Antwerp: Paul Brand.

Frye, N. 1981. *The great code: The Bible and literature.* New York: Harcourt Brace Jovanovich.

Greeley, A. M. 1972. Comment on Hunt's mythological-symbolic religious commitment: The LAM scales. *Journal for the Scientific Study of Religion* 11: 287–89.

Hogge, J. H., and S. T. Friedman. 1967. The scriptural-literalism scale: A preliminary report. *Journal of Psychology* 66: 275–79.

Howe, L. T. 1978. Religious understanding from a Piagetian perspective. *Religious Education* 73: 569–82.

Hunt, R. A. 1972. Mythological-symbolic religious commitment: The LAM scale. *Journal for the Scientific Study of Religion* 11: 42–52.

MacCormac, E. 1983. Religious metaphors: Mediators between biological and cultural evolution that generate transcendent meaning. *Zygon* 18: 45–65.

Munckhoff, M. van den. 1988. Oser's stadiamodel van religieuze ontwikkeling. Een theoretische en empirische verkenning. (Oser's stage-model of religious development. A theoretical and empirical exploration.) Master's thesis, Catholic University of Nijmegen, Nijmegen, Netherlands.

Orlowski, C. 1979. Linguistic dimension of religious measurement. *Journal for the Scientific Study of Religion* 18: 306–11.

Oser, F. K. 1980. Stages of religious judgment. *Toward moral and religious maturity*, ed. C. Brusselmans, 277–315. Morristown, N.J.: Silver Burdett.

Oser, F. K., and P. Gmünder. 1984. *Der Mensch. Stufen seiner religioösen Entwicklung. Ein strukturgenetischer Ansatz.* (Man. Stages of his religious development. A structural-developmental approach.) Zurich: Benzinger Verlag.

Oser, F. K., and K. H. Reich. 1987. The challenge of competing explanations. The development of thinking in terms of complementarity of theories. *Human Development* 30: 178–86.

Poythress, N. G. 1975. Literal, antiliteral, and mythological religious orientations. *Journal for the Scientific Study of Religion* 14: 271–84.

Reich, K. H. 1987. Religiöse und naturrwissenschaftliche Weltbilder: Entwicklung einer komplementären Betrachtungswiese in der Adoleszenz. (Religious and scientific world-views: Development of a complementary perspective among adolescents.) *Unterrichtswissenschaft* 5: 332–43.

Tillich, P. 1964. The nature of religious language. In *Theology of culture,* ed. R. C. Kimball, 53–67 New York: Oxford Univ. Press.

Vergote, A. 1984. *Religie, geloof en ongeloof. Psychologische studie.* (Religion, belief, and unbelief. A psychological study.) Antwerp: De Nederlandse Boekhandel.

What Is Psychology of Religion About? Some Considerations Concerning Its Subject Matter

Introduction

The question, What are the specimens of human behavior that the psychologist of religion is studying? is not too difficult to answer in a cultural context where the cognitive frame and behavioral patterns of an established homogeneous religious tradition are taken for granted. That was the situation when at the end of the 19th century and the first decades of the 20th, the psychology of religion was founded in Germany and the United States. Because of the dominant position of Christianity in the Western world, the psychology of religion has become mainly the psychology of Christian religion; theoretical insights, typological schemes, and measurement instruments have mainly been constructed on the basis of research among white Western Christians or subjects who grew up in a culture that had deeply been influenced by Western Christianity. Meanwhile the cultural context has changed; in a radical process of sociocultural transformations, the dominance of a Christian symbolic universe has come to an end. The number of people who in today's post-Christian era are still acquainted with and making use of Christianity's belief system, prestructured behavioral patterns, buildings, and functionaries in ordering their lives, has radically decreased. This is attended with two new phenomena: the settling down of originally non-Western religions (e.g., Islam) and unchurching on a massive scale (at least in Europe, where for an ever-increasing majority religion is something of the past).

Both phenomena should have consequences for research as well as for the writing of textbooks in the psychology of religion. The fact that I as a psychologist of religion know hardly anything about Islamic religiosity, when the number of Muslims in my country amounts to more than 2% of the population, fills me with shame. I have nothing to offer those of my students who want to investigate the religious behavior of

Muslims. We are confronted with a complete lack of literature. Neither can I tell them whether the theoretical models in their textbooks are valid for the religious behavior of subjects who profess a belief other than Christianity or Judaism.[1]

Some of the consequences, which the latter of the above-mentioned social changes should have for our discipline, will be elaborated here. First, some empirical data will be cited to argue that, if the field of vision in our discipline will remain to be confined to religion in a substantial sense, the insights that we infer from research will decrease in relevancy as they are not valid with respect to a majority of people. Second, I will address new questions with which mental health workers, psychotherapists, and medical psychologists now confront us more and more and which compel us to widen the scope of the psychology of religion and extend the domain of research to all kinds of human behavior that have to do with a search for ultimate meaning. Finally, I will anticipate some objections that might be raised to my arguments.

Threat of Irrelevancy

In several European countries the role of organized religion in the public and private domain has become marginal during the last decades.[2] With the decrease of church membership, the plausibility structure of the traditional religious worldview has disappeared. The effect of this sociocultural change can be observed in census and national survey data on religious beliefs and attitudes. For centuries the Netherlands has been a bastion of Christian faith. According to the last census (1970), 76.4% of the Dutch population belonged to one of the Christian denominations. The group of unchurched has steadily grown, however, from 17% in 1947 to 41% in 1979. The increase of this group came chiefly from the Dutch Reformed and Roman Catholic churches. Yet more striking than these disaffiliation figures is the fading away of religious worldview. In 1979, 57% of the Dutch population agreed with the statement "There is a God who wants to be a God for all of us," while 24% were uncertain or had never thought about it and 19% disagreed. The statement "Life is meaningful because of God," however,

1. The psychology of religion department in my university has started in cooperation with Islamologists some projects to investigate religious change among second-generation Islamic immigrants who are growing up in a non-Islamic cultural context as well as whether religion, compared with other factors, plays a role with respect to their subjective well-being.

2. According to recently published statistics of the Vatican, in 2000 only 21.4% of all Christians (Roman Catholic and Protestant) will live in Europe while in 1900 49.9% of them were European.

was agreed upon by not more than 26% while 50% of the population didn't agree and 24% were uncertain.

When contacts with a religious community are lacking, opportunities also are missing for reinforcement of the religious worldview that people have built up earlier in their lives. This means a decreasing chance that such a worldview will be transferred to the younger generation. This is what we observe again and again among high school and college students: the so-called first- or second-generation unchurched, the offspring of a generation who has left the church. For them the textbooks of the psychology of religion are describing the beliefs and rituals of their grandparents, religious phenomena they have never met in the environment in which they grew up. For them such a psychology of religion is a fossil from the past with no relevance at all for the present day nor the clarification of the existential meaning problems with which they or the patients, who later on will consult with them, are confronted.

The Subject of the Psychology of Religion in a Pluralistic Society

The problem that I want to discuss here concerns the definition of the subject of our discipline and the delimitation of its field of investigation. Religious behavior is generally considered the subject of our discipline, but, as we know, psychologists of religion don't agree upon the definition of religious behavior. Nobody would contend that institutional or organized religion should be the criterion; in fact, we mostly select our issues from those in the behavioral field that in the cultural context are generally categorized as religious. It can be demonstrated by the tables of content in our textbooks. That is not objectionable as long as it does not lead us to disregard types of human behavior that at first sight don't belong to this domain, but from a psychological perspective are of the same class. Especially in our pluralistic society the subject of the psychology of religion should not be confined to religious behavior in the classical sense.

For two reasons a broadening of the domain must be considered. First, there is a risk that, in case the psychology of religion should confine itself to religious behavior in the substantive sense, the empirical base of its theories will be too small. The second reason is that the subject of the psychology of religion should not be defined in terms derived from the religious field but in terms of general psychological structures and functions underlying religious behavior. As long as within a cultural context organized religion determines the ideas and behavioral patterns through which these structures and functions manifest themselves, it is evident that the religious institutions of the culture will mark the field of study of our branch. However, while functioning within psychological structures people switch to other behavioral forms and content that are not generally recognized as religious, it would stretch the identity of the psychology of religion if it should withdraw.

Let me try to be more specific. It is obvious that in traditional societies a significant function of the religious institution has always been to comfort people who are disoriented and overwhelmed with feelings of meaninglessness after confrontation with a catastrophic event, which Eliade (1952) and Turner (1968) have designated as *limit* or *liminal situations*. Through its rituals and myths religion has helped them account for the situation, to regain cognitive control and self-esteem, and to restore the outlook on a meaningful universe as well as psychological equilibrium. In every religion *salvation,* referring to being liberated from basically negative conditions such as evil, pain, finitude, and death, has been a key concept. In most religions salvation also implies the elevation of the whole world to a higher plane by restoring the original condition as described in the creation myth: a life in harmony with God, without suffering and death. When people drift away from the religious tradition, they no longer take refuge in its ritual and images when they are helpless. It is hard to believe, however, that they will no longer seek salvation.

Suffering from a life crisis is *always* related to the breakdown of a person's experience of being incorporated in a meaningful universe, as we can learn from the characteristics of the depressive disorder. Severe illness, events that destroy plans for the future, death, guilt feelings, all weaken cognitive-emotional security that is fundamental for personal identity. They remind us of the precariousness of our existence and let us know that we are unable to manage life ourselves. When confronted with the contingent character of existence, people react differently: some with feelings of loneliness, some with anxiety and depression, some with clinging to an ideology. Psychologically it is a coping problem, with a cosmic dimension, whether people turn to religion to find an answer or not. If people, for whatever reason, when they have to cope with situations that activate the basic search for ultimate meaning, don't make use of behavioral models that are presented by organized religion or that refer to a religious symbolic universe, then the psychologist of religion should study the behavior (ideas, attitudes, values, and practices) which substitute for manifest religion. Psychologically it does not make a difference whether people do or do not achieve salvation in religious-mythical images or pursue it through a religious ritual. As psychologists we primarily study mechanisms underlying concrete religious behavior. Relevant from a psychological perspective is the seeking of salvation as a cognitive-emotional dynamic of the human psyche and its expression in ideas and behavior, also when a religious-mythical worldview is abandoned.

It is my opinion that this is the behavioral domain that belongs to the psychology of religion as a psychological discipline: the need to experience oneself as a part of a meaningful universe. Traditionally, the symbols of religion have been the intermediary for such an experience, but a secular worldview can also fulfill this function. According to Erikson (1968) this basic experience should be acquired in early childhood and articulated in beliefs during adolescence as a condition for identity formation. Sense of personal identity and worldview are interrelated. Sometimes people need psychiatric help because of a crisis situation. A traumatic experience, which they could not assimilate in their worldview (to speak in Piagetian terms), has caused a breakdown of identity feelings. Coping always implies that the patient has to restructure his identity and to accommodate his worldview, which not only involves a cognitive but also a radical cognitive-emotional process.

In recent years social psychologists have become increasingly interested in these coping processes. One of the subjects of research is how victims of severe accidents and patients suffering from a life-threatening disease answer the question "Why me?" which is supposed to be life's most difficult question (Bulman and Wortman 1977; Wong and Weiner 1981; Gotay 1985). I wonder why psychology of religion textbooks and journals have not paid attention to this subject so far. In my opinion it is an outstanding example of the behavioral domain this discipline intends to study. "Why me?" is a question people ask themselves when they feel confronted with finitude. Fundamentally it is a religious question. It is the expression of a complex of cognitive needs and emotional conflicts that in the homogeneous culture of the past generally induced an appeal to religious faith and rituals in order to find salvation. Nowadays many people in these circumstances use alternative routes to salvation. Success in giving meaning to the experience of finitude without suppressing it is not the exclusive privilege of people who believe in God. It cannot be that the psychologist of religion is only interested in this behavioral situation when one specific route is chosen.

New Questions Put on Our Desk

In the foregoing paragraph I recommended, on reasons of principle, an extension of the field of study for psychologists of religion. Moreover, some facts should be mentioned that—at least in Holland—have given me cause to reconsider what at the present should be central topics for research in the psychology of religion as well as in university courses for students in this field. In the last few years a steadily growing number of clinical psychologists and other professionals working in mental health care centers are becoming aware that sometimes clients who ask for therapeutic guidance in order to be able to solve a manifest behavioral problem and to get over a psychological crisis need first of all treatment of a more fundamental problem that has to do with a feeling of existential meaninglessness and a loss of religious or other ideological orientation. The fact that mental health workers are more and more confronted with this type of failure may be a correlate of the unchurching process and one of the effects of what Allan Eister has called the severe disruption of the "orientational institutions" in society, among them organized religion. The term applies to institutions which are specifically concerned with supplying the society with its symbols and with various kinds of norms upon which all orientations depend. When, for whatever reason, such institutions don't successfully perform their function, a general sense of instability and dislocation will follow. Not everybody is equipped to cope with this problem alone and to withstand existential anxiety. Obviously this disability will sometimes interfere with the treatment of manifest symptoms of clients consulting a psychotherapist. Many psychotherapists, however, are afraid to face this dimension of their client's problem because they don't feel themselves to be capable of guiding them on this basic level. They help their clients obtain insight in their reaction patterns and attain adjustment. Questions, whether explicit or implicit, into the meaning of events and situations will remain unanswered, however. It may be considered one of the tasks of the psychologist of religion to make psychotherapists conscious of this general orientation crisis and its implication for the individual and to explain why a basic notion of existential meaning and of cosmic order is necessary for a human being in order to be able to maintain a feeling of basic trust.

In Holland cooperation is growing between clinical psychologists and psychologists of religion with respect to this task. An increasing number of practitioners in the mental health field are interested in participating in this discussion. Several fruits can be noticed already. Some training institutes for mental health workers have appointed a staff member who is expert on this borderland between worldview, meaning giving, and psychotherapy. My university undergraduate courses in clinical psychology of religion[3] have been developed for psychology stu-

3. The objective of clinical psychology of religion is the study of religious behavior from the perspective of the clinical psychological practice. It studies religion or its substitutes either as a potential determinant of behavior disorders or as the channel through which these come out or as a source for meaning and orientation. When people are disoriented or disintegrated because of severe illness or another kind of trauma, recovery of psychological well-being requires that existence is experienced as fundamentally meaningful. Clinical psychology of religion is that part of the psychology of religion that is especially focused on the interaction between ideology and mental health.

dents who later on want to work as a clinical psychologist and psychotherapist in a general hospital or mental health clinic or counseling center. The curriculum aims at preparing students to become psychologists who understand the role of meaning giving and of worldview with respect to identity and psychological well-being. In this curriculum attention is paid not only to the psychological function of belief systems, but also of rituals, symbols, and myths, the latter being tools activating imagination.

Traditionally myths and rituals have been fundamental expressions of orientation and efficacious tools in meaning giving. People who are not socialized in a religious tradition, however, no longer have these tools at their disposal. While in traditional cultures for every major life crisis there were "rites of passage" that helped the individual become reoriented in a new situation, in modern society everybody is left to himself or herself. The consequence is that many people have nothing to hang on to when they see life radically changed by a severe traffic accident or by the dying of a loved one. Some psychotherapists are rediscovering the value of old religious myths as a device for cognitive restructuring and meaning giving. Some even borrow elements from old religious rites to help clients who are suffering from a stagnating mourning process work up repressed emotions and share them (van der Hart 1984). Here myths and rituals are not mere arbitrary instruments matching the objective of behavior therapy; they are used deliberately to elicit a conversion process in which the client radically changes his self-image, worldview and value orientation. To teach students the psychological function of myths and rituals and to design quasi-experimental research in order to investigate their usefulness in psychotherapy, guidance of mourners, funerals, and so on are new tasks for psychologists of religion. Psychology of religion that is part of a facility where students are trained to become psychologists, has to contribute to those educational aims. The scientific analysis of the psychological relevance of systems of beliefs and rituals in which a symbolic universe is represented will not only give students a deeper understanding of the complicated motivational structure underlying religious behavior, but also a cognitive frame of reference enabling them to observe adequate and inadequate substitutes for religion.

Objections

Although there is general agreement among scholars concerning the impossibility of adequately defining the concept of religiosity, classifying specific psychological phenomena as religious behavior is not problematical nonetheless. Some commitment to a supernatural divine being, however little it may be, has always been the decisive criterion.

My argument to broaden the class of human behavior to be studied by the psychology of religion might raise the objection that it leads to a conceptual dilution of religion. Especially, my referring to the "Why me?" question could be interpreted as originating from two false assumptions: first, that every human being is fundamentally religious and second, that religion is nothing but a worldview. Neither of these views is endorsed by me. From a theological perspective every human being might be counted as religious. Psychologically however, this is obviously not true and not practical. My argument to consider coping behavior at an existential level as a feasible subject of the psychology of religion proceeds from the general belief that, as Pruyser (1971, 80) has written, "Religion is, psychologically, born from situations in which someone cries 'Help!'" Not less than in former days the confrontation with limits and with finitude belongs to human existence. This domain of human experience preeminently is the psychological basis of religious behavior. When people nowadays, in coping with these fundamental experiences, don't use the (ideational and ritual) symbols of religion (e.g., because they have not acquired them in a socialization process), this sociocultural circumstance should not mean that the psychologist of religion is no longer interested. If coping with limit experiences does not result in manifest religious behavior, its substitutes are not less relevant for the psychology of religion as they make clear whether and how the subject symbolizes longing to transcend the limits.

The thesis that the scope of the psychology of religion should not be restricted to religious behavior in the narrow sense but should include all human behavior that has to do with a search for ultimate meaning could be misunderstood to mean that religion is nothing but a meaning system or worldview. Vergote (Vergote and van der Lans 1986), in a plenary debate with me, has rejected this designation: "Admittedly there is a dimension of 'world-view' in all religions, for they present a conception of the place of human being in this world and they set forward some ideas of the relation between the natural world and that which in some sense is a supernatural beyond the world." But he emphasized that religions are much more than that: "They involve references to dynamic divine or, in any case, not natural and not human, somehow personal agencies who influence in some way the course of the world and of humanity. . . . In the characterization of religion as a world-view there is a hidden theory of religion: the idea that religion has its origin in the speculative mind which asks questions about the world as totality." This approach disregards the true nature of religion, according to Vergote (1986, 67). In this respect I agree with him. The objective of my argument, however, is to distinguish between the definition of religion and the definition of the subject matter of the psychology of religion. It is not my intention to reopen the discussion about the definition of religion, but about the psychological relevancy of our discipline. As psychologists we should not only be interested in the psychological aspects of religious behavior, but also in the implicit religious or quasi-religious aspects of general psychological behavior. What strikes me in psychological studies of the reactions to contingencies that radically change one's life is that cognitive-emotional processes similar to those underlying classical religious behavior, such as conversion and praying, are activated. The psychology of religion could contribute to general psychology (and improve its own theoretical weakness as well) by analyzing, on the basis of empirical research, this hardly explored domain of human behavior, by distinguishing its elements of structure and of content, and by mapping its processes in a theoretical model.

References

Bulman, R., and C. Wortman. 1977. Attributions of blame and coping in the "real" world: Severe accident victims react to their lot. *Journal of Personality and Social Psychology* 35: 351–63.

Eister, A. 1974. Culture crises and new religious movements: A paradigmatic statement of a theory of cults. In *Religious movements in contemporary America*, ed. I. Zaretsky and M. Leone, 612–27. Princeton, N.J.: Princeton Univ. Press.

Eliade, M. 1952. *Images et symboles. Essais sur le symbolisme magico-religieux.* Paris: Gallimard.

Erikson, E. H. 1968. *Identity, youth, and crisis.* New York: Norton.

Gotay, C. C. 1985. Why me? Attributions and adjustments by cancer patients and their mates at two stages in the disease process. *Social Science and Medicine* 20, no. 8: 825–31.

Pruyser, P. W. 1971. A psychological view of religion in the 1970s. *Bulletin of the Menninger Clinic* 35: 77–97.

Turner, V. 1968. Myth and symbol. In *International encyclopedia of the social sciences*, ed. D. Shils, 576–82. New York: Macmillan.

van der Hart, O. 1984. *Rituals in psychotherapy: Transition and continuity.* New York: Irvington.

van der Lans, J. 1982. Meditation: A comparative and theoretical analysis. *Annual Review of the Social Sciences of Religion* 6: 133–52.

———. 1987. The value of Sundén's role-theory demonstrated and tested with respect to religious experience in meditation. *Journal for the Scientific Study of Religion* 26: 401–12.

Vergote, A., and J. M. van der Lans. 1986. Two opposed viewpoints concerning the object of the psychology of religion. Introductory statements to the plenary debate. In *Proceedings of the third symposium on the psychology of reli-*

gion in Europe: Current issues in the psychology of religion. Ed. J. van Belzen and J. van der Lans, 67–81. Amsterdam: Rodopi.

Wong, P., and B. Weiner. 1981. When people ask "why" questions and the heuristics of attributional search. *Journal of Personality and Social Psychology* 40: 650–63.

12

C. Daniel Batson

C Daniel Batson is professor of psychology at the University of Kansas, where he has taught since 1972. He has also been a visiting professor at the University of Texas. Batson received his bachelor's degree from the University of Tennessee and his bachelor of divinity and doctoral degrees in religious education from Princeton Theological Seminary. He also obtained a doctorate in social psychology from Princeton University. Batson is a fellow of the American Psychological Association and a council member of the Society for the Scientific Study of Religion.

When Batson was at Princeton University, he worked with John Darley in the classic study "From Jerusalem to Jericho: A Study of Situational and Dispositional Variables in Helping Behavior." The study sparked in Batson an enduring interest in altruism. Seminarians at Princeton were asked to report to a certain office to participate in some research. After they arrived, they were told to go to another office to complete the study. Some were instructed to hurry; some were not. Before leaving, some read the parable of the good Samaritan; some did not. All students completed scales designed to measure their orientation to religion. On their way to the other office the seminarians had to pass through an alley in which a confederate played the role of an incapacitated individual, coughing, groaning, and sitting with his head slumped down. The dependent measure was defined as "who would stop and help." The researchers found that those who had not been told to hurry were more inclined to stop, while having or having not read the parable of the good Samaritan had no influence on the tendency to help. An intriguing personal account of the practical dilemmas encountered in conducting that research is recounted in the volume *The Research Experience* (Itasca, Ill.: Peacock, 1976), which was edited by M. P. Golden.

323

In the study with Darley, Batson conceived a new model for understanding orientations to religion. In addition to the intrinsic and extrinsic orientations made important by the work of Gordon Allport, he proposed a *quest* dimension. It is understood as an orientation to religion that goes beyond both being religious for fellowship or the sake of social contact (extrinsic religion) and being religious for inner peace or personal devotion (intrinsic religion). Quest is an orientation to religion that allows for doubt and continues to seek without having to have firm answers. It is an open, yet serious, search for the Ultimate. Batson feels that quest, which Allport implicitly included in his model, has been a neglected concept.

With W. L. Ventis, Batson coauthored *The Religious Experience: A Social-Psychological Perspective* (New York: Oxford Univ. Press, 1982), a volume noteworthy for its systematic review of all studies that have dealt with religion and mental health. No other publication has organized these studies with the same thoroughness, and the book is destined to be one of the standard texts in the psychology of religion for many years to come.

Batson's essay "An Agenda Item for Psychology of Religion: Getting Respect" begins by distinguishing between psychology by religion, religion by psychology, and psychology of religion, the latter being his main interest. He considers the psychology of religion to be in need of greater respect, which can be obtained by better theories, better research methods, and better scientific values. Though the call for better theories is not new, Batson adds his own voice by suggesting that good theory provides conceptual structure that leads to understanding, is able to be tested, and helps us answer important questions about religion. For Batson, better research methods means a departure from paper-and-pencil approaches and a greater use of behavioral indices. He maintains that the reliance of the psychology of religion on self-report is one of its major weaknesses. Finally, it is important that the psychology of religion adopt the values inherent in the scientific enterprise itself. While science values understanding more than demonstration, Batson feels that much study in the psychology of religion is undertaken to demonstrate the positive value of religion rather than to understand whether and how religion operates in life.

In the article "Religious Orientation and Helping Behavior," Batson and Gray report a study that investigated issues highlighted by the well known, earlier study known as the good Samaritan experiment. The researchers found that students who evidenced intrinsic orientations to religion were inclined to offer help to another person both when the person did and did not want it. However, students who evidenced quest orientations, those still searching for religious answers to life, offered help only when it was requested. Such findings led the authors to conclude that intrinsically oriented persons may be functioning more out of their own need to help than out of the expressed needs of others.

An Agenda Item for Psychology of Religion: Getting Respect

There are at least three distinct disciplines that lie on the interface between psychology and religion, and each is at times called psychology of religion. First, there is the practice of therapeutic psychology by religious professionals—often labeled pastoral theology or pastoral psychology. One might call this discipline *psychology by religion*. Second, there is the work of psychological theorists, especially those adopting a psychoanalytic perspective, who make statements about what is or ought to be the essence of human nature. This discipline might be called *religion (or theology) by psychology*. Third, there is the scientific study of individuals' religious beliefs and behavior, including the relationship of individual religion to other aspects of psychosocial makeup. This is the discipline I have in mind when I use the term *psychology of religion*. Doubtless [others . . .] will speak to the current state of the other two psychologies of religion.

When I reflect on the current state of the scientific psychology of religion, I have mixed feelings. I am pleased with the vitality of the discipline; lots of people are doing research in psychology of religion. But I am also troubled by what I see. At the risk of appearing overly negative, I shall restrict my comments here to what troubles me.

I think I can best explain my concerns by referring to several conversations I have had in recent months with other psychologists interested in the scientific study of religion. Remembering these conversations brings a rather odd image to mind. It is the image of a personification of the discipline of psychology of religion looking out of a television screen with sad and sloping eyebrows, saying in the words of Rodney Dangerfield, "I don't get no respect."

For over a decade, we have heard this refrain from psychologists of religion. Essays have appeared on the lack of attention given to religion in psychological texts and in major psychological journals. Informally,

From the *Journal of Psychology and Christianity* 5, no. 2 (1986): 6–11; reprinted by permission of the publisher and the author. Copyright 1986 by the Christian Association for Psychological Studies.

one hears rueful comments about lack of collegial and institutional encouragement for psychologists interested in doing research on religion. I have no reason to doubt these essays and comments. Just as the character created by Rodney Dangerfield is right in his complaint, there is probably truth in psychology of religion's complaint that it gets no—or little—respect.

But the spectre of this Dangerfieldian character prompts another observation. The character Rodney Dangerfield portrays is tragically amusing because not only does he not get respect, he does not deserve any. I fear the same is true for the psychology of religion; our discipline does not get respect, at least in part, because it does not deserve it.

Having suggested this less than flattering possibility, let me hasten to add that I identify myself as a psychologist of religion. And many of the shortcomings that limit the respect the discipline receives are as true of my work as of the work of others. Moreover, let me make a sharp distinction between the subject matter of the psychology of religion and the discipline itself. I think that the subject matter—the role of religion in individuals' lives—clearly deserves respect. It is not the subject matter but the way we are pursuing the scientific study of it that is questionable.

If our discipline is to get the respect we desire, then I think we need to make significant improvements in at least three general areas—theoretical analysis, research methods, and scientific values.

We Need Better Theories

Ever since 1969 when James Dittes published his chapter on psychology of religion in the *Handbook of Social Psychology*, and perhaps even before, there has been frequent talk about the lack of solid theory in psychology of religion. At the time Dittes wrote, and for most of the decade of the 1970s, the concern was that we were amassing large mounds of empirical observations without theoretical frameworks to render them useful. It seemed as if we had set out to build a great mansion, but rather than consulting an architect and developing a plan, we had simply called the lumberyard and stone quarry and had truckloads of materials delivered to the site. As the piles of lumber and stone became higher and higher, it became obvious that the mansion was not getting built. A plan was needed to show how the empirical pieces fit together. We heard more and more talk about the need for theory.

In the last five years, several explicit attempts have been made to apply one or another contemporary psychological theory to religion. These attempts are all to the good, but I do not believe our troubles are over. Instead, these attempts underscore that fact that it is not enough to talk about theory; it is not even enough to have theories. We need *good* theories.

I do not presume to know what makes a theory good. But I do think I can state some very general attributes common to good scientific theories:

1. The theory should provide a conceptual structure that renders the phenomenon in question more understandable than before. Simply to describe the phenomenon is not enough; a good theory helps explain it.
2. The theory should be testable—capable of being shown wrong if it is wrong. If a theory is to be scientifically useful, it should be stated with sufficient precision that one can specify empirical observations that would contradict the theory.
3. The theory should help us answer one or more important questions about the phenomenon. It should get us close to the heart of the matter, not just explain superficial aspects. To return to the construction metaphor, a good theory is "load bearing," not just a plan for some aspect of the facade.

When one applies even these very basic attributes of good scientific theories to recent attempts to introduce theory into psychology of religion, most of our attempts seem to fall woefully short of the mark. Too often, our attempts do not appear to be guided by a desire to develop empirically testable explanatory theories to answer important questions about religion. Instead, our attempts seem to be guided by our conviction that we should have theory. Desperate for a plan, we grab the top one on the architect's desk—some currently popular theory from some other area of psychology—and begin to order our boards and stone as it specifies. Working in this way, we can indeed begin to make something of our empirical observations. But such a structure is not likely to have the third attribute mentioned above; it is not likely to address really important questions about individual religion.

My intent is not to criticize the practice of borrowing theories from other areas of psychology per se. It seems both natural and appropriate that we psychologists of religion would look to existing psychological theories when attempting to introduce more theoretical sophistication into our discipline. But we must be sure that whatever theoretical analysis we employ illumines some important aspect of religious thought and behavior. There is no virtue in theory for theory's sake.

Moreover, I hope that in the future we will not only borrow theories from other areas of psychology, but also make serious attempts to develop indigenous theories. In some cases it may be possible to find an already-existing plan suited to our particular building site and needs, but in other cases it may be useful—even necessary—to develop a new plan. Whatever the source, I hope our theories will become more powerful, testable, and useful. If our discipline is to deserve respect, then we need to have more to say that is worth listening to.

We Need Better Research Methods

Closely linked to the development of better theories is the development of better empirical methods for testing these theories. In research methods, psychology of religion continues to be about 30 years behind other areas of psychology. This is not to say that there is not considerable empirical sophistication in psychology of religion; nor is it to say that there have not been important advances. But the sophistication and advances have been primarily in the area of measurement. Our research designs are often simplistic to the point of being simpleminded. By far the most popular research design in the psychology of religion is still the single-session correlational design. We measure religion—or some aspects of religion—and we measure some other psychological or social variables; then we correlate the measures. I have commented elsewhere (Batson 1977; Batson and Ventis 1982) on the weakness of correlational designs of this kind when trying to test explanatory theories and shall not repeat those comments here. I shall only observe that experimental and quasi-experimental designs, which are usually far superior to correlational designs in explanatory power, remain all too rare in psychology of religion.

There is, however, a specific problem with the way correlational designs are used in psychology of religion, one that requires further comment. The most frequently used technique for measurement in correlational studies in psychology of religion is the self-report questionnaire. Using a Likert-type scale, or some similar format, research participants are asked to indicate their agreement or disagreement with a series of statements. These may be statements about beliefs, values, attitudes, or behavior.

The problem with this type of instrument is that it fails to make a distinction between (1) what the respondent *says* he or she believes, values, and does; (2) what the respondent honestly *believes* that he or she believes, values, and does; and (3) what the respondent *actually* believes, values, and does. In some cases, the difference between these three levels of response is minor. For example, in the absence of any strong situational pressure to the contrary, we may assume that questionnaire responses about interest in religion or belief in an afterlife are reasonably accurate reflections of what the respondents actually feel or believe at the time.

But in other cases, there may be a tremendous difference. If, for example, one is interested in trying to assess the antisocial and prosocial behavior associated with various ways of being religious, then it is not enough to ask people to indicate their agreement or disagreement with questionnaire items such as, "I find racial prejudice and discrimination abhorrent," or, "It is extremely important to me to help others less fortunate than myself." There may be wide discrepancies between what people say is true of themselves on such items, what they actually believe is true, and how they behave. All major religions make rather clear prescriptions about the right answers to such questions. So there is reason to expect a positive correlation between devotion to religious teachings and more positive responses to these questions. But what does this relationship mean? It may mean nothing more than that the person knows what his or her religion teaches about these activities and can respond accordingly, regardless of whether these teachings have had any effect on the person's private attitudes or, more importantly, on the person's behavior.

It is for this reason that I strongly believe the psychology of religion needs to reexamine its use of self-report questionnaires when measuring value-laden psychological and social correlates of religion. We need to use methods that allow us clearly to distinguish between the way people present themselves, the way they honestly believe themselves to be, and the way they actually are. Specifically, if we want to know how individuals who are more or less religious in some way actually behave in value-laden areas, then I think we must take behavioral measures. We must look and see how these individuals do behave.

It is, I suspect, far from accidental that the research to date using behavioral measures to assess antisocial and prosocial behavior presents a picture of the relationship between these activities and various ways of being religious that is dramatically different from the picture presented by research using self-report questionnaires to assess antisocial and prosocial behavior. I do not wish to suggest that self-report questionnaires are of no value, but they certainly cannot be taken at face value.

Let me add that I do not believe it is enough to try to deal with this problem by introducing another questionnaire in order to measure respondents' tendency to present themselves in a socially desirable light. An increasingly popular practice is to administer the Marlowe-Crowne Social Desirability Scale (Crowne and Marlowe 1964), or some similar scale. Then, if the social desirability scale does not correlate significantly with our other measures, we conclude that self-presentation concerns are not operating. Although such a technique may have some value under some circumstances, I believe that it has been greatly overused and overvalued. There are too many different facets of self-presentation and social desirability to assume that a single scale measures them all.

Having made this pitch for a shift from our almost exclusive reliance on self-report questionnaire measures to a more balanced use of behavioral measures as well, I must admit that such a shift presents practical problems. It is usually much harder to take behavioral measures. Little is needed to administer a battery of questionnaires—copies of the questionnaires, a pencil, and a quiet place. But to take behavioral measures one must either find a situation in which the behavior in question occurs naturally with sufficient frequency, or one must create such a situation. Creating situations, whether in the field or in the laboratory, often requires experience and ingenuity. If in the laboratory, it also requires lab space and access to research participants. Although such resources are available in many college and university psychology departments, much research in psychology of religion is not done in psychology departments. Where it is done, such resources are often not available.

Because of the difficulty of doing so, behavioral measures are rarely taken in psychology of religion. The result has been a tendency to ignore the beam of measurement validity to deal instead with the mote of measurement purity. We devote much attention to improving our questionnaire measures—making them more reliable and internally consistent. This can be perfectly worthwhile, but not if we fail to confront the more fundamental problem of whether we are measuring what we want to measure. If the psychology of religion hopes to get respect, then I think it must address the fundamental problem of measurement validity as well, and soon.

We Need Better Scientific Values

This third need is, I believe, actually the most pressing. It is also the most difficult to discuss. A look at some recent developments in the scientific psychology of religion leads me to wonder whether the label *science* is really appropriate. The methods used in the discipline are scientific in that they are empirical, and the writing in the discipline is cast in a scientific mode. But rather than an honest inquiry in an attempt to understand the way religion operates in human life, I get the uncomfortable feeling that the goal for a substantial number of contributors to the discipline is to demonstrate the positive value of religion in human life.

Religion may well have positive value; if it does, then an open and honest inquiry should reveal that value. But an open and honest inquiry will occur only if we seriously entertain the possibility that religion does not have the positive value we might think it does. As Karl Popper

(1959) pointed out long ago, the key to testing a scientific hypothesis is making empirical observations in situations in which the hypothesis can show itself to be *wrong*. William McGuire (1973) nicely summarized Popper's principle of falsification:

> The scientific psychologist can offer something beside and beyond the arm-chair thinkers in that we not only generate delusional systems, but we go further and test our delusional systems against objective data as well as for their subjective plausibility. . . . Even when our theory seems plausible and so ingenious that it deserves to be true, we are conditioned to follow the Cromwellian dictum (better than did the Lord Protector himself) to consider in the bowels of Christ that we may be wrong. (452–53)

We, like Brother Juniper in Thornton Wilder's *The Bridge of San Luis Rey* (1927), need to be willing to entertain the possibility that "the discrepancy between faith and the facts is greater than is generally assumed" (164).

In too much current work in psychology of religion the researchers do not seem interested in finding out if their understanding of the role of religion in human life is wrong. Instead, they seem interested in proving their understanding right. Empirical observations are made only in situations that provide clear promise of producing evidence that supports their hypothesis.

Rather than psychology *of* religion, such work would seem to be more appropriately labeled psychology *for* religion. It involves a psychological apology for one or another particular view of religion. This work should, I believe, be sharply distinguished from a scientific psychology of religion.

But it is important to be clear about where the difference lies between this psychology for religion and a true psychology of religion. The difference is not, I think, in whether one has preconceptions or expectations about the way religion operates in human life. Anyone interested in the topic is likely to have those. Instead, the difference lies in whether one allows his or her preconceptions and expectations to be subjected to the possibility of falsification.

The scientific process of seeking falsification can be distorted in two major ways. First, we can distort the search. Intentionally or unintentionally, we can fail to ask the relevant hard questions, the answers to which might embarrass our present understanding. Failure of this kind is, I believe, amply illustrated in the questionnaire-based work concerning the relationship between different ways of being religious and antisocial or prosocial behavior. So long as we restrict assessment of antisocial and prosocial behavior to self-report questionnaire responses, we can be reasonably confident of finding positive relationships between measures of devout, sincere religious commitment on the one hand and reduced bigotry and increased brotherly love on the other.

There is a second way the scientific process can be distorted. We can distort the result of the search. Even if we ask the potentially embarrassing questions, we can fail to hear the answer given by empirical research. At the most obvious level, we can selectively perceive and report results, only taking seriously those results that support our preconceptions. One hopes this is rarely done; yet it clearly is done—most obviously in articles reviewing research on a given topic. There is another, more subtle way that we can fail to hear the answer being given. We can fail to show enough bias when evaluating research findings. No doubt it sounds heretical to suggest that we need more bias, so let me explain.

If we define bias as preference, then I think we need more bias in favor of quality research. Not all research is created equal. Yet there is a tendency in psychology of religion for reviewers of research simply to count the number of findings that support or contradict a particular hypothesis and to decide truth by majority vote. This one-study-one-vote approach may seem quite objective, but it can be quite misleading. If studies differ in quality, then this difference needs to be reflected in our assessment of what the research is saying. To once again use the example of research relating ways of being religious to antisocial and prosocial behavior, I believe that one or two studies using behavioral measures may be more informative, and so should be weighted more heavily, than several dozen studies using self-report questionnaire measures of antisocial and prosocial activities. Obviously, when quality judgments of this kind are made, there will be disagreements among different interpreters of the research. Yet, I think that such quality judgments must be made if our discipline is to deserve respect. Science is not value-free; rather, it involves adherence to a specific set of values—those directed toward enabling us to find our errors.

Having made these rather critical comments about the current state of psychology of religion, let me emphasize that these are personal views. They are not views that I would expect, or even want, everyone in the discipline to share. Moreover, I would caution against excessive "kvetching" about the right way to do psychology of religion or the right direction for the discipline to go. If it is true that one of the major agenda items for the discipline is to get more respect—both from the rest of the psychological community and from outside psychology—then we need to recognize that respect is a tricky goal to pursue. Most often, one gets respect not by seeking it but by getting on with the job and doing the job better. If and when the psychology of religion can provide those inside and outside psychology with some important, useful, and empirically-tested insights into the role of religion in human life, then we will get respect. Because then we will have done something that very much deserves it.

References

Batson, C. D. 1977. Experimentation in psychology of religion: An impossible dream. *Journal for the Scientific Study of Religion* 16: 413–18.

Batson, C. D., and W. L. Ventis. 1982. *The religious experience: A social-psychological perspective.* New York: Oxford Univ. Press.

Crowne, D., and D. Marlowe. 1964. *The approval motive.* New York: Wiley.

Dittes, J. E. 1969. Psychology of religion. In *The handbook of social psychology,* 2d ed., eds. G. Lindzey and E. Aronson, vol. 5, 602–59. Reading, Mass.: Addison-Wesley.

McGuire, W. J. 1973. The yin and yang of progress in social psychology: Seven koan. *Journal of Personality and Social Psychology* 26: 446–56.

Popper, K. R. 1959. *The logic of scientific discovery.* New York: Basic.

Wilder, T. 1927. *The bridge of San Luis Rey.* New York: Pocket Books.

Religious Orientation and Helping Behavior: Responding to One's Own or to the Victim's Needs?

R eligious teachings such as the parable of the good Samaritan admonish the faithful to help the downtrodden, sick, and troubled. The call is to be sensitive and responsive to the needs of others, not just to one's own needs. And religious individuals claim to have answered this call, for they report being more responsive than the nonreligious to the needs of others. Friedrichs (1960) found that belief in God correlated positively with self-reported charitable action. Moreover, in a Gallup poll (September 1973; see Langford and Langford 1974), 58.7% of the 526 respondents who reported having attended church in the previous 7 days said that they "almost always" took concrete action on behalf of others, whereas only 31.4% of the 862 nonattenders said that they did. Statistically, this difference was overwhelmingly significant ($p < .0001$). But although these self-reports suggest a strong desire on the part of the more devout to show greater concern and compassion, one may still wonder whether this desire is reflected in their behavior. If it is, it should be empirically observable.

The few empirical studies relevant to this question suggest that the more devout do not show greater concern and compassion. In studies correlating religious involvement with prosocial values and behavior, typical results include: the more religious were found to be less rather than more concerned about justice for racial minorities (Allport and Kramer 1946; Rokeach 1970; Rosenblith 1949), to be less rather than more free of authoritarianism and ethnocentrism (Adorno et al. 1950; Gough 1951), and to receive no higher ratings by independent judges on characteristics such as "genuine love-compassion-sympathy for others" and "being a Good Samaritan" (Cline and Richards 1965). These studies suggest that when one moves from self-reports to more valid

Coauthored with Rebecca A. Gray. From the *Journal of Personality and Social Psychology* 40 (1981): 511–20; reprinted by permission of the publisher and the authors.

objective measures, religion does not encourage compassionate responsivity to the needs of others; if anything, religion discourages it.

But such a conclusion may be premature. As has been found in research on the relationship between religion and antisocial behavior (Allen and Spilka 1967; Allport and Ross 1967; Gorsuch and Aleshire 1974), it may not be enough simply to compare the prosocial behavior of people who are more or less religious. It may also be necessary to take account of *how* people are religious (cf. Allport 1959; Rokeach 1960). The parable of the good Samaritan makes a similar point. It suggests that people can be religious in different ways—like the priest and Levite or like the Samaritan. Moreover, it suggests that these different ways can have very different behavioral implications.

We know of only one empirical study that has looked at the relationship between helping behavior and different ways of being religious, the study reported by Darley and Batson (1973). They measured three distinct ways of being religious: as a means, as an end, and as a quest. The means orientation reflected the use of religion as a means to other ends, such as social status or security (cf. Allport's extrinsic orientation; Allport 1959, 1966). The end orientation reflected a more sincere, committed approach to religion as an intrinsically valued end in itself (cf. Allport's intrinsic orientation). The quest orientation reflected an open-ended search in which religion was seen as a processs of questioning, doubting, and reexamining ultimate values and beliefs. (See Batson [1976] and Batson and Ventis [1982] for a discussion of these three ways of being religious, including information on measurement reliability and validity.)

To examine the relationship between religious orientation and helping, Darley and Batson used a research setting designed to simulate the parable of the good Samaritan: Individuals who were on their way from one building to another encountered a somewhat shabbily dressed young man slumped in an alley, coughing and groaning. Male seminary students served as subjects. Darley and Batson found that none of the three ways of being religious predicted which seminarians would stop to offer the young man help. Only a situational variable, the degree to which the seminarians were in a hurry, predicted whether they would stop.

Among those who did stop, however, religious orientation seemed to have an effect on the *type* of help offered. The end orientation correlated positively with a persistent form of help, a form that involved refusing to leave the young man, even though he stated repeatedly that he was all right, that he had already taken medication, that he just needed to rest for a few minutes, and finally, that he wished to be left alone. In contrast, the quest orientation correlated positively with a more tentative form of help, a form that seemed more responsive to the victim's statement of his desire to be left alone.

Given these results, Darley and Batson suggested that the persistent helping of the highly end-oriented subjects may have been a response to their own internal need or desire to be helpful rather than to the needs and desires of the victim. For these subjects, encountering a person in possible need seemed to trigger a preprogrammed response (e.g., taking the victim for coffee, to the infirmary, or praying for his welfare), and this response was little modified by the victim's statements about his needs. In contrast, the tentative helping of the highly quest-oriented seemed less a response to an internal need to be helpful and more a response to the expressed needs of the victim.

But as Darley and Batson were aware, this explanation of their results was entirely post hoc; moreover, another explanation was possible. Effects of religious orientation on helping may have been mediated by the perceived social appropriateness of the victim. The wishes of the shabbily dressed young man may have been ignored by higher scorers on the end orientation because they did not perceive him to be a responsible person and, as a result, did not trust him as a credible source of information about his situation. They may have thought that when he said he did not need help, he was lying, possibly because he was drunk or on drugs. Higher scorers on the quest orientation, on the other hand, may have accepted what he said because they were less sensitive to cues concerning his social appropriateness. Consistent with this alternative explanation, previous research suggests that measures of the end orientation correlate positively with a measure of concern for social appropriateness, whereas measures of the quest orientation do not (cf. Batson, Naifeh, and Pate 1978).

Present Research

The purpose of the present research was to provide new data relevant to the hypotheses that the helping associated with an intrinsic, end orientation to religion is motivated by an internal need to be helpful, whereas the helping associated with a quest orientation is motivated by a desire to relieve the expressed needs of the victim. To test these hypotheses, female subjects were confronted with a lonely young woman who said either that she did or did not want their help. We reasoned that attempts to help her when she said that she did not want help would suggest response to an internal need to be helpful rather than response to the victim's expressed need.

To test the alternative explanation, that the victim's social appropriateness mediates the effect of religious orientation on helping, the young woman's social appropriateness was also varied. In one condition, she confessed that she typically dealt with problems by praying (high social appropriateness); in the other, by drinking (low social appropriateness). It was assumed that these statements would affect her social appropriateness in the eyes of our subjects, all of whom had at least a moderate interest in religion. If the alternative explanation were correct, then when subjects were confronted with a victim of low social appropriateness, scores on the end orientation should be positively correlated with helping both when help was wanted and when it was not. But when confronted with a victim of high social appropriateness, scores on the end orientation should be positively correlated with helping only when it was wanted. Because higher scorers on the quest orientation do not appear to be especially sensitive to social-appropriateness cues, the correlations between the quest orientation and helping should be positive when help was wanted but negative when it was not in each social-appropriateness condition.

Method

Subjects

Subjects were 60 female introductory psychology students at the University of Kansas who reported at least a moderate interest in religion (34 Protestant, 20 Catholic, 6 with no religious affiliation). They participated in the study in partial fulfillment of a course requirement. Fifteen subjects were assigned to each of the 4 conditions of the 2 (victim wanted vs. did not want help) x 2 (high vs. low social appropriateness) factorial design by a randomized block procedure. Because we were interested in examining the effects of different ways of being religious, individuals who reported little or no interest in religion were not included in the sample.

Measurement of Religious Orientation

Subjects first attended a testing session where they, along with several hundred other introductory psychology students, completed a battery of questionaires. Included in the battery were the six scales used by Darley and Batson (1973) to measure religious orientation: Allport and Ross's (1967) Extrinsic and Intrinsic scales and Batson's (1976) External, Internal, Interactional, and Orthodoxy scales. Between 1 and 6 weeks after the testing session, subjects were called and invited to participate with another introductory psychology student (actually fictitious) in a study of impression formation. Everyone who was called agreed.

Procedure

When a subject arrived at the laboratory, she was ushered into a small cubicle, seated, and told that since the other student had already arrived, the study could begin. First, the experimenter (female) inquired whether the subject knew the other student, Janet Armstrong. On learning that she did not (there was no student by this name enrolled in the university at the time), the subject was given a written introduction, which described the purpose and procedure of the impression-formation study. The experimenter then left, ostensibly to give Janet the similar information.

The introduction explained that the two students would not see each other at all during the study, but would carry on a get-acquainted conversation by writing notes. The limited time available for the conversation made it necessary that one of them be designated the communicator and the other the listener. The communicator would first pass a note; then the listener would respond; and so on, through three complete rounds. The communicator would have 5 minutes to write each note; the listener, 1-1/2 minutes to write each response. It was suggested that the communicator might begin the conversation by telling something about her experiences as a college student. The listener was encouraged to respond in whatever way she would in a normal get-acquainted conversation. All notes and responses were to be sent in sealed envelopes, so that the experimenter would not be aware of what was being said. Following the conversation, the communicator would leave, and the listener would stay to report her impression of the communicator on a brief questionnaire.

After the subject had read the introduction, the experimenter returned and asked her to draw a slip to determine whether she would be the communicator or listener. The drawing was rigged so that the subject always drew the listener role, making Janet the communicator.

Assessment of subjects' self-reported helpfulness. While Janet was supposed to be writing her first note, subjects were asked to complete a brief self-perception questionnaire. This questionnaire consisted of 22 9-point trait scales (e.g., intelligent, friendly) on which subjects were to rate themselves. The experimenter explained that "we find this information helpful when we're looking at the impressions that you've formed." The purpose of the questionnaire was actually to assess the subject's self-reported helpfulness, which in turn provided some indication of their internal need to be helpful. Ratings on two traits embedded in the list, helpfulness and concern, were used for this purpose. After the subject had finished the questionnaire, the experimenter brought her the first note from Janet.

Notes from Janet. Each subject received the same three notes from Janet, except for variations necessary to introduce the experimental manipulations. By using written notes, all subjects could be presented with the same need situation. Moreover, because both manipulations were introduced through the notes and the notes that each subject received were selected by someone other than the experimenter, the experimenter was able to remain blind to experimental conditions.

The first note started with Janet's telling a little about herself: her name, that she was from Camden, Ohio, and why she was at a university so far from home. She then observed that college life was very different for her because there were so many strangers. She concluded the note by admitting that she sometimes felt lost and out of place at the university and asked if the listener ever felt that way. This question was designed to structure the subjects' responses.

In her second note, Janet wrote in more detail about her loneliness:

> I guess this being alone is really starting to get to me. Back in Camden I always had plenty of friends. There everybody knew each other. Here, you can just get lost in the crowd. I'm starting to wish I'd moved into a dorm. It might be a good way to meet other students, but I'm renting a room near campus and I have a lease so I can't move out now. My older sister warned me that dorm life is kinda crowded, noisy and unpleasant so I decided to live alone. It seems like a lot of people are from around here and already knew each other when they came and are already formed into their groups. I just don't have a friend or group of friends that I can relax and feel comfortable with. I'll bet there are some days when I don't say more than a couple dozen words to anybody. Really, I guess I've shared more with you in these two notes than with anyone else since I've been here.

Janet's third note included the two experimental manipulations.

Manipulation of the victim's social appropriateness. After restating that being alone was difficult, Janet made a comment about how she typically dealt with problems. In the *high social-appropriateness condition* she confessed, "Maybe I shouldn't mention this, but the way I usually deal with difficult situations is by praying—something I've been doing a lot lately. Like they say, things don't seem so bad when you face them with God." In the *low social-appropriateness condition* she confessed, "Maybe I shouldn't mention this, but the way I usually deal with difficult situations is by drinking—something I've been doing a lot lately. Like they say, things don't seem so bad when you see them through the bottom of a bottle."

Manipulation of desire for help. Janet then went on to observe that it might help her if she knew someone with whom she could get together and talk. In the *help-wanted condition* she said:

> I've often thought, if I could just look forward to getting together with someone—not for anything special, just coffee or a movie or something. That would sure make things better. Sitting here, I've even wondered if you'd be willing to get together a couple of times over the next few weeks.

In the *help-not-wanted condition* the note included the passage quoted above, but it was followed immediately by an expression of desire to work through the problem on her own:

> But then I thought that that would be a cop out. I think what I really need is to get my own head straight about being alone in a new place. If I don't deal with this problem on my own now—I'll just have to face it again later.

Dependent measure. The subjects' responses to Janet's third note provided the dependent measure of helping. After all the data had been collected, each third response was read by two independent judges who were blind to the subjects' experimental conditions. If the response included an explicit attempt to get together with Janet, for example, "As soon as this study is over, why don't you wait for me by the elevator?," it was coded as a helping response. If it did not include any explicit attempt to get together, it was coded not helping. There was perfect agreement (100%) between the judges on the coding of response.

First-impression questionnaire. After the experimenter collected the response to Janet's third note, the subject was asked to rate the communicator on a number of traits. Of particular interest were ratings of Janet's self-awareness, responsibility, well-adjustedness, social acceptability, and maturity. It was assumed that the social-appropriateness manipulation, if successful, would affect these ratings. Specifically, it was expected that when Janet said that she prayed, she would be rated higher on these measures than when she said that she drank.

Subjects were also asked whether the communicator had any problems and, if so, how great the need was (1–9 scale, higher numbers indicating greater need). These questions were included to check that Janet's loneliness was seen to be a problem and that her need was not perceived differently in different experimental conditions. If the experimental manipulations affected perceptions of the severity of Janet's need, a possible confounding variable would have been introduced.

Postexperimental questionnaire. Finally, subjects were given a brief questionnaire assessing how difficult and interesting they found the listener role, the degree to which they became involved in the role, and how seriously they took the task of being the listener. This questionnaire was used to check whether the experimental manipulations caused subjects to react differently to the listener role.

Debriefing. When subjects had completed the post-experimental questionnaire, they were fully debriefed. Subjects seemed readily to understand the necessity for using deception in the study, and none appeared to be upset by it. Following debriefing, subjects were thanked for their assistance and excused.

Results and Discussion

Perception of Janet's Need

On the first-impression questionnaire, subjects were asked whether the communicator had any problems and, if so, how great the need was. With the exception of one person in the high-appropriateness-help-wanted condition, all subjects said that Janet had a problem. Moreover, across all four experimental conditions Janet's need was perceived to be moderately severe, overall $M = 7.41$ on the 1–9 scale, and there were no reliable differences in perceived severity across conditions (all $Fs < 1.50$).

Effectiveness of the Social-Appropriateness Manipulation

On the first-impression questionnaire subjects were also asked to rate the communicator on a variety of traits, using 1–9 scales (e.g., 1 = irresponsible; 9 = responsible). Ratings of the communicator's self-awareness, responsibility, well-adjustedness, social acceptability, and maturity were used as a check on the effectiveness of the social-appropriateness manipulation. As expected, responses to these five items were positively correlated, rs (58) from .27 to .81, all $ps < .05$. (All significant tests are two-tailed.) Therefore, the responses were averaged to form an index of perceived social appropriateness of the communicator, with higher scores indicating greater social appropriateness. Reliability of this index was checked using Cronbach's alpha and found to be satisfactory, $\alpha = .83$. Scores on the index were then subjected to a α 2 (desire for help) x 2 (social appropriateness) analysis of variance.

The analysis revealed only one significant effect, a main effect for the social-appropriateness manipulation, F (1, 56) = 5.68, $p < .05$. As expected, when the communicator said that she dealt with her problems by praying, she was perceived to be more socially appropriate ($M = 5.51$) than when she said she dealt with her problems by drinking ($M = 4.69$). Analyses of the five individual items revealed that, although the ratings on each differed in the expected direction, differences were strongest on ratings of the communicator's responsibility, F (1, 56) = 10.78, $p < .002$, and maturity, F (1, 56) = 5.46, $p < .025$, two traits that could easily affect the credibility of the communicator as a source of information about her needs. Based on these results, we concluded that the manipulation of social appropriateness was effective.

No check was available for the desire-to-help manipulation.

Impact of the Experimental Setting

The postexperimental questionnaire was designed to assess the degree to which subjects became involved in the get-acquainted conversation with Janet. Using 1–9 scales (1 = not at all, 9 = extremely), subjects were asked to rate how difficult and how interesting they found their role as the listener, how involved they became in the role, and how seriously they took the task of being the listener. Responses indicated that subjects found it fairly easy ($M = 2.52$) and interesting ($M = 7.75$) to be the listener, that they became fairly involved in the role ($M = 6.53$), and that they took the task seriously ($M = 7.73$). Analyses of variance revealed no reliable differences across experimental conditions in response to any of these questions, suggesting that the get-acquainted-conversation format had uniform impact.

Effects of the Manipulations on Helping Behavior

The proportion of subjects helping in each experimental condition is presented in table 12.1. Although no differences were predicted across these conditions independent of the effects of religious orientation, a test for possible differences was made. A 2 x 2 analysis of variance was performed, using a normal approximation based on arc sine transformations (cf. Langer and Abelson 1972; Winer 1971, 399–400). This analysis revealed no significant effects, all Fs < 1.75. Apparently, the experimental manipulations by themselves did not significantly influence the proportion of subjects trying to help Janet; the proportion was moderately high in all four conditions.

Table 12.1

**Proportion of Subjects in Each
Condition Who Tried to Help**

Appropriateness of victim	Victim's desire for help	
	Wanted help	Did not want help
High	.73	.67
Low	.60	.47

Note: n = 15 in each condition.

But did religious orientation affect helping, and more importantly for our hypotheses, did it affect helping differently in the different experimental conditions? To answer these questions it was necessary to obtain a measure of the three ways of being religious: as a means, as an end, and as a quest.

Measuring the Three Ways of Being Religious

Correlations among the six religious orientation scales administered at the testing session are presented in table 12.2. The pattern of correlations was quite consistent with patterns found in previous research (cf. Batson 1976). The Intrinsic, External, Internal, and Orthodoxy scales were all positively correlated with one another, whereas the Extrinsic and Interactional scales had very low correlations with each of the other five scales.

Table 12.2
Intercorrelations among Six Religious Orientation Scales

Scale	1	2	3	4	5	6
1. Extrinsic	—	−.27*	.07	−.31*	.02	−.01
2. Intrinsic		—	.45**	.71***	.00	.48**
3. External			—	.61***	−.03	.56***
4. Internal				—	−.01	.55***
5. Interactional					—	−.11
6. Orthodoxy						—

Note: $N = 60$. All ps are two-tailed.
*$p < .05$. **$p < .01$. ***$p < .001$.

Next, as in previous research, scores on the six religious orientation scales were subjected to a three-factor varimax-rotated principal-component analysis. Loadings of each of the six scales on the three factors are presented in table 12.3. The factor structure reflected in table 12.3 was quite similar to the factor structures found in previous research (Batson 1976; Batson, Naifeh, and Pate 1978; Batson and Ventis 1982; Darley and Batson 1973). One factor received a single very high loading from the Extrinsic scale, a second received high loadings from the Intrinsic, External, Internal, and Orthodoxy scales, and the third received a single very high loading from the Interactional scale. Therefore, as in previous research, these three factors were named religion as means, religion as end, and religion as quest.

Individual subjects' scores on the means, end, and quest factors were computed through the use of complete-estimation factor-score coefficients. These factor scores provided the primary measures of the three ways of being religious. Because the three factors were orthogonal, each defined a dimension of religious orientation that was uncorrelated

Table 12.3
Factor Loadings for Six Religious Orientation Scales

Scale	Religious orientation factor		
	Means	End	Quest
Extrinsic	.93[a]	.01	.07
Intrinsic	−.45	.72[a]	.10
External	.26	.81[a]	.02
Internal	−.41	.81[a]	.10
Interactional	.04	−.00	.99[a]
Orthodoxy	.04	.82[a]	−.13

[a]Indicates highest factor loading for scale.

with and independent of the other two. Each subject had a score on each dimension. Moreover, since the factors were uncorrelated, how a subject scored on one factor said nothing about how she scored on the other two. A subject could score high on all three factors, low on all three, high on two and low on one, and so on. No attempt was made to type subjects as having, for example, an end orientation to religion rather than a quest orientation.

Relationship between Religious Orientation and Self-Reported Helpfulness

Having a measure of each of the three ways of being religious, it was possible to turn to the relationship between religious orientation and helping. We first considered the relationship with self-reported helpfulness. As noted earlier, survey data was revealed that frequent church attenders report greater helpfulness and concern for others. Previous research (Gorsuch and McFarland 1972) has also revealed that church attendance is positively correlated with a measure of the intrinsic, end orientation to religion. Putting these two findings together, we expected that scores on the end factor would correlate positively with self-reported helpfulness.

To provide evidence on the relationship of the three religious orientation factors to self-reported helpfulness, subjects had been asked to rate themselves on helpfulness and concern (1–9 scales; 1 = not at all, 9 =

Table 12.4

Point-Biserial Correlation of Religious Orientation Measures with Subjects' Attempts to Help

Religious orientation measure	Victim wanted help	Victim did not want help	z score
Factor			
Means	−.00	−.38**	1.47
End	.24	.27	−.08
Quest	.37**	−.32*	2.69***
Scale			
Extrinsic	−.00	−.43**	1.69*
Intrinsic	.10	.15	−.19
External	.21	.09	.45
Internal	.32*	.39**	−.29
Interactional	.36*	−.30	2.51**
Orthodoxy	.15	.32*	−.68

Note: $n = 30$ for each victim condition. ps are two-tailed.
*$p < .10$. **$p < .05$. ***$p < .01$.

extremely). Consistent with our expectations, the end factor correlated positively with the self-report of both helpfulness, r (58) = .28, $p < .05$, and concern, r (58) = .35, $p < .01$. In contrast, correlations between these traits and the means and quest factors did not differ reliably from zero. To the degree that these self-reports reflected the way subjects thought they *should* be and not just the way they were, the correlations provided evidence that higher scores on the end factor had a greater internal need to be helpful. Admittedly, however, this was an indirect measure of their internal need to be helpful.

Religious Orientation and Helping Behavior

Turning from self-reported helpfulness to behavior, the two hypotheses suggested that the end orientation would correlate positively with attempts to help Janet both when she did and when she did not want help, whereas the quest orientation would correlate positively with attempts to help when she wanted help but negatively when she did not. To test these hypotheses, point-biserial correlations between helping and the measures of the three religious orientations were computed separately for the help-wanted and help-not-wanted conditions. These correlations are presented in table 12.4.[1]

As can be seen from the table, the pattern of correlations for the end and quest factors and their related scales was generally as hypothesized: the end factor showed a weak positive correlation with helping in both the help-wanted, r (28) = .24, *ns*, and help-not-wanted, r (28) = .27, *ns*, conditions—across both conditions, r (58) = .27, $p < .04$—whereas the quest factor showed a positive correlation in the help-wanted condition, r (28) = .37, $p < .05$, and a negative correlation in the help-not-wanted condition, r (28) = –.32, $p < .09$. Similar correlations were found for the scales contributing to these two factors—the Intrinsic, External, Internal, and Orthodoxy scales for the end factor and the Interactional scale for the quest factor.

To assess the significance of the difference in the correlations when Janet did and did not want help, tests for the difference between independent correlations were computed. Consistent with the hypotheses, there was a significant change in the relationship of the quest factor to helping, $z = 2.69$, $p < .01$. Those scoring higher on this factor were more

1. Helping responses were also coded and analyzed employing four levels of helping. The correlation between this scaled measure of helping and the dichotomous measure reported in the text was quite high, $r(58) = .87$, $p < .01$, and the pattern of results was quite similar. Moreover, all effects on the scaled measure seemed to be due to differences in whether subjects tried to help. Therefore, only the dichotomous measure is reported. In addition, correlations for Protestants and Catholics were computed separately. Since the correlations for each group patterned in the same way, and correlations did not differ between groups more than would be expected by chance, religious affiliation was not included as a factor.

likely to help when Janet indicated that she wanted help, but less likely to help when she indicated that she did not. In contrast, those scoring higher on the end factor showed as strong a tendency to help when Janet said that she did not want help as when she said she did, $z = -.08$, ns. As can be seen in table 12.4, similar results were found for the scales contributing to these two factors.

No predictions had been made for the relationship between the means factor and helping. It was, however, interesting to note that although this factor was not related to helping in the condition in which Janet said that she wanted help, it was related negatively in the condition in which she said that she did not. Overall, this pattern seemed quite consistent with Allport's (1966) interpretation of the extrinsic, means orientation as one in which the individual remains focused on self-centered, egocentric needs. Higher scorers on this factor and the related Extrinsic scale were not more likely to expend effort when Janet said she wanted their help, but they were more likely to forgo the effort when she said that she wanted to work through her problem on her own.

Not only did the correlations between helping and measures of the end and quest orientation pattern as predicted, there was no evidence that the patterns were affected by the social appropriateness of the victim, for the social appropriateness manipulation produced no reliable differences in the correlations for any of the nine measures of religious orientation in either desire for help condition (all $zs < 1.0$). Apparently, the failure of the end orientation to correlate more positively with helping when it was wanted than when it was not could not be attributed to higher scorers on this orientation cuing on the social appropriateness of the person in need. Nor was there evidence that the pattern of correlations between the different measures of religious orientation and helping was a function of different perceptions of Janet's need. None of the measures of religious orientation correlated reliably with ratings of the severity of Janet's need in either the help-wanted or the help-not-wanted condition.

Conclusion and Implications

Overall, our results were quite consistent with the hypotheses that the motivation to help associated with an end orientation to religion is primarily a response to an internal need to be helpful, whereas the motivation to help associated with a quest orientation is primarily a response to the expressed needs of the victim. Across all subjects, scores on the end factor showed a weak but statistically significant positive correlation with helping, suggesting that this orientation to religion produced some motivation to help. But the correlation between this factor and helping was just as strong when the victim said that she did not want help as when she said that she did. In contrast, scores on the quest factor were positively correlated with helping when the victim said that she wanted help, but negatively correlated when she said that she did not.

Nor could this pattern be attributed to higher scorers on the end factor doubting the credibility of a socially inappropriate victim. Although ratings on the first-impression questionnaire indicated that subjects perceived the victim to be more socially appropriate in the high-appropriateness condition than in the low-, there was no evidence that learning that she prayed instead of drank affected the correlations between the measures of religious orientation and helping.

It should be pointed out that we did not actually measure the motivation lying behind subject's responses to Janet, and so we do not have conclusive evidence that those scoring higher on the end orientation were responding to an internal need to be helpful. We did, however, find some indirect evidence consistent with this possibility: the positive correlations between scores on the end factor and self-reported helpfulness and concern. To the degree that these self-reports reflected what subjects felt they *should* be and not just what they were, the correlations suggest that higher scorers on the end factor did indeed feel a greater need to be helpful.

Returning to the initial question of whether religion leads to increased responsivity to the needs of others, the present results provided no basis for determining whether being religious as opposed to not being religious leads to increased responsivity, for all of our subjects expressed at least a moderate interest in religion. The present research was designed instead to enable us to determine whether any of three different ways of being religious, as a means, as an end, and as a quest, lead to greater responsivity. For an open-ended, quest orientation to religion, the results suggest an answer of yes. When help was wanted, this orientation correlated with more helping; when help was not wanted, it correlated with less. For an extrinsic, means orientation to religion, the results suggest an answer of no, for when help was wanted, this orientation did not correlate with more helping. For an intrinsic, end orientation, the results also suggest an answer of no, for this orientation correlated only weakly with helping when it was wanted, and it correlated just as strongly with helping when it was not wanted.

Since an intrinsic, end orientation to religion is the orientation most often espoused by those who believe that religion produces prosocial consequences (cf. Allport 1966), we need to consider why this orientation seemed to lead to, at best, only weak motivation to help and, moreover, motivation that reflected little sensitivity to the expressed needs of the victim. Our findings consistently supported the explanation implicit in our first hypothesis, that this orientation is associated more with an internalized need to *appear* helpful than with a desire to respond to the needs of others.

But another possibility exists. Brickman and others (1979) have recently suggested that religious beliefs may affect perceptions of how it is possible for personal needs to be met. They suggest that devout believers, who are likely to score higher on the end orientation (cf. Batson and Ventis 1982), see individuals as powerless to meet their own needs; help must come from outside. If this suggestion is correct, then higher scorers on the end orientation may have ignored Janet's comment that she wished to deal with her loneliness on her own, not because of insensitivity, but because they believed that such an effort at self-help could never succeed. The present research provided no data either to support or contradict this alternative explanation.

Finally, it should be noted that the need situation used in the present research, as well as the need situation used by Darley and Batson (1973), required the subject to respond as an individual. Although individual response to others in need is clearly covered by religious teaching like the parable of the good Samaritan, needs in our society are often dealt with at an institutional rather than individual level. It is conceivable that involvement in institutional religion, which has been found to be closely associated with an intrinsic, end orientation (Gorsuch and McFarland 1972), may lead to an increase in institutional helping even if it does not lead to increased concern for others. In fact, there is some empirical evidence that it does (cf. Nelson and Dynes 1976). Of course, even if we were to learn that the priest and Levite in the parable of the good Samaritan passed by on the other side because they were taking contributions from the temple of Jerusalem to an orphanage down the road, it is not clear that we should excuse their lack of response to the needs of the man who fell among thieves.

References

Adorno, T. W., E. Frenkel-Brunswik, D. J. Levinson, and R. N. Sanford. 1950. *The authoritarian personality.* New York: Harper.

Allen, R. O., and B. Spilka. 1967. Committed and consensual religion: A specification of religion-prejudice relationships. *Journal for the Scientific Study of Religion* 6: 191–206.

Allport, G. W. 1959. Religion and prejudice. *Crane Review* 2: 1–10.

———. 1966. The religious context of prejudice. *Journal for the Scientific Study of Religion* 5: 447–57.

Allport, G. W., and B. M. Kramer. 1946. Some roots of prejudice. *Journal of Psychology* 22: 9–39.

Allport, G. W., and J. M. Ross. 1967. Personal religious orientation and prejudice. *Journal of Personality and Social Psychology* 5: 432–43.

Batson, C. D. 1976. Religion as prosocial: Agent or double agent? *Journal for the Scientific Study of Religion* 15: 29–45.

Batson, C. D., and W. L. Ventis. 1982. *The religious experience: A social-psychological perspective.* New York: Oxford Univ. Press.

Batson, C. D., S. J. Naifeh, and S. Pate. 1978. Social desirability, religious orientation, and racial prejudice. *Journal for the Scientific Study of Religion* 17: 31–41.

Brickman, P., et al. 1979. Helping. University of Michigan, Ann Arbor, Mich. Unpublished manuscript.

Cline, V. B., and J. M. Richards. 1965. A factor-analytic study of religious belief and behavior. *Journal of Personality and Social Psychology* 1: 569–78.

Darley, J. M., and C. D. Batson. 1973. "From Jerusalem to Jericho": A study of situational and dispositional variables in helping behavior. *Journal of Personality and Social Psychology* 27: 100–108.

Friedrichs, R. W. 1960. Alter versus ego: An exploratory assessment of altruism. *American Sociological Review* 25: 496–508.

Gorsuch, R. L., and D. Aleshire. 1974. Christian faith and ethnic prejudice: A review and interpretation of research. *Journal for the Scientific Study of Religion* 13: 281–307.

Gorsuch, R. L., and S. G. McFarland. 1972. Single vs. multiple-item scales for measuring religious values. *Journal for the Scientific Study of Religion* 11: 53–64.

Gough, H. G. 1951. Studies in social intolerance: IV. *Journal of Social Psychology* 33: 263–69.

Langer, E. J., and R. Abelson. 1972. The semantics of asking a favor: How to succeed in getting help without really dying. *Journal of Personality and Social Psychology* 24: 26–32.

Langford, B. J., and C. C. Langford. 1974. Church attendance and self-perceived altruism. *Journal for the Scientific Study of Religion* 13: 221–22.

Nelson, L. D., and R. R. Dynes. 1976. The impact of devotionalism and attendance on ordinary and emergency helping behavior. *Journal for the Scientific Study of Religion* 15: 47–59.

Rokeach, M. 1960. *The open and closed mind: Investigations into the nature of belief systems and personality systems.* New York: Basic.

———. 1970. Faith, hope, bigotry. *Psychology Today* 3: 33–37.

Rosenblith, J. F. 1949. A replication of "Some roots of prejudice." *Journal of Abnormal and Social Psychology* 44: 470–89.

Winer, B. J. 1971. *Statistical principles in experimental design.* 2d ed. New York: McGraw-Hill.

Part 6

The Social Psychology of Religion

13

Laurence Binet Brown

L aurence Binet Brown is professor and past chair in the department of psychology at the University of New South Wales, Sydney, Australia. He formerly taught in Adelaide, Australia, and in Wellington, New Zealand. He received his undergraduate training in his native New Zealand and his doctorate at the University of London. In addition to his interest in the broad field of social psychology Dr. Brown is also involved with clinical issues, especially the treatment of eating disorders. He is probably the best known of Australia's psychologists of religion; he is also a visiting fellow of Wolfson College of Oxford University and co-editor of the *International Journal for the Psychology of Religion.*

Dr. Brown's first book, entitled *Ideology,* established the theme that religious experience always occurs against the backdrop of some cultural tradition. Religious traditions such as Hinduism or Christianity, therefore, function as social ideologies, which become stimuli for social action. It is culturally impossible, according to Brown, for religions to exist without some relationship with the traditions of the society in which they are found. While it may be true that individual responses to these traditions can be in the form of affirmations or rejections, these traditions shape the foundations of thought and action in either direction nevertheless. This emphasis on cultural traditions is the essence of Dr. Brown's later book, *The Psychology of Religious Belief* (London: Academic Press, 1987), in which the importance of religion as ideology is reasserted.

In 1973, Brown edited the first of two major collections of readings in the psychology of religion. *Psychology and Religion* (London: Penguin, 1973) brings together the work of 30 of the best-known psychologists of religion from the time of William James through the 1960s. The essays were grouped under such categories as history, dimensionality and orientations, religion as a social attitude, measurement, developmental studies, experimental studies, and pathological or possibly related states, and a number of the articles have proven to be classical stimuli for current investigations. Brown's other major collection of articles, *Advances in the Psychology of Religion* (Oxford: Pergamon, 1985), brings together the presentations given at an international gathering of scholars who were invited to a conference on the psychology of religion at Wolfson College, Oxford University, in 1982.

In 1988, Brown published an introduction to the field, called *The Psychology of Religion* (London: SPCK). Another collection of essays, this one on religion, personality, and mental health, is to be published by Pergamon.

The essay on "Religious Socialization, Apostasy, and the Impact of Family Background" reports research conducted on Australian university students. The intent was to see if relations between parental and student religions that had previously been found in North America could be replicated. Apostates (those leaving religion) had power relationships with their parents. These findings are interesting because they contradict, to some degree, previous findings. The essay is a good illustration of how empirical, statistical methods can be utilized in answering difficult questions.

In the essay "Towards the Psychology of Religion," Brown is concerned primarily with the importance of methodology. He notes that while much of his research has dealt with religion, he nevertheless considers himself to be a social and general psychologist. For Brown, an important question to ask concerns the ways religious belief is maintained in modern times, when secularism and disbelief are so rampant. His conclusion is that our beliefs and disbeliefs depend on social rapport. A related interest which Brown discusses is psychological objections to and criticisms of religious belief. His discussion of the ways in which religion meets our needs and is politically useful are particularly intriguing in this regard. An especially interesting idea is Brown's comment that sociologists of religion, by their preoccupation with religion and beliefs about it as social variables have cut themselves off from the "tricky" questions that have concerned psychologists. He concludes the article by saying that understanding how people select the religious ideas they will adopt is the prime unsolved problem for psychologists working in this field. In attempting to solve the problem, Brown is looking specifically at the ways belief about prayer and its practice change across the life span of a person and vary from one religious tradition to another.

Religious Socialization, Apostasy, and the Impact of Family Background

S ome recent work in the social scientific study of religion has focused on issues related to religious socialization and "falling from the faith" (e.g., Brinkerhoff and Burke 1980; Caplovitz and Sherrow 1977; Glock and Wuthnow 1979; Hadaway 1980; Hadaway and Roof 1979; Nelson 1981; O'Hara 1980; Perry et al. 1980; Roof and Hoge 1980; Roozen 1980; Welch 1978; Wuthnow and Mellinger 1978). The present research expands the work on this topic by Hunsberger (1980, 1983), who has focused primarily on "apostates," or individuals who report being raised in a religious denomination, but who later change their religious orientation to "none."

As pointed out elsewhere (Hunsberger 1983), although some recent work on apostasy seems to have been stimulated by Caplovitz and Sherrow's (1977) investigation of apostasy among college students, their claim that apostasy represents a form of rebellion against parents and is symptomatic of familial strain and dissociation from parents has not been supported. Similarly, Caplovitz and Sherrow's claim that four particular traits (poor parental relations, symptoms of maladjustment or neurosis, a radical or leftist political orientation, and a commitment to intellectualism) are important predisposing factors for apostasy has failed to be supported. Since their original study, only "poor parental relations" has to date received any empirical support as a predisposing factor for apostasy, although this factor has been found to be only weakly related to it. In addition, Hunsberger (1983) has suggested that "poor parental relations" seems more likely to be a result than a cause of apostasy.

Hunsberger has also found that the reported emphasis placed on religion in one's childhood home is one of the best predictors of later religiosity (particularly of apostate versus nonapostate status). Apparently, apostates come from homes where religion is emphasized less

Coauthored with Bruce Hunsberger. From the *Journal for the Scientific Study of Religion* 23 (1984): 239–51; reprinted by permission of the publisher and the authors. Copyright 1984 by the *Journal for the Scientific Study of Religion*.

overall than do nonapostates, a factor ignored by Caplovitz and Sherrow in their analysis.

At the same time, Hunsberger's analyses have been restricted to a geographically confined sample of Canadian university students, and his measures have been somewhat limited in attempting specifically to test Caplovitz and Sherrow's postulations. Questions might be raised concerning the stability and generality of the factor structure derived with respect to these predictions of apostasy. Moreover, there is a need to investigate directly the importance for apostasy of a wider set of variables related to religious socialization. For example, while there seems to be general agreement that parents, church, school, and peers have an important impact influencing individuals' religious orientations (Argyle and Beit-Hallahmi 1975), apparently few studies have examined self-reports to assess the relative impact of these and other influences on religious development. In addition, while there seems to be general agreement that parents' religious orientations are particularly important factors for young people's religious development (e.g., Hoge and Petrillo 1978; Hunsberger 1980, 1983; Johnson 1973; Putney and Middleton 1961; Strommen 1963), there is less agreement concerning the relative impact of mother and father on the religious orientation of their offspring. Argyle and Beit-Hallahmi concluded that the results show the greater impact of the mother, while other authors (Hoge and Petrillo 1978; O'Doherty 1978) have concluded that fathers play the more critical role in religious development.

The present study was thus an attempt to assess and expand Hunsberger's previous findings related to apostasy and religious development with a sample of Australian university students, and further to investigate religious influences by eliciting self-reports of such influences.

Method

Eight hundred seventy-eight introductory psychology students at the University of New South Wales in Sydney, Australia, volunteered to participate in a questionnaire study as part of the regular tutorial sessions for their introductory psychology course in 1981. They completed a 15-page questionnaire, which included a wide variety of items and measuring instruments related primarily to religious background and orientation. The questionnaire took approximately 1 hour to complete.

Respondents were classified according to their present religious affiliation as defined by the questionnaire item which asked "With which religion do you presently identify yourself or think of yourself as being?" Responses to this item led to the classification of participants as Anglican, Other Protestant (primarily Presbyterian, United Church, Baptist, and unspecified Protestant, and a smaller number of Lutheran

Pentecostal, and Methodist students), Roman Catholic, Greek or Russian Orthodox, Jewish, "Personal Religion," Agnostic, or Atheist. Since 42 respondents did not fall into any of these categories, the present analyses covered a sample of 836.

Participants were defined as apostates if they reported that they had grown up in a religion, but currently reported that they did not affiliate with any formal religion.

Results

Overall, the apostasy rate in the present sample was 36%, considerably higher than the 10–20% rates found among Canadian university students in previous research by Hunsberger. Substantially different rates were noted for students reporting that they grew up in each of the religious groups. For example, the rate for Anglicans was 45%, and for Other Protestants, 43%. However, the rates for Roman Catholics, Orthodox, and Jewish groups were 33%, 31% and 13% respectively. It is to be noted that these figures do not include students who may have switched from one denomination to another, but rather students who changed from a religious affiliation to no affiliation at all.

In a series of t tests (Nie et al. 1975), it was apparent that apostates differed from nonapostates on almost all of the single items and scales included in the questionnaire. Nonapostates reported significantly higher scores than did apostates on agreement with parental religious teachings; the importance of religion in one's life; current frequency of church attendance: frequency of church attendance before the age of 15; frequency of prayer; frequency of scriptural reading; belief in God; belief in the divinity of Jesus; belief in the Bible; belief in miracles; belief in the existence of the devil; frequency of turning to religious sources for counseling; frequency of seeing both mother and father; how well the respondent gets along with both mother and father; the ability of both the mother and father to understand the respondent; how well the respondent both liked and got along with both the mother and father during childhood; reported happiness and adjustment in life; conventionalism; how well both the mother and father could represent the respondent's religious beliefs; the extent to which the respondent agrees with both the mother's and the father's position on issues of religion, the use of alcohol, premarital sex, politics, education, the importance of money, the importance of hard work, and overall philosophy of life; scales to measure Christian orthodoxy (Fullerton and Hunsberger 1982); the emphasis placed on religion in the childhood home (Altemeyer 1981); and maternal care, paternal care, and maternal overprotection (Parker, Tupling, and Brown 1979).

At the same time, apostates scored significantly higher than nona-postates on single items tapping whether or not they were living away from their parents' home; Higher School Certificate aggregate; political orientation (with more "liberal" orientations receiving higher scores on this item); political radicalism; general rebellion against parents; enjoy-ment of intellectual discussions; enjoyment in debating religious issues; self-report of intellectualism; and extent to which mother and father were upset with the respondent's present religious position. It is to be noted that all but 8 of the above t values (i.e., of the 58 tests reported above) were significant at the .001 level or better.

The only variables which revealed no significant difference between apostates and nonapostates were those dealing with sex of respondent; year in university; number of years they had lived away from parents' home; mother's and father's education level; and the father's overprotec-tiveness score (Parker, Tupling, and Brown 1979).

A factor analysis (Nie et al. 1975) was carried out on 16 variables which closely approximated the variables included in Hunsberger's (1980) previous analysis, in order to test the stability of the factor struc-ture he derived.[1] Results were very similar to the earlier analysis, with six iterative principal axes factors with eigenvalues greater than 1 being extracted from the 16 variables. When factor scores obtained from this analysis were used as the predictors in a stepwise multiple regression analysis with group (apostate or nonapostate) as the predicted variable or "outcome," results again were very similar to Hunsberger's earlier findings. That is, the factor "response to parental religious teachings" was entered into the equation first, contributing significantly to the explained variance (R-Square Change = .281, $F(7,422) = 174.80$, $p < .001$. The second variable to be entered was the factor "emphasis placed on religion in childhood" which added significantly to the explained variance, as indicated by an F test of the R-Square Change (.057), $F(8,421) = 38.93$, $p < .001$. In this analysis, a third factor also contributed significantly to the explained variance, that of "relationship with mother," (R-Square Change = .024), $F(9,420) = 17.21$, $p < .001$. The remaining 3 factors, while still contributing significantly to the explained variance, accounted for extremely small proportions of the

1. In fact, Hunsberger's (1980) original factor analysis included 17 variables, 2 of which related to reported and expected grade point average. The current study used a sin-gle measure (Higher School Certificate aggregate) in place of those variables primarily because of differences between North American and Australian educational systems in assessing cumulative student academic progress. In addition, while Hunsberger's earlier analyses involved a matched control (each apostate was matched with a nonapostate of the same sex, age, year in university, and background religion), the present multiple regression analysis controlled for these background factors statistically by entering them first (in a block) in the multiple regression analysis.

variance, "childhood relationship with father" (.007); "personal happiness and adjustment" (.005); and "present relationship with father" (.003).

In order to explore more fully the variables which might be related to apostasy and religiosity, a further analysis was carried out covering 37 variables in all (including 32 single items and 5 scale scores). These variables were subjected to a principal axes factor analysis (Nie et al. 1975), from which 11 factors were extracted which had eigenvalues greater than 1. These 11 factors were rotated suing a varimax solution. Table 13.1 presents the main items representing each factor and their loading, where only those variables with loadings of .40 or greater were included for each factor.[2] As table 13.1 indicates, the factors were interpreted as tapping dimensions of relationship with father; relationship with mother; contact with parents; emphasis placed on religion in childhood; agreement with parents on moral issues; agreement with parents on politics and education; agreement with parents on the importance of hard work; childhood relationship with parents; intellectual orientation; personal adjustment and happiness; and parental overprotectiveness.

Factor scores obtained from the above analysis were used as the predictors in a stepwise multiple regression analysis (Nie et al. 1975) with group (apostate or nonapostate) as the predicted variable. The matrix of intercorrelations is shown in table 13.2, while the results of the regression analysis are in table 13.3.

The regression analysis indicated that factor 9 (Intellectual Orientation) was entered into the equation first (after the effects of background variables [age, sex, year in university, and background religious denomination] had been removed), contributing significantly to the explained variance (.058), $F (7,341) = 22.52$, $p < .001$. The next variable to be entered was factor 4 (Emphasis Placed on Religion in Childhood) which added significantly to the explained variance, as indicated by an F test of the R-Square Change (.045), $F (8,340) = 18.49$, $p < .001$. While five further factors added significantly to the explained variance, it is clear from table 13.3 that they accounted for very little of the variance (about 1% each, as indicated by the R^2 increment).

2. This solution used a listwise deletion of missing data, thus involving an N of 355. The presentation of item loadings shows most items *once* in table 13.1. The items concerned with getting along with and liking mother in childhood loaded on both factors 2 and 8, while items regarding getting along with and liking father in childhood loaded on both factors 1 and 8. The maternal overprotection score loaded on factors 2 and 11, while paternal overprotection loaded on factors 1 and 11. Two items, political orientation (i.e., liberal-conservative) and political radicalism ("not at all" to "very"), did not load above .4 on any of the factors, and thus are not shown in table 13.1. Five additional items loaded between .3 and .4 on a second factor. All of the remaining item loadings (360) were less than .3.

Table 13.1

Items Associated with Derived Factors

Item	Factor Loading
Factor 1: Relationship with Father (33.8)[a]	
How well would you say that you get along with your (father)?	.81
How well do you feel that your (father) is able to understand you and accept you for the person you are?	.73
During your childhood, how well would you say that you got along with your (father)?	.63
During your childhood, how much would you say that you liked your (father)?	.57
Paternal Care Scale score (Parker *et al.*, 1979)	.73
Paternal Overprotectiveness Scale score (Parker *et al.*, 1979)	−.51
To what extent do you agree with your father on overall philosophy of life?	.62
Factor 2: Relationship with Mother (12.4)	
How well would you say that you get along with your (mother)?	.73
How well do you feel that your (mother) is able to understand you and accept you for the person you are?	.78
During your childhood, how well would you say that you get along with your (mother)?	.46
During your childhood, how much would you say that you liked your (mother)?	.43
Maternal Care Scale score (Parker *et al.*, 1979)	.61
Maternal Overprotectiveness Scale score (Parker *et al.*, 1979)	−.49
To what extent do you agree with your mother on overall philosophy of life?	.54
Factor 3: Contact with Parents (10.0)	
If you have moved away from your parents' home, how many years have you lived somewhere else?	−.87
How often do you usually see your (father)?	.91
How often do you usually see your (mother)?	.97
Factor 4: Emphasis Placed on Religion in Childhood (9.0)	
To what extent would you say your parents emphasized religion and religious practices as you were growing up?	.89
On the average, how often did you attend church before you reached the age of 15?	.67
Religious Emphasis Scale score (Altemeyer, 1981)	.86
Factor 5: Agreement with Parents on Moral Issues (8.0)	
To what extent would you say you agree with your mother on the use of alcohol?	.50
To what extent would you say you agree with your mother on premarital sex?	.77
To what extent would you say you agree with your father on the use of alcohol?	.49
To what extent would you say you agree with your father on premarital sex?	.79
Factor 6: Agreement with Parents on Politics and Education (7.2)	
To what extent would you say you agree with your mother on politics?	.78
To what extent would you say you agree with your mother on education?	.50
To what extent would you say you agree with your father on politics?	.71
To what extent would you say you agree with your father on education?	.50
Factor 7: Agreement with Parents on the Importance of Hard Work (5.5)	
To what extent do you agree with your mother on the importance of hard work?	.78
To what extent do you agree with your father on the importance of hard work?	.73
Factor 8: Childhood Relationship with Parents (4.3)	
During your childhood, how well would you say that you got along with your (mother)?	.57
During your childhood, how well would you say that you got along with your (father)?	.54
During your childhood, how much would you say that you liked your (mother)?	.64
During your childhood, how much would you say that you liked your (father)?	.56
Factor 9: Intellectual Orientation (4.1)	
To what extent would you say that you enjoy "intellectual" discussions?	.71
To what extent do you enjoy debating or arguing with others about religious issues?	.52
To what extent do you consider yourself to be "intellectually" oriented?	.70
Factor 10: Personal Adjustment and Happiness (3.2)	
How happy or unhappy is your life at present?	.72
How would you now describe your own personal adjustment to life?	.77
Factor 11: Parental Overprotectiveness (2.5)	
Maternal Overprotectiveness Scale score (Parker *et al.*, 1979)	.51
Paternal Overprotectiveness Scale score (Parker *et al.*, 1979)	.49

[a]Figure in brackets is the amount of variance accounted for by that factor.

Table 13.2

Intercorrelations for Group (Apostate or Nonapostate) and Factors

	F1	F2	F3	F4	F5	F6	F7	F8	F9	F10	F11
Group	.0969	.1301	.1751	.2317	.1111	.1188	.1233	.1334	−.2326	.0918	.0423
F1		.0213	.0063	.0012	.0180	.0446	.0377	.0550	−.0105	.0107	−.0377
F2			−.0045	.0079	.0445	.0188	.0364	.0584	−.0400	.0720	−.0658
F3				−.00105	−.0082	.00732	−.0170	.0243	−.0138	−.0162	.0144
F4					.0037	.0086	.0058	.0126	.0094	−.0145	.0484
F5						.0394	.0371	−.0020	−.0026	−.0279	−.0314
F6							.0524	.0034	.0066	.0014	.0036
F7								−.0166	.0254	.0178	.0583
F8									.0037	.0765	.0214
F9										.01168	−.0183
F10											−.0083

Further analyses were carried out to investigate direct self-reports of the influences in the religious development of our participants. Respondents were asked, "Which of the following had the strongest influence on your religious development? (Check *one* only)" with response categories including home, school, church, and "other (please specify)." Table 13.4 shows the percentage and frequency of choices of each of these alternatives for the nine religious orientations, and overall.

Differences among the students from different religious traditions

Table 13.3

Results of Multiple Regression Analysis

Variable	R^2	R^2 Increment	F Ratio	df	Simple R
Control variables[a]	.06458	.06458	3.93**	6,342	
Factor 9	.12252	.05795	22.52***	7,341	−.23262
Factor 4	.16779	.04526	18.49***	8,340	.23167
Factor 2	.18438	.01659	6.90**	9,339	.13005
Factor 8	.19613	.01175	4.94*	10,338	.13340
Factor 3	.20778	.01165	4.96*	11,337	.17512
Factor 5	.21837	.01059	4.55*	12,336	.11105
Factor 7	.22795	.00985	4.16*	13,335	.12331
Factor 10	.23677	.00882	3.86	14,334	.09177
Factor 1	.24438	.00761	3.35	15,333	.09692
Factor 6	.25026	.00588	2.60	16,332	.11884
Factor 11	.25032	.00006	0.03	17,331	.04226

[a]Variables of age, year in university, sex, and background religion were entered into the multiple regression equation in a block. The Simple R is not shown for these variables since the correlations available are for each of the above four variables separately rather than as a block.

***$p < .001$

**$p < .01$

*$p < .05$

Table 13.4

Frequencies and Percentages for Perceptions of "Strongest Influence" in Religious Development for Different Religious Orientations[a]

Influence	Angli-can	Other Prot.	Roman Cath.	Ortho-dox	Jewish	Agnos-tic	Atheist	Pers. Relig.	Over-all
Home	27.0	27.8	33.5	51.4	52.2	31.0	33.9	30.7	33.9
	(27)	(22)	(65)	(36)	(24)	(58)	(19)	(31)	(282)
School	30.0	12.7	46.4	20.0	21.7	33.7	33.9	29.7	31.9
	(30)	(10)	(90)	(14)	(10)	(63)	(19)	(30)	(266)
Church	21.0	22.8	5.7	12.9	0.0	12.3	8.9	4.0	10.9
	(21)	(18)	(11)	(9)	(0)	(23)	(5)	(4)	(194)
Other	22.0	36.8	14.4	15,7	26.1	23.0	23.2	35.6	23.3
	(22)	(29)	(28)	(11)	(12)	(43)	(13)	(36)	(194)
Total	100.0	100.0	100.0	100.0	100.0	100.0	100.0	100.0	100.0
	(100)	(79)	(194)	(70)	(46)	(187)	(56)	(101)	(833)

[a]Frequencies are shown in brackets immediately below each percentage. Totals may not add to 100% because of rounding.

are clearly evident. For example, substantially higher percentages of Orthodox (51.4) and Jewish (52.2) students indicated that home constituted the strongest influence, while a relatively high percentage of Roman Catholics (46.6) chose school. Similarly, Anglicans and Other Protestants indicated relatively higher percentage choices of church (21.0 and 22.8 respectively) than did the other groups, while Other Protestants and Personal Religion groups were more likely than the others to indicate that "other" influences had exerted the greatest influence on their religious development (36.8% and 35.6% respectively).

In order to investigate specific influences more directly, and to avoid forcing respondents into predetermined categories, a further open-ended questionnaire item asked, "Which three persons have had the greatest influence on your religious beliefs? Do not name the people but identify their relationship to you (e.g., mother, best male friend, high school teacher, etc.)." Table 13.5 shows the percentages and frequencies of respondents placing each of seven categories of response first (i.e., their perceived "strongest influence"). These categories included Parents (mother, father, or "parents" [unspecified]); Other Relatives (including siblings, grandparents, cousins, etc.); Friends; Teachers (including elementary, high school, university, or "unspecified" teachers); Church-Related Persons (including ministers, priests, nuns, chaplains, Sunday school teachers, retreat leaders, "God," "Jesus," etc.); No One (i.e., the respondent said that no one had had any particular influence, as opposed to those who simply did not reply to this item, and who were omitted from the frequency distribution in this table); and Self/Other (including people who said that they themselves had been influential in their religious development, or that others who could not be categorized had been particularly influential; for example, a few

Table 3.5

Frequencies and Percentages for Perceptions of Person Having Greatest Influence on Religious Beliefs for Different Religious Orientations[a]

Influence	Angli-can	Other Prot.	Roman Cath.	Ortho-dox	Jewish	Agnos-tic	Atheist	Pers. Relig.	Over-all
Parents	38.8	30.8	55.0	55.4	51.0	42.5	35.3	32.0	43.7
	(38)	(24)	(105)	(36)	(25)	(74)	(18)	(32)	(352)
Other	5.1	6.4	6.3	13.8	18.4	4.6	5.9	15.0	8.2
Relatives	(5)	(5)	(12)	(9)	(9)	(8)	(3)	(15)	(66)
Friends	23.5	35.9	10.5	1.5	12.2	13.8	9.8	16.0	15.3
	(23)	(28)	(20)	(1)	(6)	(24)	(5)	(16)	(123)
Teachers	10.2	3.8	16.2	12.3	6.1	10.9	11.8	6.0	10.6
	(10)	(3)	(31)	(8)	(3)	(19)	(6)	(6)	(86)
Church-Related Persons	17.3	20.5	8.4	9.2	6.1	7.5	7.8	15.0	11.1
	(17)	(16)	(16)	(6)	(3)	(13)	(4)	(15)	(90)
Self/Other	4.1	0.0	2.6	3.1	4.1	9.2	17.6	13.0	6.4
	(4)	(0)	(5)	(2)	(2)	(16)	(9)	(13)	(51)
No One	1.0	2.6	1.0	2.6	2.0	11.5	11.8	3.0	4.7
	(1)	(2)	(2)	(3)	(1)	(20)	(6)	(3)	(38)
Total	100.0	100.0	100.0	100.0	100.0	100.0	100.0	100.0	100.0
	(98)	(78)	(191)	(65)	(49)	(174)	(51)	(100)	(806)

[a]Frequencies are shown in brackets immediately below each percentage. Totals may not add to 100% because of rounding.

respondents mentioned well-known personalities, authors, chance meetings with a stranger, etc., as influential).

The most striking aspect of this table is the important influence that relatives, particularly the parents, were perceived to have on respondents' religious beliefs. For every religious grouping, over 30% of the respondents reported that one or both parents had been the most influential person(s); for three of the groups (Roman Catholic, Orthodox, and Jewish) the percentage is greater than 50%.

Table 13.6 shows the frequencies and percentages of respondents

Table 13.6

Frequencies and Percentages for Perceptions of Mother versus Father Having Greatest Influence on Religious Beliefs for Different Religious Orientations[a]

Influence	Angli-can	Other Prot.	Roman Cath.	Ortho-dox	Jewish	Agnos-tic	Atheist	Pers. Relig.	Over-all
Mother	24.5	14.1	31.4	46.2	30.6	27.6	21.6	20.0	27.2
	(24)	(11)	(60)	(30)	(15)	(48)	(11)	(20)	(219)
Father	5.1	12.8	12.0	7.7	14.3	13.8	11.8	11.0	11.3
	(5)	(10)	(23)	(5)	(7)	(24)	(6)	(11)	(91)

[a]Frequencies are shown in brackets immediately below each percentage.

indicating that the mother or father had the most important influence, for different religious-orientation categories.

Discussion

The percentage of apostates in this Australian sample was considerably higher than the percentages found by Hunsberger in comparable samples of Canadian university students. It would be instructive to follow these apostates in a longitudinal study to see if they maintain that status over a period of time, especially in view of the large proportion of apostates from Protestant backgrounds. It would seem difficult for these religious groups to survive apostate rates approaching 50% among their university student offspring, if such rates are maintained as these students age into their thirties.

Consistent with earlier findings (Hunsberger 1980, 1983), significant differences emerged between apostates and nonapostates for a wide variety of measures of religiosity, with the apostates being consistently "less religious" than nonapostates. In addition, apostates tended to report poorer relationships with parents, both currently and in childhood, as well as less agreement with their parents on a variety of issues such as premarital sex, politics, and education. This finding contradicts previous findings by Hunsberger (1980, 1983) of few, if any, differences on these issues. In a similar vein, the current study revealed that apostates reported different political, intellectual, and educational orientations from nonapostates, contrary to Hunsberger's previous findings.

However, this study did not employ the "matched control" technique used in Hunsberger's previous research, and the failure to control for a variety of extraneous variables may have led to the "contradictory" nature of these findings. That is, while these t tests are interesting and useful at a very basic level, they can be misleading. For example, they do not control for a variety of other factors which might be related to apostasy, such as gender (previous studies have found that more males tend to be apostates); background religion (as reported, some religions tend to be overrepresented in the apostasy column, while others tend to be underrepresented); age (apostates tend to be older), and the like. Thus the possibility arises that at least some of the differences may be attributable to biased samples (e.g., overrepresentation of females, younger people, or certain religious groups). In addition, these findings do not allow one to make relative comparisons regarding the prediction of apostate versus nonapostate status.

In order to alleviate such deficiencies, factor analysis and multiple regression analyses were carried out, which allowed statistical control of some potentially biasing variables (sex, year in university, age, and background religious denomination). The first analyses involved a factor analysis and subsequent multiple regression in an attempt to replicate Hunsberger's (1980) earlier findings. In fact, the results were very similar to the earlier findings, with two factors (response to parental religious teachings and emphasis on religion in childhood) contributing significantly to the explained variance. A third factor (relationship with mother) also contributed significantly to the explained variance, although its contribution was relatively small (2.4%). While the three remaining variables also made significant contributions to the explained variance, their contributions were too small to be meaningful (childhood relationships with father [0.7%], personal happiness and adjustment [0.5%], and present relationship with father [0.3%]). These results were thus interpreted as basically confirming the factor structure and multiple-regression analyses previously reported by Hunsberger (1980).

The expanded factor analysis (including 24 variables not included in the basic analysis described) and a multiple-regression analysis added to the preceding findings. The three variables which had contributed to the "response to parental religious teachings" factor in the initial analysis above were not included here because it was felt that they did not relate to our attempt to explain the phenomenon of apostasy. Rather, they seemed a kind of "validity check," to confirm that those who reported being apostates did in fact distance themselves from the religious teachings of their parents. The three variables that were removed from the present analyses tapped current agreement with parental religious teachings, doubt of parental religious teachings, and reaction against religious behaviors and practices.

As the results indicate, of the 11 factors generated by the factor analysis, Intellectual Orientation was entered into the multiple-regression equation first, thus making the greatest contribution to the explained variance (5.8%). It was followed closely by Emphasis Placed on Religion in Childhood which added 4.5% to the explained variance. Again, at least partially because of the relatively large sample size, five further factors added significantly to the explained variance, but they accounted for very little of the variance (about 1% each). The first of these "significant explainers" of apostasy (Intellectual Orientation) was a surprise in the light of previous research. Apparently, among this Australian student sample, items tapping self-reports of enjoyment of "intellectual" discussions, enjoyment of debating religious issues, and considering oneself to be "intellectually" oriented collectively proved to be the best predictors of apostate versus nonapostate status.

It is unclear why intellectual orientation should play such an important role in predicting apostasy in the present sample when it has consistently failed to do so in previous research (Hunsberger 1980, 1983). It is possible that the larger proportion of apostates in the present study included a relatively large number for whom intellectual pursuits served as the basis for their withdrawal from organized religion, while in previous Canadian research the smaller proportion of apostates were more affected by their religious background (Hunsberger 1980, 1983). There may well be "cultural" factors involved even though Australian and Canadian society are similar in many respects. For example, it is possible that religious identification is not so important in Australia and therefore intellectual reasons alone can offer a basis for becoming an apostate; whereas in Canada it may be more difficult to withdraw from one's religious background, so that intellectual reasons alone are not sufficient to justify such action. These possibilities involve speculation, however, and empirical work is necessary to assess them.

At the same time, the second factor entered into the multiple-regression equation was Emphasis Placed on Religion in Childhood, which explained approximately the same amount of variance (4.5%) as in previous research (Hunsberger 1980, 1983). That is, the religious environment in the childhood home apparently plays an important part in the apostasy process, such that a weaker emphasis on religion and religious practices is related to a greater probability of apostasy later in life (at least, as reported by our university students). While this factor has not accounted for large amounts of variance, and was ignored by Caplovitz and Sherrow (1977), it has consistently been a highly significant predictor of apostasy in this and in previous research by Hunsberger.

While five further factors contributed significantly to the explained variance, the contribution of each one was close to one percent of the variance. Thus, while Relationship with Mother, Childhood Relationship with Parents, Contact with Parents, Agreement with Parents on Moral Issues, and Agreement with Parents on the Importance of Hard Work cannot be ignored, their actual contribution is so small that they add little to attempts to explain the roots of apostasy as opposed to continued religious affiliation.

In light of the t tests discussed earlier, one might be led to conclude that the present findings support Caplovitz and Sherrow's (1977) conceptualization of poor parental relations, maladjustment, radical or leftist political orientation, and intellectualism as traits predisposing apostasy. However, as the subsequent factor analysis and multiple regression indicate, such a conclusion would be misleading. There *was* evidence that an intellectual orientation significantly predicted apostasy, but it is to be noted that the items loading highly on this factor involved self-perception of oneself as intellectually oriented, rather than academic success or career orientation (which apparently constituted Caplovitz and Sherrow's main measures of intellectual orientation). In addition, while factors related to parental relationships did significantly add to the explained variance, their actual contribution was negligible. And even if one considers these factors as "important" (i.e., because they were statistically significant, in spite of their very small addition to the explained variance), there is no reason to conclude that poor parental relations themselves caused apostasy. As Hunsberger (1983) has pointed out, apostasy itself could well have "caused" these poor relationships with parents. The two other "predisposing factors" posited by Caplowitz and Sherrow (maladjustment and radical or leftist political orientation) were not significant predictors of apostate status in these analyses. Thus overall, only minimal support was found for Caplowitz and Sherrow's analysis of apostasy, although emphasis on religion in childhood *was* found to be an important predictor of apostate versus nonapostate status.

Descriptive information obtained from these participants helps to elucidate the effects of different sources of religious influence during childhood. Consistent with the above finding that emphasis on religion in the childhood home was an important predictor of later apostasy-nonapostasy, participants reported overall that their "home" was the strongest influence in their religious development. However, denominational differences were apparent here, with substantially higher percentages of Orthodox and Jewish students choosing home as the strongest influence, while Roman Catholics and to a slight degree, Anglicans, were more likely to indicate "school" as the primary influence. Also, Other Protestants and Personal Religion groups reported that "other" factors had exerted the greatest influence on their religious development. Such denominational differences are obviously substantial and cannot be ignored in considering sources of religious influence.

Further open-ended questionnaire items sought to have respondents become more specific concerning the individuals who had had the greatest influence on their religious development. In this case, parents were perceived to be important influences regardless of the religious orientation of the respondents, although for some groups (Roman Catholic, Orthodox, and Jewish) more than 50% pointed to their parents as most influential. Possibly even more intriguing, in view of past conclusions that fathers are more influential with respect to children's religious development (e.g., Hoge and Petrillo 1978), was the finding that mothers were consistently reported to be more influential than fathers. Only for the Other Protestant category do fathers even come close to the mothers with respect to frequency of choices, and even there mothers were chosen more frequently than fathers.

Conclusion

Overall, the present results point consistently to the importance of the home environment (particularly the influence of parents, and especially of the mother) in influencing the *later* religious orientation (whether positively or negatively), at least when their children are university students. The evidence also indicates that respondents with the stronger emphasis placed on religion in their childhood home are more likely to remain within their childhood religious "umbrella," while those who reported a weaker emphasis were more likely to become apostates. In addition, more than 40% of all respondents reported that their parents constitute the primary religious influence, and more than 1 in 4 reported specifically that the other had the greatest influence on religious development.

Certainly, cognitive factors are important, as suggested by the present finding that intellectual orientation was related to apostate-nonapostate status. This may be seen in the light of the religious emphasis in the childhood home and of the religious traditions' norms. It would seem clear, in light of this and previous investigations, that a more thorough examination of religious socialization is in order if we are to understand the nature and the extent of influences on later religiosity and nonreligiosity.

References

Altemeyer, B. 1981. *Right-wing authoritarianism.* Winnipeg: Univ. of Manitoba.

Argyle, M., and B. Beit-Hallahmi. 1975. *The social psychology of religion.* London: Routledge and Kegan Paul.

Brinkerhoff, M. B., and K. L. Burke. 1980. Disaffiliation: Some notes on "falling from the faith." *Sociological Analysis* 41: 41–54.

Caplovitz, D., and F. Sherrow. 1977. *The religious drop-outs: Apostasy among college graduates.* Beverly Hills, Calif.: Sage.

Fullerton, J. T., and B. E. Hunsberger. 1982. A unidimensional measure of Christian orthodoxy. *Journal for the Scientific Study of Religion* 21: 317–26.

Glock, C. Y., and R. Wuthnow. 1979. Departures from conventional religion: The nominally religious, the nonreligious, and the alternatively religious. *The religious dimension: New directions in quantitative research,* ed. R. Wuthnow, 47–68. New York: Academic Press.

Hadaway, C. K. 1980. Denominational switching and religiosity. *Review of Religious Research* 21: 451–61.

Hadaway, C. K., and W. C. Roof. 1979. Those who stay religious "Nones" and those who don't: A research note. *Journal for the Scientific Study of Religion* 18: 194–200.

Hoge, D. R., and G. H. Petrillo. 1978. Development of religious thinking in adolescence: A test of Goldman's theories. *Journal for the Scientific Study of Religion* 17: 359–79.

Hunsberger, B. E. 1980. A reexamination of the antecedents of apostasy. *Review of Religious Research* 21: 158–70.

————. 1983. Apostasy: A social learning perspective. *Review of Religious Research* 25: 21–38.

Johnson, M. A. 1973. Family life and religious commitment. *Review of Religious Research* 14: 144–50.

Nelson, H. M. 1981. Religious conformity in an age of disbelief: Contextual effects of time, denomination, and family processes upon church decline and apostasy. *American Sociological Review* 46: 632–40.

Nie, N. H., C. H. Null, T. G. Jenkins, K. Steinbrenner, and D. H. Bent. 1975. *Statistical package for the social sciences.* New York: McGraw-Hill.

O'Doherty, E. F. 1978. *Religion and psychology.* New York: Alba.

O'Hara, J. P. 1980. A research note on the sources of adult church commitment among those who were regular attenders during childhood. *Review of Religious Research* 21: 462–67.

Parker, G., H. Tupling, and L. B. Brown. 1979. A parental bonding instrument. *British Journal of Medical Psychology* 52: 1–10.

Perry, E. L., J. H. Davis, R. T. Doyle, and J. E. Dyble. 1980. Toward a typology of unchurched Protestants. *Review of Religious Research* 21: 388–404.

Putney, S., and R. Middleton. 1961. Rebellion, conformity, and parental religious ideologies. *Sociometry* 24: 125–35.

Roof, W. C., and D. R. Hoge. 1980. Church involvement in America: Social factors affecting membership and participation. *Review of Religious Research* 21: 405–26.

Roozen, D. A. 1980. Church dropouts: Changing patterns of disengagement and reentry. *Review of Religious Research* 21: 427–50.

Strommen, M. P. 1963. *Profiles of church youth.* St. Louis: Concordia.

Welch, M. 1978. Religious nonaffiliates and worldly success. *Journal for the Scientific Study of Religion* 17: 59–61.

Wuthnow, R., and G. Mellinger. 1978. Religious loyalty, defection, and experimentation: A longitudinal analysis of university men. *Review of Religious Research* 19: 231–45.

Toward the Psychology of Religion

M y first studies in the psychology of religion (Brown 1962b, 1964, 1981; Wearing and Brown, 1972) concerned the relationships of personality and social attitudes with religious belief and membership. They drew on my own religious upbringing at the High Church end of Methodism and on a British academic training that still allows me to think of myself as a general and social psychologist (cf. Thouless 1958). I was greatly influenced by Thouless's (1956) textbook *An Introduction to the Psychology of Religion,* by Otto's (1923) *Idea of the Holy,* and by the fact that a majority of people in developed countries continue to claim that they are religious and remain aligned with a religious tradition, despite experts' arguments about secularization and the decline of religion. Religion is obviously an important domain in which we can apply (or develop) psychological theories about the links between individuals, institutions, and cultures, or their traditions.

Although I had hoped to show from those early studies that religious beliefs reflect personality, I could only retrieve the separate religionism factor that many others had found with broadly cast studies. I found that religious statements were found to be held more strongly than factual ones, since it may be easier to be uncertain about factual matters that are in principle verifiable. The absence of clear relationships between religious and personality measures and even the conclusion that "religious belief is a relatively isolated cognitive system . . . [that needs] strong social support for its maintenance" (Brown 1962b) might, however, have been specific to the measurement and data reduction procedures that I used, which as Dittes (1969, 618) has shown can themselves determine whether religion is found to be explicit and differentiated or subjective and diffused (and perhaps also explicit but diffused). Since other orientations to religion are possible, of which the extrinsic-intrinsic contrast is presently thought to be the most important (Donahue 1985), the problems of how religiousness can be most

From the *Journal of Psychology and Christianity* 5, no. 2 (1986): 13–18; reprinted by permission of the publisher and the author. Copyright 1986 by the Christian Association for Psychological Studies.

effectively described in psychological terms have sustained my search for a good empirical definition of it. That nonpsychologists, or lay people, use implicit theories to predict how a religious person will act and that it has only recently been acknowledged that there might be better predictors than those psychologists have developed have turned my current work, therefore, towards the "social representations" (Farr and Moscovici 1984) of religion.

As part of this search for the formative work on psychology and religion, I gathered a book of readings (Brown 1973) and then a set of papers (1985) that had been prepared for a conference in Oxford, England, of invited psychologists of religion. The various approaches in these papers show that we have not yet found a unified or general theory of religion. Despite an agreement that religion *can* be studied, differences among psychologists about what it entails are as great as those opinions among the religious people who are being studied.

To reduce the inevitable variance in religious responses, some psychologists have preferred to work within a single confessional framework. This approach has produced religious psychologies that defer to particular religious assumptions. But even in more strictly social psychological approaches to religious belief and behavior, some doctrinal content is important, since no content-free or "natural, cognitive structures" for religion, which might line up with Scott's (1969) work on the structure of concepts about nations, have yet been empirically identified. Despite animistic or ego-centric and other "primitive" forms of thinking, fear and fascination, debt and desire, myth and symbolism have all been proposed as explanations of how religious thinking might have become possible.

Having failed to find a link between religion and personality, I set out to test the validity of early arguments (Tylor [1871] 1958; Malinowski 1925) about immature thinking in religion among adults, rather than among very young children where it might simply depend on their ignorance of how to handle received doctrines. But in an examination of animistic thinking (Brown and Thouless 1965), despite extended questioning we found it impossible to decide if adults use such ideas in a playful or rhetorical manner or because they seriously believe that a bushfire, for example, is in some sense "alive." We concluded that animistic language might help solve problems and that others' misunderstandings of what it implies can easily be reconstructed by those who know the "proper" or expected answers for particular contexts or kinds of discourse. Studies of petitionary prayer (Brown and Thouless 1964; Brown 1966), therefore, found denominational rather than age-based differences in beliefs about the appropriateness of such prayers in different contexts, which is probably a result of specific religious teaching. On the other hand, age-based, but not denominational, differences were found in beliefs about the efficacy of petitionary prayers. That such apparently important issues may not be solved easily does not necessarily mean that those who believe that prayer can be effective have immature beliefs, but it might mean that we have not been asking the right questions.

We know that our social and material failures can be justified or explained in highly sophisticated ways. Psychologists of religion must always look beyond what is believed to the ways in which beliefs, and the doctrines that support them, can be justified or supported traditionally and with reference to our own experience. The basis of these explanations (which go beyond the use of attribution theory, cf. Spilka, Hood, and Gorsuch 1985) demands far more attention than it has yet been given. A sound theory of explanations could yield a more functional theory of religion than do the usual psychological measures that allow only closed, or precoded, responses. To run free format questions parallel to conventionally scaled items (Gorsuch 1984) might capture an individual's construction of religious beliefs and practice that go beyond assent to what traditions offer, and might give access to what is usually thought of as one's religious "faith." Innovative methods will be needed to resolve continuing disagreements about the most useful paradigms and theories through which to interpret religion, with the recognition that in religion, as in psychology itself, more than one perspective must be allowed.

Contrasts between literal or concrete and mythological or figurative interpretations of the meaning and application of religious doctrines or biblical stories often involve an unquestioned ideological or theological stance that depends on closed- rather than open-mindedness (Rokeach 1960) or reflects the social constraints or the context within which particular religious orientations were developed. While some claim that their religion is absolutely true, because of their experience, training, or conviction, for others the truths of religion disappear into language, depend on hope, confidence, commitment to a tradition, or aesthetic, rather than on religious responsiveness or their overriding belief in a "just world" (Lerner 1980). Only external social criteria can decide which perspective is the most mature. One step in clarifying that problem could be to explore the uses that people make of their religion, how they reconcile its claims with their other knowledge of the world, and the sanctions they find for their conclusions. In a similar way we should know how religious belief and action are welded together and where one reinforces the other. These empirical questions must be resolved with principled observations, not by continuing to indulge our flawed, participant-based theories of religion.

Those who have defected or lapsed from a religious position might be able to give more useful data about how religion works than can those who find they are not challenged by their received traditions. Moreover, religious converts have been neglected in favor of continued contrasts of those who are religious (on whatever criteria) against those who are not, or with contrasts between those with an intrinsic orientation and those with an extrinsic orientation, or between those more interested in using their religion than serving it. While experimentally manipulated comparisons allow causal inferences that cannot be drawn from correlational procedures (cf. Cronbach 1957; Deconchy 1985), meta-analyses of the results from separate correlational studies are increasingly being used to identify trends that have been independently supported (Batson and Ventis 1982; Donahue 1985).

Investigating problems like these has not, however, been the only reason for my interest in religion. I also wanted to find what support there might be for or against easy psychological criticisms and objections to religious belief (Williams 1964) and how believers come to accept or distance themselves from them. The drive there came from a remark that Gordon Allport made to me in 1964 when he said that "religion may not be psychologically interesting." I think he meant that its primary role might be in the public or social domain, or that religious *disbeliefs* are more interesting psychologically than are the beliefs which seem to shape the lives of so many people so easily. A closely related question concerns the other phenomena that religion might be compared with, as when "God" becomes an abstract source of "law and might."

Comparisons of religion with political and social ideologies, or with science as a system of explanation and control, or with sport and other leisure activities are useful but neglect the extent to which religions are appealed to for help in trouble and for sanctioning social transitions. While they are well supported in doing that, they are, nevertheless, constrained by other solutions and intellectual or social movements. Those influences and the varied uses of religion have not been well documented with psychological data, except perhaps through prejudiced or "mistaken beliefs" about the role of religion in society. The lives of religious individuals have also been neglected. Because social contexts (and religions themselves) keep changing, we ought to find some instability in the content of what is believed and in the support that is found for beliefs. But survey data show surprisingly consistent results over time within most countries (Brown 1987, 165), although there may be more explicit defections from traditional views now than there were previously and institutional structures have been made more sensitive to the constraints they impose or that are imposed on them (Brown 1988, 67). (In that sense, theories of religion are also being influenced by other intellectual movements.) While simple questions like "Do you go to church, believe in God, or keep the faith?" are sufficient filters in ordinary conversation to identify those who are religious, they cannot clarify the "deep" structures that psychologists are expected to find behind any set of religious beliefs, whether among those judged to be religiously mature or among those who are thought to be mistaken in their beliefs.

Sociologists of religion have cut themselves off from many of the tricky religious questions that have preoccupied psychologists, although Weber is said to have believed that religion has psychologically met a very general need. Their work is typified by Stark and Glock's (1968) study of religious commitment, for which they developed "on logical and theoretical grounds" measures of belief, knowledge, experience, practice (subdivided into "ritual involvement" and "devotionalism"), and the "relationships members form with their churches" (175). They concluded that, while this set of distinctions was more warranted among Catholics than Protestants, "belief orthodoxy is the best single measure [of religion], although among Catholics devotionalism is equally good" (197). Despite that, they found that "religious commitment is both logically and empirically a complex phenomenon" and that "those who seek to understand man's religiousness must study it in its full complexity" (187). Their conclusions parallel those of psychologists (Brown 1987) and emphasize that the findings of both psychologists and sociologists reflect the social, doctrinal, and traditional coherence of specific religions. Deeply psychological interpretations are less parsimonious and hard to substantiate except for those committed to nonsocial, noncognitive (and irrational) explanations. Ambiguity of religion has made it a traditional field for psychological claims about the truth or (more often) illusory nature of religious doctrines and experiences.

Furthermore Argyle and Beit-Hallahmi's (1975) and Berelson and Steiner's (1964) summaries of empirical findings in the social psychology of religion emphasize that social processes play the central role in forming and maintaining religious perspectives and participation. Psychodynamic theories about the origins of religion can hardly be taken seriously since very few people think up their own religion and most fit themselves more or less well into a received socioreligious system, with their religious and other fantasies kept hidden. When religious fantasies are exposed, they may become a target for change, or counseling. Despite that, psychologists are too often expected to look for the psychopathologies of religion leaving sociologists to deal with whatever it can achieve publicly. Yet there are few studies of "how to do things with religion" that might be in line with Austin's (1962) pragmatic emphasis on language, and we do not understand why religion does not always unmake prejudice or deal constructively with mental illness and dependency. Until the effects of belief in either an active *or* a passive God, who is inside *or* beyond and involved with individuals *or* groups, are understood, it would be sensible to step back and focus on the public uses and access to religion, asking, for example, "When and where did you last have a conversation about religion?" in order to uncover the social rules that constrain both its insiders and outsiders.

It is hard to escape pervasive social pressures towards religious "orthodoxy" (Deconchy 1980), since the rationality of any religion is socially controlled, with control that depends on each group's structure and traditions. While orthodoxy may be more obvious within Catholic than Protestant traditions, strong group pressures to conformity were shown in one of my early studies of Methodist students' attitudes (Brown and Pallant 1962). In another study, members of a religiously conservative group showed high agreement about doctrines and divergent social attitudes, while those in the Student Christian Movement were diverse with homogeneous social attitudes (Brown 1962a).

Resolving the tension between an individual's commitment to belief, practice, or experience and the "corporate commitment" that William James (1902, 491–92) recognized, which the Doctrine Commission of the Church of England in *Believing in the Church* (1981) set as a counterpoint between doctrinal and personal belief, requires answers to questions in the form "What did you do?" rather than "Why did you do it?" and the recognition that "What do you believe?" is inevitably catechetical. Leaving the Catholic Church, or the full-time ministry, may therefore be a more strident act than it would be to change from positions that are less juridical or doctrinaire. While psychologists of religion seem to assume that only one religious tradition should be adhered to at a time, studies of religious change suggest that young people who lapse are typically reacting, not so much against the implausibility of religion, as against the influence and control of their families (Hunsberger and Brown 1984).

Contemporary challenges to established religious structures by the women's movement, demands for relevance in liturgical reform, and political change that has altered the context within which religions operate have left some still hoping to preserve the received practices (cf. Welford 1948) rather than to reconstruct them. The need for change is overlooked by those who find themselves at the barricades and with hope but little optimism. Irksome conflicts over conservative or liberal reactions to such issues as whether God is female, about religion's prophetic and priestly roles, and about the place of the Holy Spirit are readily documented. Godin's (1971, 130–31) plea for a "progressive transformation of a magical and superstitious mentality" to a "sacramental life of faith," in which the numinous might be interpreted in religious *or* aesthetic terms (Back and Bourque 1970), could help us to reconstrue such issues.

The ambiguity of religion, as public or private, social or personal, secular or transcendental, made it a traditional field for psychological interpretation and study. Despite as least 90 years of empirical research on religious beliefs, once psychology emerged from theology, philosophy, and physiology, more counterintuitive questions should have been asked about religion to establish how it differs from other ideologically based movements. Agreed measures are still needed to allow separate sets of results to be compared and show how individuals cope with social and other demands and how other people may influence that. By adopting a perspective on individuals and institutions the psychology of religion could recapture Blaise Pascal's posthumously published assertion from 1670 that there are two foundations of religion, "one inward, the other outward" (1960, 128). How anyone deliberately selects from what is accessible to them is a still major but unsolved problem for psychologists of religion. That our popular conceptions of "religion" seem to have been fixed into an opposition between positive and negative evaluations of what is defined either socially or individually has not helped us to understand why so few people maintain the religious perspectives that are a resource from which many people draw support in crisis. And most of those who are religiously committed realize that they can only disclose their beliefs to others, without embarrassment, in carefully chosen contexts. Being religious entails rule-following, and that changes us more than we can change the available rules or roles. Augustine of Hippo, one of the early "psychologists," nevertheless balanced God's place in nature against a belief in man's freedom through the doctrine that God so influences that he persuades.

References

Argyle, M., and B. Beit-Hallahmi. 1975. *The social psychology of religion.* London: Routledge and Kegan Paul.

Austin, J. L. 1962. *How to do things with words.* Oxford: Clarendon Press. (Originally given as the William James lectures, 1955.)

Back, C. W., and L. B. Bourque. 1970. Can feelings be enumerated? *Behavioral Science* 15: 487–96.

Batson, C. D., and W. L. Ventis. 1982. *The religious experience: A social-psychological perspective.* New York: Oxford Univ. Press.

Berelson, B., and G. A. Steiner. 1964. *Human behavior: An inventory of scientific findings.* New York: Harcourt, Brace.

Brown, L. B. 1962a. Religious belief in two student societies. *Australian Journal of Psychology* 14: 202–9.

———. 1962b. A study of religious belief. *British Journal of Psychology* 53: 259–72.

————. 1964. Classifications of religious orientation. *Journal for the Scientific Study of Religion* 4: 91–99.

————. 1966. Ego-centric thought in petitionary prayer: A cross-cultural study. *Journal of Social Psychology* 68: 197–210.

————, ed. 1973. *Psychology and religion: Selected readings*. London: Penguin.

————. 1981. The religionism factor after 25 years. *Journal of Psychology* 107: 7–10.

————. 1985. *Advances in the psychology of religion*. Oxford: Pergamon.

————. 1987. *The psychology of religious belief*. London: Academic Press.

————. 1988. *The psychology of religion: An introduction*. London: SPCK.

Brown, L. B., and D. J. Pallant. 1962. Religious belief and social pressure. *Psychological Reports* 10: 269–70.

Brown, L. B., and R. H. Thouless. 1964. Petitionary prayer: Belief in its appropriateness and causal efficacy among adolescent girls. *Lumen Vitae Studies in Religious Psychology* 3: 91–99.

Brown, L. B., and R. H. Thouless. 1965. Animistic thought in civilized adults. *Journal of Genetic Psychology* 107: 32–42.

Cronbach, L. J. 1957. The two disciplines of scientific psychology. *American Psychologist* 12: 671–84.

Deconchy, J.-P. 1980. *Orthodoxie religieuse et sciences humaines*. Paris: Mouton.

————. 1985. Non-experimental and experimental methods in the psychology of religion. In *Advances in the psychology of religion*, ed L. B. Brown, 76–112. Oxford: Pergamon.

Dittes, J. E. 1969. Psychology of religion. In *The handbook of social psychology*, 2d ed., ed. G. Lindzey and E. Aronson, vol. 5, 602–59. Reading, Mass.: Addison-Wesley.

The Doctrine Commission of the Church of England. 1981. *Believing in the church: The corporate nature of faith*. London: SPCK.

Donahue, M. J. 1985. Intrinsic and extrinsic religiousness: Review and meta-analysis. *Journal of Personality and Social Psychology* 48: 400–419.

Farr, R. M., and S. Moscovici, eds. 1984. *Social representations*. Cambridge: Cambridge Univ. Press.

Godin, A. 1971. Some developmental tasks in Christian education. In *Research on religious development*, ed. M. P. Strommen, 109–54. New York: Hawthorn.

Gorsuch, R. L. 1984. Measurement: The boon and bane of investigating religions. *American Psychologist* 39: 228–36.

Hunsberger, B. E., and L. B. Brown. 1984. Religious socialization, apostasy, and the impact of family background. *Journal for the Scientific Study of Religion* 23: 239–51.

James, W. 1902. *The varieties of religious experience: A study in human nature*. New York: Collier.

Lerner, M. J. 1980. *The belief in a just world: A fundamental delusion*. New York: Plenum.

Malinowski, B. 1925. Magic, science, and religion. *Science, religion, and reality,* ed. J. Needham, 19–84. New York and London: Macmillan.

Otto, R. 1923. *The idea of the holy: An inquiry into the nonrational factor in the idea of the divine and its relation to the rational.* Trans. J. W. Harvey. New York: Oxford Univ. Press.

Rokeach, M. 1960. *The open and closed mind: Investigations into the nature of belief systems and personality systems.* New York: Basic.

Scott, W. A. 1969. The structure of natural cognitions. *Journal of Personality and Social Psychology* 12: 261–78.

Spilka, B., R. W. Hood, and R. L. Gorsuch. 1985. *The psychology of religion: An empirical approach.* Englewood Cliffs, N.J.: Prentice-Hall.

Stark, R. S., and C. Y. Glock. 1968. *American piety: The nature of religious commitment.* Berkeley and Los Angeles: Univ. of California Press.

Thouless, R. H. 1956. *An introduction to the psychology of religion.* 2d ed. Cambridge: Cambridge Univ. Press.

————. 1958. *General and social psychology: A textbook for students of psychology and of the social sciences.* London: Univ. Tutorial Press.

Tylor, E. B. [1871]. 1958. *Primitive culture.* [London: J. Murray.] Reprint. *Religion in primitive culture,* with introduction by P. Radin. New York: Harper.

Wearing, A. J., and L. B. Brown. 1972. The dimensionality of religion. *British Journal of Social and Clinical Psychology* 11: 143–48.

Welford, A. T. 1948. The use of archaic language in religious expression: An example of "canalised response." *British Journal of Psychology* 38: 209–18.

Williams, H. A. 1963. Psychological objections. In *Objections of Christian belief,* ed. D. M. MacKinnon, 35–56. Philadelphia: Lippincott.

14

Kenneth I. Pargament

Kenneth I. Pargament is associate professor of psychology at Bowling Green State University, Bowling Green, Ohio. He has bachelor's and doctor's degrees in clinical/community psychology from the University of Maryland and has taught psychology of religion at both undergraduate and graduate levels. Pargament was a National Institute of Mental Health postdoctoral fellow in the School of Public Health and Hygiene at Johns Hopkins University. He is a board member of Jewish Family Services of Toledo, Ohio.

Pargament is a fellow of the American Psychological Association (APA) and has been a member of the executive committee of Division 36, Psychologists Interested in Religious Issues. He has lectured widely in such places as Poland. As a frequent consultant to churches and synagogues, he is widely recognized as one of the best known psychologists of applied religion. Pargament is a member of the editorial board of the *American Journal of Community Psychology*. He has also served as editorial consultant for the *Journal for the Scientific Study of Religion, Psychological Reports,* and *Religious Studies Review.*

Pargament has published widely in the applied psychology of religion. He has been interested in assessing congregational climates, in determining the effectiveness of sermons, in measuring the religious needs of college students, and in exploring the relationship between religion and mental health. A brief survey of some of his article titles attests to his wide range of interests: "Religious Participation, Religious Motivation, and Individual Psychosocial Competence" (with R. Steele and F. Tyler), "Measuring Member Satisfaction with the Church" (with W. H. Silverman, S. M. Johnson, R. J. Echemendia, and S. Snyder), "The Resource Collaborator Role: A Model for Interactions Involving Psychologists" (with F. Tyler and M. Gatz), "Some Correlates of Sermon

379

Impact among Lay Catholics: An Exploratory Study," "Assessing the Religious Needs of College Students: Action-oriented Research in the Religious Context," and "God Help Me: Toward a Theoretical Framework of Coping for the Psychology of Religion."

Dr. Pargament has recently completed a longitudinal study of the roles religion plays in the process of coping with serious negative life events. He is currently writing a book about the psychology of religion and coping (theory, research, and practice).

In his essay "The Psychology of Religion: A Clinical-Community Psychology Perspective," Pargament discusses three major themes that have guided his work in the psychology of religion. The first is a view of religion from an individual-systems perspective. Having remained true to his training in community psychology, he has attended to the ecological/environmental factors in religious experience and behavior. He notes his long-standing interest in organizational climates as applied to religious institutions. The second theme which Pargament notes is his conviction that religion is a means of coping with the world. He writes about a novel idea, namely, that approaches to religion have both their advantages and their disadvantages. Religion is a complex phenomenon, according to Pargament, and certain persons do better in certain religious environments than in others. Finally, Pargament suggests that the applied as well as the theoretical nature of the psychology of religion has been a guidepost for him. He has been involved in action-oriented research which was focused on helping people. His involvement with religious congregations, in which he tried to link his desires to understand and to help, is a testimony to this emphasis.

In the article "The Limits of Fit: Examining the Implications of Person-Environment Congruence within Different Religious Settings," Pargament and his colleagues consider the overall impact of accommodation and agreement with the goals and behavioral expectations of religious organizations on members' satisfaction, involvement, and psychosocial competence. The results of a survey of members who did and did not "fit" with their churches revealed that those who were more accommodated evidenced lower coping skills and levels of efficacy. Utilizing systems theory, the results are considered in light of how individuals choose and are shaped by group memberships. They discuss the importance of social groups in religious identity formation and adjustment.

The Psychology of Religion:
A Clinical/Community Psychology Perspective

G ood things can come out of bad experiences. Early in my graduate student days in clinical/community psychology, I lost my
way to my first consultation appointment with the lieutenant of
the local police department. After driving around for what seemed to be
hours, I pulled into a gas station and called the lieutenant to ask for
directions. Naturally enough he asked me where I was coming from.
However, by that time I was so lost I didn't know. He said, "Well son, I
can't tell you how to get here if you don't know where you're coming
from." After I recovered from my embarrassment, I realized that, perhaps unintentionally, the lieutenant had made a powerful statement.
Since that time I have struggled to construct a map to guide me in my
work. Three major themes in particular have been very important to me
as guideposts directing my work in the area of the psychology of religion. These themes involve a view of religion from an individual-systems perspective; a view of religion as a means of coping with the
world, one which carries with it both advantages and disadvantages;
and a view of the psychology of religion as an applied as well as a theoretical field.

Religion from an Individual-Systems Perspective

James (1902) set the tone for much of the psychology of religion
when he defined religion as an individual phenomenon, that is, "feelings, acts, and experiences of individual men in their solitude" (31).
Since his time, psychologists have tended to approach religion from a
personological tradition. Through this process we have begun to
develop important insights into the complexity of individual religious
experience and its relationship to other important personal concerns

From the *Journal of Psychology and Christianity* 5, no. 2 (1986): 68–71; reprinted by permission of the publisher and the author. Copyright 1986 by the Christian Association for
Psychological Studies.

including prejudice, mental health, morality, altruism, and personality. Yet much of this work has tended to view people apart from their social context.

My own thinking and research have been heavily shaped by the ecological, or individual-systems, perspective. From this point of view, people are constantly involved in larger social situations and social systems. Over the past several years my colleagues and I have been involved in a program of research which begins to document the importance of situational and systemic factors in the psychology of religion. For example, in an effort to examine the role of churches and synagogues in the lives of their members, we recently developed a set of Congregation Climate Scales (Pargament et al. 1983). Congregation climate was defined as psychologically meaningful representations of the church/synagogue. Climate dimensions included sense of community, openness to change, social concern, autonomy, stability, activity, and personal problem solving. Through work with a variety of congregations it became clear that churches and synagogues have diverse climates or "personalities." Moreover, it became apparent that these climates hold important implications for the congregation as a whole and for the mental health of the individual member (Pargament et al. 1985; Silverman et al. 1983). We believe that this line of research begins to point to the need for a greater appreciation of social situational and systemic factors for a *psychology* of religion.

Many other interesting questions for the psychology of religion grow out of an individual-systems perspective. For example, psychologists might consider the ways in which religious institutions help or hinder members in their efforts to gain social support and solutions to problems in their lives. In a related sense it is important to consider how people develop or construct social milieu which can, in turn, enhance their own development (Pargament and Myers 1982). Psychologists might also attempt to identify those situations in which people are more likely to turn to God for help in understanding and solving problems in their lives. Initial efforts in this direction are quite promising (Pargament and Sullivan 1981; Spilka and Schmidt 1983; Gorsuch and Smith 1983). How helpful or harmful religious involvement is as a means of dealing with different situations remains an important unexplored question. However we might argue that attempts to solve problems through religious means as opposed to direct action would be particularly ineffective in situations where direct control is possible. Where direct control is not possible, religious forms of coping may be more efficacious.

Closer ties between the psychology and sociology of religion would advance the study of religion from an individual-systems perspective. There is a large body of sociological theory and research (e.g., Moberg,

Glock, Yinger, Berger, and Hoge) often overlooked yet directly relevant to psychological study. Similarly, closer ties between the psychology of religion and community psychology would be useful. For instance, recent advances by community psychology in the study of social support systems, climate, stress, coping, and problem solving suggest important directions for work in the psychology of religion.

Religion as a Means of Coping with the World: Advantages and Disadvantages

There is an interesting parallel between the history of research in psychotherapy and the history of research in the psychology of religion. Much of the early psychotherapy research focused on the question of whether psychotherapy is good for you; that is, does psychotherapy work? After much debate and study, psychotherapy researchers came to the conclusion that they were asking the wrong question. They developed for themselves a more intricate question, yet one more suited to the complexity of the psychotherapy experience: What type of therapy with what type of client offered by what type of therapist works best in what type of situation (Kiesler 1971)?

Similarly, much of the early research in the area of psychology and religion appeared to address the question of whether religion is good for you. However, it soon became clear that this question was overly simplistic. Crucial contributions were made by theorists and researchers (e.g., Allport, Glock, Spilka, and Batson) who demonstrated the multidimensional nature of religious behavior. Currently the field appears to have shifted its focus from the question of whether religion is good for you to the question of which religion is best for you. Unfortunately, the form of this latter question may also underestimate the richness and intricacy of religion.

I have tried to view religion as a complex phenomenon, one which provides a method for dealing with the world involving both advantages and disadvantages. I believe there is a growing body of literature supportive of this more intricate perspective. For example, we conducted a study which indicated that intrinsic religiously motivated congregation members generally report more favorable psychosocial competence characteristics than less intrinsically motivated members (Pargament, Steele, and Tyler 1979). This finding was not surprising. However, it oversimplified a more complex picture. When we examined the interaction between religious motivation and attendance at religious services as it relates to competence, we found that only one group indicated lower competence levels—those members who reported little intrinsic religious motivation *and* frequent church attendance. In short, a more complex analysis pointed to a more complex relationship between religion and effective functioning.

In another study, we predicted that the "fit" of church/synagogue members with their congregations would relate to a set of psychological trade-offs (Pargament, Steele, and Tyler 1979). Our prediction was supported. In contrast to members who did not fit well in their congregations, members who fit well in their congregations reported greater satisfaction with their churches and synagogues. However, members who fit well also reported significantly lower levels of efficacy and of problem-solving skills than members who fit less well. Thus both fit and lack of fit between congregation and member are associated with advantages and disadvantages.

Similarly, Batson and Ventis (1982) note that both intrinsic and quest religious orientations may carry risks and benefits for the individual. Their review of the literature leads them to suggest that while the intrinsic orientation may help "free" the individual from anxiety and fears, it may also limit his or her ability to question, change, or solve problems creatively. Conversely, they suggest that while the quest orientation may facilitate growth, change, and creativity, it may not provide a reassuring response to situations which arouse tension. These studies begin to underscore and grapple with the complexity of religious experience.

Following the historic path of psychotherapy research, future studies in psychology of religion may focus further on precise pieces of a more involved question: What type of religion held by what type of person faced with what type of life situation offer what types of advantages and disadvantages in their efforts to deal with the world? Implicit in this question is the potential value of a variety of religious experiences, rather than one type of experience or orientation alone. This question also points to the need for clearer conception and measurement of the problem-solving process. It is encouraging to note the promising efforts of several psychologists to move beyond static measures of personality, adjustment, or psychopathology to more dynamic measures of how people attempt to deal with situations in their lives (e.g., Lazarus, Spivack, Shure, and Tyler). I have also elaborated on this coping perspective in more recent theoretical and empirical studies (Pargament 1990; Pargament et al. 1988; Pargament et al., in press).

Psychology of Religion:
An Applied as Well as a Theoretical Field

Psychology and religion share an interest in helping people. Yet interactions between these two groups are typically infrequent and brief and often characterized by misunderstanding and mistrust. Resource collaboration between psychology and religion represents one antidote to this problem (Tyler, Pargament, and Gatz 1983). This process involves a recognition and sharing of the unique resources of two disciplines. Occasional exchange does take place between psychological and religious communities in the areas of psychotherapy and pastoral counseling. However, there are other important arenas for collaboration. Research represents one such arena.

I view research as an opportunity to help as well as learn something about people. This perspective has led me to a particular interest in action-oriented research which bridges applied and theoretical concerns (Matoor and Pargament 1987). For example, through our involvement with religious congregations described earlier, we developed a better understanding of churches and synagogues as human systems. We wanted to offer something to these congregations as well. Towards this end, we developed the Congregation Development Program (CDP) (Pargament et al. 1984). The CDP is a data-based change program designed to help churches and synagogues examine themselves and plan for change systematically. Congregation members complete a survey which deals comprehensively with church/synagogue life. The data are tabulated and then interpreted jointly with congregation members and leaders. Through this process a variety of congregations have been helped to define for themselves areas of strength, areas in need of improvement, and directions for change.

Thorsheim and Roberts (1983) have been involved in another action-oriented program of research incorporating applied and theoretical concerns. Practically, they developed a drug abuse prevention program in 24 Lutheran congregations which builds upon the natural support systems in these churches. Theoretically, their work has resulted in a greater understanding of social support, hope, and empowerment in these congregations.

Important research questions for psychology may also be generated by the religious community. For instance, a few years ago a minister spoke to me of his confusion about the response of a conservative religious audience to his more liberal sermons. He expected considerable dissent and negative reaction and, instead, found members complimenting him on his sermons. Conversation with the minister led to the hypothesis that some members may distort the sermon message to fit with their own religious beliefs. We developed a study of memory for religious messages which put to the test this and other predictions from cognitive psychology theory. While the results were practically relevant to religious systems, they also shed some light on how we make sense of religious material (Pargament and DeRosa 1985).

In short, a growing body of study indicates that we can assist as well as learn from those we study. Research, carefully considered and implemented, can be a basis for collaboration and mutual gain rather than suspicion and mistrust between psychology and religion. More generally, this line of work suggests that the psychology of religion is a field which has significant possibilities in both application and theory. In future years I expect to see further research in the psychology of religion which links more closely our desire for understanding with our desire to help.

References

Batson, C. D., and W. L. Ventis. 1982. *The religious experience: A social-psychological perspective.* New York: Oxford Univ. Press.

Gorsuch, R. L., and C. S. Smith. 1983. Attributions of responsibility to God: an interaction of religious beliefs and outcomes. *Journal for the Scientific Study of Religion* 22: 340–52.

James, W. 1902. *The varieties of religious experience: A study in human nature.* New York: Random.

Kiesler, D. J. 1971. Experimental designs in psychotherapy research. In *Handbook of psychotherapy and behavior change: An empirical analysis,* ed. A. E. Bergin and S. Garfield, 36–74. New York: Wiley.

Matoor, K. I., and K. I. Pargament. 1987. The roles of religion in prevention and promotion. *Prevention in Human Services* 5: 161–205.

Pargament, K. I. 1990. God help me: Toward a theoretical framework of coping in the psychology of religion. *Research on the Social Scientific Study of Religion* 2: 195–224.

Pargament, K. I., and D. DeRosa. 1985. What was the sermon about? Predicting memory for religious messages from cognitive psychology theory. *Journal for the Scientific Study of Religion* 24: 180–93.

Pargament, K. I., and J. Myers. 1982. The individual-system spiral: A foundation of value for action in community psychology. Paper presented at the American Psychological Association, August, Washington, D.C.

Pargament, K. I., and M. Sullivan. 1981. Examining attributions of control across diverse personal situations: A psychosocial perspective. Paper presented at the convention of the American Psychological Association, August, Los Angeles.

Pargament, K. I., R. Steele, and F. Tyler. 1979. Religious participation, religious motivation, and individual psychosocial competence. *Journal for the Scientific Study of Religion* 18: 412–19.

Pargament, K. I., F. Tyler, and R. Steele. 1979. Is fit it? The relationship between church/synagogue-member fit and the psychosocial competence of the member. *Journal of Community Psychology* 7: 243–52.

Pargament, K. I., S. M. Johnson, R. J. Echemendia, and W. H. Silverman. 1985. The limits of fit: Examining the implications of person-environment congruence within different religious settings. *Journal of Community Psychology* 13 (January): 20–30.

Pargament, K. I., W. H. Silverman, S. M. Johnson, R. J. Echemendia, and S. Snyder. 1983. The psychosocial climate of religious congregations. *American Journal of Community Psychology* 11: 351–81.

Pargament, K. I., J. Kennell, W. Hathaway, M. Grevengood, J. Newman, and W. Jones. 1988. Religion and the problem-solving process: Three styles of coping. *Journal for the Scientific Study of Religion* 27: 90–104.

Pargament, K. I., S. M. Johnson, R. J. Echemendia, J. Myers, P. Cook, C. McGath, W. H. Silverman, and L. Wallrabenstein. 1984. The congregation development program: A data-based change approach. *Division 36 Newsletter* 8, no. 3: 4–5.

Silverman, W. H., K. I. Pargament, S. M. Johnson, R. J. Echemendia, and S. Snyder. 1983. Measuring member satisfaction with the church. *Journal of Applied Psychology* 68: 664–77.

Spilka, B., and G. Schmidt. 1983. General attribution theory for the psychology of religion: The influence of event-character on attributions to God. *Journal for the Scientific Study of Religion* 22: 326–39.

Thorsheim, H., and B. Roberts. 1983. The "flavor" of the social ecology paradigm in use: Building on mutual social support in preventing drug abuse. St. Olaf College, Northfield, Minn. Unpublished paper.

Tyler, F., K. I. Pargament, and M. Gatz. 1983. The resource collaborator role: A model for interactions involving psychologists. *American Psychologist* 38: 388–98.

The Limits of Fit:
Examining the Implications
of Person-Environment Congruence
within Different Religious Settings

The concept of individual-systems fit has been proposed as an alternative basis for assessing and modifying the well-being of people and their settings. This perspective assumes that deficits lie neither within people nor within systems. Rather, problems follow from the incongruence or lack of fit between the needs and resources of the individual and those of the setting (Murrell 1973). Constructive change, in turn, involves a matching of individuals with suitable systems, rather than a modification of individual or systems (French, Rodgers, and Cobb 1974; Hunt 1975).

Surprisingly, in spite of its major implications for viewing and changing people and settings, the concept of fit has not generated much critical debate. Yet critical questions can be raised. For instance, does the nature of the fit between individual and system have some significance for the well-being of each? It could be argued that some types of individual-systems fit are more benign or meaningful than other types. Nielsen and Moos (1978) provide data which support this point. They found that high school students high in a preference for exploration were more satisfied and better adjusted within classrooms characterized by high exploration climates than students low in exploration preference. However, within the classes characterized by a low exploration climate, a significant relationship between exploration preference and satisfaction and adjustment did not emerge.

Questions might also be raised about the possibility of unanticipated or unintended consequences of individual-systems fit. A large body of

Coauthored with Steven Johnson, Ruben Echemendia, and William Silverman. The authors are grateful to the congregations that participated in this project. Paul Schubert of the Psychological Studies and Consultation Program in Detroit was particularly instrumental in completing this study.

From the *Journal of Community Psychology* 13 (1985): 20–30; reprinted by permission of the publisher and the authors.

research conducted within a variety of settings has pointed to positive correlations among person-environment congruence and satisfaction, adjustment, and/or performance of the individual within that setting (French, Rodgers, and Cobb 1974; Harpin and Sandler 1979; Pervin 1968). Yet the fit, or lack of fit of an individual within a setting may have different implications for other aspects of life. For example, Pargament, Tyler, and Steele (1979) found that members who fit well within their churches and synagogues were more satisfied within their congregation than members who fit less well. However, members who fit well also manifested a lower level of self-esteem and less active coping skills than those who fit less well. They suggested that the fit of an individual within a system may be associated with a set of psychological and social advantages and disadvantages.

In the present study, these critical questions about individual-systems fit are put to test within religious settings. These settings represent particularly appropriate sites for this study for several reasons: they are frequently used (approximately two-thirds of the adult population in the U.S. belongs to a church or synagogue); they vary in their needs and in the demands they make upon members; and they clearly have significance for the psychosocial well-being of the member (Moberg 1962; Pargament 1982).

One important dimension which distinguishes religious congregations is their openness to different points of view and change. Kelley (1977), for example, noted that conservative churches "do not consent to, encourage, or indulge any violation of its standards of belief or behavior by its professed adherents" (176). Other congregations tolerate and encourage diversity of opinion and behavior among members and changes within the church (McGaw and Wright 1979). Similarly, individuals vary in the degree to which they seek and tolerate different points of view and changes in their lives (Budner 1962; Frenkel-Brunswik 1949).

In this study, it was assumed that members with greater tolerance for ambiguity fit better within churches that are more open to different points of view and change than churches that are less open. Conversely, it was assumed that members with less tolerance for ambiguity fit better within churches that are less autonomous and open than more open churches. Defined in this manner, member-congregation fit was examined as it relates to three sets of variables: satisfaction with several aspects of congregational life; the level of involvement of the member in the congregation; and the psychosocial-competence characteristics of the member. Two hypotheses were studied:

1. Within churches more open to different points of view and change, members who are more tolerant of ambiguity will man-

ifest greater satisfaction, involvement, and psychosocial competence than members who are less tolerant of ambiguity.

2. Within churches less open to different points of view and change, members who are less tolerant of ambiguity will manifest greater satisfaction with and involvement in the church than members who are more tolerant of ambiguity. However, a similar inverse relationship was not predicted between tolerance for ambiguity and the psychosocial competence of the members.

In sum, this study examines the notion that the *nature* of the fit between individual and system is of significance for the individual; that is, fitting within more autonomous open churches will have different implications than fitting within less autonomous open churches. Several theorists and researchers have argued for the psychosocial value of flexible systems which allow their members to effect change and to express themselves in diverse ways (Argyris 1975; DeCharms 1968; Maslow 1965). Fit in these more open settings is expected to relate positively to indicators of member functioning within the setting (satisfaction and involvement) and to more general indicators of psychosocial effectiveness. Conversely, systems which limit the opportunities of their members to express themselves and impact on the setting have been viewed critically by social scientists (Haire 1954; Hurley 1975; Moos 1973). Fit in these less open settings is expected to relate positively to indicators of members' functioning within the setting (satisfaction and involvement). However, it is not expected to relate directly to the general psychosocial effectiveness of the member.

Method

Participants

One hundred forty-four members representing two Protestant and two Roman Catholic churches participated in this study. The sample was exclusively white, 37% male, and averaged 43 years of age.

Churches

Four churches were selected for study from a larger sample of 13 churches. The 13 churches varied considerably in terms of size, denomination, racial composition, socioeconomic status, and urban-suburban status. To control for these extraneous variables, four churches were chosen which were comparable in size, racial composition, and socioeconomic status. Two dimensions of the psychosocial climate of churches (Autonomy and Openness to Change) were used to define operationally the churches as more or less open to different points of view and change.

The two climate scales were selected from the Congregation Climate Scales developed by Pargament, Silverman, Johnson, Echemendia, and Snyder (1983). *Autonomy* measures the extent to which the church is seen as encouraging differences in ideas, beliefs, behaviors, and attitudes among members. *Openness to Change* assesses the degree to which the church is perceived as receptive to changes in programs, approaches, and ideas. A complete description of these scales as well as their psychometric properties is available (Pargament et al. 1983).

One Protestant and one Catholic church characterized by Autonomy and Openness to Change scores above the mean for the 13 congregations were defined as more autonomous and open (MAOC). Similarly one Protestant and one Catholic church characterized by Openness to Change and Autonomy scores below the mean for the 13 congregations were defined as less autonomous and open (LAOC). The use of mean climate scores for each of the four churches was based on the assumption that the members of each church would hold a similar view of their congregation. To test this assumption, homogeneity coefficients were calculated for the Autonomy and Openness to Change scales for each of the four churches (Tryon and Bailey 1970). The homogeneity coefficients ranged from .21 to .75, indicating that the members of each church shared, to at least a moderate degree, a similar perception of their congregation on these dimensions.

In table 14.1, the means and standard deviations are presented for members of the MAOC and the members of the LAOC on the two climate variables and on the measure of tolerance for ambiguity. Also shown in table 14.1 are the statistical tests of difference between MAOC and LAOC on these variables. As it indicates, the MAOC were characterized by significantly higher Autonomy and Openness to Change scores than the LAOC. MAOC members also reported significantly greater tol-

Table 14.1

Means and Standard Deviations on Climate Variables and Tolerance for Ambiguity for More Open and Less Open Churches

Variable	More open churches			Less open churches			t	df
	M	SD	n	M	SD	n		
Tolerance for ambiguity	27.88	6.01	68	25.01	6.32	76	2.78	142***
Openness to change	22.34	4.10	65	16.97	4.57	73	7.49	136***
Autonomy	26.46	4.47	63	21.57	4.68	74	6.23	135***

***p<.001.

erance for ambiguity than LAOC members. The two climate scales were significantly correlated ($r = .38$, $p < .001$), indicating that members perceiving greater autonomy in their church also perceived greater openness to change. Both climate scales were modestly correlated with the tolerance for ambiguity measure ($rs = .16$, $p < .05$).

Additional analyses revealed that the members of MAOC and LAOC churches were comparable in terms of their personal intrinsic religious orientation as measured by the Hoge (1972) Intrinsic Religious Motivation Scale. Furthermore, the two groups of churches were comparable in size proportion of male and female members, and socioeconomic status as measured by the Hollingshead-Redlich (1958) scale. However, LAOC members were significantly older ($M = 47$ years) than MAOC members ($M = 37$ years).

Measures

Tolerance for Ambiguity

The degree to which the member is able to view and deal with complex issues in flexible ways was measured by Martin and Westie's (1959) Intolerance for Ambiguity Scale. This eight-item Likert-type scale has related significantly to indices of nationalism and authoritarianism and has distinguished among racially tolerant and prejudiced adults.

Congregation Satisfaction

The satisfaction of members was measured with respect to eight aspects of congregation life: religious services, members, clergy, policies, leaders, education, facilities, and social programs. Each of the scales consists of adjectives which members characterize as descriptive or nondescriptive of that aspect of the congregation. Evidence for the reliability, convergent, and discriminant validity of these Congregation Satisfaction scales has been presented by Silverman and others (1983).

Congregation Involvement

The degree of involvement of the member in the congregation was assessed by a series of items assembled from previous studies (King and Hunt 1975; Wicker and Mehler 1971). When summed, these items formed a scale of modest internal consistency (coefficient alpha = .64).

Psychosocial Competence

Following the models of Smith (1968) and Tyler (1978), three dimensions of psychosocial competence were examined. The extent to which the individual holds favorable *self-attitudes* was measured by Rosenberg's (1965) Self-Esteem Scale. The degree to which the individual maintains a moderately optimistic *attitude toward others* and the world was assessed by Rotter's (1967) Trust Scale and the Scale of Life Satisfaction designed by Smith and Ironson (1979). Finally, the extent to which the individual *solves problems* in an active manner was measured by Tyler's (1978) Behavioral Attitudes of Psychosocial Competence (BAPC) scale. Each of these measures has demonstrated satisfactory internal consistency and significant relationships with a variety of behavioral and self-report criteria of effective functioning within diverse groups.

Procedure

The clergy from each church drew a systematic sample of 10% of the members to participate in the study with the assistance of the research group (Shaeffer, Mendenhall, and Ott 1980). The members were contacted and an evening was arranged in which the questionnaires could be administered to the entire group. The questionnaires were completed anonymously.

The participants were told that the questionnaire would assess the strengths and weaknesses of their congregation. The questionnaire consisted of three parts: (1) an assessment of the perceived psychosocial climate and member satisfaction with the church, (2) an assessment of the members' religious beliefs and practices, and (3) an assessment of the psychosocial effectiveness of the member.

Results

In this study, different relationships between tolerance for ambiguity and other measures of individual functioning were predicted for members of MAOC and LAOC. These relationships were assumed to be moderated by the nature of the church. Moderated multiple regression analyses were conducted to test this assumption (Peters and Champoux 1979). In these analyses, the satisfaction scales, level of involvement, and measures of psychosocial competence served as dependent variables. The tolerance for ambiguity scores and the dummy-coded MAOC-LAOC variable served as independent variables. They were entered into the regression equation simultaneously. The cross product of these two independent variables was then computed and treated as the interaction variable (Cohen and Cohen 1975). The interaction variable was entered into the equation last. Finally, the difference between the amount of variance accounted for in the first and second regressions was evaluated. The results of these analyses are presented in table 14.2.

Several results are of interest in this table. First, the tolerance for ambiguity scale predicted three of the four psychosocial-competence scale scores in a direct fashion. It did not, however, predict members' satisfaction scale scores. Conversely, the nature of the church (MAOC versus LAOC) predicted each of the satisfaction scale scores. Analysis of

Table 14.2

Results of the Moderated Multiple Regression Analyses

Dependent variable	Tolerance for ambiguity		More/less open churches		Cumu-lative R^2	Interaction term		Cumu-lative R^2
	ΔR^2_T	F	$\Delta R^2_{M/L}$	F		ΔR^2_m	F	
Satisfaction measures								
Members	.000	.04	.121	18.69**	.133	.011	1.83	.145
Clergy	.000	.03	.048	6.93	.049	.048	7.35**	.098
Leaders	.022	3.24	.092	13.26**	.099	.028	4.09*	.126
Education programs	.017	2.65	.160	24.59**	.161	.026	4.01*	.186
Services	.014	2.41	.196	33.70**	.196	.037	6.65*	.234
Congregation involvement	.000	.01	.009	1.15	.009	.009	.91	.016
Psychosocial competence								
BAPC	.022	3.11	.002	.28	.022	.036	5.34*	.058
Trust	.088	12.97**	.006	.89	.113	.020	3.15	.134
Self-Esteem	.073	10.84**	.003	.41	.089	.006	.87	.094
Life satisfaction	.076	11.20**	.015	2.24	.079	.039	5.95*	.118

$*p<.05$ ($F>3.92$). $**p<.01$ ($F>6.84$, $df=1.125$).
ΔR^2_T=increment in R^2 when tolerance for ambiguity is entered into the regression equation after the more/less open churches variable: $\Delta R^2_{M/L}$-increment in R^2 when more/less open churches is entered into the regression equation after the tolerance for ambiguity variable: ΔR^2_m=increment in R^2 due to the addition of the interaction term to the regression equation containing both the tolerance for ambiguity and more/less open churches variables.

the mean satisfaction scores of MAOC and LAOC members indicated greater congregation satisfaction of MAOC members on each of the five scales. However, the nature of the church did not predict the scores of the members on the psychosocial-competence scales. Neither tolerance for ambiguity nor the nature of the church emerged as a significant predictor of congregation involvement. Finally, and most central to this study, significant interaction effects were found with respect to four of the five satisfaction measures (clergy, leaders, education programs, services) and two of the four psychosocial-competence scales (BAPC, life satisfaction).[1] Thus the relationships between tolerance for ambiguity

1. As was noted earlier, members of MAOC were significantly older than members of LAOC. To assess the effects of this and other demographic variables, the moderated multiple regression analyses were recalculated with the effects of the demographic variables entered into the regression equation on the first step. The nature and size of the effects resulting from these analyses were quite similar to those reported in table 14.3.

and these dependent variables were moderated by the nature of the church.

Specific directions to these relationships were predicted within MAOC and LAOC in this study. To examine them, separate Pearson correlations between tolerance for ambiguity and the measures of satisfaction, congregation involvement, and psychosocial competence were calculated for members of MAOC and LAOC. These analysis are shown in table 14.3.

Hypothesis 1 predicted that "within churches more open to different points of view and change, members who are more tolerant of ambiguity will manifest greater satisfaction, involvement, and psychosocial competence than members who are less tolerant of ambiguity." The results in table 14.3 provide some support for this hypothesis. Within MAOC, tolerance for ambiguity related significantly to the four measures of psychosocial competence and to satisfaction with the clergy.

Hypothesis 2 predicted that "within churches less open to different points of view and change, members who are less tolerant of ambiguity will manifest greater satisfaction and involvement than members who are more tolerant of ambiguity. However, a similar inverse relationship was not predicted between tolerance for ambiguity and the psychosocial competence of the members." Modest support for this hypothesis is indicated in table 14.3. Within LAOC, greater tolerance for ambiguity

Table 14.3
Correlations of Tolerance for Ambiguity with Criteria for More Open and Less Open Churches

Tolerance for ambiguity with	Less open churches r	More open churches r
Satisfaction measures		
Member	−.08	.16
Leaders[a]	−.27	.06
Clergy[a]	−.19	.29**
Services[a]	−.26*	.18
Education programs[a]	−.24*	.11
Congregation Involvement	−.07	.10
Psychosocial competence		
BAPC[a]	−.03	.29**
Trust	.18	.41**
Self-Esteem	.21*	.35**
Life satisfaction[a]	.11	.45**

Note: n for Less Open Churches ranged from 69 to 76 depending upon number of missing cases; n for More Open Churches ranged from 61 to 68 depending upon number of missing cases. [a]Indicates a significant interaction effect for this variable in the moderated multiple regression analysis. *p < .05. **p < .01.

among members related to significantly lower satisfaction with the leaders, clergy, services, and educational programs of the congregation. Further, an inverse relation between tolerance for ambiguity and the measures of psychosocial competence did not emerge. These latter relationships ranged from a negligible correlation with the BAPC to a significant positive correlation with self-esteem.

In short, greater tolerance for ambiguity related to somewhat greater satisfaction among MAOC members while it related to lower satisfaction among LAOC members. However, while greater tolerance for ambiguity related in a consistently positive manner with the psychosocial competence of MAOC members, it did not relate inversely to the competence of LAOC members. Rather, tolerance for ambiguity was positively associated with self-esteem among LAOC members. Tolerance for ambiguity did not relate significantly to the level of congregational involvement of LAOC or MAOC members.

Discussion

This study examined the notion of individual-systems fit in critical detail within a sample of Protestant and Roman Catholic churches. Two churches were categorized as more autonomous open churches (MAOC), and two were categorized as less autonomous open churches (LAOC) on the basis of their scores on measures of the degree to which individual differences and changes in the congregation are seen as encouraged. The significant correlation between the Autonomy and Openness to Change climate scales provided further support for the use of both dimensions in the definition of the two church groups. These two groups were comparable in terms of their demographic characteristics. The groups were also comparable in their level of religious motivation and involvement in the congregation. Thus, these congregations were defined by differences in perceived autonomy and openness to change unrelated to the levels of religious commitment of the members. This latter finding was somewhat surprising in light of Kelley's (1977) assertion that religious orthodoxy is more likely to flourish within systems which discourage differences in the beliefs and practices of their members. However, these results suggest that religious commitment may be found within a variety of congregational milieu.

It was assumed that members who are able to view and deal with complex issues in flexible ways would fit more appropriately within MAOC. Conversely, members less able to deal with complexity and ambiguity were assumed to fit more appropriately within LAOC. Supporting this assumption was the significant difference among MAOC and LAOC members in their tolerance for ambiguity, a difference that suggests that these churches may selectively attract and keep members with and/or shape members toward varying tolerances for ambiguity.[2] Congregation members completed a battery of measures assessing their satisfaction with several aspects of church life, their level of involvement in the church, and their level of psychosocial competence.

Two questions regarding the nature of individual-systems fit were raised in this study. The first question concerned whether some types of fit are more benign than others. It was predicted that fit within MAOC would have uniformly positive significance for the member. In contrast, within LAOC, the positive correlates of fit were expected to be limited. The second question focused in more detail on whether the fit between an individual and system would have positive implications both in how that person functions in relation to the system and in how that person functions in life more generally. It was predicted that fit within LAOC would relate positively to the member's satisfaction with and involvement in the congregation, but not to the member's general psychosocial competence.

Modest support was obtained for both sets of predictions. Among the more autonomous open churches, a greater degree of tolerance for ambiguity was associated with significantly more active problem-solving skills, greater satisfaction with life, and higher level of self-esteem and trust in others. Satisfaction with the clergy was another significant positive correlate of tolerance for ambiguity among MAOC members. The relationships between tolerance for ambiguity and the other aspects of satisfaction and congregation involvement were positive but nonsignificant.

In contrast to the MAOC, within those churches which were less autonomous and open, greater tolerance for ambiguity among members was coupled with *lower* levels of satisfaction with the leaders, clergy, services, and educational aspects of the church. However, inverse relationships between tolerance for ambiguity and psychosocial competence did not emerge. In fact, LAOC members with greater tolerance for ambiguity reported significantly higher self-esteem.

Thus, fitting within the more autonomous open churches was associated in a uniformly positive direction with generally greater member well-being. Fitting within the less autonomous open churches, however, had mixed implications for the member. In short, the significance of fit

2. The scales that served as the basis for the definition of fit in this study were measured at the individual level. It could be argued that fit studied here reflects intraindividual discord rather than person-environment congruence. Inconsistent with this interpretation, however, is the finding that church members shared, at least in part, a similar view of their congregation. Moreover their perceptions related to other structural characteristics of the church, such as size, racial composition, and denomination (Pargament et al. 1983). Thus, while measured at the individual level, climate appears to be socially as well as psychologically relevant. Finally, it is important to note that the correlation between the climate scales and Tolerance of Ambiguity was quite modest. These findings suggest that the measures of climate and Tolerance for Ambiguity are reflective of different phenomena.

varied across the two types of churches. This is the key finding of the present study. It underscores the importance of the nature of the interaction between individual and system in evaluating the efficacy of that interaction.

Implications and Conclusions

The relationships reported in this study could have developed as the result of several possible processes. The relative fit of the member with the congregation may be shaped by his or her attitudes and involvement in the church and general psychosocial-competence attributes. On the other hand, the fit of the member with the congregation may shape the approach of the member to the church and his or her general level of effective functioning. These correlational analyses cannot substantiate either developmental interpretation. It is difficult, however, to reconcile these results with the assertion in the literature that fit invariably leads to more effective performance and greater personal well-being. In the LAOC, positive relations between member-congregation fit and psychosocial competence did not emerge.

It may be more reasonable to suggest on the basis of these results that different types of individual-system fit vary in their psychological and social value. Certain types of fit may be advantageous to both the system and its members. In this study, the nature of the fit of the member with MAOC may have allowed him or her to take advantage of the opportunities the setting provides for growth, change, and the development of individual potential. Personal congruence with other systems which enhance individuality and are open to different points of view and change may be generally desirable.

On the other hand, other types of fit may be generally destructive. While these interactions were not explored in the present study, they are easily imagined. For example, descriptions of the Jonestown tragedy point to the need of the cult members for structure, a sense of belonging, and benevolent but firm external control. The intense group cohesiveness, firm system of rules, and totalitarian leadership structure of the cult system meshed with these individual needs. While the needs and resources of members and cult, in this instance, fit, the nature of the fit was ultimately destructive to both individuals and system. Similar observations might be made regarding fit within other extremely closed systems.

Still other individual-systems interactions may have both advantages and disadvantages. The findings from the less autonomous open churches in this study offer a case in point. While fit in these churches may provide greater satisfaction for less tolerant members, it may not provide those members with the challenge necessary to stimulate more active coping skills and greater levels of self-esteem and trust in others. In this sense, the fit of the member in the less autonomous open church may occur at the expense of more generally effective living skills. Conversely, the lack of fit of members in this setting may limit the members' satisfaction with the church, yet enhance the members' self-esteem.

Advantages and disadvantages may accompany fit within other settings as well. In using correlates of individual-systems congruence *restricted to how the person functions in that setting,* this possibility has not been examined. For example, several studies have yielded positive relationships between fit and measures of performance and satisfaction of the person within those settings (French, Rodgers, and Cobb 1974; Pervin 1968). These studies have led to the conclusion that individual-systems fit is a worthwhile value. However, the use of broader criteria of functioning in these investigations could have resulted in different conclusions. It is important to note that *this* study would have also pointed to the positive value of fit in more open and less open churches if the measures of psychosocial competence had not been included. Thus, these findings suggest potentially negative as well as positive implications of fit within certain settings, particularly less open ones. More specifically, while person-environment congruence might enhance the individual's satisfaction and performance in these settings, it may restrict the individual's functioning in other areas of life.

In sum, this study points to the limits of the fit concept as an alternate basis for the definition of effective individual and systems functioning. These limits need to be explored in more depth through studies of individual-systems interactions across diverse settings. Moreover, these studies should examine the efficacy of fit through the use of a range of indicators not limited to the particular individual-systems interaction. Finally, research designs capable of clarifying the path of influence among individual, system, and interactional variables are necessary. Data from these studies may help program planners and designers avoid overly simplistic solutions or those which create as many problems as they solve. Further, they may highlight the intricate trade-offs and judgments necessary to foster persons and environments facilitative of themselves and each other. While this process may test our own tolerance for ambiguity, it may be more reflective of and suited to a complex world.

References

Argyris, C. 1975. Dangers in applying results from experimental social psychology. *American Psychologist* 30: 469–85.

Budner, S. 1962. Intolerance of ambiguity as a personality variable. *Journal of Personality* 30: 29–50.

Cohen, J., and P. Cohen. 1975. *Applied multiple regression/correlation analysis for the behavioral sciences.* Hillside, N.J.: Erlbaum Associates.

DeCharms, R. 1968. *Personal causation.* New York: Academic Press.

French, J. P., W. Rodgers, and S. Cobb. 1974. Adjustment as person environment fit. In *Coping and adaptation,* ed. G. Coelho, 316–33. New York: Basic.

Frenkel-Brunswik, E. 1949. Intolerance of ambiguity as an emotional and perceptual personality variable. *Journal of Personality* 18: 108–43.

Haire, M. 1954. Industrial social psychology. In *The handbook of social psychology,* ed. G. Lindzey, vol. 2, 1104–23. Cambridge, Mass.: Addison-Wesley.

Harpin, P., and I. Sandler. 1979. Interaction of sex, locus of control, and teacher control: Toward a student-classroom match. *American Journal of Community Psychology* 7: 621–32.

Hoge, D. R. 1972. A validated intrinsic religious motivational scale. *Journal for the Scientific Study of Religion* 11: 369–76.

Hollingshead, A. B., and F. Redlich. 1958. *Social class and mental illness.* New York: Wiley.

Hunt, D. E. 1975. Person-environment interaction: A challenge found wanting before it was tried. *Review of Educational Research* 45: 209–30.

Hurley, D. 1975. Relationship between mental health paradigm and person-power utilization in the mental health system. Master's thesis, College Park, University of Maryland.

Kelley, D. 1977. *Why conservative churches are growing.* New York: Harper and Row.

King, M. B., and R. A. Hunt. 1975. Measuring the religious variable: National replication. *Journal for the Scientific Study of Religion* 14: 13–22.

McGaw, D. B., and E. Wright. 1979. *A tale of two congregations: Commitment and social structure in a charismatic and mainline congregation.* Hartford Seminary Foundation Research Report.

Martin, J. G., and F. R. Westie. 1959. The tolerant personality. *American Sociological Review* 24: 521–28.

Maslow, A. H. 1965. *Eupsychion management.* Homewood, Ill.: Irwin-Dorsey.

Moberg, D. 1962. *The church as a social institution.* Englewood Cliffs, N.J.: Prentice-Hall.

Moos, R. 1973. Conceptualization of human environments. *American Psychologist* 28: 652–65.

Murrell, S. 1973. *Community psychology and social systems.* New York: Behavioral Publications.

Nielsen, H., and R. Moos. 1978. Exploration and adjustment in high school classrooms: A study of person-environment fit. *Journal of Educational Research* 72: 52–57.

Pargament, K. I. 1982. The interface among religion, religious support systems, and mental health. In *Community support systems and mental health,* ed. D. Biegel and A. Naperstak, 161–74. New York: Springer Publishing.

Pargament, K. I., F. Tyler, and R. Steele. 1979. Is fit it? The relationship between church/synagogue-member fit and the psychosocial competence of the member. *Journal of Community Psychology* 7: 243–52.

Pargament, K. I., W. H. Silverman, S. M. Johnson, R. J. Echemendia, and S. Snyder. 1983. The psychosocial climate of religious congregations. *American Journal of Community Psychology* 11: 351–81.

Pervin, L. 1968. Performance and satisfaction as a function of individual-environment fit. *Psychological Bulletin* 69: 56–68.

Peters, W., and J. Champoux. 1979. The use of moderated regression in job redesign decisions. *Decision Sciences* 10: 85–95.

Rosenberg, M. 1965. *Society and the adolescent self-image.* Princeton, N.J.: Princeton Univ. Press.

Rotter, J. B. 1967. A new scale for the measurement of interpersonal trust. *Journal of Personality* 35: 651–65.

Schaeffer, R., W. Mendenhall, and L. Ott. 1980. *Elementary survey sampling.* North Scituate, Mass.: Dunbury Press.

Silverman, W. H., K. J. Pargament, S. M. Johnson, R. J. Echemendia, and S. Snyder. 1983. Measuring member satisfaction with the church. *Journal of Applied Psychology* 68: 664–77.

Smith, M. B. 1968. Competence and socialization, In *Socialization and society,* ed. J. Clausen, 270–320. Boston: Little, Brown.

Smith, P., and G. Ironson. 1979. Development of the scale of life satisfaction (SOLS). Bowling Green State University, Bowling Green, Ohio. Unpublished manuscript.

Tryon, R., and D. Bailey. 1970. *Cluster analysis.* New York: McGraw-Hill.

Tyler, F. 1978. Individual psychosocial competence: A personality configuration. *Education and Psychological Measurement* 38: 309–23.

Wicker, A., and A. Mehler. 1971. Assimilation of new members in a large or small church. *Journal of Applied Psychology* 55: 151–56.

Part 7

The Integration
of Psychology and Theology

15

David G. Myers

Social psychologist David G. Myers is the John Dirk Werkman Professor of Psychology at Hope College, an institution of the Reformed Church in America, in Holland, Michigan. Since the beginning of his teaching career there in 1967, he has been chair of the department of psychology, commencement speaker, and recipient of the college's Outstanding Professor-Educator Award. His Ph.D. in psychology is from the University of Iowa.

Dr. Myers is a fellow of four divisions of the American Psychological Association, including the Division of Personality and Social Psychology (Division 8) and Psychologists Interested in Religious Issues (Division 36). He received the Gordon Allport Prize for social psychological research from Division 9, Society for the Psychological Study of Social Issues. Various colleges and universities, among them Yale and Harvard, have invited Myers to their campuses to give lectures and addresses.

Myers has published scientific articles in such journals as *Science, American Scientist, Psychological Bulletin,* and *Advances in Experimental Social Psychology* and has also published in such popular magazines as *Saturday Review* and *Psychology Today.* He has been consulting editor of the *Journal of Experimental Social Psychology* and the *Journal of Personality and Social Psychology.*

Social Psychology (2d ed. [New York: McGraw-Hill, 1988]) and *Psychology* (New York: Worth, 1986) are two major psychology textbooks authored by Dr. Myers. He has also written several books relating psychology to the Christian faith; among them are *The Inflated Self: Human Illusions and the Biblical Call to Hope* (New York: Seabury, 1980), *The Human Connection* (coauthored with Martin Bolt, Downers Grove: Inter-Varsity, 1984), and *Psychology through the Eyes of Faith* (coauthored with Malcolm Jeeves, San Francisco: Harper and Row, 1987).

The essay "The Mystery of the Ordinary" is a reprint of chapter 4 in the Myers and Jeeves volume. In this chapter, Myers observes that humans are inclined to look for evidence of the supernatural in unusual and bizarre events. He suggests, however, that the truly extraordinary and mysterious events of life can be seen in such basic psychological processes as sensation, perception, consciousness, and cognition. For Myers, further evidences of the divine are found in language acquisition, human reproduction, and human life in general.

In "Yin and Yang in Psychological Research and Christian Belief," Myers discusses polarities in both Christian beliefs and psychological dynamics which function paradoxically in our understanding of human beings. He terms these "complementary principles," citing as examples such polarities as "mind emerges from brain"—"mind controls brain" and "we are made in the image of God"—"we are finite creatures." In research evidence, the Bible, and various Christian writings, Myers finds these seemingly contradictory concepts, which he believes must be held in tension for a full understanding of human life.

The Mystery of the Ordinary

"As a rule," said Holmes, "the more bizarre a thing is the less mysterious it proves to be. It is your commonplace, featureless crimes which are really puzzling."

Sir Arthur Conan Doyle,
The Adventures of Sherlock Holmes, 1891–92

At the core of the religious impulse is a sense of awe, an attitude of bewilderment, a feeling that reality is more amazing than everyday scientific reasoning can comprehend. Wonderstruck, we humbly acknowledge our limits and accept that which we can not explain.

For many religious people the ultimate threat of science is therefore that it will demystify life, destroying our sense of wonder and with it our readiness to believe in and worship an unseen reality. Once we regarded flashes of lightning and claps of thunder as supernatural magic. Now we understand the natural processes at work. Once we viewed certain mental disorders as demon possession. Now we are coming to discern genetic, biochemical, and stress-linked causes. Once we prayed that God would spare children from diphtheria. Now we vaccinate them. Understandably, some Christians have come to regard scientific naturalism as "the strongest intellectual enemy of the church."

We can also understand why such people therefore grasp at hints of the supernatural—at bizarre phenomena that science cannot explain. Browse your neighborhood religious bookstore and you will find books that describe happenings that defy natural explanation—people reading minds or foretelling the future, levitating objects or influencing the roll of a die, discerning the contents of sealed envelopes or solving cases that have dumbfounded detectives. Whether viewed as a divine gift or as demonic activity, such phenomena are said to refute a mechanistic worldview that has no room for supernatural mysteries.

From *Psychology Through the Eyes of Faith* by David G. Myers and Malcolm A. Jeeves; reprinted by permission of Harper & Row Publishers, Inc. Copyright 1987 by Christian College Coalition.

For several reasons, most research psychologists and professional magicians (who are wary of the exploitation of their arts in the name of psychic powers) are skeptical: (1) in the study of ESP and the paranormal there has been a distressing history of fraud and deception; (2) most people's beliefs in ESP are now understandable as a by-product of the efficient but occasionally misleading ways in which our minds process information; (3) the accumulating evidence regarding the brain-mind connection more and more weighs against the theory that the human mind can function or travel separately from the brain; and, most importantly, (4) there has never been demonstrated a reproducible ESP phenomenon, nor any individual who could defy chance when carefully tested. After one hundred years of research, and after hundreds of failed attempts to claim a $10,000 prize that has for two decades been offered to the first person who can demonstrate "*any* paranormal ability*," many parapsychologists concede that what they need to give their field credibility is a single reproducible phenomenon and the theory to explain it.

We Christians can side with the scientific skeptics on the ESP issue. We can heed not only the repeated biblical warnings against being misled by self-professed psychics who practice "divination" or "magic spells and charms," but also the scientific spirit of Deuteronomy: "If a prophet speaks in the name of the LORD and what he says does not come true, then it is not the LORD's message" (18:22 GNB). We believe that humans are finite creatures of the one who declares, "I am God, and there is none like me" (Isa. 46:9 KJV). We are aware of how cult leaders have seduced people with pseudopsychic tricks. And we affirm that God alone is omniscient (thus able to read minds and know the future), omnipresent (thus able to be in two places at once), and omnipotent (thus capable of altering—or better yet—creating nature with divine power). In the biblical view, humans, loved by God, have dignity, but not deity.

If our sense of mystery is not to be found in the realm of the pseudosciences and the occult, then where? Having cleared the decks of false mysteries, where shall we find the genuine mysteries of life? We can take our clue from Sherlock Holmes, who was fond of telling people, "It is a mistake to confound strangeness with mystery. The most commonplace crime is often the most mysterious. . . . Life is infinitely stranger than anything which the mind of man could invent. We would not dare to conceive the things which are really mere commonplaces of existence."

The more scientists learn about sensation, the more convinced they are that what is truly extraordinary is not extrasensory perception, claims for which inevitably dissolve upon investigation, but rather our very ordinary moment-to-moment sensory experiences of organizing formless neutral impulses into colorful sights and meaningful sounds. As you read this sentence, particles of light energy are being absorbed by the receptor cells of your eyes, converted into neural signals that activate neighboring cells, which process the information for a third layer of cells, which converge to form a nerve tract that transmits a million electrochemical messages per moment up to the brain. There, step by step, the scene you are viewing is reassembled into its component features and finally—in some as yet mysterious way—composed into a consciously perceived image, which is instantly compared with previously stored images and recognized as words you know. The whole process is rather like taking a house apart, splinter by splinter, transporting it to a different location, and then, through the work of millions of specialized workers, putting it back together. All of this transpires in a fraction of a second. Moreover, it is continuously transpiring in motion, in three dimensions, and in color. Ten years of research on computer vision has not yet begun to duplicate this very ordinary, taken-for-granted part of our current experience. Further, unlike virtually all computers, which process information one step at a time, the human brain carries out countless other operations simultaneously, enabling us all at once to sense the environment, use common sense, converse, experience emotion, and consciously reflect on the meaning of our existence or even to wonder about our brain activity while wondering. The deeper one explores these very ordinary things of life, the more one empathizes with Job: "I have uttered what I did not understand, things too wonderful for me" (42:3 RSV).

To be sure, sometimes we use the word *mystery* not in its deep sense as when the mind seeks to fathom its brain, but rather to refer to unsolved scientific puzzles. When wonder is based merely on ignorance, it will fade in the growing light of understanding. Science is a puzzle-solving activity. Among the still unsolved puzzles of psychology are questions such as, Why do we dream? Why do some of us become heterosexual, others homosexual? and How does the brain store memories? The scientific detectives are at work on these "mysteries," and they may eventually offer us convincing solutions. Already, new ideas are emerging.

Often, however, the process of answering one question exposes more and sometimes deeper questions. A new understanding may lead to a new, more impenetrable sense of wonder regarding phenomena that seem further than ever from explanation or that now seem more beautifully intricate than previously imagined. Not long ago scientists wondered how individual nerve cells communicated with one another. The answer—through chemical messengers called neurotransmitters—raised new questions: How many neurotransmitters exist? What are the functions of each? Do abnormalities in neurotransmitter functioning predispose disorders such as schizophrenia and depression? If so, how might such problems be remedied? And how, from the electrochemical activity of the brain, do experienced emotions and thoughts arise: *how does a material brain give rise to consciousness?* Deeper and deeper go the questions, the deepest one of all being the impenetrable mystery behind the origin of the universe: *why is there something and not nothing?* (If a miracle is something that cannot be explained in terms of something else, then the existence of the universe is a miracle that dwarfs any other our minds can conceive.)

Human consciousness has long been a thing of wonder. More recently, wonder has also grown regarding the things our minds do subconsciously, automatically, out of sight. Our minds detect and process information without our awareness. They automatically organize our perceptions and interpretations. They respond (via the right hemisphere) intelligently in ways that we can explain only if our left hemisphere is informed what is going on. They effortlessly encode incoming information about the place, timing, and frequency of events we experience, about word meanings, about unattended stimuli. They ponder problems we are stumped with, and they occasionally spew forth a spontaneous creative insight. With the aid of hypnosis, they may even, on orders, eliminate warts on one side of the body but not on the other. There is, we now know, more to our minds than we are aware. And how fortunate that it should be so. For the more that routine functions (including well-learned activities such as walking, biking, or gymnastics) are delegated to control systems outside of awareness, the more our consciousness is freed to function like an executive—by focusing on the most important problems at hand. Our brains operate rather like General Motors, with a few important matters decided by the chair of the board, and everything else, thankfully, handled automatically, effortlessly, and usually competently by amazingly intricate mechanisms.

The more they explore, the more language researchers, too, have been awestruck by an amazing phenomenon: the ease with which children acquire language. Before children can add two plus two, they are creating their own grammatically intelligible sentences and comprehending the even more complex sentences spoken to them. Most parents cannot state the intricate rules of grammar, and they certainly are not giving their children much formal training in grammar. Yet before being able to tie their shoes, preschoolers are soaking up the complexities of the language by learning several new words a day and the rules for how to combine them. They do so with a facility that puts to shame many college students who struggle to learn a new language with correct accents and many computer scientists who are struggling to simulate natural language on computers. Moreover, they, and we, do so with the minimal comprehension of how we do it—how we, when speaking,

monitor our muscles, order our syntax, watch out for semantic catastrophes risked by the slightest change in word order, continuously
adjust our tone of voice, facial expression, and gestures, and manage to
say something meaningful when it would be so easy to speak gibberish.

Our womb-to-tomb individual development is equally remarkable.
What is more ordinary than humans reproducing themselves, and what
is more wonder-full? Consider the incredible good fortune that brought
each one of us into existence. The process began as a mature egg was
released by the ovary and as some 300 million sperm began their
upstream race towards it. Against all odds, you—or more exactly the
very sperm cell that together with the very egg it would take to make
you—won this 1 in 300 million lottery (actually one in billions, considering your conception had to occur from that particular sexual union).
What is more, a chain of equally improbable events, beginning with the
conception of your parents and their discovery of one another, had to
have extended backwards in time for the possibility of your moment to
have arrived. Indeed, when one considers the improbably sequence of
innumerable events that led to your conception, from the birth of the
universe onward, one cannot escape the conclusion that your birth and
your death anchor the two ends of a continuum of probabilities. What
is more *im*probable than that you, rather than one of your infinite alternatives, should exist? What is more certain than that you will not live
on earth endlessly?

Most beginnings of life fail to survive the first week of existence. But,
again, for you good fortune prevailed. Your one cell became two, which
became four, and then by the end of your first week an even more
astonishing thing happened—brain cells began forming and within
weeks were multiplying at a rate of about one-quarter million per
minute. Scientist-physician Lewis Thomas explains the wonder of that
single cell, which has as its decendents all the cells of the human brain.

> The mere existence of that cell should be one of the great astonishments
> of the earth. People ought to be walking around all day, all through their
> waking hours, calling to each other in endless wonderment, talking of
> nothing except that cell. . . .
>
> If you like being surprised, there's the source. One cell is switched on
> to become the whole trillion-cell, massive apparatus for thinking and
> imagining and, for that matter, being surprised. All the information
> needed for learning to read and write, playing the piano, arguing before
> senatorial subcommittees, walking across a street through traffic, or the
> marvelous human act of putting out one hand and leaning against a tree,
> is contained in that first cell. All of grammar, all syntax, all arithmetic, all
> music. . . .
>
> No one cell has the ghost of an idea how this works, and nothing else
> in life can ever be so puzzling. If anyone does succeed in explaining it,

within my lifetime, I will charter a skywriting airplane, maybe a whole fleet of them, and send them aloft to write one great exclamation point after another, around the whole sky, until all my money runs out. (1974, 156–57)

Human life—so ordinary, so familiar, so natural, and yet so extraordinary. Looking for mystery in things bizarre, we feel cheated when later we learn that a hoax or a simple process explains it away. All the while we miss the awesome events occurring before, or even within, our very eyes. The extraordinary within the ordinary.

So it was on that Christmas morning two millennia ago. The most extraordinary event of history—the Lord of the universe coming to the spaceship earth in human form—occurred in so ordinary a way as hardly to be noticed. On a mundane winter day at an undistinguished inn in an average little town the extraordinary one was born of an ordinary peasant woman. Like our human kin at Bethlehem and Nazareth long ago, we, too, are often blind to the mystery within things ordinary. We look for wonders and for the unseen reality—the hand of God—in things extraordinary, when more often his presence is to be found in the unheralded, familiar, everyday events of which life is woven.

References

Thomas, L. 1974. *The lives of a cell: Notes of a biology watcher.* New York: Viking.

———. 1979. *The medusa and the snail.* New York: Viking.

———. 1983. *Late night thoughts on listening to Mahler's Ninth Symphony.* New York: Viking.

Physician-scientist Thomas's collections of short essays describe scientific wonders with beautiful, awestruck prose.

Yin and Yang in Psychological Research and Christian Belief

When Christian psychologists link their profession with their faith they typically do one of three things: they analyze religious phenomena, such as conversion or prayer, through a psychological microscope; they correlate the speculations of personality theorists with the presumptions of theologians; or they propose a distinctly Christian approach to counseling or to psychological inquiry. My own interests in linking psychology and faith are rather different and for the most part arise from my involvement in the mainstream of psychological research and my vocation as a teacher of psychology. Thus my occupation—indeed my preoccupation—is to ponder two questions: What are the major insights and ideas regarding human nature that college and university students should encounter in their courses in introductory and social psychology? And, how does the human image emerging from contemporary psychology connect with Christian assumptions about human nature?

In any academic field the results of tens of thousands of studies, the conclusions of thousands of investigators, the insights of hundreds of theorists can usually be boiled down to a few overriding ideas. Biology offers us principles such as natural selection and adaptation. Sociology builds upon concepts such as social structure and social process. Music develops our ideas of rhythm, melody, and harmony.

It occurred to me when contemplating this address that many of the major insights and ideas of psychology—especially of social and cognitive psychology—could be distilled down to five pairs of complementary principles. Remarkably, these five pairs of complementary principles are paralleled in Christian thought by five pairs of theological principles.

Each psychological and theological principle represents a partial truth—an important aspect of a total system. As Pascal reminded us, no single truth is ever sufficient, because the world is not simple. Any truth

From *Perspectives on Science and Christian Faith* 39 (1987): 128–39; reprinted by permission of the publisher and the author.

separated from its complementary truth is a half-truth. It is in the union of complementary opposites—of what the Chinese called yin and yang—that one glimpses the whole reality.

Consider, first, five great principles of contemporary psychology that unite with five complementary principles, like the five fingers of the left hand clasping the five fingers of the right, to form a more complete picture of the human system. As we move along through these five pairs of psychological principles, you will, perhaps, be able to anticipate some of the Christian ideas that parallel this yin and yang of psychological research.

The Yin and Yang of Psychological Research

Brain and Mind

The explosion of recent research on genetic influences on behavior, on the influence of neurotransmitters on thought and emotion, and on the intricate links between brain structures and language, perception, and memory confirms more surely than ever that *mind emerges from brain*. My colleague Malcolm Jeeves, a cognitive neuroscientist, is unhesitating: "Every new advance in the flourishing field of neuropsychology tightens the apparent links between brain and mind" (Myers and Jeeves 1987).

Although much mystery remains, we now understand better than ever the specific brain malfunctions that cause disorders of speaking, reading, writing, or understanding language. We have glimpsed how precise surgical or chemical manipulations of the brain can manipulate thoughts, moods, and motives. We are beginning to understand the awesome process by which our sensory systems and brains decompose sensory experiences into formless neural impulses and then reassemble them into their component features and, finally, into conscious perceptions. And we are being offered new clues to the extent and the mechanisms of genetic influences upon countless traits, from emotionality to intelligence, from criminal tendencies to altruism, from gender differences to schizophrenia.

Neuroscientist David Hubel has said that "fundamental changes in our view of the human brain cannot but have profound effects on our view of ourselves and the world" (1979). The dualistic view that mind and body are distinct entities—that we are, as Descartes believed, lodged in our bodies as pilots in their vessels—seems more and more implausible. Thus psychologist Donald Hebb concludes that however implausible it may be to say that consciousness consists of brain activity, "it nevertheless begins to look very much as though the proposition is true" (1980). Mind emerges from brain.

This apparent truth is, however, complemented by another truth: *mind controls brain*. In many ways our brains function mindlessly—by automatically, effortlessly, and usually infallibly managing a myriad of routine functions. This frees our consciousness to focus, rather as the chief executive of a great country or corporation does, on the most important problems at hand. In doing so, our conscious experience directs the brain to control bodily functions in ways once thought impossible. In the burgeoning field of health psychology, for example, we are discovering the bodily consequences of stresses, be they cataclysmic events or routine daily hassles. We are learning more about the effects of emotions such as anger on a person's vulnerability to heart disease and to disorders of the immune system. We are exploring psychological techniques of pain control and stress management, and gaining clues to the control of ailments such as tension headaches and hypertension. We are glimpsing how social support or even a sense of humor helps buffer the effects of stress. These examples of "mind over body" are extensions of phenomena we frequently experience. Embarrassed, we blush. Frightened, we feel our heart pounding, our skin perspiring. Thus our first pair of complementary principles: mind emerges from brain, and mind controls brain.

Attitudes and Behavior

Among social psychology's best-known principles are those that describe the reciprocal relations between attitudes and behavior. During the 1960s, dozens of research studies challenged the assumption that people's attitudes guide their actions. But studies since 1970 have revealed conditions under which our attitudes *do* influence our actions. This is especially true when we are keenly aware of our attitudes and when other influences on our behavior, such as social pressures, are minimized. If our attitudes toward cheating, or churchgoing, or racial minorities are brought to mind in a pertinent situation—if something causes us to stop and remember who we are before we act—then we may indeed stand up for what we believe. In such situations, *attitudes influence behavior*.

But if social psychology has taught us anything during the last three decades, it is that the reverse is also true: we are as likely to act ourselves into a way of thinking as to think ourselves into action; we are as likely to believe in what we have stood up for as to stand up for what we believe. Simply put, *attitudes follow behavior*. Consider a few examples of the wide-ranging evidence:

1. In the laboratory, and in everyday situations, evil acts shape the self. People induced to harm an innocent victim typically come to disparage the victim. Those induced to speak or write statements

about which they have misgivings will often come to accept their little lies. Saying becomes believing.

2. Positive actions—resisting temptation, giving help to someone, behaving amicably in desegregated situations—also shape the self. As social psychologists predicted would happen, changes in racial behavior resulting from desegregation rulings and civil rights legislation have been followed by positive changes in racial attitudes. Evil actions corrupt, but repentant actions renew.

3. Many of today's therapy techniques make a constructive use of the self-persuasive effects of behavior. Behavior therapy, assertiveness training, and rational-emotive therapy all coax their clients to rehearse and then practice more productive ways of talking and acting, trusting that by so doing the person's inner disposition will gradually follow along.

This principle, like that of its complement, is especially valid under certain conditions—notably when people feel some choice and responsibility for their behavior rather than attributing it entirely to coercion. But most behaviors, even the enforced Nazi greeting, "Heil Hitler," do involve some element of choice. Thus, there often occur feelings of discomfort when one's behavior is out of alignment with one's attitudes. For example, historian Richard Grunberger reports that when "prevented from saying what they believed," many Germans "tried to establish their psychic equilibrium by consciously making themselves believe what they said" (1971, 27).

To repeat, two fundamental principles of social psychology are that attitudes influence behavior and attitudes follow behavior. Behavior and attitude, like chicken and egg, generate one another in an endless spiral.

Self-Serving Bias and Self-Esteem

It is widely believed that most of us suffer the "I'm not OK—you're OK" problem of low self-esteem, the problem that comedian Groucho Marx had in mind when he declared that "I wouldn't want to belong to any club that would accept me as a member." As we will see, there is evidence supporting today's conventional wisdom about the benefits of high self-esteem and positive thinking. But we moderns seem less aware of the powerful phenomenon called "self-serving bias" that has been revealed by a dozen lines of research. Consider:

1. People readily accept responsibility for their successes and good deeds, but are prone to attribute failure or bad deeds to factors beyond their control. Self-serving attributions have been observed not only in countless laboratory situations, but also with athletes

(after victory or defeat), with students (after high or low exam grades), with drivers (after accidents), and with married people as they explain their conflicts. Researcher Anthony Greenwald sums up countless findings: "People experience life through a self-centered filter" (Goleman 1984).

2. In virtually any area that is both subjective and socially desirable, most people see themselves as relatively superior. Most business-people see themselves as more ethical than the average businessperson. Most community residents see themselves as less prejudiced than their neighbors. Most people see themselves as more intelligent and as healthier than most other people. In "ability to get along with others," virtually all American high school seniors rate themselves above average and 60 percent put themselves among the top 10 percent. As Elizabeth Barrett Browning might have summarized, "How do I love me? Let me count the ways."

These observations of self-serving attributions of responsibility and self-serving perceptions of superiority are joined by other findings. Many studies indicate that we tend to justify our past actions; we have an inflated confidence in the accuracy of our beliefs and judgments; we tend to overestimate how desirably we would act in situations in which most people are known to behave less than admirably; we are quicker to believe flattering descriptions of ourselves than unflattering ones; we misremember our own past in self-enhancing ways; we exhibit a Pollyannaish optimism about our personal futures; we guess that physically attractive people have personalities more like our own than do unattractive people.

The list goes on but the point is made. At times we may disparage ourselves, especially when comparing ourselves with those who are even more successful than we are or when our expressions of self-disparagement can trigger reassuring praise from others. Nevertheless, the evidence is overwhelming: the most common error in people's self-images is not unrealistically low self-esteem, but a self-serving bias; not an inferiority complex, but a superiority complex.

The phenomenon is not only pervasive but also at times socially disruptive. For example, people who work on a group task will typically claim greater-than-average credit when their group does well and less-than-average blame when it does not. When most people in a group believe they are underpaid and underappreciated, given their better-than-average contributions, disharmony and envy surely lurk. Several studies indicate that 90 percent or more of college faculty think themselves superior to their average colleague. Is it therefore surprising that when merit salary raises are announced and half receive an average raise or less, many feel an injustice has been done them?

More dangerous yet is self-serving bias in its collective forms. Racism, sexism, nationalism, and all such chauvinisms lead one group of people to see themselves as more moral, deserving, or able than another. The flip side of taking credit for one's self-perceived achievements is to blame the poor for their poverty and the oppressed for their oppression. Samuel Johnson recognized this two hundred years ago: "He that overvalues himself will undervalue others, and he that undervalues others will oppress them."

In recognizing this principle, that *self-serving bias is powerful and perilous*, we must, however, not forget its complement: that *high self-esteem and positive thinking pay dividends.*

People who express high self-esteem—feelings of self-worth—tend to be less depressed, freer of ulcers and insomnia, less prone to drug addiction, more independent of conformity pressures, and more persistent at difficult tasks. In experiments, those whose self-esteem is given a temporary blow (say, by being told they did poorly on a test or were judged harshly by others) tend then to express heightened racial prejudice. Many clinicians believe that underneath much of the despair and psychological disorder with which they deal is an impoverished self-acceptance. For children and adults a high self-esteem can indeed be healthy.

The power of positive thoughts about oneself is also evident in the hundreds of studies that testify to the benefits of a strong "internal locus of control"—a belief in one's ability to control one's destiny. These are reinforced by hundreds more studies on the benefits of "self-efficacy," "intrinsic motivation," and "achievement motivation" and of the costs of "learned helplessness" and self-defeating thinking patterns. The moral of all these research literatures is that people profit from viewing themselves as free creatures and their futures as hopeful. Believe that things are beyond your control, and they probably will be. Believe that you can do it and maybe you will.

Of course, there are limits to the power of positive thinking. Limitless expectations may bring endless frustrations and the guilt and shame that accompany the failure to achieve what we believed was achievable—"A" grades, record sales, marital bliss.

So where do these complementary self-image principles leave us? For the individual, self-affirming thinking is often adaptive, maintaining self-confidence and minimizing depression. But it is also important to remember the reality of self-serving bias and the harm that self-righteousness can wreak upon social relationships. The question is, therefore, how can we encourage a positive self-acceptance, while not encouraging self-serving pretensions?

Situational and Personal Control

Yet another overarching principle comes to us as the greatest lesson of social psychology, that social influences are enormous. Indeed, it is difficult to overestimate the extent to which our decisions, beliefs, attitudes, and actions are influenced by our social environments. *We are the creatures of our social worlds.* Consider some everyday examples of but four phenomena of social influences.

Suggestibility

Suicides, bomb threats, hijackings, and UFO sightings have a curious tendency to come in waves. One well-publicized incident—the suicide of a famous movie star—can inspire imitation. And as we will see, copycat perceptions and actions are not restricted to crazy people. Laughter, even canned laughter, is contagious. Bartenders and beggars know to "seed" their tip or money cups with money supposedly left by others.

Role Playing

A group of decent young men volunteered to spend time in a simulated prison devised by psychologist Philip Zimbardo. Some were randomly designated as guards. They were given uniforms, billy clubs, and whistles and were instructed to enforce certain rules. The remainder became prisoners, locked in barren cells and forced to wear humiliating outfits. After a day or two of "playing" their roles, the young men became caught up in the situation. The guards devised cruel and degrading routines, and one by one the prisoners either broke down, rebelled, or became passively resigned. Meanwhile, outside the laboratory, another group of men was being trained by the military junta then in power in Greece to become torturers. The men's indoctrination into cruelty occurred in small steps. First, the trainee would stand guard outside the interrogation and torture cells. Then he would stand guard inside. Only then was he ready to become actively involved in the questioning and cruelty.

Persuasion

In late October of 1980, U.S. presidential candidate Ronald Reagan trailed incumbent Jimmy Carter by 8 percentage points in the Gallup Poll. On November 4, after a 2-week media blitz and a presidential debate, Reagan, "the great persuader," emerged victorious by a stunning 10 percentage points. The Reagan landslide made many people wonder: what qualities made Ronald Reagan so persuasive, and his audience so persuadable?

Group Influence

One of the first major decisions President John F. Kennedy and his bright and loyal advisors had to make was whether to approve a Central

Intelligence Agency plan to invade Cuba. The group's high morale seemed to foster a sense that the plan couldn't help but succeed. No one spoke sharply against the idea, so everyone assumed there was consensus support for the plan, which was then implemented. When the small band of U.S. trained and supplied Cuban refugee invaders was easily captured and soon linked to the American government, Kennedy wondered aloud, "How could we have been so stupid?"

Each of these phenomena of social influence has been "bottled up" in countless laboratory experiments that isolate their important features and compress them into a brief time period, enabling us to see just how they affect people. A few of the best known of these experiments have put well-intentioned people in an evil situation to see whether good or evil prevails. To a dismaying extent, evil pressures overwhelm good intentions, inducing people to conform to falsehoods or capitulate to cruelty. Faced with a powerful situation, nice people often don't behave so nicely.

In affirming the power of social influence, we must not overlook a complementary truth about our power as individuals: *We are the creators of our social worlds.* Social control (the power of the situation) and personal control (the power of the person) coexist, for at any moment we are both the creatures and the creators of our environment. We may well be the products of past biological and social influences. But it is also true that the future is coming, and it is our job to decide where it is going. Our choices today determine our environment tomorrow, and as we noted earlier, those who most believe in their power to influence their destinies tend most successfully to do so.

The reciprocal influences between situations and persons occur partly because individuals often choose their situations. When choosing which college to attend or which campus groups to join, a student is also choosing a particular set of social influences. Ardent political liberals are unlikely to settle in Orange County, California, join the chamber of commerce, or read *U.S. News and World Report.* They are more likely to live in San Francisco, join Common Cause, and read the *New Republic.*

Also, our expectations and behavior will modify our situations. As many recent experiments demonstrate, if we expect someone to be extroverted, hostile, feminine, or sexy, our actions toward the person may induce the very behavior we expect. The social environment is not like the weather—something that just happens to us. It is more like our homes—something we have made for ourselves and in which we now live.

Again, the reciprocal influences between situations and persons allow us to see people as either reacting to or acting upon their social environment. Each perspective is correct, for we are both the products and the architects of our social worlds.

Rationality and Irrationality

The debate over the extent of human wisdom versus the magnitude of human foolishness is long-standing. Are we, as Shakespeare's Hamlet rhapsodized, "how noble in reason! . . . infinite in faculties! . . . in apprehension, how like a god!"? Or are we, as T. S. Eliot suggested, "hollow men . . . Headpiece filled with straw"?

Research psychologists of late have produced considerable ammunition for both sides of the debate. Some of their findings lead us to marvel at our capabilities, others to be startled by our capacity for illusion and self-deception. Let's consider some of this new thinking about thinking, looking first at findings which suggest that *our cognitive capacities are awesome.*

We have been amazed by capabilities that are enabled by the human brain—a mere three pounds of tissue that contains circuitry more complex than all the telephone networks on the planet. We have been surprised at the competence even of newborn infants—at their skill in interacting with their caregivers, their ability to discriminate the sound and smell of their mothers, their abilities to imitate simple gestures. We have marveled at the seemingly limitless capacity of human memory and the ease with which we simultaneously process varied information, both consciously and unconsciously, effortfully and automatically, with each hemisphere of the brain carrying out special functions. We have wondered at our abilities to form concepts, solve problems, and make quick, efficient judgments using rule-of-thumb strategies called heuristics. Little wonder that our species has had the genius to invent the camera, the car, and the computer; to unlock the atom and crack the genetic code; to travel into space and probe the depths of the oceans.

We have also been awestruck by the ease with which children acquire language. Before children can add two plus two, they are creating their own grammatically intelligible sentences and comprehending the even more complex sentences spoken to them. Before being able to tie their shoes, preschoolers are soaking up several new words a day and grasping complex grammatical rules with a facility that humbles computer scientists as they struggle to simulate natural language. Or consider your own dimly understood capacity for language—how, in your most recent conversation, you managed *all at once* to monitor your muscles, order your syntax, watch out for semantic catastrophes that would result from a slight change in word order, continuously adjust your tone of voice and expressive gestures, and say something meaningful when it would have been so easy to speak gibberish. Indeed, it is this human capacity to do so many complex things all at once—to sense the environment, to encode information about the place, timing, and frequency of experienced events, to interpret word meanings, to use common sense, to experience emotion, and even to consciously wonder how we do it—that causes us to echo Hamlet: "how infinite in faculties! . . . how like a god!" We are indeed *Homo sapiens,* the wise species.

But the complementary truth is that our capacity for illusory thinking is equally astonishing. *To err is human.* I know from experience that one can fill a book describing our human tendencies to self-deception and false belief. Thanks to countless experiments since 1970 in the burgeoning subdiscipline of "cognitive social psychology," we have gained insight into many of the intuitive thinking patterns that, as the price we pay for their efficiency, can lead us astray. Among these reasons for unreason are the following:

1. We often do not know why we do what we do. In experiments, people whose attitudes have been changed will often deny that they have been influenced; they will insist that how they feel now is how they have always felt. When powerful influences upon our behavior are not so conspicuous that any observer could spot them, we too can be oblivious to what has affected us.

2. Our preconceptions help govern our interpretations and memories. In experiments, people's prejudgments have striking effects upon how they perceive and interpret information. Other experiments have planted judgments or false ideas in people's minds after they have been given information. These experiments reveal that just as before-the-fact judgments bias our perceptions and interpretations, so do after-the-fact judgments bias our recall.

3. We tend to overestimate the accuracy of our judgments. This "overconfidence phenomenon" seems partly due to the much greater ease with which we can imagine why we might be right than why we might be wrong. Moreover, people are more likely to search for information that can confirm their beliefs than information that can disconfirm them.

4. Vivid anecdotes and testimonies can be powerfully persuasive, often more so than factual data drawn from a much broader sample of people. This is apparently due to the attention-getting power of vivid information, and to the ease with which we later recall it.

5. We are often swayed by illusions of correlation, causation, and personal control. It is tempting to perceive correlations where none exist ("illusory correlation"), to perceive causal connections among events which are merely correlated (the "correlation cau-

sation" fallacy), and to think we can control events which are really beyond our control (the "illusion of control").

6. Erroneous beliefs may generate their own reality. Studies of experimenter bias and teacher expectations indicate that at least sometimes an erroneous belief that certain people are unusually capable (or incapable) can lead one to give special treatment to those people. This may elicit superior (or inferior) performance, and therefore seems to confirm an assumption that is actually false. Similarly, in everyday social affairs we often get what we expect.

It is important to remember that these illusory thinking processes are by-products of thinking strategies that usually serve us well, much as visual illusions are by-products of perceptual mechanisms that help us organize sensory information. But they are errors nonetheless, errors that can warp our perceptions of reality and prejudice our judgments of persons, leading us at times to act like headpieces filled with straw. By becoming aware of such tendencies we may, perhaps, also become a bit more humble about our intuitive judgments, more aware of our need for disciplined training of the mind, and more open to careful analysis and critique of our judgments. It is true that our cognitive capacities are awesome, but it also is true that to err is the most human of tendencies.

"There are trivial truths and great truths," declared the physicist Niels Bohr. "The opposite of a trivial truth is plainly false. The opposite of a great truth is also true" (McGuire 1973). Psychological inquiry illustrates Bohr's contention. Massive bodies of research indicate that mind emerges from brain and that mind controls brain; that attitudes influence behavior and that attitudes follow behavior; that self-serving bias is powerful and perilous and that self-esteem and positive thinking pay dividends; that we are the creatures of our social worlds and that we are the creators of our social worlds; that our cognitive capacities are awesome and that to err is human. To propound any one of these truths while ignoring its complement is to proclaim a half truth. It is in the union of complementary opposites, of yin and yang, that we glimpse the human reality.

Yin and Yang in Christian Belief

Although I have so far avoided any mention of Christian views of human nature, some of what I have said may have a vaguely familiar ring. And well it should, for these five complementary pairs of psychological principles parallel five pairs of Christian assumptions, do they not? Consider the following.

Body and Spirit

The emerging scientific view that we are a unified mind-brain system may pose a threat to those who, in the tradition of Plato and Socrates, believe we are a dualism of two distinct realities—a mortal body and an undying soul. But it is supportive, in its fundamentals if not its details, of the implicit psychology of the Old Testament people who were said to think with their hearts, feel with their bowels, and whose flesh longed for God. In this Hebrew view, one's *nephesh* (soul) therefore terminates at death; we do not *have nephesh* (Plato's immortal soul); we *are nephesh* (living beings).

The New Testament similarly offers us whole persons, "souls" who can eat, drink, and be merry. And it offers the hope that after death we, like Christ, will be resurrected as a perfected mind-body unit. For the Christian, death is a real enemy, not merely a "passing away" of the immortal soul as it was for Socrates drinking the hemlock. But we are promised that God will take the initiative by giving us in a new world what we do not inherently possess—eternal life.

Our minds are nothing apart from our bodies, suggests the scientific image. *We are, now and in eternity, bodies alive,* suggests the Bible. Fundamentally, both views assume—in contradiction to occult and spiritualist claims of reincarnation, astral projection, and seances with the living dead—that without our bodies we are nobodies.

Having said this, we must also add the complementary truth that in both the scientific and Christian views, something special and mysterious emerges from the unimaginably complex activity of the body. So far as neuroscientists can tell, mind is not an extra entity that occupies the brain. Yet there it is: our memories, our wishes, our creative ideas, our moment-to-moment awareness somehow arising from the coordinated activity of billions of nerve cells, each of which communicates with hundreds or thousands of other nerve cells. From the material brain there emerges the mystery of consciousness.

A scientific analogy may help us see how the properties of a whole system, such as the brain-mind system, may emerge from, yet not be reducible to, its physical parts. Physically, an ant colony is but a collection of solitary ants, each of which has a relatively few neurons strung together—a witless, thoughtless creature if ever there was one. Yet the interactions of a dense mass of thousands of ants produces a wondrous phenomenon: a collective intelligence, a social organism that "knows" how to grow, how to move, how to build. There is nothing extra plugged into the ants to create this intelligence. Yet to look no further than the individual ants would be to miss the miracle of the living colony. Likewise, to stop with the story of the brain cells would be to miss the miracle of consciousness.

Similarly, while the Bible teaches that we are bodily creatures, made from dust, it also teaches that we have the potential for something special and mysterious: *we are created for spiritual relationships*. To Paul and other biblical writers our spirituality has not to do with an invisible essence that is plugged into a bodily compartment, like a pilot in a small plane, but with the whole person in relationship with God and other persons. Theologian Bruce Reichenbach suggests that to recapture this sense of spirituality we ought to drop the term *soul* from our religious vocabulary: "Such an approach, far from destroying faith in the spiritual aspect of man, will aid in clarifying precisely wherein the spiritual lies, i.e., that it lies not in the possession of an entity, but in the style of life one leads insofar as it manifests a relation to God and to one's fellow man (1974).

Faith and Action

The social psychologist's contention that attitudes and behavior grow from each other parallels and reinforces the biblical understanding of action and faith. Depending on where we break into the spiraling faith-action chain, we will see faith as a source of action or as a consequence. Faith and action, like attitude and action, feed one another.

Much as conventional wisdom has insisted that our attitudes determine our behavior, so has Christian thinking traditionally emphasized that *faith is a source of action*. Faith, we believe, is the beginning rather than the end of religious development. For example, the experience of being "called" demonstrates how faith can precede action in the lives of the faithful. Elijah is overwhelmed by the Holy as he huddles in a cave. Paul is touched by the Almighty on the Damascus Road. Ezekiel, Isaiah, Jeremiah, and Amos are likewise invaded by the Word, which then explodes in their active response to the call. In each case, an encounter with God provoked a new state of consciousness which was then acted upon.

The dynamic potential of faith is, however, complemented by the not-so-widely appreciated principle that *faith is a consequence of action*. Throughout the Old and New Testaments we are told that full knowledge of God comes through actively doing the Word. Faith is nurtured by obedient action. For example, in the Old Testament the Hebrew word for *know* is generally used as a verb, as something one does. To know love, we must not only know about love but we must act lovingly. And to *hear* the word of God means not only to listen, but also to obey.

Likewise, we read in the New Testament that by loving action a person knows God, for "he who does what is true comes to the light" (John 3:21 RSV). Jesus declared that whoever would do the will of God would know God, that he would come and dwell within those who heed what he said, and that we would find ourselves by actively losing ourselves as we take up the cross. The wise man, the one who built his house on a rock, differed from the foolish man in that he acted on God's Word. Over and again, the Bible teaches that the gospel's power can only be known by living it.

Our theological understanding of faith is informed by this biblical view of knowledge. Faith grows as we act on what little faith we have. Just as experimental subjects become more deeply committed to something for which they have suffered and witnessed, so also do we grow in faith as we act it out. Faith "is born of obedience," said John Calvin (1975, 72; 106.2). "The proof of Christianity really consists in 'following,'" declared Søren Kierkegaard (1944, 88). Karl Barth agreed: "Only the doer of the Word is its real hearer" (Westerhoff 1971, 44). Pascal is even more plainspoken: to attain faith, "follow the way by which [the committed] began; by acting as if they believed, taking the holy water, having masses said, etc. Even this will naturally make you believe" (1965, 38). C. S. Lewis echoed Pascal's sentiments:

> Believe in God and you will have to face hours when it seems *obvious* that this material world is the only reality: disbelieve in Him and you must face hours when this material world seems to shout at you that it is *not* all. No conviction, religious or irreligious will of itself, end once and for all [these doubts] in the soul. Only the practice of Faith resulting in the habit of Faith will gradually do that. (1981, 61)

The practical implication of this faith-follows-action principle is that in church management, in worship, and in Christian nurture we need to create opportunities for people to enact their convictions, thereby confirming and strengthening their Christian identity. Biblical and psychological perspectives link arms in reminding us that faith is like love. If we hoard it, it will shrivel. If we use it, exercise it, and express it, we will have it more abundantly. In his *Cost of Discipleship*, Dietrich Bonhoeffer summarized this faith-action spiral: *"Only he who believes is obedient, and only he who is obedient believes."*

Human Pride and Divine Grace

The new research on self-serving bias is aptly summarized in a W. C. Fields quip: "Hubris is back in town." The abundant evidence that human reason is adaptable to self-interest and that our self-perceptions tend to be self-justifying echoes a very old Christian idea: that *pride is the fundamental sin*, the original sin, the deadliest of the seven deadly sins.

Unpacking this doctrine of pride, we find that it has two components. First is the assumption that self-love and self-righteous pretension are pervasive. Thus the psalmist could declare that "no one can see his own errors" and the Pharisee could thank God "that I am not like other men" (and you and I can thank God that we are not like the Pharisee). Paul assumed that our natural tendency is to see ourselves as superior when he admonished the Philippians to reverse this tendency—to "in humility count others better than yourselves" (Phil. 2:3 RSV). Likewise, he assumed self-love when he argued that husbands should love their wives as their own bodies, just as Jesus assumed self-love when commanding us to love our neighbors as we love ourselves. The Bible neither teaches nor opposes self-love; it takes it for granted.

The Christian doctrine of pride assumes, secondly, that prideful self-love can go before a fall. The Bible warns us against self-righteousness—the pride that alienates us from God and leads us to disdain one another. Pride is the fundamental sin because it corrodes human community and erodes our sense of dependence on one another and on God. The Nazi atrocities, for example, were rooted not in self-conscious feelings of German inferiority, but in Aryan pride. The arms race is fed by a national pride that enables each nation to perceive its own motives as righteously defensive, the other's as hostile. Even that apostle of positive thinking Dale Carnegie foresaw the danger: "Each nation feels superior to other nations. That breeds patriotism—and wars."

The sin that grows from human pride is an essential part of the biblical story, but it is not the whole story. In the *Interpreter's Dictionary of the Bible*, S. J. DeVries reduces the whole of Scripture to a pair of propositions: We find ourselves "in sin and suffer its painful effects; God graciously offers salvation from it. This, in essence is what the Bible is about." The salvation half of the story proclaims an unshakable basis for self-esteem: Our worth is said to be more than we appreciate, certainly more than that of "the birds of the air" and God's other creatures. It is worth enough to motivate Jesus' kindness and respect even toward those with little honor: toward women and children, Samaritans and Gentiles, leprosy victims and prostitutes, the poor and the tax collectors. Recognizing that our worth is what we are worth to God—an agonizing but redemptive execution on a cross—therefore draws us to a self-affirmation that is rooted in divine love.

Thus the Christian answer to self-righteous pride is the good news that *to experience grace is to feel accepted,* and therefore to be liberated from the need to define our self-worth in terms of achievements, or prestige, or material and physical well-being. It is simultaneously to be liberated both from our self-protective pride and our self-rejection. Recall Pinocchio. Floundering in confusion about his self-worth, Pinocchio turns to his maker Geppetto and says, "Papa, I am not sure who I am. But if I'm all right with you, then I guess I'm all right with me." In the life, death, and resurrection of Jesus, our Maker signals to us that we belong to him and that we are set right. Saint Paul, surrendering his pretensions, could therefore exult that "I no longer have a righteousness of my own, the kind that is gained by obeying the Law. I now have the righteousness that is given through faith in Christ . . ." (Phil. 3:9 GNB).

"To give up one's pretensions is as blessed a relief as to get them gratified," noted William James, "and where disappointment is incessant and the struggle unending, this is what men will always do. The history of evangelical theology, with its conviction of sin, its self-despair, and its abandonment of salvation by works, is the deepest of possible examples" (1890). There is indeed tremendous relief in confessing our limits and our pride, in being known as we are, and in then experiencing "unconditional positive regard." Having been forgiven and accepted, we gain release, a feeling of being given what formerly we were struggling to get: security, peace, love. Having cut the pretensions and encountered divine grace, we feel *more*, not less, value as persons, for our self-acceptance no longer depends exclusively upon our own virtue and achievement nor upon others' approval.

The feelings one can have in this encounter with God are like those we enjoy in a relationship with someone who, even after knowing our inmost thoughts, accepts us unconditionally. This is the delicious experience we enjoy in a good marriage or an intimate friendship, in which we no longer feel the need to justify and explain ourselves or to be on guard, in which we are free to be spontaneous without fear of losing the other's esteem. Such was the psalmist's experience: "Lord, I have given up my pride and turned away from my arrogance. . . . I am content and at peace" (131:1–2 GNB).

Divine Sovereignty and Human Responsibility

The dialectic of situational and personal control finds its Christian counterpart in the paradox of God's sovereignty and our responsibility. Attacks on the idea that we are self-made people—that thanks to our free will we are independently capable of righteousness—have come not only from social researchers but also from theologians such as Augustine, Luther, Calvin, and Jonathan Edwards. *God is ultimately in control,* they insist.

Edwards would not give so much as an inch to human free will, because to the extent that human will is spontaneous and free, God's plans become dependent on our decisions. This, said Edwards, would necessitate God's "constantly changing his mind and intentions" in order to achieve his purposes. "They who thus plead for man's liberty, advance principles which destroy the freedom of God himself," [1754] the sovereign God of whom Jesus said not even a sparrow falls to the ground apart from his will (1957; 27, 253). Nor is human will added to God's will such that the two together equal one hundred percent. Rather, agreed Saint Augustine, "our wills themselves are included in that order of causes which is certain to God." God is working in and through our lives, our choices. He is due all credit even for our faith, insisted Luther. His grace operates within the processes of nature, suggested Thomas Aquinas; God sustains and orders the natural processes that shape us.

But there can also be no doubt that the Bible assumes that *we are responsible.* We are accountable for our choices and our actions. The streams of causation run through our present choices, which will in turn determine the future. So what we decide makes all the difference. Even our decision to believe, to choose whom we will serve, is in our hands.

Everything depends on us and everything depends on God. "I . . . yet not I, but the grace of God . . ." (1 Cor. 15:10 KJV), said Saint Paul. C. S. Lewis notes that the New Testament puts these two ideas together

> into the amazing sentence. The first half is, "Work out your own salvation with fear and trembling"—which looks as if everything depended on us and good actions: but the second half goes on, "For it is God who worketh in you"—which looks as if God did everything and we nothing. I am afraid that is the sort of thing we come up against in Christianity. I am puzzled, but I am not surprised. You see, we are now trying to understand, and to separate into watertight compartments, what exactly God does and what man does when God and man are working together. And, of course, we begin by thinking it is like two men working together, so that you could say, "He did this bit and I did that." But this way of thinking breaks down. God is not like that. He is inside you as well as outside. . . . (1981)

Faced with this paradox of divine responsibility and human responsibility, or with the twin truths of social and personal control, we might think of ourselves as like someone stranded in a deep well with two ropes dangling down. If we grab either one alone we will sink deeper into the well. Only when we hold both ropes at once can we climb out, because at the top, beyond where we can see, they come together around a pulley. Grabbing only the rope of God's sovereignty or of our responsibility plunges us to the bottom of a well. So instead we grab both ropes, without yet understanding how they come together. In doing so, we may be comforted that in science as in religion, a confused acceptance of seemingly irreconcilable principles is sometimes more honest than a tidy, oversimplified theory that ignores half the evidence.

Divine Image and Finite Creature

The tension between the grandeur of our cognitive capacities and our vulnerability to error was anticipated by the psalmist. Thus he could exalt that human beings are "little less than God" in the very next breath after wondering "What is man, that thou art mindful of him?" (8:4–5 KJV). Pascal's *Thoughts* reflect a similar ambivalence. One moment we read that "Man's greatness lies in his power of thought," and the next moment that the human mind is "a cesspool of uncertainty and error" (1965, 38).

And so it is throughout the Scriptures. *We are made in the image of God,* crowned with honor and glory and given dominion over God's created world. Humanity is special. We are the summit of God's creative work. We are God's own children.

Yet we are also a part of the creation. *We are finite creatures* of the one who declares "I am God, and there is none like me" (Isa. 46:9 KJV). Loved by God, we have dignity, but not deity. Thus Karl Barth warns us never to make an idol out of our religion, by presuming our own thoughts to be God's absolute truth. Always we see reality in a mirror, dimly: "For as the heavens are higher than the earth, so are my ways higher than your ways and my thoughts than your thoughts" (Isa. 55:9 KJV).

So we see that in Christian belief, much as in contemporary psychology (see table 15.1), the whole truth seems best approximated by com-

Table 15.1
Yin and Yang in Psychological Research and Christian Belief

In Psychological Research	In Christian Belief
1. Brain and Mind	1. Body and Spirit
a. Mind emerges from brain.	a. We are, now and in eternity, bodies alive.
b. Mind controls brain.	b. We are created for spiritual relationships.
2. Attitudes and Behavior	2. Faith and Action
a. Attitudes influence behavior.	a. Faith is a source of action.
b. Attitudes follow behavior.	b. Faith is a consequence of action.
3. Self-Serving Bias and Self-Esteem	3. Human Pride and Divine Grace
a. Self-serving bias is powerful and perilous.	a. Pride is the fundamental sin.
b. High self-esteem and positive thinking pay dividends.	b. To experience grace is to feel accepted.
4. Situational and Personal Control	4. Divine Sovereignty and Human Responsibility
a. We are the creatures of our social worlds.	a. God is ultimately in control.
b. We are the creators of our social worlds.	b. We are responsible.
5. Rationality and Irrationality	5. Divine Image and Finite Creature
a. Our cognitive capacities are awesome.	a. We are made in the image of God.
b. To err is human.	b. We are finite creatures.

plementary propositions: we are, now and in eternity, bodies alive, yet we are also created for spiritual relationships; faith is a source of action and a consequence of action; pride is the fundamental sin, but grace is a key to self-acceptance; God is in control, and we are responsible; we are made in the image of God, and we are finite creatures. These Christian propositions find their counterparts in recent psychological inquiry. Both sets of propositions are the creations of human minds, mere approximations of reality that are subject to revision. Still, the parallels of content and of dialectical form are noteworthy. Because faith always seeks understanding in the language of the day, psychology can perhaps enliven ancient Christian wisdom. Perhaps it can also help us feel more comfortable with the yin and yang of truth. To ask whether it is more true that we are body or spirit, whether faith or action comes first, whether God or we are responsible, whether pride or self-rejection is the problem, or whether we are wise or foolish, is like asking which blade of a pair of scissors is more necessary. Always it is tempting when emphasizing one truth to forget the other. Martin Luther once likened us to the drunkard, who, having fallen off his horse on the right, would then proceed to fall off it on the left. In our time, at least, the cutting edge of truth seems to lie between the yin and the yang.

References

Calvin, J. 1975. *Institutes of the Christian religion.* Ed. J. T. McNeill; trans. F. L. Battles. Philadelphia: Fortress.

Edwards, J. [1754] 1957. *Freedom of the will.* Ed. P. Ramsey. New Haven: Yale Univ. Press.

Goleman, D. 1984. A bias puts self at center of everything. *New York Times,* 12 June.

Grunberger, R. 1971. *The 12-year Reich: A social history of Nazi Germany 1933–1945.* New York: Holt, Rinehart and Winston.

Hebb, D. O. 1980. *Essay on mind.* Hillsdale, N.J.: L. Erlbaum Associates.

Hubel, D. H. 1979. The brain. *Scientific American,* September, 45–53.

James, W. 1890. *The principles of psychology.* Vol. 2. New York: Holt.

Kierkegaard, S. 1944. *For self-examination and judge for yourselves.* Trans. W. Lowrie. Princeton, N.J.: Princeton Univ. Press.

Lewis, C. S. 1981. *Christian reflections.* Glasgow: Collins, Fount Paperbacks.

McGuire, W. J. 1973. The yin and yang of progress in social psychology: Seven koan. *Journal of Personality and Social Psychology* 26: 446–56.

Myers, D. G., and M. A. Jeeves. 1987. *Psychology through the eyes of faith.* San Francisco: Harper and Row.

Pascal, B. 1965. *Thoughts, 233.* Trans. W. F. Trotter. In *World Masterpieces,* ed. M. Mack, vol. 2, 38. New York: Norton.

Reichenbach, B. 1974. Life after death: Possible or impossible? *Christian Scholar's Review* 3: 232–44.

Westerhoff, J. H., III. 1971. *Values for tomorrow's children.* Philadelphia: Pilgrim Press.

16

John D. Carter

John D. Carter is professor at the Rosemead School of Psychology at Biola University, La Mirada, California. His Ph.D. in psychology is from the New School for Social Research.

Carter has been president of the Christian Association for Psychological Studies and has been active in the programs of Division 36, Psychologists Interested in Religious Issues, of the American Psychological Association. Carter currently serves as a member of the governing board of this division.

Carter's published articles indicate his major interests in the field of psychology of religion. A sampling of titles follows: "Toward a Biblical Model of Counseling," "The Nature and Scope of Integration: A Proposal" (with R. J. Mohline), "Adams's Theory of Nouthetic Counseling," and "The Psychology of Gothard and the Basic Youth Conflict seminars."

With S. Bruce Narramore Carter coauthored the widely used text *The Integration of Psychology and Theology: An Introduction* (Grand Rapids: Zondervan, 1979). In this volume he considered the important differences and similarities between scientific and religious enterprises, suggesting several models by which the two disciplines can be related: Against, Of, Parallels, and Integrates. The Carter and Narramore book has become a respected introduction to the field.

In 1981, Carter and J. Roland Fleck coedited *Psychology and Christianity: Integrative Readings* (Nashville: Abingdon). Among the articles in the volume previously published in the *Journal of Psychology and Theology* is Carter's seminal essay "Personality and Christian Maturity: A Process Congruity Model." This essay has become one of the more influential models for a growing number of researchers who are interested in the relationship between religion and psychological wholeness.

Carter's essay "Secular and Sacred Models of Psychology and Religion" provides a helpful four-category system of models of religion. In the "Against" model, either religion (in the secular version) or science (in the sacred version) is seen as untrue, and science (in the secular version) or religion (in the sacred version) is conceived to be the only valid means to truth. In the psychology "Of" religion model, psychology provides a dynamic understanding of humans as religious beings. In the psychology "Parallel" religion model, both psychology and religion provide truth, but the truths are different and unrelated. In the psychology "Integrates" religion alternative, a unified view of truth is both possible and desirable. Carter notes the sources as well as the strengths and weaknesses of each of these positions.

In his article "The Psychology of Religion: Present Concerns, Future Issues," Carter lists his present concerns as a historical theological interest in biblical psychology, an understanding of the Bible from the viewpoint of non-Western psychology, a study of spiritual direction, a probing of issues in the philosophy of science and hermeneutics, as well as a new interest in the theory and practice of psychotherapy.

He hopes in the future to complete a comprehensive bibliography of journal research literature in the field of psychology and Christianity to do further research in the relationship of religion and mental health, to develop a paradigm for the integration of faith and learning under which specific models can be subsumed, and to write a book on Christian experience.

Secular and Sacred Models
of Psychology and Religion

For the last 15 to 20 years there has been a resurgence of interest in the psychology of religion, as evidenced by such encyclopedic works as Strommen's *Research on Religious Development*. Psychology's interest in religion, which was evident during the early decades of this century (James, Starbuck, etc.), appears to have virtually died out during the 1930s and 1940s and early 1950s if the volume of publications is a criteria. Apparently, interest was rekindled at the 1959 American Psychological Association (APA) convention symposium entitled the "Role of the Concept of Sin in Psychotherapy." This renewed interest in psychology and religion by psychologists culminated two years ago in the APA's addition of Division 36—Psychologists Interested in Religious Issues.

A parallel interest in psychology's relationship to Christianity has developed in the evangelical Christian community. The growing number of books and articles and even evangelical psychological associations illustrates the evangelical psychologist's interest in psychology and Christianity (Collins 1975). This interest seems to be part of what Bloesch (1973) has called the "Evangelical Renaissance."

This article is an analysis of the four approaches, or models, by which psychologists have attempted to relate psychology to religion. It also analyzes a parallel version of these four models by which evangelical psychologists have attempted to relate to psychology and Christianity. These two analyses are called secular and sacred, respectively; they constitute the bulk of this article. Since the parallel versions of the models have developed separately, there is some difference in terminology. Psychologists have been concerned with religious phenomena and so explore religion while evangelical psychologists have been concerned

From the *Journal of Psychology of Theology* 5 (1977): 197–208; reprinted by permission of the publisher and the author. Copyright 1977 by Rosemead School of Psychology.

with Christianity and so explore psychology and Christianity rather than religion in general. The difference in terminology will be reflected in each analysis. A section comparing the two analyses, or versions, of the four models including the issues and a summary will conclude this chapter. An outline of the four secular and sacred models appears in

Table 16.1
Four Secular Models of Psychology and Religion

I. Psychology *Against* Religion
1. Science or scientific method is the only valid means to truth.
2. Truth claims other than science are destructive.
3. Religion (as myth) rather than truth is destructive.
4. Religion's destructiveness is its prohibitive or inhibitive effect on its members and society.
5. "Scientific" (valid) psychology is the solution to individual problems.
Examples: Ellis and Freud

II. Psychology *Of* Religion
1. Man is a spiritual-moral being (at least in a humanistic sense).
2. Religion, technology, science, or society which denies spirit, and thus his nature, creates pathology.
3. Most or all religions have recognized the spiritual-human quality of man and thus have the right approach.
4. The particular cultural-social-theological definition of man must be discarded in favor of a truly psychological definition of human functioning.
5. Good psychology translates the valid insights of religion into psychology and uses them for human good.
Examples: Fromm, Jung, and Mowrer

III. Psychology *Parallels* Religion
1. Religion and psychology are not related.
2. Each exists in its own sphere. One is scientific and the other is not.
3. Religion is a personal (and social) matter while psychology is intellectual and academic.
4. Both religion and psychology can be embraced. There is no conflict since they do not interact.
Examples: Thome

IV. Psychology *Integrates* Religion
1. A unifying or integrating view of truth in religion and psychology is both possible and desirable.
2. The truth or insights from psychology or religion will have some correspondence with the other discipline.
3. The truth or valid principles of religion and psychology are in harmony and form a unity.
4. Religion as socially manifested may be pathological but its intrinsic nature is not.
5. Valid religion and religious experiences are helpful in transcending the pains of existence or in assisting in the maturing process of growth.
Examples: Allport, Frankl, and Guntrip

Table 16.2
Four Models of the Scripture and Psychology

I. The Scripture *Against* Psychology

    1. Basic epistomological assumption: Revelation is against reason, i.e., the Scripture is contradictory to human thought both rationally and empirically.

    2. Soteriology and the Fall are stressed so as to eliminate and ignore creation and providence.

    3. Basic psychological assumption: The Scripture contains all the precepts of mental health.

    4. All emotional problems are spiritual problems because they result from disobedience.

    5. All problems can be solved by obedience to Scripture if the individual is confronted with a relevant passage of Scripture.

    Example: Adams

II. The Scripture *Of* Psychology

    1. Basic epistomological assumption: Human reason is more fundamental, comprehensive (technical), and contemporary than revelation.

    2. Creation and providence are stressed so as to ignore or eliminate soteriology and the Fall.

    3. Basic psychological assumption: Psychology has discovered the basic principles of emotional health, maturity, and good interpersonal functioning.

    4. Emotional problems can be solved by consulting a therapist or applying the principles of emotional maturity and good interpersonal relations.

    Examples: Relational theology

III. The Scripture *Parallels* Psychology

    1. Basic epistomological assumption: Revelation can never be reduced to reason nor can reason be reduced to revelation.

    2. God requires obedience to both revelation and reason. Hence, there is an implicit tension existing in the approach.

    3. Both creation-Providence and soteriology are stressed but they belong to different spheres.

    4. Spiritual problems should be dealt with by the pastor; emotional problems by a psychologist or psychiatrist.

    Examples: Clement (Isolation), Meehl (Correlation)

IV. The Scripture *Integrates* Psychology

    1. Basic epistomological assumption: God is the author of both revelation and reason because all truth (and truths) are God's truth and thus ultimately a part of a unified or integrated whole.

    2. Creation-Providence is stressed equally with soteriology.

    3. All problems are, in principle, a result of the Fall but not, in fact, the result of immediate conscious acts.

    4. Since values are significant both for the Christian and for therapy, a genuine Christian therapy is necessary.

    5. *Paraklesis* is the pattern for this type of therapy.

    Examples: Crabb, Hulme, van Kaam, Wagner, Carter & Mohline

tables 16.1 and 16.2 respectively. These tables must be studied in conjunction with the explanation in the text in order to fully appreciate the coherent nature of each model.

Secular Models

The four approaches psychologists have taken to psychology and religion are described as four models. Each model has its own character and pattern which have also been described in more detail and summarized in tables 16.1 and 16.2. These same four models also appear to parallel the four models that evangelical psychologists have used in their analysis of psychology and Christianity. Thus, it becomes apparent that sacred and secular versions of psychology and religion are two sides of the same model.

The first secular model is the psychology "Against" religion model. This approach holds that religion has or had a detrimental effect on mankind and on society because it is unscientific and, therefore, perpetuates myths. Hence, religion is viewed as exploiting individuals by its institutional character, that is, by its ability to control and inhibit free expression of humans in society, particularly in the area of sexual functioning. Thus, religion is viewed as being aligned with the oppressive forces in society. Secondly, as an institution in the broader sense, religion is able to reach into the individual's family life and shape his conscience so that guilt is produced with all of its detrimental and pathological effects. Thus, religion is the creator of needless, personal, emotional pain. Thirdly, religion is, at best, allowable for children and for primitive people who are not sophisticated enough to recognize its limiting function. At its worst, religion perpetuates immaturity in both a personal and intellectual sense: in the personal sense, religious views of personhood prevent autonomy and self-actualization in order to conform to the religious ideal; in an intellectual sense, religion perpetuates a view of the world and human nature which is intellectually and scientifically unacceptable. In summary, this model maintains that religion is essentially antiscientific or unscientific, that is, mythological, while psychology (as defined by the holder's view) represents a scientifically acceptable view of man, his nature, and functioning. This model is thus based on naturalism and has an antisupernaturalism stance. Freud ([1927] 1961) and Ellis (1970) are examples of this approach.

The second model is the psychology "Of" religion model. Holders of this view, like their counterpart in the Christian approach, tend to assume a mysticism, humanism, or parentheism (and sometimes a naturalism) rather than the antisupernaturalism of the "Against" model. Thus, man is a spiritual-moral being whose being needs to be free of oppressive forces whether societal, technological, or religious. Secondly, religion is good in general, that is, it is viewed as an ally or as a benign influence. Thirdly, religious metaphors or concepts are accepted and integrated in a psychological manner. The pure religious nature or content of the religious concepts are excluded or overlooked (either explicitly or implicitly), and in turn, the concepts are infused with or interpreted as having some psychological meaning derived from a particular psychological theory. The psychological benefits of religions and its functioning in healthy individuals are stressed, particularly in terms of the psychologized version of the religion(s). Jung ([1938] 1962), Fromm (1966), and Mowrer (1961) are the clearest examples of this model.

The third model—"psychology Parallels" religion—is harder to define in its secular form than in its sacred form. Holders of this view do not write specifically on their view. Rather, they are active in both spheres and may have written in both. Since the psychological community generally is unaware of the religious one and vice versa, there is little need to communicate or articulate any intellectual or rational connection of the two spheres of functioning. The view appears to be that quality functioning and productivity in both areas of endeavor are desirable, but no interaction is necessary: psychology is scientific and religion is personal (and perhaps social also). A major example provides the best articulation of this model.

Thorne (1950), for many years the editor of the *Journal of Clinical Psychology*, maintains that

> primary reliance should be placed on scientific methods when they are *validly* applicable, but that philosophy and religion also have their proper sphere of activities beyond the realm of science. (471)
>
> A distinction should be made between religion-oriented *spiritual counseling* and scientifically-oriented *personality counseling*. . . . It must be recognized in the beginning that the theoretical and philosophical foundations of spiritual and scientific approaches are basically different. (481)

While Thorne goes on to discuss the place of religion in counseling, his position is clear. Counseling, as scientifically based and grounded, is separate and even at points in opposition to religiously oriented counseling, yet there is clearly a place for religion as part of knowledge and culture. Also, its influence on certain counselees must be recognized and addressed.

The psychology "Integrates" religion model recognizes the healthy aspects of religion. It basically assumes that man needs a unifying philosophy of life and that religion, in its healthy expression, can provide an understanding of life both existentially and metaphysically which is broader than psychology. As a corollary, it assumes that religion can provide a personally integrating function in one's life, both intraspherically and interpersonally. The model also recognizes that the human condition is less than ideal and that personal and religious maturity does not automatically occur. Thus, there is unhealthy religion as well as individual and social pathology (i.e., hostility and defensiveness can occur inside as well as outside religion). Finally, a healthy religion is viewed as assisting or aiding in the transcendence of, or liberation from, pathology. Allport (1950) and Frankl (1975) are examples of this approach. Guntrip (1956, 1967) also appears to hold the Integrates' assumptions, but articulation of these implications is not developed yet.

Sacred Models

Since the original presentation of the sacred models (Carter and Mohline 1976), there have been two other attempts to define the models used in integrating psychology and Christianity (Crabb 1975; Farnsworth 1976). The former briefly outlines essentially the same four sacred models, but labels them differently and describes them in a confrontational (Against) rhetoric. The latter even more briefly outlines five models, three of which are directly equivalent to the Against, Of, and Integrates model and the remaining two which appear to be versions of the Parallels model.

As indicated above, evangelicals have used the same four models that secular psychologists have used to describe and interpret the relationship between Christianity and psychology. It should be noted that though the structure of the models is the same, the content is different and was developed independently.

The first model is the Christianity "Against" psychology approach. This model affirms that there is a radical difference between what the Bible says about man and what psychologists say. Holders of this view are either implicitly or explicitly committed to a presuppositionalism in which the unbelieving psychologists can discover no significant truths about the nature or functioning of man, especially Christian man. Secondly, they place a radical emphasis on the redemptive aspects of the Bible with a heavy stress on the difference between the believer and the unbeliever, between the old man and the new man. Thus, prayer, Bible reading, "trusting Christ," and "relying on the Holy Spirit," or a combination of these, are pursued as scriptural means for coping with life and its problems.

Thirdly, the discovery and application of God's laws from the Scriptures are stressed as solutions to all of life's problems. Thus emotional problems or "nervous breakdowns" are a result of violation of divine laws. Therapy in this approach consists largely of telling or encouraging people to follow God's requirement. While salvation by grace alone is maintained by holders of this approach, solutions to emotional difficulties come from obedience to God's laws rather than accepting God's love and grace.

Psychologically, the approach of this school of thought can be summarized by the statement, "All emotional problems are really spiritual problems." It should be noted that with few exceptions those who hold this view have no graduate training in psychology. Many evangelical psychologists would maintain that Adams's (1973) counseling techniques are representative of this approach.

The Christianity "Of" psychology model represents almost a direct antithesis of the first model discussed. This second approach also maintains that there is a difference between the Bible and the facts of science, experience, and reason, but in this case the latter is favored. The holders of this view tend to be committed to a naturalism, mysticism, or humanism rather than supernaturalism. Also, they stress the universal aspects of the Bible rather than the redemptive aspects. The Christian is not viewed as essentially different from other men, but as all other men, he is in need of the therapeutic benefits which psychology offers.

A third characteristic of the Christianity Of psychology model is its attempt to interpret the tenets of various "schools" of psychology as truly redemptive and Christian. They *selectively* translate or interpret various passages or concepts from the Bible into their particular psychology, that is, aspects of the Bible are mapped into the writings of some "school" of psychology which a particular psychologist holds. The founder of the school, be he Freud, Jung, or Rogers, becomes elevated so that what is acceptable in the Bible is what fits into the particular theory. Thus, the view to be propagated and used as a therapeutic tool is the Christianized version of some psychological theorist. Only a slightly different version of this "Christianizing" process occurs when it is not a theory but some particular principle, process, or experience which becomes the criterion, for example, group experiences or interpersonal relations, as stressed by some who take this approach. Various biblical passages are then used to give biblical sanction for the concept already accepted as true.

In its theological form, the Christianity Of psychology approach has been the position of liberalism. However, there are some current evangelicals who tend to adopt this approach. These evangelicals become so involved with accepting the client and helping him to express his repressed emotions that they ignore or implicitly deny the existence of sinful actions and attitudes. To varying degrees they reject or ignore any passages of Scripture which speak of restraint, control, commitment, or mature *Christian* living. Other evangelicals so stress some experience (for example, good interpersonal relations) that Christian experience tends to become synonymous with good interpersonal relations (Petersen and Broad 1977).

The Against and Of models just discussed represent extremes. Each has a cookie-cutter style. Onto the dough of Scripture and psychology each presses its cookie cutter. The dough inside the cutter is retained as the whole truth, and what is on the outside is rejected as false. Hence, the Against and Of models must be rejected as an inadequate approach to a Christian psychology. The remaining two approaches attempt to steer a middle course.

The third model—Christianity "Parallels" psychology—emphasizes the importance of both the Scripture and psychology, but assumes either explicitly or implicitly that the two do not interact. There are two versions of this model. The first version can be called the *isolation* version. The holders of this version maintain that psychology and the Scripture or theology are separate and there is no overlap (Clement 1974). That is, each is encapsulated, and there is no interaction because these methods and contents are different. However, since both are true, both must be affirmed but remain separate. The second version can be called the *correlation* version. Holders of this approach attempt to correlate, plug into, or line up certain psychological and scriptural concepts: for example, superego is equivalent to the conscience; it is equivalent to original sin; and empathy is equivalent to love (agape). Holders of the correlation version often assume they are integrating when in actuality they are simply lining up concepts from different spheres. The basic difference between correlating and integrating (which will become clearer after the Integrates model is discussed) is that the correlating assumes there are two things which need to be lined up and thus ignores the system or configuration of concepts in each, while the integrating assumes there is ultimately only one set (configuration) of concepts, laws, or principles which operates in two disciplines. It is the discovery of the one configuration which constitutes integration, not the lining up in concepts. Note that Farnsworth treats the correlation version as a separate model.

Correlating can be clearly seen in *What Then, Is Man?* Paul Meehl (1958), the general editor and author of several sections, outlines a solid theological view of salvation and then proceeds to discuss three psychological views of conversion and their implications for the orthodox biblical view he has just outlined. His theology never wavers, but it is as if his theology is on one side of a cliff and his psychology on the other and he is trying to build a bridge across but is not sure where to anchor the bridge on the psychological side.

Many Christian therapists either wittingly or unwittingly adopt this approach. Having been trained in the best institutions of the day, they practice the type of psychology they have learned. Being believers, they read their Bibles and attend church, but there is little if any genuine meshing of their psychology and their Christianity. Bridge building is correlating, not integrating.

The fourth model—Christianity "Integrates" psychology—basically assumes that God is the author of all truth, both the truth he has revealed in the Scripture and the truths discovered by psychology or any other scientific discipline. Hence, there is an expected congruence between Scripture and psychology because God has revealed himself in a special way in Scripture and in a general way in creation and also via his image in man (Gen. 1:26–27). Man has fallen into sin, and thus God's image in man has become marred, warped, or distorted. It is never lost, and it is being renewed through personal appropriation of salvation in Christ (Eph. 4:24; Col. 3:10). The holder of the Christianity Integrates psychology model never presumes that *all* the claims to discovered truths in psychology are genuine unless they are congruent and integratable with the Scripture, nor does he believe that certain traditional interpretations of Scripture are true either. God created psychology when he created man in his image. Man has become marred, but yet he is redeemable, and thus psychology is congruent and integratable with Christianity. This approach emphasizes both the Scripture and psychology *because they are allies*. Psychology used in this model has a small *p*, that is, it is the psychology that existed before the word was discovered, while psychology as used by the other three models has a capital *P* and refers to systems or theories. This is a critical difference.

There are many psychologists and pastoral counselors who are seeking to promote both understanding and growth in individuals. Hence, there is avaliable a vast popular literature on psychology and the Scripture. However, it is often very difficult to distinguish between the correlation version of the Parallels model and genuine integration in this popular literature because its goal is to promote practical Christian living rather than conceptual understanding. Much of the technical work exploring the nature and the content of the integration of psychology and the Scripture appears in two periodicals, The *Journal of the American Scientific Affiliation* and the *Journal of Psychology and Theology*. Many of the members of the Christian Association for Psychological Studies and the Western Association of Christians for Psychological Studies hold to the Integrates model. Crabb (1975), Hulme (1967), van Kaam (1968), and Wagner (1974) are examples of this model.

Evaluation of the Four Sacred or Christian Models

Since there is a plethora of literature currently being written on the integration of psychology and Christianity, a separate section is being given to the Christian or sacred models.

The four sacred or Christian models of psychology and Christianity just described, in reality, are only aspects of larger approaches to a Christian view of life which might be called Christianity and culture. Space does not allow for the expansion of this idea, but if the reader will substitute the word *culture* (in its anthropological sense) for *psy-*

chology in each model, he will be able to see how the four approaches to psychology grow out of four approaches to a Christian view of life.

Specifically, the Christianity Against psychology model assumes that there is no general revelation or common grace which God has revealed or given to man which can be discovered by a non-Christian psychologist. Besides running counter to systematic theology and Christian apologetics, this assumption is peculiar for two reasons. First, man was created in God's image (Gen. 1:26–27), and though marred, it has not been destroyed by the fall (Eph. 4:24; Col. 3:10). Secondly, the similar assumption does not seem to be held for medicine, economics, or physics, for example, truth which applies to Christians may be discovered by nonbelievers in these fields. Why not in psychology?

Though largely implicit, the Christianity Against psychology approach holds a surface view of sin and pathology. In practice, though not theologically, sin and pathology are reduced to symptoms. The counselee is doing, saying, or thinking the wrong things, and he is not doing, saying, or thinking the right things. Thus, therapy essentially becomes telling the counselee what the Bible says and how he or she should respond regardless of how little or much the counselor listens to the counselee. Therapy in this approach tends to become a symptoms removal or works sanctification depending upon whether it is viewed psychologically or theologically. At times, adherents to this approach sound remarkably similar to a parent lecturing an adolescent in their therapeutic techniques while the biblical emphasis on "out of the abundance of the heart the mouth speaks" (Matt. 12:34–35) or "truth in the inward parts" (Ps. 51:6 KJV) is bypassed in favor of behavioral compliance. Thus, the volume of scriptural quotation in "Christian" psychology books in no way guarantees its faithfulness to content or intent of Scripture. It is from this limited view of God's revelation in nature (man) and its limited view of sin and pathology that the Christianity Against psychology practitioner criticizes the committed Christian professionals who accept one of the latter two approaches, presuming they are taking the Of model approach. The adherents of the Christianity Against psychology approach appear to see only the scripturally invalid claims to psychological truth and thus essentially reject psychology. The adherents of the Christianity Of psychology approach appear to accept all claims to psychological truth (i.e., all claims they are committed to as valid) and thus essentially reject the integrity of Scripture.

However, since the propagators of the Christianity Against psychology approach have had almost exclusively theological rather than psychological training, they do have many helpful insights into Scripture. Their works can be read with profit (if their oppressive rhetoric can be ignored) by those professionals whose training has been exclusively psychological in nature. Furthermore, since many problems have a behavioral symptom component, the Christianity Against psychology approach helps to relieve the pressure of symptoms for many persons.

Little needs to be said concerning the Christianity Of psychology model. At best, in the opinion of those who hold this view, the Bible provides a convenient set of metaphors into which various psychological concepts can be translated. The evangelical, who operates from this approach, seems to be caught up with some psychological concepts or theoretical perspectives to such an extent that they are not able to see the larger implications of their approach. They tend to see only their favored concept or perspective in the Scripture. Thus, the totality of the biblical emphasis is limited. Ramm (1972) has described the weakness of such groups of evangelicals in a paper entitled "Is it safe to shift to an 'interpersonal theology'?"

The greatest strength of the Christianity Parallels psychology approach is also its greatest weakness. It avoids the pitfalls of the Against and Of models, but it offers no positive constructive alternatives. Many professionals who operate from this approach (especially the isolation version) have had little or no theological or biblical training but are competent psychologists. The militancy of the proponents of the Against model often has the effect of inhibiting many of this group who are searching from some biblical insight into psychology. The parallelists are aware of their own competency and the general psychological naiveté of the Against proponent and, therefore, tend to be very wary of any claims regarding the discovery of "the" biblical psychology. Other parallelists seem to arrive at their position because they believe that the laws and methods of psychology are separate from the laws and methods of theology, or economics, or any discipline for that matter. However, all disciplines are integratable in a grand Christian philosophical scheme though this integration has little to do with their therapeutic practice.

Many evangelical psychologists who are only correlating believe they are integrating. This is confusing and unfortunate. As was indicated, genuine integration involves the discovery and articulation of the common underlying principles of both psychology and the Scripture, that is, how general grace and special grace are related in reference to psychology. In addition, there are many evangelical counselors and therapists who "believe in" integration but whose therapy in no appreciative way differs from their secular colleagues except for an occasional reference to God or the Bible. It is difficult to know in what sense this kind of therapy can be called integrative or Christian, except that both therapist and client are Christians. This observation is not intended to be a pejorative comment but a descriptive categorization.

The strength and weakness of the Christianity Integrates psychology model also rests on its basic assumption: that psychology is integratable with Christianity. This is an open assumption, and the burden of proof rests on the proponent of this model. The practical proponents of this approach have proclaimed this assumption although they were not able single-handedly to supply the details. The number of articles, not to mention books, appearing in the two scholarly journals mentioned, as well as in other periodicals, suggests that the more theoretically oriented integrators are beginning to discover the details of integration. The process of integration takes time. The bulk of psychology as a discipline is less than 50 years old and much of it is less than 30 years old. Christians must study psychology and then study the Scripture to discover its psychology. Little biblical psychology will be discovered if one does not know any psychology.

The integrators tend to emphasize the inner, or depth, aspect of man as the source of both problems and health, in keeping with the biblical emphasis on the heart as the motive source of actions (Matt. 15:18–19; Luke 6:45). Also, many integrators tend to approach therapy, however, implicitly from the biblical concept *paraklēsis*, meaning support, comfort, consolation, or encouragement (exhortation). With its broad meaning, *paraklēsis* could apply to any therapy from crisis intervention to long-term analysis. *Paraklēsis* is a gift given to the church (Rom. 12:8), and the integrator presumes Christian counseling is part of the larger ministry of the church.

Thus, the Integrates model assumes a Christian view of man which includes God's special revelation in the Scripture and his general revelation in nature (Rom. 1:20; Ps. 19:1) and man (Gen. 1:27).

Table 16.2 lists five examples of those following the Integrates model. Each has a different theoretical orientation and is attempting to move from that base to an integrative one with the Scripture. Thus, the differences in style and vocabulary, one hopes, will not obscure the genuine integration in each.

Evaluation: Christian and Secular Models

This section will begin with a comparison of the two versions of each model and conclude with a discussion of a broader base of the four models.

The four sacred and secular models of psychology and religion are clearly not equally similar. The greatest difference appears in the Against model. This difference occurs because either psychology or religion is rejected in the Against model but it is the opposite part in the sacred and secular versions. However, the difference in content or orientation should not blind one to the striking equivalence in style and structure. However, the difference in content often leads the secular and sacred proponents of this model to dogmatic clashes. The difference in the Of model is much less noticeable. Both sacred and secular versions assume a humanistic-naturalistic or metaphysical view. The difference seems to be in the use of metaphors. The sacred approach predominantly uses religious metaphors, but with understood psychological meaning, while the secular approach uses psychological metaphors in such a way as to incorporate religious meanings.

The sacred and secular versions of the Parallels model are perhaps the most similar, but this model is also the least defined. It is most similar in that the central structures, religion and psychology, are separated in both versions. Because religion and/or Christianity and psychology are maintained separately, there is little definition to the model except the maintenance of the separate disciplines. However, the correlation version of the sacred Parallels model does attempt to line up the two disciplines.

There is a great deal of similarity between the secular and sacred versions of the Integrates model. There tends to be a broad philosophical or metaphysical orientation to this model. This seems to be a function of the nature of the Integrates model, which calls for an awareness and integration of two distinct bodies of knowledge. The adherents of this model seem to focus on the underlying issues in both psychology and religion without a loss of technical mastery of some area of the field of psychology. Also, the adherents' interest in a religious understanding and the integration of it with psychology are a result of personal belief, experience, and commitment.

As indicated, there have been only four approaches to the relationship between psychology and religion. Two versions of these models, sacred and secular, have been described and compared. Each version of each model (see tables 16.1 and 16.2) is founded on a relatively coherent set of assumptions. In reading and discussing psychology and religion, one should bear in mind the model which is being assumed. Since individuals implicitly hold to one of these four models, misunderstanding often occurs when another individual holds to a different model. The misunderstandings often tend to degenerate into conflicts when the nature of implicit assumptions behind the models is not recognized. Also, there are psychologists who intellectually assume one model but who are affectively committed to another.

In conclusion, the four models may be viewed as a new interpretation of an old problem: relating the secular and the sacred. *Christ and Culture* (Niebuhr 1951) describes five approaches Christians have taken in relating their religious faith to a secular world. The Christian, or religious, version of the four models, represents an application or extension of four of these approaches to psychology. Thus, relating the Christian faith to psychology is really only part of the larger problem of relating the Christian faith to the world of life and thought.

Finally, the four models may be thought of as parallel to some of the proposed solutions to the mind-body problem. How can the mind and body, two different aspects of a person, be related in one individual? How can psychology, a scientific discipline, be related to religion or Christianity, a revealed and historical faith? While there have been a number of proposed solutions to the mind-body problem, Beloff (1962) maintains the mind-body problem may be reduced to four basic solutions. The four models presented in this article appear to parallel four of these solutions. The Against and Of models appear to parallel the materialism and idealism solution. Each model denies one aspect of the problem just as materialism and idealism deny one aspect of the mind-body problem. The Parallels model seems equivalent to psychophysical parallelism. The Integrates model appears to be similar to the double aspect solution of the mind-body problem. These mind-body problem parallels are not to be thought of as total or definitive, only suggestive. Any light this suggestion throws on the relationship between psychology and religion at this primitive stage of understanding will be helpful.

References

Adams, J. 1973. *The Christian counselor's manual.* Grand Rapids: Baker.

Allport, G. W. 1950. *The individual and his religion: A psychological interpretation.* New York: Macmillan.

Beloff, J. 1962. *The existence of mind.* London: Macgibbon and Kee.

Bloesch, E. 1973. *The evangelical renaissance.* Grand Rapids: Eerdmans.

Carter, J. D., and R. J. Mohline. 1976. The nature and scope of integration: A proposal. *Journal of Psychology and Theology* 4: 3–14.

Clement, P. 1974. Behavior modification of the spirit. Paper presented at the Convention of the Western Association of Christians for Psychological Studies, May 24–25, Santa Barbara, Calif.

Collins, G. R. 1975. The pulpit and the couch. *Christianity Today* 19: 1087–90.

Crabb, L. J., Jr. 1975. *Basic principles of biblical counseling.* Grand Rapids: Zondervan.

Ellis, A. 1970. *Reason and emotion in psychotherapy.* New York: Lyle Stuart.

Farnsworth, K. E. 1976. Integration of faith and learning utilizing a phenomenological/existential paradigm for psychology. Paper presented at the Christian Association for Psychological Studies, June 25–29, Santa Barbara, Calif.

Frankl, V. 1975. *The unconscious god.* New York: Simon and Schuster.

Freud, S. [1927] 1961. *The future of an illusion.* Garden City, N.Y.: Doubleday.

Fromm, E. 1966. *You shall be as gods.* New York: Fawcett.

Guntrip, H. 1956. *Psychotherapy and religion.* New York: Harper and Row.

————. 1967. Religion in relationship to personal integration. *British Journal of Medical Psychology* 62: 423–33.

Hulme, W. 1967. *Counseling and theology.* Philadelphia: Fortress.

Jung, C. G. [1938] 1962. *Psychology and religion.* New Haven: Yale Univ. Press.

Meehl, P. 1958. *What then, is man?* St. Louis: Concordia.

Mowrer, O. H., ed. 1961. *The crisis in psychiatry and religion.* Princeton, N.J.: Van Nostrand.

Niebuhr, H. R. 1951. *Christ and culture.* New York: Harper.

Petersen, B., and S. Broad. 1977. Unmasking: an interview with Waldon Howard (including comments). *Eternity* 28 (July): 21–22.

Ramm, B. 1972. Is it safe to shift to an "interpersonal theology"? *Eternity* 23 (December): 21–22.

Thorne, F. 1950. *Principles of personality counseling.* Journal of Clinical Psychology, Brandon, Vt.

van Kaam, A. 1968. *Religion and personality.* Garden City, N.Y.: Doubleday.

Wagner, M. 1974. *Put it all together.* Grand Rapids: Zondervan.

The Psychology of Religion:
Present Concerns, Future Issues

It is a pleasure to participate in the symposium "Psychology of Religion: Present concerns, future issues." I am looking forward to reviewing the whole symposium since it will generate much interest in the field and be a stimulus to further developments.

Past Concerns

I have taken the liberty to begin this essay with a brief discussion of my past concerns because they flow so intricately with my present concerns and future issues. There have been four major issues which have occupied my attention in the past. The first has been the evaluation of Christian, or so-called biblical psychologies. These "pop" psychologies emerged suddenly in the late 1960s and continued through the 1970s, although there have been earlier anticedents (Vande Kemp 1984). Collins (1975) has described these emergent psychologies in general while I evaluated two in detail: Bill Gothard and his Basic Youth Conflict seminars and Adams's theory of nouthetic counseling (1974c, 1975, 1976). Secondly I have been occupied with the concept of processes of maturity from both a biblical and psychological perspective (1974a). The New Testament concept of *telos* and its usage seems very similar to Jung's concept of individuation and Rogers's concept of self-actualization (Carter 1974b). Oakland (1974) has observed a similar connection to Maslow's concept of self-actualization.

Thirdly, models or types of psychology of religion have been a preoccupation of mine for a long time. In 1977 I developed a four-category system of secular and sacred models of psychology of religion labeled "Against," "Of," "Parallels," and "Integrates." Partly through my preoccupation with models and partly as an alternative to the so-called bibli-

From the *Journal of Psychology and Christianity* 5, no. 2 (1986): 20–24; reprinted by permission of the publisher and the author. Copyright 1986 by the Christian Association for Psychological Studies.

cal psychologies, I developed a biblical model for counseling based on the New Testament concepts of the flesh and the spirit (1980). My fourth concern has focused on the psychology of religion in general and its corollary, the theology of psychology. Together these concerns have been called the *integration of psychology and theology* (Carter and Mohline 1976; Carter and Narramore 1979; Fleck and Carter 1981) while others have referred to it as *psychotheology* (McLemore 1976; Stern and Marino 1970). This latter or fourth concern is broader than the previous three and reflects in a philosophy-of-science sense what Barbour (1974) in *Myth, Models, and Paradigms,* following Kuhn (1970), would call a paradigm, while the first three concerns are model related, that is, more particular, concrete, and potentially testable in that they organize data or generate hypotheses.

Present Concerns

Presently my concern with evaluating biblical psychologies has peaked or rather is culminating in a small monograph on Jay Adams's theory of nouthetic counseling. This work is a summary and analysis of Adams's nouthetic theory and a critical evaluation from a biblical evangelical perspective, which Adams has asked to be the exclusive criteria for judging his work. I still have some interest in a biblical psychology, but in a historical theological sense. However, more significantly, I have come to view the Bible in a non-Western perspective. It reflects a psychology which is Third-World oriented or primitive in an anthropological sense. This is why attempts to write a biblical psychology will fail unless based on cultural understanding with a non-Western worldview. Traditional (Western) theology and anthropology should be used only for comparative purposes. The possible outcome of this line of thinking will be discussed in the next section.

My concern with the topic of spiritual and psychological maturity is also fading. There are probably several reasons for this. I feel relatively satisfied with my contribution to the issue, and thus it has lost some of its challenge for me. On the other hand, the issue is by no means fading as an issue for the psychology of religion. It remains a continuing concern although it seems to have become pluralized, that is, there seems to be an increasing exploration of spirituality within specific religious traditions. There is a sense in which my interest in maturity has only shifted to an interest in spiritual direction which goes by various names, such as discipleship, healing, healing of the memories, Christian counseling or therapy depending on the particular religious (or secular) tradition in question and whether health or restoration is stressed.

My interest in models or model building has remained, but it has generalized to a concern for the philosophy of science and hermeneu-

tics in both a psychological and a philosophical sense. However, as I
have attempted to expand the foundation of my Integrates model of the
psychology of religion in the introduction to *Psychology and Christianity*
(Fleck and Carter 1981) and in my reply to DeVries (Carter and Narramore 1984), I realized that a framework or a meta-theory of the psychology of religion was being developed. Hence what I was trying to
articulate was a paradigm for looking at the psychology of religion, that
is, a paradigm in Kuhn's (1970) sense. Therefore, my interest in models
(for example, Against, Of, Parallels and Integrates) is becoming fused
with my interest in the broader questions of the relationship of psychology and religion as disciplines, as ways of experiencing the world, and
as ways of conceptualizing the world.

A new interest in the theory and practice of therapy has developed
recently. The newer movement in psychoanalytic theory called object
relations theory has captured my attention. It grows out of the writings
of Fairbairn (1952), Guntrip (1961), and Kohut (1977) and is a depth-
interpersonal-self theory within the psychoanalytic perspective (Hedges
1983; Greenberg and Mitchell 1983). My interest in this developing psychoanalytic perspective seems to parallel an interest by analysts in religions (Meissner 1983; McDargh 1983; Lovinger 1984). My curiosity in
psychoanalysis was originally kindled by the Dutch theologian-analyst
Heije Faber's (1975) work on psychoanalysis and religion. As an outgrowth of this interest I am working on developing a book of readings
on psychoanalysis and object relations theory of psychology of religion.
This will probably be squeezed in between the first and second or the
second and third projects described below. The practice side of therapy
has also led me to become interested in the development of God concepts and the experience of God as it manifests itself clinically. In a
developmental sense this therapeutic interest is probably an outgrowth
of my previous interest in spiritual maturity.

Future Projects

As of the moment I can see four projects on the horizon. These projects do not correspond directly to my past concerns but rather grow
out of my interests in models and the paradigm of integration. I will
discuss them in the order of remoteness in time. Of necessity the clarity
and specificity of the projects will become increasingly lost to a general
conception.

The first project grows out of my long-standing interest in the psychology of Christianity and the integration of psychology and theology.
I am developing a comprehensive bibliography of journal literature in
this field from 1970 to the present. This literature is being put on the
computer and will be available for interested persons in the field.

Access will be through a key-word search service. The first phase of this extensive project will focus on the empirical studies, that is, studies which have collected data. This phase at present contains over 600 titles. The announcement of the search service will be published in the *Journal of Psychology and Theology* sometime in the fall or winter of 1985. Dissertations will be the second phase of this service and should be complete during 1986, well before the later phases of this project. The additional domains of this literature (theoretical, clinical, and social) will be added to the search service as they are completed. Obviously this project will generate many specific papers and studies by both my students and myself.

Two particular areas of investigation have begun to emerge for me from the literature search project. Allport (1966) has described intrinsic-extrinsic religious orientation and Allen and Spilka (1967) have described committed-consensual religion. Considerable empirical literature has emerged around these concepts. The issue which is arising for me concerns the nature of these constructs. Are they orientations to types of religion or are they motivation? If motivation, how do they relate to the rest of human personality? In addition, how many orientations or motivations exists? Fleck (1981) has argued for three—intrinsic-committed, consensual and extrinsic—with good theoretical but weaker empirical support. Spilka, Hood and Gorsuch (1985) have presumed there are just two—intrinsic-committed and extrinsic-consensual—though the research basis for this is unclear.

The second issue emerging from the literature research is whether religion promotes or hinders mental health. The literature is filled with many conflicting findings. Perhaps the most important single issue is to review the methodological adequacy of this research in order to determine what the literature is validly saying about mental health and religion. This literature is filled with many speculative and clinical discussions which lack any valid empirical basis. Batson and Ventis (1982) have begun this task, as have Spilka, Hood and Gorsuch (1985), but what these studies lack is a sound methodological critique of the literature on this topic. However, I do not fault them as they have begun the task which in my judgment is the biggest single task in the field of psychology of religion: a systematic and thorough methodological critique to determine what can be said with some degree of confidence.

However, the larger purpose of the computer search project is to promote growth and understanding in the field of psychology of religion since there is no one abstracting service or centralized source for the field where scholars and researchers can gain access to all of the pertinent literature.

My second future project will be a series of articles or monographs attempting to define integration as a paradigm which can organize many existing "models of integration." Although some of the particulars have formed in my thinking, space does not allow me to discuss the details except to say that I view integration as a paradigm in a broad Kuhnian sense of paradigm as discussed by Barbour (1974) and as general propositions as discussed by Larzelere (1980). There appear to be several aspects to this task: (1) analyzing and discussing various approaches relevant to the philosophy of the social sciences, (2) describing the paradigm itself, and (3) discussing some of the particular details or aspects of the paradigm. To date I have not done any writing on the philosophy-of-science aspect of this project. The articulation of the paradigm itself I see growing out of what I have called the Integrates model (Carter 1977) and expanded in my introduction to *Psychology and Christianity* (Fleck and Carter 1981). Some of the detail of this paradigm I see growing out of the common conceptual dynamics between psychology and theology described in "The Nature and Scope of Integration" (Carter and Mohline 1976). Probably the first paper in this group will deal with the relationship of sin to psychopathology, which has occupied my thinking for some time.

Still further in the future and, like a helix, I feel my thinking will probably return to theological anthropology, only at a higher and more mature level. My sense is that some of the separate threads of interest in models and paradigms, biblical thought, and theology will converge into a theological anthropology of experience. I am currently negotiating the revision of one of the older biblical-theological psychologies. This will stimulate and enrich my current thinking in the psychology of religion and my integrative interest expressed in the literature search. Reading these old biblical psychologies is like reading Plato and Aristotle. It does not turn one into a fourth-century B.C. Greek philosopher, or even into a Platonist or Aristotelian, but it does stimulate my thinking and reduces my tendency to arrogance, the arrogance of a 20th-century psychologist who thinks that he and his colleagues have original, fundamental, and permanent solutions to the problem in the psychology of religion.

Finally, when I am very old and I hope much wiser, I envision a comprehensive work on the psychology and theology of religious or Christian experience. It would include a grounding in the philosophy of sciences and a section on personality theories and their implicit assumption about the nature of human nature and conclude with a discussion of the nature of experience and its implications for religion and theology. Reviewing my position and current interests as well as my projected future ones has been a stimulating and a growth-producing experience.

References

Allen, R. O., and B. Spilka. 1967. Committed and consensual religion: A specification of religion-prejudice relationships. *Journal for the Scientific Study of Religion* 6: 191–206.

Allport, G. W. 1966. The religious context of prejudice. *Journal for the Scientific Study of Religion* 5: 447–57.

Batson, C. D., and W. L. Ventis. 1982. *The religious experience: A social-psychological perspective*. New York: Oxford Univ. Press.

Barbour, I. 1974. *Myths, models, and paradigms. The nature of religious and scientific language*. New York: Harper and Row.

Carter, J. D. 1974a. Maturity: Psychological and biblical. *Journal of Psychology and Theology* 2: 89–96.

———. 1974b. Personality and Christian maturity: A process congruity model. *Journal of Psychology and Theology* 2: 190–201.

———. 1974c. The psychology of Gothard and the Basic Youth Conflict seminars. *Journal of Psychology and Theology* 2: 249–59.

———. 1975. Adams's theory of nouthetic counseling. *Journal of Psychology and Theology* 3: 143–55.

———. 1976. Nouthetic counseling defended: A reply to Ganz. *Journal of Psychology and Theology* 4: 206–16.

———. 1977. Secular and sacred models of psychology and religion. *Journal of Psychology and Theology* 5: 197–208.

———. 1980. Toward a biblical model of counseling. *Journal of Psychology and Theology* 8: 43–52.

Carter, J. D., and S. B. Narramore. 1979. *The integration of psychology and theology: An introduction*. Grand Rapids: Zondervan.

———. 1984. Beyond integration and back again: A reply to DeVries. *Journal of Psychology and Christianity* 3, no. 2: 49–59.

Carter, J. D., and R. J. Mohline. 1976. The nature and scope of integration: A proposal. *Journal of Psychology and Theology* 4: 3–14.

Collins, G. R. 1975. Popular Christian psychologies: Some reflections. *Journal of Psychology and Theology* 3: 129–32.

Faber, H. 1976. *The psychology of religion*. Philadelphia: Westminster.

Fairbairn, W. 1952. *An object-relations theory of personality*. London: Kegan Paul.

Fleck, J. R. 1981. Dimensions of personal religion: A trichotomous view. In *Psychology and Christianity: Integrative readings*, ed. J. R. Fleck and J. D. Carter, 66–80. Nashville: Abingdon.

Fleck, J. R., and J. D. Carter, eds. 1981. *Psychology and Christianity: Integrative readings*. Nashville: Abingdon.

Greenberg, J. R., and S. A. Mitchell. 1983. *Object relations in psychoanalytic theory*. Cambridge: Harvard Univ. Press.

Guntrip, H. 1961. *Personality structure and human interaction.* New York: International Universities Press.

Hedges, L. E. 1983. *Listening perspectives in psychotherapy.* Northvale, N.J.: Aronson.

Kohut, H. 1977. *The restoration of the self.* New York: International Universities Press.

Kuhn, T. S. 1970. *The structure of scientific revolutions.* Chicago: Univ. of Chicago Press.

Larzelere, R. 1980. The task ahead: Six levels of integration of Christianity and psychology. *Journal of Psychology and Theology* 8: 3–11.

Lovinger, R. J. 1984. *Working with religious issues in therapy.* New York: Aronson.

McDargh, J. 1983. *Psychoanalytic object relations theory and the study of religion: On faith and the imaging of God.* Lanham, Md.: Univ. Press of America.

McLemore, C. 1976. The nature of psychotheology: Varieties of conceptual integration. *Journal of Psychology and Theology* 5: 217–20.

Meissner, W. W. 1983. *Psychoanalysis and religious experience.* New Haven: Yale Univ. Press.

Oakland, J. 1974. Self-actualization and sanctification. *Journal of Psychology and Theology* 2: 202–9.

Spilka, B., R. W. Hood, Jr., and R. L. Gorsuch. 1985. *The psychology of religion: An empirical approach.* Englewood Cliffs, N.J.: Prentice-Hall.

Stern, E. M., and B. Marino. 1970. *Psychotheology.* Paramus, N.J.: Paulist Press.

Vande Kemp, H. 1984. *Psychology and theology in Western thought, 1672–1965: A historical and annotated bibliography.* In collaboration with H. N. Malony. Bibliographies in the History of Psychology and Psychiatry: A series. Millwood, N.Y.: Kraus International.

17

Gary R. Collins

G ary R. Collins is professor of counseling and psychology and dean of the Institute for International and Multicultural Counseling at Liberty University in Lynchburg, Virginia. Prior to this appointment, he was professor of psychology at Trinity Evangelical Divinity School, Deerfield, lllinois, and taught at Bethel College (Minnesota) and Conwell School of Theology. Since 1980 Collins has served as adjunct instructor at the United States Air Force Chaplain School at Maxwell Air Force Base in Alabama. A native Canadian, he received undergraduate and master's degrees from McMaster University and the University of Toronto. He earned the Ph.D. in clinical psychology from Purdue University and engaged in further study at Western Baptist Seminary and the University of London.

Collins is past president of the American Scientific Affiliation, an interdisciplinary group of Christian scientists. In 1984, he was awarded the William Bier Award for outstanding achievement in applied psychology of religion by Division 36, Psychologists Interested in Religious Issues, of the American Psychological Association.

Known as a stimulating presenter and provocative thinker, Dr. Collins travels overseas frequently to conduct training workshops in Christian counseling for armed forces chaplains and other groups. He has had a strong interest in making general psychology understandable and palatable to religious persons.

Collins has authored over 30 books, several of which have been written for counselors. *Christian Counseling: A Comprehensive Guide* (Waco, Tex.: Word, 1980) is a widely used volume for undergraduate, seminary, and lay counselor training. *Can You Trust Psychology?* (Downers Grove: Inter-Varsity, 1988) gives Christian answers to many of the questions raised by students and by critics of psychology. Dr. Collins writes the

457

monthly *Christian Counseling Newsletter* and is general editor of Word Books' Resources for Christian Counseling—a series of 35 professional books written by experts in counseling.

Other writings by Collins has been directed toward rethinking the theoretical relationships between psychology and theology. *The Rebuilding of Psychology: An Integration of Psychology and Theology* (Wheaton: Tyndale, 1982) is a good example of his thinking. This volume recounts the history of psychology and notes its dependence on the philosophical assumptions of the natural sciences. Collins suggests that these assumptions were affirmed by the founders of modern psychology in an effort to make the study of human behavior respectable. Collins boldly proposes that these are not the only assumptions which can provide a foundation for psychology and that we rebuild psychology on a new foundation: the foundation of the Bible and Christian revelation. This foundation includes assumptions that all truth is God's truth, that there is general and special revelation, and that empiricism must be expanded to include religious experience and other sources of knowledge.

In the article "Moving through the Jungle: A Decade of Integration," Collins suggests that those who have been trying to integrate psychology and theology have been carving out an entirely new field. While the psychology of religion is not new, the attempt to integrate is novel. After reviewing articles printed in the first 40 issues of the *Journal of Psychology and Theology*, Collins concludes that there is a need to clarify integration goals, retain an evangelical theology, sharpen integration assumptions, focus on the practical, evaluate the trends, sharpen the focus, and admit the importance of personal applications.

In "The Psychology of Religion Today," Dr. Collins notes that very early he decided to be a committed Christian first and a competent psychologist second—a combination he has not found incompatible. He identifies the following as those issues and questions that have most interested him: why people are religious, how we can account for individual differences in religious beliefs and practices, how religion relates to counseling, how religion relates to popular psychology, and whether religion should be used apologetically.

In issuing a challenge to his fellow psychologists of religion, Collins says it is they who must demonstrate that the field is a legitimate, respectable, and practical part of general psychology. In the future he feels the psychology of religion should be a vehicle for greater understanding of guilt management, of the influence of values on behavior, of the effect of religion on psychopathology and of the study of the church as a social institution. He further proposes that the psychology of religion become an agency for social change. And Collins hopes these prospects for the future can be met while avoiding three potential pitfalls: sloppy and dull writing, scientism that excludes nonempirical evidence, and unadmitted prejudgments that influence studies and research.

Moving through the Jungle:
A Decade of Integration

S everal years ago, near the time when the *Journal of Psychology and Theology* (referred to in this article as the *Journal*) began publication, I discussed integration with a seminary colleague who is well known as an evangelical theologian. My friend suggested,

> Christians in psychology are pioneers. Much of the scholarly work in theological and biblical disciplines is a refinement of what already has been discovered, a retreading of well traveled paths, and an avoidance of investigative routes that others have found to be "deadends." In contrast, those who want to integrate psychology with theology or biblical studies are carving new pathways. Such people are like explorers standing at the edge of a jungle with a machete, but with no real sense of where or even how to cut through the brush.

The imagery is picturesque (and I suspect my mind has added a few embellishments over the years), but the point is basic: integration is a new field, and the people who read or write in journals such as this one often are still "finding their way." We are still refining methodology, deciding which issues are important, determining what needs to be done, and sometimes evaluating whether the effort is worth all of our work, or even possible.

Like the laborer with the machete, however, there is value in stopping periodically to examine our work, to see where we have failed or made progress, and to ponder our next moves.

Such self-examination should start with a reminder that the relationship between psychology and religion has been studied for decades— long before the *Journal* began publication. Freud, Jung, James, Hall, Fromm, Allport, Mowrer, and a host of lesser-known people pondered the psychology-religion interface, before most of us were born. The theological and psychological perspectives of these early pioneers were

From the *Journal of Psychology and Theology* 11 (1983): 2–7; reprinted by permission of the publisher and the author. Copyright 1983 by Rosemead School of Psychology.

diverse, and "integration" was rarely a goal in their work. Most sought to understand—and sometimes to explain away—religious attitudes and behavior. Nevertheless their exploratory efforts can give insight into useful methodology, the influence of assumptions, the selection of issues to be considered, and the practical implications of our work. Carefully written critiques which summarize, evaluate, and help readers learn from the work of others have appeared in the *Journal*, but to avoid the mistakes of others and to clarify issues for future investigation, it is essential that we know more about the historical roots of the psychology-theology interaction.

In preparing this article, I reviewed all 40 issues of the *Journal* thus far. I had planned to categorize the articles under headings such as historical overviews, integration theory, psychopathology, pastoral counseling, and articles on the self, but after a couple of frustrating hours, I abandoned the project. The articles which have appeared in this publication are so diverse that they almost defy classification. Reports of research and historical evaluations have been interspersed with literature reviews and papers on such diverse topics as spiritual conflict, nouthetic counseling, homosexuality, the mental health of Jesus, communication theory, feminism, holiness, demon possession, loneliness, urban ministries, cognitive theory, hypnosis, grace, inner healing, counselor education, systems theory, and masturbation. It could be argued that such diversity is healthy, especially in these early stages of our work. Psychology is a complex field concerned with numerous issues, and it is not surprising that the *Journal* covers a variety of topics.

Is it possible, however, that we are too diverse? The 40 journals on my desk leave me with the feeling that we may be settling for a shotgun approach, moving in various directions at the same time, but with few clear goals, in spite of the carefully stated "publications policy" which appears on the back cover of each issue.

So where do we go from here? The editors' invitation to prepare an evaluation of the *Journal*'s first decade has stimulated me to make several observations about the task of integration and the future of this publication. I emphasize that these are only the opinions of one person, and they are not listed in any special order of importance.

Clarifying Our Goals

On the front cover, each issue of this journal is described as "An Evangelical Forum for the Integration of Psychology and Theology." Fleck and Carter (1981) have noted that there is no particular significance to the term *integration*. The word has been used, especially in evangelical circles, to describe the relationship between psychology and Christianity, but it does not imply the fusion of two fields into a third discipline, the reduction of psychology to "nothing but" religion (or vice versa), or the lining up of psychological terms alongside somewhat similar Christian concepts and calling the result "integration." Some have suggested that other terms would be better, that it would be more precise to talk about the "synthesis," "interaction," "dialogue," or "interface" between psychology and Christianity. These newer terms may be more accurate, but they have not come into wide use, and it now seems unlikely that we ever will shift to a new terminology. We are left, then, with the difficult task of defining integration both conceptually and operationally.

Integration is an emerging field of study. It seeks (a) to discover and comprehend truth about God and his created universe by using scientific methods (including empirical, clinical, and field observations) and the hermeneutically valid principles of biblical interpretation, (b) to combine such findings, when possible, into systematic conclusions, (c) to search for ways of resolving apparent discrepancies between findings, and (d) to utilize the resulting conclusions in a way which enables us to more accurately understand human behavior and more effectively facilitate the changes which help individuals move towards spiritual and psychological wholeness. All will not agree with this statement of purpose, but surely there is value in pondering what we mean by integration and considering what our integrative efforts should seek to accomplish.

In a thoughtful book published several years ago, Crabb (1977) wrote about "spoiling the Egyptians," taking insights from psychology and making use of those concepts which are compatible with Christian presuppositions and scriptural teaching. In his analysis, however, Crabb did not describe how we go about this task. Like many others, including me, he has written about the need for integration but has said little about the process and methodology of integrating Christianity and psychology. In contrast Farnsworth's recent article (1982) on the "conduct of integration" is a move in the direction of considering how we approach the integrative task.

In the coming decades, I suggest that we could benefit from additional articles on the meaning, purposes, and methodology of integration. We are unlikely to make significant progress in this field if we have only foggy ideas about these basic issues. We cannot reach the goals of integration if we do not know what the goals are or if we are not even sure that our integration work is worth doing.

Retaining Our Theology

This journal exists as "an evangelical forum" for integrating psychology and theology. Regretfully, the term *evangelical* has become confused during the past decade. It would be difficult to find a definition which all would accept but surely one foundation of evangelicalism is an acceptance of the Bible as the authoritative Word of God. Evangelicals who write about psychology and religion differ from Freud, James, Ellis, and others in that we accept the Scripture as God's only written revelation to the human race. The Bible is more than an interesting piece of literature. It is a book of truth which teaches us about God, gives unique insights into human nature, and makes personal claims on our lives.

Since the founding of the *Journal* I have been listed as a "contributing editor." This means that I am asked, at times, to review and critique submitted articles before the editorial committee makes a final decision concerning publication. Within recent years I have noted that some of these articles reflect a drift away from the evangelical position which makes the *Journal* unique.

Surely, no one would like to see this publication move to a narrow fundamentalist position, but neither would it be beneficial to have this become a journal of psychology and religion-in-general. To their credit the editors have kept the *Journal* on a course which might be described as "broadly evangelical." I would hope that this distinction would be maintained.

One way to retain the present theological perspective is to have more articles written by persons who are theologically trained. That is a difficult goal to accomplish. Few people have dual training, and it appears that psychologists and others in the professional helping disciplines are more interested in integration than are theologians. Perhaps readers of the *Journal* should insure its greater circulation among theologians. We need more articles like Smith's controversial appraisal of integration (1975). We could benefit from the input of people like McQuilkin (1975) and others who are active in organizations such as the Evangelical Theological Society.

In the meantime, those who might tend to be critical of periodic theological or hermeneutical naivete in the *Journal* should ponder how they could do better or how they could help psychological writers to be more sophisticated theologically.

Sharpening Our Assumptions

In the first issue of this journal and in two subsequent publications (Collins 1973, 1977, 1981), I proposed that productive integration must start with a consideration of the assumptions in which psychology and theology are constructed. Some readers challenged the proposal that psychology should be rebuilt on biblically based assumptions, but there has been little criticism of the idea, proposed by a number of writers, that all scholarly activity is based on presuppositions which must be acknowledged, described, and clarified. Several years ago, Wertheimer (1972) wrote that psychologists simply cannot avoid making at least implicit statements concerning a number of semiphilosophical issues. Such issues involve almost every psychological question or investigation, and where psychologists stand on them is shaped by or shapes their psychological thinking in many important ways.

Wertheimer identified 10 fundamental presuppositional questions which every psychologist should consider: (a) Are humans masters or victims of their fate? (b) Are humans basically good or basically evil? (c) Should our research focus on holistic issues or on the smaller elements which make up the whole? (d) Is behavior best explained by physiology or by psychological "mental" explanations? (e) Should we look at behavior subjectively or objectively? (f) In explaining behavior is it better to search the past or to concentrate on the present? (g) Are personality, capabilities, and behavior influenced more by nature or by nurture? (h) Do we aim for theories which are simple or complex? (i) In our research should we strive for precision or for a broader richness? (j) Should we concentrate more on theory or on data collection? Wertheimer notes correctly that these issues have existed for centuries. They represent ends of continua and not "either-or" categories. They also are issues which should be considered in detail from a Christian perspective.

Sharpening our assumptions must be a continual process, discussed at least periodically within the pages of the *Journal*. But it is not a process which should consume so much attention and effort that we never turn to the research or to the practical applications which grow out of the assumptions.

Focusing on the Practical

Considering the present widespread interest in Christian counseling (including pastoral counseling), it is surprising that no nationally recognized, high-quality evangelical counseling journal exists. Christian counselors must get information from secular journals, books, or occasional articles in *Leadership* or *Christianity Today*.

The *Journal of Psychology and Theology* does publish practical articles and the publications policy clearly indicates that applied papers are welcome. Nevertheless the major emphasis in the *Journal* appears to be theoretical. I suspect that relatively few pastors or full-time professional care givers find the articles to be of practical help in their counseling work. It would be helpful to see more of an applied perspective in this publication.

But what is the major purpose of the *Journal?* Clearly it is not intended to be a "how-to-do-it" guidebook. If we had more emphasis on the practical, there would be less room for theoretical articles or for research reports. Even now it is possible that the editors receive few well-written manuscripts that are both practical in emphasis and sound in psychological and theological scholarship. Instead of more practical emphasis in this publication, perhaps there is need for a new periodical with an applied emphasis which would stand alongside the present *Journal.*

Even if most practical articles were to be published elsewhere, in one applied area the *Journal* must take leadership. We must give more attention to the previously mentioned issue of integration methodology. How do we do integration? What skills and methods are involved? Who is qualified to work in this area? What are the dangers or sources of error? Must we develop techniques that differ from the established methods in psychology and theology? Most of us agree that assumptions are important, and many recognize the value of integration, but how we approach the integrative task could be a major emphasis of this *Journal* in the coming decade.

Evaluating the Trends

The field of psychology is so diverse and popular that fads and emerging trends appear often in both professional and nonprofessional circles. Some of these contemporary movements fade quickly, but others persist, exert a major influence, and merit careful, fair evaluation. Carter's analysis of the Gothard seminars (1974), his appraisal of nouthetic counseling (1975), and the Alsdurf and Malony (1980) critique of Stapleton's "inner healing" are examples of critiques written from psychological and theological perspectives.

It is difficult for any one person to be aware of all psychologically oriented trends, and it is even harder to know how these movements should be evaluated. What is happening at present, for example, in the field of community psychology, and how could this movement be critiqued? How do we evaluate the boom in lay counseling, the emergence of church counseling centers, the growing self-help movement, or the interest in cross-cultural psychology? This is neither a political nor a social psychology publication, but is there room in the *Journal* for competent and balanced analyses of social issues such as the influence of the Moral Majority, the antinuclear movement, the electronic church, the apparent increase in mate beating, the interest in occult phenomena, or the emergence of psychology among Christians in non-American cultures?

I hesitate to make predictions about future trends, but it appears that religious experience may become an issue of increasing interest. At the turn of the century, the early pioneers in this field wrote about the psychology of conversion, faith healing, and worship. These still are significant issues, and so are glossolalia, parapsychology, demon possession, and altered states of consciousness. During the past decade articles have appeared dealing with many of these topics, but few are of an "overview and critique" nature.

Articles designed to help readers keep abreast of emerging trends might be interspersed with articles suggesting methodology for evaluation. How do we evaluate religious experience or new movements from a psychological and theological perspective? College students are not the only people who might like an answer to that question.

Sharpening the Focus

The second issue of the *Journal* (April 1973) was a special issue commemorating the work of Paul Tournier at the time of his 75th birthday. The Fall 1983 issue focused on psychology and missions. Between these two issues there have been no clear special emphases. Each issue is a collection of articles, usually on a variety of unrelated topics.

Clearly this reflects an editorial policy which has worked well in the past, but would there be value in devoting, say, half the articles in each future issue to a special topic? Other journals do this, and for me, at least, it adds interest. In addition to missions, could there be issues of the *Journal* devoted to topics such as Christian theories of counseling, the psychology of worship, values, sex counseling, parapsychology, spiritual maturity, pastoral psychology, the nature of persons, or psychological perspectives on hermeneutics and apologetics?

I realize that this is easier to propose than to accomplish. It is easy for a critic to say what should be in a journal; it is much more difficult for editors to find appropriate high-quality articles. The *Counseling Psychologist* advertises coming special issues in advance, solicits relevant articles, and appoints a guest editor for each issue. As a staff decision, *Leadership* editors decide on the topic for each issue and invite qualified writers to prepare articles. These are printed alongside unsolicited manuscripts. Could the *Journal* develop similar policies?

Perhaps this is the point to make a comment about research. It is my impression that the overall quality has not been good. The desire to include empirical research in this *Journal* is admirable, but surely no research is better than poor research. The quality in the future should be better, and sharper.

Admitting the Personal

Integration can be an aloof, intellectual enterprise, mentally challenging but personally irrelevant. Carter and Narramore (1979) challenge this impersonal perspective with the proposal that in addition to

> the relating of secular and Christian concepts . . . integration is also a way of living and a way of thinking. In fact, it seems to us that very little conceptual integration is possible without a degree of personal integration. . . . It is far too easy to ensconce ourselves securely behind the walls of our theological or psychological professionalism in order to avoid facing the truth about ourselves and consequently being open to new perspectives. . . .
>
> As Christians our aim must not be simply to pursue isolated intellectual understanding. The clear message of Scripture is that God intervened in history to change lives. . . . Integrative efforts come alive when we recognize their eternal aspect and see our work as part of humanity's God-ordained task of reconciling men to God, themselves, and others. (117–18, 121)

This viewpoint is not typical of the unbiased perspective which most professional journals seek to attain. Total objectivity is impossible, however, and it is more honest intellectually to admit our values and to state them openly than to pretend that we are completely objective or neutral.

Most of the writers in this journal would claim to be Christians, and as such we cannot deny the personal relevance and spiritual implications of our integrative work. This, of course, does not need to be stated in every article, but perhaps it should be mentioned occasionally and remembered frequently.

In his perceptive volume on the Christian mind, British critic Harry Blamires ([1963] 1978) proposed that we need to "think Christianly," viewing all issues from a Christian perspective and in terms of the human being's "eternal destiny as the redeemed and chosen child of God" (42). Blamires assumes that there is nothing that one can experience, however "trivial, worldly, or even evil," which cannot be thought about "Christianly."

Is it possible that we who work in this field and read the *Journal* can learn to "think Christianly" and "think psychologically" about our academic interests, our counseling, our world, and our personal lives? Such thinking, if done carefully, can give rise to high quality articles which will continue to enrich the pages of the *Journal* and will contribute to the continuing movement through the jungle of psychology-theology issues.

References

Alsdurf, J., and H. N. Malony. 1980. A critique of Ruth Carter Stapleton's ministry of "inner healing." *Journal of Psychology and Theology* 8: 173–84.

Blamires, H. [1963] 1978. *The Christian Mind.* Reprint. Ann Arbor, Mich.: Servant.

Carter, J. D. 1974. The psychology of Gothard and the Basic Youth Conflict seminar. *Journal of Psychology and Theology* 2: 249–59.

———. 1975. Adams's theory of nouthetic counseling. *Journal of Psychology and Theology* 3: 143–55.

Carter, J. D., and S. B. Narramore. 1979. *The integration of psychology and theology: An introduction.* Grand Rapids: Zondervan.

Collins, G. R. 1973. Psychology on a new foundation: A proposal for the future. *Journal of Psychology and Theology* 1: 19–27.

———. 1977. *The rebuilding of psychology: An integration of psychology and theology.* Wheaton: Tyndale.

———. 1981. *Psychology and theology: Prospects for integration.* Nashville: Abingdon.

Crabb, L. J., Jr. 1977. *Effective biblical counseling.* Grand Rapids: Zondervan.

Farnsworth, K. E. 1982. The conduct of integration. *Journal of Psychology and Theology* 10.

Fleck, J. R., and J. D. Carter. eds. 1981. *Psychology and Christianity: Integrative readings.* Nashville: Abingdon.

McQuilkin, J. R. 1975. The behavioral sciences under the authority of Scripture. Paper presented at the Evangelical Theological Society, December, Jackson, Miss.

Smith, C. R. 1975. What part hath psychology with theology? *Journal of Psychology and Theology* 3: 272–76.

Wertheimer, M. *Fundamental issues in psychology.* New York: Holt, Rinehart and Winston.

The Psychology of Religion Today

Are graduate students still required to memorize Edwin Boring's *History of Experimental Psychology*? Early in my doctoral program, I was required to read and digest the Boring book (the author's name fit his volume perfectly) and then to pass a multiple-choice test on its contents.

I failed.

On the second attempt, I barely managed to pass, and only then did approval come to move ahead with the doctoral program. In the opinion of the man who chaired the psychology department, knowing the history of one's discipline was a crucial prerequisite for any kind of psychological training.

Edwin Boring's book is almost 800 pages in length, but this massive history of psychology devotes only four lines to the psychology of religion. In describing the life of G. Stanley Hall, Boring noted—almost in passing—that Hall had an "old interest" in the psychology of religion and that he published a book which "brought to him the *odium theologicum*" (1950, 523). Hall, of course, helped to found the American Psychological Association and served as its first president. I suspect he would have been happy to see Division 36 come into existence.

Would Boring have felt the same? His scholarly book demonstrated that the psychology of religion had been largely ignored during much of the history of our discipline. Boring, himself, overlooked important contributions by early scholars, and the subject still appears to be on the fringes of mainstream psychology today.

But there are signs of change. This volume is an example, and the participants have been asked to give personal observations on "present concerns and future issues" in the psychology of religion. "Note the issues that have been of consuming interest to you," we were instructed. "Assess their importance to the present and project yourself into the future—indicating the direction the field should take." These three topics—consuming interests, present issues, and future directions—will

From the *Journal of Psychology and Christianity* 5, no. 2 (1986): 26–30; reprinted by permission of the publisher and the author. Copyright 1986 by the Christian Association for Psychological Studies.

comprise the major portions of this paper. I will begin and conclude with a few personal observations about the field.

A Personal Starting Point

When Professor Boring wrote his famous history, apparently many psychologists believed that ours is a neutral science and that psychologists could work without being influenced by their biases, values, hopes, or beliefs. Such a viewpoint is not widely held today. Complete neutrality is impossible. Nowhere is that more apparent, perhaps, than in issues surrounding religion.

Many years ago, I decided to strive to be a committed Christian first and a competent psychologist second. From my perspective these two goals are compatible. Nevertheless, this ordering of priorities means that my personal religious beliefs and values are the prime molders of my thinking, life goals, professional work, and "consuming interests." This will be clear in the selection of issues to be discussed in the following paragraphs.

Consuming Interests

Some of the issues and questions that interest me have been of concern to psychologists for many years. Most of them still do not have clear answers, and it would seem that many have practical as well as scholarly implications.

1. Why are people religious? Freud sought to answer this question in his controversial interpretations of anthropology and personal dynamics (1913, 1927). More recent writers have looked to social learning theory or to studies of cognitive and moral development. Even with this progress, however, there still are many questions about why people believe as they do, why some people are religious while others are not, and why some forsake the faith while others grow spiritually and maintain a consistent involvement with their religion.

Freud's prediction of the demise of religion has not come to pass. Psychological studies of religion should continue to investigate the reasons for this continuing interest. Why is there persisting and widespread involvement with religious beliefs and behaviors?

2. How do we account for individual differences in religious beliefs, commitment, experiences, and practices? This is closely related to the first question. It acknowledges that some people are casually or externally religious but that others are more personally committed. Some have a religion that is highly intellectual and logical while others prefer

more experiential beliefs. Some choose to be Pentecostals but others become Methodists or "Moonies."

Issues such as these have practical relevance for religious educators, counselors, and parents. They also could interest any curious student of individual differences who wonders about the "why" of human behavior.

3. How does religion relate to counseling? For many counselors and their clients, religion is rarely discussed, and then only if the client raises the issue or acknowledges its importance.

But religion has great relevance to guilt management, forgiveness, bitterness, interpersonal tension, life planning, existential concerns, feelings of helplessness, morals, values, and other issues. If the counselor believes that God exists, is powerful, and cares about human problems, can the counselor be internally consistent and a responsible people helper if he or she deliberately avoids discussions of the theological issues that could be of great help to the client? Have Christians in the counseling room become double-minded counselors who compartmentalize their beliefs and their therapies? Unlike many of our secular colleagues, have we become afraid to raise the very issues that can most help our clients?

It is true that counselors face these questions more often than those who are interested primarily in a scholarly study of the psychology of religion. I suspect there needs to be mutual work on these issues however, especially since many psychologists have a personal and professional interest in both areas.

4. How does religion relate to popular psychology? In a recent paper, Bregman (1985) discusses the view that for many people, popular psychology has tended to replace traditional religion. "Why is the religion of psychology so plausible and appealing to so many persons today?" Bregman asks. "Popular psychology—particularly as available to nonspecialists and in the form of guidance, self-help and 'how to do it' books—sees itself as uncovering the real essence of what religion ought to be."

This is an issue that should be of concern both to the theologically minded and to psychologists of religion. Why do many people shun the teachings of religion or the words of Scripture and instead look for meaning and practical help in the writings of popular psychology? Is this because the church has lost its relevance or its ability to meet human needs? Has psychology really become our new religion—one that proposes the worship of self instead of the worship of God (Vitz 1977)? If so, why is this happening?

5. Should there be a psychological apologetic? Apologetics is a discipline that seeks to give reasonable arguments in support of the faith; it is a field of theology that defends the faith against its critics and accusers. Historically, Christian apologists have attempted to present

the gospel in terms that contemporary people can understand and have given answers to those who question Christianity in terms of the prevailing wisdom of the time.

I am no more than a casual reader of Christian apologetics. I have wondered, however, if many modern apologists spend time and great amounts of energy finding answers to questions that almost nobody is asking. It could be argued that some of the major challenges facing the church today come from those who seek to undermine basic Christian doctrine by providing psychological solutions to problems, psychological explanations of religious experience, and psychological alternatives to traditional religion. Why, then, do many modern apologists seem to be unaware of the psychological challenges to the faith and disinclined to build a psychologically-sophisticated apologetic? It is unlikely that a non-Christian specialist in psychology of religion will be concerned about apologetics, but what about Christians with an interest both in the Great Commission and in psychology?

Current Issues

After a half-century of neglect by all but a few creative psychologists, the psychological study of religion now shows signs of resurrected vigor. The creation of the American Psychological Association Division 36 (Psychologists Interested in Religious Issues) was a significant step in that direction. Nevertheless, there are challenges ahead. The prejudices of antireligious psychologists must be countered, and we who are in this field have a responsibility to show that the psychology of religion is a legitimate, respectable, and potentially practical part of psychology. Let us consider each of these.

1. The psychology of religion is a *legitimate* area for study. If psychologists are interested in human behavior, values, subjective experiences, interpersonal relationships, social groups, motivation, perception, or defenses, then how can we ignore the ways in which religion influences millions of people in these and related areas? To ignore or to casually—and sometimes flippantly—dismiss the influence of religion is to cast aside a significant area of human behavior. Is it possible that those who resist this field of study are not as enlightened and scientifically honest as they are intolerant and perhaps threatened by studies of religion?

2. The psychology of religion is a *respectable* area for study. In psychology, as in most other disciplines, one does not gain lasting respect by rhetoric. Psychology of religion will gain respect as it carefully builds a body of research, a well-written and clearly documented literature, and a core of models and theories that are concise, logical, factually

based, and free from sweeping generalizations, rigid conclusions, and appeals to undocumented personal experiences and "testimonies."

I believe we are making excellent progress in these areas. Recent textbooks such as those of Paloutzian (1983), Byrnes (1984), Meadow and Kahoe (1984), and Spilka, Hood, and Gorsuch (1985) give evidence of the vigor and increasing scientific and scholarly respectability of the psychological study of religion.

3. The psychology of religion is a *practical* area for study. Recently, one of my former students applied for a doctoral internship in the counseling center of a large Big-Ten university. The interviewing committee noted that he had a degree from a theological school, and some were concerned that he might be "weird" or "fanatical." When my student demonstrated that he was a committed believer but also a competent counselor, he was accepted into the internship program and welcomed with an interesting comment from the counseling center director.

"We need counselors who understand religion," he said. "Most of our training ignores religion, so we don't know what to do with religious clients or with those who have religious questions and struggles."

The psychology of religion, when linked with the psychology of counseling, can help to produce therapists who have dual competence and are able to meet needs that religiously unsophisticated counselors cannot handle. To give high-quality counselor training in these two related areas surely must be one of the major current issues facing our field.

Coming Indications

Where do we go from here? What are some future possibilities for the psychology of religion?

As we move toward the end of this century, I would hope to see the psychology of religion moving to

> become an academic subdiscipline that is increasingly accepted and recognized as a valid and scholarly part of psychology;
>
> become an avenue for increasing our understanding of such issues as guilt management, the development and influence of values, the effect of religion on psychopathology and on maturity, the role of religious concepts in therapy, religion and the church as social institutions, and the contribution of religion to life management or to the search for meaning in life;
>
> become an aid to effective counseling, especially with clients who are religious, have religious struggles, or grapple with such existential

issues as problems of meaninglessness, guilt, alienation, uncertain values, or grief;

become an apologetic resource for Christians and for others who seek answers to religious questions or who attack those who are believers; and

become an agency through which social change and improvement may come to society. Religion and psychology, especially social psychology, both deal with issues of poverty, crime, injustice, ignorance, intolerance, and similar social issues. Can psychology of religion make a contribution to the understanding and alleviation of such social injustice?

A Personal Postscript

I am encouraged by the recent history of the psychology of religion. This, I believe, is one of the frontier areas of psychology, and it can be exciting for any of us to be "part of the action." In the years ahead, however, I would hope that the psychology of religion could avoid three potential problem areas that have bogged down and ossified some other subspecialities in psychology.

First, I would hope that we could avoid dull, sloppy writing. Graduate students, and too many of their professors, still seem to equate "scholarly" with long drawn-out sentences, complicated terms, and boring writing. It is hard to believe that anyone could take an exciting topic like the psychology of religion and make it dull. But some do that very well. Can't we be scholarly, knowledgeable, and interesting too? Can this be one field in psychology where the writing is clear, bright, and free from academic deadness? Too many English teachers have let us reach adulthood and graduate schools with no ability to write. Surely no one is a scholar who fails to communicate clearly.

Second, I would hope that we can be scientific but not so narrow that we exclude all evidence that cannot fit our scientific molds. As a part of scientific psychology, the psychology of religion must be scientific. But let us not assume that science is the only source of knowledge and factual data. We can become narrow and inaccurate when we cast aside such sources of information as the teachings of tradition, the sacred writings, the insights of literary observers, or the experiences of deeply religious believers. A field that accepts only rigidly measured scientific data is a narrow field indeed. As Wertheimer noted several years ago (1972) we must be careful not to completely sacrifice richness on the altar of precision.

Finally, I would hope that we don't become so aloof and objective that we fool ourselves into believing that our own values and beliefs have no influence in our studies. In his now classic study of religion, Allport (1950) wrote that his approach was psychological: "I make no assumptions and no denials regarding the claims of revealed religion. Writing as a scientist I am not entitled to do either." I doubt that such neutrality is possible, and it may not even be desirable. Far better, I suggest, is the honest acknowledgement of our beliefs, values, and assumptions. These influence how we study our subject matter and how we interpret data. By admitting our biases and deliberately seeking to control them, we are better able to get a fuller and more complete psychological understanding of religion and religious behavior.

Edwin Boring might not have liked such suggestions, but the history of psychology now appears to be taking some new directions. Perhaps we need some new assumptions and new methods. As an emerging discipline, the psychology of religion may be one of the freshest, more relevant, more interesting, and potentially useful subdivisions of psychology. For me it is already much more of a "consuming interest" than the dull facts that I had to read about when I first became a graduate student.

References

Allport, G. W. 1950. *The individual and his religion: A psychological interpretation*. New York: Macmillan.

Bregman, L. 1985. Popular psychology, inner experience and non-traditional religiousness. *Psychologists Interested in Religious Experience Newsletter* 10 (Spring).

Boring, E. G. 1950. *A history of experimental psychology*. New York: Appleton-Century-Crofts.

Byrnes, J. F. 1984. *The psychology of religion*. New York: Free Press.

Freud, S. 1913. *Totem and taboo*. London: Routledge and Kegan Paul.

———. 1927. *The future of an illusion*. Garden City, N.Y.: Doubleday.

Meadow, M. J., and R. D. Kahoe 1984. *Psychology of religion: Religion in individual lives*. New York: Harper and Row.

Paloutzian, R. F. 1983. *Invitation to the psychology of religion*. Glenview, Ill.: Scott, Foresman.

Spilka, B., R. W. Hood, Jr., and R. L. Gorsuch. 1985. *The psychology of religion: An empirical approach*. Englewood Cliffs, N.J.: Prentice-Hall.

Vitz, P. C. 1977. *Psychology as religion: The cult of self-worship*. Grand Rapids: Eerdmans.

Wertheimer, M. 1972. *Fundamental issues in psychology*. New York: Holt, Rinehart and Winston.

Part 8

General Psychology
and the Psychology
of Religion

18

Raymond F. Paloutzian

Raymond F. Paloutzian is professor and chair of the department of psychology at Westmont College, Santa Barbara, California. In the past he has taught at Scripps College and the University of Idaho. He has twice been a visiting professor at Stanford University and was a visiting research psychologist at the University of California, Santa Barbara. He received the Ph.D. in psychology from the Claremont Graduate School.

Paloutzian has served in various capacities in Division 36, Psychologists Interested in Religious Issues, of the American Psychological Association. He presently is a fellow of the division and a member of the division's executive committee. He is also a consulting director editor for several professional journals.

Dr. Paloutzian is the author of *Invitation to the Psychology of Religion* (Glenview, Ill.: Scott, Foresman, 1983), a small volume that is one of the best introductory texts available today. It covers almost all major issues in the field and can be used with anthologies of readings in both graduate and undergraduate classes. Paloutzian has also had the distinction of writing the only section on the psychology of religion ever to appear in a major introductory psychology text. It appears in the 10th edition of Philip G. Zimbardo's *Psychology and Life* (Glenview, Ill.: Scott, Foresman, 1979).

Several research areas have attracted Paloutzian's attention and effort over the years, including conversion and purpose in life, intrinsic-extrinsic religious orientation, the social behavior of retardates, and brain mechanisms' control of sexual behavior in rats. With a rigorous experimental bias, Paloutzian conducts his research. In one of his major areas of interest, spiritual well-being, he collaborated with Craig Ellison to construct and standardize one of the principal scales to measure this dimension, the Spiritual Well-Being Scale. His most recent studies have concerned the role of unmet desires and expectations for social contact in loneliness. He is broadly interested in the interaction between cognitive, physiological, and social processes. Whether by style or habit, Paloutzian is one to try things. He always has a small team of research students working with him, as he eagerly inspires them to do the same.

In the article "Purpose in Life and Value Changes Following Conversion," Paloutzian reports a study, conceived within the framework of a cognitive-need theory, in which he compared recent and long-term converts to nonconverts. Converts evidenced a greater sense of meaning in life than nonconverts. The values given more weight by those exhibiting greater purpose in life include salvation and cleanliness while those with lower purpose put more value on comfort, happiness, freedom, and mature love.

Paloutzian's essay "Psychology of Religion as a Medium of Communication with General Psychology" is grounded in the thesis that scholars in the field should use their studies as vehicles for relating to the general psychological world. He suggests that the idea of a "crucial experiment," in which the highest methodological standards would be followed and the research related to basic theory, should be revived and executed. Two possible barriers to the success of the endeavor exist, however. The first is that few psychologists are interested in religious behavior as the focus of their professional work. The second is that most psychologists view the psychology of religion as a branch of applied, rather than basic, psychology. Paloutzian, suggesting that the solution is to do basic research on issues of applied relevance, proposes that the psychology of religion become more a subset of social and personality psychology than simply an isolated discipline unto itself.

Purpose in Life and Value Changes Following Conversion

B y intuition, one might suppose that complete personal changes, such as those that occur in religious conversion, would be rare. We tend to think that people have stable traits and that they continue to be about the same as they have been. Yet, in recent years, millions of such profound and sometimes paradoxical changes have occurred in people's lives. This includes people turning to born-again religion, faith healing, the transcendental meditation variety of Hinduism, mysticism, and varieties of Eastern religions (Gallup 1977–78), as well as to several new cults (Stoner and Parke 1977). The obvious question is, How does this happen? What personal, social, or cognitive needs are being met? One possible answer is that religious conversion satisfies a motive for meaning in life. This article is concerned with the relation between such conversion and the experience of meaning or purpose in life. It addresses the questions of how the sense of purpose in life changes over time following conversion, what values are associated with purpose in life, and what specific components of the sense of purpose in life mediate the changes.

Theoretical statements addressing these issues have varied. Psychoanalytically oriented writers have assumed that conversion has an emotional base (i.e., that some type of emotional need is satisfied by conversion). (For an overview of these theories see Scobie [1975] or Argyle and Beit-Hallahmi [1975].) The initial idea behind the present study was derived from a different, more cognitive model. This model fuses Frankl's (1975) view that a mature religious sentiment helps satisfy the "will to meaning," with what I call a cognitive-need theory. The idea is that people have cognitive needs to perceive wholeness, pattern, purpose, or meaning in the stimuli that confront them—much the same as the Gestalt principle of closure. This theory says that when people are confronted with perceiving themselves in relation to the whole of life,

From the *Journal of Personality and Social Psychology* 41 (1981): 1153–60; reprinted by permission of the publisher and the author. Copyright 1981 by the American Psychological Association.

or the cosmos, they have a need to complete the picture, as it were, in order to perceive purpose or meaning in life. Adopting an encompassing religious worldview would be a way of meeting this need. One implication of this idea is the hypothesis that converts would score higher on a measure of perceived purpose in life than nonconverts.

Prior research has yielded only a few studies bearing on this hypothesis. High scores on Crumbaugh and Maholick's (1969) Purpose in Life (PIL) Test have been reported for students who rank ordered the religious value of salvation highly in Rokeach's (1973) Value Survey (Crandall and Rasmussen 1975): a group of trainees in a congregation of Dominican Sisters (Crumbaugh, Raphael, and Shrader 1970), a group of "active and leading Protestant parishioners" (Crumbaugh 1968), and people who believe that they have been "saved" by placing faith in Jesus Christ (Soderstrom and Wright 1977). Four studies (Bolt 1975; Crandall and Rasmussen 1975; Paloutzian, Jackson, and Crandall 1978; Soderstrom and Wright 1977) reported data associating high PIL with an intrinsic religious orientation (Allport and Ross 1967). Finally, Paloutzian and Ellison (1982) report findings associating intrinsic religious orientation with greater spiritual well-being and existential well-being and less loneliness. Though none of these studies were designed to test the effects of conversion per se, to the extent that the religious subjects in those studies were religious converts, the findings, like the cognitive-need theory, suggest higher PIL in converts.

In the present study, the prior research and the general hypothesis that converts would experience more meaning were extended in three ways. The first concerns the dimension of time. In none of the prior research was any assessment made of how long the subject held his or her belief. Thus, both brand-new converts and long-time believers could have been grouped together and treated as if they were the same. This procedure might have obscured important differences between new and old believers in the extent to which PIL is experienced and in the factors that mediate the experience. For example, new converts may be very strong and full of fervor in their newfound belief, whereas older converts may have become stale. On the other hand, new believers may be uncertain as to the reality or permanence of their commitment because they are wrestling with doubt, whereas long-time believers may have resolved these doubts long before. Such possibilities suggest that there may be instability in PIL over time from the point of conversion onwards. At least two predictions about the shape of the PIL function over time following conversion are possible: (a) PIL could quickly rise to a peak and then gradually decline, due to initial excitement which would then dissipate or (b) PIL could begin low and then gradually incline as the belief becomes more securely held and/or doubts have been reasoned through. These two time-course hypotheses were explored in the present study.

The second extension of prior work does not directly concern the effects of conversion per se, but instead concerns the relation between PIL and values. Crandall and Rasmussen (1975) studied PIL as related to only Rokeach's (1973) 18 terminal values. The present study extends this to the question of the relation between PIL and Rokeach's 18 instrumental values. Therefore, in addition to exploring how PIL is associated with specific ends that people would like to attain, the present study tests whether PIL is associated with the means by which people pursue those ends.

The third extension concerns the question of what specific facets of PIL mediate any obtained changes in total PIL as a function of time from conversion. Though the rationale for the present study was based on a cognitive-need model, PIL, as conceived of by Frankl and as measured by Crumbaugh and Maholick's (1969) test, is a broader concept composed of a variety of specific elements. For example, the PIL test contains questions about sense of excitement, clear goals, sense of responsibility, seeing a reason for existing, belief in own freedom to choose, being prepared and unafraid of death, and a sense of personal control. Some of these elements are cognitive, and some are emotionally toned. The present study allowed for examining whether any changes over time in total PIL are due to an increase or decrease in all elements as a whole, or whether a particular subset of PIL items contributes to the effect.

A large evangelistic meeting provided a natural experiment for the exploration of the above questions. PIL and value measures were obtained from two control groups of nonconverts and from four groups of believers at varying amounts of time following their own conversions.

Method

Subjects and Design

The subjects were 91 students in a large ($N = 400$) introductory psychology course at the University of Idaho. They were approximately equally divided by sex, came from predominantly white, rural, and generally Christianized backgrounds, and participated voluntarily and anonymously. The 51 experimental subjects were those who indicated that they were Christian believers, as reflected in their responses to a questionnaire item (described in a following paragraph). Data for the 40 control subjects were based on a random sample of questionnaires from the rest of the students in the class.

The subjects self-selected into six groups. The two control groups were those who answered no ($n = 24$) or not sure ($n = 16$) to being a convert. The four experimental groups were those who indicated having been believers for up to 1 week ($n = 11$), between 1 week and 1 month ($n = 10$), between 1 and 6 months ($n = 8$), and 6 months or longer ($n = 22$).

Questionnaire

The questionnaire consisted of three parts. Part 1 was the Purpose in Life Test (Crumbauch and Maholick 1969). This test contains 20 questions, each answered on a 1–7 scale. A high PIL score represents a high sense of meaning; a low PIL score indicates some degree of existential frustration or lack of perceived meaning.

Part 2 was a list of Rokeach's (1973) 18 terminal and 18 instrumental values, in that order. Though Rokeach has subjects rank order these values, time constraints in the present study required that a quicker rating procedure be used. Each subject rated each value on a 7-point scale according to the degree to which the value was important as a guiding principle in his or her own life.

Part 3, on the back of the questionnaire, contained the item from which subjects would be classified as converts or nonconverts and from which amount of time since conversion would be assessed. To be consistent with and closely mirror the message and tone of the evangelistic presentation, subjects were asked to indicate whether they had "made a decision to trust Jesus Christ" or "received Jesus Christ into heart and life" as personal Savior and Lord. Subjects could indicate "yes," "no," or "not sure." Those who answered "no" and "not sure" were considered nonconverts. Those who answered "yes" were considered converts and were asked to indicate how much time had elapsed since they made their initial commitment. They could indicate "within the past week," "between 1 week and 1 month ago," "between 1 and 6 months ago," or "6 months or longer."

Procedure

Questionnaires were completed in class 5 days after the evangelistic meeting. No mention of the evangelistic meeting was made. The occurrence of the evangelistic meeting made the study possible by raising the probability that there would be a larger-than-normal number of new (1 week or less) believers in the large psychology class. Subjects in the other three convert groups would have been converted in their own way and time.

The evangelistic meeting itself, at which an undetermined number of the 1-week believer group would have been converted, was an illusionist show combined with a talk given by the illusionist. The talk was a simple statement of the belief system to be espoused and can be best characterized as a rational appeal. At the close of the meeting, after the speaker concluded his lecture and encouraged people to become believers, the audience was invited to adopt the belief. People were not asked to go forward or to make any other public display indicating conversion. Converts were asked to indicate their decision by checking the appropriate box on comment cards distributed to the audience after the service.

Results

Purpose in Life

To detect whether there were any significant differences in PIL between groups, the PIL scores were submitted to a one-way (6-group) analysis of variance. The analysis was significant, F (5, 85) = 5.5, $p <$ .001. The mean PIL scores are presented in table 18.1. Looking across the top row of table 18.1 reveals that within 1 week following conversion, the PIL mean rises sharply to a peak. Within 1 month it drops down to a level comparable to that of the nonconverts. Within 6 months it goes back up to a moderately high level, and then stabilizes at that level at 6 months or longer from conversion.

Table 18.1
Purpose in Life Scores as a Function of Time from Conversion

		Condition				
	Nonconverts			Converts		
Purpose in life	No	Not Sure	1 week	1 week to 1 month	1 to 6 months	6 months or longer
M	101.4	107.8	118.8	108.5	114.9	114.7
SD	12.1	10.4	6.6	13.5	9.6	11.4
n	24	16	11	10	8	22

Post hoc probing of the differences between means was accomplished with the Scheffé procedure. The major findings from the Scheffé tests are that (a) the combined convert groups scored higher on PIL than the combined nonconvert groups ($p <$ .01), (b) the 1-week convert group scored higher on PIL than the nonconvert groups ($p <$ .03), and (c) the 6-month and 6-month-or-longer convert groups scored higher on PIL than the nonconvert groups ($p <$ .03). The drop in PIL for the 1-week to 1-month convert group was marginally significant ($p <$ .05 by a regular t test). The significance of the analysis of variance and the post hoc contrasts suggest that the obtained set of PIL means reflects a similar pattern present in the population.

Values and Purpose in Life

The relation between PIL and values was assessed in two ways. The first procedure was to calculate the correlations between the raw value ratings and the PIL scores. These relationships are summarized in table 18.2. It is clear from table 18.2 that the majority of values are significantly associated with PIL and that the correlations generally fall in the moderate range. None of the correlations is strikingly large. Note, however, that all of the correlations are positive ($z = 6.0$, $p < .00001$), suggesting that this overall pattern of relationships reflects a similar pattern in the population. Therefore, it appears that a general sense of values is associated to a moderate degree with a general sense of purpose.

Table 18.2
Correlations between Value Ratings and Purpose in Life Scores

Terminal values	r	Instrumental values	r
A comfortable life	.19	Ambitious	.37***
An exciting life	.22*	Broadminded	.37***
A sense of accomplishment	.21*	Capable	.30**
		Cheerful	.35***
A world at peace	.20	Clean	.37***
A world of beauty	.29**	Courageous	.23*
Equality	.28**	Forgiving	.43***
Family security	.38***	Helpful	.39***
Freedom	.16	Honest	.32**
Happiness	.14	Imaginative	.30**
Inner harmony	.14	Independent	.22*
Mature love	.20	Intellectual	.28**
National security	.17	Logical	.31**
Pleasure	.12	Loving	.27**
Salvation	.37***	Obedient	.38***
Self-respect	.36***	Polite	.39***
Social recognition	.27**	Responsible	.44***
True friendship	.31**	Self-controlled	.35***
Wisdom	.23*		

*$p < .05$. **$p < .01$. ***$p < .001$.

The second procedure for assessing the relation between PIL and values was designed to yield ordinal information more directly comparable to prior research. Because prior research was concerned with the ordinal relation of values to PIL, the next question for data analysis is, Which values receive relatively more weight for subjects high versus low in PIL? Because the value rating procedure used in the present study does not assess the relative weight assigned to specific values, a transformation of the value rating scores was necessary. The individual value rating scores were transformed into deviations from the subject's own mean value rating. Then the relative weight assigned to each value was contrasted for subjects high versus low on PIL. The top and bottom thirds of the PIL scores were selected for comparison, and Mann-Whitney U tests were conducted for each value on the corresponding value deviation scores. These analyses showed that five terminal values and one instrumental value were significantly related to PIL. Two values were given relatively more weight by subjects high in PIL—the terminal value of salvation ($p < .04$) and the instrumental value of being clean ($p < .04$). Four values were given relatively more weight by subjects low in PIL—the terminal values of comfort ($p < .05$), happiness ($p < .04$), freedom ($p < .02$), and mature love ($p < .01$).

Item Analysis

To detect whether a particular subset of PIL items was responsible for the significant effect across groups for total PIL, the PIL scores were submitted to an item analysis. Whether items responded to groups in different ways was explored by two overall analyses, along with tests on individual items. First, the overall significance of the set of 20 items was assessed by a multivariate analysis of variance among the six groups. This analysis approached, but did not reach, conventional levels of statistical significance, $F (100, 322) = 1.19$, $p < .13$. This result suggests that, though PIL totals differ markedly by groups, it is unclear whether specific items are responsible for the PIL total effect. Second, to confirm the above results, the data were also analyzed by a repeated measures analysis of variance (6 groups x 20 items), with the items serving as the repeated measures factor. This analysis yielded a significant main effect for groups, $F (5, 85) = 5.9$, $p < .001$, which corresponds to the overall significance for PIL totals across groups. The items effect was also significant, $F (19, 1,615) = 7.3$, $p < .001$. Of greater importance for the item analysis is the significant Group x Item interaction, $F (95, 1,615) = 1.5$, $p < .003$, which suggests that subjects responded differently to items by group.

Because the multivariate analysis and the interaction term of the repeated measures analysis yield different results, and because the multivariate test is the more inclusive and is less subject to violations of assumptions, the item analysis must be interpreted with caution. The significant effect for PIL totals cannot be reliably attributed to a specific subset of items. The results are, however, suggestive. Therefore, the following analyses of specific items are presented for documentation and to suggest lines of future research.

Follow-up analyses probed the significance of each item across groups. A separate one-way (6-group) analysis of variance was conducted on the scores for each of the 20 items on the PIL Test. These analyses revealed that scores for nine items showed significant variation across groups. Mean scores for these items are presented in table

Table 18.3

Mean Scores for Purpose in Life Items Significantly Associated with Time from Conversion

| | | | | Condition | | | |
| | Nonconverts | | | Converts | | | |
Item content	No	Not sure	1 week	1 week to 1 month	1 to 6 months	6 months or longer	F
1. Usually bored vs. enthusiastic	5.17	5.50	6.00	5.30	5.62	5.68	2.97*
2. Life seems exciting vs. routine	4.96	5.19	6.00	5.60	5.63	5.68	2.77*
5. Every day is new vs. the same	4.88	5.00	6.09	5.40	5.38	5.95	3.96**
9. Life filled with despair vs. good things	5.04	5.44	6.09	5.10	6.13	5.77	4.22**
10. My life worthwhile vs. worthless	5.33	5.56	6.36	5.60	6.38	5.77	3.13**
11. See a reason for why I exist	4.46	5.12	6.09	5.50	6.62	5.64	5.89***
12. The world confuses me vs. fits meaningfully	4.17	4.94	5.45	5.10	5.50	5.32	3.91**
15. Prepared and unafraid of death vs. frightened	4.13	3.75	5.45	5.30	5.88	6.00	7.39***
19. Facing daily tasks is pleasure vs. painful	4.75	5.00	6.09	5.30	5.38	5.59	4.44**

Note: All items are scored so that a higher number represents more meaning. *$p<.03$. **$p<.055$. ***$p<.0001$.

18.3. Looking across the rows in table 18.3 reveals that, for most items, the scores rise and fall in a reversal pattern similar to the pattern for PIL total scores. As compared to the nonconvert group, scores for the 1-week group rise to a peak, then drop for the 1-week to 1-month group, and then rise again for the 6-month groups. Some of the items show slight variations in this general reversal pattern.

Item 15, which asks about fear of death, shows a unique pattern. Except for one minor reversal, mean scores for this item incline markedly and continually from the nonconvert groups to the 6-month-or-longer group.

Discussion

Purpose in Life

The general hypothesis that converts perceive more meaning in life than nonconverts is supported by the present research. However, this general hypothesis must be modified to account for the fluctuation in PIL over time following conversion. The data in the present study suggest that within a week following the commitment, the sense of meaning rises sharply to a peak. This peak is followed within a month by an experiential dip. PIL then increases again and stabilizes at an intermediately high level within 6 months following conversion. This reversal pattern for PIL scores suggests that the elevation in perceived meaning in converts is unstable during the period shortly following conversion.

One interesting aspect of the data is the low PIL score for the 1-month convert group. This drop in PIL may be very important psychologically because it is at approximately the same PIL level as that for the "not sure" nonconvert group. Such an experiential dip may represent a period of reassessment of one's decision to adopt the belief, during which time the convert gains understanding, assurance, and stability of the decision. Assuming that the new converts do not drop out and in essence return to the control groups, this period of reassessment is followed by a return to a higher level of meaning after assurance is gained and doubts have been reasoned through.

There are some interesting points of correspondence between the present data and those of prior research. First, Crumbaugh (1968) found that college undergraduates averaged 108.5 on the PIL Test. The present sample of nonconverts scored nonsignificantly lower than Crumbaugh's. Thus, it can be inferred that the present sample of nonconvert undergraduates is at a normal level on the PIL scale. Second, the peak effect that occurred within 1 week from conversion could reflect a psychological state of high motivation analogous to that in Crumbaugh, Raphael, and Shrader's (1970) sample of Dominican Sisters, who also scored close to 120 on the PIL Test. Third, it is interesting to note that the PIL level at which the converts stabilized after 6 months is almost exactly the same as that for Crumbaugh's (1968) group of "active and leading Protestant parishioners": both groups scored 114.

The results of the item analysis are a clue to the kinds of cognitive and emotional processes that mediate the reversal pattern in PIL total scores. Examination of those PIL test items whose scores were elevated for the 1-week group indicates that some of those items connote a sense of excitement (e.g., Items 1, 2, 5, and 19) and some are more cognitively toned (e.g., Items 10, 11, and 12). All of the items show a drop for the 1-month group, and most of the items show an increase for the 6-month group. These findings suggest that both cognitive and emotional responses contribute to the total PIL effect. The specific subset of PIL items that produce this effect cannot be determined with certainty, however, due to the marginality of the overall tests in the item analysis. Therefore, the results of the item analysis should be interpreted as suggestive, not conclusive. The process by which PIL fluctuates must be understood through future research.

Values and Purpose in Life

In regard to the value-PIL relationships, the general positive relation between values and PIL makes intuitive sense. We would expect those who value things more to experience a greater sense of purpose.

The results of the ordinal analyses, however, are less straightforward. Both the inverse relation between comfort and PIL and the positive relation between salvation and PIL replicate prior findings (Crandall and Rasmussen 1975) and argue against a materialistic philosophy of life. It is especially intriguing, however, that the values of happiness, freedom, and mature love would all be given more weight by subjects low in PIL. At first glance at these findings, I am pressed to ask, "Don't people with high PIL value happiness, freedom, and love?" It seems to me that they probably do. This paradoxical relation is more understandable when one realizes that subjects were asked to consider these values as if they were actual guiding principles in their own lives, as opposed to valuing them abstractly. People who strive directly for happiness, freedom, and love may miss their goal and, consequently, feel less fulfilled. It is as though they miss these end states by trying hard to find them. On the other hand, as has been stated by Frankl (1963), people whose attention is directed toward more spiritual goals gain a sense of meaning as a by-product.

Limitations and Directions

The cross-sectional design of the present study includes built-in limitations that suggest that generalities be drawn carefully and that indicate where further study is needed. The key limitation is that, as in the case in any cross-sectional study, subjects could not be randomly assigned to groups. The converts in the present study made their commitments in their own way and time. Therefore, we must assume that any important differences between specific modes of acquiring belief or between general conversion types (i.e., sudden, gradual, unconscious; Scobie 1975) were balanced out across groups. Some of those in the present 1-week convert group made their commitments under the unique circumstances of the campus evangelistic meeting; it could be that conversions occurring under other circumstances would not produce the 1-week peak effect. Future research must resolve this issue, preferably with a repeated measures design in which scores are obtained from subjects before conversion and at several points in time after conversion. Similar data for people with different conversion types would also be informative.

Two additional types of research questions are raised by the present study. First, what other types of changes in life produce PIL effects similar to those in the present study? Does it have to be a personal choice to believe a life-encompassing system or world-view, or will any major change produce the same effect? Second, what other effects follow from conversion besides changes in PIL? Certainly, the obtained changes in fear of death need to be probed with additional research. Also, the behavioral effects that follow from conversion deserve research attention. Finally, the relative weights given to cognitive and emotional factors as both causes and consequences of conversion need to be explored.

References

Allport, G. W., and J. M. Ross. 1967. Personal religious orientation and prejudice. *Journal of Personality and Social Psychology* 5: 432–43.

Argyle, M., and B. Beit-Hallahmi. 1975. *The social psychology of religion.* London: Routledge and Kegan Paul.

Bolt, M. 1975. Purpose in life and religious orientation. *Journal of Psychology and Theology* 3: 116–18.

Crandall, J. E., and R. D. Rasmussen. 1975. Purpose in life as related to specific values. *Journal of Clinical Psychology* 31: 483–85.

Crumbaugh, J. C. 1968. Cross-validation of Purpose in Life Test based on Frankl's concepts. *Journal of Individual Psychology* 24: 74–81.

Crumbaugh, J. C., and L. T. Maholick. 1969. *The Purpose in Life Test.* Munster, Ind.: Psychometric Affiliates.

Crumbaugh, J. C., M. Raphael, Sr., and R. R. Shrader. 1970. Frankl's will to meaning in a religious order. *Journal of Clinical Psychology* 26: 206–7.

Frankl, V. 1963. *Man's search for meaning: An introduction to logotherapy.* New York: Washington Square Press.

———. 1975. *The unconscious god.* New York: Simon and Schuster.

Gallup, G. 1977–78. *Religion in America: The Gallup opinion index.* Princeton, N.J.: Princeton Religion Research Center.

Paloutzian, R. F., and C. W. Ellison. 1982. Loneliness, spiritual well-being, and the quality of life. In *Loneliness: A sourcebook of current theory, research, and therapy,* ed. L. A. Peplau and D. Perlman, 224–37. New York: Wiley, Interscience.

Paloutzian, R. F., S. L. Jackson, and J. E. Crandal. 1978. Conversion experience, belief system, and personal and ethical attitudes. *Journal of Psychology and Theology* 6: 266–75.

Rokeach, M. 1973. *The nature of human values.* New York: Free Press.

Scobie, G. E. W. 1975. *Psychology of religion.* New York: Halsted Press.

Soderstrom, D., and W. E. Wright. 1977. Religious orientation and meaning in life. *Journal of Clinical Psychology* 33: 65–68.

Stoner, C., and J. Parke. 1977. *All God's children: The cult experience—salvation or slavery?* New York: Penguin.

Psychology of Religion as a Medium of Communication with General Psychology

Introduction

Psychologists of religion should want to do at least two things: (a) do the best research they can in order to advance our knowledge of the psychological bases of religious belief and behavior and (b) influence general psychology through their research. The first of these two goals is a "given." Everyone will agree that we should produce scholarship of high quality so that we can attribute more truth value to the knowledge we claim to have. The second of these goals, however, is less obvious and may not draw widespread agreement from the full spectrum of psychologists of religion. "Knowledge for knowledge sake," some would say. It is not really our task to influence others.

At least four possible responses to the idea of influencing general psychology through psychology of religion research are identifiable. One response is *laissez-faire:* Let's not concern ourselves with it. We should conduct business as usual and assume that as psychology matures it will automatically incorporate psychology of religion material into its mainstream. A second response is *isolationist:* We should not try to actively engage ourselves in the general psychology enterprise because the essence of the thing we study is "higher" than or at least different from behavior in general. Because psychology of religion studies variables that are "basically unique" (Dittes 1969), it is a field unto itself. It is simply not necessary for the field to become part of mainstream psychology. A third response is *defeatist:* Our efforts to see the psychology of religion become part of mainstream psychology have not succeeded in the past, and psychology still appears to have an antireli-

From the *Journal of Psychology and Christianity* 5, no. 2 (1986): 62–66; reprinted by permission of the publisher and the author. Copyright 1986 by the Christian Association for Psychological Studies.

gious bias (Argyle and Beit-Hallahmi 1975; Ragan, Malony, and Beit-Hallahmi 1980; Spilka, Hood, and Gorsuch 1985). Therefore, we should stop kidding ourselves and simply accept that this field will always be considered a second-rate, "taboo topic" in mainstream psychology. A final response is *progressive:* Let us take the present status of the psychology of religion as a challenge and see how far we can move it into the mainstream in our generation. This is my point of view.

A Crucial Experiment: An Analogy on Which to Build

Progress to Date

Doing research in the psychology of religion is a mixed blessing. On the positive side, we look at the past 20 years and see obvious, major advances in the field: formation of American Psychological Association Division 36, Psychologists Interested in Religious Issues, more official program time given to this topic at professional meetings, and the recent publication of five major books in the area by standard psychology textbook publishers (Batson and Ventis 1982; Byrnes 1984; Meadow and Kahoe 1984; Paloutzian 1983; Spilka, Hood, and Gorsuch 1985) following many years when an author simply could not get a major publisher to even consider the topic. We have also seen the first appearance of a section on the psychology of religion in an introductory psychology book (Zimbardo 1979),[1] and in the last 6 years the publication of articles on psychology of religion topics in the personality section of the *Journal of Personality and Social Psychology* and in the *American Psychologist* (Gorsuch 1984). I feel gratified by these developments. The psychology of religion has come a long way.

Yet, those who are active researchers in the field are painfully aware of the need for scholarship that advances the field in its own right, and which creates and extends its involvement in the parent discipline. These areas of need are challenges to spark what could be the field's most creative and influential period. Our field has recently turned a corner; a major task is directly ahead.

In order to accomplish this, however, our research must be linked to the central lines of theory and research in other areas of psychology and be published in psychology's main lines of communication. Such scholarship would constitute a joint "crucial experiment"—a collective effort to significantly influence general psychology through psychology of religion research.

1. Unfortunately, this section was dropped in the subsequent edition of the book due to space considerations.

How a Crucial Experiment Works

Every student of experimental psychology[2] learns about a long list of investigations which, in a step-by-step way, are supposed to lead that student's mind one step further into psychological truth. Along the way, the student learns about the crucial experiment—that clever, ingenious arrangement of experimental treatments which, if executed correctly and without bias, would forever answer the question of which of two opposing explanations for some phenomenon is correct. The key point for our consideration is that crucial experiments influence the field.

There are at least two uses of the concept of crucial experiment in psychology. One use is highly specialized: a laboratory procedure designed to test predictions from two opposing theories. For example, the classic studies of place learning versus response learning in rats (e.g., Kimble 1961) are of this type. The other use is more general: any investigation that makes a major statement or that dramatically illustrates a point, especially if its point is at first nonobvious but becomes widely accepted. Asch's (1952) demonstration of conformity pressures, Milgram's (1963, 1965) demonstration of the power of authority, and Zimbardo and others' (1973) prison simulation demonstrating the power of situations to regulate behavior are of this latter type. We ought to construe the psychology of religion as large-scale crucial experiment of this second type.

How do such pieces of scholarship come to have effects that endure? In the studies cited above from social psychology, at least three conditions were met: (a) the studies either tested an idea or produced results that were not the obvious or mundane, not the old "I could have told you *that* from common sense" notion; (b) the studies tested ideas that were not utterly foolish or ridiculous; (c) rather, they tested ideas and produced results that were "nonobvious but plausible," results which were discrepant from what is predicted based on our intuitive judgment or common sense, but which are more believable once we understand the power of social force to control behavior. It is this last effect—the dramatic difference between what we predict based on intuitive judgment versus the behavior of the subjects in these studies—that enables research of this type to have enduring effects on psychology.[3]

We should be creating scholarship in the psychology of religion after the above pattern in order to make a statement to general psychology that will affect the field and leave its own lasting and central contribu-

2. I entered this field as a student of experimental and physiological psychology.

3. Though I used examples from my own field, social psychology, to illustrate the above argument, equally important and enduring examples are readily available in almost any subfield of psychology. Major breakthroughs contributed by Freud, Piaget, Skinner, Bandura, the Gestaltists, and others could be cited.

tion. What this statement should look like, and how it should be communicated, is what needs to be clarified.

Basic Research with Applied Focus

Is the Psychology of Religion Too Applied?

There are two possible barriers to the success of such efforts. One of them is unavoidable. It is simply that religious belief and behavior are the focus of our scholarship. By definition, its "barrier" is part of the essence of our challenge to produce the kind of research that will speak to the parent discipline. The second barrier is avoidable if we approach our topic of study in a strategic way. This view presupposes that psychology of religion is best understood as an area of applied psychology. The paradox, however, is that much of the influential work in psychology has come from basic research. Traditionally in academic circles, basic research has been considered better, purer, and more valuable than applied research. Though there has been some lessening of this attitude, it still prevails. It also poses a barrier to the acceptance of an applied field like the psychology of religion.

My suggested strategy is not that we do applied research, but that we do basic research on issues of applied relevance. For example, we can do research on issues at the interface between religion and current theory in general psychology. Suggested topics include the cognitive and motivational processes associating forms of religiousness and behavior, the implications of attribution processes for religion and the construction of meaning, the mechanisms of religious control and freedom, developmental perspectives on religiousness, and errors in judgment based on religious interpretations of causality.

Each of these topics can be approached as an area of basic research. Yet each one has an analog in social, personality, developmental, or cognitive psychology. Each one applies a question from another area of psychology to its counterpart in the psychology of religion. The implication is that basic research can be done on the psychology of religious manifestations of these issues. Such work is an important component of our efforts to contribute to general psychology and increase the involvement of psychology of religion material with that of its mainline counterparts.

Other subfields are in a position similar to the psychology of religion, yet each has gained acceptance in the mainstream. For example, work on the psychology of sex roles, organizational behavior, and race prejudice all emerged out of a concern for applied issues. But each area has become established in the mainstream partly because scholars in that area did basic theoretical work within the bounds of that applied topic.

That is, the work was basic in that it tested hypotheses derived from general psychological theories; it was also work on a topic of applied concern. These examples illustrate how the right mix of both a basic and an applied focus in the psychology of religion can ease assimilation of the field into the mainstream.

Psychology of Religion as a Subset of Social and Personality Psychology

My own attempt to apply the above argument is that I view psychology of religion as a subset of social and personality psychology. This view evolved as I considered questions elementary to social and personality psychologists: Why and how do people respond to social pressure? What is the relation between attitude, personality, and behavior? What are the nature and limits of persuasion? Where does social influence end and personal choice begin? How do people form and sustain beliefs, and how do they guide morally relevant behavior, prosocial and antisocial?

Examining these questions led me to conclude that each one either involves religious issues or could be applied to the religious instance. The result was my view that the psychology of religion is an arena where we apply the concepts, theories, questions, and methods of social and personality psychology to the case of religious belief and behavior.[4] Many topics in psychology of religion fit squarely within this domain. For example, religion has been treated as an attitude, and the intrinsic and extrinsic religious orientation dimension has been considered to be a reflection of a personality dimension. But the nature of attitudes and personality dimensions are basic questions in social and personality psychology. Many of the issues with which the psychology of religion deals are in essence those that are central to personality and social psychology. They are expressions of those issues in the psychology of religion realm.

Therefore, within the boundaries of the psychology of religion it is possible to do research that broadens, illuminates, challenges, and extends lines of inquiry on basic processes in personality and social psychology. Doing this enables us to speak from within those fields and enhances our ability to make the contribution that is needed.

Conclusion

Doing research in the psychology of religion is like conducting a crucial experiment: the need is clear, the scholarship can speak to ques-

---

4. This logic is easily extended. Ideas from many areas, such as cognitive, motivation, and developmental psychology, can be applied to the religious case.

tions central to psychology, and psychology of religion's potential ties with other areas of psychology are in place and ready to be developed. Also, there is now a critical mass of scholars in this area, and our methodologies and ability to conduct programmatic research have advanced to an acceptable level. Our next task is to produce the scholarship that will enable the psychology of religion to make its needed contribution in the discipline.

References

Argyle, M., and B. Beit-Hallahmi. 1975. *The social psychology of religion.* London: Routledge and Kegan Paul.

Asch, S. E. 1952. *Social psychology.* Englewood Cliffs, N.J.: Prentice-Hall.

Batson, C. D., and W. L. Ventis. 1982. *The religious experience: A social-psychological perspective.* New York: Oxford Univ. Press.

Byrnes, J. F. 1984. *The psychology of religion.* New York: Free Press.

Dittes, J. E. 1969. Psychology of religion. In *The handbook of social psychology,* 2d ed., G. Lindzey and E. Aronson, vol. 5., 602–59. Reading, Mass.: Addison-Wesley.

Gorsuch, R. L. 1984. Measurement: The boon and bane of investigating religion. *American Psychologist* 3: 228–36.

Kimble, G. A. 1961. *Hilgard and Marquis' conditioning and learning.* New York: Appleton-Century-Crofts.

Meadow, M. J., and R. D. Kahoe. 1984. *Psychology of religion: Religion in individual lives.* New York: Harper and Row.

Milgram, S. 1963. Behavioral study of obedience. *Journal of Abnormal and Social Psychology* 67: 371–78.

———. 1965. Some conditions of obedience and disobedience to authority. *Human Relations* 18: 57–75.

Paloutzian, R. F. 1983. *Invitation to the psychology of religion.* Glenview, Ill.: Scott, Foresman.

Ragan, C. P., H. N. Malony, and B. Beit-Hallahmi. 1980. Psychologists and religion: Professional factors and personal belief. *Review of Religious Research* 21: 208–17.

Spilka, B., R. W. Hood, Jr., and R. L. Gorsuch 1985. *The psychology of religion: An empirical approach.* Englewood Cliffs, N.J.: Prentice-Hall.

Zimbardo, P. G. 1979. *Psychology and life.* 10th ed. Glenview, Ill.: Scott, Foresman.

Zimbardo, P. G., C. Haney, W. C. Banks, and D. Jaffe. 1973. The mind is a formidable jailer: a Pirandellian prison. *New York Times Magazine,* 8 April.

19

Jean-Pierre Deconchy

Jean-Pierre Deconchy is professor of social psychology at the University of Paris, where he is also director of the laboratory in social psychology. He has lectured in Canada, Italy, Belgium, Portugal, Spain, and Poland. Deconchy's doctorates are in experimental social psychology and the humanities. He was the first head of research at the National Center for Scientific Research in France. In 1967 Dr. Deconchy received the Five-Year Prize of Religious Psychology awarded by the International Commission of Scientific Religious Psychology located in Luxemburg. In 1973 he received the bronze medal of the National Center for the Scientific Research for the psychological and psychophysiological sciences.

Deconchy's main subject of research has been the social monitoring of beliefs, which has led to an experimental study of culturally specified religious beliefs. He is particularly interested in how religious beliefs relate to such issues as abortion, artificial insemination, and genetic engineering. Deconchy has participated in a number of international conferences on the psychology of religion, including those meeting at Oxford University in England and at the Catholic University in Nijmegen, the Netherlands. He has published over 120 articles and books.

In the article "Rationality and Social Control in Orthodox Systems," Deconchy considers the intricate connection between what people say they believe and the function those beliefs serve in maintaining cultural adjustments. He suggests that fitting in with one's tradition is at least as important a rationale for religious beliefs as asserting their absolute truth. Challenges to orthodox beliefs are always experienced, according to Deconchy, as a threat to society as well as to unquestionable truth. In an outline of current research projects, Deconchy identifies the interac-

497

tion of differing religious ideologies within a culture as an important research topic.

In his essay "Equipping the Psychology of Religion with a Theoretical Framework," Deconchy argues, along the lines of William James, that religious systems are not different from other human systems in the processes involved. The systems differ only in subject matter. However, he concludes that religious systems can demonstrate very little empirical support and therefore become ideologies, which are affirmed more by passion than by logic. If the psychology of religion ignores these facts, it will do so to its own peril. Deconchy evaluates the social psychological theory of attribution as the most promising for furthering the psychology of religion.

Rationality and Social Control
in Orthodox Systems

A social psychologist sometimes selects as his field of research attitudes and interactions which are invested with powerful personal implications and strong ideological connotations. If at the same time he is determined not to study them in isolation from the complex social systems in which they are produced, he is confronted by a number of difficulties, many of which are by no means merely methodological. Two of these difficulties are particularly important. One of them is that the trends of thought which dominate social psychology tend to conceive of interactions between individuals or between subgroups as if they were enacted outside of the framework of institutional and ideological systems, and yet it is the salience and the regulating power of these systems which determine the fact that we are dealing with "interactions" rather than with something like "inter-reactions." The second difficulty is that, in the course of their historical development and in order to ensure their survival, these systems had to attempt to gain their legitimacy. This has been the case even on the cognitive level in the sense that the institutional and ideological systems constructed models of explanation which would enable them to become socially accredited and long-lived. Consequently, the social psychologist often finds it difficult to resist the temptation to accept uncritically the explanatory models and concepts which these systems use in achieving their self-acceptance and their acceptance by others. As a result, these concepts and models are often accorded a degree of heuristic significance and epistemological rigor which is not warranted in view of the *ideological* function which they fulfil for the system.

It is said that words are rarely innocent: concepts are *never* innocent. It is the task of a researcher to present in an axiomatic form, with the help of his own procedures and in the light of his objectives, the concepts and the models through which a social system attempts to ana-

From *The Social Dimension*, vol. 2, edited by Henri Tajfel; reprinted by permission of Cambridge University Press. Copyright 1984 by Maison des Sciences de l'Homme and Cambridge University Press. This essay was translated from the French by Henri Tajfel.

lyze its own functioning for purposes of its self-legitimation; if the researcher's independent work is not done, we risk constructing a form of knowledge which would itself become an inherent part of the sociocognitive ideological field that is presumed to be the object of our exploration.

In its concern with orthodoxy, the present chapter will attempt an experimental operationalization of the concept and a translation into scientific terms of the social functioning it represents. Orthodoxy is a concept which has often remained ambiguous and inexplicit, particularly in its application to the thinking and research about religious behavior. It has never been adequately operationalized, no more so in sociology (Davidson and Quinn 1976) than in social psychology, and it has virtually never been the subject of theories which had a direct and specific relevance to it.

Introduction

The Term Orthodoxy

Extension and Current Usage

The term *orthodoxy* mainly applies to individual and social data relating to one particular area of culture: the religious. It is also occasionally applied to political data (e.g., Murvar 1972) with reference to a particular ideological system and, less frequently, to a system of social customs. Thus, Bailey (1972) wrote about "racial orthodoxy," and for Bourdieu and Passeron (1970) the "orthodoxy" of the secondary and higher systems of education is one of the social factors which contribute to the maintenance (reproduction) of a society. The term also sometimes refers to an area of scientific practice such as the classic use and stereotype of concepts (Atkinson 1971); the dominant tendencies in a scientific discipline (Teilhet-Waldorf [1979] wrote about "anthropological orthodoxy"); the purity and rigor of a theoretical paradigm (Friedrichs [1974] referred to "behaviorist orthodoxy"); or the traditional and politically respectable forms of a social theory oriented towards action (Golding [1974] criticized the "theoretical orthodoxy" involved in the conception of natural and economic development). In general, the use of the term retains a "religious" flavor, particularly so as in its more recent versions it has rarely been subjected to a genuine operationalization.

Inside religious systems, the term *orthodoxy* presents a number of special characteristics. In most cases it refers to an ethnographic description of a particular group, with an approximate analysis of the stock of beliefs of which this group undertakes the cognitive and social management. It is essentially a descriptive tool which does not supply a theory of the internal functioning of ideological groups. For example, it was not included in the great dictionaries of theology (Godin 1972), nor does it appear in the vocabulary of the latest council of the Roman Catholic Church (Chenu 1974). Its earlier use, initiated in the fourth century in order to designate the correct Christian attitude in the face of errors contradicting the "authentic" Christian faith, has been abandoned little by little, at least in the Western church.

In social psychological research, the term is used to apply to social indicators which are virtually the same as those just described. The question therefore arises whether this kind of use of orthodoxy enables the research to establish its distance from the orthodox epistemology, so that it can become independent of an ideological system which finds its self-legitimation in its social functioning and in the beliefs which are controlled by this functioning.

In social psychology, the term *orthodoxy* was rarely used outside of the Christian and Jewish contexts with, in addition, some occasional uses in the oriental context (Brandon 1970; Das and Singh 1975). Most of the time the term is employed as if it were self-explanatory, in the sense of encompassing the modalities of adherence to a corpus of beliefs and of insertion into a social group inside which these beliefs were created. People who are considered orthodox are those who give their adherence to the doctrinal items which are deemed to be characteristic of the group (either a priori, e.g., Gregory 1957; Stewart and Webster 1970; or by experts, e.g., Brown 1962). A good example of this conception was provided in the well-known "index of orthodoxy" (Glock and Stark 1966; Stark and Glock 1968).

Although the term refers most often solely to the "intellectual" dimensions of adherence to, and insertion in, religion and it has been at times explicitly distinguished from ritual conformity (Allport 1954), it has also been related in some research to forms of ethical conduct (e.g., Greeley and Rossi 1968; Danesimo and Laxman 1971) or to a distribution of the roles played in civic and religious contexts (e.g., Baer and Mosele 1971). Thus, *orthodoxy* has served as not much more than a shorthand reference to religious adherence and the membership of a religious group. It is likely that, with this background of its use, if it were to be operationalized it would find itself very closely related to various models of social behavior dealing with conformity.

The Articulation of the Concept

It is true, however, that there has also been some more interesting research which has attempted to distinguish between various specific forms of orthodox functioning. These attempts have been, more often than not, purely semantic, but sometimes they have also included distinctions which could be operationally useful. For example, in Jewish orthodoxy, distinctions have sometimes been made between its "modern" and "traditional" forms (Heilman 1977), and also "ultra-orthodoxy" (Hoffnung 1975). Some authors have distinguished within the same system beliefs which are "orthodox" and those which are "compulsory" (Thouless 1954), or the "orthodox" and the "liberal" expressions of the same system of beliefs (Stewart and Webster 1970). These typologies are suggestive, but they still remain merely descriptive. In some approaches which could be described as more clinical, the notion of orthodoxy was conceptualized with more precision. Orthodoxy was conceived in them as one of the "dimensions" of religious attitudes or behavior. This was the case in, for example, the work of Lenski (1961), in which "orthodoxy" was presented as an alternative to "devotionalism."

In sum, the theoretical roots of the use of the term *orthodoxy* in social psychology have gone no deeper than was the case in sociology. The work has consisted of little more than a simple transcription of some elements of the semantic system used and controlled by the religious groups for their own purposes. The conceptual distance, mentioned earlier in this chapter, has not been achieved; nor have there been serious attempts to validate the conceptual tools used by these groups by referring them to social and psychosocial mechanisms which might be involved rather than just relating them to words. The work of analyzing these mechanisms, whose aim it is to exert by means of words certain types of control within a particular social system, has not been done.

The itinerary followed by Rokeach (1954, 1960) in his work on this subject seems to us to have opened new possibilities (for an earlier discussion, see Deconchy 1970). "Ethnocentrism," as it was defined by Adorno and others (1950), was concerned with certain forms of social interaction, actual or potential. In considering ethnocentrism as no more than a facet of a more general mental rigidity which mainly affects intellectual operations, Rokeach "socialized" these operations at the same time as he "intellectualized" social interactions. A closer look at these notions about rigidity reveals their limitations, which appear when Rokeach attempts to establish a relationship between his views about social interactions between individuals and his perspectives upon ideological systems which have a vast scope and a profound impact. His arguments tend to imply that it is not possible to separate actions of an ideological nature from the social systems which support these actions and are supported by them. It is true that Rokeach did not pursue this argument to its conclusion. In establishing the concept of dogmatism he fashioned a tool which is of an unquestioned usefulness for the establishment of a *social epistemology* of ideological actions and attitudes. He has done this by focusing upon two ideas: the first, that every belief is an integral part of an individual or a social system outside of which it is hardly conceivable; and the second, that is a systematic analysis the structure of the system is capable of yielding more information than the contents of the beliefs.

The main questions with which this chapter is concerned are as follows: what are the characteristics of the sociocognitive field which enable these beliefs to remain tenable despite their divergence from what is habitually referred to as "rationality" and, conversely, what is the nature of the sociocognitive strategies enabling the "believers" to endow this field with an institutional consistency which has an exceptional stability? In dealing with these questions, it would be difficult to follow closely the sequence of theorizing proposed by Rokeach. His concept of dogmatism was applied at the individual and at the group levels. He detected a convincing isomorphism in the social context between the dogmatism of individuals and the dogmatism of groups, as if there existed here some kind of a "pre-established harmony." But he rarely attempted to operationalize the concept at the level of the individual/group articulation, or—a better expression—of the individual-group totality *(totalité)*. This is probably so because he refused to make a choice between the individual and the group as a focus for operationalizing the concept of dogmatism. As they were both initially conceived in a parallel fashion, Rokeach finally gave priority to the study of the dogmatic individual (mainly in the earlier period of his work) and was able to construct an attitude scale which made it possible for him to engage in experimental studies.

Our choice has been to adopt a definition of the notion of *orthodoxy* which is located at the point of articulation between the individual and the group. It has not been our main purpose to provide a description of the modes of adherence to particular doctrine and of the interactions between beliefs and customs which might be characteristic of a particular group. Instead, the aim was to study some of the forms of social functioning intervening in the establishment of a sociocognitive field which is "ideological"; that is, a field in which the main items of information are held to be "true" although they are not capable of being validated through the use of hypothetico-deductive or experimental methods and one in which it is taken for granted that all of the information is, in some way, already available in its essential form and is supplied prior to any investigation, an interaction, and even any possible innovation.

The Concept of Ideological Orthodoxy

Definitions

We shall refer to an *individual* as orthodox if he accepts, or even requests, that his thoughts, his language, and his behavior be regulated by the ideological group to which he belongs, and particularly so by the power apparatus of that group.

We shall refer to a *group* as orthodox if it ensures this type of regulation and when the axiological and technological basis of this regulation is itself part and parcel of the doctrine accepted by the group.

An orthodox *system* consists of all the social and psychosocial arrangements which regulate the activity of the orthodox individual in an orthodox group.

Thus, the concept of *orthodoxy* jointly defines the notion of an orthodox individual and of an orthodox group, considering them as an organic whole. As such, it is not conceived as an *attitude* in the usual sense of the term. It refers to the status of an individual as well as to the function and the social control which he exerts in a strongly institutionalized and hierarchical social system; in this system, to each type of power there corresponds a particular type of knowledge or lack of knowledge. To take one example: in a social system such as the Roman Catholic Church, a priest need not be either authoritarian or dogmatic in the sense given to these terms by Adorno and Rokeach. A strict application of terms in the framework of the above definitions means that the priest cannot *not* be orthodox. This is so as soon as he assumes within his church a certain status which is recognized as such, even if he enacts it in ways which are relatively marginal or audacious. Even then, he attributes to himself, in one form or another, a certain power of providing information which is explicitly recognized as his prerogative. This power, which may also be moral or ritualistic, derives from his status, and he evaluates it with reference to an ideological background controlled by the hierarchical group to which he belongs. All this being the case, he enters the logic of an orthodox system.

In a system of this kind, the processes of influence—whatever they may be—are relevant not only to beliefs, values, and attitudes, but also to the social characteristics and the social functioning of the system as a whole, which are often considered as external to the doctrine. As suggested by the second of the definitions formulated above, the orthodox beliefs also include the social system (the "Church," the "Party," the "School") which presents itself as a guarantee and a support of the values and beliefs around which the group has forged its consensus. Thus, the orthodox beliefs apply also to the interactions and modalities of interaction programed by the system. In an orthodox system one is not really a believer unless one also "believes" in the social system, in the basic rectitude of what it has instituted, and consequently in the existing distribution of powers and roles. It will thus be seen that, in such a system, it is sometimes more crucial to believe in the social regulation which has been programed than in the object and the specific contents with which the regulation and the program are concerned. A few examples of this will be given later in the chapter.

Limitations

The definitions proposed earlier would lead to the inference that all ideologies (and all systems of social representations which cannot be validated in a hypothetico-deductive or experimental way, and yet claim to supply information which is "objectively" and "necessarily" true) must end up as orthodoxies. This could be so for orthodoxies of all kinds: philosophical, religious, political, or artistic. There could also exist a scientific orthodoxy if and when claims are made that scientific research must be inserted, a priori and without any possible revision, into certain institutional structures which regulate the ways in which research is conducted, and that there can be no acceptable methodology outside of the principles which have been accredited by these institutional structures.

Although it is true that ideologies can contribute to the construction of various kinds of orthodoxy, they cannot be fully subsumed under the concept of orthodoxy. A phase when all information is regulated and the consequent distribution of social roles is a matter of simple reproduction can sometimes be succeeded by a phase in which the information is dislocated and the distribution of roles loses its acceptability. This happens in periods of agitation in which cognitive and linguistic elements of a quasi-prophetic nature contribute to the social climate. In many cases all this occurs *inside* the ideological field without deviance from the contents of the ideology being involved. It is not the contents or the object of the beliefs managed by the orthodox system which are being attacked by those who protest; it is the type of social regulation which this system has imposed upon the essential beliefs of the group and which has caused these beliefs to lose their significance, their flavor, and also very often their political potentialities. The messianic or prophetic protesters accuse those who are in control of the orthodox system of having trivialized the initial values and intuitions. They wish to reintroduce the contents and the significance, which the system has managed to control and to master to such an extent that its adherents have come to believe more in its institutions than in its values. It is, of course, probable that once the protesters have won their case they would re-introduce regulations and a structure which would resemble the previous situation.

This oscillation between orthodoxy and a movement which could be called a "prophetic and messianic agitation" was described above in "diachronic" terms. In fact, this interplay between orthodox structures without contents and contents which escape the structures also occurs synchronically. An important aspect of the self-legitimation of an orthodox system is that it often harks back to its early times, which are said to have been exemplary—it was then neither a system nor was it orthodox—but which are now gone and finished. As a result, orthodox control is often inescapably counteracted by social and cognitive forces which demonstrate simultaneously its legitimacy and its factitious character. This is why, in systems of this kind, the affirmations and the contesting of beliefs can never result in forms of influence which are unidirectional; we have shown this elsewhere (Deconchy 1975) in discussing standpoints taken by minorities. These paradoxical forms of social counter influence must be taken into account in research on the subject. If they are not, the concept of orthodoxy will become no more than a simple imitation of models of conformity or of majority influence, in which the functions served are supposed to be those of reducing dissonance, establishing congruence, or reinstating balance.

Specifications

It would be beyond the scope of this chapter to describe all the theoretical reasons which led to the conclusion that religious orthodoxies represent more clearly than do other ideological systems the type of functioning which is our concern here. It will be seen later that the work done by our research team enabled us to confirm that this was the case. Amongst ideological systems, religious ideologies are probably the only ones which explicitly admit—even proclaim—the nonrationality of their essential beliefs. There are also reasons to believe (see Deconchy 1980, 1–19) that the Roman Catholic Church has probably brought this logic of orthodoxy to its strictest form.

A series of experiments, some of which will be outlined below, was conducted in certain sectors of the Roman Catholic Church consisting of what we shall call the "lower fringe of its power apparatus" (priests, teachers of catechism, monks, nuns, seminarists). The aims of the experiments were to operationalize the concept of orthodoxy and to make explicit the modes of functioning to which the concept refers. We were able to do this research at a time (1966–72) when the Catholic Church was going through an intense crisis of conscience, identity, discourse, and control. This crisis led, in the groups referred to above, to some degree of fluidity in the ways they functioned and enabled us to elicit, for the purpose of our studies, some changes of position which could be empirically detected. At the same time, the crisis caused the groups to be willing to confront scientific information against which they had been immunized for a long time. The physical conditions of this work, as well as its methodological and ethical problems, are described and debated elsewhere (Batson 1977, 1979; Deconchy 1976, 1977, 1978b, 1980; Yeatts and Asher 1979). Some examples of this research, outlined below, aimed to describe certain modes of functioning which are, in our view, fairly characteristic of the kind of system concerning us here (Deconchy 1971). The purpose of others was to construct a theory of the paradoxical—yet essential—interplay of belief, rationality, and social control which are inherent in an orthodox system (Deconchy 1980).

Influence, Authority, and Social Representations of the Group in an Orthodox System

The range of positions which can be taken in an orthodox group about information which is consensual is neither infinite nor indefinite. It is not infinite because it is agreed—and this is one of the fundamental elements of the consensus—that all basic information is already available. The only innovations which are doctrinally legitimate are those which would provide more ingenious formulations or which would introduce more coherent arrangements of the corpus of doctrine. It is not indefinite, in the sense that social interactions which would lead an orthodox individual to vary his viewpoints are strictly regulated by the group. We are not dealing here with social interactions in which only the relations between individuals matter. Instead, there is the establishment of a system of social programing of attitudes, opinions, and viewpoints held by individuals who are always defined by the positions they occupy in the system of which they are merely points of relay. We shall illustrate some of these points with examples from research (Deconchy 1971).

The Experimental Situation

This will be described in a simplified form. The experiments were inserted into the activities of a course of study during which representatives of the lower fringe in the power apparatus of the Catholic Church worked under the direction of teachers of theology and experts in the human sciences. The purpose of the course was to adapt the teaching of catechism, and in particular its linguistic expression, to new situations which the students were likely to encounter during their ministry. In view of the nature of the course, it was therefore completely natural that (1) there was intervention by "experts" who, in a Catholic context, are never just cognitive experts but also social actors functioning as representatives of the power apparatus of the group; (2) there were hints of hesitations, or even of variations, in the manner of formulating the beliefs; and (3) some experimentation was involved, since the experts in the human sciences were suggesting that this was useful for the progress of the course.

The subjects were presented with a list of 18 propositions. These propositions reproduced some classic beliefs of the group in a form which was either direct or contradictory and intentionally ambiguous. The statements, selected with the help of the people responsible for the course, were expected to elicit an approximately equal number of agreements and rejections in the population of our subjects. The subjects were not, however, simply requested to agree or disagree with the statements.

In the first phase, they were asked to sort the statements into four categories: *Position A:* "I believe it, and all those who wish to be members of my church must also believe it"; *Position B:* "I believe it, but someone who does not could still be a member of my church"; *Position C:* "I do not believe it, but someone who does could still be a member of my church"; *Position D:* "I do not believe it, and someone who does could not be, in any circumstances, a member of my church." Of these four categories, A and D can be considered as "extreme," while B and C are "liberal."

In the second phase, new information was supplied to the subjects, who were now randomly divided into several groups. Some of them were given a document which was supposed to have been prepared by the group of theologians who taught in the 6-week course, one of whom was, incidentally, of world renown. This document specified the position of the (theological) authority in relation to each of the propositions and stated that this was the "'viewpoint' of the church." In the document the 18 propositions were classified as "compulsory" (dogmatic), "free" (left to individual analysis), or "forbidden" (heretical). In order to guarantee the credibility of the procedure, care was taken that the positions adopted by the authority were only moderately discrepant from those which the majority of the subjects were likely to adopt. For purposes of replication, two documents were used; each was given to a separate group of subjects.

Another group of subjects was informed about the result of an opinion poll which was supposed to have been conducted with a very large sample of Catholic respondents culturally similar to the subjects. This document was prepared in the same way as the one described above, so that for each of the propositions one of the positions (A, B, C, or D) was supposed to have been adopted by a very large majority of the fictitious respondents. Here also, as above, the procedure was replicated with two other groups of subjects, for whom different documents were used.

The procedures just described were a part of a more complex experimental sequence which need not be described here. The study was conducted with the full agreement of the people responsible for the course. The subjects were debriefed at the end of the experiments and were informed about the early results as soon as they became available.

Hypotheses and Results

In a very brief summary, the two procedures (information deriving form authority and from the results of the opinion poll) had effects which were nearly identical, although it seems that the latter procedure had a little less influence than the former on the subjects' positions.

It is not surprising that the classic forms of functioning were found to operate in these siltations. In the four groups, the extreme positions (A and D) resisted more strongly than did the liberal positions (B and C) interventions which were contradictory to them. The more an intervention was dissonant with the subjects' initial position, the stronger was its capacity to elicit various degrees of conformity. This result was to be expected as we were careful to ensure that the situations were credible, in the sense that they did not create extreme forms of dissonance.

The existence of two forms of functioning was established; they both appear to be fairly characteristic of the system we were studying.

The High Cost of Acquisition

The orthodox subject, who wishes to remain within the system and has institutional support for doing so, tends to conform to a pre-established corpus of beliefs. It is taken for granted that nothing genuinely new can be added to this and that nothing essential can be abandoned. There exists, however, the possibility of slight modifications which derive from information and suggestions supplied by the programing center of the hierarchical group.

But these modifications are not all of equal urgency. In a climate of peaceful orthodoxy, when there are no apologetic or inquisitorial activities, to remain silent is to be acquiescent. It is then less important and socially less desirable to proclaim openly and publicly one's orthodoxy than not to admit to heterodoxy; in other words, it is less important to say what one is supposed to say than not to say what should not be said.

This appears clearly to be the case when the sequence *Initial position 1—Intervention—Subsequent position 2* is examined separately for each of the four groups in using the total of the 2,412 cases of propositions x subjects. A proposition which was initially adopted (A or B) is more often abandoned as the result of an intervention in which this proposition is presented as heterodox than a proposition which was initially rejected (C or D) is adopted as a result of an intervention which presents it as being orthodox. It is remarkable that this dissymmetry was found not only in the conforming types of response which were adopted by a large majority of the subjects; "it also appeared when the subjects were out-bidding" the interventions proposed to them and in cases of increased rigidity. In the latter instances, when an intervention of type C or D was confronted with an initial position of liberal agreement, B, the subject finally adopted the extreme orthodox position, A; or when an initial position of liberal disagreement, C, was confronted with an intervention of type B or A, the subject moved to the position D of extreme rejection. A detailed analysis of these responses showed that they were not due to exceptional strategies of a few isolated subjects but are probably typical of closed social systems in which all of the essential information is considered as taken for granted.

The Integrity of Orthodoxy

We have argued earlier that, in an orthodox system, the role of social control is in some ways more essential than the contents and the meaning of the information for the sake of which this control is exerted. Regulation of group membership does not fully encompass the notion of social control, but it is one of its principal aspects, and it is at this level that complex strategies are usually developed.

The results of our experiments clarify these processes. When the four groups are considered separately, as soon as an initial extreme agreement (Position A) becomes a rejection as a result of the intervention by one or the other of the programing centers, this rejection is more often expressed in its extreme form (Position D) than in its liberal form (Position C), even when the extreme position was not suggested by the intervention. Conversely, when an initial extreme rejection (Position D) is transformed into agreement, this is more often expressed in its extreme form (Position A) than in its liberal form (Position B). In other words, *social regulation* (which operated here in an all-or-none fashion) is more resistant to the programing interventions than the *meaning* attributed by the subjects to the information which they are offered. We are confronting here a situation in which, as one moves from one proposition to another, their nearness or the distance between them is decoded more in terms of the social control which is at the background of the propositions than as a function of their informational content. Exaggerating a little, one could summarize as follows: What does it matter if changes occur in what one says or believes as long as the modalities of social control remain stable? What does it matter if information contains contradictions or does not make sense, as long as the system of social control remains coherent and is capable of imposing itself? In the studies described above, this was the case for the extreme positions, but we have also been able to show that the same applied at the level of the liberal positions (Deconchy 1971).

The relevance of these results to the central theme of this chapter—the interplay of rationality and social control inside orthodox systems—concerns the role played by social control in the functioning of these systems. It appears that this role is so fundamental that it exceeds in its essential functions the role played by social control in other forms of institutional cooperation in which the object of consensus is merely technological or rational.

Religious Orthodoxy and the Norms of Generic Rationality

Whatever may be the ideology of an orthodox system, the statements around which the group establishes its consensus and organizes its corpus of beliefs manage to escape the habitually accepted norms of rationality such as those which function in the sciences. This is particularly so in ideological systems of a religious nature, in which this departure from rationality is often explicitly adopted and even proclaimed. More subtle forms of this escape from rationality are used in other types of ideological systems. Our major hypothesis can be stated as follows: *The power of social control in an orthodox system is due to its functions. It prevents the adherents of the system from realizing the gap that exists between the beliefs to which they subscribe and the usually accepted norms of rationality.* If this is the case, then one should be able to show that when this gap becomes more apparent to the adherents, the orthodox group should attempt to strengthen its hold over the sociocognitive field which it controls. In contrast, when this control weakens, the rational fragility of the beliefs should become more apparent.

The experimental paradigm we have used (in social and ideological conditions identical to those described earlier) was organized around three parameters: the perception, or its absence, of the gap between accepted beliefs and rationality; the rigor, as perceived by the subjects, of the rules governing the membership of the system (this reflects, but not exhaustively, the notion of social control); and finally, the perception, or its absence, of defects within the corpus of beliefs which the system has often managed to endow, over a period of time, with a very high level of technicality. The cohesion, which is often remarkable, of this corpus is due to the formal virtuosity of the logical framework holding together its various parts, while each of them is basically irrecoverable through rationality. At the same time, a number of beliefs inserted into the corpus provide the doctrinal justification of the processes of social and cognitive control expected by the system.

In *secure orthodoxy,* when there is no urgent need for apologetics, polemics, or inquisitorial confrontations, the divergence from norms of rationality is not necessarily perceived. In such cases, the ideological statements are manipulated as if the information which they are supposed to convey was no more problematic than statements which can be rationally validated—for example, statements in mathematics. The corpus of beliefs is perceived as unified and having no internal weaknesses. There is therefore no contradiction for the orthodox subject between the significance of any of the individual statements and the global significance of the doctrinal system. The conception of the rules of membership would include here the entire range, from the acceptance of dogma to the anathema of heresy, while at the same time leaving open the possibility of a controlled liberalism. We have been able to show (Deconchy 1971) that in such situations the orthodox subject is able to organize functionally in this way his conception of a particular statement around the three parameters described earlier.

The situations of *threatened orthodoxy* bring to the surface the compensating play of regulation through social control (e.g., rules governing membership) and of perception of rational fragility. The details of experimental procedures, which can be described here only in part, can be found in Deconchy (1980).

Through a rational polemic, which was carefully dramatized, students of theology who were following a course in the human sciences were shown that statements in which they believed could not be reconciled with the generally accepted notions of rationality. As a result, two patterns of response appeared. In one of them there was a more marked reliance upon a stricter regulation of group membership (a large number of agreements with a liberal position were transferred to agreements with an extreme position). The other pattern consisted of strengthening the conception the subjects had of the perfect internal coherence of the orthodox corpus of beliefs (certain internal weaknesses, initially detected, disappeared after a second reading of a text which followed the polemical discussion). In other identical situations, the subjects were informed that "in the view of a number of experts and according to the results of an opinion poll," the beliefs to which they subscribed were not as important for the rigorous regulation of their group membership as they had naively and spontaneously thought. They were thus led, on the one hand, to perceive more clearly the divergences between these beliefs and the norms of rationality; on the other hand, they had to moderate the views they had previously held about the perfect internal coherence of the orthodox corpus of beliefs (some inconsistencies, not previously detected, appeared at the second reading which followed the controversy).

In the same conditions, in which a theological polemic was also introduced, the subjects were shown that weaknesses existed in the orthodox corpus to which they subscribed. In this way, as they were forced to see more clearly the strain that their beliefs imposed upon norms of rationality, they were also led to adopt a stricter conception of the rules of membership.

As already mentioned, all these experimental interventions were made with the agreement of the people directing the course and were followed by postexperimental debriefing.

These results seem to show that the hypothesis which predicts that, in an orthodox system, the rational fragility of information will be compensated by an increased rigor in the regulation of the system and can account for some of the modes of functioning released by threats and attacks against the integrity of the system. The results we obtained lead to the conclusion that the effects of threat, when they apply to what has been called here a "threatened orthodoxy," are not unidirectional. As long as the system endures, the attacks which are directed against the nonrationality of the beliefs held by the subjects do not have any marked effects. They are counterbalanced by an appeal for stricter social control (an appeal which is both organizational and doctrinal). In contrast, there is no direct compensation for attacks directed against the various aspects of social control. These attacks result in a clearer perception of the rational fragility of the beliefs, and this entails, in turn, all the risks of decay which can be brought about by the cumulative effect on the system of both these injuries to its integrity.

These results can contribute in some measure to a better understanding of certain macroscopic forms of functioning. For example, there are social systems in which everything possible is done to create an institutional atheism through methodical demonstration of the "nonscientific" nature of religious beliefs. Despite all these efforts, religious beliefs manage to survive for long periods of time, and religion is lived and experienced in forms which are more dogmatic and is organized according to stricter social models (as, for example, in rituals) than in situations where attacks of this kind are not usual. One can also understand why it is that the institutional leaders of a church (or a party which aims at establishing its hegemony) show long-lasting resistance to the idea of obtaining reliable statistics about those who respect the canonical obligations (such as attending Mass or the Sunday service). If the numbers turned out to be less impressive than imagined by the adherents, the canonical norms would appear as exerting a weaker social control of actual or potential adherents than expected, and this, in turn, could be associated with a risk of a more critical analysis of the relevance of the information conveyed through beliefs, now seen as being less powerfully controlled than had previously been thought. Another example: it is understandable that groups which are the most rigid in their orthodoxy react to suggestions about modernization, changes, and adaptations by setting a higher value on rituals which have become out-of-date. It was correct to think—as some did with anticipation, and some in fear of consequences—that the Catholic Church, in authorizing its priests to exert some measure of ritual liberalism, even if only on points of detail, was initiating a process which logically would result in questioning of the church's theology of priesthood and even of the relevance of the priest's status.

Religious Orthodoxy and the Effects
of Specific Scientific Information

The sociocognitive strategies which our research has been able to articulate were elicited in situations in which the orthodox subjects were confronted with a generic form of rationality. The subjects take their distance from this rationality when they explicitly admit that the information which they accept is at odds with its norms and principles. But at the same time they are fascinated by it, since they need it in order to provide an organizing logical framework for the information on which is based the social control of their system.

This situation defines its own research problem. What would be the cognitive strategies employed by the same subjects when, instead of being confronted with generic rationality, they would have to come to terms with a specific form of scientific information? The information in this case had to do with their own ways of functioning and acting as orthodox subjects enclosed within an orthodox system.

Using situations similar to those previously described, we attempted to find out in what ways the subjects would remain orthodox after they had been informed about the results of our experimental work, and when the theoretical framework of this work was also outlined to them. The subjects whom we have been able to reach in our research (from the lower fringe, as described earlier) are usually quite willing to be exposed to some form of initiation into the human sciences. This willingness is based on the idea—on the whole rather vague—that the human sciences might be of help to them in improving the quality of their pastoral work. They are therefore, in principle, receptive to the information. There was the possibility that once this information had been communicated to them, they would not be able to resort to the latent and classic epistemology which they normally use in order to authenticate their system of beliefs, since they were provided with evidence that social control is used by the system so as to obscure the nonrational nature of these beliefs.

Thus, these subjects were presented with experimental results selected from those previously mentioned, together with an analysis of the theoretical background of the research, the parameters around which it had been organized, and a description of the research methods. All this taken together amounts to demystifying the experiments—as is often done for obvious ethical reasons in research conducted in other circumstances. Although the earlier experiments were done with other subjects, they were still conducted within the same system, and thus the presentation of the results showed directly to the subjects the artificial character of the epistemology inherent in the system, the role played by this epistemology in the conception the system has of itself, and also the role it plays in the adherents' way of thinking about the system.

In an experimental situation of this kind, the orthodox system is driven to a position in which it is not able to seek, as it normally does, the foundation of its beliefs in its traditional and implicit epistemology. We expected that, consequently, there would be displacement of the consensus, even at the fringes of the system, and that this displacement would result in somewhat more independence from the social and cognitive controls programed by the system and supporting it. A wider latitude would have to be given to the counterinfluences which are always present but which are normally controlled and subdued. Some concessions would have to be offered to the social and cognitive restlessness against which the system is immunized in conditions of peaceful orthodoxy. These concessions would protect from the unrest those areas of the cognitive and social order which still clearly remained under control.

A series of experiments was conducted, each with a different group of subjects. In addition to the theoretical background, they were presented with the results of two of the experiments from amongst those outlined above. One of them was the study in which the perception of the rational fragility of a particular belief led the subjects to strengthen their faith in the internal cohesion of the doctrinal corpus as a whole. The second was the study in which the perception of new defects in the coherence of the doctrinal corpus as a whole elicited a clearer perception of the rational fragility of a particular belief.

Information of this kind modified the subjects' beliefs in the sense that they became in some ways more utopian. Some subjects said that they were more convinced than ever before that little by little, as time goes by, in some indefinite future, the believer will be able "really to understand" the "true" and "real" meaning of such-and-such particular belief. Others resorted to a form of eschatology, in the sense that they were now more convinced than ever before that what they called "the end of time" would bring with it a radical transformation of the profound significance of their beliefs. Others still reported a conviction held more strongly now than before. This was the view that, precisely because the cognitive procedures are so uncertain, the future role played by the mystics in the study of beliefs would become more important than the role of theologians and of the institutional hierarchy.

The educational methods the subjects planned to use in their pastoral teaching lost some of the rigor and technicality which are usually adopted in a climate of traditional orthodoxy. Thus, after having been confronted with the scientific information described earlier, the subjects evaluated more positively than they did before the effectiveness of using pictorial examples which are not metaphorical in order to make children understand the various beliefs in the catechism which these examples are supposed to illustrate (Deconchy 1978a). Other subjects assigned a more important educational role to gestures and to nonverbal and audiovisual methods. The apologetic procedures which, in a climate of orthodoxy, usually follow the path of proof and demonstration, were now seen as capable of being modified. More often than before the subjects said that "unconscious" factors should be involved in order to achieve an understanding of beliefs since, in the last analysis, faith is more firmly based upon affectivity than upon rationality.

In that milieu from which the subjects with whom we worked came, the classic orthodox strategies are strongly marked by their reliance upon a monolithic social background and institutions which are firmly hierarchical. In the studies with which we are now concerned, the subjects were led to consider the potential epistemological value of social contexts which offered more differentiation and variety. Thus, after scientific information had been given to them, they evaluated more positively the role that "small, informal, and fraternal communities" could play in contributing to a genuine understanding of the beliefs which were the basis of their formation (Deconchy 1975).

It appears, therefore, that the subjects and the system of which they are a part use as a safeguard some of the "restless" social forms and forces against which they are habitually immunized. It would not be prudent, however, to interpret these evasive tactics as a weakening of the system and of the conceptions which it legitimizes or as a mellowing in its exercise of control. These displacements toward the fringes of the system, the aim of which is to find new foundations and a new locus for the theoretical interpretation of beliefs, are also programed and they are a part of the ideological capital which is managed by the system. What basically happens in this kind of situation is that certain conceptions about the historical origins of the system, which precede the formation of its orthodoxy are brought back into circulation and reactivated; for example, the original intuitions, cognitive turbulence, modes of social conduct which are dissenting or even revolutionary, the flavor and the fervor of social processes characteristic of minorities, prophecies, and messianism which are visionary and appealing. There is a risk in all this that the system might reintroduce into its functioning a heightened significance of certain preorthodox conceptions which were often turbulent and which the orthodox social control managed to assimilate in a paradoxical way by causing them to sink into oblivion, but this risk is carefully kept under control and it is probably no more than temporary.

It will be obvious that instances of this reactivation of original conceptions are not confined to the kind of situations we have used and to the effects of scientific information which intervened in them. There are other ways of trying to reinstate the initial conceptions and intuitions of orthodoxies through demystifying various aspects of the orthodox social control. Our main purpose was to show—starting from one particular point of view—that the conformity which appears inherent in the very notion of an orthodox system can certainly not be accounted for solely in terms of psychosocial processes conceived as being unidirectional.

Conclusion

Starting from the notions summarized in this chapter, the research on the interplay between rationality, belief, and control in closed social systems is proceeding at present in three directions:

1. When an ideological system of the kind we have explored here has not succeeded in imposing its hegemony upon the society as a whole, it must come to share certain social interactions with other coexisting systems. These systems might occasionally become isomorphic, and the interactions may be diverse and complex, interactions such as, for example, open conflict, cold war, ecumenical activities, a historical compromise, etc. These various ideological systems, which interact and confront each other, differ at the cognitive level—which has been our concern in this chapter—in the sets of meanings and values which they convey; but sometimes they are very similar in the social structures which they have created for themselves. When social control is used in this type of interaction, it is probably as complex and differentiated in such cases as it is in the internal sociocognitive management of the orthodox system. We are now studying these modes of functioning as they relate to the cognitive strategies adopted by Catholic churchmen when they are confronted with conceptions of Marxist origin (Deconchy 1976–77).

2. The introduction of generically considered rationality in our experimental manipulations elicited a strengthening of the social control. The introduction of information which dealt specifically with the functioning of the subject and of the ideological group led to other forms of displacement. This information was validated through research which consisted of experiments. We have been able to show that scientific information validated in this way had effects which were more disturbing for the orthodox system than was the case for information based only on a descriptive and correlational study of a set of empirical data (Deconchy 1980). Further research will therefore deal with the various modes of conflict which develop between the latent epistemology used by an orthodox system for purposes of self-legitimation and the diverse methodologies employed by the natural and the human sciences.

3. The reactivation of some of the original conceptions and beliefs contributes to disturbances in an orthodox system, as the system is then led back towards less controlled, or even uncontrolled, forms of social functioning. Another theme of present research is the study of the ways in which an orthodox system programs for its adherents strategies of immunization or of strictly limited exposure to the return of its own original contents and meanings which—paradoxically—can contribute to the destruction of the system, its modes of control, and its corpus of beliefs.

References

Adorno, T. W., E. Frenkel-Brunswick, D. J. Levinson, and R. N. Sanford. 1950. *The authoritarian personality.* New York: Harper.

Allport, G. W. 1954. *The nature of prejudice.* Cambridge, Mass.: Addison-Wesley.

Atkinson, D. 1971. *Orthodox consensus and radical alternative: A study in sociological theory.* London: Heinemann.

Baer, D. J., and V. E. Mosele. 1971. Political and religious beliefs of Catholics and attitude toward involvement in the Vietnam War. *Journal of Psychology* 78: 161–64.

Bailey, T. 1972. *Race orthodoxy in the South,* 2d ed. New York: Neale.

Batson, C. D. 1977. Experimentation in psychology of religion: An impossible dream. *Journal for the Scientific Study of Religion* 16: 413–18.

———. 1979. Experimentation in psychology of religion. Living *in* or *with* a dream? *Journal for the Scientific Study of Religion* 18: 90–93.

Bourdieu, P., and J. C. Passeron. 1970. *La reproduction: Éléments pour une théorie du système d'enseignement.* Paris: Éditions de Minuit.

Brandon, S. G. F. 1970. *A dictionary of comparative religion.* New York: Scribner.

Brown, L. B. 1962. A study of religious belief. *British Journal of Psychology* 53: 259–72.

Chenu, M. D. 1974. Orthodoxie-orthopraxie. In *Le service théologique dans l'église.* Paris: Éditions du Cerf.

Danesimo, A., and W. A. Laxman. 1971. Catholic attitudes and beliefs in transition: a decade study of a Jesuit college. *Psychological Reports* 28: 247–50.

Das, J. P., and P. S. Singh. 1975. Caste, class, and cognitive competence. *Indian Educational Review* 10: 1–18.

Davidson, J. D., and G. J. Quinn. 1976. Theological and sociological uses of the concept orthodoxy. *Review of Religious Research* 18: 74–80.

Deconchy, J.-P. 1970. Milton Rokeach et la notion de dogmatism. *Archives de sociologie des religions* 30: 3–31.

———. 1971. *L'orthodoxie religieuse: Essai de logique psychosociale.* Paris: Éditions Ouvrières.

———. 1975. L'image des "Communautés de base" comme support cognitif pour des croyanes menacées dan leus fondements "rationnels"? In *Changement social et religion*, 285–307. Lille, France: Editions CISR.

———. 1976. Expérimentation et processus d'influence idéologique dans les groupes réels. *Psychologie Française* 21: 281–6.

———. 1976–77. Régulation et signification dans un cas de compromis idéologique (ecclésiastiques catholiques et propositions marxistes). *Bulletin de psychologie* 30: 436–50.

———. 1977. La psychologie sociale expérimentale et les comportements religieux. *Annual Review of the Social Sciences of Religion* 1: 103–32.

———. 1978a. Étude expérimentale d'un phénomène de contre-emprise sociale: Le recours à un matériel esthétique comme support cognitif pour des croyances menacées dans leurs fondements rationnels. *Archives de sciences sociales des religions* 45: 117–43.

———. 1978b. L'expérimentation en psychologie de la religion. *Archives de Sciences sociales des religions* 46: 176–92.

———. 1980. *Orthodoxie religieuse et sciences humaines*. Paris: Mouton.

———. 1981. Laboratory experimentation and social field experimentation An ambiguous distinction. *European Journal of Social Psychology* 11, no. 4: 323–49.

Friedrichs, R. W. 1974. The potential impact of B. F. Skinner upon American sociology. *American Sociologist* 9: 3–8.

Glock, C. Y., and R. Stark. 1966. *Christian beliefs and anti-Semitism*. New York: Harper.

Godin, A. 1972. Orthodoxie religieuse et psychologie sociale. *Nouvelle revue théologique* 104: 620–37.

Golding, P. 1974. Media role in national development: Critique of a theoretical orthodoxy. *Journal of Communication* 24: 39–53.

Greeley, A. M., and P. H. Rossi. 1968. *The education of Catholic Americans*. New York: Doubleday.

Gregory, W. E. 1957. The orthodoxy of the authoritarian personality. *Journal of Social Psychology* 45: 217–32.

Heilman, S. C. 1977. *Inner and outer identities: Sociological ambivalence among modern Orthodox Jews*. Flushing, N.Y.: Queens College.

Hoffnung, R. A. 1975. Personality and dogmatism among selected groups of Orthodox Jews. *Psychological Reports* 37: 1099–1106.

Lenski, G. 1961. *The religious factor: A sociologist's inquiry*. New York: Doubleday.

Murvar, V. 1972. Non-theistic systems of belief. *American Behavioral Scientist* 16: 169–84.

Rokeach, M. 1954. The nature and meaning of dogmatism. *Psychological Review* 61: 194–204.

———. 1960. *The open and closed mind: Investigations into the nature of belief systems and personality systems*. New York: Basic.

Stark, R., and C. Y. Glock. 1968. *American piety: The nature of religious commitment.* Berkeley/Los Angeles: Univ. of California Press.

Stewart, R. A., and A. C. Webster. 1970. Scale for theological conservatism and its personality correlates. *Perceptual and Motor Skills* 30: 867–70.

Teilhet-Waldorf, S. 1979. Anthropological orthodoxy: A case of reverse ethnocentrism? *Human Organization* 38: 416–20.

Thouless, R. H. 1954. *Authority and freedom: Some psychological problems of religious belief.* London: Hodder and Stoughton.

Yeatts, J. R., and W. Asher. 1979. Can we afford not to do true experiments in psychology of religion? *Journal for the Scientific Study of Religion* 18: 86–89.

Equipping the Psychology of Religion with a Theoretical Framework

In these few pages, each contributor is asked to say what are his main preoccupations within the framework of his scientific work. The task would be impossible without mentioning at the outset a certain number of data that underlie these preoccupations, data ranging from a description of the concrete sites where the work is carried out to the initial epistemological concepts, which, of course, would remain to be axiomatized, and all this without going into an analysis of personal experiences, for which this is not the place.

As far as my own scientific work is concerned, I think a certain number of preliminary data which explain these preoccupations must be mentioned, but without implying that I consider these preoccupations to be the only ones that are possible, thinkable, and fundamental.

Some excellent pieces of work (Beit-Hallahmi, 1977; Ragan, Malony, and Beit-Hallahmi 1980) have put the interest aroused by religion, professional training and practices, and religious commitment in perspective. For my own part, I am not interested primarily, still less exclusively, in the study of religious data. As a social psychologist of the experimental kind, it is an interest in the interactions at work in complex social systems that led me to study so-called religious systems among others and in comparison with other systems. We have tried to tackle these complex social systems (which may or may not be religious), and we are seeking to construct theories about their foundations at several levels: the interplay of the regulatory mechanisms (hold on adherents and social control that support and organize these systems) the genesis (management and decline of representations, beliefs, and diversified symbolisms enshrined in them) and the cognitive strategies aimed simultaneously at accrediting the social "legitimacy" of the system and the "truth" of the information regulated by that system. As can be seen, our approach—and we make this choice in full awareness of its limitations—bears only slightly on the affective, the lived, and the experiential. Moreover, it goes without saying that when we are working on

This essay was translated by Mary Turton.

"religious" data we come up against all the methodological, theoretical, and epistemological problems raised by experimental social psychology and the "state of crisis" that is habitually being diagnosed in that psychology.

It follows, nevertheless, that our research work rests on three assumptions (at least!), and of course it is neither unthinkable nor forbidden to axiomatize them. Stated briefly, as we shall do, they may appear provocative, whereas all we are doing is outlining the epistemological climate of my own scientific work (which is not the whole of my life!) or, if you like, the theoretical backdrop to the most operational aspects of that work.

On the one hand, religious systems and the interactive strategies enshrined in them, both for individuals and for the social field governed by these systems, are psychosocial facts like any others which, up to a point, do not essentially (in the etymological sense of the word) require either a methodology or a theory intrinsically different from those at work on other social facts.

On the other hand, a scientific project dealing with religious data is not essentially different from scientific projects dealing with other data. Its methodological and theoretical demands are those that define the nature of scientific research and those alone (see Spilka, Hood, and Gorsuch 1985). As far as we are concerned, we are not convinced that it is possible to "integrate" psychology and religious or theological discursiveness in a potentially unified language.

Finally, in order firstly to avoid the psychographic or ethnographic style but above all to provide the conditions necessary for constructing a theory (or theories) in the psychology of religion, it seems to us that religious systems must first be plunged (in the mathematical sense of the word) into the whole of which they are logically and epistemologically a part, namely ideologies (a concept), by the way, that has so far been very poorly operationalized and, for that reason, gives rise to much reaction. In other words, it would seem to us to be detrimental—returning to the classic terminology—to seek to establish their specific difference before trying to establish what accounts for their next higher genus *(genus proximum)*.

Rightly or wrongly, we think these three axioms may help to bridge the theoretical gap that continues to affect the psychology of religion and hold it back to the point of paralysis in its effort to acquire the status of a scientific discipline. With Spilka, Hood, and Gorsuch (1985), we think that not only does a scientific psychology of religion rest on the observation of "data that are public . . . and reproducible" but that "we must have theories, ways of organizing our thoughts and ideas so that the data we collect make sense" (3).

It is true that the theoretical penury of what we shall nevertheless lump together under the name of psychology of religion is recognized by everyone (to draw attention to it nowadays is prosaic, Hood and Morris 1983), although this lack is not always deplored. This weakness is often ascribed, either as cause or effect, to the real or supposed difficulty, not to say impossibility, of resorting to experimental techniques in this field (Warren 1977; Batson 1977; Deconchy 1977, 1978a). In saying this, we are thinking less of the absence of theories bearing specifically on psychosocial phenomena labelled as "religious" than of the reluctance of researchers to apply to these phenomena theoretical models, however transitory, which have stood the test in other sectors. We may wonder if this reluctance, considered from a functional and not necessarily apologetic angle, does not stem from the fact that the great majority of researchers in the psychology of religion remain very close to personal religious preoccupations, on the one hand, and to pastoral practices seeking their own foundations and effectiveness on the other. Indeed, it is by no means impossible that, concerning the way religions function, the theory and epistemology underlying psychology of religion are seen as being in competition with the modes of validation and legitimization, themselves religious, that in any given system of beliefs authenticate the firm foundation of those beliefs. An attempt has even been made to demonstrate this experimentally (Deconchy 1980).

It follows that a certain number of strategies for substituting or even getting around the problem might be brought into play: apology on the part of a psychographic or sociographic research that has little aptitude or desire to generalize and so to theorize; the notion that, once it is set in motion, the theoretical effort should concentrate on what makes religious interactions and cognitions peculiar in relation to other interactions and cognitions; the recurring temptation to introduce a stereotyped model of two religions, one of which might perhaps be more suitable than the other to be the subject of scientific (and therefore theoretical) investigation and the other, the "better," more "true," more "profound," more "lived" religion, being beyond the scope of such analysis. Here we have a typology that is clearly not based on a scientific approach alone but is at least a function of an anthropology that tends to be isomorphic with the one suggested by the term *religion* itself. What comes to mind—and this remark is in no way derogatory—is the operative pairing of extrinsic/intrinsic, the fluctuations of which should be analyzed in the work of its originator (Allport 1954, 1960, 1966; Allport and Ross 1967); we think perhaps, too, of other pairs: "committed" and "consensual" (Allen and Spilka 1967, for example), "mythological" and "symbolical" (Hunt 1972), "behavioral" and "ideational" (Himmelfarb 1975), "acted out" and "internalized" (Roof 1979, analyzing Himmelfarb 1975). These distinctions that perhaps give birth to the idea of two types of psychology (Sullivan 1962), of research strategy (Havens 1961), or indeed of measurement (Dittes 1971).

Be that as it may, until quite recently any appeal to theoretical models available elsewhere has been extremely scanty. Batson (1977) considered that only Dittes (1969) and Proudfoot and Shaver (1975) had conquered this reluctance. At the same time (Deconchy 1977) we were adding to this an occasional recourse to the theory of cognitive dissonance (Guthrie and Marshall 1966; Lee and Doran 1973; Batson 1975b; Adam 1974; Hsieh 1976; Dunford and Kunz 1973; Brock 1962; not forgetting, of course, Festinger, Riecken, and Schachter 1956!). From that time on, a whole spate of literature was appearing on the analysis of religious attitudes around the notion of "locus of control," more perhaps from the angle of a differential psychometry than from recourse to the foundations and theoretical potentials of the notion introduced by Rotter (see nomenclature in Deconchy 1978b).

Quite recently, however, it is undeniable that a desire for theory has become more clearly discernable in scientific production, with a reference (variously modulated and still rather scattered) to theories available in social psychology: social categorization (Saigh, O'Keefe, and Antoun 1984; Yinon and Sharon 1985); social influence (Mugny and Perez 1985); theory of aggression (Kanehar and Merchant 1982); models of the S-R type (Unger 1978) or the S-O-R type (Malony 1977, 1985). But it is on the lines of the theory of attribution, meritoriously opened up by Proudfoot and Shaver (1975) and, laterally, by Batson (1975a) that the theoretical breakthrough, after tentative beginnings, is currently most evident and, in our view, most promising (Ritzema 1983; Ritzema and Young 1983; Gorsuch and Smith 1983; Spilka and Schmidt 1983; Spilka, Shaver and Kirkpatrick 1985; Brown 1987), until it has become the key to an exhaustive presentation of the psychology of religion and its objectives in the excellent work of Spilka, Hood, and Gorsuch (1985).

In this leaning of the subdiscipline toward theory creation, we must make sure at the very moment when we experience the bias that on leaving the mainstream of the psychology of religion we do not set off up a blind alley. This would be the case if we confined ourselves to resorting half-heartedly to a theory whose aims and scope would tend naturally toward generalization. The risk then would be of appealing only to theoretical "allegories" and not to theoretical creativity itself: allegories are suggestive but their implications would culminate in a reasoned classification of cultural raw material without considering the modalities and laws that produced it.

Allegorical use of a particular theoretical system is sometimes explicitly assumed and then leads to descriptions and suggestive analyses. It brings order to a wealth of raw material without attempting to isolate its laws of production. We may think, for example, (although they are very varied in tone and substance) of the works of Carroll (1979), Brams (1980), or Ashbrook (1984): the first resorts to a rhetoric born of the theory of cognitive dissonance for a renewed reading of the Old Testament; the second organizes interactions between God and men as they appear in the Scriptures by a vertiginous application of game theory; in the third, a typology of all theological propositions is created by means of behavioral models assumed respectively by the left and right hemispheres of the brain. This is a happy return on the part of theoretical insight to a tool kit that generates a content analysis of a very particular type.

There are perhaps slightly more ambiguous situations in which the wish to theorize is explicitly stated and remains probably within the potentialities and obligations of theory creation. In fact this may be the case in the current vogue for resorting to the theory of attribution, where it seems to us that what is produced does not fully measure up to what the theory requires. We should indeed begin by asking ourselves what are the conditions of form and material on which recourse to the theory of attribution could truly be based in the psychology of religion; in spite of the remarkable quality of the book by Spilka, Hood, and Gorsuch (1985), the answer is not fully apparent (Deconchy 1987).

In a first analysis, concerning an event that happened to me, what is needed is to know how, within some eventual scientific reflections, I attribute the causes of the event to my own dispositions and my own actions, to the interplay of natural forces and determinisms at work in the species (a type of attribution, incidentally, that has received little study), to external social and environmental influences and, in the case of psychology of religion, to the action and intentions of a "God," whom it is clearly impossible to locate or track down empirically. This was indeed the way the first authors tackled it, either by open questions or by closed questions.

But where can we find in current works on the theory of attribution a study of the cognitive strategies according to which the subject, faced with the task of explaining causally how certain events that happen to him are produced, creates loci of attribution which depend neither on being located empirically nor on a hypothetico-deductive type of logic and yet refer to an unverifiable ontology? In fact, the first works on the psychology of religion confine themselves to seeing whether and how often subjects accept as their own a proposition inculcated in them by the dominant culture, namely, that "God" is the (efficient, sufficient, auxiliary, and so on) cause of a certain number of things. They observe—and compute—the number of times subjects resort linguistically to a certain available cultural language. Of the cognitive mechanisms that contribute to generating the representation of a "being" who is causative in this sense and to placing the imaginary in an ontological position, we are almost totally ignorant. A psychology of religion that is truly "theorizing" in its aims should not only work to establish and elucidate these mechanisms but should also give to the theory of attribution, observed from its most general angle, a dimension that it lacks so far, namely, the ability to theorize about mechanisms and strategies which conjointly (in parallel or in alternation), with the resort to empirically detectable dispositional or situational data, create ontological loci of causal production that derive neither in fact nor "doctrinally" from empirical analysis of the data. Against this position two others arise which are paradoxical: one which resorts to a possible rationality of "rational proofs" of the existence of God on the basis of empirical data and by that route to persistent, although outmoded, apologetics; the other which confers a quasi-empirical quality on religious experience, pushing the problem of locating the causes to which that experience is attributed a notch farther away.

The very great difficulty of applying available theoretical models to religious experience (and to the strategies that support it as well as those to which it leads) is clearly apparent. When Jones works at centering attributive strategies on the image of the intention of an interactor, with what or with whom are we dealing in religious attribution, which might derive more or less closely from empirical discoverability? When Kelly considers the attributing subject as proceeding from a sort of spontaneous analysis of covariance between the effects of three factors (consensus, differentiation, and consistence), how can its "content" be transferred to a field of representations devoid of empirically locatable correlates? If, in order to explain this, we had to resort only to the pregnancy of a particular cultural language, the desire to theorize would by that very fact fall back into the field of a taste for description, even if, slightly better modeled. But, in a way, the appeal to a theory (in this case of attribution) would then in its turn depend on "allegory."

References

Adam, J. P. 1974. La culture religieuse au secondaire. Esquisse d'un cadre de'analyse psycho-sociale. *Cahiers de pastorale Scolaire* (Sherbrooke, Quebec, Canada) 5: 105–15.

Allen, R. O., and B. Spilka. 1967. Committed and consensual religion: A specification of religion-prejudice relationships. *Journal for the Scientific Study of Religion* 6: 191–206.

Allport, G. W. 1954. *The nature of prejudice*. Cambridge, Mass., Addison-Wesley.

———. 1960. *Personality and social encounter*. Boston: Beacon Press.

———. 1966. The religious context of prejudice. *Journal for the Scientific Study of Religion* 5: 447–57.

Allport, G. W., and J. M. Ross. 1967. Personal religious orientation and prejudice. *Journal of Personality and Social Psychology* 5: 432–43.

Ashbrook, J. B. 1985. *The human mind and the mind of God: Theological promise in brain research.* New York: Univ. Press of America.

Batson, C. D. 1975a. Attribution as a mediator of bias in helping. *Journal of Personality and Social Psychology* 32: 176–84.

―――. 1975b. Rational processing or rationalization? The effect of disconfirming information on a stated religious belief. *Journal of Personality and Social Psychology* 32: 455–66.

―――. 1977. Experimentation in psychology of religion: An impossible dream. *Journal for the Scientific Study of Religion* 16: 413–18.

Beit-Hallahmi, B. 1977. Curiosity, doubt, and devotion: The beliefs of psychologists and the psychology of religion. In *Current perspective in the psychology of religion,* ed. H. N. Malony, 381–91. Grand Rapids: Eerdmans.

Brams, S. J. 1980. *Biblical games: A strategic analysis of stories in the Old Testament.* Cambridge, Mass.: MIT Press.

Brock, T. C. 1962. Implications of conversion and magnitude of cognitive dissonance. *Journal for the Scientific Study of Religion* 1: 199–203.

Brown, L. B. 1987. *The psychology of religious belief.* London: Academic Press.

Carroll, R. P. 1979. *When prophecy failed: Cognitive dissonance in the prophetic tradition of the Old Testament.* New York: Seabury.

Deconchy, J.-P. 1977. La psychologie sociale expériementale et les comportements religieux. *Annual Review of the Social Sciences of Religion* 1: 103–32.

―――. 1978a. L'expérimentation en psychologie de la religion. *Archives des sciences sociales des religions* 46: 176–92.

―――. 1978b. La théorie du "locus of control" et l'étude des attitudes et des comportements religieux. *Archives de sciences sociales des religions* 46: 153–60.

―――. 1980. *Orthodoxie religieuse et sciences humaines.* Paris: Mouton.

―――. 1987. Théories et allégories en psychologie de la religion. *Archives des Sciences sociales des religions* 64: 179–92.

Dittes, J. E. 1969. Psychology of religion. *The handbook of social psychology,* 2d ed., eds. G. Lindzey and E. Aronson, vol. 5, 602–59. Reading, Mass.: Addison-Wesley.

―――. 1971. Two issues in measuring religion. In *Research on religious development,* ed. M. R. Strommen, 78–106. New York: Hawthorn.

Dunford, F. W., and P. R. Kunz. 1973. The neutralization of religious dissonance. *Review of Religious Research* 15: 2–9.

Festinger, L., H. W. Riecken, and S. Schachter. 1956. *When prophecy fails: A social and psychological study of a modern group that predicted the destruction of the world.* New York: Harper.

Gorsuch, R. L., and C. S. Smith. 1983. Attributions of responsibility to God: An interaction of religious beliefs and outcomes. *Journal for the Scientific Study of Religion* 22: 340–52.

Guthrie, G. M., and J. F. Marshall. 1966. Cognitive dissonance among protestant fundamentalists. *Pennsylvania Psychiatric Quarterly* 6, no. 2: 11–25.

Havens, J. 1961. The participant's vs. the observer's frame of reference in the psychological study of religion. *Journal for the Scientific Study of Religion* 1: 79–87.

Himmelfarb, H. 1975. Measuring religious involvement. *Social Forces* 53: 606–18.

Hood, R. W., Jr., and R. T. Morris. 1983. Towards a theory of death transcendance. *Journal for the Scientific Study of Religion* 22: 353–65.

Hsieh, T. 1976. Missionary family behavior: Dissonance and children's career decision. *Journal for the Scientific Study of Religion* 4: 221–26.

Hunt, R. A. 1972. Mythological-symbolic religious commitment: The LAM Scales. *Journal for the Scientific Study of Religion* 11: 42–52.

Kanehar, S., and S. M. Merchant. 1982. Aggression, retaliation, and religious affiliation. *Journal of Social Psychology* 117: 295–96.

Lee, J. L., and W. J. Doran. 1973. Vocational persistence: An exploration of self-concept and dissonance theories. *Journal of Vocational Behavior* 3, no. 2: 129–36.

Malony, H. N., ed. 1977. *Current perspectives in the psychology of religion.* Grand Rapids: Eerdmans.

———. 1985. An S-O-R model of religious experience. In *Advances in the psychology of religion,* ed. L. B. Brown, 113–26. Oxford: Pergamon.

Mugny, G., and J. A. Perez. 1985. Influence sociale, conflit, identification. *Cahiers de psychologie sociale* 26: 1–13.

Proudfoot, W., and P. Shaver. 1975. Attribution theory and the psychology of religion. *Journal for the Scientific Study of Religion* 14: 317–30.

Ragan, C. P., H. N. Malony, and B. Beit-Hallahmi. 1980. Psychologists and religion: Professional factors and personal belief. *Review of Religious Research* 21: 208–17.

Ritzema, R. J. 1983. Research methodology for studying attributions to supernatural causality. *Journal of Psychology and Theology* 11: 48–50.

Ritzema, R. J., and C. Young. 1983. Causal schemata and the attribution of supernatural causality. *Journal of Psychology and Theology* 11: 36–43.

Roof, W. C. 1979. Concepts and indicators of religious commitment: A critical review. In *The religious dimension: New directions in quantitative research,* ed. R. Wuthnow, 17–45. New York: Academic Press.

Rotter, J. B. 1966. Generalized expectancies for internal versus external control of reinforcement. *Psychological Monographs* 80: 28.

Saigh, P. H., T. O'Keefe, and F. Antoun. 1984. Religious symbols and the WISC-R performance of Roman Catholic parochial schools students. *Journal of Genetic Psychology* 145: 149–66.

Spilka, B., and G. Schmidt. 1983. General attribution theory for the psychology of religion: The influence of event-character of attributions to God. *Journal for the Scientific Study of Religion* 22: 326–39.

Spilka, B., R. W. Hood, Jr., and R. L. Gorsuch. 1985. *The psychology of religion: An empirical approach.* Englewood Cliffs, N.J.: Prentice Hall.

Spilka, B., P. Shaver, and L. A. Kirkpatrick. 1985. A general attribution theory for the psychology of religion. *Journal for the Scientific Study of Religion* 24: 1–20.

Sullivan, J. E. 1962. Two psychologies and the study of religion. *Journal for the Scientific Study of Religion* 1: 155–64.

Unger, J. 1978. Is religion a system of adaptation? In *Psychological studies on religious man,* ed. T. Kallstad. Stockholm: Almqvist and Wiksell.

Warren, N. C. 1977. Empirical studies in the psychology of religion: An assessment of the period 1960–1970. In *Current perspectives in the psychology of religion,* ed. H. N. Malony, 93–100. Grand Rapids: Eerdmans.

Yinnon, Y., and I. Sharon. 1985. Similarity in religiousness of the solicitor, the potential helper, and the recipient as determinants of donating behavior. *Journal of Applied Social Psychology* 15, no. 8: 726–34.

Part **9**

Clinical Psychology of Religion

20

L. Rebecca Propst

L
Rebecca Propst is associate professor of psychology at Lewis and Clark College, Graduate School of Professional Studies, Portland, Oregon. Prior to this, Dr. Propst was assistant professor of psychology at Ohio University. She has also lectured in the department of medical psychology at the Oregon Health Sciences University. Her doctorate in clinical psychology is from Vanderbilt University.

Propst has been active in Division 36, Psychologists Interested in Religious Issues, of the American Psychological Association. She was a member of the advisory board of the Institute for Religion and Wholeness. A contributing editor of the *Journal of Psychology and Theology,* Propst has also reviewed articles for the *Journal for the Scientific Study of Religion,* the *Personality and Social Psychology Bulletin,* and the *Journal of Social and Clinical Psychology.*

Dr. Propst has done seminal work on the treatment of depression utilizing religious ideas. Her research has compared those treated with cognitive behavioral therapy mode with religious imagery to those treated without religious imagery. She is presently engaged in an extensive follow-up study of 60 clinically depressed patients in which she is assessing the effect of this treatment on the persons' religious values. Propst's study of these dynamics is considered to be one of the best empirically based investigations of the use of religious resources.

A sampling of titles of Propst's published articles attests to the breadth of her interests: "A Comparison of the Cognitive Restructuring Psychotherapy Paradigm and Several Spiritual Approaches to Mental Health," "Predictors of Coping in Divorced Single Mothers," "Spiritual Practice and Psychotherapy," and "The Comparative Efficacy of Religious and Nonreligious Imagery for the Treatment of Mild Depression

533

in Religious Individuals." The last mentioned article, and work Propst presented in a paper at the 1984 meeting of the Society for Psychotherapy Research are discussed in the most recent edition of the *Handbook of Psychotherapy and Behavior Change* (New York: Wiley, 1986) by Allen Bergin and Sol Garfield.

Psychotherapy in a Religious Framework: Spirituality in the Emotional Healing Process (New York: Human Sciences, 1987) represents Propst's most recent work and is the most comprehensive text in the area of the integration of psychology and theology. In the book she has linked some of the insights and empirical findings of the literature of cognitive-behavioral psychotherapy with some of the theological insights of Karl Barth, the literature of the Christian mystical tradition, and contemporary liberation theology.

In the article "Servanthood Redefined: Coping Mechanisms for Women within Protestant Christianity," Propst notes the double bind into which women are put by the traditional expectation that they should be self-denying at the same time as they are encouraged to be self-determining and self-efficacious. She deals with this issue as it is manifested by Christian women who come for psychotherapy. Propst describes characteristics of the self-efficacious person and illustrates how they are compatible with the goals of Jesus for human life.

In her essay "The Psychology of Religion and the Clinical Practitioner" Dr. Propst relates her long-standing interest in the impact which religion can have on psychotherapy and the emotional healing process. This has involved her in psychotherapy outcome research, an area in which very little work, other than by Propst herself, has been done. According to Propst, research on religion's influence on counseling has been hampered by the reluctance of funding agencies to support these studies and by a weak commitment to scientific methodology on the part of religious counselors.

Another consuming interest for Propst has been in the relationship of adjustment and spirituality. This has led her to a study of active coping versus passive acceptance modes of relating to life and the way in which persons handle anger. She discusses control of impulses and the studies which indicate that well-being is related to personal control. Propst also reports her growing interest in Christian admonitions about how to react when others do one wrong. She notes that while most mental health professionals advocate assertion, this seems to be in contrast to what Jesus teaches. Propst sees the need to investigate sex differences in these matters.

Servanthood Redefined:
Coping Mechanisms for Women
within Protestant Christianity

One of the chief tenets of Christian behavior is the notion of servanthood. Though the emphasis put on this concept has varied throughout the centuries, the Christian community has often been at its best when it has viewed itself as a servant of others. Servanthood within the Christian context has meant self-surrender or self-denial for God or others. This concept may cause difficulty for women, however, who are also expected to be more self-denying than the rest of society by the rules of that society. For example, women are expected to give up their names, suppress their needs for the needs of their husbands, or passively assent to all decisions.

This stance can obviously cause difficulties as the recent work in learned helplessness and personal efficacy (Bandura 1979) suggests. Those who allow themselves to be controlled by others, whether within the marriage relationship or in the larger community, often suffer from higher levels of depression or stress.

Recent work in psychotherapy research coupled with feminism has laid greater emphasis on women's self-determination and greater self-efficacy. This work, however, has led to a double bind for Christian women who desire earnestly to live their faith. Should they assert themselves and push their needs forward, or should they give up their rights to others as Christianity would suggest? This dilemma is very real for many women in psychotherapy whose faith is important for them.

The tension between the supposed demands of self-determination and ideal Christian behavior manifests itself in the therapy context via many emotions. Such women may feel angry at such a double bind. This anger, in turn, leads to guilt and thus to depression. They feel somewhat irritated by the demand that they feel totally involved and satisfied in the role in which they find themselves. They often report

From the *Journal of Pastoral Counseling* 26, no. 1 (1982): 14–18; reprinted by permission of the publisher and the author.

that the work is unsatisfying. On the other hand, they do not feel justified in complaining and thus experience guilt for their complaints, because "surely the work in which they are engaged is important." Certainly, their religious faith teaches that caring for the helpless (such as children) is important. Yet, on the other hand, they do not feel very important when they are engaged in the work. These women may be led to devalue their activities, because, on the one hand, religious leaders may verbally assent to the importance of such activities. On the other hand, these same religious leaders, however, do not have time for such activities in their own lives, thus communicating that such activities are not indeed valuable. Christian women are thus trapped by the double messages they receive. They would like to step out of some of their unsatisfying roles, but feel guilty for their wishes to do so.

The present paper will discuss the basic elements of self-efficacy theory as proposed by Bandura (1979). Some channels within the Christian tradition for applying these elements of self-efficacy theory for women will then be presented.

Bandura (1979) suggests that the perception of self-efficacy is one of the best predictors not only of psychological health, but also of performance on tasks. He differentiates the self-efficacy paradigm from the learned helplessness paradigm in the following manner. According to Bandura, self-efficacy refers to the individual's expectations that she has the competency to accomplish a certain necessary activity. Learned helplessness, on the other hand, refers to the notion that regardless of the individual's competency or ability to execute a certain necessary task no rewards will be forthcoming, even if the task is executed (Seligman 1975).

In the former paradigm, individuals may give up trying because they seriously doubt that they can realize the required level of performance, whereas, in the latter paradigm, individuals may be assured of their capabilities, but give up because they expect their efforts to produce no results in an environment that is unresponsive or is consistently punishing. The paradigm of principal interest in the present paper is the self-efficacy paradigm, in which individuals seriously doubt their capabilities to perform certain required activities.

Bandura asserts certain characteristics of individuals who have a sense of self-efficacy. First, the individuals are persistent because they feel that, based upon past experiences, their capabilities will eventually bring about the desired result. The second characteristic of individuals with high self-efficacy is a sense of internal control. The individuals perceive that they are the determiners of what happens to them, rather than the environment. A third characteristic of individuals with a strong sense of self-efficacy is the ability to select the environments they will expose themselves to. To understand why this is important, we must understand again the difference between outcome expectations which are derived from the learned helplessness model and efficacy expectations which are derived from Bandura's self-efficacy model. In the former model the central notion is that outcomes, regardless of one's capabilities, will not be forthcoming from an environment. In this case, the individuals develop a sense of helplessness because they have learned that their outcomes are independent of their responses. Regardless of their competency, the desired outcomes would not come forth from the environment. Self-efficacious persons in this circumstance are then able to exercise enough control to attempt to change environments. They will choose activities and an environmental setting which will give them better rewards or outcomes.

A fourth characteristic of self-efficacious persons relates to the preceeding notion. Essentially these individuals will choose their own activities which they desire to engage in. They will usually weigh the pros and cons and make choices based upon their own personal goals. It is their own personal goals and not pressures from the environment which will dictate choice of activities. The final characteristic of self-efficacious individuals is the possession of a strong sense of competency. Competency in Bandura's model is not the ability to perform a fixed act but is rather a generative capability. More specifically, the competent individual is able to organize component skills into courses of action in accordance with certain rules and strategies. Competent individuals, therefore, have certain learned and internalized rules and strategies to guide their actions, and to constantly generate the required new behaviors.

Given the characteristics of self-efficacious individuals, it would seem that religious individuals and in particular religious women would find it difficult to be self-efficacious, especially with the admonition to "give up oneself" and the prescription that one should "give God the credit" for one's accomplishments. Indeed, sometimes in working with them within a therapy context I have often found such women hesitant to take credit for accomplishments because they sincerely feel that would be wrong. Furthermore, I have often found such women hesitant to change their environment because they feel they should accept what God has brought their way. This passivity and resignation may be the result of one of two processes. On the one hand, passivity and resignation may be a cognitive set which they acquired early in life, and their Christian faith may accord them a justification for that. On the other hand, however, the resignation or passivity may be a conscious attempt to adapt themselves to what they perceive are the demands of Christianity. Christianity does provide, however, a model for self-efficacious coping which women can freely adapt to their own concerns.

The therapeutic solution is to encourage women with a cognitive behavioral framework to look back into the roots of their religious tradition in an attempt to integrate the demands of self-denial via self-surrender and the demands of self-affirmation via personal efficacy. The model presented is that of Jesus as a decision maker who made choices of self-giving rather than as one who allowed those choices to be dictated to him by society. Indeed the model is of one who risked societal displeasure (and the displeasure of the religious authorities) in order to pursue his own personal destiny. The model is still one of servanthood, but servanthood resulting from a sense of personal vocation and not from intimidation by the social forces, servanthood from an internal locus of control not an external locus of control.

This article will now discuss the various characteristics of the self-efficacious individual and relate these to the notion of the model of Jesus as a decision maker, and then show how some of these ideas can be made to apply to women within the Christian community.

One of the crucial characteristics of the self-efficacious individual is a sense of internal control. Jesus demonstrates this par excellence. Even in the face of very overwhelming odds, he continues to assert that he makes the decisions. For example, with reference to his death, there is very much the concept of internal control. In the face of a hostile environment, he says, "No one takes my life from me, I lay it down myself" (John 10:18). His overall sense of the work also allows him to be free of the power of intimidation. When he was brought before a hostile religious authority, he asserted, "You could have no control over me, unless it was given to you" (John 19:11).

Jesus also very much portrayed the self-efficacious individual by his activities. He continually did not allow himself to be pressured by his environment into an activity that was not on his agenda. This included pressure from his disciples or even his closest friends. For example, in the Gospel of Mark, one of his disciples remarks that people are looking for him and that he needs to go back to a certain locale and take care of some of the sick people there. He remarks instead that he must go on to another city, because that will be more consistent with his purposes. He did not allow himself to be pressured by even seemingly good activities. This pressure is certainly very similar to the pressure which religious women receive.

Another activity of Jesus which places him in the category of the self-efficacious individual is the ability to change environments when one environment becomes unresponsive to his efforts. He did not feel a need to try to make every environment respond positively. He was very fond of saying, "A prophet is without honor in his own country" (John 4:44). If people did not respond or show respect, he went to another locale and essentially communicated that there were too many other good things to do to be concerned with those that were uninterested in him.

Finally, we may notice that Jesus had a perceived competency which certainly led to a persistence of what he was about in the face of difficult odds. He persisted, whether it was in caring for the needs of a large number of people or going to a location to which he was determined to go (Jerusalem) despite opposition from even his best friends.

These notions of the self-efficacy of Jesus can provide a very helpful model for Christian women, who often find themselves unable to do the various things which perhaps their tradition via the model of Jesus could encourage them to do.

One very destructive phenomenon existing today in the Christian community which has often been the undoing of a number of depressed Christian women whom I have counseled is the proliferation of a number of "how to" books for Christian women. Usually these books, patterned somewhat after the "total woman" books, describe the types of activities in which the women would be able to engage. They speak of the virtues of the immaculate house or the elaborately prepared meals, or the latest set of disciplines they should follow. Often what happens, however, is the women find themselves unable to live up to these ideals which they feel other women are able to achieve. Such perceived failure on their part results in guilt, anxiety, depression, and/or anger. They begin to question their Christianity. They feel the books should be taken seriously. After all, they are written by Christians. Furthermore, some of the notions in the books are often reinforced by well-meaning Christian friends.

A helpful therapeutic approach with such depressed women is not to eliminate their value systems, but, on the contrary, to find within them a marvelous sense of liberation for these women. A helpful homework assignment for some of these women is to ask them to go through one of the Gospels and write down, for example, the number of instances in which Jesus found himself opposed to the loaal religious authorities or the number of instances in which he was criticized by his friends or disciples for his seemingly un-Christian behavior. They could even find examples of schedule interruptions which he used in a positive sense. I find that most women gain an immediate sense of release from such activities.

Some women also feel very unhappy in certain circumstances because they may feel a loss of self-respect. They feel, however, it would be improper to leave that situation. They feel that they should instead learn to accept it. The realization that Jesus often went to another situation in which he could be more effective is often liberating for them.

Communicating that a sense of internal control is also proper for these women is crucial. It is, in fact, probably one of the most important therapeutic activities needed. This sense of control or accomplishment can be communicated experientially via behavior assignments. A sense of accomplishment goes a long way towards giving one a sense of internal control.

Interestingly, the notion of self-control can be seen as integral to the notion of "being made in God's image" and can be presented as such. To be more specific, the idea or concept of the image of God as it is often presented by Scripture is not clearly discussed. In the Christian Scriptures the idea of the image of God is used in a dynamic sense to refer to the ability to be in relationship not only with others but with oneself. The uniqueness of being human and in God's image is therefore the notion of being able to hold dialogue with oneself or others. This is the ability to step outside of oneself and question oneself. This idea was clearly presented by, for example, Reinhold Niebuhr in his book *The Nature and Destiny of Man* (1964). Now it is very interesting that the idea of holding dialogue with oneself and stepping outside of and transcending one's environment is very similar to the idea of cognitive self-control via what one says to oneself. Most of the cognitive therapists such as Rehm, Beck, Ellis, or Meichenbaum assert that one gains control of concepts and a sense of self-control via being able to examine and transform one's thoughts. There is thus a control of one's internal thoughts.

I find that defining the growth of a self-consciousness and a self-dialogue as realizing the image of God very therapeutic for these women. They are encouraged to examine and argue with their maladaptive thoughts which they may have adopted from others, using Jesus as a model. A stronger religious self-definition results, but this is a religious self-definition that is indeed a self-definition and not "another's" definition. The person that results is not necessarily a selfish individual like one that may be generated by, for example, the Gestalt therapy emphasis on the increased sense of self. There is, rather, a giving self, as Jesus was, but one that gives in terms of one's own goals, purposes, and strategies.

References

Bandura, A. 1979. Reflections on self-efficacy. In *Annual review of behavior therapy*, ed. C. Franks and G. T. Wilson, 137–91. New York: Brunner-Mazel.

Niebuhr, R. 1964. *The nature and destiny of man*. New York: Scribner.

Seligman, M. 1975. *Helplessness: On depression, development and death*. San Francisco: W. H. Freeman.

The Psychology of Religion and the Clinical Practitioner

An examination of the impact which religion may have on psychotherapy and the emotional healing process is a fascinating and important concern for one such as myself who claims to be both a serious religious practitioner (Christian) and a clinician. My interest in this question extends in several directions. Most recently, my interest has focused on whether or not the individual's religious faith or spirituality can be a useful tool in the actual psychotherapy process itself. This interest has meant working in the area of psychotherapy outcome research. Additional questions which also seem worthy pursuits in an examination of the spirituality-mental health relationship include the role of anger in the individual's spirituality and the issue of whether the individual shall be primarily passively accepting or actively assertive.

Answering the question of whether or not the individual's personal spirituality and religious beliefs systems can be a useful helping tool in the psychotherapy process is really a question of passionate concern to most practitioners of religion. Most Christians, as well as those individuals of other faiths, feel strongly that their faith is an active contributor to their mental health. The recent upsurge of interest in Christian and pastoral counseling centers attests strongly to the belief in the emotional healing powers of Christian spirituality. Indeed, a large segment of the Christian laity usually demand a Christian counselor. One of the most common comments heard in some Christian circles, is, "Of couse, if I needed counseling, I would want only a Christian counselor!"

Given this urgent concern that spiritual values play a role in the counseling arena, the question of the hour is, Does the active inclusion of spiritual issues and concerns in the counseling process affect the probability of a successful outcome of that counseling? One would think there would be abundant research answering this question in the literature. Unfortunately, this is not the case. To the author's knowledge

From the *Journal of Psychology and Christianity* 5, no. 2 (1986): 74–77; reprinted by permission of the publisher and the author. Copyright 1986 by the Christian Association for Psychological Studies.

there has never been a full-blown outcome study published in any of the standard clinical journals answering this question. To my knowledge, an analogue psychotherapy study by the author (Propst 1980) is still the only study in the literature which attempts to probe the actual impact of spirituality on the psychotherapy process.

It is too often just assumed that spiritual values are important in counseling and psychotherapy. This may not always be the case. For example, an interesting paper by Spero (1981) actually found that the ability of the therapist to convey sensitivity and genuine acceptance (all considered important ingredients in the therapeutic mix) was actually hindered when the client and the therapist shared the same religious values. Spero further contends that the client is less able to perceive the therapist's sensitivity and genuine acceptance when religious values are shared with the therapist. In actuality, most of the contentions of religious practitioners that spirituality leads to a better format for solving one's problems is based on anecdotal evidence or personal observations. This type of evidence, however, has its problems. Not only is such evidence subject to the biases and blind spots of the practitioner, but it is usually discounted by nonreligious practitioners.

The lack of research examining the role of spirituality in the psychotherapy process probably results from at least two phenomena. First, research support, in the form of grants, is difficult if not impossible to obtain. Psychotherapy research, due to its complexity, time, and personnel demands, is a very difficult undertaking without such support. It appears to this writer, at least, that federal agencies have become even more nervous about the role of religion in mental health because they have in the past run into hostilities and even law-suits from some Christian groups who have challenged their support of research on such techniques as Transcendental Meditation on the grounds that it violates the separation of church and state. Consequently, any variables related to religion will be approached quite cautiously in the future by these funding agencies.

A second factor which may be contributing to a paucity of psychotherapy outcome research in this area may be a weak commitment to the scientific method on the part of religionists and clinicians. One suspects that some practitioners of religion secretly may fear that science will discover some fact that will destroy their faith, or at least their view that religious belief is an indispensable part of mental health. Perhaps they have not yet come to appreciate the dictum that "all truth is God's truth." One suspects this fear of the more conservative practitioners of religion. The more liberal practitioners also have their problems with science. They suspect science of dehumanizing the individual and speaking about that individual in only cold objective categories, when what is needed is a more humanistic perspective on the person.

Both groups, however, can rest assured that at least, thus far, their worse fears have not been confirmed. Jerome Franks (1982) in speaking about the present status of outcome research, has stated that "thus far, we have found that the most important determinants of psychotherapy success seem to be the personal qualities of the patient and the therapists and their interactions rather than the therapeutic methods" (283). Additionally, Franks has reiterated an earlier position of his that perhaps the greatest contributor to emotional dysfunction is some type of demoralization. He states also that perhaps the most fruitful way to success is to focus on the individual's personal belief systems and the healing abilities of the therapist. I think both conservative and liberal religionists would find Frank's statements heartening.

The question of how much the individual's spirituality can contribute to her or his emotional or physical healing is certainly a consuming question for religious practitioners. Furthermore, several reports have indicated that when people have had emotional problems 42% to 60% have turned first to clergy to counsel (Brown 1969; Scarlett 1970). Such facts indicate that this issue should be spoken to in a scientific manner, now while the psychotherapeutic Zeitgeist is open to innovations.

It may be that there is a more primary question that must be answered before we can pursue the role of spirituality in the emotional healing process. Perhaps before one can know if spirituality can contribute to the healing process, one must ascertain whether that particular spirituality in question has the ingredients that are said to be part of mental health. Recently, there has been increased interest in the general relationship between religiosity and mental health. Allen Bergin (1983), in a meta-analysis of this literature, suggests that both religion and mental health are multidimensional phenomena. Any analysis of the relationship between these variables would lead to mixed results unless the separate dimensions of each of the variables were examined.

In my clinical experience I have found two dimensions which are important in both the individual's spirituality and his or her mental health. In some cases, these concerns may appear to conflict in the spiritual and psychological spheres of the individual's existence. These dimensions are (1) the passive acceptance versus the active coping dichotomy of human existence and (2) the individual's relationship and acceptance of anger in his or her life. Any integrative endeavor which attempts to seriously embrace both spirituality and emotional health in the individual must take seriously these concerns.

The mental health literature is replete with theories and empirical studies which state that perceptions of uncontrollability in the individual's life lead to decreased mental health, decreased persistence, and even depressed affect (see Rothbaum, Weisz, and Snyder [1982] for a review of this literature). This theme has come forth from Bandura's self-efficacy formulations, from Seligman's learned helplessness research, and from the attribution research. Those individuals with an external locus of control—those who see circumstances, chances, and powerful others as controlling outcomes—are, in general, more likely to manifest emotional dysfunction.

Spiritual practitioners of all stripes, however, maintain that passivity must play an important role in the individual's consciousness. An example of such a sentiment might be, "I must let go and let Jesus do it. I must not try to cope with my problems myself, but instead have faith that God will intervene." Those psychologists of religion who assert that this is a parody of Christianity miss the point of some of Jesus' central assertions about saving one's life and therefore losing it, and giving up one's life so that it can be found. This sentiment of passivity or acceptance is also found in the mystical literature. Saint John of the Cross asserts that one must wait in the passivity of the dark night for one's beloved. Saint John of the Cross, in his book *The Dark Night of the Soul*, also states that the soul, when confronted with this dark night which has come from God, should remain in interior quiet, because God is indeed dealing with him or her despite the individual's lack of knowledge of that fact.

This tension between passive acceptance and waiting which plays an active role in Christian spirituality and the active coping advocated by the current research in coping and psychopathology must be resolved. Recent work by Pargament, Sullivan, Tyler, and Steele (1982) may be a beginning state in this direction. They found that a moderate sense of control by God coupled with a high sense of personal control was related to high levels of well-being. However, they also found that a high sense of control by God when coupled with moderate levels of control by powerful others and chance and a lower sense of personal control was also related to higher well-being. They suggested that it is the benevolence and coherence of an explanatory framework rather than its internality or externality, which may have the greatest coping significance for the individual. This line of research needs to be extended more firmly into more significant clinical areas, such as psychopathology.

A third question I have recently become interested in is the role of anger in the individual Christian's life. The specific question is, What should one do, if someone has wronged you? When should one be assertive, and when should the wrong be quietly accepted? Any serious reading of the Sermon on the Mount should make it apparent to the casual observer that Christianity has a problem here that Christian psychologists have sloughed off or have largely ignored. For the most part, the contemporary Christian culture has opted to go with the assertiveness option, rather than turning the other cheek.

Contemporary evangelicalism, with its emphasis on slick marketing techniques, the American success story, and the support of military spending, is a good example of the assertiveness option. These churches have begun to emphasize the *imago dei* which is present in the individual, but have often neglected the Sermon on the Mount. The Anabaptist churches, on the other hand, with their strong emphasis on the Sermon on the Mount as a source of doctrine, have tended more to opt for the "turning of the cheek option" and the principles of the Sermon on the Mount. There has been less of an emphasis there, however, on the *imago dei* and the self-esteem of the individual.

Some groups who emphasize corporate power and assertion (building the kingdom of God, defending Christian America, and aggressive evangelism techniques) also paradoxically emphasized the lack of power and assertions of rights for some of their weaker or more disenfranchised members, such as women. Women are often reminded of Jesus, who did not push for his rights. Some groups who vehemently emphasize their right as Christians to defend their country by military build-up and war, if necessary, often reject women's claims for more power and control as un-Christian because they are defending their rights and Christians should not assert their rights. This split view of the appropriate use of power and assertion in some segments of the Christian church is a fascinating psychological phenomenon and deserves further study. It may promise to generate some very powerful insights into the relationship between Christian spirituality and mental health.

The split view of power and assertion in the Christian church points to another issue deserving of study. More specifically, those groups which have such a split view of men's and women's roles should provide an interesting microcosm for the study of the impact of sex roles on mental health. Indeed, it may be that the relationship between mental health and religious belief may need to be qualified by moderator variables. This moderator variable may be sex. If, as the literature suggests, a more assertive life stance is necessary for mental health, those segments of the religious community who are denied this assertive life stance may manifest the most psychopathology.

This brief paper has focused primarily on the need for research which examines the impact of religious faith and commitment on variables and processes of interest to the clinician. More specifically, the impact of the individual's spirituality on the process and outcome of psychotherapy needs to be more closely examined. A second focus of research which would greatly aid clinicians in their treatment of religious clients would be a fuller investigation into the passive-active coping dichotomy, which is a strong theme in Christian spirituality, and its impact on mental health. Two subareas of investigation in this area include the role of anger in the Christian's life and the impact of sex roles on the relationship between religious commitment and mental health.

References

Bergin, A. E. 1983. Religiosity and mental health: A critical reevaluation and meta-analysis. *Professional Psychology, Research and Practice* 14: 170–84.

Brown, B. 1969. Emerging community mental health settings: The clergy's role in social movements. Talk given before Task Force on Religion and Mental Health in the Community National Council of Churches, February, Philadelphia.

Franks, J. 1982. The present status of outcome research. In *Converging themes in psychotherapy research,* ed. M. R. Godfried, 281–90. New York: Springer Publishing.

Pargament, K., J. Sullivan, F. Tyler, and R. Steele. 1982. Patterns of attribution of control and individual psychosocial competence. *Psychological Reports* 51: 1243–52.

Propst, L. R. 1980. Comparative efficacy of religious and nonreligious imagery for the treatment of mild depression in religious individuals. *Cognitive Therapy and Research* 4: 167–78.

Rothbaum, F., J. Weisz, and S. Snyder. 1982. Changing the world and changing the self: A two-process model of perceived control. *Journal of Personality and Social Psychology* 42: 5–37.

Scarlett, W. 1970. The clergyman's role and community mental health. *Mental Hygiene* 54: 378.

Spero, M. 1981. Countertransference in religious therapists of religious clients. *American Journal of Psychotherapy* 35: 565–75.

21

Edward P. Shafranske

E dward P. Shafranske is associate professor in the Graduate
School of Education and Psychology at Pepperdine University,
Los Angeles. He is a clinical psychologist with special interest
and training in psychoanalytic psychology. Prior to his appointment at
Pepperdine, Dr. Shafranske was a clinician in the clinical counseling
services of the University of San Diego, where he also taught in the
graduate program in practical theology. He received the doctorate in
psychology from United States International University.

Dr. Shafranske has been active in Division 36, Psychologists Interested in Religious Issues, of the American Psychological Association
and has served on the division's executive committee since 1987. He has
been newsletter editor and chair of the division's committees on clinical
training and continuing education and is chair of the division's task
force on religious issues in clinical psychology training. Shafranske has
presented papers on psychology and religion at state, regional, and
national psychology association programs. In 1990 he was cochair of a
national conference on the Reality of Evil: Implications for Pastoral
Counseling and Clinical Psychology.

Dr. Shafranske has also been chair of the task force on spirituality
and psychotherapy of the California State Psychological Association. As
chair of that task force, he conducted research leading to the publication of "Factors Associated with the Perception of Spirituality in Psychotherapy" (*Journal of Transpersonal Psychology* 16 [1985]: 231–41,
with R. L. Gorsuch) and "Clinical Psychologists' Religious and Spiritual
Orientations and Their Practice of Psychotherapy" (*Psychotherapy* 27
[1990]: 72–78, with H. N. Malony). These articles are the most thorough
surveys of the religious backgrounds of therapists and of their sense of

the importance of religion in psychotherapy to be found in recent professional literature.

In the article "Clinical Psychologists' Religious and Spiritual Orientations and Their Practice of Psychotherapy," Shafranske and Malony report a survey of clinical psychologists regarding the impact of religion on their practice of psychotherapy. The majority utilized interactions of a religious type and reported spiritual concerns in their own lives. While almost all of them indicated they were raised in an organized religion, less than half remained active. These findings are similar to those reported by the authors in an earlier survey of California psychologists.

In the essay "The Dialectic of Subjective Historicity and Teleology," Shafranske concludes that psychology and religion both speak to the basic need of human beings to find a meaningful identity in existence. He discusses the parameters involved in this pervasive human struggle to find meaning and he explores the importance of "remembering" to this process. Shafranske conceives of faith as a process whereby the paradox of doubt and the necessity of self-affirmation join. He concludes his philosophical discussion by relating these various ideas to the task of clinical psychology.

Clinical Psychologists' Religious and Spiritual Orientations and Their Practice of Psychotherapy

Recent contributions (Lovinger 1984; Spero 1985; Quackenbos, Privette, and Klentz 1986) have noted the relevance of examining religious and spiritual issues as approached by the profession of psychology and, in particular, in respect to the practice of psychotherapy. This attention to religious and spiritual issues is based on an appreciation of the influential role religious beliefs, traditions, and experiences serve in the lives of persons. Religious and spiritual dimensions are posited to be significant constituents of human experience and as such fall within the legitimate purview of psychology (Allport 1950; Hall 1904; James 1902). Within clinical psychology this interest is based on the acknowledgment of the value of taking religious factors into account in psychological assessment and in psychotherapy (Lovinger 1984). Feifel proposed almost 30 years ago that "regardless of our own religious or non-religious commitments or attitudes we need to accept and understand the individual's religious situation as a significant area in [his or her] life" (1958, 565).

A review of the literature suggests that religious variables affect the utilization of psychological services and may influence the process of psychotherapy (Hillowe 1985; Worthington 1986). In light of these findings it appeared relevant to ascertain clinical psychologists' orientations to religious and spiritual issues and the effect their orientations have on their practice of psychotherapy. Past research suggested that psychologists, in general, affiliate with and participate in organized religion to a lesser degree than the general population (Ragan, Malony, and Beit-Hallahmi 1980). However, studies of California and Wyoming clinical psychologists found that psychologists, in general, address spiritual and religious issues in their personal lives, appear to respect the function religion serves in others' lives, and exhibit competence in dealing with

Coauthored with H. Newton Malony. From *Psychotherapy* 27 (1990): 72–78; reprinted by permission.

549

religious and spiritual issues in psychotherapy (Shafranske and Gorsuch 1985; Shafranske and Malony 1985; Elkins and Shafranske 1987).

This study examined the nature of clinical psychologists' religiousness and spirituality, their attitudes toward religiousness, their utilization of interventions of a religious nature in psychotherapy, and their training regarding religious and spiritual issues. As used in this study, *religiousness* is defined as adherence to the beliefs and practices of an organized church or religious institution, and *spirituality* is defined as those more personal practices of a religious nature which may or may not emanate from a particular religious institution.

Method

Subjects

A sample of 1,000 clinical psychologists was randomly selected from the 1987 membership, of the American Psychological Association (APA), Division 12, Division of Clinical Psychology. Four hundred nine surveys were completed and returned; this represents a 41% return rate. The respondents were 107 females (26%), 299 males (73%), and 3 no response (1%). Their average age was 48 years with a range from 29 to 88 years. Ninety-six percent possessed doctoral degrees of which 93% were granted by APA-approved psychology training programs. The theoretical orientations of the subjects, as reported on a forced-choice item, were psychoanalytic—135 subjects (33%); cognitive—121 subjects (30%); learning theory—68 subjects (17%); humanistic—50 subjects (12%); and eclectic—27 subjects who gave multiple responses (7%). There were 8 subjects who gave no answer (2%).

Materials

A survey method was utilized in this research. The instrument consisted of a 65-item questionnaire which included (1) demographics; (2) an ideology orientation scale adapted from Lehman (1974) which measured degrees of belief in a personal God; (3) External, Internal, and Quest scales which measured dimensions of religiousness (Batson and Ventis 1982); (4) items which measured attitudes towards religion and psychology and clinical training experiences; (5) a scale which assessed attitudes and practices regarding specific counseling interventions; and (6) a case study which investigated clinician bias with respect to the religious client.

Procedure

The sample clinical psychologists were mailed invitations to participate in the study, the research instrument, a nonparticipant response form, and a stamped, addressed return envelope. A second follow-up mailing and non-participant bias check were completed to insure the representativeness of the findings. We received 409 completed questionnaires and 116 non-participant forms. Five research packets were returned, 3 with no forwarding address, 1 indicating the subject was disabled, and 1 indicating the subject was recently deceased.

In an attempt to assess the representativeness of the findings, we asked those subjects choosing not to complete the questionnaire to answer a six-item nonparticipant survey. The subjects were 74% male and 26% female in the participant group and 75% and 25% respectively in the nonparticipant group; a chi-square analysis did not indicate a significant difference between the subjects with respect to sex. No significant difference was found between the participant and nonparticipant groups with respect to attitudes regarding religion's or spirituality's being within the scope of psychology. The groups differed, however, in the degree to which they declared spirituality as relevant in their personal lives, x^2 (2, $N = 525$) = 9.01, $p < .05$; spirituality as relevant in their professional lives, x^2 (2, $N = 525$) = 6.90, $p < .05$; and involvement in organized religion, x^2 (4, $N = 525$) = 20.266, $p < .001$. It may be construed from these comparative data that the findings of this survey skew towards a positive bias in regards to personal religiousness and spirituality and may over-estimate the degree to which psychologists, in general, involve themselves with religious or spiritual issues within their professional practice of psychology. These findings, as might be hypothesized, suggest that those with a sensitivity towards religious and spiritual concerns were more apt to choose to participate in the study and those without were less inclined to complete the questionnaire.

Results

Ideology

The subjects were asked to select a brief orientation which most nearly reflected their own from six ideological positions that ranged from the position that notions of the position of God or the transcendent are illusions to belief in a personal God. These data, represented in table 21.1, may be summarized into the following framework: 163 (40%) endorsed an orientation that affirms belief in a personal, transcendent God; 123 (30%), an orientation that affirms a transcendent dimension in all nature; 106 (26%), the position that all ideologies are illusion although they are meaningful; and 8 (2%), the position that all ideologies are illusion and are irrelevant to the real world.

The subjects, in general, appeared to view religious beliefs and questioning as valuable. Two hundred seventeen subjects (53%) rated having

Table 21.1
Ideological Orientations

Ideological Statement	N	%
There is a personal God of transcendent existence and power whose purposes will ultimately be worked out in human history.	121	29.6
There is a transcendent aspect of human experience which some persons call God but who is not imminently involved in the events of the world and human history.	42	10.3
There is a transcendent or divine dimension found in all manifestations of nature.	85	20.8
The notions of God or the transcendent are illusory products of human imagination; however, they are meaningful aspects of human existence.	106	25.9
The notions of God or the transcendent are illusory products of human imagination; therefore, they are irrelevant to the real world.	8	2.0
No Response	9	2.2

religious beliefs as desirable for people in general; 57 subjects (14%) rated this as undesirable; and 135 subjects (33%) expressed a neutral position. Two hundred sixty-six subjects (65%) reported spirituality as personally relevant. Of the subjects 59% (N = 240) disagreed with the statement, "Whether I turn out to be religious/spiritual or not doesn't make much difference to me." Two hundred twenty-two subjects (54%) reported that "my religious or spiritual development has emerged out of my sense of personal identity." These data suggest that psychologists, in general, value the religious or spiritual dimension.

Affiliation with Organized Religion

Of the subjects 97% (N = 397) reported to have been raised within a particular religion regardless of their degree of involvement. This is in contrast to current affiliation with organized religion which is 70.4% (N = 288) regardless of involvement and 40.8% (N = 167) if the criteria includes regular participation. The average attendance of a religious service is under two times per month; 48.6% (N = 199) reported no attendance. Twenty-nine subjects, or 7.1%, reported disdain and a negative reaction to religion. Table 21.2 presents the degree of affiliation in organized religion; table 21.3 presents the religious institutions in which the subjects were raised or currently identify with. These findings support past research which indicated that psychologists were relatively uninvolved in organized religion (Ragan, Malony, and Beit-Hallahmi 1980).

Fewer than one in five subjects (N = 72, 18%) agreed that organized religion was the primary source of their spirituality. The majority of the subjects (N = 207; 51%) characterized their spiritual beliefs and practices as an "alternative spiritual path which is not a part of an organized religion." For some the eschewing of organized religion may be in

Table 21.2

Affiliation and Involvement in Organized Religion

Degrees of Affiliation	N	%
Active participation, high level of involvement	74	18.1
Regular participation, some involvement	93	22.7
Identification with religion, very limited or no involvement	121	29.6
No identification, participation or involvement with religion	91	22.2
Disdain and negative reaction to religion	29	7.1
No Response	1	.2

response to negative experiences in the past or socialization away from institutional involvement. Twenty-five percent ($N = 101$) reported that they felt negative about past religious experiences.

Table 21.3

Religious Affiliations

Religion	Childhood N	Childhood %	Present N	Present %
Roman Catholic	90	22.0	57	13.9
Jewish	83	20.3	64	15.6
Methodist	48	11.7	23	5.6
Protestant	44	10.8	9	2.2
Episcopal	22	5.4	21	5.1
Baptist	20	4.9	9	2.2
Presbyterian	20	4.9	23	5.6
No Religion	12	2.9	122	29.8
Lutheran	11	2.7	8	2.0
Christian	7	1.7	4	1.0
Church of Latter-day Saints	7	1.7	2	.5
Mennonite	6	1.5	1	.2
Congregational	5	1.2	3	.7
Unitarian Universalist	4	1.0	18	4.4
United Church of Christ	4	1.0	3	.7
Other (1% or less of sample)	26	6.3	42	10.2

Dimensions of Religiousness

Batson and Ventis (1982) proposed a three-dimensional model of ways of being religious: the means, ends, and quest orientations. The means orientation, as measured by the External scale, refers to the degree to which an individual's external, social environment has influenced his or her personal religiousness. This perspective views religious fervor as shaped by social needs for affiliation and interpersonal relations. The ends orientation, as measured by the Internal scale, refers to the function of religion in providing clear answers to existential questions. The quest orientation, as measured by the Interactional scale, refers to the degree to which an individual's religiousness involves an open-ended dialogue with existential issues. Although based on the seminal work of Allport and Ross (1967), Batson and Ventis (1982) departed from specific intrinsic-extrinsic research in their effort to create a framework of conceptualizing religiousness as one dimension with dichotomous poles.

The dominant religious orientation of the subjects was assessed utilizing the External, Internal and Interactional scales as criteria; 90 subjects (22%) were not assessed because they left one or more items within one of the scales unanswered. Of the assessment group 45% were found to be within the quest dimension, 32% within the means, and 23% within the ends dimension. A chi-square analysis found that the sex of the subject did not significantly influence the form of religiousness. These data suggest that for a relatively large group of psychologists their form of religiousness is based upon an appreciation of religious questioning.

Clinical Practice and Training

Relevance of Religion

The data suggest that these psychologists, in general, view spiritual and religious issues to be relevant in their work as clinicians. Seventy-four percent ($N = 303$) disagree that "religious or spiritual issues are outside the scope of psychology" (15%, [$N = 63$] agree; 11% [$N = 43$] neutral). Sixty percent ($N = 245$) reported that clients often express their personal experiences in religious language, and approximately half of the therapists estimated that at least 1 in 6 of their client population presents issues which may involve religion or spirituality. Fifty-two percent ($N = 214$) reported spirituality as relevant in their professional life. Sixty-seven percent ($N = 273$) agreed with the statement, "Psychologists, in general, do not possess the knowledge or skills to assist individuals in their religious or spiritual development." Approximately one-third ($N = 141$) of the clinical psychologists expressed personal competence in counseling clients regarding religious issues and matters of spirituality.

Religious Interventions

Although it appears that these clinical psychologists, for the most part, view religious and spiritual issues as within the legitimate focus of clinical psychology, there is a divergence of opinion as to the importance of these concerns and the appropriate manner which they should be addressed. Sixty-four percent (*N* = 263) reported that the religious backgrounds of clients influence the course and outcome of psychotherapy. Eighty-seven percent (*N* = 356) believe that it is appropriate for a psychologist to know the religious backgrounds of their clients (7% [*N* = 28] disagree; 6% [*N* = 25] neutral). Fifty-nine percent (*N* = 242) support the use of religious language, metaphors, and concepts in psychotherapy (26% [*N* = 105] disagree; 15% [*N* = 62] neutral). Fifty-five percent (*N* = 225) agree that it is inappropriate for a psychologist to use religious scripture or texts while conducting psychotherapy (33% [*N* = 135] disagree; 12%, [*N* = 48] neutral). Sixty-eight percent (*N* = 278) agree that it is inappropriate for a psychologist to pray with a client (19% [*N* = 79] disagree; 13% [*N* = 52] neutral). These data suggest that as the counseling interventions become more explicitly religious and participatory in nature the attitudes of the clinicians become less favorable. The subjects were asked in addition to expressing their attitudes to identify the behaviors which they have performed in conducting psychotherapy.

These clinicians' behaviors paralleled their attitudes (see table 21.4). As the interventions became more explicitly religious in nature (e.g., praying with a client), the frequency of the behavior decreased. The data suggests that the majority of the subjects seems cognizant of the religiousness of their clients and utilize religious language and concepts. The data may suggest that although psychologists might possess

Table 21.4

**Therapist Interventions of a
Religious Nature in Psychotherapy**

Behavior	Performed		Not Performed	
	N	%	N	%
Know clients' religious backgrounds	372	91	37	9
Pray with a client	30	7	379	93
Pray privately for a client	98	24	311	76
Use religious language or concepts	235	57	174	43
Use or recommend religious or spiritual books	129	32	280	68
Recommend participation in religion	147	36	262	64

opinions regarding their clients' religiousness or share in the belief orientation, they tend to not participate or actively seek to influence their clients' lives in this regard. Seventy-three percent ($N = 299$) disagreed that it would be appropriate for a psychologist to recommend to a client that he or she leave a religion if the psychologist assessed it to be hindrance to the client's psychological growth. Thirty-six percent ($N = 147$) have recommended participation in a religion in the course of psychotherapy; 64% ($N = 262$) have not.

Attitudes and behaviors regarding interventions of a religious nature are primarily influenced by the clinician's personal view of religion and spirituality rather than by their theoretical orientation in psychology. The subject's personal experience of religion significantly correlated with their attitudes and behaviors regarding interventions of a religious nature. The data reflected a positive correlation between affiliation and participating in organized religion and the performance of the aforementioned interventions ($r = .27$). The more negatively the subjects viewed religious experiences in their past, the less likely they were of utilizing interventions of a religious nature ($r = .16$). The type of religiousness also influenced the therapist's view of their competence to provide counseling regarding these religious and spiritual issues. Therapists whose predominant religiousness was assessed as ends orientation expressed the highest degree of competence in knowledge and skills $F (2, 398) = 8.39, p < .001$.

Attitudes Toward Religious Clients

An additional aim of this study was to investigate the presence or absence of bias towards clients holding a religious perspective. A case study was presented to the subjects in which the variable of religious participation was manipulated. Fifty percent of the sample received the "religious" client (RC) case study and 50% the "nonreligious client" (NRC) case study. The nonreligious client was not presented as anti-religious; rather, religiosity was not mentioned. All other details in the cases were identical (see Appendix A). The subjects were asked to assess the likelihood that the client would make substantial progress in psychotherapy and to estimate the number of therapy sessions that would be required for the client to make substantial progress. There was no significant difference in the assessment of substantial progress between the RC and the NRC cases for the sample as a whole and within the psychoanalytic, learning theory, humanistic, cognitive, and eclectic subgroups. Although differences were found between the estimates of the sessions required for substantial progress for the RC and NRC cases, when the data were analyzed controlling for the effect of the therapists' personal orientations towards religion, no significant difference was found. A positive correlation was found, however, between the psychologist's attitudes toward religious concerns and their estimate of likelihood for progress in psychotherapy for both the RC and NRC cases $(r = .14)$.

Education and Training

The findings of this study suggest that the majority of the subjects view religious and spiritual issues as relevant in their practice of clinical psychology and to varying degrees utilize interventions of a religious nature. It was important, therefore, to assess the educational and training opportunities which prepare psychologists to deal with these issues. Five percent ($N = 20$) reported that religious and spiritual issues were presented in their training; 12% [$N = 48$], sometimes; 45% [$N = 185$] rarely and 38% [$N =156$] never. Fifty percent ($N = 204$) expressed satisfaction with their training, and 35% ($N = 143$) did not. It should be noted that this should not be taken as a measure of the quality of or an assessment of preparation to deal professionally with religious or spiritual issues. To illustrate, those who view religious and spiritual issues as irrelevant to clinical psychology rate their satisfaction highly in that no training in these area occurred. This was intended to provide a global measure of overall satisfaction with clinical training as it has existed and was not intended to reflect a measure of its quality with respect to these issues.

Other educational experiences were investigated. Approximately 10% of the subjects had some degree of theological training; 10% were current members of APA Division 36, Psychologists Interested in Religious Issues. The degree of background in the area of psychology and religion was also assessed by asking the subjects to note which, if any, of three seminal texts in the field (as selected by the 1987 executive committee of APA Division 36) and one popular text they had read. One hundred fifty-five, or 38%, of the subjects had read William James's *Varieties of Religious Experience;* 79, or 19%, Gordon Allport's *The Individual and His Religion;* 14, or 3%, Paul Pruyser's *A Dynamic Psychology of Religion;* and 136, or 33%, the popular text M. Scott Peck's *The Road Less Traveled.* Fifty-six percent ($N = 228$) had read at least one of the above mentioned books. These data suggest that psychologists, in general, receive limited education and training in the area psychology and religion.

Of the subjects 54% rated the psychology of religion as desirable in the education of a clinical psychologist; 29% ($N = 118$) rated this as undesirable; and 17% ($N = 68$) were neutral. Sixty-two percent ($N = 253$) indicated that clinical supervision and training in dealing with religious and spiritual issues with clients were desirable; 24% ($N = 97$) rated these as undesirable; and 14% ($N = 59$) were neutral.

Discussion

The analysis of respondent bias indicated that the findings as projected to the population of clinical psychologists skew towards a greater affinity and receptivity to religious and spiritual issues than actually exists. The conclusions of this study should, therefore, be read with that acknowledgment and should be applied conservatively.

These psychologists appear to value the role religious and spiritual issues serve in human existence. The majority holds religious beliefs and affiliate to some degree with organized religion. Fewer than one in five, however, declare organized religion to be their primary source of spirituality. Approximately one-fourth report negative feelings regarding religious experiences in their past.

Psychologists' personal orientations toward religiousness and spirituality were the primary determinants of their clinical approach to these issues in professional practice. Personal attitudes as contrasted with clinical training appear to shape the clinician's therapeutic intervention with clients. These results replicate, in part, the findings of Hillowe (1985), which point to a personal bias that may affect the therapeutic course and outcome with religious clients.

Although the majority asserted that psychologists possessed the knowledge and skills to assist clients with respect to religion and spirituality, about one-third of the subjects expressed personal competence in doing so. This is perhaps a favorable finding for the profession—that the majority do not express such competence—in light of the limited education and clinical training in psychology and religion which the subjects reported. Education and training within the area of psychology and religion appear to be very limited; 85% reported the frequency of discussion of these topics to be rare or never.

This study had as its intent an examination of psychologists' religious and spiritual orientations and their practice of psychotherapy. The findings of this national study of clinical psychologists were, in general, similar to the result of previous studies of California and Wyoming psychologists (Shafranske and Gorsuch 1985; Shafranske and Malony 1985; Elkins and Shafranske 1987). This study taken within the context of previous data suggests that clinical psychologists appreciate religious and spiritual concerns, view religious and spiritual issues as relevant to clinical practice, utilize interventions of a religious nature to varying degrees, and receive limited training with respect to religious and spiritual issues. The findings that the majority of clinicians view clients as presenting issues which may involve religion or spirituality, the evidence that clinical interventions are based primarily upon personal conviction rather than professional training experiences, and the limited training that clinicians reportedly receive point to the need for the profession to reflect upon its fundamental attitudes toward religion and spirituality. In conclusion, these preliminary findings suggest that religious and spiritual orientation affects to some extent clinical psychologists' attitudes and their therapeutic interventions which may impact the process and outcome of psychotherapy.

References

Allport, G. W. 1957. *The individual and his religion: A psychological interpretation*. New York: Macmillan.

Allport, G. W., and J. M. Ross. 1967. Personal religious orientation and prejudice. *Journal of Personality and Social Psychology* 5: 432–43.

Batson, C. D., and W. L. Ventis. 1980. *The religious experience: A social-psychological perspective*. New York: Oxford Univ. Press.

Elkins, D. N., and E. P. Shafranske. 1987. Attitudes toward religion, spirituality, and psychotherapy: A comparison of California and Wyoming psychologists. Paper presented at the annual meeting of the California State Psychological Association, February, Coronado, Calif.

Feifel, H. 1958. Introduction to the symposium on the relationship between religion and mental health. *American Psychologist* 13: 565–66.

Hall, G. S. 1904. *Adolescence*. New York: Appleton.

Hillowe, B. V. 1985. The effect of religiosity of the therapist and patient on clinical judgment. Ph.D. diss., Institute for Advanced Studies, Adelphi University, Garden City, N.Y.

James, W. 1902. *The varieties of religious experience: A study in human nature*. New York: Longmans.

Lehman, E. H. 1974. Academic discipline and faculty religiosity. *Journal for the Scientific Study of Religion* 13: 205–20.

Lovinger, R. J. 1984. *Working with religious issues in therapy*. New York: Aronson.

Quackenbos, S., G. Privette, and B. Klentz. 1986. Psychotherapy and religion: Rapprochement or antithesis? *Journal of Counseling and Development* 65: 82–85.

Ragan, C. P., H. N. Malony, and B. Beit-Hallahmi. 1980. Psychologists and religion: Professional factors and personal belief. *Review of Religious Research* 21: 208–17.

Shafranske, E. P., and R. L. Gorsuch. 1985. Factors associated with the perception of spirituality in psychotherapy. *Journal of Transpersonal Psychology* 16: 231–41.

Shafranske, E. P., and H. N. Malony. 1985. California psychologists' religious and spiritual orientations and their practice of psychotherapy. Paper presented at the annual meeting of the American Psychological Association, August, Los Angeles.

Spero, M. H., ed. 1985. *Psychotherapy of the religious patient.* Springfield, Ill.: C. Thomas.

Worthington, E. L., Jr. 1986. Religious counseling: A review of published empirical research. *Journal of Counseling and Development* 64: 421–31.

"Religious" and "Nonreligious" Clients
Case Studies

Mary is a 26-year-old doctoral candidate in mathematics. Her presenting complaint is that she is having difficulty reading, studying, and concentrating because she has become increasingly preoccupied with thoughts that she cannot dispel. She now spends hours each night reviewing the day's events and endlessly tries to correct in her mind any mistakes that she might have made. She runs over every event, asking herself if she had behaved properly or said the right thing. It is not unusual for her to look at the clock after such a period of rumination and find, to her surprise, that 2 or 3 hours had elapsed.

Mary is single, has never had a steady boyfriend, and accepts dates rarely, anticipating that men will find fault with her and drop her. She has few friends and describes herself as a child being a fearful, quiet girl. She has always been an A student and is recognized as being gifted in mathematics. Her parents she describes as "doting" on her and as having high expectations of her. Mary says that she has always felt a sense of trust and security that comes from a belief in her intellectual worth and academic accomplishments, . . .

Religious Client

from a belief in God, and from a feeling that things happen according to God's plan. Her few social contacts are other members of the religious congregation to which she belongs. Her two "good friends," whom she sees occasionally, are members with her of a Bible study group . . .

561

Nonreligious Client

and from a feeling that "things happen for the best." Her few social contacts are with the other members of the mathematics department. Her two "good friends," whom she sees occasionally, are members with her of the university's Mathematics Club . . .

She avoids other social contacts because she feels that she has "nothing to offer" and would be rejected anyway.

The Dialectic
of Subjective Historicity and Teleology:
Reflections on Depth Psychology
and Religion

Consciousness, Dostoyevsky declared, was the worst misfortune to befall humankind (1960, 50). For the unique nature of human consciousness compels *Homo sapiens*, unlike other earthly beasts, to consider the fact of their being in the world and to assert personal meaning within the broad horizon of human experience. Mythology, literature, music, and art from throughout antiquity, artifacts both profound and simple, bespeak the universal attempt to assert a sense of personal identity within the cosmos. Among the *tasks of existence*, the provision of a meaningful context through which to live out existence stands out as a vexing challenge which is uniquely human. The endeavor to discover the personal within the vastness leads to doubt and faith, despair and integrity. Dostoyevsky's disdain is made intelligible in light of the burden consciousness places upon the individual: to find an ontological home.

It is my view that depth psychology and religion necessarily intersect on this ontological pilgrimage. As complementary disciplines, each offers an essential contribution to the existential task of creating meaning. Lived experience and faith become intertwined as personal identity is forged into a sense of self. Psychology attempts to discern meaning within the history of the subjective experience of the individual. Religion offers a teleological perspective, a beacon which articulates a sense of perspective and direction. It is my thesis that meaning emerges out of the meeting of individual historicity and teleology. This paper presents an overview of the dialectic of subjective historicity and teleology and posits implications of such a perspective for the clinical psychologist.

563

Historicity and the Process of Remembering

The apprehension of meaning appears within an ever-evolving historical context. Through the process of remembering the person reflects upon his or her life experience and grasps a sense of meaning out of the many strands of lived experience. Psychotherapy, as the principal therapeutic and research application of depth psychology, was founded upon the appreciation of the constituent role of remembering in the formation of personal identity.

Meaning, as created in the moment of remembering, is rooted in an individual's historicity, that being, the authentic telling of the experience of being in the world. By this I wish to convey that an individual's history is neither a static compendium nor a mere collection of events. Rather, it is a psychodynamic gestalt of the subjective meanings created by the individual. Borrowing from the contributions of Spence (1982), I posit that the person's remembering of history is always a narrative truth, a construction of history, rather than a simple recounting of what happened or historical truth. The distinction between subjective and objective history is rendered moot in the appreciation that personal history is a hermeneutic enterprise.

History, as an interpretation of life experience, is constructed by the person through conscious and unconscious processes. In keeping with this view, I prefer to use the term *subjective historicity* to emphasize the dynamic nature of our remembering of the past and to distinguish this process from the solely biographical, conscious events that are commonly described as a person's history. The life of the individual is more than the sum of life events; an obituary can never do justice to the subjective historicity of a person.

The remembering and articulation of subjective historicity reveals meaningful aspects of the person's lived experience. The collaboration of subjective historicity and teleology forms a dialectic, a dynamic interchange of perspectives. This dialectic shapes the aperture through which historical events are apprehended and become weaved into the ever-evolving tapestry of subjective historicity. Through an individual's conscious, preconscious, and unconscious remembering, the subjective history of the individual unfolds. Further, such remembering, which exists within the context of teleology, constitutes the ontological bedrock upon which existence is lived.

On Remembering

I intend *remembering* to serve as the referent of both conscious and conscient processes. Reflection and the articulation of meaning may be viewed as the conscious constituents within the topography of the experience of remembering. The inner organization of remembering, which prompts the appearance of memory and association, lies shrouded within preconscious and unconscious domains. Loewald (1978) refers to such preconscious forms of mentation as conscient processes.[1]

Remembering is suggested to be a class of phenomena which incorporate both conscious and conscient aspects toward the aim of disclosing the subjective historicity of a person. Remembering plays an essential role in the formation of meaning as presented in the thesis of this paper. The subjective historicity of the individual in consort with consciously held beliefs and a conscient sense of teleology evoke a sense of personal meaning. Our discussion of remembering appropriately commences with what is conscious.

Conscious Processes

Conscious remembering, or what could be called reflecting, brings to mind experiences that have contributed to the life of the individual. Such remembering goes beyond the chronicling of life events. Reflection attempts to address history within a broadened context. For in such recollection life experience is assimilated and accommodated into a more comprehensive picture. This can be readily observed within clinical work. A memory which the patient presents is ripe with significance which goes beyond the simple description of a past event.[2] This offering to the therapeutic enterprise articulates the individual's subjective experience of past events and relationships, of the present relationship with the therapist, and of the possibilities anticipated in the future. Such remembering, of course, is not limited to the consultation room. It is discerned in any process of remembering in which historical events are revealed within a personal, subjective context.

Such contextualization of experience enlarges the event to include meanings beyond the moment. Seemingly isolated experiences become wed to the past and to the future. Implicit and explicit belief systems provide the basic models in which the meaning of experience is apprehended. Explicit belief systems are those patterns of perception and thought which articulate assumptions and attributions about the nature of existence. Shared belief systems form the basis of philosophical and religious thought and establish institutions which define the culture in which individual identity takes root.

1. I acknowledge the tautology that is inherent in positing the involvement of the unconscious in remembering; the proof for its existence lies in its very inaccessibility. In my view, however, proof abounds of such a region or mode of mental functioning as evidenced in dreams and in the vicissitudes of everyday life.

2. Modell (1990), in discussing Freud's concept of *Nachträglichkeit*, suggests that remembering is best understood as a dynamic process in which a "retranscription" of memory occurs. In this view, the context of frame contributes to the formation of memory.

Conscient Processes

Of particular interest for depth psychology, and the primary focus of this paper, is the role of implicit belief systems in the creation of personal meaning. The existence of such implicit or unconscious systems may be intuited in the "simple" act of remembering. Consider the following questions: Is our remembering haphazard and random? Or does our remembering present a coherent narrative of the self? It is my view that it is the latter. In the process and contained within the content of remembering lies the enduring appreciation of the experience of the self. Prior to conscious mentation experience is apprehended and organized. This process serves as a precursor to conscious articulation. Remembering, as one form of free association, is in fact not free but rather is the product of such preconscious mentation, for memory, in the service of the formation of self-identity, involves a delimiting selection of life experience. What is remembered, collected out of a seemingly infinite source of experience, discloses meaning in the appearance of the specific memory. The significance of the memory lies in both the content of the memory and in the underlying process which freely located it within the subjective historicity of the individual. It is my view, and, is in keeping within the psychoanalytic tradition, that the content of the memory derives its relevance from the dynamic production of the memory at that specific moment. The noetic quality emerges from those conscient processes which intuit the meaning of the memory and imbue its relevance in the act of remembering. By this I intend to introduce the preconscious and unconscious determinants in the act of remembering and to hypothesize a critical bridge between conscious and conscient processes.

Remembering is a process through which the subjective historicity of the individual is revealed vis-à-vis the unique selection of life experience for the content of remembering. The production of a memory expresses in symbols the nascent sense of meaning which coalesces within the complexity of unconscious. The process of remembering serves to illuminate the dimly shrouded sense of self which exists meta-psychologically beneath the conscious articulations of the meaning of the self.

In remembering, discrete moments of experience become yoked for a common purpose: the elucidation of personal meaning. Seemingly disparate experiences in fact do become associated in a meaningful manner through their revelation in dreams, associations, and memories. Through such mentations extending upward in topography to conscious remembering, the person meets the nascent self in evolution. Such phenomena freely appear within consciousness as harbingers of meaning (if we have the eyes to see and the ears to listen). As if to weave a coherent pattern out of the threads of experience, the conscient processes seem to present the subjective historicity to the individual.

This presentation of subjective historicity contains the constituents of the individual's fundamental sense of self.

This emergent, evolving sense of self lies beneath conscious experience within the domain of the conscient. The self which was born out of early experience within the "nursing couple" (Winnicott 1958) experiences and comes to apprehend an aesthetic of being. This aesthetic conveys a sense of value and identity to the child and anchors his or her own sense of meaning about existence. This aesthetic of being is communicated to the nascent self through the mother's handling and ministrations during infancy. As Erikson (1950) described, the child comes to apprehend the world with a sense of basic trust or mistrust. Drawing upon the work of Bollas (1987), I suggest that such an aesthetic of being becomes the salient feature of the conscient life of the individual and is the foundation upon which later life events are experienced and a sense of personal meaning is articulated.

I have proposed that meaning and personal identity are revealed through the elucidation of subjective historicity in the act of remembering. Depth psychology mirrors remembering as a valued activity of the psyche and promotes such activity in providing the unique context of psychotherapy. Psychotherapy not only provides a setting but also presents a technique for the exploration and confrontation of resistances and impediments to remembering.

Teleology and the Process of Faith

Personal meaning seen solely as a product of subjective historicity would render the future an illusion; the future would be encapsulated by the finitude of the past. Personal destiny would be limited to variations on the theme of repetition. If human consciousness were so limited, such would be human fate. Human consciousness, however, extends not only from the present into the past but also thrusts existence into the eternal. By eternal I refer to that which is beyond the past and the present, as the "counterpart to history and time" (Loewald 1978, 62). The sense of the future in personal history, I posit, is fantasized out of a sense of the eternal. It is in the appreciation of the eternal that the self can emerge out of the shadows of the past. This source of meaning is the teleological.

Teleology refers to that which one is called to become. It offers a vision of destiny which, while affirming personal freedom, proposes a comprehensive order to existence. Teleology is apprehended through an act of faith, for its verification is not derived so much out of the finite empirical experiences of the past, but rather is held by virtue of trust and commitment. Meissner wrote that "faith reaches beyond the illumination of reason into the darkness of paradox . . . [It is] the highest human passion—touching life at every point of our essential existence, transcending the calculations and illusions of worldly wisdom, grasping and immersing itself in the finitude of life (beyond withdrawal from the finite in resignation), triumphing over the dread that permeates man's existence" (1987, 91–92).

Teleology is inseparable from the act of faith. Through faith the individual extends the contextualizing of personal existence beyond subjective historicity, beyond what has been personally experienced, to the domain of the eternal, to the possibilities of human existence. Meaning is discovered not only in what has been but also in the becoming of existence.

Sources of Teleology

Our apprehension of teleology arises out of both conscious and conscient processes. Through reflection the individual considers the multitude of belief orientations that attempt to articulate a comprehensive order of the universe. Such an enterprise, although described here as a seemingly abstract, intellectual exercise, is nonetheless vital to the individual and provides the cornerstone for the foundation upon which existence is lived out. Culture provides the individual with a coherent set of beliefs and a supportive community which establishes a rudimentary sense of teleology. The child is initially provided with a foundation of beliefs which suggest the nature and possibilities for existence. Clearly religious institutions provide articulate systems of belief and community support to sustain and maintain the faith commitment of the individual. Through conscious reflection the person scrutinizes the tenets of faith in light of their subjective historicity. A teleological stance is adopted by the person by faith which serves as the integrating structure of life experience. As Meissner noted, "Faith comes to play a more or less central role in shaping the responses and initiatives that determine the course of human life" (1987, 117).

Teleology is also influenced by conscient processes. The individual may experience a mode of mentation, commonly referred to as "religious" or "mystical" experience, that transcends ordinary consciousness and contradicts usual conceptualizations of the world. Loewald suggests "that [such] 'intimations of eternity' bring us in touch with levels of our being, forms of experiencing and of reality that themselves may be deeply disturbing, anxiety provoking to the common-sense rationality of everyday life" (1978, 69). Within such moments our subjective historicity may be touched by a sense of the eternal. The import of such conscient experiences may lie in the very confrontation of the limits of our personal history juxtaposed with the eternal.

Personal meaning and identity becomes formed by an act of faith in which the subjective historicity of the individual becomes contextualized within the broadened context of eternity. This contextualization occurs through both the integration of a conscious belief-driven teleological system and preconscious intimations of the eternal.

Implications for Clinical Psychology

It has been proposed that meaning emerges out of the meeting of subjective historicity and teleology. Through conscious and conscient processes the self discloses an appreciation of both what has been and what can become. A dialectic exists in which the history of the subjective life of the person influences the breadth of the teleology and the teleology affects the ongoing subjective historicity of the individual. The depth psychologist participates with the patient in his or her creation of meaning in both acknowledging the truth of the patient's subjective historicity and in addressing the teleological dimension which includes religious orientation. The focus on the history of the subjective life of the patient is well established in clinical literature. The latter role of addressing the teleological has been less emphasized.

For the individual whose subjective historicity bears the scars of abuse and for whom trust has been violated, a sense of hopefulness, an inviting teleology of the possible, is rarely established. In fact, the teleology often does not possess the spirit of the eternal but rather is reduced to an impotent, lifeless teleology in which the future lies only in the shadows of the past. The therapist stands at the fulcrum of subjective historicity and teleology in acknowledging the truth of the past and in presenting the possibility of a revisioned teleology. The therapeutic relationship is the context through which the subjective historicity and the teleological meet, for within its bounds lies the struggle between conflicted repetitious phenomena and the possibility for the patient to experience hitherto new ways of perceiving and of being in the world. In transference the subjective historicity of the patient is not so much remembered as it is expressed within the therapeutic relationship. The teleological stance in resistance is thus limited to a repetition of the past. It is as if the patient only exists within the subjective historicity devoid of a teleology that bears any imprint of the eternal. Through respectful confrontation and exploration the therapeutic enterprise encourages resolution through a sensitive appreciation of historicity and the creation of more life-giving teleology. This relationship does not so much provide a corrective emotional experience as much as it provides a context for a revisioning of teleology through the lived experience of authentic, impassioned concern and respect for the subjective historicity of the patient. In addition to the focus on the subjective historicity of the patient the therapist may explore the religious belief systems which contribute to the teleological dimension of the patient's sense of meaning. It is within this context that ontological, religious themes become relevant for the progress of psychotherapy, for, as has been proposed, the teleological dimension contributes significantly to the individual's sense of meaning and shapes the ongoing formation of subjective historicity.

In conclusion, depth psychology and religion contribute to an understanding of the life of the self as it is revealed in subjective historicity and teleology. The clinician is enabled to assist the patient through the exploration of both conscious and conscient processes in the subjective historicity and teleology out of which personal meaning is expressed.

References

Bollas, C. 1987. *The shadow of the object.* New York: Columbia Univ. Press.

Dostoyevsky, F. 1960. *Notes from the underground.* In *Notes from the underground, Poor people, The friend of the family: Three novels,* trans. Constance Garnett, with general introduction by Ernest J. Simmons, 25–140. New York: Dell.

Erikson, E. 1950. *Childhood and society.* New York: Norton.

Loewald, H. 1978. *Psychoanalysis and the history of the individual.* New Haven: Yale Univ. Press.

Meissner, W. 1987. *Life and faith.* Washington, D.C.: Georgetown Univ. Press.

Modell, A. H. 1990. *Other times, other realities.* Cambridge: Harvard Univ. Press.

Spence, D. 1982. *Narrative truth and historical truth: Meaning and interpretation in psychoanalysis.* New York: Norton.

Winnicott, D. W. 1958. Paediatrics and psychiatry. In *Collected papers. Through paediatrics to psychoanalysis,* 157–73. London: Tavistock.

22

Allen E. Bergin

Allen E. Bergin is professor of psychology and director of a program in clinical psychology at Brigham Young University in Provo, Utah. Previously, he was director of the Values Institute, a research program directed toward the study of the development of values in human beings. For 11 years, before going to Brigham Young, Dr. Bergin was professor of clinical psychology at Teachers College in New York City. He has lectured widely in the United States and overseas. He was a fellow in the Psychiatric Institute of the University of Wisconsin. He is listed in *American Men and Women of Science, Who's Who in the East,* and *Who's Who in the West.* His doctorate is from Stanford University.

Dr. Bergin is a diplomate in clinical psychology of the American Board of Professional Psychology and a fellow of both Division 12, Clinical Psychology, and Division 36, Psychologists Interested in Religious Issues, of the American Psychological Association. He has been president of the Society for Psychotherapy Research as well as of the Association of Mormon Counselors and Psychotherapists. Bergin is a manuscript reviewer for 12 journals, including *Psychotherapy: Theory, Research, and Practice, Journal of Abnormal Psychology, Journal of Consulting and Clinical Psychology,* and *Contemporary Psychology.*

In 1980, Dr. Bergin wrote the first of many articles on values in psychotherapy. Entitled "Psychotherapy and Religious Values," this essay in the *Journal of Consulting and Clinical Psychology* promoted a discussion of religious values that is ongoing in the professional literature. He has followed up this article with others such as "Religious and Humanistic Values: A Reply to Ellis and Walls," "Religiosity and Mental Health: A Critical Re-evaluation and Meta-analysis," "Values and Evaluation, Therapeutic Change," "Religious Values and Human Behavior," "The

571

Three Contributions of the Spiritual Perspective to Counseling," and "Religious Orientation of the Therapist."

With Sol Garfield, Bergin coedited the *Handbook of Psychotherapy and Behavior Change: An Empirical Analysis* (New York: Wiley, 1986), which has now gone into its third edition. This book, the standard for the profession, has been designated as a citation classic by the Institute for Scientific Information and has been listed among the 25 most frequently recommended books by departments of psychology. Bergin has coedited five other volumes pertaining to psychotherapy.

In "Proposed Values for Guiding and Evaluating Counseling and Psychotherapy," Bergin reports a survey of opinions of mental health professionals regarding the values that enhance mental health. He notes that there is a growing and wide consensus that it is important for the therapist to be explicit about his or her values. Values provide a frame of reference for helping others regulate their life-styles. Without question, clients should be encouraged to be self-determining. One way that therapists can foster this is by helping their clients make distinctions between what is universally true and what is only culturally acceptable.

In "Religious Life-Styles and Mental Health," Bergin and his colleagues report in-depth interviews with two groups of students who differed from each other in terms of whether their religious development had or had not been interrupted by periods of doubt or apostasy. While the mental health of those whose development was uninterrupted was greater, their religious development was less than that of students whose development had been interrupted. This study was part of a larger investigation of the relationship of life-styles to adjustment.

Proposed Values for Guiding and Evaluating Counseling and Psychotherapy

It is widely agreed that values influence every phase of psychotherapy, from theories of personality and pathology, the design of change methods, and the goals of treatment, to the assessment of outcomes (Bergin 1980b; Beutler 1979; Graham 1980; Rosenbaum 1982; Wallach and Wallach 1983). Values in this context are orienting beliefs about what is good for clients and how that good should be achieved. Value decisions affect both specific aims, such as symptom removal, and general aims, such as life-style changes. It is the thesis of this article that because values are necessarily embedded in the treatment process, they should be made explicit and should be openly used to guide and evaluate change.

There is currently, however, only a limited consensus about which values to endorse. Disagreements arise because of differences in theoretical orientation, personal philosophy, religion, and cultural, ethnic, or national background (Bergin 1983a; Strupp and Hadley 1977; Sue 1983). Although there is a trend in Western nations toward distinctly humanistic and naturalistic therapeutic philosophies consistent with the scientific secularism that dominates Western education, a strong countertrend exists within more theistic and conservative communities. Even secular society, however, is showing a strong trend to reconsider spiritual perspectives, as evidenced in part by renewed attention to various philosophies and religions (Bergin 1980b).

Given the great diversity of value positions within both the secular and spiritual orientations, there now exists a wide array of value themes that can and do influence the thinking of psychotherapists. This diversity has led many professionals to avow a belief in ethical relativism. Such a position, however, is fraught with logical inconsistencies (Bergin 1980a, 1980b, 1980c; Kitchener 1980a, 1980b). It is difficult to reconcile the notion that there are lawful behavioral consequences of one's actions. Although *cultural* relativism clearly exists (i.e., cultures differ in

From *Counseling and Values* 29, no. 2 (1985): 99–116; reprinted by permission of the publisher. Copyright 1985 by the American Association for Counseling and Development.

values), *ethical* relativism does not follow from this fact. The values of differing cultures are not equally healthy (Maslow 1971).

In an attempt to achieve some coherence in this domain, I synthesized a set of values rooted in Judeo-Christian traditions that I felt were related to mental health and social integration (Bergin 1980b). My intent was to clarify and make explicit my own views as well as values implicit in the writings of other professionals and to contrast them with some of the values common in the clinical literature.

My outline included such values as self-control; commitment to marriage, family life, and fidelity; forgiveness as an aid in psychological healing; acceptance of guilt, suffering, contrition, and restitution when one's behavior has harmed others; love and self-transcendence or self-sacrifice as opposed to a sole focus on self-actualization; and the importance of spiritual knowledge.

I also proposed testable hypotheses, such as:

1. In communities that provide the combination of a viable belief structure and a network of loving, emotional support there should be manifest lower than normal rates of emotional and social pathology and physical disease.
2. Those groups that endorse high standards of impulse control should have lower than average rates of alcoholism, drug addiction, divorce, emotional instability, and associated interpersonal difficulties.
3. A stable marriage and family life should constitute a psychologically and socially benevolent state. As the percentage of persons in a community who live in such circumstances increases, social pathologies should decrease and vice versa. (Bergin 1980b, 102–3)

In response to that article, I received about 1,000 requests for reprints, many of which included comments about the values listed. Although the remarks showed a strong divergence of opinion about the theistic and spiritual themes (Ellis 1980; Walls 1980), they also showed surprising support for many of the core values I proposed.

Excerpts from some of these positive responses—views rarely expressed in professional publications—show the importance of a viewpoint to be presented later that may otherwise seem inconsistent with professional opinion. They are represented by the following sample of extracts from letters, which are quoted with the permission of the writers:

Ellen Berscheid, professor, Department of Psychology, University of Minnesota:

I congratulate you for saying what I believe has needed to be said for a long time. . . . I very much hope that this paper will, in retrospect, be considered one of the most important to have been published in the area in the new decade.

Ted Lorei, Health Services Research and Development Service, Veterans Administration, Washington, D.C.:

I think this is a landmark article that says several things that many people must have been thinking for years. You have done us all a great service.

Lise Wallach, lecturer, Department of Psychology, Duke University:

. . . am extremely sympathetic with the hypotheses you describe.

Karl Menninger, The Menninger Foundation, Topeka, Kansas:

I commend you on your excellent article.

Richard Jessor, Institute of Behavioral Science, University of Colorado:

Although not in agreement with much of your position, I do appreciate your bringing it clearly before psychologists. And I do share your concern for making explicit the values that necessarily underlie and guide not only psychotherapy but psychological work as a whole. That religious values are or can be among those is difficult to dispute.

Dorothy Fahs Beck, director of Counselor Attitude Study and consultant on evaluation research, Family Service America:

I am also wondering whether you consider that maintenance of the obviously desirable value patterns that you outlined as necessarily dependent on a theistic orientation. . . . Would it perhaps be possible, using the findings of science on child development, family systems, and the like, to provide an alternate philosophic base that would still support the value positions you outlined?

Paul Vitz, professor, Department of Psychology, New York University:

I found it important, interesting, and quite heartening. I hope it receives wide circulation.

Hans Strupp, professor, Department of Psychology, Vanderbilt University:

On the whole, I am very much in agreement although we may differ on some aspects. . . . Major values in human relations are woven into various religious systems, and they seem to be universally true regardless of what a therapist's attitude toward a Supreme Being might be.

Robert Sears, professor, Department of Psychology, Stanford University:

I enjoyed your article thoroughly. With your memories of 20 years ago, unrefreshed by more recent contact with me, you will be surprised to know that I agreed heartily with most of what you said. That is, I agree that for the therapist it is important to have his values as explicit as possible and the patient's values should also be explicit. . . . In some places you seem to be talking theism versus atheism. In others, there is some implication of more specific "good and bad" principles. . . . In this connection, let me tell you a quick story. In the 1930s, no instructor in psychology could avoid being an amateur psychotherapist for university students. There were no psychiatrists, no counseling services. We all did it as just part of our university service. I suppose I spent as much as 5 or 6 hours a week doing what we would now call psychotherapy. To this day I remain proudest of my accomplishment in dealing with a young devout orthodox Jewish boy who was suffering severe conflicts about his religious role and the relation of his Jewish beliefs to some of the issues that he was having to face in classes (not mine). The satisfying outcome was that he returned to his orthodox views, without further conflict, and ultimately became a rabbi. . . . The other kinds of values seem more pertinent to me, even in research. Inescapably they enter into the ways in which questions are asked and the methods by which answers are sought. . . . I do believe that every psychological researcher should be familiar with his own value system.

Albert Bandura, professor, Department of Psychology, Stanford University:

Whether it be the role of religious values in the science and practice of psychology, humanism, radical behaviorism, or social learning theory, such ideas touch the lives of people in the field because certain proponents were willing to state them, whatever the reactions of others might be. It is through writings such as yours that religious values will receive greater consideration in psychotherapy.

Carl Rogers, Center for Studies of the Person, La Jolla, California:

I don't disagree as much as you might think. . . . I do believe there is some kind of a transcendent organizing influence in the universe which operates in man as well. I lean toward the notion that perhaps this force is a struggling force and that we are a part of the struggle to make the universe a better place to live in. . . . My present, very tentative, view is that perhaps there is an essential person which persists through time, or even through eternity . . . your value system is a little too narrow to suit me, but at least it is yours. . . . I had to smile the other day when talking to Mwalimu Amara. . . . He told me that when he gets to feeling depressed, he reads some of "the gospels by Rogers." When the people around laughed at his remark, he said, "Well, this guy has been writing religious stuff for many years, and it's about time that he admits it."

In addition to such comments, I was surprised by positive comments from several practicing psychoanalysts who I had assumed would look upon these matters from a more Freudian perspective.

In concluding this list of quotations, I refer to a comment by Gary Walls (1980), who published a critique of my paper on values. In a letter responding to my reply to his critique, he said:

Although the differences among us were clearly drawn, the corresponding overlap points to the possibility of fruitful discussion among different viewpoints. The contribution of this interchange I think is to dispel the notion that dogmatic opposition and stubborn, unreflective allegiance to a given point of view is a necessary stance in order to maintain ideologically pure and self-consistent ethical systems. An open system is not necessarily ethically relativistic or neutral, but acknowledges human fallibility. . . . Although I myself do not endorse theism, I feel comfortable that if its cause is furthered in a scholarly manner . . . it will prove to be a strong positive force (along with "Positive" humanism) in the advancement of ethically sound psychotherapy practice.

Like the others, he feels it is important to be specific about values, to endorse constructive values, and to study the results of adopting such values. This article is thus a response to the stimulus, provided by his and the other letters, to develop a more explicit therapeutic value orientation. What follows is merely a beginning, and it emphasizes points of agreement rather than disagreement. I feel it is important to temporarily set aside disputes about controversial values and their origins (Bergin 1983a)—which could lead to endless and unfruitful debates—and instead establish areas of agreement. We might thereby provide common reference points that will stimulate further development of therapeutically relevant values and enhance both theory and practice.

This brings me to the most difficult part of this article—outlining a set of values, concerning which I believe there is a reasonable consensus among counselors and psychotherapists, even though it has been hidden over the years by arguments that no common ground exists and that we can legitimately operate only on the unstable foundation of relativism.

I base this outline on my reading of the therapy and personality literature, on correspondence, on discussions at conferences with colleagues in North and South America and European countries, and on doctoral dissertation research I helped supervise (Billington 1983; Lilienfeld 1966; Vaughn 1971). The outline is my personal interpretation and synthesis from these sources. In addition, I compared my outline with Rokeach's (1973) 18 terminal and 18 instrumental values and with Shostrom's (1966) Personal Orientation Inventory values, resulting in further adjustment and integration.

I recognize, of course, that there may be high agreement on a value that may, in fact, lack validity. Nevertheless, it seems important to consider values espoused by a large proportion of professionals who systematically observe the behavior of many people.

It should also be pointed out that many important values are omitted from the discussion that follows. Values such as political freedom, equal opportunity, nondiscrimination, and freedom from poverty certainly influence mental health, but to discuss them would take us far beyond the focus of this article. Also omitted are numerous values about which there are continuing controversy and disagreement. Although these issues are worthy of continued exploration, such a debate could not be contained in one article.

Twenty-three value statements have been clustered under seven headings, representing my distillation of consensus values from the sources noted above. It is proposed that counselors and psychotherapists should collaborate with clients in working together to achieve the following goals which are hypothesized to enhance mental health:

I. Freedom, Responsibility, and Self-Regulation
   A. Freedom of choice via improving the person's range of alternatives and capacity to act well at choice points.
   B. Freedom from coercion, abuse, manipulation, and the inhibiting effects of symptoms.
   C. Personal independence and autonomy.
   D. Personal responsibility for one's actions and their effects on oneself and others.
   E. Self-control and discipline in order to achieve or live congruently with ideals, values, principles, or goals.
II. Love and Relationships
   A. The capacity to give and receive love and affection. This includes caring, trust, commitment, loyalty, nurturant support, and the ability to develop fulfilling emotional and physical intimacy.
   B. Effective interpersonal relationship skills, especially the capacity to resolve conflict.

    C. The ability to forgive others, even those who have inflicted pathologizing experiences on oneself.

    D. The ability to make restitution for negative consequences of one's influence and to forgive oneself for past mistakes.

    E. Commitment to family needs and growth.

    F. Fidelity and loyalty in marriage.

    G. Empathic sensitivity to the feelings of others and an ability to express one's feelings accurately and constructively.

    H. Effective participation in a large or small mutually supportive social network with a sense of community or group identification.

III. Identity

    A. The ability to prize one's own human dignity and self-worth as one deserving of esteem from others and oneself.

    B. The ability to be introspective and reflective in order to achieve deepened self-awareness, including sharing self-knowledge with others.

    C. Engagement in a continuing process of self-development or actualization of capacities.

IV. Truth

    A. The ability to be honest, authentic, and open.

    B. A rational view of the personal and interpersonal world, extending to a value on knowledge and truth.

V. Values

    A. A belief in some set of universal values.

    B. Establishment of an active, orienting set of goals derived from one's values.

VI. Symptom Management

    A. Ability to be flexible in order to cope with the vicissitudes of life.

    B. Ability to relieve distress and symptoms by means of coping strategies for managing reality stresses and for obtaining appropriate need satisfactions.

VII. Work

    A. Ability to work productively, achieve, and attain competencies.

Each of these values is stated as a positive declaration, indicating that endorsing and living according to the value is likely to enhance mental health. It is assumed, then, that assisting clients to recognize the value of such guiding constructs can aid positive change processes. This is likely to be especially relevant to counseling situations where psychopathology is not too extreme. Where pathology is severe, technical interventions that are not particularly value laden must be used to bring the client toward a more rational condition before values can be used effectively. Discussing values is a fairly cognitive process that assumes a client's capacity for self-management is relatively intact. Deep emotional conflicts or serious conditioned reactions, then, should be partially alleviated before focusing on issues of life-style and self-regulation.

Values and Life-Styles

Life-styles issues are central to this discussion. Values guide life-styles, and life-styles have mental health consequences, just as they have physical health consequences. This concept is analogous to the trend in behavioral medicine that has identified life-style variables as important correlates of medical symptoms (Matarazzo 1982). In biological disorders, it has become more evident that broad spectrum interventions may be as efficacious as single, precise interventions. For instance, nutritional and exercise habits, use of drugs, alcohol, nicotine, and caffeine, the quality of air and water, all have wide-ranging effects and correlate with a wide variety of disorders. As these broad life-style matters are brought into appropriate regulation, many types of problems are prevented or disappear without specific intervention.

Similarly, many values imply a frame of reference for guiding behavior and regulating life-style so as to prevent or ameliorate psychopathologies and thus avoid the need for an endless array of precise technical interventions. Specific interventions are, of course, essential in many instances, but prevention and amelioration through modified life-style is certainly preferable.

Implications for Practice and Research

A variety of values have been listed, and their relevance has been briefly explained. It is important to examine the question of how adopting and applying them might influence practice and research. The first issue in that application is how to use values without infringing on the client's self-determination.

Therapist Values and Client Self-Determination

There is a difference of opinion about whether therapists should influence client values. No matter how much therapists may agree on what behaviors are mentally healthy, many believe it is unethical to influence clients toward specific values. This argument is based upon a traditional view, first advanced by Freud, that therapeutic treatment is a technical matter that should be kept value-free. Good technique frees clients from symptoms that inhibit their agentive capacities, permitting them to make rational life decisions on their own. The therapist makes no judgment about these life decisions but is content to provide competent professional service. This view emphasizes relieving distress as its highest value and regards moral choices as irrelevant, much as a physician might relieve a bank robber's pain from a gunshot wound without considering the morality of the robber's life-style.

Although this position regarding psychotherapy was virtually demolished by Perry London 20 years ago (1964) and has been eroded further by numerous leading writers such as Erich Fromm, Albert Ellis, Carl Rogers, and others (Bergin 1980c; Kitchener 1980a), it still has merit because great care must be taken to avoid negative consequences when overtly dealing with values in therapy sessions.

Clients who are in pain become easily dependent on their therapists and are vulnerable to their influence and authority (Frank 1973). This position can easily be abused by therapists who may take advantage of clients for the purpose of promoting their personal value agendas. Such therapist behavior should be shunned because a client's mental health cannot be advanced by giving up autonomy. It is a very delicate matter to preserve the client's autonomy while at the same time dealing with the inevitable value issues that arise during the change process. That is probably why the most common value found in the therapeutic literature concerns enhancing the client's freedom.

At the same time, therapists who emphasize freedom to the exclusion of the other values listed in the outline because they wish to keep the treatment setting value-free are taking an extreme position that is difficult to defend. Indeed, empirical studies show that therapists do not remain value-free in their verbal behavior even when they intend to do so (cf. Bergin 1980b).

In the process of treating clinical disorders, therapists inevitably have to make important choices about how to best optimize a client's functioning. It is at these decision points that therapists and clients must collaborate in arriving at goals that will facilitate change. The professional values that underlie such choices are often implicit because they are buried in theories and technical jargon. Also, we are usually not trained to elicit and help clarify client values.

It is vital that we be more explicit about values because we use them, however unconsciously, as a means of therapeutic change. Although we may have been hesitant about this for fear of becoming manipulators of morals, being explicit actually protects clients. The more subtle our values, the more likely we are to be hidden persuaders. The more open we are about our views, the more choice clients will have in electing to be influenced or not be influenced.

Even trying to avoid a particular value choice by being noncommittal amounts to taking a value position. Our silence, for example, may be seen as consent for a particular line of action. Behavior therapy and other active therapies have made it clearer than ever before that as therapeutic agents we try to influence people in certain directions that we value and that we believe will benefit the client or others involved (Begelman 1975).

Although we have to be patient while people struggle with their choices and may have to watch them make bad decisions without interference, it is irresponsible to fail to inform them of our educated opinions about the alternatives. Like good teachers or parents, we should at times instruct carefully. We need to be honest and open about our views, collaborate with the client in setting goals that fit his or her needs, and then step aside and allow the person to exercise autonomy and face consequences. Our expertise, therefore, should help shape the goals of treatment according to our best judgment of how the disorder can most effectively be modified and how the change can best be maintained. To do less than this is to pretend we do not care about the outcome or to expend effort on behalf of goals we do not value, which is self-defeating.

Enhancing Freedom

Clients would not be clients if they had not already lost a measure of autonomy. Enhancing their capacity for agentive choice and self-regulation is therefore a major, if not *the* major, goal of professional assistance. Clients are, however, frequently like children in that their disturbances make them vulnerable and dependent on the benevolent care of a stronger person. A client is unlikely to become fully functioning without passing through a critical period of reliance on the therapist's support and guidance. This dependency must, of course, be temporary, and it must be used in the service of ultimate independence. It is comparable to the psychoanalytic concept of "regression in the service of the ego," a notion supported by reports showing that a child cannot become a fully functioning, autonomous adult without first passing through a period of deep trust and dependence on a nurturant figure (Erikson 1963).

Regardless of what kind of therapy is employed and whether it is acknowledged, this dependency process occurs. It is a natural, socially pervasive process that therapists should not fear. During this phase two things are happening: symptoms are being alleviated and new insights or cognitive controls are taking over the person's attitudes, values, and life-style. These are inevitable processes that cannot be stemmed by the therapist's retreating into "techniques" or a laissez-faire relativism. They are normal processes to be used wisely and carefully. No better comparison can be made than to that of good parenting: trust is established; guided growth is stimulated; values are conveyed in a gentle, loving, and respectful way; the person being influenced becomes stronger, more assertive, and independent; the person learns ways of clarifying and testing value and life-style choices; the influencer decreases dependency nurturance and external advice, and continues to be available with such resources, while the person experiments with new behaviors and ideas until becoming a mature and autonomous identity. This process in a client-therapist relationship makes symptomatic changes enduring and allows for future growth, adaptation, and change.

The concept being offered as the "freedom value," then, is that therapy may be construed as a method of enhancing a persons' freedom or range of alternatives at a choice point. We achieve this in part by eliminating symptoms and in part by assisting with value-based cognitive reconstructions.

If we endorse a value such as enhancing freedom of choice, train therapists in such thinking, and help clients understand that we are aiming at their general capacity to choose and to act on behalf of those choices, the psychotherapy situation is put in a very broad context. We no longer are focusing solely on the simple technology of symptom relief, but we are promoting a greater good—the liberation of a personality from inhibiting and distressing effects and the formation of new internal guidance mechanisms.

The therapist's temporary ascendancy is thus in the service of the client's becoming an autonomous, fully functioning person. The client then becomes able to consider a range of alternatives for optimal fulfillment at any choice point. Although this is not a new idea (cf. Rogers 1961), construing it this way broadens our perspective and puts the psychotherapy situation in the context of an effort to activate people's agentive capacities to an optimal level.

Love, Relationships, and Fidelity

This is perhaps one of the most important dimensions in all of psychology. We can see its influence particularly in child rearing and in psychotherapy. As counselors and therapists, we often see the destructive effects of the absence of love and the harmful influence of isolation, deprivation, humiliation, rejection, punishment, and abuse. Indeed, parents' incapacity to love may be the single most pervasive pathologizing factor in human psychology. If we can consider the source of depressions, anxieties, phobias, obsessions, family conflict, schizoid withdrawal, and sexual dysfunctions, we easily conclude that hateful, punitive actions, even momentary or sporadic, can profoundly affect the developing person.

We are also well aware of the importance of a caring, nurturing quality in our behavior as psychotherapists which, as Carl Rogers has so well outlined, can be a powerful therapeutic antidote for such experiences (1957). It is caring about our clients that sets the stage for reforming personality, restoring ego strength, and increasing capacity to function interpersonally. Of equal importance is the power of teaching, training, and otherwise assisting the client in learning to become a loving person despite having been a victim of early abusive experiences.

Just how to implement the value of love in a therapeutic situation, however, is not always easy. In many marital conflict situations, for example, love brought the couple together, but conflicts occur that erode that love. The question becomes how to reintroduce love to help resolve the conflicts. We might consider that love demands a certain amount of self-sacrifice and thus might teach a client how to extend love to a spouse in the face of hostility, pettiness, or disloyalty (Erikson 1963). Encouraging a client to exercise such self-control, denying his or her own needs for a time, may prove to be powerfully therapeutic in the long run. The eventual quality of the couple's capacity to love might increase dramatically if self-sacrifice is effective in conveying to the partner a sense of deep loyalty and commitment, despite the partner's weaknesses and difficulties.

Discussion of this kind of commitment arose in relation to the question of marital fidelity at the International Conference on Psychotherapy in Bogota, Colombia, where portions of this article were delivered. At a luncheon following my presentation, in which I argued that there were moral absolutes, Sol Garfield was asked by a participant whether he believed there are absolutes. He said he believed in "moderation in all things," with the exception of fidelity, which he said he considered absolute. Philip Kendall, at the time from the University of Minnesota, then related that he was gratified to hear our views because he and his wife had held to the same position despite widespread rejection of the idea by young friends with whom they were associated in the 1970s.

Discussions with many other people have revealed a hidden professional consensus on this issue that has been obscured by popular writings of a few authors whose books have been widely quoted. Also, a pilot values survey by Jensen (1984) showed that about three-fourths of nearly 100 mental health professionals in the Seattle area endorse fidelity.

Although it is not new to argue this position, it also is not routine to train new therapists to think in such value-laden terms. Helping them learn the skill of instructing their clients in ways of thinking about values and showing clients that there are connections between values and mental health consequences is a substantial innovation. Considering values helps both therapist and client to think about treatment outcomes in the broad terms of modifying life-style rather than in the usual short, narrow terms of simple relief from distress or symptom removal.

Universals versus Relativism

Strupp's comment earlier in this article that "major values . . . seem to be universally true regardless of what a therapist's attitude toward a Supreme Being might be" has been echoed by many others. Maslow was among the strongest advocates of such a view. He declared that "instead of cultural relativity, I am implying that there are basic underlying human standards that are crosscultural—psychologists who advocate moral and cultural relativism are not coming to grips with the real problem" (Goble 1971, 92).

Ethical relativism is not consistent with the idea that there are laws of human behavior (Kitchener 1980a). Human growth is thus likely regulated in part by moral principles comparable in exactness with physical or biological laws, a position adeptly argued by Campbell (1975).

Some writers, however, object to this thesis on the grounds that its absolutistic tendencies are tainted by an authoritarian, narrow, and judgmental frame of reference that is incompatible with personal freedom (Ellis 1980). This dichotomizing of lawfulness and freedom is, however, oversimplified. Obedience to moral law is, in principle, no different from obedience to physical laws. We are free to launch a space shuttle into orbit only as we precisely obey the natural principles that make it possible. It may be that behavioral laws are just as precise and obedience to them just as essential to obtaining desirable and predictable consequences. The freedom to self-actualize, for example, is predicated on obedience to the laws by which self-actualization is possible. Thus, the thinking that pits conformity to moral law against individual freedom, and then repudiates all favorable references to ethical universals, is inconsistent and misleading (Bergin 1980c).

If we take seriously the probable existence of universals, as a large proportion of clinical thinkers do, then the importance of guiding constructs for orienting one's choices and goals becomes more evident. It seems that the laws pertinent to how we should live have much to do with the way we construe the world, how we activate our agentive capacities, and the responsibility we take for the ways in which we act.

Such patterns of cognitive evaluation and choosing we observe regularly in our clients as we discern the causes of their pain and suffering, as well as the changes that bring relief and hope. Our awareness that certain principles underlie the processes of disturbance and therapeutic improvement anchors the way we think about therapy and the way we influence clients' views about how they might regulate their lives. This, then, provides them with cognitive structures for organizing the behavior being suggested by the therapist.

A good example of the application of the concept of universals is in therapeutic attempts to promote self-control. Enhancing self-control of impulses or addictions is critical in modern practice. Such self-regulation must be guided by beliefs that the regulation is valuable, that it leads to long-term consequences beneficial to the client and to those who are important to the client. In this respect, the therapist is in the role of a teacher or instructor who is trying to help the client reconstruct the world and incorporate in the new construct system values concerning intrapsychic and interpersonal consequences of behavior.

Endorsing such values and making them explicit helps both the therapist and the client to realize that self-control can be guided in terms of possible universal themes. Self-discipline can never be optimally successful unless a commitment is made to values, and that commitment can be stronger and more lasting if the client feels he or she is committing to something that is lawful and moral—not just because somebody said so but because it is built into the universe and is part of our nature.

Research and Theory

Empirical Studies of Values, Life-Styles, and Mental Health

This article is conceptual in nature and must be considered as a set of educated hypotheses. Much empirical work is needed to explore the implications suggested by them. Several studies are under way that test questions raised here. Jay Jensen (1984), for instance, is doing a doctoral dissertation under my supervision that involves a national survey of mental health professionals to determine their opinions about the values in the outline and a number of other values. We are also doing a longitudinal study of life-styles that examines relationships between values and mental health. Pertinent completed studies done by others are also being reviewed. It is clear that careful, unbiased studies are needed to move forward in this area.

Cognitive Theory and Values Research

The notion that the ways in which people construe their experience are powerful mediators of the quality of their adjustment is an integral feature of the cognitive revolution that is sweeping through the therapeutic scene. Because values are cognitive constructs, they lend themselves to the same types of inquiries as other cognitions and can be researched in the same way.

The works of Bandura (1982), Beck (1976), Ellis (1973), and many others have been exemplary in facilitating work in this area, although Kelly's psychology of personal constructs long preceded the modern work and is still the most elegant of the cognitive theories (Kelly 1955;

Leitner 1981). The proposals in this article fit well in these cognitive trends and should be further examined within that context, while also recognizing that cognition clearly is not the only important feature of pathology, therapeutic change, or values.

Measurement Studies

Another important potential of values research involves developing measurement techniques for assessing values specifically pertinent to mental health. A mental health values inventory would provide a means of operationalizing definitions and conceptions of mental health in new ways. We could then estimate where a person stands on such variables. We would then also have a presumably valid means of estimating changes in values. This could assist assessment before and after therapy. The former would help us diagnose the client and the latter would help us estimate the effectiveness of therapy in relation to the kind of life-style dimensions that might make changes lasting. A preliminary measurement enterprise along such lines is now being explored by our research group. The evaluation of therapeutic outcomes could thus be markedly affected. We might find, for instance, that symptoms improve while the persons' life-style simultaneously becomes negative in some respect (Bergin 1983b). For instance, some reports indicate that sex therapy may improve a person's sexual performance but also deteriorate his or her relationship if special attention is not given to the kind of life-style values outlined here.

Values Research and Theory as a Major Trend

There are numerous additional efforts in theory and research that have significant implications for therapeutic practices that explicitly address issues of values. Without attempting to list a comprehensive bibliography, the following are noted as a sample of important work that might be pursued further. These illustrate a major trend in the literature.

Seymor Post's book *Moral Values and the Superego Concept in Psychoanalysis* (1972) as well as Lovinger's *Working with Religious Issues in Therapy* (1984) and Will's paper (1981) provide useful introductions to psychodynamic perspectives on values matters. Perry London's *Modes and Morals of Psychotherapy* (1964) provides a classic, penetrating view of therapists as promoters of values, while C. Marshall Lowe's treatise (1976) shows just how pervasive such phenomena are. The 1979 Nebraska Symposium on Motivation (Howe and Page 1980) concerned theory, research, and measurement of beliefs, attitudes, and values; a book entitled *Ethics and Values in Psychotherapy: A Guidebook*, edited by Max Rosenbaum (1982), addresses values issues in the context of practice; a book entitled *Exploring Human Values: Psychological and Philosophical Considerations* (1981), by Kalish and Collier, deals with many conceptual issues; and a 1980 special issue of the journal *Psychotherapy* (Graham 1980) dealt entirely with values. The writings of Thomas Szasz also provide provocative reading on these topics (Szasz 1974, 1978; Szasz and Nemiroff 1963). Other important sources include Cross and Khan (1983), Kessel and McBrearty (1967), Khan and Cross (1984), and Vardy and Kay (1982).

These authors and editors are struggling with the same issues discussed in this article. They suggest that values have an undergirding and overarching influence on our field, an influence of which we have sometimes been deliberately ignorant.

Readers may not agree with all I have asserted here, but the points discussed are eminently subject to definition, description, measurement, research, and testing. I hope further examination will occur and that it will provoke us to reconsider the gravity of what we do when we try to influence a human life.

Obviously, this article provides only a beachhead in a territory yet to be fully explored. Dozens of values have not been mentioned that may have strong implications for healthy functioning. The fact that psychotherapy, as we know it, has been formulated mainly in the secular centers of Western Europe and North America induces a cultural narrowness about values and mental health that will have to be broadened as this work continues. Nevertheless, we have to begin somewhere with the best estimates we have as to which values lead to which consequences.

When we reconstrue the psychotherapist's role partly as one of evaluating and guiding value decisions, we therefore have to do so tentatively and with an awareness that we are entering a sensitive domain. But it is a domain through which I believe we are likely to have a more positive and lasting influence. In effect, this means bringing values into our traditional empirical and rational framework so that the essentially spiritual variables that are reflected in value dimensions can be integrated within the traditional scientific modes to which we are already dedicated. Despite the imperfections and struggles we must deal with in such a challenging task, the possible results provide considerable incentive. Hopefully, many persons of diverse persuasions and backgrounds will collaborate in progressing towards this higher synthesis.

References

Bandura, A. 1982. Self-efficacy mechanism in human agency. *American Psychologist* 37: 122–47.

Beck, A. T. 1976. *Cognitive therapy and the emotional disorders.* New York: International Universities Press.

Begelman, D. A. 1975. Ethical and legal issues of behavior modification. In *Progress in behavior modification,* ed. M. Hersen, R. M. Eister, and R. M. Miller, vol. 1, 259–89. New York: Academic Press.

Bergin, A. E. 1980a. Behavior therapy and ethical relativism: time for clarity. *Journal of Consulting and Clinical Psychology* 48: 11–13.

———. 1980b. Psychotherapy and religious values. *Journal of Consulting and Clinical Psychology* 48: 95–105.

———. 1980c. Religious and humanistic values: A reply to Ellis and Walls. *Journal of Consulting and Clinical Psychology* 48: 642–45.

———. 1983a. Religiosity and mental health: A critical re-evaluation and meta-analysis. *Professional Psychology Research and Practice* 14: 170–84.

———. 1983b. Values and evaluation, therapeutic change. In *Therapeutic behavior modification,* ed. N. J. Helm and P. E. Bergin, 9–14. Berlin, East Germany: VEB Deutches Verlag der Wissenschaften.

Beutler, L. 1979. Values, beliefs, religion, and the persuasive influence of psychotherapy. *Psycho-therapy: Theory, Research, and Practice* 16: 432–40.

Billington, L. 1983. Psychotherapy outcome as a function of client-therapist values relationship and client values change. Ph.D. diss., Fuller Theological Seminary, Pasadena, Calif.

Campbell, D. T. 1975. On the conflicts between biological and social evolution and between psychology and moral tradition. *American Psychologist* 30: 1103–20.

Cross, D. G., and J. A. Khan. 1983. The values of three practitioner groups: Religious and moral aspects. *Counseling and Values* 28: 13–19.

Ellis, A. 1973. *Humanistic psychotherapy: The rational-emotive approach.* New York: Crown.

———. 1980. Psychotherapy and atheistic values: A response to A. E. Bergin's "Psychotherapy and religious values." *Journal of Consulting and Clinical Psychology* 48: 635–39.

Erikson, E. H. 1963. *Childhood and society.* 2d ed. New York: Norton.

Frank, J. D. 1973. *Persuasion and healing.* Baltimore: Johns Hopkins Univ. Press.

Goble, F. G. 1971. *The third force: The psychology of Abraham Maslow.* New York: Pocket Books.

Graham, S. R., ed., 1980. Values in psychotherapy [Special issue]. *Psychotherapy: Theory, Research and Practice* 17, no. 4.

Howe, H. E., and M. M. Page, eds. 1980. *Nebraska symposium on motivation, 1979.* Lincoln: Univ. of Nebraska Press.

Jensen, J. P. 1984. *Mental health values of professional therapists: A national interdisciplinary survey.* Pilot data, Psychology Department, Brigham Young University, Provo, Utah.

Kalish, R. A., and K. W. Collier. 1981. *Exploring human values: Psychological and Philosophical Considerations.* Monterey, Calif.: Brooks-Cole.

Kelly, G. A. 1955. *Theory of personality: The psychology of personal constructs.* 2 vols. New York: Norton.

Kessel, P., and J. F. McBrearty. 1967. Values and psychotherapy: A review of the literature. *Perceptual and Motor Skills* 25: 669–90.

Khan, J. A., and D. G. Cross. 1983. Mental health professionals: How different are their values? *American Mental Health Counselors Association Journal* 6: 42–51.

———. 1984. Mental health professional and client values: Similar or different? *Australian Journal of Sex, Marriage, and Family* 4: 71–78.

Kitchener, R. F. 1980a. Ethical relativism and behavior therapy. *Journal of Consulting and Clinical Psychology* 48: 1–7.

———. 1980b. Ethical relativism, ethical naturalism, and behavior therapy. *Journal of Consulting and Clinical Psychology* 48: 14–16.

Leitner, L. M. 1981. Psychopathology and the differentiation of values, emotions, and behaviors: A repertory grid study. *British Journal of Psychiatry* 138: 147–53.

Lilienfeld, D. M. 1966. The relationship between mental health information and moral values of lower class psychiatric clinic patients and psychiatric evaluation and disposition. Ph.D. diss., Columbia University, 1965. *Dissertation Abstracts* 27: 610b–11b.

London, P. 1964. *The modes and morals of psychotherapy.* New York: Holt, Rinehart and Winston.

Lovinger, R. J. 1984. *Working with religious issues in therapy.* New York: Aronson.

Lowe, C. M. 1976. *Value orientations in counseling and psychotherapy: The meanings of mental health.* 2d ed. Cranston, R.I.: Carroll Press.

Maslow, A. H. 1971. *The farther reaches of human nature.* New York: Viking.

Matarazzo, J. D. 1982. Behavioral health's challenge to academic, scientific, and professional psychology. *American Psychologist* 37: 1–14.

Post, S. C., ed. 1972. *Moral values and the superego concept in psychoanalysis.* New York: International Universities Press.

Rogers, C. R. 1957. The necessary and sufficient conditions of therapeutic personality change. *Journal of Consulting Psychology* 22: 95–103.

———. 1961. *Becoming a person.* Boston: Houghton Mifflin.

Rokeach, M. 1973. *The nature of human values.* New York: Free Press.

Rosenbaum, M. 1982. *Ethics and values in psychotherapy: A guidebook.* New York: Free Press.

Shostrom, E. L. 1966. *Personal Orientation Inventory manual.* San Diego: Educational and Industrial Testing Service.

Strupp, H. H., and S. M. Hadley. 1977. A tripartite model of mental health and therapeutic outcomes. *American Psychologist* 32: 187–96.

Sue, S. 1983. Ethnic minority issues in psychology. *American Psychologist* 38: 583–92.

Szasz, T. S. 1974. *The myth of mental illness: Foundations of a theory of personal conduct.* Rev. ed. New York: Harper and Row.

———. 1978. *The myth of psychotherapy: Mental healing as religion, rhetoric, and repression.* Garden City, N.Y.: Doubleday.

Szasz, T. S., and R. A. Nemiroff. 1963. A questionnaire study of psychoanalytic practices and opinions. *Journal of Nervous and Mental Diseases* 137: 209–21.

Vardy, M. M., and S. R. Kay. 1982. The therapeutic value of psychotherapists' values and therapy orientations. *Psychiatry* 45: 226–33.

Vaughn, J. L. 1971. Measurement and analysis of values pertaining to psychotherapy and mental health. Ph.D. diss., Columbia University. *Dissertation Abstracts International* 32: 3655B–56B.

Wallach, M. A., and L. Wallach. 1983. *Psychology's sanction for selfishness.* San Francisco: W. H. Freeman.

Walls, G. B. 1980. Values and psychotherapy: A comment on "Psychotherapy and religious values." *Journal of Consulting and Clinical Psychology* 48: 640–41.

Will, O. A., Jr. 1981. Values and the psychotherapist. *American Journal of Psychoanalysis* 41: 203–10.

Religious Life-Styles and Mental Health: An Exploratory Study

This study is part of a series of inquiries in which the relation of values to mental health were examined (Bergin 1980a, 1983, 1985; Bergin, Masters, and Richards 1987; Jensen and Bergin, 1988). In this article, we examine religious aspects of life-styles and their relation to mental functioning in a sample of religious college students.

Our reviews of previous work in this area (Bergin 1983; Donahue and Bergin 1987) and our own experiences in studying these problems left us dissatisfied. Many studies have been done, but the overall picture of the phenomenon and the principles operating therein are ambiguous and inconclusive. Debates over the role of religion in mental health have therefore been difficult to resolve (Bergin 1980a, 1980b; Ellis 1980; Walls 1980).

There are two ways out of the empirical and conceptual difficulties facing researchers. One is to become much more precise in measuring and differentiating the religious dimension so that the ambiguities in global, undifferentiated assessments of this complex of psychosocial variables can be avoided. Progress is being made in this direction (Batson and Ventis 1982; Bergin, Masters, and Richards 1987; Donahue 1985; Kahoe and Meadow 1981).

The other avenue is more difficult. It involves a deeper, more naturalistic, and more descriptive immersion in the phenomena than can be achieved by the typical large-sample correlational or factor-analytic study of scores on paper-and-pencil instruments. We chose this avenue. Although we gave up a degree of precision by doing so, we felt that this would be offset by the benefit of a more penetrating exploration of processes that are still poorly understood.

Consequently, we elected to study a modest-sized sample descriptively, using an intensive (Chassan 1979) research approach to generate

Coauthored with Randy D. Stinchfield, Thomas A. Gaskin, Kevin S. Masters, and Clyde E. Sullivan. From the *Journal of Counseling Psychology* 35, no. 1 (1988): 91–98. Copyright 1988 by the American Psychological Association.

hypotheses concerning the role of religious life-styles in mental health. Therefore, we present interesting trends that expand on previous data, without suggesting that we have made definitive tests of specific hypotheses.

Questions Explored

Previous data, already alluded to, led us to believe that religiousness might have both costs and benefits for psychological functioning, depending on how it operates in the individual's life. Consequently, we explored how different elements of religious life-styles related to quality of mental functioning.

Because our participants followed a comparatively regulated life-style entailing considerable self-discipline, we were interested in whether there would be benefits or significant psychological costs in connection with such high levels of self-control. We also explored the possible consequences that might emerge when the individual's strict morality was compromised, as well as possible antecedents of the choice to violate a moral standard. It was also our intention to explore and describe the participants' religious experiences: What were they like, and what role did they play in adjustment? Finally, we addressed issues of personal growth and therapeutic change.

Method

Participants

The sample was composed of 60 undergraduate dormitory residents (27 men and 33 women) who regularly attended a student ward (congregation) of 163 members of The Church of Jesus Christ of Latter-day Saints (Mormon) on the Brigham Young University (BYU) campus. The median age of subjects at the beginning of the study was between 18 and 19 years. Subjects were primarily freshmen (42) and sophomores (11) from white, middle-class families who came largely from urban areas. Half were from the West (9 from California, 9 from Utah, 7 from Oregon, and 5 from Washington), and half came from 15 other states, Canada, and West Germany. They had an average high school grade point average of 3.51 out of 4.00. (The BYU average for incoming freshmen was 3.34 in 1984.) Ten were enrolled in the university honors program.

Participants were solicited through individual letters, announcements placed on bulletin boards, and a verbal announcement given prior to a church meeting. Participation was voluntary, but sample selection was influenced by the fact that the principal investigator was also the bishop (lay pastor) of the ward.

We originally debated whether to use a different ward or a random sample of dormitory residents but chose to use the principal investigator's ward because it provided a unique opportunity for the kind of intensive study that we envisioned. A relationship of trust was already established that could yield the kind of disclosure and commitment to participation that is necessary for such research.

Of the 163 members, 76 began the test and interview procedures, but 16 dropped out because of time constraints. To compare the characteristics of the 16 dropouts, the 87 nonparticipants, and the 60 remaining participants, the principal investigator and his two counselors in the ward bishopric did the ratings (independently). The drop-outs turned out to be very similar to the participants, so we made careful comparisons only of participants versus nonparticipants.

Participants, in contrast to nonparticipants, were rated as better adjusted ($M = 4.5$ vs. 4.0 on a 5.0 scale), more spiritually committed (4.2 vs. 3.6), and closer to the bishop (4.0 vs. 2.9). They were also more likely to have been missionaries (22% vs. 9%), to seek the counsel of clergy (36% vs. 21%), to be converts (12% vs. 2%), and to attend church regularly (96% vs. 80%). Thus, they were somewhat more religious and had a closer relationship with the principal investigator than did nonparticipants; this was considered an advantage, however, for an intensive study of the more religious students.

The potential for biases in and abuses of the special relationship between the principal investigator and the participants was guarded against by appointment of a special oversight committee cochaired by a church leader and the dean of students. A majority of interviews and all testing were done by non-Mormon research team members. The entire procedure was also thoroughly reviewed by the university's Human Subjects Review Committee. A further protection against biases or distortions in the study as a whole was that our research team membership averaged 50% non-Mormon. These team members made critical evaluations during every phase of the research.

Religious Life-Style

The participants structured their lives in conformity with the typical Latter-day Saints (LDS) behavioral pattern. All of them held unpaid volunteer positions in the ward, such as teachers, leaders, social activities or sports directors, service project coordinators, musicians, and records and financial clerks. Time commitments to these responsibilities ranged from about 2 to 10 hours per week, in addition to attendance at 3 hours of Sunday meetings. Nearly all subjects addressed the congregation during the weekly Sacrament Meeting in a brief sermon at least once during the year. The ward is a social system of activity and mutual help. It is, in a sense, a large family—not always a completely happy family but, nevertheless, a relatively close social network.

In addition to donating time to ward responsibility and activity, the participants (with few exceptions) donated generously of their funds and also followed standard Mormon strictures, such as chastity, abstinence from alcohol, tobacco, tea, coffee, and nonprescribed drugs; daily private prayer; regular scripture reading; and participation in a weekly Family Home Evening.

They were at the same time lively and in many respects typical American college students. They acted out ordinary dormitory pranks and played loud music. They included jocks, modern dancers, and scientific intellectuals. They had their share of roommate conflicts, broken engagements, and individual problems. Although the research team saw them as a cut above the average, we also viewed them as normal young adults who were in the processes of adjustment and transition regarding many of the primary dimensions of their lives.

Procedure

The subjects read and signed an extensive informed consent form that was cosigned by a witness. Two interview guides, specifically designed by us for this study, were used in 1- to 2-hour semistructured interviews that elicited details of life history, values, life-style, personal conflicts, and religious experiences. One year later (winter-spring 1985), we were able to contact two–thirds of the original subjects and conducted follow-up interviews with them. Subjects were administered a battery consisting of a biographical inventory, the Minnesota Multiphasic Personality Inventory (MMPI), Eysenck Personality Inventory (EPI), California Psychological Inventory (CPI), Tennessee Self Concept Scale (TSCS), the Allport Religious Orientation Scale (ROS), and other experimental value inventories that are not part of this report.

Four of the seven research team members studied the interviews and life histories of a sample of the participants, and through group discussion, derived a set of prominent themes concerning the students' values and life-styles. Careful individual reviews preceded the group sessions in which interpretive theses were proposed. The main themes stood out relatively well, and a fairly rapid consensus concerning them evolved. This was perhaps the most creative and important phase of the study. These themes, or dimensions, provided a way of classifying the subjects' experiences into categories that appeared to be significant and relevant to the purposes of the study.

The categories were Religious Development, which included two possible ratings: (a) continuous, in which religiousness developed consistently and smoothly over the life span, and (b) discontinuous, in which religious involvement varied significantly between high and low over time; Impact of Religion on Adjustment, which included four possible ratings: (a) no obvious impact, (b) reinforcement of developmental trends, in that religious influences complemented and supported family values and family relationships during the subject's socialization, (c) compensating, in which religion had a positive impact, prompting improved functioning following or during distress, and (d) deleterious, in which religion had a negative impact, prompting deterioration in functioning; and Religious Experiences, which included two possible ratings: (a) intense, in which frequent or strong religious experiences were reported by the subject, and (b) mild, in which mild to moderate degrees of religious experiences were reported. (All these definitions are elaborated in this article.)

The selection and definition of these dimensions were based on judgments by the researchers and are original to the study. They are part of the exploratory purpose of the project and require cross-validation in further research.

Each interviewer categorized his own interviewees according to this schema. The interviews and histories of a sample of two-thirds of the cases were then subjected to an independent rating by a group of four persons, two of whom had done interviews and ratings on their own cases and two of whom had done neither interviewing nor rating. If the group rating was discrepant from that of the interviewer, a consensus rating was made after discussion. The initial attempts at categorizing, prior to using the consensus rule, yielded 95% agreement on Religious Development ratings, 89% on Impact of Religion on Adjustment, and 89% on Religious Experiences. Because all ratings were dichotomous, 50% agreement would occur by chance. The category Impact of Religion became dichotomous because ratings occurred in only two of the four categories, namely, reinforcement of developmental trends and compensating. Procedures were invoked to control for biases in the ratings, including bringing in one reliability rater who had no previous acquaintance with the study and one who had done no interviews and no ratings but who helped define the categories.

The rating scheme provided profiles of the religious life-styles of the subjects that allowed for useful subgroupings of the sample. The test scores of these subgroups were then compared.

Subgroups

The analyses that follow are based on subgroupings of the 60 participants according to the foregoing categories. A subgroup of 44 out of 60 was identified by continuous religious development over their life spans, as opposed to 16 who experienced discontinuous development. These 44 appeared to come from orthodox families who followed the

LDS life-style and who integrated religion with most other aspects of life. Of the 44 continuous subjects, 42 were also rated as reinforcing. The impact of institutionalized religion on their lives simply reinforced developmental religious trends established within the family. Of these people, 33 also reported mild religious experiences during their lives that seemed well integrated with other aspects of their development. These 33 constituted what we labeled a continuous-reinforcing-mild subgroup.

The other group of 16 subjects manifested a different style. All were actively involved and committed in church at the time of the study, but their religious development was rated as discontinuous because of significant fluctuations in religious involvement and commitment over their life spans. Of these people, 7 also reported that religion tended to have a compensating effect on problems that they had experienced during their lives. Of these 7 subjects, 5 also reported having intense religious experiences that seemed to make decisive differences in their lives. These 5 constituted a discontinuous-compensating-intense subgroup.

Several other small subgroupings occurred. They appeared to be less significant than the foregoing, and analysis of them was beyond the scope of this brief article.

Results

Table 22.1 summarizes the mental measurements for the entire sample of the study ($N = 60$). Mean scores on the MMPI for this sample were within the normal range on all scales, in comparison with other samples in this age group (Colligan et al. 1983), and were similar to profiles compiled by Judd (1986) from previous studies of LDS (at BYU), Catholic, Protestant, and Jewish groups. In the light of these data, our sample may be surprisingly representative of lower division BYU undergraduates and, possibly, other normal college samples.

There was no evidence of unusual defensiveness or faking on the validity scales. The relatively high group mean on the Hypomania scale is common among college-student populations and is likely to be more indicative of a generally high level of activity than of pathology.

Distributions on the other personality scales were also typical, and some means appeared to be slightly above average in the positive direction, as might be expected from this somewhat selective sample. Scores on the Religious Orientation Scale were higher than usual on the Intrinsic dimension and lower on the Extrinsic.

Table 22.1 also shows that those with continuous religious development generally appeared to be more mentally healthy than the discontinuous group. Out of 15 clinical scores (8 MMPI, 3 CPI, 3 TSCS, and 1

Table 22.1

Means and Standard Deviations for the Total Sample and Subgroups

Scale	Research sample (n=60)		Continuous (n=44)		Discontinuous (n=16)		t
	M	SD	M	SD	M	SD	
MMPI							
L	51	8.3	52	8.0	48	8.5	1.74
F	55	5.0	54	5.0	57	4.7	1.95
K	58	7.7	58	7.3	57	9.0	0.64
Hypochondriasis	53	8.8	52	8.3	53	10.3	0.07
Depression	48	7.7	47	6.2	51	10.4	1.59
Hysteria	56	7.4	56	7.7	57	6.8	0.37
Psychopathic Deviate	58	9.8	55	6.9	66	11.9	3.56**
Masculinity and Femininity	56	12.7	57	12.6	52	12.7	1.28
Paranoia	55	7.7	54	8.2	58	5.4	2.35*
Psychasthenia	58	8.5	57	6.9	62	11.0	1.79
Schizophrenia	59	8.8	57	6.9	65	11.3	2.39*
Hypomania	63	9.8	62	10.0	63	9.3	0.18
Social Introversion	50	8.0	50	8.6	49	6.1	0.47
CPI (Crites, Bechtoldt, Goodstein, & Heilbrun, 1961)							
Factor 1 (Compliance)	48	8.3	49	7.7	46	9.4	1.33
Factor 2 (Mastery)	53	7.8	53	8.4	55	5.4	1.37
Factor 3 (Adjustment Level)	54	8.1	54	8.0	52	8.3	0.94
TSCS							
Total Positive	53	8.5	55	7.8	49	9.4	2.20*
General Maladjustment	49	7.9	47	7.1	53	9.1	2.04*
Personality Integration	57	8.5	58	8.8	54	7.0	1.75
EPI							
Extroversion (E)	13	3.7	13	4.0	14	2.8	0.56
Neuroticism (N)	8	4.1	8	3.8	10	4.7	1.51
ROS							
Extrinsic	23	5.4	24	5.1	22	6.2	0.92
Intrinsic	38	5.0	38	4.6	37	6.0	0.97

Note: Minnesota Multiphasic Personality Inventory (MMPI), California Psychological Inventory (CPI), and Tennessee Self Concept Scale (TSCS) are all based on a standardized mean of 50 and a standard deviation of 10. Eysenck Personality Inventory (EPI) Form A means and standard deviations, respectively, for American college students are 13 and 4 for E and 11 and 5 for N. There are no national norms for the Religious Orientation Scale (ROS). A fairly representative sample, taken from Purdue University undergraduates, yielded a mean Extrinsic score of 29 and a mean Intrinsic score of 28 (Donahue, 1985).

Scores for men and women were lumped together because (a) they were equally respresented in the two groups (55% female in the continuous group and 56% in the discontinuous group) and (b) there were no significant differences between their mean scores on any scales except MMPI Masculinity and Femininity and EPI Neuroticism. Sex differences, therefore, cannot account for the significant differences obtained.

*$p<.05$ (continuous vs. discontinuous). **$p<.01$ (continuous vs. discontinuous).

EPI), the continuous group was slightly better on 14, a highly significant statistical trend when considered in terms of a nonparametric
"sign" test or binomial distribution. Five of these were statistically significant on *t* tests: MMPI Psychopathic Deviate, Paranoia, and Schizophrenia and Tennessee Self Concept Scale Total Positive and General
Maladjustment.

Analyses similar to those presented in table 22.1 but not included
here were conducted on other subgroupings, such as discontinuous and
compensating (*n* = 7) versus continuous and reinforcing (*n* = 42) and
continuous-reinforcing-mild (*n* = 33) versus discontinuous-compensating-intense (*n* = 5).

All these comparisons showed the same pattern of differences, and
all of them favored those with continuous religious development, mild
religious experience, and reinforcing impact of religion on development
and adjustment. Although the continuous-discontinuous variable alone
appeared to account for most of the variation in the cases, the largest
number of statistically significant differences occurred between the
small, homogeneous groupings of continuous-reinforcing-mild and discontinuous-compensating-intense. Although these final classifications
yielded small subgroups, they also provided the kind of context for discovery that we were looking for. These people proved highly interesting,
and the following cases illustrate their life-styles and dynamics.

Cases

We begin with two female subjects, L and S, who manifested the
continuous and reinforcing style with mild religious experiences; we
conclude with two male subjects, E and G, who manifested the discontinuous, compensating style with intense religious experiences.

We chose these individuals for this report because their histories highlighted the differing styles. There is no special significance in the fact
that the continuous examples are female and that the discontinuous
ones are male. Their stories simply are most informative concerning the
two modes. Of the 5 discontinuous-compensating-intense subjects, 2
were female, and 3 were male. Of the 33 continuous-reinforcing-mild
subjects, 16 were female, and 17 were male.

Case L. L is a 19-year-old woman who rated her parents, family, and
church as the strongest influences on her life-style, and this has been so
for as long as she can remember. She described the parenting she
received as high on both control and warmth and not involving physical
punishment. Her parents served as examples; she felt that she was
allowed both to make mistakes and to live with consequences; and her
parents reprimanded her verbally and explained to her. She plans to
raise her children in the same way.

Religion is the major guideline in her life. She stated that the Scriptures guide every aspect of her life, which makes her feel happy and successful. She considers such a life-style to be a "nonfail" way of living and adds, "Having the gospel in my life makes me happy—it gives me perspective; I know who I am, where I am going, and I know the overall plan. I am a child of God so I realize my worth."

L has a very optimistic outlook on life. She stated, "I see such futility in being unhappy—there is no advantage to it. I don't need sympathy—I get my attention by being active, confident, and happy. I have nothing to be unhappy about. I feel free to do what I want to do and I feel freedom in living the principles of the gospel. I know I am pleasing people who are important to me."

Interviews, tests, and life achievements show L to be functioning extremely well in every aspect of her life. Overall, her psychological functioning is above average: she is interpersonally skillful, affectively integrated, a high achiever, and a leader who is popular with her peers. There was no evidence of crises of belief, parental relationships, or identity in her history. She lives a well-regulated but not overcontrolled life in which self-discipline is balanced with self-expression. In her case, a religious life-style and positive mental health seem to be totally integrated.

Case S. S is an 18-year-old woman who also grew up in a traditional Mormon family reflecting typical Mormon values and life-style characteristics. Her case, however, illustrated the presence of disturbing trends within an otherwise standard moral and spiritual life pattern. Although she was close to both parents during childhood, tensions between her parents during her adolescence caused her to shift her loyalty more toward her mother. The emotional alienation from her father also was accentuated by his dealing with other children in the family very sternly. This frightened her, and she developed a pattern of conformity rather than risk the punishments that other siblings experienced because of their resistance and rebellion.

She has been a consistent leader in high school, college, church, and community activities. She is a high achiever and has maintained a high grade point average. She said, "It feels good to plan and to succeed in achievements." She rarely does anything on impulse. Generally, she is respected for her organizational abilities and efficiency, but these sometimes also seem to trigger resentment in others. This may occur because she does not express emotions readily and because it is hard for her to show weaknesses. She makes it easy for others to envy her productive life-style and to feel somewhat distant from her. Although she does have a few close friends, intimacy is not easy for her.

Making moral decisions or maintaining self-control in the face of temptations is no problem. She described herself as organized, responsible, self-controlled, calm, and emotionally cool. This coolness is a reflection of high self-control and perhaps fear of intense emotion. She perceives being very emotional as dangerous and as possibly leading to disorganization, and therefore, she tends to squelch feelings that might produce conflict or deep encounters with another person. At times, however, she becomes somewhat depressed and has especially difficult times over the conflict between her parents. When this happens, she tends to pray, which she says makes her feel peaceful and calm. She reports that her church is the most stable thing in her life in the light of the family problems and that it keeps her strong and helps her have a more optimistic perspective.

It appears that religious influences have helped her develop a regulated and productive life-style that helps her manage disruptive feelings and provides her defenses against disturbing trends. At the same time, religion has tended to reinforce perfectionistic tendencies that limit her capacity to experience emotion in a complete way or to deepen relationships and approach new crises in a flexible manner. Although her test profiles and life-style are similar to those of Case L, this outward picture of health obscures a vulnerability to depression and a rigidity that may make future adaptability difficult.

Case E. E is a 24-year old man. In contrast to the first two cases, E grew up in a Mormon family that was totally inactive as far as church commitments were concerned. He reported a great deal of chaos and some violence within his family, with a resulting lack of group cohesion and a personal sense of alienation from them. In elementary school, he felt that both his peers and teachers used him as a scapegoat. He performed at a very low level and was considered by a teacher to be mentally retarded. He became rebellious, angry, and involved in lying, stealing, fighting, and similar minor antisocial behavior. At about age 9, he had a dramatic moral and religious self-confrontation experience while lying in bed thinking about his situation. He began to attend church by himself, even though his family did not support him. He became involved in the church social system, developed friendships, and became better adjusted to society and his family. This trend culminated at about age 14 or 15 when he was elected president of his junior high school student body.

When he entered high school, he began to sing and play in a rock band and participated with its members in a variety of minor antisocial behaviors. There was a corresponding decline in spirituality and religious behavior. After about 1 year, he again felt a need to change his life and involved himself in church activities and had several intense religious experiences. Subsequently, he graduated successfully from high school, went on a mission for his church, attended college, married, and held a number of leadership positions in the campus community.

He has graduated from college with good grades, has three children, and has accepted a position with a corporation in the Midwest.

E described a number of intense religious experiences, taking place over a period of years and continuing to the present. He described these as powerful emotional experiences that changed his life at critical points. He noted that they seemed to stabilize his sense of direction and give him a feeling of confidence.

In an interview focused on these experiences, E reported that they made him feel warm, happy, and peaceful, with a sense of joy. At times, he was emotionally moved to the point of tears. For instance, in one of his religion classes during junior high school, he reported feeling the spirit within himself "really strong." He said, "It was like it was not even me; it wasn't even my conscious thinking. It just lifted me out of the chair and I went to the front of the room and bore my testimony [i.e., testified of his spiritual experiences during a testimony session]." He also reported a time on his mission when he was praying and felt what has been referred to as the "still, small voice." He said, "I knew very clearly that my prayer had been answered. It was a voice in my mind. It was like someone talking to me, yet it was in my mind." He also described feelings like burning or warmth within his body, especially through his chest and stomach.

In our study, reports of such religious experiences seemed to be more characteristic of adult converts and people like E, who grew up in the church setting but had a discontinuous pattern of religious development. Those who grew up in the church in a more benevolent, ordinary setting tended to report more mild and calm religious experiences, perhaps because there were no major crises that called for a dramatic response or resolution.

On the basis of several such reports during interviews, we identified such experiences as compensating in the sense that they seemed to compensate for deficiencies in life that moved the individual to a level of adjustment beyond what might have been expected. The compensating potentiality of religious experiences thereby became one of the major hypotheses generated by our explorations, and it is consistent with previous studies on conversion (cf. Bergin 1983; Hood 1974).

Case G. G is also a 24-year-old man. He is a sensitive, thoughtful, and conscientious person who has found meaning for a difficult life in religion. He had been troubled by many forms of substance abuse, depression, sexual promiscuity, insecurity, lack of self-esteem, and lack of meaning or purpose to his life. After an LSD trip (which prompted a depressed state) and his father's death, he experienced a crisis and became preoccupied with the meaning of existence and his purpose in life. He began to feel that God was trying to lead him out of trouble, and he turned to religion for answers.

Later, Mormon missionaries visited him and his roommate, and both converted and joined the church. G interprets these events as divine intercessions in answer to his prayers. Still feeling unworthy of the Lord's blessings, G served as a missionary for 1-1/2 years and returned feeling renewed.

An earlier theme in G's life was a lack of parental guidance and a susceptibility to peer pressure. G enjoyed the freedom but was disturbed by a lack of direction and meaning. His parents provided him with a measure of love but not with specific principles or values to guide his life, so he searched and found both social structure and personal meaning in a new religion.

G's life-style changed drastically with his religious conversion, and this transformation is one of the predominant themes in his life. He is no longer involved in drug abuse or sexual promiscuity and does not suffer from depression. He has direction and goals to strive toward and has found meaning and purpose in his existence. He has also developed social skills, is respected by his peers, and has selected a career goal.

Although both E's and G's MMPI profiles were slightly elevated, other tests and interview evaluations showed them to be considerably stabilized.

Discussion

Conformity of Life-Style to Religious Standards

A recurring finding from the interview data was that nearly all the subjects in the continuous-reinforcing subgroup of 42 cases displayed a remarkable adherence to parental and church values and norms. This was demonstrated by the subjects' (a) report that parents and church had the most pervasive influence on their life-style, (b) acceptance of parental and church teachings, (c) resistance to peer influences that oppose parental and church standards, (d) life-style of personal restraint of impulses and family and church participation, and (e) stated desire to please parents and church figures.

There are a number of explanations for this: First, these students are relatively young and may not have individuated themselves fully from their parents; second, they may have thoughtfully and intentionally assimilated and integrated the values of their elders into their life-style; third, conformity to parental and church norms is highly valued and is reinforced, whereas the cost of nonconformance is high, including potential loss of parental acceptance and approval, loss of in-group peer approval, and disciplinary action by church or university; fourth, because their religious affiliation places them in a cultural subgroup and in some settings an out-group, they have an unusually strong identification with the subgroup and their parents. As one subject stated, "My friends may come and go, but my family will always be there."

Overall, this disciplined and emotionally interdependent life-style was associated with better mental health on both test data and interview assessments. High degrees of self-control were not associated with a cost in level of adjustment. This pattern reflects a degree of family cohesion and loyalty to traditional ideals that is more characteristic of an earlier era. The processes of Mormon socialization appear to stimulate the development of a sense of personal identity that is strongly linked to group identity.

In this connection, we noted little evidence of identity crises among the continuous group. It is as though their identification with family and church values progressed smoothly into young adulthood. Although they seemed to be developing the kind of mature identity described by Erikson (1968), they were getting there by a different process from the crises described by him. Theirs involved mutual affection between parent and child and joint participation in a variety of activities. On the other hand, the discontinuous subjects' histories appeared to be more consonant with Erikson's seminal descriptions.

Although it was found that those whose life history reflected the continuous developmental pattern appeared to be better adjusted than those who manifested the discontinuous pattern, it is not possible to make statements about whether religion caused this difference, because familial factors in the adjustment of the participants were so intertwined with religion that the religious element could not be isolated from other influential factors. It appeared, however, that familial influence in the continuous group involved both high parental control (behavioral standards) and high parental affection, whereas subjects in the discontinuous group frequently reported that the parenting they received lacked control, affection, or both.

That continuous religious development is associated with better functioning is a finding worthy of description and further investigation. From a theory-building point of view, the idea that the developmental dimension is the major variable is interesting because it is long lasting and pervasive and includes powerful social influences. For those individuals whose religion was positively integrated into their family life and their own emerging life-styles, it seemed to provide a source of stability that in turn was related to better adjustment.

At the same time, the less-adjusted subjects in the discontinuous group appeared to have their adjustment level boosted considerably by intense religious experiences. These were like Maslow's (1968) peak experiences, especially those he described as "acute identity experiences" (103), with the addition of a specific sense of contact with God and a transforming of motivation and life-style as a result. Such therapeutic personal changes have also been documented by Linton, Levine, Kuechenmeister, and White (1978) and compared with equally profound but nonreligious transformations. The former tend to yield new levels of self-regulation, contentment, and group identification, whereas the latter yield more self-expression, exploration, and individualism.

Guilt and Adjustment

Some subjects occasionally deviated from their moral standards. Those who did so appeared to be a more disturbed subgroup on the tests, and in interviews they reported more conflicted relationships with their parents than did the other participants.

When asked how they dealt with violations of their consciences (or church standards) and consequent feelings of guilt, a minority answered that they used the church-prescribed practice of confession and repentance. For the others, responses were diverse: waiting until their feelings of guilt subsided; attempting to convince themselves that what they had done was really not that bad, that is, not a transgression; doing something righteous to balance their account and to alleviate their feelings of guilt; promising themselves (and God) that they would avoid it the next time; punishing themselves by calling themselves self-deprecating names and feeling bad for 1 or 2 days; trying not to think about it; and avoiding spiritual contexts because they felt unclean.

These practices represent a variety of defense mechanisms (e.g., denial, suppression, rationalization, and reaction formation), the purpose of which is to defend the integrity of the self-concept. We hypothesized that these people have defined themselves as righteous, and that therefore, evidence to the contrary (transgression) threatens the integrity of their self-image. To follow the practice of confession and repentance would be to acknowledge unrighteousness, which is contrary to their righteous self-identity. This problem appears to reflect a conflict produced in vulnerable people by the subculture's putting emphasis both on maintaining an external image as a righteous person and on honest self-disclosure. It pits an extrinsic norm against an honest, intrinsic style.

An Intrinsically Religious Group

This sample scored high on intrinsic and low on extrinsic religious orientation (Allport and Ross 1967; Donahue 1985). The mean scores were nearly identical to those obtained from other samples of Mormon students (Bergin, Masters, and Richards 1987) and somewhat similar to those obtained from samples of conservatively religious individuals who are not Mormon (Bolt 1977; Shoemaker and Bolt 1977). Thus, the sample represents a conservative religious life-style marked by an intrinsic orientation, which is characterized by those who internalize beliefs and live by them. Religion is for them an end. The opposite, extrinsic orientation, is characterized by people who use their religion as a means of obtaining status, security, self-justification, and sociability. This approach is basically utilitarian.

As in previous research (Bergin, Masters, and Richards 1987), we also found overall psychological adjustment of such an intrinsic group to be normal. The mean values on all reported measures were well within normal limits, and some tended toward above-average levels. This supports other findings and runs counter to the notion that religiousness is necessarily correlated negatively with mental health (Bergin 1983).

Limitations

This project was primarily hypothesis generating and allowed the research team freedom to attempt to discover rather than test, but this introduced some limitations:

1. The data gathered during interviews was based on memories and perceptions of the subjects themselves rather than on objective indexes of their life-styles.
2. Although church members' trust in the principal investigator yielded many volunteers for an arduous series of tasks, it also caused biases in the sample. It encouraged participation by the more religious members and possibly discouraged participation by those who felt some alienation from the church. Indeed, this sample and the university population generally provide few rebels or drop-outs. Studying the life-styles and mental health of a less committed sample is a prime task for the future.
3. The small number of subjects in certain classifications reduces the certainty with which generalizations can be made.
4. Finally, because of the homogeneity of the sample, a restricted range of scores on the tests often occurred. This was particularly true of the Religious Orientation Scale. Generalizations from such a sample are necessarily limited, although the main goal of deriving fertile hypotheses from intensive analyses of a small group was achieved.

Hypotheses and Implications for Research and Practice

1. Future research should explore the hypothesis that religious factors, independent of variation in family stability, contribute to adjustment of offspring. In our sample, family and religious variables could not be disentangled.

2. Follow-up and cross-validating comparisons of the continuous-reinforcing-mild life-style with the discontinuous-compensating-intense life-style should also be done. It appears that the individuals in the continuous subgroup come from more stable backgrounds. They should show greater stability over the long term, but some of them may be dependent on family and religious support and not resilient outside of that context.

On the other hand, the discontinuous group appeared less stable and more vulnerable to stress, but it may include individuals who, by virtue of their personal conviction and conversion of life-style, may be more resilient. Are the effects of their compensating experiences enduring and integrative?

3. Our findings suggest that religiousness can be correlated with benevolent development and identity formation and that high levels of self-control are not necessarily associated with lower levels of adjustment. On the other hand, vulnerable individuals may interpret religious pressures to conform to high standards in a detrimental way. We hypothesize that the healthy features of intrinsic religiousness will be better actualized when the institutional and familial environments allow for honest recognition and acceptance of moral imperfections, thus emphasizing growth relative to moral principles rather than an outward perfectionism that reinforces rigidity and ensures lowered adaptability.

4. Given a strict morality, compromises and deviation within the group as a whole are inevitable. Our findings suggest the hypothesis that more disturbed individuals compromise more readily, that compromises deepen distress, and that the individuals involved experience more conflict with parents than do the noncompromisers. We also infer that self-regulation comes more naturally and readily for the noncompromisers, whereas it is a more salient struggle for those who eventually deviate.

5. All the preceding points provide potentially valuable insights for counselors concerning the vicissitudes of conservatively religious students' life-styles. Our findings suggest that such students, including those with turbulent histories involving intense religious experiences, can be comparatively normal, or at least, their religious interests and aspirations can be used on behalf of adjustment counseling, provided that the emphasis is on growth rather than external appearances. The continuous-discontinuous distinction may also be useful in diagnosis and counseling.

Because psychologists tend to be less religious than the U.S. norm (Jensen and Bergin, 1988), our results have the important implication that counselors need to be tolerant of religious students and not to automatically interpret their religiosity negatively.

Also pertinent to counseling is the fact that our descriptions of differing modes of religiousness can be put into developmental perspective. The intrinsic, the continuous, and the nondefensive modes appear to be higher levels of functioning. We did not measure other presumably high-level dimensions, such as quest (Batson and Ventis 1982) or religious autonomy (Kahoe and Meadow 1981), but these, like our dimensions, can be compared with other views of positive growth, such as those of Maslow (1968), Erikson (1968), Kohlberg (1969), Fowler (1981), Perry (1970), and Loevinger (1976). Conceptually, correlations between religious development and these other developmental schemes can be articulated and applied in the counseling setting. Our guess is that trying such articulation in practice and research will show that religious development is most successful when it partakes of both the religious dimensions we have described and the dimensions defined by these other theorists.

6. Diverse life-styles, religious and nonreligious, need to be compared and correlated with indexes of disturbance and health in order to extend the small set of suggestive findings reported here.

References

Allport, G. W., and J. M. Ross. 1967. Personal religious orientation and prejudice. *Journal of Personality and Social Psychology* 5: 432–43.

Batson, C. D., and W. L. Ventis. 1982. *The religious experience: A social-psychological perspective.* New York: Oxford Univ. Press.

Bergin, A. E. 1980a. Psychotherapy and religious values. *Journal of Consulting and Clinical Psychology* 48: 95–105.

———. 1980b. Religious and humanistic values: A reply to Ellis and Walls. *Journal of Consulting and Clinical Psychology* 48: 642–45.

———. 1983. Religiosity and mental health: A critical re-evaluation and meta-analysis. *Professional Psychology: Research and Practice* 14: 170–84.

———. 1985. Proposed values for guiding and evaluating counseling and psychotherapy. *Counseling and Values* 29: 99–116.

Bergin, A. E., K. S. Masters, and P. S. Richards. 1987. Religiousness and mental health reconsidered: A study of an intrinsically religious sample. *Journal of Counseling Psychology* 34: 197–204.

Bolt, M. 1977. Religious orientation and death fears. *Review of Religious Research* 19: 73–76.

Chassan, J. B. 1979. *Research design in clinical psychology and psychiatry.* 2d ed. New York: Wiley, Halsted Press.

Colligan, R. C., D. Osborne, W. M. Swenson, and K. P. Offord. 1983. *The MMPI: A contemporary study.* New York: Praeger.

Crites, J. O., H. P. Bechtoldt, L. D. Goodstein, and A. G. Heilbrun, Jr. 1961. A factor analysis of the California Psychological Inventory. *Journal of Applied Psychology* 45: 408–14.

Donahue, M. J. 1985. Intrinsic and extrinsic religiousness: Review and meta-analysis. *Journal of Personality and Social Psychology* 48: 400–19.

Donahue, M. J., and A. E. Bergin. 1987. Religion, personality and life style: Review and meta-analysis. Unpublished manuscript, Search Institute, Minneapolis.

Ellis, A. 1980. Psychotherapy and atheistic values: A response to A. E. Bergin's "Psychotherapy and religious values." *Journal of Consulting and Clinical Psychology* 48: 635–39.

Erikson, E. H. 1968. *Identity, youth, and crisis.* New York: Norton.

Fowler, J. W. 1981. *Stages of faith: The psychology of human development and the quest for meaning.* San Francisco: Harper and Row.

Hood, R. W., Jr. 1974. Psychological strength and the report of intense religious experience. *Journal for the Scientific Study of Religion* 13: 65–71.

Jensen, J. P., and A. E. Bergin. 1988. Mental health values of professional therapists: A national interdisciplinary survey. *Professional Psychology* 19: 290–97.

Judd, D. K. 1986. Religious affiliation and mental health. *Association of Mormon Counselors and Therapists Journal* 12: 71–108.

Kahoe, R. D., and M. J. Meadow. 1981. A developmental perspective on religious orientation dimensions. *Journal of Religion and Health* 20: 8–17.

Kohlberg, L. 1969. Stage and sequence: The cognitive-developmental approach to socialization. In *Handbook of socialization theory and research,* ed. D. A. Goslin, 347–48. Chicago: Rand McNally.

Linton, P. H., L. Levine, C. A. Kuechenmeister, and H. B. White. 1978. Lifestyle change in adulthood. *Research communications in psychology, psychiatry and behavior* 3: 1–13.

Loevinger, J. 1976. *Ego development.* San Francisco: Jossey Bass.

Maslow, A. H. 1968. *Toward a psychology of being* 2d ed. New York: Van Nostrand.

Perry, W. G., Jr. 1970. *Forms of intellectual and ethical development in the college years: A scheme.* New York: Holt, Rinehart and Winston.

Shoemaker, A., and M. Bolt. 1977. The Rokeach value survey and perceived Christian values. *Journal of Psychology and Theology* 5: 139–42.

Walls, G. B. 1980. Values and psychotherapy: A comment on "Psychotherapy and religious values." *Journal of Consulting and Clinical Psychology* 48: 640–41.

Name Index

Subject Index

617